Mammals
of Illinois

Published in cooperation with the
Illinois Department of Energy
and Natural Resources

and its divisions, the
Illinois State Museum

and the
Illinois State Natural History Survey

Mammals
of Illinois

Donald F. Hoffmeister
Museum of Natural History
University of Illinois

UNIVERSITY OF ILLINOIS PRESS
Urbana and Chicago

Library of Congress Cataloging-in-Publication Data

Hoffmeister, Donald Frederick, 1916-
    Mammals of Illinois / Donald F. Hoffmeister.
        p. cm.
    "Published in cooperation with the Illinois Department of
Energy and Natural Resources and its divisions, the Illinois
State Museum and the Illinois State Natural History Survey."
    Bibliography: p.
    Includes index.
    ISBN 0-252-01515-0 (alk. paper)
    1. Mammals—Illinois. I. Title.
QL719.I2H65 1989
599.09773—dc19   87-29516
                                                          CIP

This book is dedicated to Illinois:
its land and its inhabitants, large and small,
of today and tomorrow and time beyond recall.

Contents

Color illustrations (following page 142):

Preface

In 1945, my interest in Illinois mammals was aroused when as a young faculty member at the University of Kansas I helped a new graduate student, E. Lendell Cockrum, work on his mammalian distribution maps for Illinois. At the time, I had started a faunal study of the mammals of Kansas and young Cockrum was studying the mammals of Illinois. With my move in 1946 to the University of Illinois, I began to work earnestly on the mammals of Illinois and Cockrum continued my work on Kansas mammals. Since that date, I have worked with and on the mammals of this state as well as on numerous other projects.

The very next summer (1947) field work was started in Illinois as four of us collected specimens and made observations on mammals. Included in this first field trip were Charles McLaughlin, later to become director of the San Diego Natural History Museum, Paul Parmalee, later to become director of the Frank H. McClung Museum, University of Tennessee, and William Robertson, now of the United States National Park Service. Each year, a number of undergraduate and graduate students working with mammals at the University of Illinois have, as part of their training, collected specimens, accumulated life history data, analyzed population sizes and fluctuations, and made general observations in Illinois. Specimens of Illinois mammals at all or nearly all institutions housing such collections have been examined. Colleagues throughout the state and from adjacent states have shared their information with me, and hopefully this report is the better for it.

This report will never be complete, regardless of the effort devoted to it. New mammals, such as the cotton rat, will move northward into the state in the not too distant future. The ranges of all species are continuously changing, some only slightly, but others drastically. Examples of the latter are the western harvest mouse and the coyote. There may be counties from which specimens of some "common" species have not been collected, but that does not mean they do not occur there. It has been deemed not necessary to collect in every county. Thus, new "county records" or first reports for some counties will continue to be found and these are to be expected.

When I came to Illinois in 1946, only two trained mammalogists were working on Illinois mammals. Today (1986) nearly a score are studying our mammals. Nevertheless, much remains to be learned about many aspects of Illinois mammals, especially as regards the life history of some of our most common species, the summer and winter ranges of our bats, areas of sympatry between the northern and southern short-tailed shrews, the ecology of coyotes and coyote-dog hybrids, to mention a few. It is important to study the rare or uncommon species, such as the white-tailed jack rabbit and the red squirrel, but more information on the common species may be even more important.

Acknowledgments

Many persons have assisted in many ways with specimens, research, financial assistance, and suggestions that have made possible the completion of this book. Attempts will be made to acknowledge all of this help, but some individuals will inadvertently be omitted.

For nearly forty years, at the University of Illinois, many students in classes in mammalogy have collected specimens in Illinois. It is not possible to name all the students involved. Numerous graduate and honors students have provided data also. Included among these are: Mary Adam, Donald Allison, Elsie P. Anderson, Larry Beasley, Richard Bein, Leslie Burger, Robert Calef, Steven Carothers, Robert Chiasson, Wayne H. Davis, Victor Diersing, Dean Ecke, Lance Scott Ellis, Ben Fawver, Lowell Getz, John S. Hall, Sadako Hayase, Robert G. Hoffmeister, Ann V. Holmes, Charles Hume, Carl Jacoby, Neil Jensen, Edward Kirby, Hedda Kurapkat, William Lidicker, Elliot Magidson, Robert Martin, Lowell Miller, Iyad A. Nader, Anthony Nusbaumer, Belva Pearson, Carlos Pinkham, David J. Schmidly, Dean Schneider, William Severinghaus, Patrick Shields, H. Duane Smith, Dana Snyder, Leslie Swartz, Julius Swayne, Luis de la Torre, James Wallace, Graydon Ware, Ralph Wetzel, Raymond Will, John Winkelmann, David Wright, Robert E. Wrigley, Nancy Van Cura, Richard Van Gelder, and Earl Zimmerman.

Various faculty members working with mammals have provided help and information: George Batzli, Lowell Getz, and M. Raymond Lee at the University of Illinois; Harlan Walley at Northern Illinois University; Harold Broadbooks at Southern Illinois University, Edwardsville; Willard Klimstra, William George, and George Feldhamer at Southern Illinois University, Carbondale; Dale E. Birkenholz, Illinois State University; John Warnock, Western Illinois University; Richard Andrews, Eastern Illinois University; Glen Sanderson, Stephen Havera, and Bruce Brown, Illinois Natural History Survey.

The Illinois Department of Conservation has assisted in many ways with this state-wide project. Through the former director, David Kinney, the Department made available grants that enabled Dr. Victor Diersing to examine specimens in numerous museums, Peter Goodin to review the large numbers of books on the early history of Illinois, including hundreds of county reports, provided for the detailed preparation of the distribution maps by Dorothy M. Smith and Marilyn O'Hara, and for the preparation of some of the illustrations. This financial assistance is acknowledged with many thanks. Many persons from the staff of the Department of Conservation have provided valuable information on Illinois, and I would especially thank George F. Hubert, Jr., Carol Mahan, and Michael Sweet. Woodrow and Lois Goodpaster collected in critical areas in Illinois through financial assistance by the Department of Conservation. Dr. J. Purdue of the Illinois State Museum has provided valuable data. The final draft of the manuscript was carefully reviewed by Dr. John O. Whitaker, Jr., Indiana State University, and Dr. Jerry R. Choate, Fort Hays State University. Their suggestions are greatly appreciated.

Dr. Victor Diersing was closely associated with this study in its early stages, especially in examining and measuring specimens in collections and preparing some analyses of geographical variation. This help is greatly appreciated. The art work was done by Alice Prickett, Carol Kubitz, and Harry Henriksen. Most of the manuscript was typed by Arlene Webb; several other persons worked on finishing it, especially Jane Feilen. Their help is greatly appreciated.

The Illinois Department of Energy and Natural Resources, the Illinois State Museum, and the Illinois Natural History Survey, through Drs. Don Etchison, Bruce McMillan, and Loring Nevelin, respectively, provided funds to assure the production of the book. The University Research Board provided monies for the completion of necessary art work. The Museum of Natural History and the Department of Ecology, Ethology, and Evolution provided the author with the necessary freedom and assistance to complete the manuscript. The manuscript was completed and submitted in April 1986. Attempt was made to incorporate as much as possible of the data on Illinois mammals up to that time. Only a limited amount could be added after that date.

The many collections from which we have examined specimens are listed under Methods and Plan (p. xv). We thank the persons in charge of these collections.

Introduction

Mammals are not a conspicuous part of the Illinois landscape, but that does not mean that they are rare or absent. Indeed, in any acre of Illinois countryside, there may be a score of mammals of several different species. Mammals are inconspicuous because they are mostly nocturnal and of small size. Of the 62 species in Illinois, only 10 are diurnal. Only one species can be regarded as of large size (the white-tailed deer) and only nine of medium size: opossum, beaver, coyote, red fox, gray fox, raccoon, badger, river otter, and bobcat. Of the species of mammals in Illinois, 84 percent are nocturnal or subterranean and 68 percent are rat-size or smaller. At an earlier time, additional large-sized species were present: bison, elk, mountain lion, and bear, and additional medium-sized species: timber wolf, wolverine, fisher, and porcupine. All of these species are now gone from Illinois.

Mammals in Illinois live in a variety of habitats. Some live almost entirely below the surface of the ground: eastern moles and plains pocket gophers; some mostly in water: river otters, beavers, and muskrats; some are adept flyers: 13 species of bats; some are good climbers: tree squirrels, flying squirrels, and golden mice.

Mammals have unique behavioral and physiological adaptations. Bats navigate through forests and caves and hunt insects by using sonar or echolocation. A bat released in a building will not fly into a closed window because it perceives the sound waves reflected from the clear glass. Some mammalian species in Illinois conserve energy in the winter by hibernating when food is in short supply or not available. This is especially true for some kinds of bats, and for woodchucks, ground squirrels, and jumping mice. Those bats that do not hibernate may migrate to the south of Illinois in the fall and north again in the spring.

Some mammals have selective diets. Bats feed almost exclusively on flying insects. Shrews and moles feed on ground-dwelling insects and mollusks. Rice rats may prey upon minnows and young turtles. Mink prey extensively on muskrats, and a favorite food of raccoons is crayfish.

Because of the central geographical position of the state of Illinois, certain species that have their principal centers of distribution elsewhere do extend into Illinois. Eight species of southern or southeastern distribution reach the state; six species that are primarily western reach the state. To put it another way, eight southern species and six western species are part of the Illinois fauna. The same is true for several northern species. Just as interestingly, in the near future three species that are primarily southern may extend their ranges into the state at any time and six species that are northern may do the same, for they occur so near to Illlinois that this seems inevitable unless dramatic environmental changes take place.

The mammalian fauna has been altered in Illinois since European man first arrived. Some think it has been changed so drastically they despair that man's activities will eliminate many more species. As a matter of fact, relatively few species have been extirpated in the state — elk, bear, bison, wolf, and mountain lion, and some species that never were abundant, including the porcupine and cotton mouse. A few species that have been nearly eliminated but re-introduced are probably more abundant now than ever before; these include the white-tailed deer and the beaver. Many species have prospered by European man's activities, such as plowing the prairies and converting these into shortgrass pastures, opening the forests, forming badlands from strip-mining, providing roadside refuges that are left uncut, and building lakes and drainage canals. Some species that have profited from this are the red fox, coyote, badger, eastern cottontail, and western harvest mouse. Programs of setting aside lands for permanent nature preserves, including natural areas, wooded areas, and railroad rights-of-way, as well as caves and abandoned mine shafts, and of protecting and maintaining these areas in as natural a condition as possible, will go a long way toward preventing the elimination of additional species of mammals.

Methods and Plan

This book attempts to give a detailed account of those mammals that are present in Illinois in the twentieth century, with descriptions, comparisons, distribution including maps, life history, and ecological data. Also included is information on those mammals that were present prior to this century and as far back as the arrival of Europeans in the 1600's. A brief characterization of the climate, soils, and vegetation in Illinois, especially as it affects the mammals, is included together with information on fluctuations and abundance of mammals and an account of those mammals that have been recently extirpated as well as those that are presently endangered or threatened.

Distribution maps are based upon those specimens that have been examined, as well as upon some published records that appear to be authentic. On the maps, each locality of occurrence is given a number, and this same number appears under records of occurrence. When several listed localities fall within the area covered by one numbered dot, each of these localities is given the same number but is further distinguished by letters. For example, in Champaign County, four localities may fall within a single dot: 14A, 2½ mi N Urbana; 14B, 2 mi NW Urbana; 14C, Urbana; 14D, ½ mi S Urbana. All are under dot 14. An example of this is found under *Blarina Brevicauda,* locality 50 for Fulton County. Localities are arranged by counties, more or less in a series of horizontal rows, running from west to east. The order of sequence of the 102 counties in Illinois is shown on the map on page xvii and is listed on the same page. An alphabetical listing of the counties, and their numbers in the above sequence, is given on page xvi. For some species, the number of localities for specimens examined may exceed 99. In that case, the numbering starts again with "1." An example of this can be seen in Map 8.5 for *Blarina brevicauda.* County names are abbreviated on the maps.

The distribution of each species within the United States is given as a supplement to its distribution in Illinois. Maps are given without longitudinal and latitudinal coordinates. The map on page xvii does, however, show these degree marks.

For those species of bats that may be migratory, the date of capture of some specimens that were examined is given under *Records of occurrence.* These dates may also serve to indicate when bats are in or out of hibernating chambers.

Dental formulae are usually presented in this fashion: 3/3, 1/1, 4/4, 2/3 (as in *Canis*) or 1/1, 0/0, 1/1, 3/3 (as in *Tamias* and others). This indicates, in order, the number of upper and lower incisors, canines, premolars, and molars in each half of the jaw. Thus, in the example for *Canis* there are 3 upper and 3 lower incisors, 1 upper and 1 lower canine, 4 upper and 4 lower premolars, and 2 upper and 3 lower molars on one side of the upper and lower jaw. For the total number of teeth, this would be multiplied by two. For *Canis* there would be a total of 42 teeth, 20 above and 22 below.

Keys for identification of species are arranged near the groups of mammals that they are intended to serve. If descriptions for taking cranial measurements are not found in the text, reference can be made to Hoffmeister (1986) under the appropriate genus or species as to how they were made.

Many diagnostic and key characters for the identification of species are based on external measurements, such as length of hind foot, ear, or tail. It is critical that these measurements are taken (and recorded on the specimen label) accurately, for differences between species may be only a few millimeters. Hind foot is measured from the back of the heel to the tip of the longest claw. Tail length is from the tip of the tail bone (the last caudal vertebra), not the longest hairs on the tip, to the place where the tail vertebrae join the sacral vertebrae. These measurements are further discussed in the *Glossary* (p. 323).

In the synonym in the species accounts, the recognized name combination is followed by the name of the author responsible for the name. An example is *Sorex cinereus*

cinereus (p. 60), where Kerr is responsible for the name *cinereus*. In the 1925 reference, Jackson was first to recommend that *cinereus* of Kerr not be used in combination with *arcticus*. Thus, Jackson's name is separated from *cinereus* with a comma. In 1985, the International Code of Zoological Nomenclature, Third Edition, says (Article 51 B, i) that the separation be with something other than a comma or parentheses. Some mammalogists are using colons; unfortunately some use nothing. Until this procedure has become standardized with mammals, I shall continue to use a comma.

Sources for the information on mammals in Illinois between 1650 and 1900 are described in the section Early History of Mammals in Illinois (p. 27). The difficulty of evaluating these data that are based on the use of ill-defined common names is discussed therein.

Numerous museums have been visited for study of specimens or have loaned material, or both. These are referred to—in the text and under specimens examined—by certain acronyms which are as follows:

AM   American Museum of Natural History, New York
BM   Burpee Museum of Natural History, Rockford
CAS Chicago Academy of Sciences
CU   Cornell University, Ithaca
EIU Eastern Illinois University, Charleston
EU   Eureka College, Eureka
FM   Field Museum of Natural History, Chicago
FS   Florida State Museum, University of Florida, Gainesville
IDC Illinois Department of Conservation, Springfield
ISM Illinois State Museum, Springfield
ISU Illinois State University Collection, Normal
KC   Knox College Collection, Galesburg
KU   Museum of Natural History, University of Kansas, Lawrence
MCZ Museum of Comparative Zoology, Harvard
MSU Michigan State University, East Lansing
NHS Illinois Natural History Survey, Champaign
NIU Northern Illinois University, DeKalb
NW   Northwestern University, Evanston
SIC Southern Illinois University, Carbondale
SIE Southern Illinois University, Edwardsville
SRL Cooperative Wildlife Research Lab, Carbondale
TU   Tulane University, New Orleans
UI   University of Illinois Museum of Natural History, Urbana
UM   University of Michigan Museum of Zoology, Ann Arbor
US   U.S. National Museum of Natural History (includes U.S. Biological Survey Coll.), Washington
WIU Western Illinois University, Macomb
WG   William George Private Collection, Carbondale

Counties of Illinois arranged alphabetically, followed by numbers as indicated on the map on facing page.

County	No.	County	No.
Adams	40	Lee	10
Alexander	100	Livingston	36
Bond	70	Logan	46
Boone	4	McDonough	28
Brown	42	McHenry	5
Bureau	18	McLean	37
Calhoun	52	Macon	61
Carroll	7	Macoupin	57
Cass	44	Madison	69
Champaign	49	Marion	79
Christian	59	Marshall	33
Clark	68	Mason	43
Clay	81	Massac	102
Clinton	77	Menard	45
Coles	65	Mercer	16
Cook	13	Monroe	75
Crawford	74	Montgomery	60
Cumberland	66	Morgan	54
De Kalb	11	Moultrie	62
De Witt	47	Ogle	9
Douglas	64	Peoria	32
Du Page	14	Perry	88
Edgar	67	Piatt	48
Edwards	84	Pike	51
Effingham	72	Pope	98
Fayette	71	Pulaski	101
Ford	38	Putnam	19
Franklin	89	Randolph	87
Fulton	30	Richland	83
Gallatin	95	Rock Island	15
Greene	55	St. Clair	76
Grundy	22	Saline	94
Hamilton	90	Sangamon	58
Hancock	26	Schuyler	41
Hardin	99	Scott	53
Henderson	25	Shelby	63
Henry	17	Stark	31
Iroquois	39	Stephenson	2
Jackson	92	Tazewell	35
Jasper	73	Union	96
Jefferson	80	Vermilion	50
Jersey	56	Wabash	86
Jo Daviess	1	Warren	27
Johnson	97	Washington	78
Kane	12	Wayne	82
Kankakee	24	White	91
Kendall	21	Whiteside	8
Knox	29	Will	23
Lake	6	Williamson	93
La Salle	20	Winnebago	3
Lawrence	85	Woodford	34

Counties of Illinois arranged by sequential numbers as given on the map.

1. Jo Daviess	52. Calhoun
2. Stephenson	53. Scott
3. Winnebago	54. Morgan
4. Boone	55. Greene
5. McHenry	56. Jersey
6. Lake	57. Macoupin
7. Carroll	58. Sangamon
8. Whiteside	59. Christian
9. Ogle	60. Montgomery
10. Lee	61. Macon
11. De Kalb	62. Moultrie
12. Kane	63. Shelby
13. Cook	64. Douglas
14. Du Page	65. Coles
15. Rock Island	66. Cumberland
16. Mercer	67. Edgar
17. Henry	68. Clark
18. Bureau	69. Madison
19. Putnam	70. Bond
20. La Salle	71. Fayette
21. Kendall	72. Effingham
22. Grundy	73. Jasper
23. Will	74. Crawford
24. Kankakee	75. Monroe
25. Henderson	76. Saint Clair (or St. Clair)
26. Hancock	77. Clinton
27. Warren	78. Washington
28. McDonough	79. Marion
29. Knox	80. Jefferson
30. Fulton	81. Clay
31. Stark	82. Wayne
32. Peoria	83. Richland
33. Marshall	84. Edwards
34. Woodford	85. Lawrence
35. Tazewell	86. Wabash
36. Livingston	87. Randolph
37. McLean	88. Perry
38. Ford	89. Franklin
39. Iroquois	90. Hamilton
40. Adams	91. White
41. Schuyler	92. Jackson
42. Brown	93. Williamson
43. Mason	94. Saline
44. Cass	95. Gallatin
45. Menard	96. Union
46. Logan	97. Johnson
47. De Witt	98. Pope
48. Piatt	99. Hardin
49. Champaign	100. Alexander
50. Vermilion	101. Pulaski
51. Pike	102. Massac

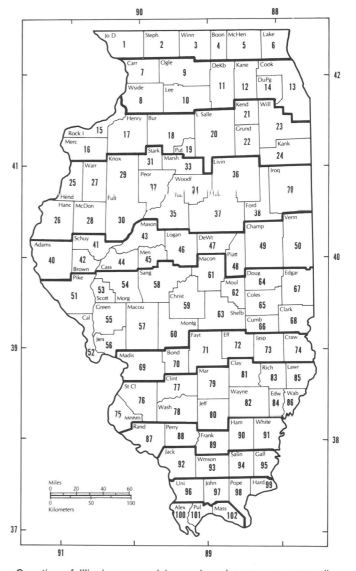

Counties of Illinois arranged in numbered sequence, generally west-to-east and north-to-south. The first and northern tier includes counties 1 to 6; next, counties 7 to 13, and so forth. Throughout the text, records under *Specimens Examined* are arranged by counties in this numerical sequence.

History of Mammal Study in Illinois | 1

People in Illinois have always been interested in mammals as a source of food, a source of fur and hides, and as a source of pleasure in photographing and hunting them. Few people, however, recorded information on the life history, identity, and distribution of mammals until the 1900's. A variety of pre-1900 reports about mammals in the state were made by observers passing through, or by early explorers. These were casual observations, usually of non-scientific quality.

In the 1850's, Robert Kennicott of West Northfield, a suburb of Chicago, published a catalogue of the mammals of Cook County (1855) and on mammals of Illinois that were injurious or beneficial to the farmer (1857, 1858). Robert Kennicott was the son of John Kennicott, M.D., and, although without formal advanced schooling, was trained in Washington, D.C., by Spencer F. Baird, Jared P. Kirtland, and Philo Hoy. In the Trans actions of the Illinois State Agricultural Society for 1853–1854, Robert's mammals of Cook County comprised a mostly unannotated list, prepared at the request of the corresponding secretary of the Society. Kennicott stated (1855): "nearly all the species named I have observed myself. A few I have given on the authority of John K. Clarke, who was one of the first settlers in the county. . . ." In 1855, Robert worked as an unsalaried employee of the Illinois Central Railroad to survey the natural history along the right-of-way between Chicago and Cairo. Baird encouraged Robert Kennicott in these endeavors by having him spend one winter in Washington to arrange the specimens he had collected (Hendrickson, 1970) and urging him to publish his material in the United States reports of the commissioner of patents.

In 1861, Cyrus Thomas published a "catalogue" of species of mammals found in Illinois (1861) which was only a list taken largely from the earlier reports of Robert Kennicott. Following this report by Thomas, no reports of any significance on Illinois mammals appeared until 1910.

C. K. Worthen of Warsaw, Illinois, was a taxidermist in the late 1800's and early 1900's. He prepared many specimens that are preserved in scientific collections and many are mentioned in the literature. Nearly every specimen is labelled Warsaw. For comments about specimens collected by Worthen, see the account of the genus *Canis.*

In 1910, Frank E. Wood published a monograph on the mammals of Champaign County, but in fact did not restrict himself to Champaign County. Also included were such mammals as red squirrels, golden mice, eastern wood rats, swamp rabbits, and pocket gophers, all of which are unknown in Champaign County. In 1910, Arthur H. Howell reported on collections of mammals that he had made in Illinois in 1909. Howell preserved specimens of 19 species from various parts of the state, and these are housed in the U.S. Natural History Museum. Howell collected on the following dates in 1909: Alexander County, McClure (May 13, June 17–18); and Olive Branch (May 8, May 14–21); Union County, Wolf Lake (May 24–25); Pope County, Golconda (June 20–21); Johnson County, Reevesville (June 22); Gallatin County, Shawneetown (June 18); Jersey County, Riehl Station (May 30); Marion County, Odin (June 5); Richland County, Olney (June 7–8); Edgar County, Kansas (June 10–11). This must be regarded as the first scholarly account based upon specimens that were permanently preserved—although Howell did draw some false conclusions, based upon hearsay or on casual observations. He says (1910:31) that pocket gophers, *Geomys bursarius,* occur as far as Odin and near Olney, apparently based on evidence of mounds and not actual specimens, and that spotted skunks, *Spilogale putorius,* "undoubtedly range north as far as southern Illinois. They are reported to be fairly common at Golconda, Illinois . . . " (1910:32). Howell saw or preserved no specimens.

An excellent account of "The Mammals of Illinois and Wisconsin" was published in 1912 by Charles B. Cory, curator of zoology at the Field Museum. Species were characterized, information on their life history given when available, subspecies discussed, the range in northeastern United States and southern Canada given, and well illustrated. Specimens examined were also listed. So good was this account that nothing more appeared until 1941, when Necker and Hatfield published an up-to-date checklist of the species in Illinois.

Some of the significant, subsequent papers on Illinois mammals include: mammals of the Chicago region by Gregory (1936), area surveys such as Layne (1958a&b) on southern Illinois, Anderson (1951) on Fulton County, Klimstra (1969) on the Pine Hills, Brown and Yeager (1943) and Mohr (1943) on Illinois furbearers, and Hoffmeister and Mohr's (1957) field guide for the state. In more recent years, a number of articles and studies have appeared that deal extensively with one or another species of mammal found in the state. Reference is made to these papers in the species accounts.

Physical Geography and Relation to Mammals | 2

Physiography

The state of Illinois is largely an elevated plain that tilts slightly from the north to the south. The plain is dissected by streams which were large at an earlier time and cut wide channels, even shallow valleys, through the deep soils. These channels are bordered with bluffs which in turn are cut through by smaller, tributary streams. In general, the plain is at an average elevation of 600 feet, but in southernmost Illinois it has declined to a 300-foot elevation, more or less.

The northern part of the state, here defined as being delimited at the south by the Shelbyville moraine of the Wisconsin glaciation of about 20,000 years before present, consists of deep dark soils, rich in organic material (Map 2.1). In this area, tree growth is limited mostly to stream valleys, eroded bluffs, and various recessional moraines. The Illinois prairie grown with tall prairie grasses occupied much of this area, and it has now been converted, almost entirely, to crop and farmlands.

The southern part of the state south of the Shelbyville moraine has soils that are less pervious, with a tight clay subsoil, and the area lacks deep dark soils.

Three areas in the state remained unglaciated during the Pleistocene: part of Jo Daviess County, part of Calhoun County, and the southernmost part of Illinois, namely the Shawnee Hills and the southern section of the Ozark Uplift (Map 2.2). These sites are the most rugged in Illinois, with rocky strata projecting above the glacial till. Jo Daviess County contains a driftless or unglaciated area of dissected dolomite and shale, with natural caves as well as mine shafts. The unglaciated parts of southern Illinois are mostly Pennsylvanian sandstone that contains sinkholes, caves, and mine shafts.

In the late 1700's, about 57 percent of the state was prairie, consisting of grasses of varying heights up to five feet, and 43 percent was forest. The acreage of forest at that time was estimated to be 15,273,000 (Telford, 1927). By the early 1800's it may have been reduced to about 14,000,000 acres (King and Winters, 1952). Map 2.3 shows the extent of the forest about 1820. Between 1800 and 1820, the human population in the state increased from around 3,000 to 55,000, and by 1830 to 160,000. By the early 1920's, the acreage of forest was about 3,000,000. Vestal (1926) prepared a map of the forest areas around 1926 and this is reproduced in Map 2.4. By 1974, the forests were even more greatly reduced, as indicated by the satellite imagery shown in Map 2.5.

In 1850, there were about 12,000,000 acres of farmland in Illinois; by 1900, 33,000,000 acres. Man's activities in harvesting lumber and clearing forested areas for living have greatly influenced the open-areas and altered the biota. Other activities such as strip-mining have resulted in altered terrain and a change in faunal succession. Graber and Graber (1963) point out that in little more than 100 years, the Illinois landscape changed from a few relatively high-density habitats to the diversified and managed habitats of the early 1900's. Now, the habitats include plowed fields, row crops, pastureland, fencerows, orchards, and the "wastelands" from strip-mining, as well as unmanaged habitats such as increased forest-edge. The vast amount of land that has been converted into crop land or pasture land or has been used for our expanding cities is indicated by the non-forested area as shown in Map 2.5 based upon a survey of the mid-1970's. "Natural" conditions of a prairielike habitat are to be found in a few private or public areas and along some abandoned railroad rights-of-way. Those changes in prairie conditions can be noted by comparing the map for 1820 (Map. 2.3) with that for 1974–1976 (Map 2.5). These changes have affected numerous kinds of mammals, some adversely and some beneficially. Species such as the eastern mole, *Scalopus aquaticus,* and deer mouse, *Peromyscus maniculatus,* have had a reduction in their distribution and numbers. But no prairie species has been eliminated by this reduction of prairie within the state.

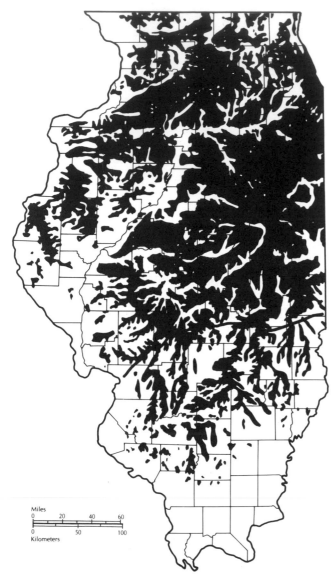

Miles
0   20   40   60
0   50   100
Kilometers

Map 2.1. Tallgrass prairie (shaded) in Illinois as known in the 1920's (Vestal, 1931), including farmland. This includes the Grand Prairie and part of the Southern Till Plain, together with prairies named by Vestal as Mendota, Shannon, Bushnell, and Carthage.
  The Grand Prairie is separated from the Southern Till Plain approximately at the heavy line.

Miles
0   20   40   60
0   50   100
Kilometers

Map 2.2. Forests of two non-glaciated areas in Illinois: Jo Daviess Hills or Wisconsin Driftless and Ozark or Shawnee Hills. The non-glaciated area in Calhoun and Pike counties is also shown.

Climate

Illinois has relatively uniform temperature, rainfall, snowfall, and frost-free days throughout the state, with a trend from north to south in all features. Temperature averages from 46° to 48° F in northernmost Illinois to 58° to 60° F in the southernmost part. Frost-free days number about 160 in the north, 200 or more in the south. Precipitation varies from 32 to 34 inches in the north to 46 inches or more in the south.

Approximately 4,000 to 6,000 years ago there was a warmer, drier period than what presently exists in Illinois. From 4,000 years ago to the present, the climate has undergone no drastic changes although the weather may vary widely from year to year.

Southernmost Illinois is only 490 miles from the Gulf of Mexico and thus the side effects of cyclonic activity can be felt in this area. Precipitation is higher in winter and early spring as a result, but from April to September the precipitation is much the same as farther north.

Soils

In Illinois, soils were developed either under prairie vegetation or under forest vegetation, although soils along major waterways (Mississippi, Ohio, Illinois, Wabash rivers) were formed primarily from alluvium. Soils resulting from prairie vegetation or heavy grasses are dark-colored since they are high in organic matter and usually the subsoils are moderately to rapidly permeable.

Soils developed under forest vegetation are light-colored since they are low in organic matter, and usually the subsoils are slowly or only moderately permeable. At the forest edges there may be dark-colored soils where the forest has started to invade the prairie.

Dark soils are mostly north of an east-west line that runs across Illinois from Edgar County to Jersey County. South of this line some soils that developed under heavy grasses may be light-colored to medium-colored and with only slowly permeable subsoil. These two areas and the division between them is indicated on Map 2.1.

Species of mammals whose distribution in Illinois may be correlated with dark soils with readily permeable subsoils are the masked shrew (*Sorex cinereus*), thirteen-lined ground squirrel (*Spermophilus tridecemlineatus*), and Franklin's ground squirrel (*Spermophilus franklinii*). It is possible that these soils favorably affect the distribution of these species also: plains pocket gopher (*Geomys bursarius*), meadow vole (*Microtus pennsylvanicus*), and badger (*Taxidea taxus*).

Species whose distribution may be correlated with light-colored soils developed primarily under forest conditions are southeastern shrew (*Sorex longirostris*), southern short-tailed shrew (*Blarina carolinensis*), and eastern chipmunk (*Tamias striatus*).

Vegetative and Geographical Divisions

Within the state of Illinois, certain natural areas can be distinguished and characterized by their vegetation, soils, topography, and glacial history. Basically these are areas of prairie with grasses and few or no trees and of wooded or forested areas that are in bottomlands or hill country. Most of the original prairie has disappeared and most of the forests have been cut. Different investigators have subdivided these vegetative-geographical areas in different ways and applied a variety of names to them. Two divisions, prairie and forest, with some of their subdivisions are discussed here.

Prairie Division. This is a damp prairie with such plants as big bluestem, little bluestem, Indian grass, prairie dropseed, switch grass, and prairie dock. Shrubs include prairie willow, dwarf pussy willow, spirea, prairie rose, and wolfberry. Most of these prairie areas are poorly drained, and the soil is high in organic material.

One of the largest segments of this area is the *Grand Prairie Division* (Fig. 2.1). Originally a wet prairie with tall grasses and deep, dark soil, this division included wooded river bottoms and some sand areas. The Grand Prairie Division is located north of the Shelbyville Moraine. South of this moraine is the so-called *Southern Division* or *Southern Till Plain Division* which contained prairie areas with the characteristic prairie vegetation, but they were less mesic and the soils were lighter in color and not as deep. Sandy prairie areas are scattered throughout the state. Along and near the Mississippi River in Jo Daviess and Carroll counties and along parts of the Illinois River are areas sometimes called the *Sand Prairie* (Fig. 2.2). At other places along the Mississippi River there are sandy areas, especially in Henderson and Mercer counties. Extensive areas of sand occur along the Illinois River.

Forest Divisions are more varied than prairies, with original forests ranging from white pine and Canada yew to bald cypress, beech, and basswood.

The driftless areas—that is, those sections free of Pleistocene glaciations—were forested, as were the river bottoms. Parts of the driftless areas are given such names as the *Wisconsin Driftless Division* or the *Jo Daviess Hills* (Fig. 2.3). The *Mississippi Border* has been subdivided into the *Upper, Middle,* and *Lower Mississippi River Bottomlands Divisions* (Map 2.6). Prairies are present within the wider, mostly wooded, bottomlands of the larger rivers.

The *Rock River Hill Country Division* contained white pine along with oaks, maples, walnuts, and some Canada yews and yellow birches.

Forests in the bottomlands (Fig. 2.4) of much of the Mississippi, Illinois, and Wabash rivers consisted of silver maples, American elm, white ash, pin oaks, locusts, sycamores, and black walnut. In the southern portions of the Mississippi and Wabash rivers, there were beech, tulip, honey locust, red buckeye, mixed in with a variety of oaks, sweet gum, hickories, and other trees.

The *Shawnee Hills Division,* which is sometimes referred to as the *Ozark Hills Division,* although the latter is preferably restricted to the hills bordering the lower parts of the Mississippi River, consists of the non-glaciated Cretaceous hills of southern Illinois (Fig. 2.5). The soil is shallow in most places. The vegetation included such items as blackjack and scarlet oaks, red cedar, pignut and bitternut hickories, together with a variety of other oaks, sugar maples, and black walnut. The Ozark Hills contained a few shortleaf pine (*Pinus echinata*). South of the Shawnee Hills, the rolling country adjacent to the Ohio River now or at an earlier time had such unique plants as screw stem (*Bartonia paniculata*), netted chain-fern, silverbell tree (*Halesia carolina*), Spanish oak, chestnut, and cucumber tree. This area is referred to as the *Tertiary Border* or the *Coastal Plain Division.*

The northeastern corner of the state, radiating southwestward from Lake Michigan, has sometimes been called the *Northeastern Morainal Division.*

Fig. 2.1. Grand Prairie of central and northern Illinois, as exemplified by this remnant of big bluestem. (From Evers and Page, Illinois Nat. Hist. Survey Biol. Notes, 100. 1977)

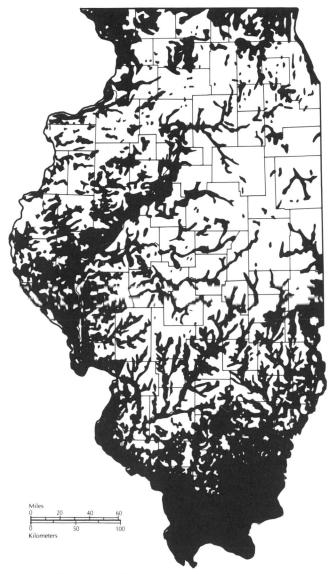

Map 2.3. Distribution of forest (shaded), and prairie and unforested areas of Illinois about 1820 (modified from Anderson, 1970).

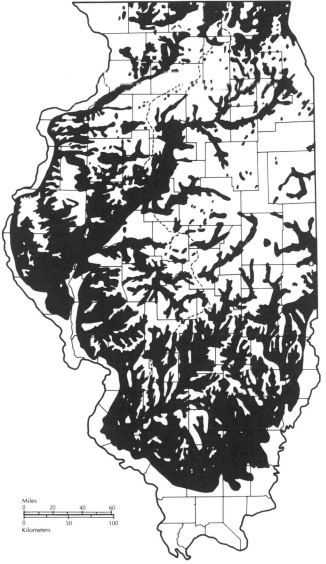

Map 2.4. Forested parts of Illinois as shaded, exclusive of the Jo Daviess Hills or Wisconsin Driftless and the Ozark or Shawnee Hills (see Map 2.2) in the 1920's according to Vestal (1931). Vestal distinguished three divisions of forest, as shaded: Grand Prairie Forest (northeast); Western Division Forest (west); Southern Division Forest (south).

Fig. 2.2. Sand Prairie as found along parts of the Mississippi and Illinois rivers and shown here near Kilbourne, Mason Co., Illinois. (From Evers and Page, Illinois Nat. Hist. Survey Biol. Notes, 100. 1977)

Fig. 2.3. Jo Daviess Hills or Wisconsin Driftless Area as shown in Apple River Canyon State Park, Jo Daviess County. The hills have oaks, basswood, hop hornbeam, as well as white pines and Canada yew. (From Evers and Page, Illinois Nat. Hist. Survey Biol. Notes, 100. 1977)

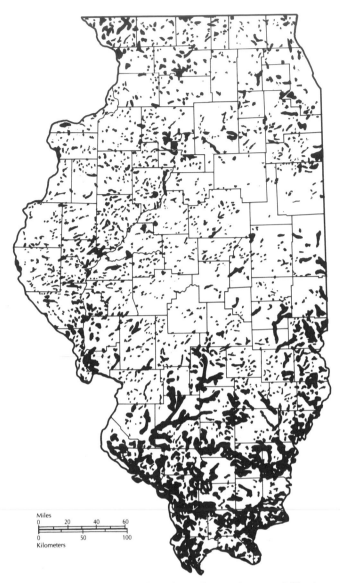

Map 2.5. Forested (shaded) and non-forested areas of Illinois as determined by ERTS imagery 1974-1976. Nearly all of the non-forested (unshaded) area presently represents either croplands or pasturelands, with a small percentage in urban developments and a few lakes.

Map 2.6. Border areas along the major waterways in Illinois have characteristic riparian forest species of plants. These areas are: Mississippi Border, although this area extends partway up the Illinois River; Tertiary Division or Coastal Plain Division, along or near the Ohio River; Wabash Border (after Vestal, 1931).

Relationship of Mammals to Physiographic Features

The physiography of Illinois still retains some aspects of the conditions found in the state when European man first arrived, but much has been altered through subsequent human activities. Forests have been removed to make more farmlands, wet areas have been drained, resulting in drier fields, drainage ditches have provided new waterways, mine shafts have provided additional retreats for some mammals, and streams have been dammed to make new lakes.

In southernmost Illinois, some of the original cypress swamps and the shortleaf pine habitat still persist. Such habitats are suitable for the rice rat, cotton mouse, golden mouse, swamp rabbit, and eastern wood rat. The presence of these species is also influenced by the proximity of this area to the south central states. As mentioned elsewhere, it is anticipated that the cotton rat will be present in southern Illinois before too long.

In northern Illinois, with much of the original forest that contained white pines now removed, some mammalian species typical of this habitat still persist, such as the red squirrel, pygmy shrew, masked shrew, and least weasel.

The prairie species of mammals have suffered the least of any group in Illinois because prairie conditions, although greatly altered, have been supplemented with the formation of new farmlands. Under these circumstances, some species have extended their ranges, including the plains pocket gopher, meadow vole, and western harvest mouse. Other species have seemingly become more abundant, such as the coyote, badger, red fox, thirteen-lined ground squirrel, and eastern cottontail.

The development of drainage ditches has provided additional habitat for muskrats, mink, and raccoons. New lakes have done the same for beavers. Mines and mine-shafts have provided retreats and hibernacula for some species of bats.

Because of the geographically central location of Illinois, some mammalian species are present because of the habitat and the proximity of the state to faunas to the north or other directions. Eight northern species of mammals reach their southern limits of distribution in Illinois (Map 2.7). Seven species of southern affinities

have their northern limits of distribution in Illinois (Map 2.8), and for two more shrews—*Sorex hoyi* and *S. cinereus*—the southeastern segments of their ranges reach their northern limits in the state. Three western mammalian species reach their eastern limits either in Illinois—white-tailed jack rabbit (*Lepus townsendii*)—or just slightly beyond Illinois in Indiana, western harvest mouse (*Reithrodontomys megalotis*), and plains pocket gopher (*Geomys bursarius*) (Map 2.9).

Certain species of mammals seem restricted to or delimited by certain ecological divisions of the state. Some of these are:

Ozark or Shawnee Hills (and possibly Coastal Plain Division)
    Oryzomys palustris, marsh rice rat
    Peromyscus gossypinus, cotton mouse
    Ochrotomys nuttalli, golden mouse
    Neotoma floridana, eastern wood rat

Tertiary Border and Wabash Border
    Sorex cinereus (southern segment), masked shrew

Grand Prairie Division, including Northeastern Morainal Division and Western Forest-Prairie Division
    Microtus pennsylvanicus, meadow vole
    Mustela nivalis, least weasel

Northeastern Morainal Division
    Sorex hoyi (northern segment), pygmy shrew

Grand Prairie and northward
    Spermophilus tridecemlineatus, thirteen-lined ground squirrel
    Spermophilus franklinii, Franklin's ground squirrel

Dark- or light-colored soils developed primarily from medium- and fine-textured outwash (Fehrenbacher et al., 1967), east and south of Illinois and Kankakee rivers
    Geomys bursarius, plains pocket gopher

Southern limits of Northern Coniferous Forest remnants
    Tamiasciurus hudsonicus (former range), red squirrel

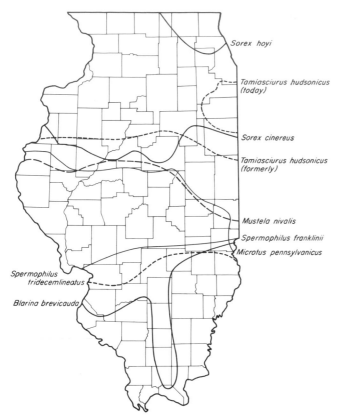

Map 2.7. Southern limits of distribution of northern species of mammals in Illinois.

Map 2.8. Northern limits of distribution of southern species of mammals in Illinois, other than bats. *Sorex hoyi* and *S. cinereus* are northern species but their distribution in Illinois shown here represents northern limits of southern segments of their ranges.

Map 2.9. Western species of mammals that attain their eastern limits of distribution in Illinois (*Lepus townsendii*) or those that nearly do so, extending slightly into Indiana.

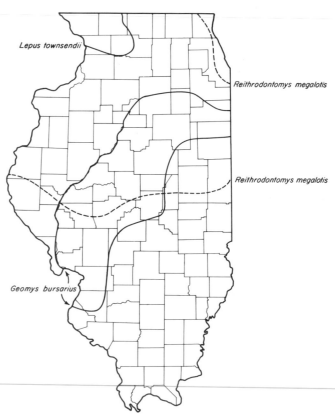

Fig. 2.4. Bottomland Forest as shown here along the Middle Fork of the Vermilion River, Vermilion County. The area contains various oaks, maples, sycamores, locusts, ash, basswood, dogwood, sassafras, and beech. (From Evers and Page, Illinois Nat. Hist. Survey Biol. Notes, 100. 1977)

Fig. 2.5. Shawnee or Ozark Hills of southern Illinois, as shown at Bell Smith Recreational Area, Pope County. The forest consists of beech, hard maples, birch, alder, willow, and several species of oaks. (From Evers and Page, Illinois Nat. Hist. Survey Biol. Notes, 100. 1977)

Game and Fur-bearing Mammals | 3

Game mammals are those usually sought after for food and are taken usually by gun or bow and arrow. Furbearers are those mammals having hides that have monetary value as fur pieces. These are usually taken by trapping, but they sometimes are taken by gun.

Game and fur-bearing mammals in Illinois are identified by the Illinois revised statutes, Chapter 61, Wildlife Code, Article II, Section 2.2. These are arranged here in the same phylogenetic order in which they are presented in this book.

Game Mammals

Eastern cottontail	*Sylvilagus floridanus*
Swamp rabbit	*Sylvilagus aquaticus*
*White-tailed jack rabbit	*Lepus townsendii*
Woodchuck	*Marmota monax*
Gray squirrel	*Sciurus carolinensis*
Fox squirrel	*Sciurus niger*
White-tailed deer	*Odocoileus virginianus*

Fur-bearing Mammals

Virgina opossum	*Didelphis virginiana*
Beaver	*Castor canadensis*
Muskrat	*Ondatra zibethicus*
Coyote	*Canis latrans*
Red fox	*Vulpes vulpes*
Gray fox	*Urocyon cinereoargenteus*
Raccoon	*Procyon lotor*
Least weasel	*Mustela nivalis*
Long-tailed weasel	*Mustela frenata*
Mink	*Mustela vison*
*Badger	*Taxidea taxus*
Striped skunk	*Mephitis mephitis*
*River otter	*Lutra canadensis*
*Bobcat	*Felis rufus*

Those species marked with an asterisk (*) have no open season and are protected under the provisions of the Endangered and Threatened Species regulations (p. 19). In addition, the statutes have a category of non-game and non-fur-bearing mammals entitled *Other Mammals* which is designed to protect species that are on the Endangered and Threatened Species list plus the flying squirrel, *Glaucomys volans*.

Regulations on the taking of game and fur-bearing mammals in Illinois are issued annually by the Illinois Department of Conservation as to when these animals can be taken and the daily- and possession-limits of each. The gun-hunting of deer is the shortest season, being not more than 10 days by law and usually only six days. The longest hunting seasons are for coyotes and skunks, which are closed only during deer season. The trapping seasons for these two species are much shorter. Current regulations, including season length, hours of hunting, and limits of take can be obtained from the Illinois Department of Conservation, Springfield, or its regional offices.

For many years, the white-tailed deer has been the prize game mammal for hunters in Illinois. The increase in abundance of this species during this century is chronicled in the section on deer (p. 314). In Illinois, more individuals hunt cottontails and tree squirrels than deer, and the takes are usually high.

The fur trade was an important source of revenue and activity in the settlement of Illinois. Reports of early explorers and fur trappers are discussed in the section "Early History of Mammals in Illinois" (p. 27).

In present times, muskrats and raccoons were the furbearers most often taken in the late 1970's and early 1980's. For example, in 1979–1980, the estimated annual harvest indicates that 90 percent of the take was muskrats (49%) and raccoons (41%). At other times, the take of muskrats and opossums was much greater and that of raccoons much smaller.

The number of animals harvested and the proportion of one species to another varies from year to year. This depends on many factors: some species are more abundant (e.g., the increase in coyotes and beavers) and others may

Table 3.1. Estimated annual fur harvest for 25 years between 1934 and 1983. The estimates are derived from a variety of sources and these are so designated. Such numbers as "34" refers to the 1934-1935 trapping season. There are conflicting estimates for 1938 and both series of estimates are given. Most early reports made no distinction between red foxes and gray foxes, so these are reported as "foxes."

	34(1)	35(2)	36(2)	37(2)	38(2)	38(3)	39(2)	41(4)	42(5)	47(5)	49(6)	50(6)
Muskrat	255,978	173,004	213,840	323,895	413,823	884,395	729,077	307,179	249,100	730,476	344,312	460,027
Mink	16,080	11,412	12,312	21,593	33,239	53,723	48,581	18,880	19,362	60,345	30,734	31,623
Raccoon	4,470	4,212	6,281	26,734	30,732	42,412	314,577	20,245	27,130	96,936	81,818	71,040
Red fox						10,674						
Foxes	3,450	2,661	1,944	3,926	10,292		10,760	6,232	16,636	30,842	11,191	14,255
Gray fox						4,328						
Opossum	26,838	29,277	22,680	25,519	97,755	244,242	132,585	61,897	94,774	121,202	68,790	47,871
Striped skunk	18,240	17,965	11,016	30,426	47,338	49,640	45,263	21,103	22,580	18,373	11,816	6,582
Weasel						8,889				3,384	442	1,145
Beaver												
Coyote												

(1) Anon (1935) (2) Anon (1939) (3) Brown and Yeager (1943) (4) Anon (1946) (5) Ashbrook (1948) (6) Ashbrook (1955) (7) Anon (1964) (8) Anon (1965) (9) Anon (1966) (10) Hubert (1984)

Table 3.2. Average prices paid for furs for some Illinois furbearers for 21 years between 1929 and 1983. Prices are determined in a variety of ways. For 1929-1937, prices are based on #1 medium pelts (Mohr, 1943); 1938-1939, on average of a large series (Brown and Yeager, 1943); 1962-1968, based on average fur prices for species in Missouri (Anon, 1960's); 1975-1983, average for all sizes and grades (as supplied by Illinois fur buyers, Hubert, 1984).

	1929(1)	30(1)	34(1)	35(1)	36(1)	37(1)	38(1)	39(2)	62(3)
Muskrat	1.00	0.60	0.70	0.60	0.75	0.60	0.80	1.00	0.90
Mink	7.00	3.50	4.00	3.50	6.50	5.50	7.00	6.00	10.60
Raccoon	5.50	3.00	2.50	2.50	3.50	3.50	2.00	2.00	1.95
Red fox	10.00	3.30	3.30	2.50	3.50	2.80	3.00	2.75	1.25
Gray fox	5.00	3.50	1.00	1.30	1.40	1.40	1.75	1.75	
Opossum	0.40	0.35	0.25	0.25	0.30	0.30	0.20	0.20	0.40
Striped skunk	2.40	1.20	0.90	0.90	1.00	0.75	0.75	1.00	0.55
Weasel	0.25	0.25	0.25	0.25	0.25	0.25	0.35	0.35	0.75
Beaver									4.70
Coyote							2.00	2.00	0.55

(1) Mohr (1943) (2) Brown and Yeager (1943) (3) Anon (1964) (4) Anon (1965) (5) Anon (1966) (6) Anon (1970) (7) Hubert (1984)

have been reduced by overcropping and destruction of habitat. Economic conditions may cause more persons to turn to trapping as a supplemental income at certain times. As farms get larger, there are fewer farm boys to do trapping. Fashion trends make the hides of certain species more valuable at some times than at others, and trappers seek these species according to demand. Weather conditions may affect the taking of some species. Attitudes about trapping may discourage some persons. Because of some or all of these factors, the annual fluctuations in total number of furs taken or in the numbers taken of a particular species do not necessarily reflect an accurate population size.

Prices of furs have fluctuated with demands. During some years, long-haired furs were popular (as the period of coonskin coats); at other times, short-haired furs such as mink were popular. Price fluctuations also can be influenced by furs that are not prime, and thus less

desirable. Trapping seasons are established with the hopes that most furs will be harvested after the animals have completed their molt and the pelts thus are prime. To bring the greatest revenue, pelts should be prepared in such a way as to avoid improper cuts, poor stretching, and greasy conditions. In Illinois, most fur buyers would prefer to purchase the unskinned animal from the trapper and do the skinning and preparation themselves.

The annual fur harvest for most years from 1934 to 1983 is given in Table 3.1. The fur take for any species is affected by many factors, including those discussed above. The accuracy of these estimated figures is not known; some were published anonymously. The figures are derived mostly from those provided by the United States Fish and Wildlife Service and by George Hubert of the Illinois Department of Conservation. I have greater confidence in the estimates provided by Hubert (1984) for the years 1975 to 1983. One can note that the number

51(6)	62(7)	63(8)	64(9)	68(9)	75(10)	76(10)	77(10)	78(10)	79(10)	80(10)	81(10)	82(10)	83(10)
574,665	207,586	103,289	129,944	94,251	445,737	256,315	300,314	422,354	460,674	421,585	325,415	297,872	248,146
33,944	8,416	4,917	6,589	3,175	18,009	14,253	12,910	19,814	22,971	26,607	24,478	17,768	16,056
80,807	88,522	61,758	83,066	49,429	310,593	187,377	237,315	292,728	381,006	314,777	314,963	292,189	203,633
					11,247	7,206	9,715	13,582	14,136	13,965	13,533	9,780	8,719
6,399			1,136	2,159									
					7,132	6,166	9,086	9,525	10,547	8,716	7,649	5,943	4,152
31,887	8,675	2,132	4,337	3,459	49,874	42,153	46,198	25,097	38,626	46,710	55,729	35,548	22,289
4,662	547	122	200	150		821	1,503	1,633	3,111	1,625	840	341	137
428	64	40	41	6	181	311	147	147	145	85	53	74	60
			1,342	345	2,337	1,548	2,425	3,386	7,345	7,338	4,145	2,517	2,742
					2,833	3,882	7,678	9,891	9,831	8,412	10,390	8,180	7,289

63(4)	64(5)	68(6)	75(7)	76(7)	77(7)	78(7)	79(7)	80(7)	81(7)	82(7)	83(7)
1.15	1.02	0.97	2.90	4.44	5.10	5.00	6.35	6.50	4.30	2.75	3.15
10.30	7.90	8.21	6.00	13.95	13.20	15.20	20.15	18.90	17.45	13.90	15.15
1.15	1.60	3.11	14.00	17.17	18.00	27.25	25.50	19.40	22.50	14.55	13.15
1.40	1.00	6.64	34.00	45.61	47.45	61.50	48.40	44.80	46.75	30.40	30.90
	0.50		16.00	27.67	31.05	42.95	43.80	36.40	28.75	26.35	27.35
0.35	0.30	0.59	1.10	1.21	2.05	2.65	3.35	1.45	1.05	0.95	0.85
0.45	0.45	0.81	1.00	2.25	2.20	2.55	2.60	2.00	2.15	1.50	1.55
0.75	0.50	0.42	0.50	0.54	0.60	0.65	0.50	0.60	0.50	0.50	0.65
5.60	5.13	8.73	4.50	7.00	7.00	7.25	14.40	10.60	6.40	4.95	5.45
0.50	0.50		8.00	16.07	16.75	31.35	22.85	19.25	24.45	13.85	9.40

of furs of nearly all species increase by nearly sixfold in Hubert's estimates. This in part accounts for the large increase in the value of the total, annual fur take beginning in 1975 (Table 3.3).

The prices that probably were paid for most furs taken for the years 1929 to 1983, with some years unknown, are given in Table 3.2. Some of these data are those given by the U.S. Fish and Wildlife Service, some for prices paid in Missouri for 1962–1964 and 1968 since they are not available for Illinois, and some by George Hubert. The table indicates that from 1975 on, the prices for certain furs increased markedly: raccoon, red fox, gray fox, and coyote.

Table 3.3 shows that the cropping of furs in Illinois has been a multimillion dollar revenue since at least 1975, and probably was for several years before that.

Table 3.3. Total value for furs harvested in Illinois per year as based on average fur prices (Table 3.2) and estimated annual take (Table 3.1).

1934	$ 285,224	1975	$ 6,333,636
1935	182,818	1976	5,179,851
1936	283,841	1977	6,960,463
1937	445,389	1978	12,039,572
1938	704,951	1979	14,718,081
1939	1,745,707	1980	10,603,487
		1981	10,106,683
1962	542,474	1982	5,931,455
1963	243,570	1983	4,188,314
1964	342,464		
1968	291,488		

Endangered and Threatened Mammals in Illinois | 4

Various plants and animals are protected by federal and state laws that are usually referred to as the endangered and threatened species acts. The federal "Endangered Species Act" of 1973 defined an *endangered species* as "Any species which is in danger of extinction throughout all or a significant portion of its range. . . . " A *threatened species* was defined as "Any species which is likely to become an endangered species within the foreseeable future throughout all or a significant portion of its range."

Two mammalian species in Illinois are included on the Federal Endangered Species list:

Myotis sodalis, Indiana myotis
Myotis grisescens, gray myotis

No mammals in this state are regarded as threatened species on the federal list.

The State adopted its own Illinois Endangered Species Protection Act in 1977. By this Act, the State has redefined endangered and threatened species for Illinois. A *"State Endangered Species"* is defined as "Any species which is in danger of extinction as a breeding species in Illinois." Included as endangered are these species of mammals:

Myotis sodalis, Indiana myotis
Myotis grisescens, gray myotis
Lepus townsendii, white-tailed jack rabbit
Neotoma floridana, eastern wood rat

A *"State Threatened Species"* is defined as "Any breeding species which is likely to become a state endangered species within the foreseeable future in Illinois." In this category are these species of mammals:

Ochrotomys nuttalli, golden mouse
Oryzomys palustris, marsh rice rat
Lutra canadensis, river otter
Felis rufus, bobcat

By state law, species are included in the official list when they meet one or more of the following criteria:

1) Species included in the Federal list of Endangered or Threatened species.

2) Species proposed for Federal Endangered or Threatened status which occur in Illinois.

3) Species which formerly were widespread in Illinois but have been nearly extirpated from the State due to habitat destruction, collecting, or other pressures resulting from the development of Illinois.

4) Species which exhibit very restricted geographic ranges of which Illinois is a part.

5) Species which exhibit restricted habitats or low populations in Illinois.

6) Species which are significant disjuncts in Illinois, i.e., the Illinois population is far removed from the rest of the species' range.

Not listed for Illinois is *Tamiasciurus hudsonicus,* red squirrel. This species is present but so poorly established in Illinois in the 1980's that it might well be included on the State Endangered Species list.

Of the eight species (nine with *Tamiasciurus hudsonicus*) included in the Illinois list, none would meet the definitions of the federal list except for the two *Myotis.* Throughout all or a significant portion of their range, the other species are not in danger of extinction. As a matter of fact, some of them are so numerous in parts of their range as to be considered pests.

Perhaps a better way to recognize endangered mammals in Illinois would be to establish another category for those species which are not abundant because only a portion of their range extends into Illinois (Peripheral). Also they may be extending their ranges into habitat that is only marginally suitable for the species, and this may be a limiting factor. These species would not necessarily be uncommon in other parts of their range. Endangered and threatened species would be defined as they presently are.

Endangered species of mammals:

Myotis sodalis, Indiana myotis
Myotis grisescens, gray myotis

Lutra canadensis, river otter
Felis rufus, bobcat

Threatened species of mammals:

Myotis austroriparius, southeastern myotis
Sylvilagus aquaticus, swamp rabbit

Peripheral, not abundant, species of mammals in Illinois:

Sorex hoyi, pygmy shrew
Plecotus rafinesquii, Rafinesque's big-eared bat
Tadarida brasiliensis, American free-tailed bat
Lepus townsendii, white-tailed jack rabbit
Tamiasciurus hudsonicus, red squirrel
Oryzomys palustris, marsh rice rat
Peromyscus gossypinus, cotton mouse
Ochrotomys nuttalli, golden mouse
Neotoma floridana, eastern wood rat

Numbers, Populations, and Fluctuations of Illinois Mammals

In any given area, mammals both small and large seem to be uncommon and sparse, especially in comparison with birds. This is accentuated by the fact that most mammals are nocturnal. Thus it is necessary to observe or census the mammals at night as well as in the daytime. Furthermore, numbers of individuals of any species differ during the year and for some, the numbers fluctuate greatly from one year to the next.

Numbers of mammals of all species in Illinois are probably somewhere between 5 and 25 individuals per acre (12–62 per hectare). Population sizes can be determined in a variety of ways: indirectly by counting houses, mounds, holes, tracks, and so forth, and directly by trapping, either by live-trapping or snap-trapping. With live-trapping, mammals can be marked and released, thus not disturbing their home ranges or territories. There are disadvantages, including the fact that some species are trap-shy, and it may take an unusually long time to trap all of the animals in a given area. With snap-trapping, mammals are removed from the area, which in turn encourages other individuals to move in, which affects the census. To reduce the amount of ingression, plots selected for analysis by snap-trapping are usually circular in outline. Mammals that are trap-shy are less likely to avoid snap traps. The entire trapping period probably should be completed in three days or less to avoid ingression.

For 23 years, students and workers in the Museum of Natural History at the University of Illinois trapped a circular acre for three days with approximately 100 snap traps in an ungrazed, bluegrass area adjacent to the river bottomlands at Allerton Park, near Monticello, Piatt County. Trapping was in late October or early November each year. The number of small mammals caught varied from a low of 4 to a high of 54 (Table 5.1 and Fig. 5.1): the average for one acre over the 23 years was 20.40. The actual number was probably less than this because some animals outside the plot may have moved in and been counted. The habitat of this acre was influenced by natural succession and, by the end of the trapping years, it had become invaded with larger bushes and small trees (Fig. 5.2). As a result, the number of *Peromyscus leucopus* increased in the trapping area.

The same type of survey was conducted for 23 years in a woodland (Fig. 5.3) near the Sangamon River, Allerton Park, Piatt County. The number of animals trapped varied from a low of 6 to a high of 49 (Table 5.2 and Fig. 5.4). The average take for one acre over the 23 years was 20.65, but the actual number was probably smaller.

In an ungrazed prairie in Fulton County (½ mi N Norris), similar snap-trapping by Elsie Anderson and her students produced the following numbers of small mammals per acre: 54 (Oct. 1949), 64 (Feb. 1950), 73 (Oct. 1950), 52 (Feb. 1951), and 39 (Sept. 1951).

In a timberland in Fulton County (2½ mi NE Norris), Anderson's trapping produced the following numbers of small mammals per acre: 15 (Oct. 1949), 12 (April 1950), 5 (Jan. 1951), 27 (May 1951), and 17 (Oct. 1951).

Snap-trapping in the Allerton Park area for grassland and woodland, as previously described, yielded the most mammals the first night, fewest the third night. In the woodland, 52.5 percent were caught the first night; then 29.9 and 17.6 percent, respectively. In the grassland, 44.3, 29.7, and 26.0 percent, respectively.

Stickel's (1946) field research in Maryland revealed that there was a large discrepancy in population numbers when mammals are censused by snap- and live-trapping. A 17-acre area live-trapped for seven days showed a density of between 6 and 7 *Peromyscus leucopus;* a circular acre within the 17-acre tract snap-trapped for three nights produced 23 *P. leucopus.* Will (1962) did a similar analysis in a woodland in northeastern Effingham County, Illinois, where he live-trapped 13.9 acres for nearly two months and snap-trapped a central acre for three nights. Live-trapping indicated approximately 2 small mammals per acre; snap-trapping, 6 per acre. When he excluded *Blarina* and *Tamias striatus,* and thus restricted the count to *Peromyscus leucopus,* the adjusted

Table 5.1. Mammals snap-trapped in a circular acre of ungrazed grassland at Allerton Park, Piatt County, each fall for 23 years. The trapping was for three consecutive nights and approximately 100 traps were set each night.

Total	Microtus ochrogaster	Synaptomys cooperi	Peromyscus leucopus	Peromyscus maniculatus	Cryptotis parva	Blarina brevicauda	Mus musculus	Microtus pinetorum	Date
51	10	35	6	0	0	0	0	0	Nov 1946
10	0	9	0	0	1	0	0	0	Nov 1947
6	0	4	0	0	2	0	0	0	Oct 1948
22	5	0	0	0	12	0	5	0	Oct 1949
20	1	2	0	0	16	0	1	0	Oct 1950
6	2	0	0	0	2	0	2	0	Nov 1951
49	33	1	3	0	12	0	0	0	Nov 1952
15	9	2	1	1	2	0	0	0	Nov 1953
7	0	1	2	0	1	0	0	3	Nov 1954
14	4	4	0	0	6	0	0	0	Nov 1955
26	1	6	3	0	10	0	6	0	Nov 1956
37	9	6	5	0	1	0	16	0	Nov 1957
7	4	2	0	0	1	0	0	0	Oct 1958
8	1	5	1	0	1	0	0	0	Nov 1959
28	5	6	4	0	7	0	6	0	Oct 1960
54	19	8	19	0	6	1	1	0	Nov 1961
4	0	1	2	0	0	0	1	0	Oct 1962
20	9	2	3	0	3	0	3	0	Nov 1963
22	7	0	8	0	2	1	4	0	Oct-Nov 64
23	2	0	18	0	1	0	2	0	Nov 1965
				No Trapping					1966
15	6	0	1	0	5	1	2	0	Nov 1967
14	6	0	5	0	1	0	2	0	Nov 1968
11	3	0	6	0	0	0	2	0	Nov 1969

Table 5.2. Mammals snap-trapped in a circular acre of woodland at Allerton Park, Piatt County, each fall for 23 years. The trapping was for three consecutive nights and approximately 100 traps were set each night.

Total	Peromyscus leucopus	Blarina brevicauda	Microtus pinetorum	Mus musculus	Glaucomys volans	Cryptotis parva	Date
7	1	3	2	0	1	0	Nov 1947
7	3	2	0	0	2	0	Oct 1948
9	2	4	0	1	2	0	Oct 1949
14	6	6	2	0	0	0	Oct 1950
7	7	0	0	0	0	0	Nov 1951
29	17	8	2	0	2	0	Nov 1952
9	7	1	0	0	1	0	Nov 1953
29	23	0	6	0	0	0	Nov 1954
15	12	0	2	1	0	0	Nov 1955
30	25	1	4	0	0	0	Nov 1956
37	26	1	1	9	0	0	Nov 1957
10	6	2	0	2	0	0	Oct 1958
8	6	0	0	0	2	0	Nov 1959
30	22	5	1	1	1	0	Oct 1960
35	28	1	2	0	3	1	Nov 1961
21	15	2	0	4	0	0	Oct 1962
17	16	0	0	1	0	0	Nov 1963
38	35	1	0	1	1	0	Oct-Nov 64
49	39	3	6	0	1	0	Nov 1965
37	28	3	1	2	3	0	Nov 1966
6	3	0	2	0	1	0	Nov 1967
17	13	1	1	2	0	0	Nov 1968
14	9	2	2	1	0	0	Nov 1969

population densities for *P. leucopus* were 0.5 for live-trapping and 1.5 for snap-trapping.

Goodnight and Koestner (1942) in trapping near Seymour, Champaign County, found that snap- and live-trapping gave nearly comparable results. Their plots, however, were only 62½ meters by 10 meters. Wetzel's (1949) doctoral research in east central Illinois showed that the two trapping methods provided nearly the same densities for *Peromyscus leucopus*.

Numbers of animals of a particular species in a given area can be greatly influenced by alterations of the habitat also. Such changes over a 50-year period following strip-mining in Vermilion County, Illinois, as shown in Fig. 5.5 illustrate this. Not only were numbers affected, but some species dropped out entirely, and others invaded the changed area.

Dr. Lowell Getz and his students have been live-trapping various habitats in the University of Illinois Biological Research Area, including the Trelease Prairie area and the Phillips Tract—both located northeast of Urbana. The numbers of voles of the species *Microtus ochrogaster* and *M. pennsylvanicus* that they have deduced as occurring in these places in 14 years' time are shown in Figs. 5.6–5.8. In a bluegrass area (Fig. 5.6) that they studied the common plants were bluegrass, dandelion, and nightshade. Both species of *Microtus* lived there at certain times. Usually the number of voles per hectare was less than 80 (less than 32 per acre). More than 125 *M. ochrogaster* per hectare (more than 51 per acre) were taken in 1972–1973 and in 1985. About 80 *M. pennsylvanicus* per hectare (32 per acre) were taken in 1978–1979. The tallgrass areas (Fig. 5.7) they studied contained lespedeza, ironweed, Indian grass, bluestem, and goldenrod. In these, *Microtus pennsylvanicus* was the predominant species. Numbers of voles per hectare were usually less than 70 (fewer than 28 per acre). In this habitat more than 125 *M. pennsylvanicus* per hectare (more than 51 per acre) were taken in 1980–1981. Not included in these population counts are such other small species as short-tailed shrews, western harvest mice, and white-footed mice that could have been present.

Populations of small mammals, especially microtine rodents, may fluctuate greatly in numbers from year to year. If these fluctuations occur in a set pattern, they may be referred to as cycles. The buildup in numbers to a peak and the crash afterward may happen rather rapidly. Cycles are often said to repeat every three to four years, but the length of such cycles may be variable. Such fluctuations are thought to occur in synchrony over a large area, but it appears that in Illinois there may be little synchrony. Cycles may be affected by food availability, weather, predation, and the stresses of overcrowding.

Getz et al. (1987) found that there were several "highs" and "lows" in a population of prairie voles, *Microtus ochrogaster*, during a 14-year period. The highs do not

show any pronounced synchrony or cycle. Highs were most extreme in 1972–1973 and 1984–1985, with moderate highs in 1975–1976 and 1981 (Fig. 5.8). In 1972–1973, the Getz study reported 240 prairie voles per hectare (97 per acre); in 1984, 268 per hectare (108.5 per acre); in 1985, 491 per hectare (199 per acre).

In Fulton County, 1 mi W Canton, Elsie Anderson, using snap traps, found a peak density of 134 prairie voles, *Microtus ochrogaster*, per acre in an uncut, luxuriant cover of bluegrass in an orchard, in January 1950. In 1946, Hoffmeister (1947) found a peak in numbers of

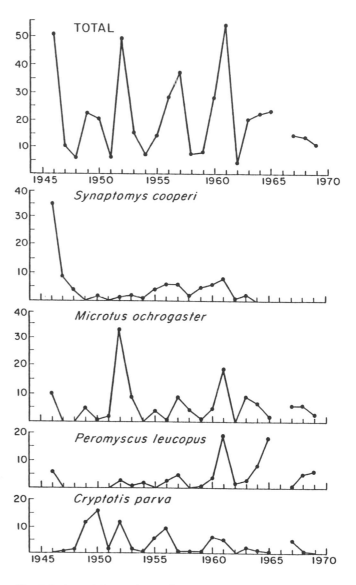

Fig. 5.1. Annual fluctuations of numbers of certain species of mammals caught in a circular acre each fall from 1946 to 1969 in the grassland at Allerton Park, Piatt County. The numbers caught are given on the vertical axis; the year caught, horizontal axis. The total number is given in the graph at the top. So few *Peromyscus maniculatus*, *Blarina brevicauda*, and *Microtus pinetorum* were taken that they are not included. See Table 5.1 for *Mus musculus*. Trapping was not done in 1966.

Fig. 5.2. (Above) Grassland area, Allerton Park, near Monticello, Piatt County, snap-trapped annually for 23 years. Top picture was taken in 1954; bottom, in 1964. Note the invasion of brushy and woody plants into the grassy area. Species found commonly in this habitat are prairie vole (*Microtus ochrogaster*), white-footed mouse (*Peromyscus leucopus*), southern bog lemming (*Synaptomys cooperi*), and least shrew (*Cryptotis parva*).

Fig. 5.3. (Below) Woodland area, Allerton Park near Monticello, Piatt County, snap-trapped annually for 23 years. This is open timber with much leaf mold. Species commonly found in this area are northern short-tailed shrew (*Blarina brevicauda*), white-footed mouse (*Peromyscus leucopus*), pine vole (*Microtus pinetorum*), southern flying squirrel (*Glaucomys volans*), and an occasional fox squirrel (*Sciurus niger*).

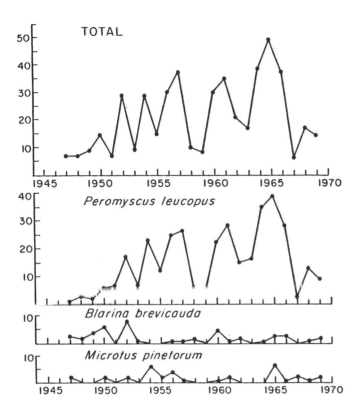

Fig. 5.4. Annual fluctuations of numbers of certain species of mammals caught each fall from 1947 to 1969 in a circular acre in the woodlands at Allerton Park, Piatt County. Numbers caught are given on the vertical axis; year caught, horizontal axis. The total number is given in the graph at the top. So few *Mus musculus, Glaucomys volans,* and *Cryptotis parva* were taken that they are not included (see Table 5.2).

Synaptomys cooperi at 35 per acre, based on snaptrapping, in the bluegrass at Allerton Park, Piatt County.

Trapping for 24 years in bluegrass and woodlands at Allerton Park shows (Figs. 5.1-5.4) relative abundance and fluctuations of species in each situation. In the bluegrass, eight species were captured, but three were taken in 3 years or less (*Peromyscus maniculatus, Microtus pinetorum, Blarina brevicauda*). Numbers of all species were high in 1946, 1952, 1957, and 1961 (Table 5.1 and Fig. 5.1). Population highs for various species are noted in these years: *Synaptomys cooperi,* 1946; *Microtus ochrogaster,* 1952, 1961; *Peromyscus leucopus,* 1961, 1965.

Woodland populations might not be expected to show as much fluctuation as grassland. Nevertheless, there are certain highs (Table 5.2 and Fig. 5.4): 1952, 1954, 1957, 1961, 1965. All of this variation is indicative of that displayed by *Peromyscus leucopus.*

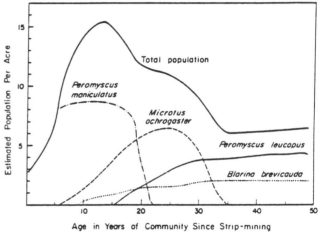

Fig. 5.5. (Above) Changes in the population numbers and species structure with successional change in vegetation during 50 years following strip-mining. (Adapted from Wetzel, 1958:268)

Fig. 5.6. (Below) Population size and fluctuations in numbers of prairie voles, *Microtus ochrogaster,* and meadow voles, *Microtus pennsylvanicus,* in a bluegrass area 10 km NE Urbana. The population size was determined by live-trapping. (From Getz et al., 1987)

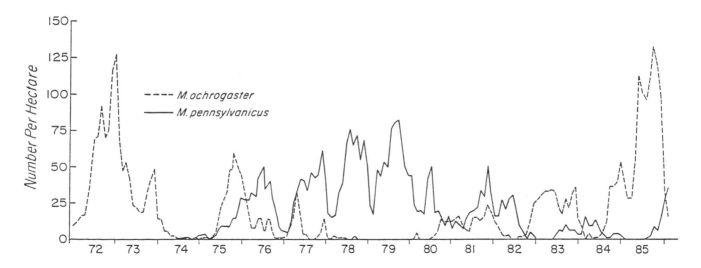

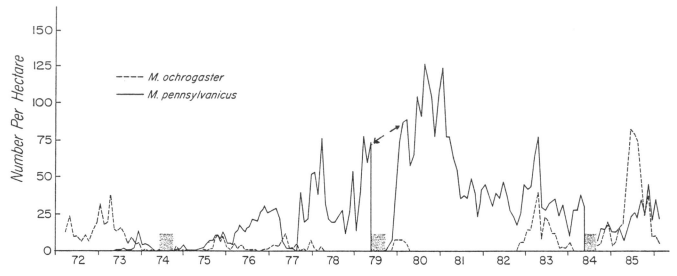

Fig. 5.7. Population size and fluctuation in numbers of prairie voles, *Microtus ochrogaster,* and meadow voles, *Microtus pennsylvanicus,* in a tallgrass area 10 km NE Urbana. The three stippled segments represent time periods when the area was burned. The population size was determined by live-trapping. (From Getz et al., 1987)

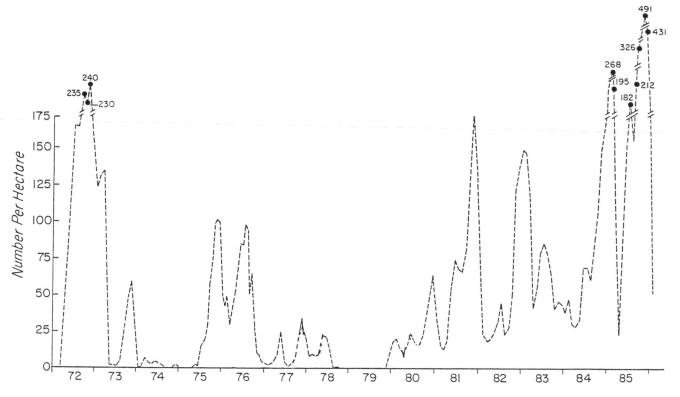

Fig. 5.8. Variation in numbers of prairie voles, *Microtus ochrogaster,* during 14 years as determined by live-trapping in a field of alfalfa and forbs 10 km NE Urbana. Years are indicated on the horizontal axis. Note large numbers of voles in 1972-73 and 1984-85 with minor increases in 1975-76 and 1981. Meadow voles, *Microtus pennsylvanicus,* were present in small numbers from 1975 to 1980. (From Getz et al., 1987)

Early History of Mammals in Illinois: 1650–1900

Early explorers or travelers while residing in or passing through Illinois often left accounts of their observations, including comments in varying depth and accuracy about the mammals. Many persons have prepared histories of individual counties within Illinois that in a few cases contain natural history information on mammals. These reports and volumes are housed in the University of Illinois Library's Illinois Historical Survey Collection. The material prior to 1900 was examined most extensively, much of it being painstakingly reviewed by Mr. Peter Goodin for me.

Some accounts are not dated or they make reference only to "the early days." Data without dates are not often used. References to a particular species may be difficult to interpret because common or vernacular names were not standardized. The greatest confusion is with the cats, the coyotes versus wolves, and the deer-elk complex.

Many of the county histories contain accounts of the mammals that appear to be stock pieces; that is, the terminology in numerous accounts is much the same, as if it had been copied and without verification. Examples of this are such vague statements as "We had the American elk" or "The gray wolf may still exist within our limits." Such statements are of little value in interpreting the early history of Illinois mammals.

One gets the general impression from these accounts that some especially heavy snowfalls occurred and that these were disastrous to big game species. Apparently one such heavy snowfall around 1763 greatly depleted the bison. Subsequently, many bison bones could be found in parts of Illinois. Another severe snow apparently occurred sometime around 1830–1831.

Another fact emerges. Many species were decimated between the mid and late 1800's. This must have been the result of man's uncontrolled hunting and trapping, together with the effect of his altering the landscape and fencing.

Bison or Buffalo

In the early literature, bison were referred to as buffalo, oxen, pisikious, or Illinois cattle. Because of their size and unique features, they probably were never mistaken for other mammals.

In 1673, Father Marquette during his descent of the Mississippi River found buffalo in good numbers at a place north of Rock Island (latitude 40°28') in July. He said they grazed upon the banks of the river and he saw 400 in one herd (French, 1846). In another account of Marquette's travels (Thwaites, 1900) it is noted that the missionaries when coming down the Mississippi River found a change in vegetation and topography at about 42° latitude and saw only deer and cattle [=bison] below that point. Of the Illinois River they said, "We have seen nothing like this river that we enter, as regards its fertility of soil, its prairies and woods, its cattle [=bison], elk, deer, wildcats . . . and even beaver" (p. 161). Marquette's party killed buffalo and deer for meat on their trips. Buffalo were abundant along the Illinois River throughout the 1700's. Deschamps said that in the late 1700's, when going up the river near Peoria he was nearly swamped in his canoe by a herd of buffalo swimming across the river (Matson, 1872).

In December 1679 and January 1680, Sieur de La Salle traversed and explored the valley of the Illinois River. La Salle and his party knew that buffalo were plentiful but they could not find enough for meat, presumably because the Miami Indians had fired the prairie in their autumn hunt (Hennepin, 1880). Hennepin describes such a hunt. "When they [the Miamis] see a herd, they gather in great numbers, and set fire to the grass every where around these animals, except some passage which they leave on purpose, and where they take post with their bows and arrows. The buffalo, seeking to escape the fire, are thus compelled to pass near these Indians, who sometimes kill as many as a hundred and twenty in a

Fig. 6.1. Bull bison. (From Garretson, The American Bison, New York Zool. Soc.)

day . . ." (p. 143). Hennepin traveled from Fort Miamis at the mouth of the Chicago River to the village of the Illinois Indians, on the Illinois River, in December 1679, and found an innumerable quantity of wild bulls [=bison]. In 1668, Pierre Liette joined a group of Illinois Indians for a five-week buffalo hunt near the Illinois River (Quaife, 1947). More than 1,200 buffaloes were killed.

In southern Illinois, bison were abundant in the early 1700's. A good account of this is given by Moyers (1931) where he points out that from early 1703 until April 1704, a party of French hunters worked the Big Muddy (=Au Vase) and Wabash rivers, as well as the Tennessee, Cumberland, and Castor rivers and Apple Creek and took the skins from 13,000 bison. This number may be subject to question, but the hunters apparently encountered many bison. The hides were cached in depots where they could be reached by small boats and taken to a larger receiving area. Several of the depots were located in Illinois: Bel Garde near the mouth of Massac Creek, one at Francefort (=Frankfort), at or near Kingkaid Hill in Jackson County, and possibly at Stone Fort, Saline County (Moyers, 1931:64). These depots were guarded by four or five French soldiers. Moyers (1931:64) points out that the "Francefort depot, with its little rifle-pits, was near, or upon, one of the largest buffalo trails of southern Illinois. That trail . . . may be seen today a mile west of West Frankfort. . . . The buffalos roamed the great forest southward, frequented the salt springs, and wandered northward far up the Grand Trace."

In the early 1700's, there were reports of bison throughout much of Illinois. For example, Kip (1866:38–39) refers to a letter from Father Rasles of October 12, 1723, which says, "Of all the nations of Canada, there are none who live in so great abundance of everything as the Illinois. . . . Not a year passes but they (the Indians) kill more than a thousand buffaloes. From four to five

thousand of the latter can often be seen at one view grazing on the prairies."

J. A. Allen (1876) reviews some of the records for the early 1700's. Father Marest saw bison along the Kankakee River in 1712; Charlevoix in 1721 found bison along the Illinois River below the junction of the Kankakee River; Vandreuil in 1718 found them on the bluffs of the Rock River. Charlevoix makes some interesting observations on their habitat along the Illinois River. "In this Route we see only vast Meadows, with little clusters of Trees here and there, which seem to have been planted by the Hand; the Grass grows so high in them, that one might lose one's self amongst it; but everywhere we meet with Paths that are as beaten as they can be in the most populous Countries; yet nothing passes through them but Buffaloes, and from time to time some Herds of Deer, and some Roe-Bucks."

In writing about Kaskaskia in 1750, Father Villier (Thwaites, 1900, vol. 69) says "It is usually necessary to go [from Kaskaskia] . . . seven or eight [leagues] to find oxen." Beckwith (1879:210) quotes George Croghan as making the following entry in his journal of June 18–19, 1765, of travels from Vincennes to Quiatanon:

We traveled through a prodigious large meadow, called the Pyankeshaws' hunting ground. Here is no wood to be seen, and the country appears like an ocean. The ground is exceedingly rich and partially overgrown with wild hemp. The land is well watered and full of buffalo, deer, bears, and all kinds of wild game. [Continuing for June 20–21] . . . We passed through some very large meadows, part of which belonged to the Pyankeshaws on the Vermilion River. The country and soil were much the same as that we traveled over for these three days past. . . . The game is very plenty.

In 1763, Hicks (1877:29) in writing about the history of Kendall County says that "the snow fell, it is said, twelve feet deep—the severest winter ever known—and the buffaloes, cut off from their supplies, wholly perished." In an account of the history of Kane County, Wilcox (1904:624) reported on an Indian story about a winter of incredible snow and spring flooding that accounted for the extinction of the bison, but gave no date for the story. In the winter of 1806–1807, thousands of bison in the Mississippi Valley perished. Marsh (1978) in reviewing a family history of Mercer County says the buffalo could swim the Mississippi River but herds sometimes broke through the ice in the winter. He goes on to say that the family journal records that 7,380 carcasses of bison were counted on the shore of the river on May 2, 1807, having fallen through the ice the preceding winter. In a history of Kankakee County (Honde and Klasey, 1968), it is recorded that the Indians told the early settlers that buffalo in Illinois were killed by the tens of thousands during the hard winter of 1779–1780.

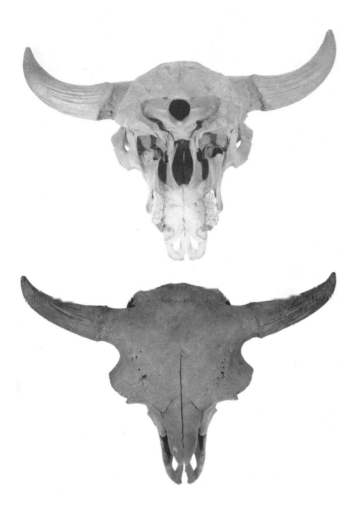

Fig. 6.2. Skull without horn-sheaths of *Bison bison* found near the Rock Island railroad bridge over Camping Run, near Wyoming, Stark Co., Illinois, in 1924. This partially mineralized skull was discovered when the bridge was washed out by floods. The skull must be that of a native bison that died in Illinois in the early 1800's. The specimen, obtained by Mr. E. E. Brown, is in the University of Illinois Museum of Natural History. Greatest length of the skull is 525 mm.

By the beginning of the nineteenth century, the number of bison in Illinois was greatly reduced. Probably the combination of severe winters in the late 1700's and early 1800's and the hunting of these animals with rifles led to their decimation. Alvord (1965) in writing about the Illinois country of 1673 to 1818 said that bison disappeared in the first decade of the nineteenth century. Schoolcraft (1825:205) wrote, "It is but a few years since this last-mentioned animal [bison] was quite common on these plains. . . . There is not now an animal of this species existing, in a native state, between the Ohio and Mississippi." In the 1800's, there were published reports of bison bones found in good numbers in many counties in Illinois. In Bureau County, Matson (1872:313) observed, "In the early settlement of the country, buffalo bones were plenty on the prairies, and at three different places in this county, acres of ground were covered with

them, showing large herds had perished. Skulls of buffaloes, with the horns still on, were frequently found. . . ." Although there is no date, this must have been about 1815. The history of the bison in Illinois was well reviewed by an anonymous writer in 1837:

> The buffalo has entirely left the limits of the state. . . . This animal . . . so late as the commencement of the present [19th] century, was found in considerable numbers; and traces of them are still remaining in the buffalo paths, which are to be seen in several parts of the state. These are well-beaten tracks, leading generally from the prairies in the interior of the state to the margins of the large rivers, showing the course of their migrations as they changed their pastures periodically, from the low marshy alluvion, to the dry upland plains. Their paths are narrow, and . . . the animals travelled in single file through woods . . . (Anon, 1837:38).

Probably all native, wild bison were exterminated in Illinois before 1830, brought about by a number of factors, the most important of which was hunting pressure. Before European men arrived, Indians had difficulty killing buffalo, but once they had rifles, they were highly successful hunters. They sought the hides for trade for blankets, beads, axes, ammunition, and other items. The Indians rarely saved more than the tongue from the buffalo to eat. Also, many of the early settlers had much spare time and employed themselves hunting, especially bison and deer. Furthermore, as was noted earlier, adverse weather with heavy snows at the end of the 1700's and into the early 1800's killed off many bison.

Elk

Elk were known to early explorers and settlers as stags, cerfs, or elk. Sometimes it is difficult to be certain whether the early writers meant elk, *Cervus elaphus(=Cervus canadensis)*, or deer, *Odocoileus virginianus*.

In 1673, Father Marquette's party found that elk were common along the Illinois River (Thwaites, 1900, vol. 59). In 1712 "the plains and prairies [on either side of the Illinois River] are all covered with buffaloes, roebucks, hinds, stags . . ." according to Father Marest. In writing about the area of Union County of 1795, Andre Michaux (1795:72) noted, "My guide killed an Elk called Cerf by the Canadians and French of Illinois . . . Its antlers are twice the size of those of the European stags . . . This animal has canine teeth in the upper and lower jaw. . . ." There are relatively few references about elk in the literature of the 1700's, but they indicate that elk were present and not reduced in numbers. In 1778, a Captain Hutchens prepared a map on which he made notes along the Illinois River that read "Innumerable Herds of Buffaloe, Elk, & Deer feed here" (Taylor, 1979:5). There are some accounts which indicated that heavy snows in the 1760's may have been detrimental to this species.

Fig. 6.3. Elk—young, doe, and bull from left to right—roaming in a parklike zoo near Elgin, Illinois. Photograph by Charles Hume.

In the early 1800's, elk were still present. In 1811–1813, both elk and buffalo were present in Edwards County (J. Woods, 1822, in Thwaites, 1904). But Maximilian, in writing about the area of the Wabash River in 1832–1833, said elk together with buffalo, beaver, and bear had been extirpated. Elkhorn Grove and Creek were reportedly named for the large number of elk antlers found there before 1828. In the history of Kendall County (Hicks, 1877) it was reported that elk disappeared about 1818. The trade in elk hides ceased in Will County about 1820. By 1831, elk were gone from Peoria County (May, 1968). A history of Massac County indicated that by 1837 the buffalo was extinct and bear and elk were seldom seen (May, 1955:21), but a few elk persisted until as late as 1855, for one was killed at Tucker's Mill in "Lower Massac" (Page, 1900:65). In Jackson County, elk reportedly were extinct about 1835.

Elk were uncommon and probably nearly gone in northern Illinois by the 1820's and in southern Illinois by the 1830's.

White-tailed Deer

Deer in Illinois were referred to by early explorers and settlers by a variety of names: deer, roebuck, dwarf deer, chevreuil. Furthermore, it is not always certain when early writers were referring to white-tailed deer or to elk. Sometimes the reference was to deer and roebuck in the same sentence.

Nearly everywhere that the explorers of the 1600's reported bison, they also reported deer. Both of these animals were important food sources, but the writers seemed more impressed by the bison, perhaps because of their size and unique appearance. Throughout the 1700's there seemed to be no great decrease in numbers of deer. Father Rasles in writing in 1723 about the Illinois country said that roebucks were seen in vast herds and that Indians killed more than a thousand each year (Kip, 1866) and Father Villier noted that near Kaskaskia deer . . . "abound in all seasons, except near the inhabited portions" (Thwaites, 1900:143, vol. 69).

In 1820 in Edwards County, deer were present but they were more numerous in 1818 than in 1820 (Woods, 1822). J. Woods goes on to say (pp. 289–290), "Deer are not very numerous. I suppose, I have seen about 100, but never more than five or six together. [Woods expected them to be in large herds like buffalo.] I bought several in the winter, the greater part without their skins, at one dollar each, but one or two higher; one weighed more than 100 lb. weight. They generally weigh from 60 lb. to 100 lb. A good skin is worth 50 cents; their horns, though large, are of no value here." In Hancock County,

1,052 deer skins were received at the Fort Edwards trading post in 1818; 3,296 skins in 1819 (Hancock Co. 1968). One early settler wrote that there was no necessity for serving a single meal in his house without wild honey and either fresh or dried venison. In 1848, venison taken locally was selling in the markets of Chicago at three cents a pound. The killing of large numbers of deer can be found in many accounts. For example, in the history of Livingston County (Livingston County, 1878), there is an account of one man and his son killing more than a thousand deer in the early 1800's. Deer were not bringing in much money, for in 1834, 75 of them, consisting of skins and "hams" only, were sold for $60 in Ottawa.

In Franklin County around 1860, hunters turned to hunting deer from horseback and using dogs. Several riders would close in on an area and shoot the deer as they attempted to escape (Gallatin County, 1887).

F. C. Piatt (1883) in his account of the history of Piatt County said that 11 fawns were captured and shipped to New York in 1856. There was no indication of the survival or fate of these deer.

In the late 1800's, the deer population declined rapidly. Whereas many deer were seen in Lee County in the mid-1800's, they were an "impossible sight" in 1893. Partridge in writing about the history of Lake County (Bateman and Selby, 1902:623) noted that deer "increased after Indians left, but finally were killed off" with a few persisting in the O'Plain [?] Woods even as late as 1871. "Deer were abundant as late as 1850 [in Will County]. They disappeared rapidly after that because settlers came in immediately following that date. Firearms and dogs were destructive . . ." (Mane, 1928:145). Deer were extinct in Kendall County in the early 1870's (Bateman and Selby, 1914, 620, vol. 2). By 1902, deer were so scarce in Brown County that the hunting season was closed (Brown Co., 1972). They may have been scarce for several years *before* 1902, also. Bradsby (1885) reported that "Locust Spring was the last spot in the county [Bureau] with deer" but he does not give a date. In Champaign County, deer were "nearly or quite extinct" by 1860 (Bateman and Selby, 1905:699), but there was evidence that some were still seen that winter. In Madison County, deer were "still occasionally seen as late as 1860" (Norton, 1912:184).

The history of white-tailed deer in Illinois from the late 1800's until the present time is reviewed also under *Remarks* in the account of *Odocoileus virginianus*.

Black Bear

Bears were called only bears in the early literature and they were not confused with other species of mammals. Thus when early writers referred to bears there is little doubt about what they meant. It seems, however, that bears were *expected* in Illinois, and were taken for granted, although not much was said about them other than their being present or absent.

Bears were used by early explorers and settlers as a source of food and hides. Reports indicate that Indians rarely used bears as food but they did use the canine teeth in necklaces and perhaps also the claws.

Father Binneteau in his account of the Illinois country of 1699 (in Thwaites, 1900, vol. 65) stated that for the early explorers the ox (=bison), bear, and deer were the main meats. In the same publication, Father Gravier in 1700 reported seeing more than 50 bears in one day along the Mississippi River between the present sites of St. Louis and Cairo. The few reports that we have from the 1700's all indicate that bears were present and in some cases in great numbers or they "abound" except near settlements. As late as November 6, 1834, a black bear was shot "on the south branch above Madison Street" in Chicago (Goodspeed and Healey, 1909:107).

In the early 1800's, Birbeck (1818:115) in writing about his travels in and around Edwards County said, "We saw no bears, as they are now [August 1] buried in the thickets, and seldom appear by day; but, at every few yards, we saw recent marks of their doings, 'wallowing' in the long grass, or turning over the decayed logs in quest of beetles or worms. . . ."

Bears were encountered in much of Illinois until near the mid-1800's. Bears were extinct in Peoria County in 1831, and were extirpated along the Wabash River by 1852–1853. The last one killed in Bond County was in 1821. Bears were seen as late as 1855 in Massac County, and they were thought to be extinct in Madison County by 1866.

In most places in Illinois in the 1850's or slightly before, bears were sufficiently rare that if one were seen or reported, it caused considerable interest.

Fig. 6.4. Black bear, *Ursus americanus*. Photograph by John L. Tveten.

Fig. 6.5. Mounted specimen of a wolf, *Canis lupus,* in the University of Illinois Museum of Natural History. Specimen from Minnesota.

Wolf

Many early reports—and even certain more recent reports—on mammals encountered in Illinois made no distinction between wolves, *Canis lupus,* and coyotes, *Canis latrans.* I am regarding most references in the early literature to grey (or gray) wolves, timber wolves, or true wolves as *Canis lupus* and references to prairie wolves or small wolves as *Canis latrans.* Some accounts refer to three kinds of wolves in the state: timber or black wolf, gray wolf, and prairie wolf or coyote. In such cases, I assume the first two references are to *Canis lupus.* When the reference is only to "wolf," I have analyzed the description and when possible have assigned the reference to either *C. lupus* or *C. latrans.* In many cases, however, it is impossible to do this and the reference is not considered in the discussion.

In 1818, Hubbard (1911:119) reported that a large female timber wolf and her cubs attacked a squaw near Peoria. In the 1830's, John Dixon who ran the Dixon ferry on the Rock River said, that "wolf" pelts brought from twenty-five to thirty-three cents and that over a five-year span, 50 wolf hides were sold (Barge, 1918:71). In another account of Lee County, "In those early days [late 1830's] the wolves were in great number" and one doctor reportedly put strychnine into balls of bread or meat and threw them to the wolves that followed him on his rounds (Smith, 1893:284). A similar account is given for Grundy County.

In an account of a family in Mercer County, probably about 1853, reference is made to both timber wolves and coyotes (Marsh, 1978:39). In a history of Du Page County, there is an account of wolves and wolf hunting about 1846 (Richmond, 1876), but it is not certain whether this pertains to *Canis lupus* or *Canis latrans.*

In 1826, wolves were said to be so numerous in Woodstock Township, Schuyler County, "that they would chase the dogs clear to the cabin door..." (Schuyler-Brown cos., 1882). In Livingston County, both wolves and coyotes were present in the early 1800's. In an account of Clark County, Perrin (1883) says that the large timber wolf was the prevailing species in Darwin Township, but it is not clear what year he refers to. It apparently was in the first half of the 1800's.

In some parts of Illinois bounties were offered for wolf and coyote scalps, but no distinction between the two species was made. In a history of Madison County (Madison, 1882:128) one reads "On December 30th, 1815, a wolf scalp law was enacted. One of the stipulations of this law made it necessary for applicants for premiums to solemnly swear that they had never willingly spared the life of a 'bitch wolf' with a design to increase the breed."

In a history of Coles County, Wilson (1906:621) stated that the "panther, wildcat, the black timber wolf, large gray wolf, and, in vastly large numbers, the prairie wolf or coyote" were present. This reference must have been for a period in the early 1800's. The same relationship of numbers was true in Effingham County, with prairie wolves (=coyote) more common. The attacks on cattle and horses in cold weather must have been made by *Canis lupus.*

The laws of the Illinois Territory in the early 1800's encouraged the killing of wolves (species not specified). In 1822, an act of law read as follows:

AN ACT to encourage the destruction of Wolves.
Sec. 1. *Be it enacted by the people of the state of Illinois represented in the general assembly,* That the person who shall kill the greatest number of wolves, not less than sixty, within this state, between the fifteenth day of April one thousand eight hundred and twenty-three, and the fifteenth day of November, one thousand eight hundred and twenty-four, shall be entitled to the sum of two hundred dollars; and the person who shall kill, within the time aforesaid, the greatest number of wolves, not less than ten, within the limits of any one county in this state, shall be entitled to the sum of twenty dollars: *Provided,* that when it shall appear that two or more persons applying for the same

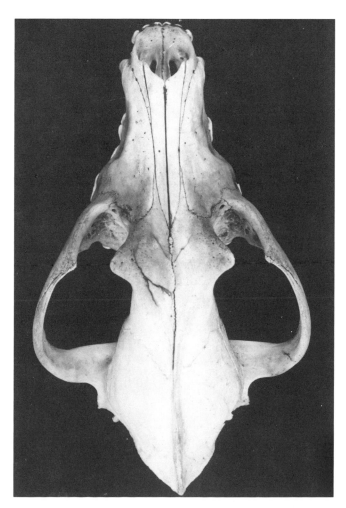

Fig. 6.6. Photograph of skull of *Canis lupus,* Four Town Lake, St. Louis Co., Minnesota. No. 1148, University of Illinois Museum of Natural History. Sex unknown; 252 mm greatest length of skull.

premium, have killed, as aforesaid, an equal and the highest number of wolves, such premium shall be divided equally among such persons.

Sec. 2. *Be it further enacted,* That it shall be the duty of every person wishing to obtain any of the above premiums, to take the scalps with the ears entire, to the clerk of the county commissioners' court of the county in which he resides, which clerk shall administer to him an oath or affirmation in the following form, to-wit: "I, A.B. do solemnly swear, (or affirm, as the case may be,) that the scalps now presented by me, are the scalps of wild wolves, which have been killed by me, within the limits of this state, (or this county, as the case may require,) since the fifteenth day of April, one thousand eight hundred and twenty-three." And whoever shall take such oath or affirmation, knowing it to be false, shall be deemed guilty of perjury, and shall suffer such punishment as is now, or may be hereafter prescribed by law for persons guilty of wilful and corrupt perjury; and it shall be the duty of said clerk to destroy said scalps, and to give to such person taking such oath or affirmation a certificate. . . .

By 1825, the premium for each wolf was only one dollar, but the county commissioner could raise it to two dollars, with the county picking up the difference. In 1837, the Act read that "big wolves" of six months or older receive one dollar, each wolf of six months or younger, fifty cents, and prairie wolves fifty cents. In 1839, the premiums went to two, one, and one dollar, respectively. According to Auditor's Report for Illinois, the following amounts were paid out by the State for wolf counties: 1830, $32.21; 1837, $13.00; 1838, $390.50; 1839, $709.00; 1840, $2,578.50; December 1, 1820 to December 1, 1842, $12,037.00; 1842–1844, $4,057.00; 1844–1846, $405.50, 1846–1848, $63.50; 1848–1850, $13.00; 1850–1852, $2.00.

These figures indicate that wolves, both *Canis lupus* and *Canis latrans,* were disappearing or becoming scarce, interest in collecting them was waning, or that the state was going out of the bounty business. Perhaps all three factors were involved.

In my estimation, wolves, *Canis lupus,* disappeared from Illinois sometime before 1860. References to wolves in Illinois, including figures on bounties paid for wolves, in the late 1800's are actually to coyotes, which have usually been called prairie wolves in this state. The reference by Cory (1912) to wolves in Illinois in the early 1900's must certainly be to large coyotes. If there have been any wolves in Illinois in the 20th century, they must have been imported from outside of the state and have escaped into the wild.

Coyote

As pointed out in the account on "Wolf," it is difficult in many instances to determine if early references to wolves were for prairie wolves (=coyotes), *Canis latrans,* or grey or timber wolves, *Canis lupus.*

A report of 1750 (Father Villier in Thwaites, 1900:209, vol. 69) of the area near Kaskaskia noted that there were numbers of wolves which were much smaller than those of Europe and much less daring. J. Woods' (1822) account of travels in the early 1800's in Edwards County mentions wolves that howled at night, but these actually may have been coyotes.

Early observers were aware of the fact that the coyotes in Illinois were of large size and larger than individuals in the Southwest. For example, in the history of Kane County (Wilcox, 1904:624) it was pointed out that "Prairie wolves were very numerous, but they should not be confounded with the coyotes of the western plains. They were much larger and bolder than the latter. In size they were midway between the timber wolf and coyote." In the mid-1800's, an account of Grundy County said, "The wolves were of the coyote species . . . and a bounty was early offered by the county for their scalps" (Ulbrich, 1968:265).

It is difficult to know whether the references are to coyotes or wolves, or both, that were so abundant in some localities in the mid 1800's that the county governments offered bounties. For example, in Bureau County, "in 1851, a bounty of $1.50 was offered on wolf scalps" (Bradsby, 1885:280). Probably the bounty was paid on either species—coyote or wolf—that was brought in.

Matson (1867:15) in writing about Bureau County said, "the big black and gray wolves were occasionally seen; but the greatest pests were the prairie wolves, they were very plenty, and their howling could be heard almost every night. They lived on the prairie, and would come forth at night and attack sheep, pigs, etc. They have about all disappeared." Baldwin (1877:516) in discussing the fauna of La Salle County says that

the prairie wolf here found their natural habitat, and existed by thousands. They are a bold, impudent, and mischievous animal, living on rabbits, birds, lambs, pigs, poultry, green corn, watermelons, berries, and almost every thing that comes in their way. They burrow in the ground usually or some high ridge of the prairie, to rear their young, having from six to ten at a litter . . . Hunting them on horseback, with dogs and grayhounds [sic] to lead, was exhilarating sport . . . and if the wolf [=coyote] did not reach the covert of a thicket or timber, was pretty sure to yield up his skin.

This account, published in 1877, went on to say that "the prairie wolves are not yet exterminated."

Mountain Lion and Bobcat

It is difficult to determine whether some of the earlier references in the literature about Illinois are to *Felis rufus*, bobcat, or to *Felis concolor*, mountain lion. For example, in 1677 Father Allovey in writing about the Kaskaskia Indians says they hunted "the Wildcat, a species

of tiger" and in 1669, Father Binneteau says that such animals as "wildcats, lynxes, . . ." were present. In 1688, Pierre Liette (In Quaife, 1947:102) hunted with the Indians for five weeks and describes an animal which probably was a mountain lion.

We also killed some animals which the Illinois and Miami call Quinousaoveia, which signifies the big tails, as they have tails more than two feet long, a head like that of a cat, a body about three feet long, a very lank belly and long legs, and fur reddish and very short. They move faster than any other beast for two or three arpents [about 386 to 579 feet]. If they were as common as wolves we should not see so many bucks in that country, for they live only on these.

The animal that is known by such names as mountain lion, cougar, or puma in many parts of its range was almost always called a panther by the early settlers in Illinois. Sometimes it was called catamount or painter. By the 1800's, most reports seemed to distinguish between panthers, *Felis concolor*, and wildcats or lynxes (=bobcats), *Felis rufus*.

Mountain Lion

By the early 1800's, Woods (1822, in Thwaites, 1904:288) says "Of panthers I have seen nothing, and hear but little; a noted hunter told me, he had followed hunting steadily (an American phrase) for twenty years and had never seen one; but that others, who had hunted but little, had sometimes killed one. It is said to be a fierce animal." Hubbard (1911) in describing the winter fare in 1818–1819 along the Illinois River mentioned venison, racoon, panther, bear, and turkey.

A Panther Creek in St. Marys Township of Hancock County was named for a panther supposedly killed here (Hancock County, 1968). In 1857, a panther was sighted in Henderson County (Mercer-Henderson County, 1882). In an account of the Spoon River country, there is a comment that "Father was not what you might call a great hunter but he killed a few catamounts and many wildcats . . ." (Spoon River, 1970:14). In Christian County in 1825, a hunter killed a panther that was described as nine feet from nose to tip of tail and which was the source for the naming of Panther Creek in that county (Drennan and Broverman, 1968). About 1823, a panther was seen at a sugaring camp in Vermilion County (Beckwith, 1879). The history of Madison County (1882) included reports that panthers were present in the county as late as 1850, but in another place (page 544), it stated, "The neighbors said of him, that he killed several bears and panthers in this neighborhood [Saline Township], and the three pointed out to me where he shot the last panther, in 1818." This same account recorded that in Alhambra Township, Madison County, one man killed seven panthers in the winter of 1817.

Panthers in the early 1800's were reported from Coles, Jasper, Bond, Marion, Lawrence, Gallatin, Pope, and Massac counties, but numbers or other comments were not given.

Late records of mountain lions (panthers) include one of "about 1858" near Brownsville (Husband, 1973:4). Cory (1912:282) gave reports of one killed in Macoupin County in 1840 and one east of Thebes, Alexander County, around 1862. Cory was skeptical of a report of one panther seen in Pope County in 1905, as I would be also. Mane (1928:147) stated in his history of Will County that panthers were absent there by 1870. Probably all panthers or mountain lions were exterminated in Illinois before 1870.

Bobcat

Bobcats were referred to by the early settlers as wildcats or lynxes, and rarely as bobcats. In the early literature, there are several references to wildcats and lynxes, as if the writer was referring to *Felis rufus* and *Felis lynx*. For example, in Kendall County, there is a statement that "wild cat and lynx . . . have been known here" (Hicks, 1877); in Lake County, "Wild cats and lynx were frequently killed" (Bateman and Selby, 1902). Other accounts will list a series of animals in which wildcats and lynxes are included. An example of this is in the history of Bond County which "abounded in all of the wild animals common in this latitude — bears, panthers, lynxes, wolves, catamounts, wild cats, deer . . ." (Perrin, 1883). There is no reason to believe that these writers had any basis for differentiating between *Felis rufus* and *Felis lynx* and I am not convinced that the Canada lynx, *Felis lynx,* was ever present in Illinois.

In the early literature that we surveyed, bobcats (wildcats) were reported from 43 counties in Illinois. These tended to be in those counties with heavy timber stands, especially along the major waterways, although bobcats probably did occur in every county of the state in the 1700's and early 1800's.

A history of Hancock County (1968) indicates that in 1819 at Fort Edwards, 51 wildcat skins were handled at the post. At Dixon's ferry trading post, Lee County, between 1830 and 1835, only nine wildcat pelts were handled, and these sold for twenty-five cents each (Barge, 1918:37).

Bobcats were greatly reduced in numbers in the state about the time the mountain lion disappeared. The "last one" was killed in De Kalb County around 1885, were absent in La Salle County before 1877, were present in Piatt County until 1860, to mention a few reports. They probably persisted in low numbers in various parts of the state until the mid-1900's. See further comments in the account of *Felis rufus* (p. 311).

River Otter

In 1832, Maximilian, Prince of Wied, reported that river otter were common in the Wabash River, probably from its mouth to above New Harmony, Indiana. (Thwaites, 1843). Otter were reported as abundant in Clark County in the early 1800's but a specific locality is not given.

Reports of otter in the Ohio River are not well known to me. May (1955) and Page (1900) in histories of Massac County indicate that otter were present in the early days, but are not specific as to date or place. J. W. Allen (1949) indicates that otter were present at an earlier time in Pope County.

River otter were most abundant along the Mississippi River and records from trading posts in this area indicate this. At Fort Edwards, Hancock County, 26 otter skins were handled at the post in 1818; 33 in 1819. Morgan (1968) says that the otter furs exported from Illinois trading posts in 1816 was 400.

River otter were well distributed along the Illinois River. Early reports indicate their presence in numerous counties bordering this river: Will, Grundy, La Salle, Bureau, Peoria, Fulton, Mason, Schuler, Brown, and Jersey. They were also present along the Kankakee River.

Otter began to disappear in the mid-1800's. During these years, such reports appear as "have almost disappeared [1872]" in Bureau County, "seldom seen now [1877]" in La Salle County, "extinct in the county" [Schuyler and Brown counties before 1882], "very rare" but still found [Piatt County, 1883], otter "rarely seen" [Randolph, Perry, and Monroe counties, 1883], "present locally until about 1860 [Whiteside County]," and "observed as late as 1850's [Kane County]."

Badger

Judging from the early literature, badgers occurred as far south in Illinois as Brown, Piatt, and Vermilion counties before the 1850's. Furthermore, they must have occurred near the Indiana line because Jones (1911) in a history of Vermilion County says that badgers "were also plenty" and infers that this is in the mid-1850's. Several counties north of these counties reported badgers.

Accounts of the early history of Christian and Madison counties indicate that badgers were present, but these accounts appear to be copied from some other source and do not represent factual information based upon actual records for the counties. A history of St. Clair County (Bateman and Selby, 1907) indicated that badgers were present, but these comments may not be specifically for St. Clair County.

Beaver

Wherever there was ample water, beaver were common in Illinois at the time of settlement of this country by Europeans. The unrestrained taking of beaver resulted in their decline in the late 1800's, however, and by the early 1900's they were nearly or entirely exterminated. Cory (1912:161) wrote that "at the present time they are practically exterminated in Illinois, although it is probable that a very few individuals may exist in the extreme southern portion of the state."

Marquette in commenting about his second trip in Illinois in 1674–1675 said the Indians gave beaver skins as gifts (Thwaites, 1900:177). Intensive trapping of beaver in Illinois did not begin until the late 1700's and early 1800's. The pressure by European trappers to get as many beaver as possible probably stimulated the Indians into seeking them more intensively.

It is reported (Belting, 1948) that in the 1700's an inventory for one trapper at the time of his death indicated that he had taken 4,443 pounds of beaver. At the Fort Edwards trading post, Hancock County, 199 beaver pelts were handled in 1819. Beaver taken on the Rock and Mississippi rivers in 1831 brought $2 a pound (Barge, 1918).

Before the interior swampy parts of the state were ditched and drained, beaver were present. In writing about Champaign County, Cunningham (1905) reported that beavers and beaver dams were found by the earliest comers. Wood (1910:536) said, "There was an extensive dam on the South Fork a few miles above Urbana, and several others, less generally known, on the lower part of the Salt Fork." In the early 1800's, Birbeck (1818) found that a swamp north of Old Shawneetown "is only passable for man over the dams made by beavers."

By the late 1800's, repeated references to the disappearance of the beaver are found. These include: "Early settlers claimed that beavers . . . were present locally until about 1860" [Whiteside County]; "trappers extirpated him many years ago" [Kendall County, 1871]; extinct by 1831 [Peoria County]; disappeared about 1900 [Carroll County]; beaver disappeared before 1912 [Madison County].

Porcupine

Porcupine remains have been found in Illinois in a cave deposit near Columbia, Monroe County (Meyer Cave). At least 10 individuals were recovered (Parmalee, 1967:121). Also, remains were found in the Archaic Indian Riverton Site, 2 miles northeast of Palestine, Crawford County (Parmalee, 1963).

Because of these prehistoric records of porcupine in Illinois as well as early records for Indiana (Lyon, 1936), probably northeastern Iowa (Bowles, 1975) and southernmost Wisconsin (Jackson, 1961), I expected to find references in the literature to porcupines in Illinois in the late 1700's or 1800's. Such is not the case, however.

Early histories of counties in Illinois where one might expect porcupines to be present make no mention of them. Many accounts enumerate not only large mammals, but smaller ones also, such as "gray gophers" and "striped gophers" [=ground squirrels], rats, mice, moles, tree squirrels, but no porcupines. We have looked especially at reports of those counties which were heavily wooded.

Kennicott (1858:91) stated that he was "not aware that it [the porcupine] has been observed in Northern Illinois, though it is said to inhabit Whiteside county and the banks of the Illinois River." In my own survey, however, I can find no proof of its presence in Whiteside County nor along the Illinois River.

Lyon in his account of the mammals of Indiana (1936) gave a map of published records with dates of observation. Within 40 miles of Illinois, eight Indiana counties were reported to have porcupines, and the years of their reported presence were 1832, 1834, 1837, 1882, 1884, and 1910.

Some early histories of Illinois not seen by us may verify the presence of porcupines within historic times in Illinois.

Pleistocene and Holocene Mammals Known from Illinois

Mammalian remains are known in Illinois from the Pleistocene (often called the Ice Age) and Holocene (mostly the last 10,000 years and when early man was present). The remains are known as fossilized skeletal material or as remains from archaeological sites.

The Pleistocene in Illinois consisted of four glacial stages of extreme cold with nearly all or only parts of the state covered with ice and snow. Between these four periods there were three major interglacial periods with much warmer climates and much free water, producing rivers and lakes. Although some kinds of mammals lived in Illinois during periods of glaciation, such as the muskox, mammoth, and mastodon, most flourished in the interglacial periods.

The deeper valleys in Illinois were trenched at the close of the first (Nebraskan) and second (Kansan) glacial periods (Frye et al., 1965). Nebraskan glaciers entered Illinois only in the western part. Kansan glaciers entered

Fig. 6.7. Giant ground sloths, *Megalonyx jeffersonii* (Desmarest), were the size of bison, fed on vegetation, and were related to the armadillos and anteaters. (From Hoffmeister and Mohr, 1957. Charles A. McLaughlin)

Illinois on both the west and east, and were not extensive in the state. The third period of glaciation, the Illinoian stage, covered much of Illinois. The final glaciation, the Wisconsin stage, was extensive in northern Illinois, extending as far south as the Shelbyville moraine. This stage of glaciation may have persisted in the state until as recently as 15,000 years before the present. In its retreat, this glaciation deposited the remnants of at least 30 moraines. By 10,000 years before the present, the topography in Illinois may have been much as it is today, but climatic conditions may have varied considerably since that time.

Megalonyx jeffersonii (Desmarest), Giant ground sloth

Giant ground sloths are members of the order Edentata or, as they are often called, the order Xenarthra. Included in the order are the armadillos, anteaters, and sloths. Many of the species lack teeth. When a few premolars and molars are present, these teeth lack enamel and have a single root. Giant ground sloths were of large size, being as large as bisons, and often supported themselves on their hind legs and broad tail while feeding on leaves and twigs at some distance above the ground. The toes were heavily clawed.

Some records of occurrence include: Champaign, Champaign Co. (Hay, 1914:128); Glen Carbon, Madison Co. (UI): Urbana, Champaign Co. (Hay, 1923); 1 mi S Ashmore, Coles Co. (FM).

Castoroides ohioensis Foster, Giant beaver

Giant beaver were especially large rodents and were thought to be more than eight times the bulk of the present-day beaver, *Castor canadensis*. They apparently looked like modern beaver but had shorter legs. The structure of the incisor teeth indicates that they were not good chiselers or gnawers and they probably fed on softer materials, much like muskrats do, rather than cutting trees. These giant beavers preferred lakes and ponds formed by retreating glaciers and therefore were not dam-builders.

Some records of occurrence include: New Bedford, Bureau Co. (UI); Bellflower, McLean Co. (UI); Galena, Jo Daviess Co. (Hay, 1914:468); 1 mi S Ashmore, Coles Co. (FM).

[The publication by Bader and Techter (1959) of a list of fossil mammals of Illinois included *Canis mississippiensis*, wolf, which some persons thought was allied to the dire wolf, *Canis dirus*. I found no evidence to justify the inclusion of the species for Illinois. Galbreath (1938:309) refers an upper canine tooth tentatively to *Ursus horribilis*, grizzly bear, but I doubt the presence of this animal in Illinois.]

Mammut americanum (Kerr), American mastodon

American mastodons are elephant-sized with well-developed upper tusks that tend to be almost parallel with each other (not greatly curved outward), teeth with distinctive cusps that are opposite one another, column-like legs, and extended proboscis.

The habits of the mastodon must have been much the same as those of present-day elephants. They apparently were browsers, feeding on leaves and branches.

Records of remains of *Mammut americanum* are common in Illinois and the species may well have occurred in every county at one time. Some records are: North Alton, Madison Co. (UI); Easton, Mason Co. (UI); Calhoun Co. (UI); St. Claire Co. (UI); Roberts, Ford Co. (UI); 2 mi W Canton, Fulton Co. (UI); 5 mi S Rossville, Vermilion Co. (UI); Mattoon, Coles Co. (UI); Hume, Edgar Co. (UI); 2½ mi E Farmer City, De Witt Co. (UI); 1 mi S. Ashmore, Coles Co. (FM).

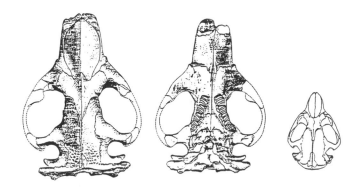

Fig. 6.8. Skull of giant beaver, *Castoroides ohioensis*, from near Bellflower, McLean County, Illinois (in collection of University of Illinois Museum of Natural History). A skull of the present-day beaver, *Castor canadensis*, is shown for comparison. All skulls are drawn to the same scale. Greatest length of the skull of *C. ohioensis* is 296 mm. Drawings of *C. ohioensis* are modified from Stirton, 1965.

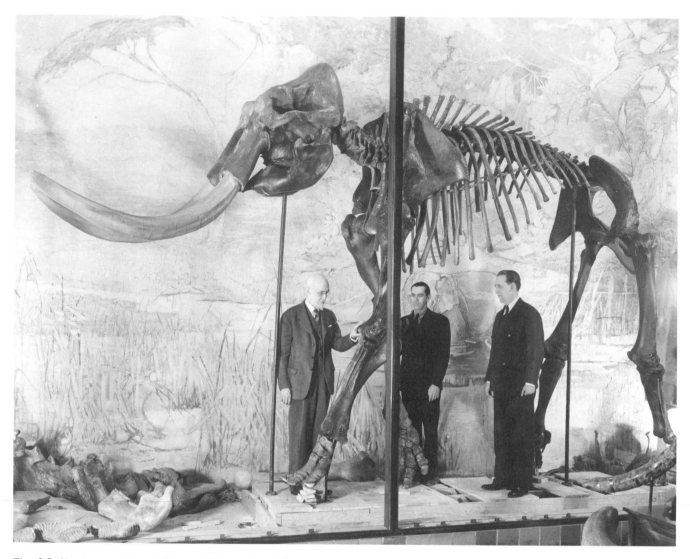

Fig. 6.9. Nearly complete skeleton of *Mammuthus jeffersoni* collected at Kewanee, Henry Co., Illinois. The articulated mammoth skeleton is shown here being placed on display in the University of Nebraska State Museum. Photograph courtesy of the University of Nebraska State Museum.

Mammuthus jeffersoni (Osborn) and *Mammuthus primigenius* (Blumenbach), Mammoth

Mammoths were as large, or larger, than present-day elephants, tusks in the upper jaw bowed outward but curved inward near the tips; cheek teeth consisted of a number of transverse plates, each plate containing enamel, cement, and dentine.

Two species apparently lived in Illinois and they are distinguishable by the number of plates in the tooth. Since most reported finds are not identified as to species, I have not attempted to discuss the two separately.

The feeding habits of mammoths must have been much the same as present-day elephants because their teeth are so similar.

Mammoths were widespread in Illinois. Some known records of occurrence are: Calhoun Co. (UI); Toledo, Cumberland Co. (UI); 2 mi E Champaign, Champaign Co. (UI); Morton, Cumberland Co. (UI); Near Rossville, Vermilion Co. (UI); 2¾ mi S, 1 mi W Pekin, Tazewell Co. (UI); Lacon, Marshall Co. (UI); ½ mi E Belleview, Calhoun Co. (UI).

Equus complicatus Leidy, Horse

Remains of the horse, consisting mostly of a few teeth, have been referred to the species *Equus complicatus*. This species was much like the present-day horse *Equus caballus*. It is not clear whether they should be called *E. complicatus* or *E. caballus*.

Record of occurrence: Bond Co. (Hay, 1914:178).

Fig. 6.10. American mastodons, *Mammut americanum* (Kerr), were the size of elephants, to which they were closely related, and were common throughout the Illinois area during the Pleistocene. (From Hoffmeister and Mohr, 1957. Charles A. McLaughlin)

Fig. 6.11. Slightly larger than mastodons, mammoths had heavy, often curved tusks. Their cheek teeth consisted of a number of fused, transverse plates. (From Hoffmeister and Mohr, 1957. Charles A. McLaughlin)

Platygonus compressus LeConte, Peccary

Piglike mammals referred to the species *Platygonus compressus* looked much like hogs but had longer legs and were about 2½ ft high at the shoulders.

These peccaries apparently were present in parts of Illinois after the last or Wisconsin ice-sheet.

Specimens have been reported from near Galena, Jo Daviess County, and Alton, Madison County.

Cervalces sp., Stag-moose

An animal with features of both a moose and an elk, known as *Cervalces*, reportedly was present in Illinois at the end of the last glaciation. Antlers were moose-like but the face was much like an elk. Stag-moose were especially long-legged. Remains referred to this genus have been found 7 mi E Springfield, Sangamon Co. (ISM); Ashmore, Coles Co. (FM).

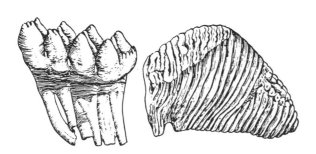

Fig. 6.12. Cheek tooth of mastodon (left) and mammoth (right). The mastodon tooth has distinct cusps; the mammoth, a series of fused transverse plates. Illinois State Geological Survey. (From Hoffmeister and Mohr, 1957)

Rangifer sp., Caribou

Remains have been found near Alton, Madison Co., that have been referred to *Rangifer*. These could be referrable to a form described from near Muscatine, Iowa, and called *Rangifer muscatinensis* Leidy.

Antilocapra americana (Ord), Pronghorn

Pronghorns have never been reported in Illinois and not observed closer than westernmost Iowa. Fryxell (1926:333) reported on a horn he found at Moline, buried in 18 inches of alluvium. Fryxell points out that this horn may have been brought here by early Indian traders. The horn seemingly showed no fossilization. For some reason, Bader and Techter (1959) included this species in their list of fossil mammals of Illinois.

Symbos cavifrons (Leidy), Musk-ox

Extinct musk-oxen of the species *Symbos cavifrons* were the size of cattle, with the horns rising immediately behind the eyes and directed outward, slightly downward, and forward. In all likelihood they had a long, shaggy coat of hair. (Fig. 6.13, p. 40.)

Symbos remains have been found in states surrounding Illinois and as far south as Arkansas. Some records of Illinois occurrence are Bondville, Champaign Co. (UI); Bellflower, McLean Co. (UI); Sec. 27 (NW ¼), T 11 N, R 4 W, Lawrence Co. (SIC).

Bison sp., Bison

Remains of fossil *Bison* have been found in Illinois and states adjacent to it, and referred to the species *B. occidentalis*, *B. antiquus*, and *B. bison*. Remains of a

Fig. 6.13. Extinct musk-ox, *Symbos cavifrons* (Leidy), that lived in Illinois during the Pleistocene. (From Hoffmeister and Mohr, 1957. Charles A. McLaughlin)

bison much larger than the present-day bison have been found near Alton, Madison Co., and are probably referrable to *B. occidentalis*. Some other remains found in the state are probably referrable to *B. bison*.

Archaeological investigations in Illinois have produced a variety of mammalian species over the period of time occupied by man, namely from about 10,000 years before present until now. These species designations are based on identifiable skeletal remains that were found in association with Indian artifacts. With a variety of objects present at a site, it usually is possible to date the age of the site.

Skeletal parts of mammals may be present in these sites for a variety of reasons: they are the remnants of foods eaten by the Indians; they are parts such as teeth and claws used in necklaces or ornaments; they are the remains of mammals that died within the Indian dwellings. There is no assurance that the mammalian remains came from the site where they were found. The Indians may have captured the animals some miles distant and brought them, alive or dead, to their village. Or, the Indians may have traded with other groups, sometimes removed by a considerable distance, for a mammal, or parts thereof. Where the remains are found in a cave or shelter, there is the possibility that the owls may have transported the material there, although they could have caught the mammals several miles away. Also, the absence of a given

species of mammal in an Indian site may be the result of a native taboo against catching such animals rather than its absence from the fauna. Or, it may be that methods of recovering materials from sites has overlooked some species. This is especially true for small species, such as bats and shrews.

Most recently, Purdue and Styles (1986) have reviewed the distribution of mammals in Illinois during the Holocene. Table 6.1 based on their work summarizes the periods when remains of mammals have been recovered. However, this table does not show that, for some time-periods, species were found at numerous sites; in some cases, only at one site. The table also does not show the localities where species were found in the state at a given time. Reference should be made to the Purdue-Styles paper with their distribution maps.

Certain species in Table 6.1 need comment and clarification. *Sigmodon hispidus*, cotton rats, and *Spilogale putorius*, spotted skunks, are not known to have ever occurred in Illinois. Records for the two species are from the Modoc Rock Shelter, only a few miles from the Mississippi and Missouri rivers. These species may have been brought there from outside Illinois by owls that regurgitated them at their roost, or by native traders. However, wood rats, *Neotoma floridana*, have been reported from Modoc Rock Shelter and from Meyer Cave. If this southern species extended this far north at one time and rice rats, *Oryzomys palustris*, as far north as near Peoria, then it is possible that *Sigmodon hispidus* was present in southern Illinois in the early Holocene.

Pocket gophers, *Geomys bursarius*, have been reported from several localities throughout the Holocene. One of these, Napolean [*sic*] Hollow, is west of the Illinois River, but close to the river, and pocket gophers may have been transported from across the river by Indians. Thus, the distribution of *Geomys bursarius* in Illinois is probably as it is explained in the species account on page 185.

Listed in Table 6.1 are those species of mammals for which there is sufficient evidence for dating their period of occurrence. For example, remains of wood rats of the species *Neotoma floridana* are known from Meyer Cave, Monroe County, and Modoc Rock Shelter, Randolph County, but the precise time of their occurrence at these sites is not clear. *Neotoma floridana* is not included in the list.

Table 6.1. Known, dated occurrences of mammals at archaeological sites in Illinois in the Holocene. The heavy line indicates the presence of the species in a given time period. Sites are grouped into eight climatic episodes (from Pre-boreal/Boreal to Neo-boreal) or eight cultural stages (from Early Archaic to Oneota/Historic). The probable time span for each episode or cultural stage is given in years before present. Data from Purdue and Styles (1986).

Time periods (years before present): 10000-8500, 8500-5000, 5000-2800, 2800-1700, 1700-1300, 1300-800, 800-400, 400-100

Species:

- Didelphis virginiana
- Blarina sp.
- Cryptotis parva
- Scalopus aquaticus
- Sylvilagus floridanus
- Sylvilagus aquaticus
- Tamias striatus
- Marmota monax
- Spermophilus tridecemlineatus
- Spermophilus franklinii
- Sciurus carolinensis
- Sciurus niger
- Tamiasciurus hudsonicus
- Glaucomys volans
- Geomys bursarius
- Castor canadensis
- Oryzomys palustris
- Peromyscus sp.
- Sigmodon hispidus+
- Microtus pennsylvanicus
- Microtus ochrogaster/M. pinetorum
- Ondatra zibethicus
- Synaptomys cooperi
- Zapus hudsonius
- Erethizon dorsatum*
- Canis latrans
- Canis lupus*
- Vulpes vulpes
- Urocyon cinereoargenteus
- Ursus americanus*
- Procyon lotor
- Mustela frenata
- Mustela vison
- Martes americana*
- Martes pennanti*
- Taxidea taxus
- Mephitis mephitis
- Spilogale putorius+
- Lutra canadensis
- Felis concolor*
- Felis rufus
- Odocoileus virginianus
- Cervus elaphus*
- Bison bison*

* Species not present today in Illinois.
+ Species not known to have been present in Illinois in the last 500 years.

Extirpated and Possible Species in Illinois | 7

Species of Possible Occurrence in Illinois, Past or Future

At least 15 species of mammals are known to occur now or to have occurred in the past within 100 miles of Illinois (Map 7.1). Of these 15 species, 8 are primarily northern species, 2 are western, and 3 are southern. An additional species, *Plecotus townsendii,* is found both east and west of the southern tip of Illinois, and this wide-flying bat probably has traversed the state.

Sorex fumeus, Smoky shrew

A smoky shrew, *Sorex fumeus,* was taken at Racine, Wisconsin, in 1853, and the specimen is in the National Museum of Natural History. This is the only specimen known from Wisconsin. In 1981, nine smoky shrews were collected in the Harrison-Crawford State Forest, Crawford Co., Indiana (Mumford and Whitaker, 1982), which is approximately 60 miles east of the Illinois state line.

Sorex fumeus can be distinguished from other Illinois long-tailed shrews, genus *Sorex,* by its larger size, longer tail (usually more than 38 mm), and dark underparts (same color as back).

Sorex arcticus, Arctic shrew

The arctic shrew, *Sorex arcticus,* has been taken at several localities in Dane and Dodge counties, Wisconsin. Larger than the three species known to occur in Illinois, *S. arcticus* in winter pelage has a unique color pattern. There is a band of black down the back; the sides are brownish; the underparts may be the same shade of brown or lighter.

Condylura cristata, Star-nosed mole

Star-nosed moles, *Condylura cristata,* are known from numerous localities in northern Indiana, and Mumford and Whitaker's (1982) map shows that they have been taken as far west as Laporte County. They are also known

from central Wisconsin. This species has many features of the eastern mole, *Scalopus aquaticus,* but *C. cristata* differs noticeably in having a unique fringe of short, fleshy tentacles at the tip of the snout around the nostrils and in having a much longer, fleshy tail.

There are reports that this mole has been in Illinois, but none is based on preserved specimens, photographs, or identification by a mammalogist. F. E. Wood (1910:588) remarked of the species, "So far as known it is nowhere common in Illinois, but is found in the northern part of the state." He went on to say that a dead specimen was found in the vicinity of Urbana by Frank Smith. At one time Smith was associated with the Museum of Natural History and if he had thought it truly was a star-nosed mole, I believe he would have saved some part of the specimen.

Cory (1912) thought that star-nosed moles were found as far south in Illinois as Edgar County but saw only a specimen collected at Warsaw, Illinois, by C. K. Worthen, a professional taxidermist. Worthen put his address on every specimen he prepared, regardless of where it was collected. I do not regard the Worthen record of *Condylura* as being from Warsaw.

Kennicott (1858:101) lists this species in his report but says, "I am informed . . . that it has been captured in parts of Northern and Middle Illinois. I learn, moreover, that, in Edgar county, where it is not very rare, it has been observed inhabiting the prairie." Obviously, Robert Kennicott had not seen a star-nosed mole from Illinois.

There is a possibility that at one time star-nosed moles may have lived in the marshy, boggy areas near Lake Michigan, near the Indiana or Wisconsin border, but I am not convinced that they ever were present in Illinois.

Myotis leibii, Small-footed myotis

Small-footed myotis, *Myotis leibii,* are known to inhabit caves in central Kentucky and in southeastern Missouri. There is a good possibility that this species

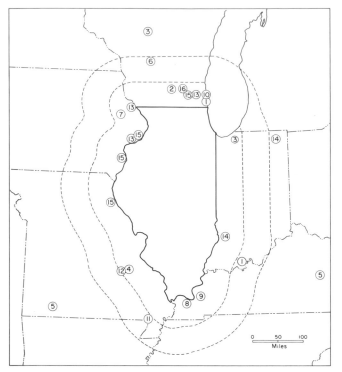

Map 7.1. Records of occurrence of species that may have appeared in the past or may be discovered in the future in Illinois. Numbers on the map refer to the localities outside of Illinois where the species has been taken. The last recorded dates of capture at these localities, if known, are given in parentheses. The outer line is 100 miles beyond the Illinois boundary; the inner, 50 miles.

1. *Sorex fumeus*, smoky shrew (Wisc., 1853; Ind., 1983)
2. *Sorex arcticus*, arctic shrew (1931)
3. *Condylura cristata*, star-nosed mole (Wisc., before 1914; Ind., 1942±)
4. *Myotis leibii*, small-footed myotis (1949)
5. *Plecotus townsendii*, Townsend's big-eared bat
6. *Eutamias minimus*, least chipmunk (present time)
7. *Perognathus flavescens*, plains pocket mouse (1957)
8. *Reithrodontomys humulis*, eastern harvest mouse (1950)
9. *Sigmodon hispidus*, hispid cotton rat (present time)
10. *Clethrionomys gapperi*, southern red-backed vole (1898)
11. *Myocastor coypus*, nutria
12. *Canis rufus*, red wolf
13. *Mustela erminea*, ermine (1972)
14. *Gulo gulo*, wolverine (before 1900)
15. *Spilogale putorius*, eastern spotted skunk (present time)
16. *Felis lynx*, lynx (1907)

may occur at some times in the caves or rocky outcrops of southern Illinois.

The species can be recognized by the small hind feet, light brown color, flattened skull, and keeled calcar.

Plecotus townsendii, Townsend's big-eared bat

Townsend's big-eared bat, *Plecotus townsendii*, is known to occupy caves in central Kentucky and in the Ozark Plateau of Missouri and Arkansas. There is a possibility that the species could and may occupy caves in southern Illinois from time to time.

Plecotus townsendii differs from Rafinesque's big-eared bat, *Plecotus rafinesquii*, in having whitish rather than tan underparts, gray rather than brown fur on the back, long hairs on the toes, and bicuspid upper incisors.

Eutamias minimus, Least chipmunk

Of all the mammals discussed here, the least chipmunk, *Eutamias minimus*, may have the least likelihood of having been present in the past or of being present in the future. These chipmunks live in coniferous or mixed conifereous-hardwood forests, usually where the forest growth is not too dense. Observers should have noticed and recorded them if least chipmunks were present in Illinois, but such does not seem to have been the case.

Least chipmunks are present at Camp Douglas, Juneau Co., Wisconsin. They look something like eastern chipmunks, *Tamias striatus*, but the dark dorsal stripes extend to the base of the tail, the three most dorsal stripes are separated by light stripes, not dark gray stripes, the white stripes on the sides of the face are more pronounced, and the animal overall is much smaller.

Perognathus flavescens, Plains pocket mouse

The plains pocket mouse, *Perognathus flavescens*, occurs as far east in Iowa as 2 mi W Center Point, Linn County, and Backbone State Park, Delaware County, within 30 miles of Illinois (Bowles, 1975:81), and northern Missouri (Schwartz and Schwartz, 1981:173). These mice live in the loess soils which are grassy and not heavily grazed. These heteromyid rodents are characterized by their relatively long hind legs, small size but long, nearly hairless tail, and yellowish colored upper parts. The Mississippi River may be a barrier to the eastward spread of this species. When the river is frozen over, these mice are in hibernation.

Reithrodontomys humulis, Eastern harvest mouse

A specimen of the eastern harvest mouse, *Reithrodontomys humulis*, was collected on March 11, 1950, by William B. Robertson 6⅘ mi E Paducah, Livingston Co., Kentucky. This species should be looked for along the north side of the Ohio River in Illinois.

Reithrodontomys humulis has all the features characteristic of the genus as defined on page 199. It differs from *R. megalotis* in its darker coloration and in certain features of the dentition.

Sigmodon hispidus, Hispid cotton rat

Hispid cotton rats, *Sigmodon hispidus*, were present at the Tennessee-Kentucky line, in the Mississippi River

Fig. 7.1. Hispid cotton rat, *Sigmodon hispidus*, from Reelfoot Lake, Tennessee. Photograph by W. W. Goodpaster.

Valley, in the late 1940's. The first specimens were taken in Kentucky in 1964 in Lyon County according to Barbour and Davis (1974:190) and they indicate that by 1974 *S. hispidus* was "well established and fairly common in the Purchase and the Land Between the Lakes." The cotton rats live in grassy or weedy places, along roads, fields, or the edges of woods. They make indistinct runways. These rats should be looked for on the northern side of the Ohio River in Illinois. Such streams as the Kansas and Mississippi rivers have not been barriers to the dispersal of these cotton rats, so the Ohio River should not be either.

Hispid cotton rats are smaller than eastern wood rats, *Neotoma floridana,* and have less hairy tails. They are heavier-bodied and shorter-tailed than rice rats, *Oryzomys palustris*. Hispid cotton rats might be confused with barn rats from which they differ in having a dorsal coloration that is mottled or flecked rather than uniformly dusky or yellowish gray, tail less scaly and lighter-colored below, and hind feet shorter; there are also various cranial differences.

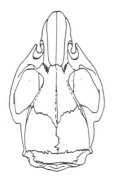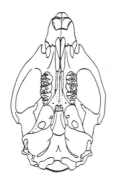

Fig. 7.2. *Sigmodon hispidus,* dorsal and ventral views of skull, Yuma County, Arizona, 38974 UI. Female, 25.3 mm greatest length.

Clethrionomys gapperi, Southern red-backed vole

Southern red-backed voles, *Clethrionomys gapperi,* are reported in Wisconsin as close as Oak Creek, Milwaukee County, and Beaver Dam, Dodge County (Jackson, 1961). In this area, they inhabit coniferous or deciduous woodlands in areas that are moist, with moss-covered rocks or logs or tamarack bogs. For some reason, Jackson regards the record from Beaver Dam as "accidental."

Adult *Clethrionomys gapperi* can be told from all other microtines in Illinois by the reddish color on the dorsum.

Myocastor coypus, Nutria

The nutria, *Myocastor coypus,* is a South American hystricomorph rodent which has gone feral (wild) in many places in the United States. Nutria has been exploited in Illinois as a fur farm animal that can be raised inexpensively out-of-doors and in turn produces valuable fur. The demand for and the monetary value of the pelts has been so low as to cause many nutria-farmers to give up on the undertaking. Some have released the animals and they may become established in the wild. The specimen caught along a creek in a muskrat set on January 10, 1961, at Divernon, Sangamon County, and preserved at Illinois State Museum, may have been such an animal that had gone feral. On December 12, 1983, a nutria was found dead on the road on the main dam of Rend Lake, 3½ mi NW Benton, Franklin Co., Illinois, according to a report given me. The specimen was deposited in the collections at Southern Illinois University.

The nutria is an aquatic animal, much like a beaver or muskrat, and intermediate in size between the two. It differs from both by having a round tail.

Canis rufus, Red wolf

The red wolf, *Canis rufus,* may have occurred at an earlier time in the Ozark Uplift of southern Illinois. Red wolves at one time were fairly common in the Ozark Highlands of Missouri and may have moved into Illinois.

A specimen of red wolf labeled as Warsaw, Hancock Co., Illinois, is in the American Museum. The authenticity of this record is discussed in the section for the genus *Canis* (p. 263).

Mustela erminea, Ermine

The ermine, *Mustela erminea,* formerly called the short-tailed weasel, has been taken in southern Wisconsin and eastern Iowa. These records are from Pewaukee, Waukesha Co., Wisconsin (Jackson, 1961) and Dodge Township, Dubuque Co., and vicinity of Stockton, Muscatine Co., Iowa (Bowles, 1975). Since these animals cover a considerable distance in their normal movements, they should continue to move closer to and even into Illinois. They may already be in Illinois, but not recognized. A report of an ermine from near Bondville, Champaign County, was published by Long (1968:140) but he published a correction (1969:334) indicating the specimen was a long-tailed weasel. Ermines and long-tailed weasels, *Mustela frenata,* are much alike, and male ermines are about the same size as female long-tailed weasels. A detailed comparison of long-tailed weasels and ermines is given in the account of *Mustela frenata.*

Specimens of weasels from along the east side of the Mississippi River north of Pike County, and from the northern counties along the Wisconsin line need to be identified accurately to ascertain the status of *Mustela erminea.*

Gulo gulo, Wolverine

Wolverines, *Gulo gulo,* but sometimes referred to as *Gulo luscus,* have not been reported within historic times in Illinois, but there are two records for Indiana and one for central Iowa. E. R. Hall (1981:1009) records this species from Washington Township, Noble Co., and near Edwardsport, Knox Co., both in Indiana, and Mumford and Whitaker (1982:3) indicate that the last report for Indiana was in 1852. Bowles (1975:129) regards the Iowa specimen as accidental, having been transported into the state in 1960. Two lower jaws of wolverine from an Indian mound in the Havana Mound Group, Mason County, may have been the remains of animals that were traded by local Indians bartering with other Indians to the north or east, or they may represent remains of specimens taken in Illinois. This species is included only because it "may possibly have occurred in Illinois in the past."

Spilogale putorius, Eastern spotted skunk

Eastern spotted skunks, *Spilogale putorius,* should be in Illinois, but we have no proof of any in the state for at least the last 125 years. Spotted skunks have been present in eastern Iowa, where they are locally known as civets or civet cats, for a long time. Nearly every county bordering the Mississippi River in Iowa has spotted skunks (see Bowles, 1975: Fig. 52) and in my experiences they are common to abundant in most of these counties. Spotted skunks must have arrived much later in Wisconsin, for Jackson (1961) knew of only two records, one collected in 1957 in St. Croix County and one near the Illinois state line, taken at Fort Atkinson, Jefferson County, in 1955.

There are various reports of spotted skunks in Illinois but none can be verified by preserved specimens. Arthur Howell (1910:32) wrote that "the spotted skunks undoubtedly range north as far as southern Illinois. They were reported to be fairly common at Golconda, Illinois. . . ." B. H. Bailey (1916:290) reported that a Mr. C. H. Swift of Sabula, Jackson Co., Iowa, had "personally trapped two specimens of the little spotted skunk on the Illinois side of the Mississippi River north of Savannah [=Savanna, Carroll Co., Illinois] twenty years ago." In his 1959 study, Van Gelder did not regard *S. putorius* as being present in Illinois.

Remains of spotted skunks, consisting of parts of one maxillary and seven dentaries, were found in the Modoc archaeological site, 2 mi NW Modoc, Randolph Co., Illinois. This is within four miles of the Mississippi River and parts of Missouri where spotted skunks are known to occur. The age for some materials found at the Modoc site is between 5,100 and 8,500 years before the present. In reporting upon these, Parmalee and Hoffmeister (1957) said, "It is impossible to be sure if the spotted skunks represented by these remains come from the immediate vicinity of the Modoc site, but judging from other remains, one would be inclined to think so."

Spotted skunks are much like striped skunks but are considerably smaller, each side of the body has two broken or interrupted white stripes rather than only one, and the tail is much shorter, with no white on its sides but a small white tip.

Felis lynx, Lynx

Lynxes (*Felis lynx*), also known by the scientific name of *Lynx canadensis,* at an earlier time were found as far south in Wisconsin as Jefferson and Sauk counties (Jackson, 1961). There is no reason to believe that in the 1800's this species was present in northern Illinois. It is, however, difficult to ascertain if observers were making a distinction between lynxes and bobcats (*Felis rufus*). Kennicott (1855:579) did include this species in his list of Mammals of Cook County, but without any comment. A lynx differs from the bobcat in its larger size, longer ear tufts, tip of short tail black all around, larger feet, and in certain features of the basicranial region of the skull (see pp. 311 and 312, Figs. 8.142B and 8.143).

Non-native mammals that are sometimes held as pets in Illinois—but that may escape but do not necessarily become established—are the armadillo, axis deer, various species of monkeys, gerbils, and hamsters.

Extirpated Species That Have Disappeared in Illinois within Historic Time

This section discusses those species of mammals that were present when Europeans arrived in Illinois and within the last 350 years, but are no longer present.

Erethizon dorsatum, Porcupine

The porcupine, *Erethizon dorsatum,* may have been present in Illinois before the forests were so extensively decimated. In 1857, Kennicott wrote (1858:91) "I am not aware that it has been observed in Northern Illinois, though it is said to inhabit Whiteside county and the banks of the Illinois River." Cory (1912:255) writes, "I have been informed that years ago it was occasionally found in Jo Daviess County, but upon investigation the evidence proved unsatisfactory. Nevertheless, Mr. Edward Grimm of Galena writes me, he believes it was formerly found in that county [Jo Daviess]." Mumford and Whitaker (1982:3) thought that the last record of the porcupine in Indiana was about 1918. The last record in Illinois was probably much earlier than this. Parmalee (1967) found remains of at least 10 porcupines in the bone deposit of Meyer Cave, Monroe County. These may date back to about 2,000 years before present. In an Archaic Indian site near the Wabash River, at Riverton, 2 mi NE Palestine, Crawford County, a skull and four mandibles were recovered (Parmalee, 1963).

Canis lupus, Wolf

The wolf, sometimes called the timber wolf or gray wolf, *Canis lupus,* at one time was abundant and widespread in Illinois. For a detailed account, see the section *Early History of Mammals in Illinois* (p. 32). Probably all wolves were gone from Illinois before the 1860's.

Numerous bounties have been paid on wolves in Illinois since that date. The name prairie wolf is often applied to the coyote, *Canis latrans,* and bounties may have been paid on these as "wolves." As a general rule it might be said that canids weighing less than 50 pounds are coyotes or dogs. Adult Illinois wolves would weigh well over 50 pounds.

Parmalee (1959) was of the opinion that Indians seldom killed wolves, and he remarked that remains of wolves have been found in only nine Indian sites in Illinois (as of 1959).

Ursus americanus, Black bear

Black bears, *Ursus americanus,* may never have been abundant in Illinois and were greatly reduced in numbers by the 1850's (Kennicott, 1859:251). Cory writes (1912:398) that "there have been rumors of Bears having been seen in the swampy country in extreme southern Illinois as late as 1885 or 1890, but the evidence is unsatisfactory." He goes on to say that a Mr. C. J. Boyd of Anna said the last bear was killed about 1860 in the hills near Alexander County.

In 1966, a black bear was killed in the Big Muddy River Bottoms near Waltonville, Jefferson County, according to various newspaper accounts of June 5, 1966, and Klimstra and Roseberry (1969). At that time it was also reported that several persons thought there were other black bears in the Shawnee National Forest area. If black bears are present at times in southern Illinois, they must represent emigrants or introductions, for the population there was extirpated in the 1800's. Thomas wrote in 1861 that the black bear "is occasionally seen in the southern part of the State. Although once found in considerable numbers, is now supposed to be a visitant from Missouri, when seen."

Indians in Illinois within historical times used bears for food; earlier Indians apparently sought and used the canine teeth, mandibles, and crania (Parmalee, 1959).

Martes americana, Marten

There was a skeleton of a marten, *Martes americana,* in the Chicago Academy of Sciences, labelled "Illinois," according to Cory (1912:385). Kennicott (1859:243) makes the vague statement that "it has been seen, occasionally, in Northern Illinois."

Martes pennanti, Fisher

The presence of the fisher, *Martes pennanti,* is based on the statements of Kennicott. Specimens from Illinois are not known to be present in any collections. Kennicott (1855:578) says in his list of mammals of Cook County that the fisher "used frequently to be seen in the heavy timber along Lake Michigan" and in his account for the state says (1859:241) "It has been found, within a few years, in Northern Illinois, and appears to be an inhabitant of the woods, alone."

One of the principal sources of food for the fisher is the porcupine and the presence of the fisher may depend in part on the number of porcupines also present.

Some 450 to 800 years ago, fisher may have been present near the Cahokia Middle Mississippi Site near East St. Louis because remains of this animal have been found in the middens (Parmalee, 1957; Baker, 1941). The lower jaw of a fisher was found at a Middle Mississippi village site west of Clear Lake Slough, Cass County (Parmalee, 1960).

Felis concolor, Mountain lion

Mountain lions, *Felis concolor*, were more commonly called cougars or panthers in Illinois. By the end of the 1800's, *Felis concolor* had been extirpated. See the section on *Early History of Mammals of Illinois* (p. 34) for additional information.

Cervus elaphus, Elk

Elk, or wapiti, as they *should* be called, *Cervus elaphus* (=*Cervus canadensis*), ranged widely in the state until the early 1800's and by the middle of that century had been almost extirpated. Also see the section on *Early History of Mammals of Illinois* (p. 30).

Bison bison, Bison

Bison or buffalo, *Bison bison,* sometimes referred to by early explorers as oxen, were present in fair numbers on some of the prairies of Illinois. For a detailed discussion of their distribution and disappearance, see the account under *Early History of Mammals of Illinois* (p. 27).

Checklist of Species and Subspecies

MARSUPIALIA: Marsupials
  Didelphidae: Opossums
    Didelphis virginiana, Virginia opossum
      virginiana

INSECTIVORA: Insectivores
  Soricidae: Shrews
    Sorex cinereus, Masked shrew
      cinereus
      lesueurii
    Sorex longirostris, Southeastern shrew
      longirostris
    Sorex hoyi, Pygmy shrew
      hoyi
      winnemana
    Blarina brevicauda, Northern short-tailed shrew
      kirtlandi
    Blarina carolinensis, Southern short-tailed shrew
      carolinensis
    Cryptotis parva, Least shrew
      parva
  Talpidae: Moles
    Scalopus aquaticus, Eastern mole
      machrinus

CHIROPTERA: Bats
  Vespertilionidae: Vespertilionid bats
    Myotis lucifugus, Little brown myotis
      lucifugus
    Myotis sodalis, Indiana bat
    Myotis austroriparius, Southeastern myotis
    Myotis grisescens, Gray myotis
    Myotis keenii, Keen's myotis
      septentrionalis
    Lasionycteris noctivagans, Silver-haired bat
    Pipistrellus subflavus, Eastern pipistrelle
      subflavus
    Eptesicus fuscus, Big brown bat
      fuscus
    Lasiurus borealis, Red bat
      borealis

Lasiurus cinereus, Hoary bat
  cinereus
Nycticeius humeralis, Evening bat
  humeralis
Plecotus rafinesquii, Rafinesque's big-eared bat
  rafinesquii
  Molossidae: Free-tailed bats
    Tadarida brasiliensis, American free-tailed bat
      mexicana

LAGOMORPHA: Rabbits
  Leporidae: Rabbits and hares
    Sylvilagus floridanus, Eastern cottontail
      mearnsii
    Sylvilagus aquaticus, Swamp rabbit
      aquaticus
    Lepus townsendii, White-tailed jack rabbit
      campanius

RODENTIA: Rodents
  Sciuromorph Rodents
    Sciuridae: Squirrels, woodchucks, chipmunks
      Tamias striatus, Eastern chipmunk
        striatus
        griseus
      Marmota monax, Woodchuck
        monax
      Spermophilus tridecemlineatus, Thirteen-lined ground squirrel
        tridecemlineatus
      Spermophilus franklinii, Franklin's ground squirrel
      Sciurus carolinensis, Gray squirrel
        carolinensis
      Sciurus niger, Fox squirrel
        rufiventer
      Tamiasciurus hudsonicus, Red squirrel
        loquax
      Glaucomys volans, Southern flying squirrel
        volans

Geomyidae: Pocket gophers
 Geomys bursarius, Plains pocket gopher
  illinoensis
Castoridae: Beaver
 Castor canadensis, Beaver
  subsp?
Myomorph Rodents
 Muridae: Rats and mice
  Cricetinae: New World rats and mice
   Oryzomys palustris, Marsh rice rat
    palustris
   Reithrodontomys megalotis, Western harvest
    mouse
     dychei
   Peromyscus maniculatus, Deer mouse
    bairdii
   Peromyscus leucopus, White-footed mouse
    leucopus
   Peromyscus gossypinus, Cotton mouse
    megacephalus
   Ochrotomys nuttalli, Golden mouse
    lisae
   Neotoma floridana, Eastern wood rat
    illinoensis
  Microtinae: Voles and lemmings
   Microtus pennsylvanicus, Meadow vole (mouse)
    pennsylvanicus
   Microtus ochrogaster, Prairie vole
    ochrogaster
   Microtus pinetorum, Pine vole
    auricularis
    scalopsoides
   Ondatra zibethicus, Muskrat
    zibethicus
   Synaptomys cooperi, Southern bog lemming
    gossii
  Murinae: Old World rats and mice
   Rattus rattus, Black rat
    subsp.?
   Rattus norvegicus, Norway rat
    subsp.?

Mus musculus, House mouse
 subsp.?
Zapodidae: Jumping mouse
 Zapus hudsonius, Meadow jumping mouse
  intermedius
  americanus

CARNIVORA: Carnivores
 Canidae: Coyotes, wolves
  Canis latrans, Coyote
   thamnos
  Vulpes vulpes, Red Fox
   fulva
  Urocyon cinereoargenteus, Gray fox
   cinereoargenteus
 Procyonidae: Raccoons, ringtails
  Procyon lotor, Raccoon
   lotor
   hirtus
 Mustelidae: Skunks, weasels, and allies
  Mustela nivalis, Least weasel
   allegheniensis
  Mustela frenata, Long-tailed weasel
   noveboracensis
  Mustela vison, Mink
   letifera
   mink
  Taxidea taxus, Badger
   taxus
  Mephitis mephitis, Striped skunk
   avia
  Lutra canadensis, River otter
   lataxina
 Felidae: Cats
  Felis rufus, Bobcat
   rufus

ARTIODACTYLA: Even-toed Ungulates
 Cervidae: Deer and allies
  Odocoileus virginianus, White-tailed deer
   virginianus (?)

Species of Possible Occurrence in Illinois (Past or Future)

Sorex fumeus, Smoky shrew
Sorex arcticus, Arctic shrew
Condylura cristata, Star-nosed mole
Myotis leibii, Small-footed myotis
Plecotus townsendii, Townsend's big-eared bat
Eutamias minimus, Least chipmunk
Perognathus flavescens, Plains pocket mouse
Reithrodontomys humulis, Eastern harvest mouse

Sigmodon hispidus, Hispid cotton rat
Clethrionomys gapperi, Southern red-backed vole
Myocastor coypus, Nutria
Canis rufus, Red wolf
Mustela erminea, Ermine
Gulo gulo, Wolverine
Spilogale putorius, Eastern spotted skunk
Felis lynx, Lynx

Species Extirpated in Illinois within Historic Time

Erethizon dorsatum, Porcupine   *Martes americana,* Marten   *Cervus elaphus,* Elk or wapiti
Canis lupus, Timber wolf   *Martes pennanti,* Fisher   *Bison bison,* Bison
Ursus americanus, Black bear   *Felis concolor,* Mountain lion

Order Marsupialia, Marsupials

Primitive mammals that give birth to immature young that continue to develop within a pouch (marsupium); have relatively small braincase, angular process of lower jaw inflected, bullae poorly developed, milk (deciduous) teeth retained in adulthood; in the female, the terminal portion of each uterus differentiated as a vagina, resulting in two lateral vaginae; in the male, the bifid penis permits deposition of sperm in the lateral vaginae.

Family Didelphidae, New World Opossums

Teeth totaling 50; dental formula 5/4, 1/1, 3/3, 4/4; incisors small; feet with five separate toes, large toe of hind foot opposable; tail prehensile. Represented in Illinois by genus *Didelphis.*

Didelphis, Opossums

Diagnosis. A didelphid marsupial of medium to large size as characterized under the species *Didelphis virginiana.*

Comparisons. One other species of *Didelphis* (*D. marsupialis*) occurs in North America. *D. virginiana* differs from the Mexican and Central American *D. marsupialis* in having its head more whitish, lacrimal bone rounded posteriorly, and chromosome with an FN of 32 rather than 20.

Didelphis virginiana, Virginia opossum

Range. Throughout the state. See Map 8.1.

Diagnosis. A large-sized marsupial (weight about 4 to 8 lbs); tail nearly as long as the body, nearly naked, and thicker and darker at the base; legs short, giving the animal a squat appearance; ears large and bare; first toe of hind foot clawless and opposed to other toes to aid in grasping; skull with marsupial features of inflected angular process of mandible; braincase relatively small; sutures not obliterated even in old individuals; five upper and four lower incisors.

Color. The overall color is a grizzled effect since the underfur is mainly white, although lightly tipped with black; this is overlaid with scattered gray, black, or white guard hairs. The face is mostly whitish, the feet blackish, and the inner side of the ears blackish. Opossums have two color phases, grayish and blackish, but the blackish phase is not common in Illinois specimens. One specimen taken in Champaign County is all white, except the ears, which are blackish. We have a similar albinistic specimen from Clermont County, Ohio.

Dental formula. 5/4, 1/1, 3/3, 4/4.

Chromosomes. 2N=22. Three pairs of large-sized subtelocentrics; three pairs of medium-sized subtelocentrics, four pairs of medium-sized acrocentrics; X chromosomes, medium to small submetacentric; Y, small acrocentric.

Comparisons. Didelphis virginanus differs from all other Illinois mammals in the characteristics given for the Marsupialia as well as the Didelphidae. The opossum is not to be confused with the raccoon, from which it differs in having a nearly naked tail, whitish face, nearly naked ears, clawless and opposable big toes; much smaller braincase, inflected angular process of mandible, and five upper and four lower incisors.

Growth. At birth, opossums weigh between 0.10 and 0.20 gms; at 10 days, 0.9 gms; 20 days, 1.7 gms; 60 days, 25.0 gms; 100 days, 125 gms. (Petrides, 1949:369). The changes in total length and weight through the first 11 months of age are shown in Fig. 8.3A.

Secondary sexual variation. In the 17 cranial measurements given by A. L. Gardner (1973) for opossums from Texas, males averaged larger than females in all but one dimension (postorbital constriction) and were significantly larger in 11 measurements. Hamilton (1958) observed that males average about 32 percent heavier than females.

General Remarks. Although opossums are often regarded as tropical or semi-tropical animals, they do well in Illinois, being abundant in most places. They are part

Fig. 8.1A. Virginia opossum, *Didelphis virginiana.* Photograph by W. W. Goodpaster.

of a group of primitive mammals that include kangaroos and koalas. They have a unique reproductive system and post-embryonic development. Although opossums may be less active in winter than in summer, they do not hibernate. Their death-feigning behavior is unique among Illinois mammals. Their habits of moving into urban areas—to take advantage not only of food sources in the form of garbage and dog food, but also numerous shelters—make them conspicuous to many persons who come in contact with them or their signs.

It is not clear whether opossums were present in Illinois in the mid-1600's when Marquette, La Salle, and other explorers visited the state. Their early reports do not mention animals that can be recognized as opossums. Baldwin (1877) in writing about La Salle County for a time period that was probably in the early 1800's observed that "The opossum, the only American marsopial [*sic*] are found in quite limited numbers. It is said that they were not here before the settlement and fore some years after."

Habitat

Opossums live in a variety of habitats: wooded areas, especially along or near streams or waterways; brushy fencerows and ditches; under or around buildings and shrubs on the farm or in the city. In wooded areas, the opossums may forage and wander beyond the cover where their dens are usually located.

Habits

Virginia opossums may be relatively bold or conspicuously sluggish animals, or both, for they amble along slowly, apparently disdainful of trouble. This behavior is partly compensated for by their ability to feign death or play dead when trouble confronts them. Also, they will hiss, growl, and bare their teeth to intimidate an enemy. But if they elect to flee, they can run at a good rate. Friction ridges on the feet, the opposable hallux, and the prehensile tail aid in climbing.

Opossums are principally nocturnal. Their nightly foraging often takes them to roads where they may feed on other animals killed by moving vehicles. In turn, the slow-moving opossums may be killed. Occasionally, opossums are seen in the daytime, more often in the wintertime when they are searching for food or shelter.

Den or nest sites are in or under brushpiles and debris, in culverts, hollow down-logs, cavities in standing trees, or burrows. When street and highways crews fell trees in summer, either in or outside of towns, opossums are often found living in dens within these trees. Nests are made of dry grasses, leaves, or nearly any dry plant material or shredded paper. Nesting material is grasped by the front feet and passed under the body where the tail curls around it and then carries it to the nest site. One animal "may transport as much as eight mouthfuls at once with its tail and carry additional material in its mouth" (Schwartz and Schwartz, 1981:24).

The opossum's ability to withstand subzero temperatures (F°) has surprised numerous workers. Nevertheless, they seemingly do well in the coldest parts of Illinois, although their ears and tails frequently suffer permanent damage from frostbite. The opossum has been slow in its northward spread and it is believed that cold temperatures may be a controlling factor. For comments on the early occurrence (pre-1900's) of opossums in Illinois see above, and Table 6.1, page 41.

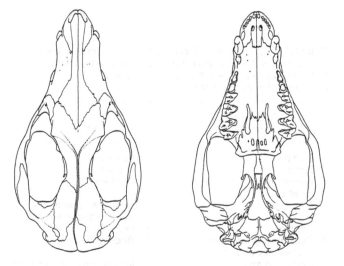

Fig. 8.1B. *Didelphis virginiana,* dorsal and ventral views of skull. Kaskaskia Island, Randolph Co., Illinois, 59869 UI. Sex unknown, 115.9 mm greatest length.

Food

The opossum has been called an opportunistic omnivore. Animal material is the preferred food. In southern Illinois, 76.2 percent of the food volume was animal material, 23.8 percent plant material (Stieglitz and Klimstra, 1962) in 131 individuals. At different times of the year and under varying circumstances, the percentage and composition of foods eaten varies. In areas where waterfowl are hunted, the diet may be heavy in ducks and geese that are recovered as carrion from dead and unclaimed waterfowl during the hunting season. On some occasions the diets are heavy in grasshoppers, earthworms, road-killed animals, or garbage. Much of the opossum material found in digestive tracts of animals from southern Illinois was probably the result of grooming and ingestion of hair. In these same animals it was evident that in late summer opossums relied primarily on plant foods, but as winter came on, mammals, birds, and reptiles were more heavily used.

In central Missouri, Reynolds (1945) found that from fall to spring the food of opossums was by frequency in 259 scats and volume of content of 68 stomachs, given in parentheses, as follows: insects, 87.6 percent (34.2 percent); invertebrates other than insects, 32.4 (4.5); mammals, 28.2 (32.3); birds and eggs, 8.9 (4.9); reptiles, 18.9 (10.0); fruits, 50.6 (6.8); and grains and miscellaneous seeds, 12.7 (7.3).

In 83 Indiana opossums, mammal remains totaled 22.2 percent; birds, 21.3; insects and other invertebrates, 25.3; vegetation, 19.0; and garbage, 3.1 (Whitaker, et al., 1977).

Opossums probably are incapable of catching adult, healthy cottontails and most tree-roosting birds. These items are generally obtained as carrion. Smaller mammals can be captured in nests or burrows and opossums effectively hunt for amphibians and reptiles, as well as many invertebrates.

Reproduction

Opossums breed in late January and in February; most breed again in May. Two litters of young per year is the usual pattern, and the number of young varies considerably. Within the pouch where the young are nursed there are nine to 17 teats, with the usual number 13. In central Illinois, the average litter size was 7.9 (Holmes and Sanderson, 1965). In central Missouri, the average was 8.9 (Reynolds, 1945). One female is known to have given birth to 25 young (Reynolds, 1952:157). Parturition of the young occurs at 13± days after copulation and insemination.

Young are exceedingly immature at birth, with an average weight of 0.16 gm (=0.0056 oz). They move by swimming motions from the vulva to the pouch, and usually some young do not make it to the pouch. Only

Table 8.1. Foods as determined by digestive tract analysis of 131 opossums in southern Illinois. (From Stieglitz and Klimstra, 1962:199)

Food Item	Per Cent Volume		Per Cent Frequency of Occurrence	
ANIMAL FOODS	76.2		100.0	
Mammals		48.7		76.3
Opossum		16.3		52.7
Cottontail		14.7		15.3
Prairie Vole		6.4		5.3
Other Mammals		11.3		18.5
Birds		14.5		19.1
Domestic Chicken		7.1		4.6
Grackle		4.7		2.3
Other Birds		2.7		3.1
Reptiles		1.6		14.5
Amphibians		3.0		5.3
Frogs		2.5		3.8
Toads		0.5		1.5
Fishes		0.1		1.5
Unidentified Scales				
Insects		6.3		93.1
Scarabacidae Larvae		2.0		11.5
Short-horned Grasshoppers		1.5		54.2
Unidentified Lepidoptera Larvae		0.9		9.2
Other Insects		1.9		—
Other Invertebrates		1.9		—
Earthworms		1.3		3.8
Snails		0.5		31.3
Miscellaneous Invertebrates		0.1		—
Undetermined Animal Materials		0.1		2.3
PLANT FOODS	23.8		100.0	
Persimmon		8.1		21.4
Pokeberry		5.1		25.2
Grapes		1.8		11.5
Tree Leaf Fragments		1.3		87.0
Corn		1.1		3.1
Other Plant Foods		6.4		—

Table 8.2. Major groups of food consumed by opossums in descending order of importance in central Missouri with frequency of occurrence based on 259 scats, and volume on 68 stomachs. (Reynolds, 1945:372)

Frequency of Occurrence	Volume
1. Insects	1. Insects
2. Fruits	2. Mammals
3. Invertebrates (other than insects)	3. Reptiles
4. Mammals	4. Cultivated grains and miscellaneous seeds
5. Reptiles	5. Fruits
6. Cultivated grains and miscellaneous seeds	6. Birds and eggs
7. Birds and eggs	7. Invertebrates (other than insects)

Fig. 8.2. Newborn opossums in a teaspoon (above); an enlarged view, below. (From Hartman, Possums, Univ. Texas Press, 1952)

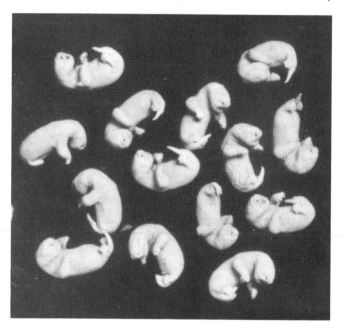

the forelimbs are capable of movement at the time of birth. The young become firmly attached to a nipple within the pouch. They may abandon the pouch anytime between the 60th and 100th day. There is some mortality of the young while they are growing within the pouch. In central Illinois, Sanderson (1961:24) found a 12 percent mortality. In an Ohio population of opossums, Petrides (1949) found that 75 percent of the known mortality occurred among young animals in the pouch, and the probable life expectancy was 1.33 years.

Populations and Home Range

In central Illinois in an area of oak-hickory forest and floodplain bordering the Sangamon River, the population of opossums in midsummer was about 300 per square mile, with the estimated numbers fluctuating in various years. In 1958, the population was estimated at 259 per sq mi; 1959, 419; 1960, 138; 1961, 261 (Holmes and Sanderson, 1965). In Carroll County, in an area that would be considered poor habitat for opossum, with 98 percent of the land under cultivation and with trees in farmyards and a few scattered willows, Osage orange, box elder, and cherry, there were an estimated 10 opossums per square mile (Verts, 1963:128).

The home ranges of opossums are often of a size to fit the shape of small areas of available habitat. Most are elongate, but probably vary in size and shape at different times of the year.

Variation within the Species

Aging of the specimens. Animals at approximately three months of age have a dental formula of 5/4, 1/1, 2/2, 0/0; at four months, 5/4, 1/1, 3/3, 1/2; at five to 8½ months, 5/5, 1/1, 3/3, 2/3; at seven to 11 months, 5/4, 1/1, 3/3, 3/4; at 10 months or more, 5/4, 1/1, 3/3, 4/4 (Petrides, 1949). There is some overlap in the age

Table 8.3. External and cranial measurements (in mm) of individual, male and female, *Didelphis virginiana* from Illinois. All specimens are in age classes 4 to 6 (see text).

Locality	Total length	Tail length	Head-body length	Hind foot length	Ear length	Greatest length skull	Condylo-basal length	Palatal length	Zygo-matic length
MALES									
Champaign Co.	800	310	490	65	50	124.85	123.1	70.2	73.0
"	752	286	466	70	45	117.5	116.0	68.3	66.3
"	795	330	465	71	50	—	—	70.8	—
Stephenson Co.	813	275	538	74	52	125.6	122.15	72.6	—
FEMALES									
Champaign Co.	765	280	485	64	48	111.9	109.5	65.6	56.95
"	786	306	480	70	52	115.55	114.8	68.4	60.25
Jo Daviess Co.	701	278	423	62	44	106.1	104.6	63.9	56.6
Du Page Co.	685	270	415	65	50	98.0	96.5	60.2	52.6
Fulton Co.	744	302	442	59	55	105.8	104.5	63.7	56.3
"	770	300	470	70	51	119.9	117.8	72.2	61.0
"	784	310	474	70	54	113.35	110.0	65.6	60.8

categories. Animals are placed in age groups, as in Table 8.3 (p. 54), following this classification in Gardner (1973): Age 4 has M_4 and the permanent premolars in position; Age 5 has all teeth erupted but M^4 has little wear; Age 6 has M^4 moderately to excessively worn.

Methods of measuring skulls. Gardner (1973) gives a series of 17 measurements of the cranium and lower jaw and defines how these are taken. Most are standard measurements. Breadth across molars is across M^3. Breadth of braincase is behind the zygomatic arches anterior to the lateral expansion of the lambdoidal crests. Breadth of palatal shelf is the free extension. Breadth of rostrum is taken at the junctures of the maxillofrontal suture and the lacrimal.

Didelphis virginiana virginiana Kerr

1792. *Didelphis virginiana* Kerr, The animal kingdom . . . p. 193. Type locality, Virginia.

Range. Throughout the state (see Map. 8.1).

Diagnosis and Comparisons. D. v. virginiana is of large size with a relatively shorter tail than adjacent subspecies.

Remarks. One specimen from Jo Daviess County has the last upper molar in an abnormal position, pointing backward rather than downward. It probably never would have occluded with the lower molars.

Records of occurrence. SPECIMENS EXAMINED, 90. **Jo Daviess Co.:** [1] 3½ mi S, 2 mi E Apple River Canyon, 1 (UI). **Stephenson Co.:** [2] 3 mi W Freeport, 1 (UI). **Lake Co.:** [3b] Waukegan, 2 (CAS); [4a] Deerfield, 1 (CAS); [4b] Highland Park, 2 (FM). **Ogle Co.:** [5] 1 mi S Byron, 1 (NIU). **De Kalb Co.:** [6a] 5 mi N De Kalb, 1 (NIU); [6b] 2 mi N De Kalb, 1 (NIU). **Kane Co.:** [7a] St. Charles, 1 (CAS); [7b] near St. Charles, 1 (ISM). **Cook Co.:** [8a] Glencoe, 1 (FM); [8b] Evanston, 1 (FM); [8c] Niles, 1 (FM); [9] Chicago, 1 (FM); [10] 1 mi S Palos Hills, 1 (UI); [11] Hazelcrest, 1 (FM). **Du Page Co.:** [12] Glen Ellyn, 1 (UI), 1 (NIU); [13] Naperville, 1 (FM). **Bureau Co.:** [15] 2 mi NE Mineral,

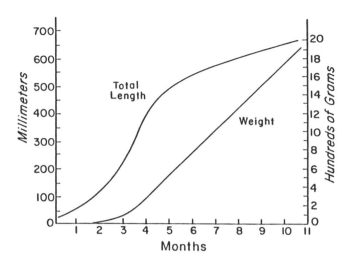

Fig. 8.0A. Growth in opossums in total length and weight as based upon tagged wild opossums. (After Petrides, 1949)

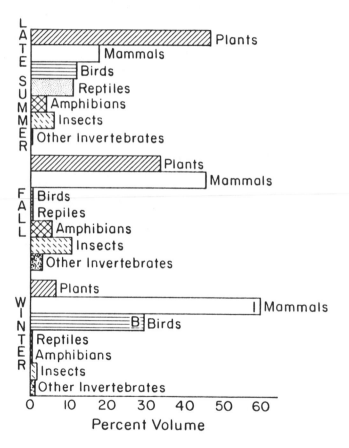

Fig. 8.3B. Major food groups of 131 opossums in southern Illinois at different times of the year: late summer, fall, winter. (After Stieglitz and Klimstra, 1962)

Inter-orbital const.	Post-orbital const.	Breadth across canines	Breadth across molars	C-M⁴ length
25.2	10.85	26.5	35.8	47.3
25.1	10.0	20.7	35.4	50.5
—	—	21.5	34.0	48.9
25.7	12.5	21.6	37.8	48.5
20.9	11.2	19.75	33.3	46.2
22.5	11.7	21.5	35.0	46.75
20.6	11.3	18.15	34.0	—
20.0	11.2	17.55	33.1	43.2
21.0	11.3	18.8	34.1	45.1
24.7	12.55	21.0	34.8	45.65
22.2	11.4	19.3	35.2	46.3

DeDecker Farm, 1 (UI). **Hancock Co.:** [17] Warsaw*, 2 (US). **Fulton Co.:** [18] 2 mi S Farmington, 1 (UI); [19a] 1 mi W Canton, 2 (UI); [19b] Canton, 1 (UI). **Livingston Co.:** [20] 6 mi S Dwight, 1 (NIU). **McLean Co.:** [21] 4 mi NW Hudson, 1 (ISU); [22] 1 mi E Normal, 1 (ISU). **Champaign Co.:** [24a] 3 mi N. Mahomet, Sangamon River, 1 (UI); [24b] 5 mi NW Champaign, 1 (UI); [25a] ½ mi N Urbana, 1 (UI); [25b] Champaign, 5 (UI); [25c] Urbana, 8 (UI); [25d] 3 mi E Urbana, 1 (UI); [25e] S Urbana, 1 (UI); [25f] 2 mi S Champaign, 1 (UI); no specific locality [not plotted], 1 (UI). **Morgan Co.:** [26] 6 mi SW Ashland, 1 (UI).

Macoupin Co.: [27] 3 mi E Virden, 1 (ISM); [28] 8 mi E Carlinville, 1 (SIE). **Sangamon Co.:** [30a] Springfield, 1 (SIC); [30b] 3 mi SE Springfield, 2 (ISM); [30c] South Fork Sangamon River, near Rochester, 1 (ISM). **Cumberland Co.:** [31] 3 mi SE Neoga, 1 (UI). **Madison Co.:** [32a] 4 mi S Godfrey, 1 (SIE); [32b] Alton, 1 (SIE); [33] 7 mi S Bunker Hill [labelled Macoupin Co.], 1 (SIE); [34a] 4 4/10 mi W Edwardsville, 1 (SIE); [34b] Edwardsville, SIU campus, 1 (SIE). **Bond Co.:** [35] 6 mi W, 1 mi N Greenville, 1 (UI). **Jasper Co.:** [36] Bogota, 4 (FM). **Saint Clair Co.:** [37] 4 mi N Mascoutah, 1 (UI); [38] Belleville, 1 (US), 1 (SIE). **Clinton Co.:** [39] 6 mi E Jamestown, 1 (SIE). **Marion Co.:** [40 Odin, 1 (FM). **Jefferson Co.:** [41] T3S, R3E, Sec. 18, 1 (SRL); no specific locality [not plotted] 1 (SRL). **Randolph Co.:** [42] Kaskaskia Island, 3 (UI). **Perry Co.:** [43] no specific locality, 1 (SIC). **Franklin Co.:** [44] 2 mi S West Frankfort, 1 (NIU). **Hamilton Co.:** [45] 3 mi S McLeansboro, 1 (UI). **Jackson Co.:** [46] near Ava, 1 (SRL); [47] 3 mi N Murphysboro, 1 (SIC); [48] 1 mi W Carbondale, 1 (SIC). **Saline Co.:** [50] no specific locality, 1 (UI). **Union Co.:** [51] 6 mi W Jonesboro, 1 (FM). **Alexander Co.:** [52] Olive Branch, 1 (US), 2 (FM).

Additional records. **Lake Co.:** [3a] Illinois Dunes State Park [=Illinois Beach State Park], 1 (FS). **Henry Co.:** [14] Kewanee (Necker and Hatfield, 1941:41). **Will Co.:** Romeoville (Necker and Hatfield, 1941:41). **Ford Co.:** [23] Piper City (Necker and Hatfield, 1941:41). **Champaign Co.:** [25b] Champaign, 1 (UM). **Macoupin Co.:** [29] Mount Olive, 1 (FS). **Williamson Co.:** [49] Herrin (Necker and Hatfield, 1941:41).

———

*Worthen specimens.

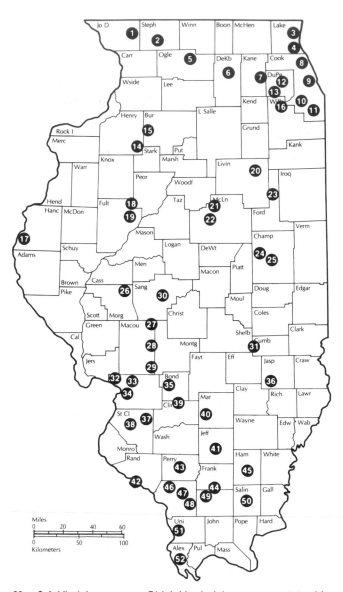

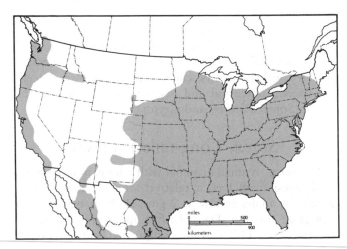

Map 8.1. Virginia opossum, *Didelphis virginiana,* occurs statewide; records of occurrence are numbered (see text *Records of occurrence*). The subspecies is *D. v. virginiana.* The distribution of the species in the United States is shaded.

Order Insectivora, Insectivores

The majority are small nocturnal mammals with long, pointed noses, small eyes, sharply cusped teeth, some of which are single-cusped, others multicusped; sutures of skull disappear early; tympanic bone usually ring-shaped; no inflated auditory bulla. Consists of seven or eight living families—depending on one's interpretation—and numerous extinct families.

KEY TO INSECTIVORA (SHREWS AND MOLES) IN ILLINOIS

1a. Total length more than 140 mm; forefeet greatly enlarged, paddle-shaped, and larger than hind feet; eyes not visible externally; skull with zygomatic arches TALPIDAE
Sculopus aquaticus, p. 78

1b. Total length less than 140 mm; forefeet not greatly enlarged and smaller than hind feet; eyes small but visible; skull without zygomatic arches SORICIDAE 2

2a. First upper incisors with medial tines (see Fig. 8.5); postmandibular foramen usually absent; length of tail more than 45 percent of body length SOREX 3

2b. First upper incisors without medial tines; postmandibular foramen usually present; length of tail less than 36 percent of body length BLARINA, CRYPTOTIS 5

3a. In lateral view, only three upper unicuspids are readily evident, as third unicuspid is flattened and disklike and fifth unicuspid is small and often hidden (see Fig. 8.4); medial tines between large upper incisors lengthened (see Fig. 8.5)
Sorex hoyi p. 64

3b. In lateral view, five upper unicuspids evident, but fifth is reduced in size; medial tines between upper incisors present but not lengthened 4

4a. Tail usually 30 mm or more; hind foot usually 11 mm or more; third upper unicuspid usually larger in lateral view than fourth (see Fig. 8.4); breadth across fourth unicuspid less than length of unicuspid toothrow *Sorex cinereus* p. 58

4b. Tail usually 29 mm or less; hind foot usually 10 mm or less; third unicuspid usually smaller in lateral view than fourth; breadth across fourth unicuspid more than length of unicuspid toothrow *Sorex longirostris* p. 61

5a. Five upper unicuspids, with four readily visible in lateral view; color of dorsum blackish; greatest length of skull 18.0 mm or more *Blarina* 6

5b. Four upper unicuspids, with only three readily visible in lateral view (see Fig. 8.4); color of dorsum brownish or brownish gray; greatest length of the skull less than 18.5 mm
Cryptotis parva p. 74

6a. Greatest length of skull 21.3 mm or more; braincase breadth 11.6 mm or more; head-body length 81 mm or more; weight 13.5 gms or more
Blarina brevicauda p. 67

6b. Greatest length of skull 20.7 mm or less; braincase breadth 11.4 mm or less; head-body length less than 81 mm; weight 13.4 gms or less
Blarina carolinensis p. 72

Family Soricidae, Shrews

Small insectivores, including the smallest terrestrial mammals; nose long and flexible, ears short, feet small; skull with elongated rostrum, no zygomatic arch; first incisor enlarged, other incisors, canines, and premolars (except the fourth) unicuspid and peglike. Represented by the genera *Sorex*, *Blarina*, and *Cryptotis*.

Sorex, Long-tailed shrews

Diagnosis. A small mammal with a long, pointed nose; small eyes; small feet; a relatively long tail; small ears; weight of adults as low as 2 gms; skull triangular, with elongated rostrum (Fig. 8.4); five upper unicuspids, but the third and fifth may be compressed and reduced in size; cranium with incomplete zygomatic arches; no auditory bullae; tympanic bone ringlike; braincase relatively large; color variable, but usually brownish gray above and slightly lighter below.

Dental formula. 3/1, 1/1, 3/1, 3/3.

Comparisons. Sorex differs from *Blarina* in having a longer tail, both actually and relative to the head-body length; tail usually more than half the body length rather than less than one-third the body length; color brownish rather than blackish; underside of tail noticeably lighter than top; skull shorter (greatest length less than 16.5 mm) and narrower (braincase breadth less than 8.5 mm).

Sorex differs from *Cryptotis* in having a longer tail, both actually and relative to the head-body length; upper

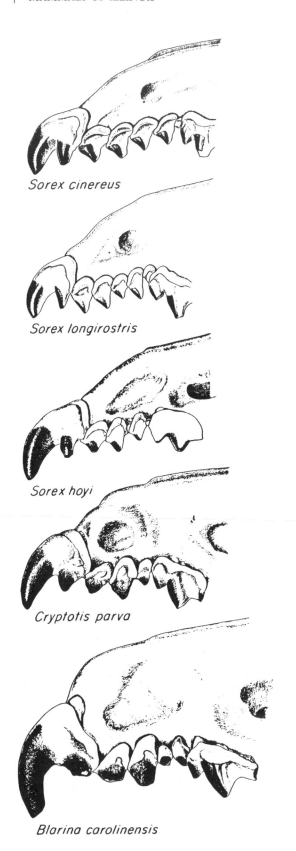

Fig. 8.5. Upper incisors of *Sorex* with medially located tines, smaller in *Sorex cinereus* and *S. longirostris* (left), larger in *S. hoyi* (right).

jaw has four obvious unicuspids plus a small fifth one, rather than only three unicuspids, with the small fourth one hidden from view; large upper incisors touching at midline rather than with a gap.

Secondary sexual variation. No significant secondary sexual differences in size were noted in any samples of *Sorex*. Males and females are combined.

Aging. Shrews that are young can be told from old animals by the position of the cingulum of upper incisor one, relative to the alveolus. In young animals the cingulum is oppressed to the dentary. With increasing age and growth, the root increases in length and pushes the cingulum away from the alveolus. An increase in distance between the alveolus and cingulum is directly correlated with an increase in age.

For some cranial measurements, as well as total length, there are significant differences between animals less and more than one year old. Diersing (1980:79) points out that in 13 of 28 characters in *Sorex hoyi*, there are significant differences.

Sorex cinereus, Masked shrew

Range. Northern third of state and southern part near the Wabash River and near junction of the Mississippi and Ohio rivers. See Map 8.2.

Diagnosis. A soricid of the subgenus *Otisorex* characterized by no postmandibular canal on the inside of the lower jaw; a pigmented ridge on the lingual side of the unicuspids, running from the apex to the cingulum; length of tail usually 30 mm or more; hind foot usually more than 10 mm; third unicuspid usually as large or larger than fourth; secondary cusp of incisor one is large.

Color. Dorsum brownish black to almost black; feet tan or dusky. Molting apparently occurs in late March and early April and females may molt later than males.

Comparisons. Sorex cinereus needs comparison with three other small shrews: *Sorex longirostris, S. hoyi,* and *Cryptotis parva*. It differs from *Cryptotis parva* in the characters given under *Sorex* for telling these two genera apart (p. 57).

S. cinereus differs from *S. longirostris* as follows: unicuspid 3 usually as large or larger than unicuspid 4

Fig. 8.4. Lateral view of rostral part of skull of five shrews in Illinois. Note differences in the number and size of the unicuspid (small) teeth.

Fig. 8.6A. Masked shrew, *Sorex cinereus*. (From Hoffmeister and Mohr, 1957. Photograph by Ernest P. Walker, Smithsonian Institution, Washington, D.C.)

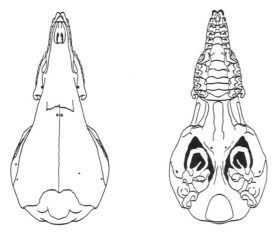

Fig. 8.6B. *Sorex cinereus,* dorsal and ventral views of skull; 1 mi W Park Ridge, Cook Co., Illinois, 56225 UI. Female, 16.1 mm greatest length.

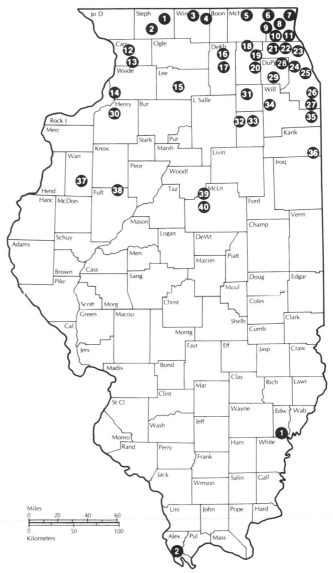

Map 8.2. Distribution of the masked shrew, *Sorex cinereus*. The subspecies in northern Illinois is *S. c. cinereus;* in southern Illinois, *S. c. lesueurii*. Numbers are referenced in *Records of occurrence.* The distribution of the species in the United States is shaded.

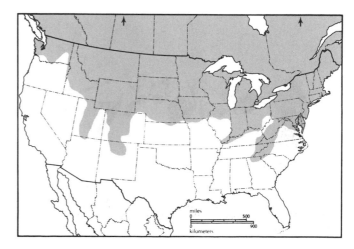

(Fig. 8.4), rather than smaller; tail usually 30 mm or more, rather than less; hind foot usually 11 mm or more, rather than less; secondary cusp on incisor 1 larger and directed slightly more forward; length of unicuspids 1–5 greater than the breadth across unicuspids 4, as measured across the outside, whereas in *S. longirostris* less (Fig. 8.5). This latter character indicates that the rostrum of *cinereus* is relatively long and narrow; of *longirostris,* short and broad.

S. cinereus differs from *S. hoyi* as follows: four or five unicuspids easily visible in lateral view, whereas only three are readily visible because of crowding and compression; unicuspid 3 about same size as unicuspid 4 rather than very small and disklike; unicuspid 5 small but not minute; hind foot longer, usually more than 10.5 mm rather than less.

Secondary sexual variation and aging. See account of the genus *Sorex.*

Remarks. The long-tailed shrews obtained in northern Illinois in all probability will be the masked shrew. There is one record for the pygmy shrew (*Sorex hoyi*) within

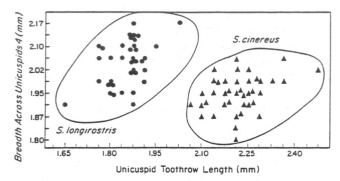

Fig. 8.7. Scattergram comparing length of unicuspid toothrow and breadth across upper unicuspids 4 in *Sorex longirostris* and *S. cinereus* for Illinois specimens.

the northern segment of the range of *S. cinereus*. The long-tailed shrews of central and southern Illinois in all probability will be the southeastern shrew, *S. longirostris*, but there are at least two records of *S. cinereus* within the range of *S. longirostris*.

Habitat

Masked shrews prefer damp, even wet, places where there is a good ground cover. For example, one was taken in a dense stand of grass and weeds near a railroad right-of-way that was damp, not wet. Of 11 others taken in Iroquois County, four were taken in sedge meadows, three in shrub prairie, three in flatwoods, and one in a mesic sand-prairie (Mahan and Heidorn; 1983 *MS*). In the damp and marshy areas of Goose Lake Prairie, Grundy County, masked shrews were fairly abundant. From 1969 to 1973, Birkenholz (1973) found them to be the third most abundant mammal at Goose Lake Prairie, next to the meadow vole, *Microtus pennsylvanicus*, and the short-tailed shrew, *Blarina brevicauda*. In McLean County, specimens have been taken in an old brome-grass meadow.

In southern Illinois, masked shrews live in even damper situations. Five specimens were collected near Miller City, Alexander County, along a manmade drainage ditch that ran through a forest of gum, oak, and ash. When we dug down only a few inches in the soil we reached the water table and there were numerous small pools of standing, surface water among the tree stumps and logs.

In Indiana, masked shrews were taken in tamarack bogs, swampy deciduous woods, fencerows bordering bluegrass fields, border of a bald cypress pond (Mumford and Whitaker, 1982:99). In Wisconsin, Jackson (1961:29) adds these habitats: alder thickets and spruce-cedar swamps.

Habits

These mammals are primarily nocturnal. Although the species is not uncommon in many parts of northern Illinois, little is known of its habits within the state. At

a site 2.2 mi SW Middle Grove, Fulton County, one sunken can intended to catch shrews caught six adult male masked shrews in one night. Overall, some 22 masked shrews were taken at this locality in a relatively short period of time.

Because these mammals have such a high metabolic rate, they require a relatively large amount of food. Therefore, in live traps or sunken can traps they usually die of starvation in a short time.

Food

The stomachs of Illinois masked shrews have not been examined for food contents. However, they feed extensively on insects and other invertebrates. In New York, the percentage by volume in the stomachs of 62 masked shrews was 65 percent for insects; for all invertebrates, at least 80 percent (Hamilton, 1930:36). In Indiana, the stomachs of 50 masked shrews by volume consisted of more than 98 percent invertebrates, with only small amounts of *Endogone* and other vegetable material (Whitaker and Mumford, 1972a). These authors concluded that masked shrews seldom ate earthworms, in contrast to the feeding habits of some larger species of shrews.

Reproduction

Breeding occurs in late March or early April, and perhaps at other times of the year. Two Illinois specimens taken on April 14 carried embryos. In Indiana, two females taken April 5 were lactating, and pregnant females were taken in mid-May (Mumford and Whitaker, 1982:101). The gestation period is about 18 days and litter size runs from four to eight embryos. Young are foraging for themelves in mid-June because animals we have collected on June 12 are young of the year, to judge from the lack of wear on the teeth. We suspect that animals must be in their second year to bear young. One female specimen from Edwards County has three pair of inguinally situated mammary glands.

Variation

Two subspecies are known in Illinois.

Sorex cinereus cinereus Kerr

1792. *Sorex arcticus cinereus* Kerr, The animal kingdom . . . , p. 206. Type from Fort Severn, Ontario, Canada.
1925. *Sorex cinereus cinereus*, Jackson, J. Mamm., 6:56.

Range. Northern third of state as far south as Fulton and McLean counties.
Diagnosis. A medium-sized subspecies; small in breadth across M^2-M^3, long unicuspid toothrow, short molariform toothrow.
Comparisons. For a comparison with *S. c. lesueurii*, see that account.

Records of occurrence. SPECIMENS EXAMINED, 119. **Stephenson Co.:** [1] 1½ mi NW Dakota, 1 (UI); [2] 3 mi W Freeport, 1 (UI). **Winnebago Co.:** [3] 3 mi W of South Beloit, 1 (SRL); [4] 2 mi E Roscoe, 1 (UI). **McHenry Co.:** [5] 1 mi W Hebron, 1 (SRL). **Lake Co.:** [6a] Chain-of-Lakes State Park, 6 (IDC); [6b] Lake Villa, 1 (NIU); [6c] Fox Lake, 3 (FM); [6d] Pistakee Bay, 2 (FM); [7a] Camp Logan, 9 (FM); [7b] Zion City [=Zion], 1 (CAS); [7c] Beach, 1 (CAS); [8] Grayslake, 1 (CAS); [9] Volo Bog, 3 (ISM); [10] Lake Zurich, 1 (NHS); [11a] Lake Forest, 1 (FM); [11b] Prairie View, 1 (CAS); [11c] Highland Park, 1 (CAS); [11d] Deerfield, 2 (CAS). **Carroll Co.:** [12a] ¼ mi W Mt. Carroll, 1 (UI); [12b] Mt. Carroll, 1 (UI); [12c] Carroll Twp., 1 (NHS); [13] Fairhaven Twp., 1 (NHS). **Whiteside Co.:** [14] 5 mi W Erie, 1 (UI). **Lee Co.:** [15] Amboy, 1 (UI). **De Kalb Co.:** [16a] 6 mi N De Kalb, 1 (NIU); [16b] 5.7 mi N De Kalb, 1 (NIU); [16c] 5 mi N De Kalb, 1 (NIU); [17a] 2 mi N De Kalb, 1 (NIU); [17b] De Kalb, 1 (NIU). **Kane Co.:** [18] 7.3 mi W, 4.8 mi N Elgin, 1 (UI); [19a] Elgin, 1 (UI); [19b] Bowes, 1 (CAS); [20] near St. Charles, 1 (ISM). **Cook Co.:** [21a] Barrington, 1 (UI); [21b] Crabtree Farm Nature Center (Forest Preserve), 1 (ISM); [21c] near Palatine, 1 (FM); [22a] 4 mi N Des Plaines, on Hwy 45, dam no. 2, 2 (UI); [22b] 3 mi N Des Plaines, 3 (NHS); [23a] Glencoe, 1 (CAS); [23b] West Northfield, 2 (US); [23c] 1 mi E Golf, 1 (UI); [23d] Evanston, 1 (FM); [23e] 1 mi W Park Ridge, 2 (UI); [23f] Niles Center [=Niles], 1 (CAS); [24] River Forest, 1 (CAS); [25] Chicago, 1 (FM); [26a] Chicago, Calumet River Preserves, 2 (UI); [26b] Calumet Lake, 1 (CAS); [26c] Calumet City, 1 (CAS); [27] Chicago Heights, 3 (FM). **Du Page Co.:** [28] 2 mi N, 1 mi W Bensenville, 1 (UI); [29] 1 mi W Lisle, 1 (UI). **Henry Co.:** [30] 10 mi N, 1 mi E Cambridge, 1 (KU). **Kendall Co.:** [31] Yorkville, 4 (UI). **Grundy Co.:** [32] 6 mi W Morris, 3 (UI); [33a] Morris, 1 (UI); [33b] Goose Lake Prairie, 2 (ISU). **Will Co.:** [34] 4 mi W Joliet (Backroad), 1 (KU); [35] Crete, 1 (ISU). **Kankakee Co.:** [36] 6 mi E St. Anne, 1 (UI). **Warren Co.:** [37] 5 mi NE Roseville, 1 (WIU). **Fulton Co.:** [38] 2.2 mi SW Middlegrove, 22 (UI). **McLean Co.:** [39] 2 mi NW Hudson, 2 (ISU); [40] ¼ mi E [Jct.] Rts 55 and 51, Normal, 1 (ISU).

Sorex cinereus lesueurii (Duvernoy)

1842. *Amphisorex lesueurii* Duvernoy, Mag. Zool. d'Anat. Comp. et Paleont., 1842:33. Type locality fixed as New Harmony, Posey Co., Indiana (see Diersing and Hoffmeister, 1981:7).

1942. *Sorex cinereus lesueurii*, Bole and Moulthrop, Sci. Publs. Cleveland Mus. Nat. Hist. 5:95.

Range. Edwards and Alexander counties, southern Illinois.

Diagnosis. A subspecies of *S. cinereus* of medium to large size, skull large, broad across M²M² and M³M³, long molariform toothrow, short unicuspid toothrow.

Comparisons. S. c. lesueurii differs from *S. c. cinereus* in being broader across molars, having a longer molariform toothrow, but a shorter unicuspid toothrow. If length of molariform toothrow is plotted against breadth

across toothrows, there is more than an 80 percent separation of the two subspecies.

Records of occurrence. SPECIMENS EXAMINED, 6. **Edwards Co.:** [41] 2 mi N Grayville, adjacent Mud Creek, 1 (UI). **Alexander Co.:** [42] 1½ mi E, ½ mi S Miller City, 5 (UI).

Sorex longirostris, Southeastern shrew

Range. Illinois, south of a line from northern Hancock County across to northern Vermilion County (Map 8.3).

Diagnosis. A soricid of the subgenus *Otisorex* characterized by length of tail being usually less than 30 mm, hind foot usually 10 mm or less; third unicuspid usually smaller than fourth, secondary cusp on incisors one not especially large and may project slightly posteriorly; tail narrow in diameter and not especially well haired.

Color. Dorsum reddish brown, but variable and indistinguishable in color alone from *Sorex cinereus* (p. 50).

Comparisons. S. longirostris differs from *S. cinereus* as pointed out in the account of that species (p. 58). The diagnosis above for *S. longirostris* emphasizes features for separating *longirostris* from *cinereus*. The rostrum is broad and this is shown by the breadth across unicuspids 4 and breadth across the upper toothrows. In *S. longirostris* (in contrast with *S. cinereus*), the breadth across unicuspids 4 is greater than the length of the unicuspid toothrow.

S. longirostris differs from *S. hoyi* in the same way that *S. cinereus* does. See the account of the latter species (p. 59).

Secondary sexual variation and aging. See account of the genus *Sorex* (p. 57).

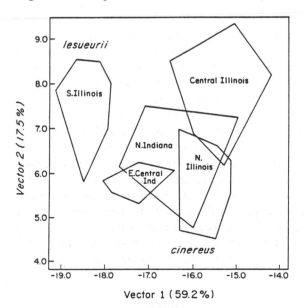

Fig. 8.8. Canonical variate analysis of samples of *Sorex cinereus* from Illinois and Indiana. The lines connect the peripheral specimens of each geographical sample.

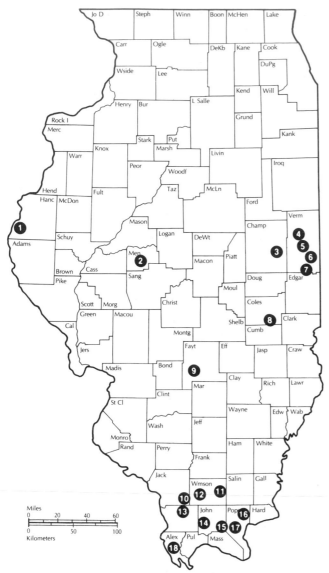

Map 8.3. Distribution of the southeastern shrew, *Sorex longirostris*. The subspecies is *S. l. longirostris*. Numbers are referenced in *Records of occurrence*. The distribution of the species in the United States is shaded.

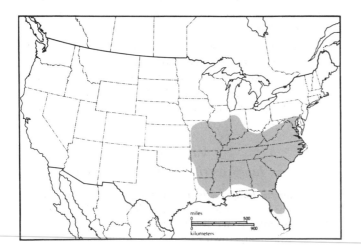

Remarks. Sorex longirostris is the long-tailed shrew of the southern half of Illinois, although there also are two records of *S. cinereus* from the south—one each in Alexander and Edwards counties. At no place, however, have the two species been taken together. Near Terre Haute, Indiana, the two species have been taken in the same field (Mumford and Whitaker, 1982) and there is the distinct possibility that the two may be taken in this fashion in McLean, Vermilion, Edwards, and Alexander counties, in Illinois.

In some cases, the size of the third unicuspid—smaller than the fourth unicuspid—does not serve to distinguish *S. longirostris*. For example, in 28 specimens of *longirostris*, 23 have the third unicuspid smaller and in one specimen both unicuspids are the same size. When there is doubt about the size of the third unicuspid, recourse should be made to measurements that indicate the relatively shorter (than in *cinereus*) rostrum in *S. longirostris*. For example, the length of the unicuspid toothrow is less than the breadth across the labial sides of unicuspids 4 (the reverse is true in *S. cinereus*). The length of the unicuspid toothrow is less than 2.0 mm; in *S. cinereus*, more than 2.1 mm.

E. R. Hall (1981:31) shows the range of this species in northeastern Illinois, apparently based on a record that he lists as "Pistakee Lake." I know of no specimens of *S. longirostris* from such a locality; I have seen two specimens of *S. cinereus* from Pistakee Bay, Lake County (see *S. c. cinereus* under *Records of occurrence*, p. 61).

The specimen of *S. longirostris* taken on July 6, 1983, at the Phillips Research Tract, Champaign County, represents the first specimen from this area or from Champaign County. Trapping of small mammals has been underway for about 40 years at Trelease Grasslands, across the road from Phillips, and for about 12 years at Phillips Tract, yet no long-tailed shrews have been caught previously.

Sorex longirostris is reported from a bone deposit in Meyer Cave, 4 mi SSW Columbia, Monroe County. This is a natural entrapment of mammals caused by their dropping down a shaft with no escape. The remains in this cave are thought to date from as much as 2,000 years before the present. Parmalee (1967:136) reported 27 individuals represented in the bone material. This cave is approximately 78 mi WSW of the currently known occurrence of the species near Vandalia.

Habitat

Southeastern shrews are found in a variety of habitats in Illinois. These include grassy and weedy areas in a woods near a stream (Middle Fork of the Vermilion River), restored tallgrass prairie (Phillips Research Tract, east of Urbana), grassy fields adjacent to a pond (Jackson and Union cos.), cypress woods with temporary standing

Fig. 8.9A. Southeastern shrew, *Sorex longirostris.* (From Hoffmeister and Mohr, 1957. Photograph by K. Maslowski and W. W. Goodpaster)

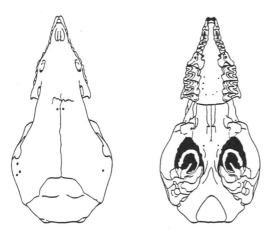

Fig. 8.9B. *Sorex longirostris,* dorsal and ventral views of skull; 1 4/5 mi NE Collison, Vermilion Co., Illinois, 55287 UI. Male, 15.4 mm greatest length.

water (Johnson Co.), among grasses, multiflora rose, blackberries, and river birch (Pope Co.).

In northeastern Missouri, these shrews were found in grassland usually near wooded areas or fencerows (Mock and Kivett, 1980). In Indiana, southeastern shrews have been taken from a variety of habitats (Mumford and Whitaker, 1982:104) much the same as in Illinois.

Habits

Southeastern shrews are seemingly easy prey for predators. In Union County, William George recovered 25 of these shrews caught by his domestic cats. Along the Little Vermilion River, 5 mi SE Georgetown, Vermilion County, John Laughnan's cat has caught at least eight. An immature shrew, possibly dropped by a predator, was picked up along a road 4 mi E Eddyville, Pope County (Klimstra and Roseberry, 1969:413). Because most of these shrews are brought in by the cats during the daytime and in unspoiled condition, one might conclude that the

shrews are diurnal in their activities or are easy to hunt out and catch, or both. Mumford and Whitaker, (1982:105) regard this shrew as "partially diurnal" with one worker observing one during the day at the edge of a woods and catching it when it crawled beneath some bark. Others were caught in sunken can traps in the daytime.

The shrews are known to produce a "bird-like series of very soft chirps" and "the echolocation frequency was recorded at 22,000 cycles per second" (French, 1980).

Southeastern shrews readily find their way into sunken can traps. We have been successful in catching these shrews in this way in Illinois, and workers in other mid-American states have also. These shrews were regarded by Hoffmeister and Mohr (1957) as one of the least-known mammals in the state, and represented by less than 12 specimens. Now, I know of 65 in collections and another dozen or so that are mentioned in the literature. *S. longistrostris* is probably no more abundant today, but we have perfected methods of collecting the species. French (1980) stated that on two study plots in Alabama, the population of southeastern shrews was estimated at 30 per hectare and 44 per hectare, respectively.

Food

Foods eaten by southeastern shrews in Illinois have not been determined. French (1980) reported the results of examination of 102 shrew stomachs from Vigo County, Indiana; 73 percent of the food consisted of spiders, lepidopteran larvae, crickets, beetles, and harvestmen. Seven stomachs (also from Indiana) analyzed by Whitaker and Mumford (1972a) contained mostly spiders, slugs, snails, lepidopteran larvae, vegetation, and centipedes.

Reproduction

On April 11, a female southeastern shrew was caught that carried five embryos and on June 4 another with four. These two were apparently overwintering females. Two specimens taken on September 18 and September 22 each had four embryos and probably were young of the year. French (1980) found pregnant females from March 31 to October 6. Apparently, females born in the spring can produce a litter by fall and some do so. It is not known if overwintering females produce two litters per year. French (1980) gives the number of embryos as 3.9 (1–6).

Variation
Sorex longirostris longirostris Bachman

1837. *Sorex longirostris* Bachman, J. Acad. Nat. Sci. Phila., 1, 7(2):370. Type locality Hume Plantation, swamps Santee River [=Cat Island, mouth Santee R.], Georgetown Co., South Carolina.

Range. As given for the species (p. 61 and Map 8.3).

Diagnosis and Comparisons. A medium-sized subspecies, reportedly smaller than *S. l. fisheri* from the Dismal Swamp, Virginia, hind foot usually 10 mm or less, unicuspid toothrow length usually less than 2.0 mm.

Records of occurrence. SPECIMENS EXAMINED, 64.
Hancock Co.: [1a] Warsaw, Geode Park, 1 (WIU); [1b] Kibbe Pond, 1 (WIU). **Menard Co.:** [2] 3 mi E Petersburg, 1 (ISM), 2 (UI). **Champaign Co.:** [3] Phillips Research Tract, Urbana, 1 (UI). **Vermilion Co.:** [4a] 1⅛ mi NE Collison, 16 (UI); [4b] 1 mi W Higginsville, 1 (UI); [5] 3.6 mi N, 1½ mi W Hillery, 1 (UI); [6] Forest Glen, near Westville, 1 (UI); [7] 5 mi SW Goergetown, 3 (UI). **Coles Co.:** [8a] 2 mi S Charleston, 1 (UI); [8b] Fox Ridge, 1 (NHS). **Fayette Co.:** [9] 2½ mi SW Vandalia, 1 (UI). **Williamson Co.:** [11] 1.2 mi E Crab Orchard, 1 (SRL); [12] Crab Orchard Lake Wildlife Refuge, 7 (WG). **Union Co.:** [13a] 2 mi N Cobden, 1 (WG); [13b] 2 mi NE Cobden, 1 (WG); [13c] 1½ mi N Cobden, George's Farm, 14 (WG); [13d] 1 mi N Cobden, 1 (WG); [13e] T12S, R1W, Sec. 4, 1 (SRL); no specific locality [not plotted] (Klimstra and Roseberry, 1969:413). **Johnson Co.:** [15] Reevesville, 1 (MCZ), 3 (FM). **Pope Co.:** [17] 2 mi E, ½ mi S Dixon Springs, 3 (UI). **Alexander Co.:** [18] Olive Branch, 3 (FM).

Additional records. **Jackson Co.:** [10] 6½ mi S Carbondale, McGuire's Orchard Farm (W. G. George, 1977:1). **Johnson Co.:** [14] Bird Spring Swamp (George, 1977:2). **Pope Co.:** [16] 4 mi E Eddyville (Klimstra and Roseberry, 1969:413).

Sorex hoyi, Pygmy shrew

Range. Known only from the northeastern corner (near Palatine, Cook County) and southeastern corner (Wabash County) of the state.

Diagnosis. A small soricid of the subgenus *Microsorex* with the third unicuspid small and disklike, fifth unicuspid minute, median tines on large upper incisors long; postmandibular foramen absent, mental foramen usually located ventral to M_1.

Color. Brownish to brownish black on dorsum, lighter on venter. The color seems more like that of *Sorex longirostris* and less dark than in *Sorex cinereus*, but the sample of *S. hoyi* is small.

Comparisons. *Sorex hoyi* differs from *S. cinereus* and *S. longirostris* in having a small disklike third unicuspid, a minute fifth unicuspid, and well-developed median tines between the upper incisors. When seen in lateral view, there appear to be only three unicuspids rather than five, and when viewed from the front, the median tines between the large upper incisors are much longer.

S. hoyi differs from *Cryptotis* and *Blarina* in the generic differences given on pages 74 and 66 respectively. Outstanding differences are the relatively longer tail of *S. hoyi*.

Secondary sexual variation and aging. See account of the genus *Sorex* (p. 57).

Remarks. *Sorex hoyi* has most often been referred to as *Microsorex hoyi*, a member of a distinct genus. Diersing

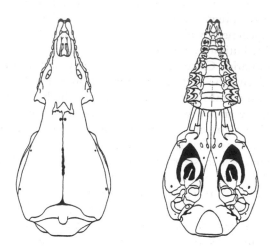

Fig. 8.10. *Sorex hoyi*, dorsal and ventral views of skull. Sioux Narrows, Ontario, Canada, 38958 UI. Sex unknown, 16.2 mm greatest length.

(1980) felt that the phylogenetic and systematic relationships would best be served if *Microsorex* were considered a subgenus of *Sorex*, most closely allied with the subgenus *Otisorex*. This arrangement is followed here.

Sorex hoyi was reported from a skull fragment from the bone deposit of Meyer Cave, 4 mi SSW Columbia, Monroe County, by Parmalee and Munyer (1966:82). The fragment consisted of part of the rostrum, with "both I and Pm³" and a lower left jaw. This record is far outside of the expected range of the species at the present time.

Habitat

Pygmy shrews in Illinois probably live in wooded areas or in grassy places adjacent to woods. They probably require fallen and rotting logs or some forest-floor litter. The specimen taken in Cook County was captured in a garage in mid-winter and it may have been forced indoors by a heavy coating of ice out-of-doors (Sanborn and Tibbitts, 1949). In Iowa, two pygmy shrews were taken in a bluegrass field, ungrazed for four years, adjacent to a lake (Bowles, 1975). In Wisconsin, one was taken in a hemlock forest under a rotten log, three in hardwoods on clay soils, one among dense pines, and still another in mixed forest with ferns. Whitaker (personal communication) informs me that nearly 100 were taken under logs in dense forests of the unglaciated hills of south central Indiana.

Habits

This is the rarest of the shrews in Illinois, being known by only two specimens. Nonetheless, when collecting techniques are improved and sunken can traps are used more often, and when we are more familiar with the habitat requirements of the species, it may be that many more specimens will become available and their habits and distribution better known.

In Ontario, Canada, a captive pygmy shrew was as active during the daytime as at night (Prince, 1940). When it slept, the limbs were drawn up under the body. When awake, the animal was active most of the time. It held the tail straight out or slightly curved upward when it ran. Prince says that this shrew jumped out of a 4½ inch container, which seems remarkable for an animal with such short legs. Saunders (1929) had one escape over the edges of a tub three or four inches high.

The sounds made by these shrews have been described as short, sharp squeaks as the animal moved around the cage (Prince, 1940) and "whispering and whistling infinitely high" notes (Saunders, 1929). Also, pygmy shrews emit a very powerful, musky odor, especially when agitated. Saunders (1929) went on to say that this shrew often sat up on its hind legs, kangaroo-fashion.

Pygmy shrews are reported to be active the year around, having been trapped on the snow and in runways through the snow (Long, 1974).

Food

In southern Indiana, pygmy shrews fed on insect larvae, spiders, adult beetles, and ants, to judge from stomach analyses of 63 individuals (Whitaker and Cudmore, 1988). Prince (1940), during a 10-day period, fed a captive shrew the carcasses of 20 *Sorex cinereus,* one *Peromyscus,* one *Clethrionomys,* and the carcass of one *Sorex hoyi.* Saunders (1929) found that his shrew pulled below ground all food items offered — raw fish, raw meat, earthworms — but did not necessarily eat all of these.

Reproduction

A specimen in Clay County, Iowa, was reported as carrying seven embryos on July 18. Gunderson and Beer (1953) made the statement, without giving any data, that "several litters are born each year." Long (1974), however, said there is no evidence for more than one litter per year. A male specimen in our collection from Minnesota had enlarged testes on May 14; a female also in our collection from near Pinawa, Manitoba, on September 15 was lactating.

Variation

Two subspecies are recorded from the state according to the revisionary studies of Diersing (1980). In earlier literature, these shrews were reported under the name *Microsorex* (see discussion above under *Sorex hoyi* p. 64).

Sorex hoyi hoyi Baird

1858. *Sorex hoyi* Baird, Mammals, *in* Repts. Expl. Surv., 8:32. Type locality Racine, Racine Co., Wisconsin.

Map 8.4. Known records of the pygmy shrew, *Sorex hoyi.* Two subspecies occur in Illinois: *S. h. hoyi* to the north; *S. h. winnemana,* south. Numbers are referenced in *Records of occurrence.* The distribution of the species in the United States is shaded.

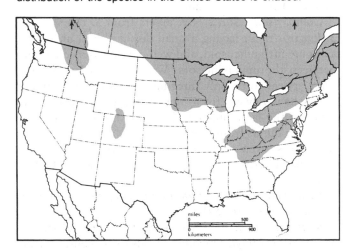

Range. Known only from northeastern corner of state near Palatine (Map 8.4).

Diagnosis. A subspecies of large size, both externally and cranially; weight 4.05 (1.6–7.3) gm.

Comparison. S. h. hoyi differs from *S. h. winnemana* in larger size externally, longer skull, and longer toothrow.

Remarks. Diersing (1980:98) in revising *Sorex hoyi* emphasizes how much larger *S. h. hoyi* from Palatine, Cook County, is than a specimen of *S. h. winnemana* from Wabash County. In the former, the length of the upper molariform toothrow is 3.79 mm; in the latter, 3.30 mm; in the length of the unicuspid toothrow, 1.76 mm vs. 1.50 mm.

Records of occurrence. SPECIMENS EXAMINED, 1. **Cook Co.:** [1] near Palatine, 1 (FMNH).

Sorex hoyi winnemana (Preble)

1910. *Microsorex winnemana* Preble, Proc. Biol. Soc. Wash., 22:101. Type from bank of Potomac R., near Stubblefield Falls, 4 mi below Grand Falls, Fairfax Co., Virginia.

1925. *Microsorex hoyi winnemana,* Jackson, Proc. Biol. Soc. Wash., 38:126.

1980. *Sorex hoyi winnemana,* Diersing, J. Mamm., 61:98.

Range. Known only from southeastern corner of state in Wabash County (Map 8.4).

Diagnosis. A subspecies of *S. hoyi* of small size, both externally and cranially; weight of two specimens, 1.5 gm and 2.3 gm; relatively broad palate.

Comparisons. S. h. winnemana differs from *S. h. hoyi* as given in the latter account (p. 65).

Remarks. This small, southern race of *S. hoyi* probably never has intergraded with *S. h. hoyi* in Illinois. In all likelihood, intergradation has occurred through the eastern subspecies, *S. h. thompsoni.*

The specimen from Wabash County in the U.S. National Museum of Natural History has no specific locality. It was in a jar containing several specimens preserved in alcohol, but was the only *Sorex hoyi* in the jar.

This specimen is considerably smaller than the one from near Palatine and was referred to this subspecies by Diersing (1980).

Records of occurrence. SPECIMENS EXAMINED, 1 **Wabash Co.:** [2] no specific locality, 1 (US).

Blarina, Short-tailed shrews

Diagnosis. Shrews that are large-bodied but have short tails; for Illinois specimens the length of tail is 28 mm or less; tail length amounts to about 35 percent of the body length; fur blackish or grayish black, being only slightly lighter on the venter; first two upper unicuspids relatively large in comparison with next two (unicuspid 3 and 4); fifth unicuspid minute and usually not visible in lateral view; skull appears rugose in contrast with other shrews.

Dental formula. 3/1, 1/1, 3/1, 3/3. In the upper jaw there is a large falciform tooth, five unicuspids, and four

Table 8.4. External and cranial measurements (in mm), with mean, minimum and maximum, and one standard deviation, of three species of *Sorex.* Superscripts indicate sample less than N.

Species & Subspecies	Locality	N	Total length	Tail length	Body length	Hind foot length	Greatest length	Braincase breadth	Maxillary breadth
S. cinereus cinereus	N. Illinois: top 3 tiers of counties	16	85.4 73-96 7.60	33.4 27-36 2.90	52.0	11.07 10-12 0.59	15.24[13] 14.6-15.6 0.28	7.52[10] 7.4-7.8 0.13	4.21 3.95-4.5 0.15
" " "	Fulton County	21	90.9 85-98 3.20	34.5 30-39 2.50	56.4	11.14 10-12 0.48	15.33[16] 14.7-16.1 0.38	7.72[15] 7.4-8.1 0.19	4.16 3.9-4.3 0.11
S. cinereus lesueurii	Alexander & Edgar counties	5	88.4 79-98 6.50	36.0 32-40 3.08	52.4 47-58 3.91	11.20 11-12 0.45	15.65[3] 15.25-16.0 0.38	7.38[3] 7.15-7.7 0.28	4.14 3.89-4.45 0.27
S. longirostris longirostris	Vermilion County	20	82.9[14] 72-94 5.46	29.2[14] 27-32 1.19	53.7	9.9 9.0-10.5 0.39	14.32[17] 13.91-14.9 0.26	7.47[12] 7.3-7.7 0.13	4.37 4.2-4.5 0.12
" " "	Alexander, Johnson, Union, Williamson counties	19	80.6[19] 72-92 5.59	27.4[18] 24-30 1.85	53.2	9.7[19] 9.0-10.5 0.54	14.06[6] 13.61-14.55 0.32	7.35[7] 7.11-7.48 0.14	4.27[13] 4.15-4.41 0.09
S. hoyi hoyi	near Palatine, Cook County	65567[1]	77	27	50	9	—	—	—
S. hoyi winnemana	Wabash County	154175[2]	—	—	—	—	12.7	6.4	3.9

[1] Field Museum   [2] U.S. Natl. Museum

multi-cusped premolar-molars; lower jaw with a falciform tooth, two unicuspids, and three multi-cusped premolar-molars.

Comparisons. For a comparison with *Sorex,* see account of that genus (p. 57). Trenchant differences are the large body, tail that is only 35 percent or less rather than more than 50 percent of the body length, and differences in proportions of the unicuspids.

For a comparison with *Cryptotis,* see account of that genus (p. 74).

Secondary sexual variation. Analyses of 232 specimens from Champaign County for two external and 10 cranial measurements showed that there were no significant differences between males and females, but males average slightly larger than females (Ellis et al., 1978). In statistical analyses, the sexes are treated together.

Aging. Animals can be placed in categories based on wear of the teeth. Ages were thus assigned to these categories relative to dates of capture and based on the studies of O. P. Pearson (1945) and Choate (1972). It should be noted that wear on the teeth may be affected by what the animals have been eating.

1–2 Months: No wear on unicuspids or on cusps of molariform teeth.

2–5 Months: Unicuspid 1 and 2 blunt; slight wear on protocone and hypocone of P^4, M^1, M^2.

6 Months: Unicuspid 1 nearly level with posterior section of I^1, paracone of P^4 blunt; moderate wear of other cuspid.

1 Year: Unicuspids rounded and showing moderate to heavy wear; protocone and hypocone on upper molariform teeth nearly flat; M^3 worn nearly flat.

More than one year: Actually two categories can be designated. One has unicuspid 2 worn nearly to the level of unicuspid 1; dark pigment is mostly gone from all teeth. The other (older) specimens show much wear on all teeth and dark pigment is almost entirely lacking.

Remarks. Two species of *Blarina* are found in Illinois: *B. brevicauda* and *B. carolinensis.*

Molt. Molting in Illinois shrews has not been followed, but in Wisconsin Jackson (1961:43) reported that there are two molts annually in *Blarina brevicauda*—a spring molt from May through July and a fall molt from late August until early October. Jackson says the molt usually starts on the shoulders and back and proceeds forward, backward and then downward. Probably the number and sequence of molts is the same in *Blarina carolinensis.* In Louisiana, Lowery (1974:75), in writing about *carolinensis,* observed, "Winter pelage is slightly darker than that of summer, which is browner, less slaty gray."

Specimens of *Blarina* frequently are abnormally colored in that some specimens are piebald or whitish. One specimen taken in Illinois is piebald and another appears a dirty white because the bases of the hairs have a grayish pigmentation.

Blarina brevicauda, Northern short-tailed shrew

Range. Central and northern Illinois, north of a line running through St. Clair and Fayette counties, but also present in south central Illinois in Franklin and Johnson counties (Map 8.5, p. 71).

Diagnosis. A large but variable species of *Blarina;* in Illinois the body averages more than 85 mm, hind foot averages 13 mm or more, skull long, with the greatest length usually more than 22 mm and occipito-premaxillary length more than 21 mm, skull broad across the maxillary region and cranium, toothrow long (Table 8.5, p. 70).

Color of dorsum blackish; venter somewhat lighter, with more brownish cast. Fur of back and sides often has an iridescence. In some specimens the underside of the tail may be lighter than the top; in others, the tail is uniformly blackish all around.

Weight averages about 18.5 gms, with extremes of 13.5 to 24 gms.

Chromosomes. Reported to have a 2N of 48, 49, or 50, and a FN of 48 (Lee and Zimmerman, 1969).

Comparisons. *B. brevicauda* differs from *B. carolinensis* in larger body (probably if specimens are accurately measured, there would be no overlap in head-body length, with *brevicauda* 81 mm or more, *carolinensis* less than

Toothrow length	Unicuspid toothrow length	Complex toothrow length	Breadth across toothrows	Breadth across unicuspids[4]
5.80	2.24	3.73	3.74	2.00
5.6-5.95	2.1-2.4	3.5-3.8	3.6-4.0	1.9-2.1
0.09	0.05	0.07	0.10	0.05
5.75	2.21	3.73	3.74	1.93
5.5-6.1	2.1-2.5	3.6-3.9	3.55-3.9	1.8-2.1
0.14	0.10	0.08	0.07	0.07
5.69	1.98	3.83	3.90	1.91
5.31-6.06	1.83-2.17	3.63-4.04	3.70-4.08	1.70-2.10
0.32	0.14	0.17	0.18	0.14
5.32	1.86	3.65	4.01	2.05
5.2-5.5	1.76-1.94	3.5-3.8	3.8-4.2	1.91-2.17
0.09	0.04	0.08	0.11	0.07
5.24[13]	1.82[14]	3.62[15]	3.98[13]	2.03[12]
4.94-5.46	1.65-2.02	3.44-3.74	3.85-4.08	1.92-2.17
0.15	0.09	0.08	0.08	0.07
5.3	1.8	3.8	4.2	—
4.6	1.5	3.3	3.6	1.98

Fig. 8.11A. Northern short-tailed shrew, *Blarina brevicauda*. (From Hoffmeister and Mohr, 1957. Photograph by Ernest P. Walker, Smithsonian Institution, Washington, D.C.)

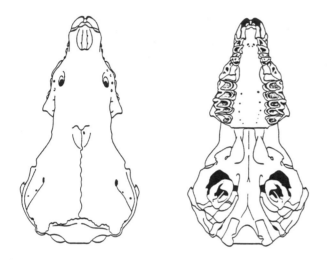

Fig. 8.11B. *Blarina brevicauda*, dorsal and ventral views of skull. Indian Creek, 3 mi E Petersburg, Menard Co., Illinois, 59244 UI. Male, 23.6 mm greatest length.

81 mm); heavier (weight 13.5 gms or more, rather than 13.4 gms or less); hind foot longer (averaging about 14.5 mm vs 11.5 mm); skull longer (no overlap in greatest length and occipito-premaxillary length); skull broader (no overlap in maxillary and cranial breadth); mandible longer and higher (no overlap); for chromosomes, 2N usually 48 rather than 46 and FN 48 rather than 44.

Remarks. In many habitats, *B. brevicauda* is one of the most abundant mammals. This is especially true of forested areas where there is a heavy leaf-cover on the forest floor.

At Meyer Cave, Monroe County, located on the bluffs of the Mississippi River Valley, 4 mi SSW Columbia, Parmalee (1967) reported that the remains found in the cave were of both *B. brevicauda* and *B. carolinensis* (listed as *Blarina brevicauda carolinensis*). This site is about 17 miles west of the known presence of *B. brevicauda* in that part of the state (1½ mi S Freeburg, St. Clair Co.) and 30 miles northwest for *B. carolinensis* (½ mi W

Marissa, St. Clair Co.). Although we have tried unsuccessfully to trap *Blarina* in the general vicinity of Meyer Cave, there is a good possibility that one or both species will be taken here. The material that Parmalee identified represented a period of perhaps 2,000 years before the present, and consisted of remains of animals that had fallen into this cave and were unable to escape. *B. carolinensis* may have been more abundant in this area, for Parmalee recovered jaws of 134 *B. carolinensis* and 93 *B. brevicauda*.

Figures 8.12 and 8.13 are scattergrams comparing length of hind foot and greatest length of skull in the two species. In Fig. 8.12, forty specimens chosen at random of each species are compared. In Fig. 8.13, specimens are compared at places where they are known to occur close together.

Habitat

Short-tailed shrews live in a variety of habitats in Illinois but are most numerous in wooded areas with a heavy ground-litter of decayed leaves. This habitat is enhanced if there are numerous, well-decayed logs on the forest floor. If the leaf substrate has innumerable runways, which can be recognized if one's heel sinks into the ground on nearly every step, there is an excellent chance that short-tailed shrews, white-footed mice, pine voles, and eastern moles are present. All of them may use these just-below-the-surface runways.

Short-tailed shrews may also live in grassy areas along fencerows or in open woodlands. In 1954, I started trapping in mature stands of bluegrass along the edge of a forested area. Trees began to invade this grassland more and more and by 1961, the first short-tailed shrew was caught. In some wooded areas, we find *Blarina* to be more abundant on the grassy fringes than within the woods proper.

In central Fulton County, short-tailed shrews outnumbered white-footed mice in a trapping census during a period of 1½ years (31 *Blarina* to 26 *Peromyscus leucopus*). The habitat was in an 80-acre hardwood forest with little underbrush but much down timber and a thick cover of leaves and leaf mold.

Habits

The foraging behavior of these shrews was observed by Wilfred Osgood and Tappan Gregory in upper peninsular Michigan on a rainy afternoon in late May. Gregory writes (1936:29):

... we came on two of these little shrews at close range. They were foraging. Their motions were lightning fast and they covered the ground rapidly, poking vigorously under leaves in search of insects, turning this way and that, tumbling over twigs and stems. We thought they might come together and watched for interesting developments, but their courses did not bring them within five feet of each other. Relying on their poor sight, we moved close. The nearer of the two found food and ate rapidly, using its forefeet to assist in the operation. It came up to Dr. Osgood's shoe, looked under the toe, followed along the edge of the sole the full length of the shoe, occasionally aiding its progress with one foot on the shoe, and then continued on its hunt, undisturbed. We stamped two or three times rapidly, and squeaked and the shrew dashed under the leaves, returning our squeaks. We approached the second shrew and squeaked again, whereupon its also retired hastily, but in silence.

Short-tailed shrews depend more on their hearing than their sight. Some sounds that they produce are audible; others are inaudible to us and are probably used by these shrews in echolocation. Ultrasonic clicks are emitted to determine barriers up to 2 ft (61 cm) away and to distinguish the nature of certain barriers (Tomasi, 1979:751). The glands on the sides of the body produce a musky secretion that must be important in marking territories, runways, and burrows. Their sense of smell must be acute enough to distinguish variations in the odors produced by different individuals. It has been suggested that males produce this musk all year long but females only during the non-breeding season (Mumford and Whitaker, 1982:110).

Tappan Gregory of the Chicago Academy of Sciences gives an interesting observation of a shrew which his dog caught alive at Northfield Township, Cook County, and

which we rescued, apparently unharmed. It was placed in a pan with sides high enough to prevent escape, given some bacon and moved into the sun to be photographed. The bacon was eagerly devoured, but before long the shrew was seized with a fit and rolled over and over very rapidly for several seconds, perhaps half a minute, then lay on its side and stiffened out, quivering. A short session in the shade and a dash of cold water soon brought it around and when released it scuttled off as though none the worse for its experience. (1936:29)

During periods of low temperature, short-tailed shrews enter a state of torpor, with a decrease in body temperature, metabolic rate, and locomotor activity. Animals may shake as a means of raising body temperature after a deep sleep.

Reproduction

Our evidence for shrews breeding in Illinois is meager. All too often specimens are not examined for the presence of embryos. Only six specimens have been recorded as with embryos, with a mean of 5.2 (3–7). Six were recorded as lactating. From this it appears there are pregnant or lactating females from April to July and from September to November. In Ohio, Gottschang (1981:24) stated that shrews breed from the latter part of March through the second week in October. In Indiana, Mumford and

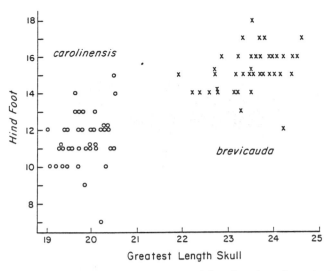

Fig. 8.12. Comparison (in mm) of hind foot length and greatest length of skull in *Blarina carolinensis* (sample of 40) and *B. brevicauda* (40) from various places in Illinois.

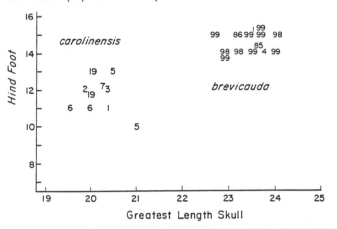

Fig. 8.13. Comparison (in mm) of *Blarina brevicauda* and *B. carolinensis* from localities where the two species are in close proximity. Numbers indicate localities as listed in Specimens Examined and on maps. Areas are in Macoupin Co. (*brevicauda* #85, 86 vs. *carolinensis* 1); Madison and St. Clair cos. (98, 99 vs. 2, 3, 5, 6); Clinton and Fayette cos. (1 vs. 7); Johnson Co. (4 vs. 19).

Whitaker (1982:112) thought there were breeding peaks from March through May, and to a lesser extent in the fall. The gestation period is 21 to 22 days and the young at birth are helpless, pink, and wrinkled. The nest usually consists of shredded leaves, some grasses, and any other available soft material. It is not certain how long young are nursed or how long they remain in the nest, without foraging for themselves. Ellis et al. (1978:307) believed that the animals have reached adult size at the time they leave the nest and forage for themselves.

Food

Short-tailed shrews feed almost exclusively on invertebrates, especially earthworms, snails, slugs, and almost

Table 8.5. External and cranial measurements (in mm), with mean, minimum and maximum, and one standard deviation, of two species of *Blarina*.

Species & Subspecies	Locality	N	Total length	Tail length	Body length	Hind foot length	Greatest length	Occipito-premaxillary length	Braincase breadth	Maxillary breadth	Inter-orbital breadth	Complex toothrow l. p^4-M^3
B. brevicauda kirtlandi	Chicago area	21	115.1 85-146 12.23	21.50 14-30 3.74	92.7 71-107 9.66	14.4 12-16 1.33	23.7 22.9-24.4 0.60	22.7 21.8-23.6 0.64	12.7 12.3-13.0 0.11	8.0 7.7-8.5 0.23	5.8 5.5-6.0 0.14	6.3 6.0-6.5 0.14
" "	W. Champaign Co.	88	114.6 104-125 5.02	23.8 20-28 1.83	92.3 79-105 5.72	14.95 13-18 0.84	23.6 22.1-25.2 0.56	22.7 21.3-24.2 0.56	12.6 11.6-13.8 0.39	8.0 7.3-8.5 0.19	5.8 5.3-6.2 0.19	6.4 5.6-6.8 0.19
B. carolinensis carolinensis	Pope Co.	29	91.3 79-103 6.26	19.6 11-23 2.65	71.7 60-82 5.88	11.2 7-14 1.51	19.9 19.1-20.7 0.38	19.1 18.2-19.8 0.38	10.5 10.1-11.2 0.27	6.7 6.2-7.0 0.22	5.2 4.9-5.9 0.16	5.5 5.0-5.7 0.16
" "	Alexander & Union cos.	35	88.0 77-98 5.61	18.4 12-25 2.85	69.8 59-84 5.92	11.7 10-15 1.18	19.9 19.1-20.7 0.47	19.0 18.2-19.8 0.47	10.4 10.0-10.8 0.24	6.7 6.5-7.0 0.18	5.1 4.8-5.4 0.18	5.4 5.2-5.7 0.18

any available insects or insect larvae. Plant material is sometimes eaten, but this may have been consumed accidentally while feeding on some invertebrate. In Indiana, Whitaker and Mumford (1972a) found that the fungus *Endogone* was sometimes found in the stomachs. In 125 stomachs, however, earthworms were found to comprise more than one-third of the items, and these made up about 50 percent of the bulk.

Dana Snyder analyzed the stomachs of nine short-tailed shrews taken in east central Illinois from February to April (Snyder, 1947). In seven animals he found remains of gastropods; in one, spiders; insects in only four. Probably gastropods were more readily available than insects at this time of the year.

Shrews are notorious for being ravenous feeders. If food is available, they are said to eat more than their body weight each day. Edgren (1948) found that a shrew weighing 14.8 gms consumed an average of 25.6 gms of food and 9.1 cc of water per day for several days. There are many other similar reports of food consumption. Actually, shrews require a considerable amount of water; much of it is supplied by the kinds of food they eat and this is supplemented with free water when available. Also, the oxidation of the fatty foods they ingest provides more water. It has been suggested that during some severe periods in the winter, short-tailed shrews may supplement their diet with seeds as the only source of available food.

In captivity, short-tailed shrews will do well on a diet consisting of hamburger, ground liver, dry dog meal, and water, mixed to a hamburger consistency (O. P. Pearson, 1950:351). This can be stored in a refrigerator and provided in proper amounts daily.

Fighting

All shrews, but especially *Blarina*, have a reputation of being ferocious fighters. Some reports indicate that short-tailed shrews attack and kill wild healthy animals that are as large or larger than themselves. For example, Maurer (1970:549) uncovered beneath a bale of hay an adult *Blarina* and a juvenile *Microtus pennsylvanicus* "furiously fighting with their mouths and forefeet. At least one vocalized three or four times before I caught them both." Maurer thought that one had invaded the others territory and brought about a provoked attack. Frequently, when *Blarina* and mice are placed in small, caged quarters, the *Blarina* will kill the other animal. However, Michael Piotrowski in our laboratories gave *Blarina* the opportunity to prey on the young of *Microtus ochrogaster*. *Blarina* killed only one young during 12 trials with a total of 21 young available. On one occasion, a female *Microtus* removed a young to a new spot within the experimental room in a rather exposed place and left it there for 23 minutes. On several occasions a *Blarina* came within 5 cm of the young but moved no closer; three times it sniffed the young and then moved away; six times the shrew retreated when the infant vole moved suddenly. After this, the female *Microtus* dashed out, grabbed the young, and returned it to the nest.

Variation

From one to three subspecies of *Blarina* are reported in Illinois E. R. Hall (1981) recognizes three: *brevicauda*, *kirtlandi*, and *carolinensis*, but does not recognize *B. carolinensis* as a distinct species. Some other workers would call the large, *brevicauda*-like shrews in Illinois *Blarina kirtlandi* (Graham and Semken, 1976). Ellis et al. (1978) regard the large short-tailed shrews in Illinois as referable to *B. brevicauda kirtlandi*.

Blarina brevicauda kirtlandi Bole and Moulthrop

1942. *Blarina brevicauda kirtlandi* Bole and Moulthrop. Sci. Publ., Cleveland Mus. Nat. Hist., 5:99. Type from Holden Arboretum, Lake and Geauga cos. line. Ohio.

Range. As given for the species (p. 67 and Map 8.5).

Diagnosis and Comparisons. A subspecies of *B. brevicauda* of medium size, being smaller than *B. b. brevicauda* in having a smaller body, hind foot, and in skull length and breadth.

Remarks. Although specimens of *B. brevicauda* from northwestern Illinois are slightly larger than others, they are referred to *B. b. kirtlandi* and not to the larger *B. b. brevicauda*. The shift or step in the clinal variation from the smaller *kirtlandi* to the larger *brevicauda* occurs in the area of the Mississippi River.

Records of occurrence. SPECIMENS EXAMINED, 642.

Jo Daviess Co.: [1] 1 mi W ½ mi S Menominee, 1 (SRL). **Stephenson Co.:** [2] 3 mi W Orangeville, 1 (SRL); [3a] 2 mi NE Rock Grove, 2 (UI); [3b] ½ mi W Davis, 2 (UI). **Winnebago Co.:** [4] 2 mi E Roscoe, 1 (UI); [5] Rockford, 3 (UI); [6] 4¾ mi E, 3½ S Rockford, 1 (UI). **Boone Co.:** Davis Slough [not located, not plotted], 1 (UI). **McHenry Co.:** [8] 2 mi E Union, 1 (UI). **Lake Co.:** [9a] Camp Logan, 6 (FM), [9b] Waukegan, 1 (US); [10a] Fox Lake, 27 (FM); [10b] 3 mi NW Volo, 2 (ISU); [10c] Volo Bog, 2 (ISM); [11] Grayslake, 1 (CAS); [12a] 3 mi W Wauconda, 1 (UI); [12b] 1 mi N Lake Zurich, 1 (NIU); [13a] Prairie View, 2 (CAS); [13b] Highland Park, 6 (CAS), 3 (FM); [13c] Deerfield, 3 (CAS). **Carroll Co.:** [14] Mississippi Palisades State Park, 2 (UI); [15] Mt. Carroll, 4 (UI). **Whiteside Co.:** [16a] 1 mi E Erie, 1 (NIU); [16b] 2 mi S Erie, 1 (NIU). **Ogle Co.:** [17] White Pines State Park, 2 (UI). **De Kalb Co.:** [18a] ¾ mi NNE Genoa, 1 (UI); [18b] ¼ mi NE Genoa, 1 (UI); [19a] 5.7 mi N De Kalb, 1 (NIU); [19b] 5 mi N De Kalb, 1 (NIU); [19c] 2 mi E De Kalb, 1 (NIU); [19d] De Kalb, 2 (US), 7 (NIU); [19e] 1 mi SE De Kalb, 1 (NIU); [20] 7 mi W De Kalb, 1 (NIU). **Kane Co.:** [21a] 2.4 mi W, ½ mi N Elgin, 1 (UI); [21b] Bowes, 1 (CAS); [22a] St. Charles, 4 (ISM); [22b] 2¼ mi W, ½ mi S Batavia, 1 (UI); [23b] Sugar Grove, 1 (CAS).

Cook Co.: [24a] West Northfield, 4 (US); [24b] 3 mi N Des Plaines, 1 (UI); [24c] 1 mi W Park Ridge, 1 (UI); [25a] River Forest, 1 (CAS); [25b] Riverside, 1 (UI); [25c] Hollywood [=Brookfield], 1 (UI); [25d] Lyons, 1 (UI); [25e] La Grange, 1 (UI); [26] Chicago, Jackson Park, 7 (FM); [27a] Oaklawn, 1 (NIU); [27b] Worth, 1 (FM); [27c] Palos Park, 1 (CAS), 4 (UI); [28] Lemont, 1 (CAS); [29a] SW Hazelcrest, 2 (UI); [29b] Homewood, 1 (CAS), 3 (FM), 1 (UI); [29c] Chicago Heights, 1 (NIU), 1 (FM), 1 (UI); Sokol Camp [location?], 1 (UI). **Du Page Co.:** [30a] 2 mi W Lombard, 1 (UI); [30b] 1½ mi SW Villa Park, 1 (UI); [31] Naperville, 1 (FM); [32] Downers Grove, 5 (UI). **Rock Island Co.:** [33] Rock Island, 1 (UI); [34] 12 mi S Moline, 1 (UI). **Henry Co.:** [35] 5 mi E Colona, 5 (UI). **Bureau Co.:** [36] Ohio, 1 (UI). **La Salle Co.:** [37a] 2 mi N La Salle, 1 (UI); [37b] 2 mi SE Utica, 1 (UI). **Kendall Co.:** [38] Yorkville, 1 (UI). **Grundy Co.:** [39a] 6 mi W Morris, 1 (UI); [39b] Morris, 2 (UI); [39c] 6 mi W, ½ mi S Morris, 2 (UI); [40] Goose Lake Prairie State Park, 1 (ISU), 1 (UI). **Will Co.:** [42] Wheatland Twp., 1 (FM); [43] Romeoville, 1 (UI); [44] New Lenox, 1 (UI). **Kankakee Co.:** [45] 6 mi E St. Anne, 1 (UI). **Hancock Co.:** [46] Warsaw*, 3 (US). **Warren Co.:** [47a] 1 mi W Roseville, 1 (UI); [47b] ½ mi W Roseville, 2 (UI). **Knox Co.:** [48] 4 mi S Victoria, 1 (UI). **Fulton Co.:** [49] 10 mi NW

* Worthen specimens.

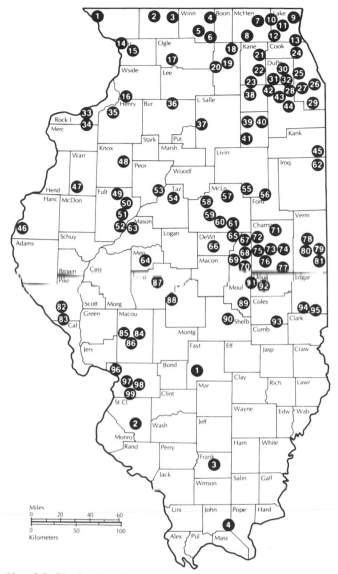

Map 8.5. Distribution of the northern short-tailed shrew, *Blarina brevicauda*. The subspecies is *B. b. kirtlandi*. Numbers are referenced in *Records of occurrence*. The distribution of the species in the United States is shaded.

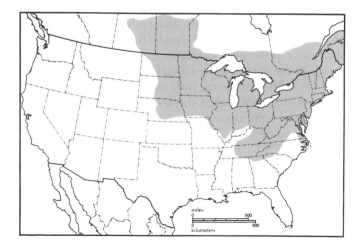

Canton, 2 (UI); [50a] 3 mi N Canton, 1 (UI); [50b] 2 mi W Canton, 1 (UI); [50c] 1 mi W Canton, 5 (UI); [50d] ½ mi W Canton, 2 (UI); [51] Bryant, 2 (UI); [52] 6 mi NNW Havana [labelled Mason Co.], 1 (UI). **Peoria Co.:** [53] Peoria, 1 (UI). **Tazewell Co.:** [54] 1 mi N Morton, 2 (UI).

Livingston Co.: [55] 2 mi S Fairbury [uncatalogued alcoholic], 1 (UI); [56] 7 mi E, 1 mi S Strawn, 12 (UI). **McLean Co.:** [57] 1 mi E Lexington, 1 (UI); [58a] 3 mi NW Hudson, 2 (ISU); [58b] 4 mi N Normal, 3 (ISU); [58c] 2½ mi N Normal, 2 (UI); [58d] 2 mi N Normal, 1 (ISU); [59a] 1 mi N Normal, 1 (ISU); [59b] Normal, 2 (ISU); [59c] 2 mi W, ½ mi S Normal, 2 (UI); [59d] Bloomington, 1 (ISU), 1 (UI); [59e] 5 mi SE Bloomington, 2 (UI); [60a] 3½ mi N, 3 mi W Le Roy, 1 (UI); [60b] 3 mi NW Le Roy, 1 (UI); [60c] 1 mi N, ½ mi W Le Roy, 1 (UI); [61a] 5 mi ENE Le Roy, 1 (UI); [61b] 2 mi E Le Roy, 1 (UI). **Iroquois Co.:** [62a] T29N, R11W, sec. 22, 2 (UI); [62b] 1 mi W Donovan, 1 (UI). **Mason Co.:** [63a] 4 mi NNE Havana, 1 (UI); [63b] 5 mi NE Havana, 1 (UI). **Menard Co.:** [64] 3 mi E Petersburg, Indian Creek, 2 (UI). **De Witt Co.:** [65] ½ mi S Farmer City, 1 (UI); [66] 2 mi E Clinton, 1 (UI). **Piatt Co.:** [67a] 2½ mi W Mansfield, 3 (UI); [67b] 1½ mi E Mansfield, 2 (UI); [68a] 2 mi N White Heath, 1 (UI); [68b] Monticello, 1 (UI); [69] 5 mi W, 2½ mi S Monticello, Allerton Park, 16 (UI); [70] 3 mi N Bement, 1 (UI).

Champaign Co.: [71] ¾ mi E Rantoul, 1 (UI); [72a] 15 mi NW Champaign, Hart Woods (3½ mi NE Mahomet), 82 (UI); [72b] 2 mi NE Mahomet, 1 (UI); [72c] Mahomet, Sangamon River, 6 (UI); [73a] 5 mi N Urbana, 2 (UI); [73b] 4 mi N Urbana, 1 (UI); [73c] 4 mi N, 1½ mi E Urbana, 1 (UI); [73d] 4 mi NW Urbana, 1 (UI); [73e] Brownfield Woods [=2 mi N, 2½ mi E Urbana], 10 (UI); [73f] 2 mi N Urbana, 13 (UI); [73g] 1⅛ mi N Urbana, 2 (UI); [73h] Urbana, Busey Woods, 5 (UI); [73i] Urbana Wildlife Area, 2 (UI); [73j] Urbana, Trelease Woods, 3 (UI); [73k] 4 mi NE Urbana, Trelease Prairie, 5 (UI); [73l] ¾ mi N, 3 mi E Champaign, 1 (UI); [73m] 3 mi ENE Urbana, 1 (UI); [73n] Champaign, 10 (UI); [73o] 3 mi E Champaign, 1 (UI); [73p] ¼ mi S Champaign, 1 (UI); [73q] Urbana, 6 (UI); [73r] ¼ mi S Urbana, 1 (UI); [73s] 2 mi E Urbana, 4 (UI); [73t] 2½ mi E Urbana, 1 (UI); [73u] 3 mi E Urbana, 1 (UI); [73v] 3½ mi E Urbana, 1 (UI); [73w] 1 mi W Mayview, Mayview Prairie, 13 (UI); [73x] 4 mi E Urbana, 1 (UI); [73y] ½ mi W Mayview, 1 (UI); [73z] 5 mi E Urbana, 2 (UI); [73aa] ½ mi S Champaign, 2 (UI); [73bb] 1 mi S Champaign, 13 (UI); [73cc] 1 mi S Urbana, 1 (UI); [73dd] 2 km S Champaign, 1 (UI); [73ee] 2½ mi SW Champaign, 1 (UI); [73ff] 2 mi S Champaign, 7 (UI); [73gg] UI Agricultural Area [=1 mi S UI campus], 2 (UI); [73hh] Urbana, Orchard S campus, 1 (UI); [73ii] 2 mi S Urbana, 1 (UI); [73jj] 2½ mi S Champaign, 1 (UI); [73kk] 2½ mi E, 2 mi S Urbana, 1 (UI); [73ll] 3 mi S Champaign, 3 (UI); [73mm] 3 mi S Urbana, 1 (UI); [73nn] 5 mi E Savoy, 1 (UI); [74a] 6 mi E Urbana, 3 (UI); [74b] ½ mi W St. Joseph, 1 (UI); [74c] 1 mi E St. Joseph, 2 (UI); [75a] 3½ mi W Champaign, 8 (UI); [75b] 1 mi E Bondville, Kaskaskia River, 2 (UI); [76a] 5 mi S Champaign, Willard Airport, 3 (UI); [76b] 1 mi S Savoy, 6 (UI); [77] 7 mi SE Philo, 2 (UI).

Vermilion Co.: [78a] 2 mi NE Collison, 1 (UI); [78b] 1⅘ mi NE Collison, 2 (UI); [78c] 1 mi W Higginsville, 18 (UI); [78d] ¼ mi E, ¼ mi S Higginsville, 7 (UI); [78e] 2½ mi E, ½ mi S Collison, 19 (UI); [78f] 1 mi S, 3 mi E Collison, 3 (UI); [78g] 2½ mi N, 1¾ mi E Newtown, 3 (UI); [78h] 2 mi N, 1½ mi E Newtown, 3 (UI); [78i] 1¼ mi W, ½ mi S Snider, 8 (UI); [78j] ½ mi S, ½ mi E Newtown, 8 (UI); [79a] 1½ mi NE Danville, 1 (UI); [79b] ½ mi NE Danville, 1 (UI); [79c] 3 mi Danville, 1 (UI); [79d] 4 mi SE Danville, 2 (UI); [80a] Kickapoo State Park, 1 (FM), 1 (UI); [80b] 6/10 mi E Muncie, 1 (UI); [80c] 2 mi SE Muncie, 1 (UI); [80d] 4 mi S Oakwood, 1 (UI); [81a] 4½ mi E, 2¼ mi S Westville, 1 (UI); [81b] 3⅘ mi E, 2⅖ mi S Westville, 3 (UI). **Pike Co.:** [82a] 3½ mi S Pittsfield, 8 (UI); [82b] 5 mi N Pleasant Hill, 1 (SIE); [83] 2 mi W Nebo, 3 (UI). **Macoupin Co.:** [84] ½ mi E Carlinville, 1 (SIE); [85] 1½ mi NW Chesterfield, 1 (UI); [86a] 2 mi NE Beaver Dam State Park, 1 (UI); [86b] 4 mi N Plainview, 1 (SIE). **Sangamon Co.:** [87] Springfield, 1 (ISM). **Christian Co.:** [88] 4 mi WSW Edinburg, 1 (UI). **Moultrie Co.:** [89] 3 mi E Sullivan, 1 (UI). **Shelby Co.:** [90] 3½ mi NE Shelbyville, 1 (UI). **Douglas Co.:** [91] Atwood, 1 (NHS); [92] 6 mi N Arcola, 1 (UI). **Coles Co.:** [93] Fox Ridge State Park, 1 (NHS). **Edgar Co.:** [94] 8 mi SW Paris, 2 (UI); [95] 6 mi S Paris, 2 (UI). **Madison Co.:** [96] Alton, 2 (SIE): [97a] 1 mi NE Edwardsville, 1 (SIE); [97b] 5 mi W Edwardsville, 1 (SIE); [97c] Edwardsville, 2 (SIE); [97d] Edwardsville, SIU campus, 1 (SIE); [97e] ½ mi S Edwardsville, 1 (SIE); [98] 1½ mi SE Kuhn, 3 (UI); [99a] 1½ mi SE Glen Carbon, 1 (UI); [99b] 1½ mi E Collinsville, 4 (UI); [99c] 2 mi E Collinsville, 2 (UI); ½ mi W Eden [not located, not plotted], 1 (UI). **Fayette Co.:** [1] 2½ mi SW Vandalia, 1 (UI). **St. Clair Co.:** [2] 1½ mi S Freeburg, 1 (SIE). **Franklin Co.:** [3] Benton, 1 (UI). **Johnson Co.:** [4] ½ mi E Grantsburg, 1 (UI).

Additional records. **McHenry Co.:** [7] Wonder Lake, 2 (FS). **Lake Co.:** [13b] Highland Park, 2 (FS). **Kane Co.:** [23a] 2 mi W Sugar Grove, 1 (UM). **Grundy Co.:** [41] Verona (Harty, 1981 in litt.). **McLean Co.:** [59d] Bloomington, 8 (UM).

Blarina carolinensis, Southern short-tailed shrew

Range. Southern Illinois, south of a line running through Macoupin and Wayne counties (Map 8.6, p. 73).

Diagnosis. A small species of *Blarina,* characterized by small body (averaging less than 75 mm); short hind foot (averaging 12 mm or less); skull short, with the greatest length usually less than 21 mm and occipito-premaxillary length less than 20 mm, narrow across the maxillary region and the cranium (Table 8.5); toothrow short. Weight averging about 9.6 gms with extremes of 7 to 13 gms.

Color. Dorsum and venter much the same as in *B. brevicauda* (p. 67).

Chromosomes. In Illinois, 2N = 46; FN = 44. Specimens from outside of Illinois show Robertsonian polymorphism.

Comparisons. In Illinois *B. carolinensis* differs from *B. brevicauda* in its smaller size and in the 2N and FN of chromosomes. See *B. brevicauda* for a detailed comparison and Figs. 8.11A and 8.11B.

B. carolinensis differs from *B. hylophaga* (as defined and delimited by George et al., 1981, 1982) in its smaller size, both externally and cranially, and in chromosomal differences, including a 2N of 46 (sometimes 37, 38, or 39) vs 2N of 52 and a FN of 44 (sometimes 45) vs FN of 60 or 61, respectively.

Growth. As pointed out in the account of the genus, *B. carolinensis* reaches adult size at or near the time when it leaves the nest and forages for itself.

Remarks. Most workers have regarded all of the specimens of *Blarina* in Illinois as referable to *B. brevicauda.* When the individual, age, secondary sexual, and geographical variations are taken into account, it is clear that two separate units—species—of *Blarina* are found in Illinois (Ellis et al., 1978). Ellis et al. used the name *B. carolinensis* for the small-sized species in southern and south central Illinois.

Earlier accounts referred to specimens in this part of the state as *B. brevicauda* or *B. brevicauda carolinensis.* More recently, George et al. (1981) have recognized another small species, *B. hylophaga,* which supposedly is found in most of Missouri. This species is recognized principally on chromosomal differences. The *Blarina* in southern Illinois are not referable to *hylophaga* but to *carolinensis,* according to information provided me by M. R. Lee.

Habitat

Specimens in the Pine Hills, Wolf Lake, and LaRue Swamp area of Union County were "taken in the drier woodland and open, grassy field communities of the lowlands" (Klimstra, 1969:3). They were also taken "in surface runways in a variety of grassy situations and in subsurface burrows in mature oak-hickory woodlands" (Layne, 1958a:222). In Pope County, we took specimens in a variety of habitats from grassy fields to open woods to dense thickets with a heavy cover of briars and honeysuckle. We caught southern short-tailed shrews in the same sunken cans where we caught *Sorex longirostris* at 2 mi E, ½ mi S Dixon Springs, Pope County. This was in debris adjacent to a drainage ditch. Blackberries, wild rose, and various grasses together with river birch were present.

Mammals associated with southern short-tailed shrews in Illinois includes *Microtus ochrogaster, Ochrotomys nuttalli, Sorex longirostris, Synaptomys cooperi,* and *Peromyscus leucopus.*

Reproduction

Little is known about the reproduction of the species in Illinois or if it differs from that of *Blarina brevicauda.* Five of our specimens are listed as pregnant; eight as lactating. In April, three are pregnant, four lactating; May, one pregnant; June, one pregnant; September, one pregnant, two lactating; October, one lactating. I suspect that young are born from March to June and again in the fall. Those animals bearing young in the fall are probably females born the same spring.

Our pregnant females have an average of 5.4 (5–6) embryos. Layne (1958a:222) reports a female with three embryos taken April 3.

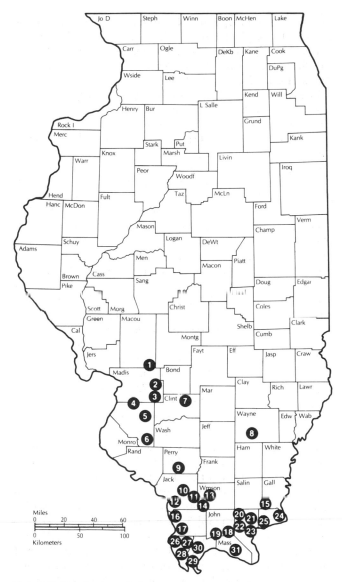

Map 8.6. Distribution of the southern short-tailed shrew, *Blarina carolinensis.* The subspecies is *B. c. carolinensis.* Numbers are referenced in *Records of occurrence.* The distribution of the species in the United States is shaded.

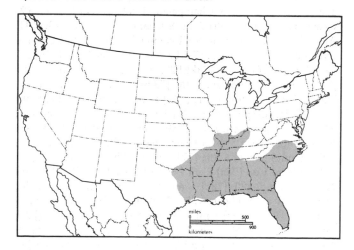

Population

Southern short-tailed shrews are common to abundant in southern Illinois. In Union County, Klimstra (1969) found the species to be the second most abundant small mammal (next to white-footed mice) in 1961. In the vicinity of Dixon Springs, Pope County, we have always found these shrews to be common. A student found one freshly dead in a field there. It could have been abandoned by a predator, or it could have died of natural causes.

A short-tailed shrew at Lake Glendale, Pope County, served as food for a sunfish, *Lepomis cyanellus* (Huish and Hoffmeister, 1947). It is not certain if this shrew was swimming in the lake of its own volition or if it accidentally fell in. *B. carolinensis* is sufficiently small that it could be swallowed by a sunfish.

Variation

Blarina carolinensis carolinensis (Bachman)

1837. *Sorex carolinensis* Bachman, J. Acad. Nat. Sci. Phila., 1, 7(2):366. Type locality eastern South Carolina.
1857. *Blarina carolinensis*, Baird, Mamm. Expl. and Surv. . . . , 1857:45.

Range. As given for the species (p. 72 and Map 8.6).
Diagnosis and Comparisons. A subspecies of large size for *B. carolinensis,* both externally and cranially.
Remarks. The range and characters of *B. carolinensis* are poorly understood at the present time. Therefore, it is difficult to make a diagnosis and comparisons. As presently understood, there may be four subspecies of *B. carolinensis: B. c. carolinensis, B. c. minima, B. c. shermani,* and *B. c. peninsulae.* Specimens in southern Illinois appear to average larger in many measurements than specimens of the other subspecies.

Records of occurrence. SPECIMENS EXAMINED, 213.
Macoupin Co.: [1] 3½ mi E, 4½ mi S Wilsonville, 1 (UI).
Madison Co.: [2] 3½ mi WSW Grantfork, 1 (UI); [3a] E edge Highland, 1 (SIE); [3b] 3½ mi W Highland, 1 (UI). **St. Clair Co.:** [4] Collinsville, 1 (SIE); [5] 9 mi E Belleville, 3 (UI); [6a] East of Peabody's River King Mine, Pit 3, E of Athens, 1 (UI); [6b] ½ mi W Marissa, 3 (UI). **Clinton Co.:** [7] 4 mi NNE Carlyle, Eldon Hazlet State Park, 2 (UI). **Wayne Co.:** [8a] 2 mi ENE Sims, 1 (UI); [8b] 3 mi S, 3 mi E Sims, 1 (UI); [8c] 3 mi E, 4 mi S Sims, along Skillet Fork, 1 (UI). **Perry Co.:** [9] Pyatts Striplands, 1 (SRL). **Jackson Co.:** [10c] Murphysboro, 1 (SRL); [10b] 1 mi E Murphysboro, 2 (SIC); [11a] Carbondale, 6 (SRL); [11c] Carbondale, Thompson Lake, 1 (SRL); [11d] 1½ mi S Carbondale, 1 (SIC); [11e] T9S, R1W, Sec. 28, 6 (UI); [12a] 9 mi SW Murphysboro, 1 (UI); [12b] near Grand Tower, T10S, R3W, Sec. 18, 1 (UI); Quail Area [location?], 1 (SRL). **Williamson Co.:** [13] 6 mi S Herrin, 1 (UI); [14] W side Little Grassy Lake, 3 (UI), 1 (SRL). **Gallatin Co.:** 3 mi N Karbers Ridge, High Knob [labelled Hardin Co.], 1 (UI). **Union Co.:** [16a] Pine Hills Recreation Area, 1 (UI); [16c] 8 mi N Ware, Pine Hills, 2 (UI); [16d] 2 mi SE Aldridge, Pine Hills, 1 (UI); [16e] 3 mi N Wolf Lake, 1 (UI);

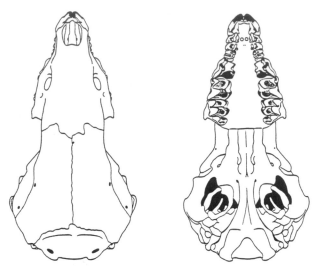

Fig. 8.14. *Blarina carolinensis,* dorsal and ventral views of skull; 2½ mi S Olive Branch, Alexander Co., Illinois, 52607 UI. Male, 20.6 mm greatest length.

[16f] 3 mi NNW Wolf Lake, 1 (NIU); [16g] Wolf Lake, 1 (US); [17a] 3 mi SE Ware, 1 (UI); [17b] 6 mi S, 2 mi E Ware, 4 (UI); [17c] 6 mi S, 3 mi E Ware, 1 (UI); no specific locality [not plotted], 1 (US).
Johnson Co.: [18] Reevesville, 5 (FM); [19] 1 mi S Foreman, 2 (UI). **Pope Co.:** [20a] ½ mi E McCormick, 1 (SRL); [20b] 2 mi SE McCormick, 1 (FS); [21] 3 mi E Eddyville, 1 (UI); [22a] 1 mi S, ½ mi E Glendale, 1 (UI); [22b] 3¾ mi N Dixon Springs, 1 (UI); [22c] 1½ mi S Glendale, 21 (UI); [22d] 2½ mi S Glendale, 2 (UI); [22e] 2½ mi S, ½ mi E Glendale, 15 (UI); [22f] 2 mi E, ½ mi S Dixon Springs, 6 (UI); [23a] 3.8 mi W Golconda, 4 (UI); [23b] Golconda, 1 (UI), 3 (FM), 1 (US). **Hardin Co.:** [24] 3 mi E Lamb, 1 (UI); [25a] 1 mi S Eichorn, 2 (UI); [25b] Rosiclare, 8 (FM). **Alexander Co.:** [26] Cypress Jct. [=McClure], 1 (US); [27a] 3 mi W Tamms, Sandy Creek, 3 (UI); [27b] Tamms, 1 (SRL); [28a] ½ mi NNW Olive Branch, 1 (SRL); [28b] Olive Branch, 33 (FM), 2 (US); [28c] 2 mi S Olive Branch, 1 (UI); [28d] 2½ mi S Olive Branch, 23 (UI); [28e] 3 mi S Olive Branch, 2 (UI); [28f] Miller City, 4 (UI); [28g] 1½ mi E Miller City, 1 (UI); [28h] 1½ mi E, ½ mi S Miller City, 2 (UI); [29] 5 mi N Cairo, 1 (ISU). **Pulaski Co.:** [30] T15S, R1W, Sec. 16 [labelled Alexander Co.], 1 (UI). **Massac Co.:** [31a] 4 mi NE Metropolis, 1 (SIC); [31b] 2 mi N Metropolis, 1 (SIC); [31c] 1½ mi N Metropolis, 1 (SIC); [31d] ½ mi ENE Metropolis, 1 (SRL).

Additional records. **Jackson Co.:** [11b] Carbondale, SIU campus, 1 (FS). **Union Co.:** [16b] Aldridge, Pine Hills, 1 (FS). **Alexander Co.:** [27b] Tamms, 3 (FS).

Cryptotis, Least shrews

Diagnosis. Least shrews are short-bodied, with a short tail; length of tail in Illinois specimens 20 mm or less, and usually less than 19 mm; weight in Illinois specimens usually less than 6.7 gms; four unicuspids in each upper jaw but only three visible in lateral view; skull not rugose; color brownish or brownish gray; underparts about the same color as dorsum only lighter.

Dental formula. 3/1, 1/1, 2/1, 3/3, consisting of a large falciform tooth, four unicuspids, and four premolars-molars in each upper jaw; a large falciform tooth, two unicuspids, three premolars-molars in lower jaw.

Comparisons. Cryptotis is a short-tailed shrew that differs from the other genus of short-tailed shrews, *Blarina,* as follows: color brownish or brownish gray rather than blackish; three unicuspids visible in lateral view (and fourth present) rather than four unicuspids visible in lateral view (and fifth present); skull less rugose; in central and northern Illinois tail length is shorter (19 mm or less rather than 20 mm or more for *Blarina brevicauda*).

Cryptotis parva, Least shrew

Range. Throughout Illinois.

Diagnosis. A small species of *Cryptotis,* but *C. parva* is the only species occurring in the United States (others in Mexico and Central America); characters as given for the genus; tail about one-third body length. In Illinois, weight in non-pregnant animals is usually less than 6.7 gms.

Chromosomes. Cryptotis parva in Missouri is reported to have a 2N of 52 and FN of 50 with all autosomes acrocentric (Hsu and Benirschke, 1970a).

Comparisons. Cryptotis parva is the only species of the genus in the U.S. and needs no comparisons with Central American species.

Secondary sexual variation. In a sample of 82 specimens, differences between the sexes for cranial and external measurements were checked by Choate (1970:215). He found a significant difference only in length of maxillary toothrow, and suggested that the sexes be treated together.

Aging. Four age categories were recognized by Choate (1970:214)—from young with no wear on the teeth and juvenile pelage to old adult with cutting surfaces of the teeth well-worn. Among the four age categories, he could find no significant differences except in length of maxillary toothrow. All animals are included in the analyses of measurements.

Molt. The most complete analysis of molt is by Choate (1970:217). He found that the post-juvenile molt to winter pelage begins on the venter or above the rump, progresses rapidly on the venter and on to the dorsum, with the top of the head the last to molt. Post-juvenile molt to summer pelage is more irregular. Adult-pelage molt in the fall is like the post-juvenile winter molt. Adult-pelage spring molt usually begins on the head and progresses ventrally and posteriorly, with the rump molting last.

Pfeiffer and Gass (1963:427) stated that least shrews caught at Carbondale and kept in captivity "molted

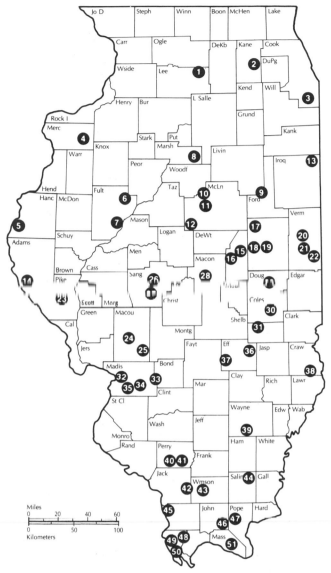

Map 8.7. Distribution of the least shrew, *Cryptotis parva.* The subspecies is *C. p. parva.* Numbers are referenced in *Records of occurrence.* The distribution of the species in the United States is shaded.

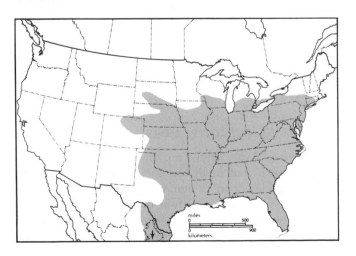

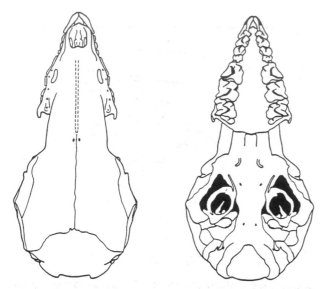

Fig. 8.15. *Cryptotis parva,* dorsal and ventral views of skull. Dixon Springs, Pope Co., Illinois, 57849 UI. Male, 17.0 mm greatest length.

without regard to season." However, these workers did not know about the sequence of molt reported at a later date by Choate.

Habitat

Least shrews seem not to be abundant in any habitat in Illinois, but prefer grassy or weedy fields. For example, in Piatt County in central Illinois, for three days annually we trapped a one-acre plot that was primarily bluegrass, intermixed with thistle, *Erigeron,* with some small trees, including cherry and haw, nearby. During a period of 23 years, we caught 105 least shrews, or 4.57 per year. In a hardwood forest, made up primarily of white oaks, red oaks, and maple, with some shagbark hickory, not more than a half-mile away, we caught only one least shrew in the same length of time. The fact that we did catch one is interesting because here it was in association with pine mice, short-tailed shrews, and flying squirrels. In Fulton County, a bit of what was called "original prairie" along a slightly used railroad right-of-way was inhabited by least shrews. Parts of the area had bluegrass; others were primarily sunflowers, two- to three-feet-tall weeds, and occasionally blackberries.

In southern Illinois, least shrews have been taken in short-grass fields, in brome sedge, and in ravines with weedy substrates and overhanging vegetation. I have seen them in the damp basements of houses, perhaps attracted there by the presence of spiders and water bugs.

In general, least shrews avoid woody areas and fields that are exceedingly brushy.

The underground burrow system and nest of a least shrew was excavated on the south campus of the University of Illinois on October 15, 1957. The burrow

system was in a cut, bluegrass field near some apricot trees. Small holes, about the size of crayfish holes, led to underground burrows that were never more than six inches below the ground surface. Burrows were followed for about seven feet in total, but no part of the system was straight; the burrows may have been even longer, but it was impossible to follow them in the dry, hard soil.

At one place the burrow became larger and a nest about the size of a baseball was found. A least shrew was seen just beyond, and it had apparently been frightened away. Construction of the nest was not elaborate and there were no finer fibers lining it.

Near the nest, the ground of the burrow was noticeably darker, seemingly stained, and with an ammonia-like odor. This area appeared to be the toilet area of the burrow system and it probably had been used by several shrews over a good many generations. In this same area, *Microtus ochrogaster* and *Spermophilus tridecemlineatus* are present. Numerous ants traversed the burrows, and these might be one source of food.

Least shrews are known to build and use nests beneath debris on the ground or under the roots of grasses and weeds. We suspect that they may use the underground burrows of voles and bog lemmings also, and construct nests therein.

Food

Little is known about the food habits of least shrews in Illinois. Mohr (1935) found one shrew in Illinois had fed on chinch bugs and a spider, and Layne (1958a) found that three in southern Illinois had eaten earthworms, various insects, and some unidentified arthropods. In Indiana, Whitaker and Mumford (1972a) found that least shrews fed extensively on the larvae of lepidopterus insects, earthworms, and spiders, as well as the internal organs of different kinds of insects. Plant material was 5.6 percent, but the stomach of one specimen was entirely filled with seeds and flower parts. Least shrews are reported to incapacitate grasshoppers and crickets by biting their legs or head, sometimes several times.

Reproduction

Young are born in both the spring and fall in Illinois. Two least shrew specimens taken in April were pregnant. A female taken at Carbondale in March was nursing four young (Pfieffer and Gass, 1963). In September, two females were lactating and one in October was pregnant. The two spring pregnancies were overwintering adults, judging from tooth wear. The October pregnancy was of a female born in the spring.

The females had 4, 6, and 7 embryos. Whitaker (1974) gives the mean for number of embryos at 4.9 (2–7) and the number of young in 16 litters as 4.5 (2–7). The gestation period is about three weeks. Young develop rapidly and by two weeks after birth are fully haired and have eyes open. By one month of age, the young have attained adult weight.

Populations

Although least shrews are seemingly not abundant anywhere, this may be a reflection on our ability to capture them. For example, large numbers of *Cryptotis parva* have been entrapped in Meyer Cave in Madison County during a period of many years. Parmalee (1967:135) stated that 1,049 individuals were identified, and perhaps more individuals were represented but not identified. If we used more effective methods of trapping for least shrews we might find that they are more abundant than we think.

In our 23-year censusing of an acre in central Illinois (Allerton Park), sometimes in three days of trapping we caught no least shrews; once we caught 18. In two other years, we caught 12, once 10; otherwise it was 7 or fewer. Since least shrews are reported to get along better with each other than most shrews, and several may occupy the same nest, it may be that instances of larger catches actually represent taking several animals from one or two nest areas.

Variation

Many workers recognize two subspecies of *Cryptotis parva* in Illinois: *C. p. parva* (eastern Nebraska) and *C. p. harlani* (New Harmony, Indiana). We compared 12 specimens from eastern Nebraska, 21 from western Illinois, 28 from eastern Illinois, 16 from southern Illinois, and 12 from western Indiana.

A canonical variate analysis of all individuals was run and plotted (Fig. 8.16). An area of one standard deviation around the mean for each geographical sample overlaps one or more areas for other samples. There is such an overlap of individuals and populations that there appear

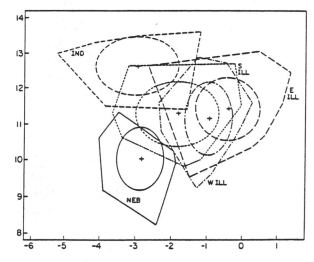

Fig. 8.16. Canonical variate analysis of five populations of *Cryptotis parva:* western Indiana (12 specimens), eastern Nebraska (12), western Illinois (21), southern Illinois (16), eastern Illinois (28). For each population, peripheral specimens are connected; the enclosed ellipse is one standard deviation from the mean. Note how all of the samples overlap.

to be no significant differences among the five geographical samples.

A discriminant function analysis (Fig. 8.17) shows much the same overlap among specimens from the five geographical areas.

I find no basis for regarding *Cryptotis parva harlani* as a distinct subspecies.

Cryptotis parva parva (Say)

1823. *Sorex parvus* Say, in Long, Account . . . Rocky Mts., 1:163. Type from W bank Missouri River, near Blair, Washington, Co., Nebraska.
1842. *Brachysorex harlani* Duvernoy, Mag. de Zool. de. Anat. Comp. . . . , 25:40. Type locality New Harmony, Posey Co., Indiana.

Table 8.6. External and cranial measurements (in mm), with mean, minimum and maximum, and one standard deviation, of *Cryptotis parva parva*.

Locality	N	Total length	Tail length	Body length	Hind foot length	Greatest length	Braincase breadth	Maxillary breadth	Toothrow length	Unicuspid toothrow length	Complex toothrow length	Breadth across toothrows	Breadth across unicuspid 4's
W. central Illinois	21	77.1 68-89 5.94	15.8 12-19 2.04	61.3	10.0 9-11 0.56	15.1 14.3-15.92 0.43	7.9 7.58-8.45 0.26	5.1 4.80-5.47 0.21	5.8 5.32-6.11 0.20	1.8 1.61-1.99 0.10	4.1 3.82-4.35 0.14	4.7 4.39-5.06 0.19	2.2 2.06-2.55 0.13
E. central Illinois	28	75.3 66-90 5.17	15.6 11-19 1.81	59.7	10.1 9-13 0.82	15.3 14.6-15.75 0.36	7.9 7.6-8.27 0.16	5.2 5.02-5.32 0.10	5.8 5.40-6.15 0.16	1.9 1.61-2.02 0.10	4.2 3.86-4.42 0.13	4.8 4.50-4.99 0.12	2.3 2.06-2.46 0.11
Southern Illinois	16	73.7 63-87 6.12	15.9 13-20 1.96	57.8	10.4 9-11 0.61	15.5 15.03-15.92 0.04	8.0 7.7-9.15 0.13	5.2 4.91-5.43 0.15	5.9 5.62-6.03 0.11	1.9 1.72-1.99 0.08	4.2 4.09-4.31 0.07	4.9 4.65-4.99 0.11	2.3 1.99-2.40 0.13

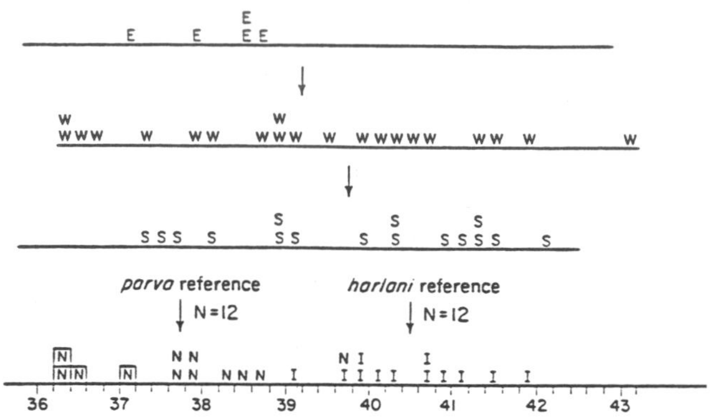

Fig. 8.17. Discriminant function analysis of five populations of *Cryptotis parva:* I, western Indiana; N, eastern Nebraska; W, western Illinois; S, southern Illinois; E, eastern Illinois. The reference sample of *C. p. parva* from Nebraska and *C. p. harlani* from Indiana are on the lower line; those from Illinois on the lines above. Note the overlap between *parva* and *harlani.*

1858. *B*[*larina*]. *eximius* Baird, Mammals, in Repts. Expl. Surv., 8:52. Based on two specimens: one from De Kalb Co., Illinois; one from St. Louis, Missouri.

1912. *Cryptotis parva,* Miller, Bull. U.S. Nat. Mus., 79:24.

Range. Throughout Illinois (Map 8.7).

Diagnosis. A small to medium-sized subspecies, with a short hind foot, short skull, and short to medium-length toothrows.

Remarks. Specimens from southernmost Illinois average a little larger than those in central Illinois (Table 8.7) but the differences are minimal. Southern Illinois specimens have somewhat shorter bodies and slightly longer hind feet.

Records of occurrence. SPECIMENS EXAMINED, 193. **Lee Co.:** [1] Kyte River, 5 mi S Rochelle, 1 (SRL). **De Kalb Co.:** [2] Cortland, 1 (US); no specific locality [not plotted], 1 (US). **Cook Co.:** [3] Homewood, 2 (FM). **Mercer Co.:** [4] ½ mi E, 1½ mi S Viola, 2 (SRL). **Hancock Co.** [5] Warsaw, 3 (FM). **Fulton Co.** [6a] ½ mi N Norris, 7 (UI); [6b] 3 mi N Canton, 1 (UI); [6c] 1 mi W Canton, 5 (UI); [6d] 2½ mi E Canton, 2 (UI); [7] near Dickson Mounds, 1 (ISM). **Marshall Co.:** [8] Toluca, 1 (ISU). **Livingston Co.:** [9] 7 mi E, 1 mi S Strawn, 2 (UI). **McLean Co.:** [10] 3 mi NW Hudson, 1 (ISU); [11a] 4 mi N Normal, 1 (ISU); [11b] 2½ mi N Normal, 1 (ISU); [11c] 1 mi N Normal, 3 (ISU); [11d] 1 mi W Normal, 1 (ISU); [11e] ½ mi E Bloomington, 1 (ISU); [12] 1½ mi N McLean, Funk's Forest, 1 (UI). **Iroquois Co.:** [13] 5 mi E Beaverville, 1 (UI). **Adams Co.:** [14] 3¼ mi S Payson, 1 (UI). **Piatt Co.:** [15] White Heath, 1 (UI); [16a] 1½ mi ENE Cisco, RR right of way, 3 (UI); [16b] Allerton Park, 34 (UI). **Champaign Co.:** [17] Fisher, 1 (UI); [18] Seymour, 2 (UI); [19a] Trelease Woods, 3 mi E, 1 mi N Urbana, 8 (UI); [19b] Phillips Tract, 1 (UI); [19c] Trelease Grassland, 5 mi NE Urbana, 3 (UI); [19d] Trelease Prairie, 4 mi NE Urbana, 2 (UI); [19e] 1⅛ mi N Urbana, 1 (UI); [19f] Urbana, 7 (UI); [19g] Mayview Prairie, 4 mi E Urbana, 3 (UI); [19h] SW Champaign, 1 (UI); [19i] Ill. Central RR, 1½ mi SW U of I, 1 (UI); [19j] Ill. Central RR, 2 mi S Champaign, 1 (UI); [19k] 2½ mi S Urbana, 2 (UI); [19l] Urbana Twp. [Wildlife] Area, 2½ mi E, 2½ mi S Urbana, 1 (UI).

Vermilion Co.: [20a] 1⅘ mi NE Collison, 1 (UI); [20b] 1 mi W Higginsville, 1 (UI); [20c] 2 mi N, 1½ mi E Newtown, 1 (UI); [20d] 1¼ mi W, ½ mi S Snider, 3 (UI); [21a] ½ S, ½ mi E Newtown, 3 (UI); [21b] Kickapoo State Park, 1 (UI); [22] 3⅘ mi E, 2⅖ mi S Westville, 5 (UI). **Pike Co.:** [23] Pittsfield, 2 (UI). **Macoupin Co.:** [24a] 3 mi NE Beaver Dam State Park, 1 (UI); [24b] 2 mi NE Beaver Dam State Park, 2 (UI); [24c] 1 mi NE Beaver Dam State Park, 1 (UI); [25] ¼ mi S Benld, 1 (SIE). **Sangamon Co.:** [26] Springfield, 1 (ISM); [27a] Chatham, 1 (ISM); [27b] 1 mi N Glenarm, 1 (ISM). **Macon Co.:** [28] 2.3 mi W Decatur, 1 (UI). **Douglas Co.:** [29] 2 mi SW Camargo, Embarrass River, 1 (UI). **Coles Co.:** [30] Charleston, 1 (NHS), 2 (UI). **Cumberland Co.:** [31] 6 mi NW Toledo, 1 (NHS). **Madison Co.:** [32a] 2 mi S Roxana, 1 (SIE); [32b] 3 mi W, 1 mi S Edwardsville, 1 (SIE); [33] 3 mi E, 0.3 mi S Grantfork, 1 (SIE); [34] 3 mi NE Troy, Silver Creek, 1 (UI); [35] 2 mi NE Glen Carbon, 1 (UI). **Effingham Co.:** [36] T8N, R7E, Sec. 32, 1 (UI); [37] 3 mi S Altamont, 1 (UI). **Crawford Co.:** [38] Flatrock, 1 (CAS). **Wayne Co.:** [39] 3 mi E, 4 mi S Sims, along Skillet Fork River, 1 (UI). **Perry Co.:** [40] Striplands Res. Area, 1 (SRL); [41] 2 mi W Du Quoin, 1 (SIC). **Jackson Co.:** [42] Carbondale, 1 (SIC). **Williamson Co.:** [43] Crab Orchard Lake Refuge, 6 mi S Herrin, 1 (UI). **Saline Co.:** [44] 2½ mi NW Eldorado, 1 (SIE). **Union Co.:** [45a] Pine Hills, 8 mi N Ware, 1 (UI); [45b] Wolf Lake, 4 (CAS). **Johnson Co.:** [46a] Grantsburg, Bay Creek, 1 (UI); [46b] ½ mi E Grantsburg, 2 (UI); [46c] Reevesville, 2 (FM). **Pope Co.:** [47a] 1 mi S, ½ mi E Glendale, 1 (UI); [47b] 1½ mi S Glendale, 3 (UI); [47c] 2½ mi S, ½ mi E Glendale, 1 (UI); [47d] Dixon Springs, Glendale Lake, 1 (UI). **Alexander Co.:** [48] Tamms, 1 (SRL); [49] 3¼ mi NNW Olive Branch, 1 (SRL); [50a] Olive Branch, 12 (FM); [50b] 2½ mi S Olive Branch, 4 (UI); [50c] Horseshoe Lake, 1 (UI). **Massac Co.:** [51] 4 mi NE Metropolis, 1 (SIC).

Additional records. **Piatt Co.:** [16b] Allerton Park, 1 (FS). **Alexander Co.** [50d] Cache, 1 (FS).

Family Talpidae, Moles

Medium-sized insectivores with enlarged forefeet; front legs developed for digging and pushing; eyes usually reduced or absent; pinna of ear absent; nose long and flexible; cranium with zygomatic arches; first upper incisors long and flat. Represented in Illinois by the genus *Scalopus.*

Fig. 8.18. Frontal view of live eastern mole, *Scalopus aquaticus*. Note broad forefeet, prominent nose, and reduced eyes. Photograph by K. Maslowski and W. W. Goodpaster.

Scalopus, Eastern mole

Diagnosis. A talpid in which the eyes are absent externally, nose snoutlike and naked; palms of forefeet broader than long with toes well clawed and webbed; hair short but plush, color usually blackish, grayish black, or brownish black.

Dental formula. 3/2, 1/0, 3/3, 3/3.

Chromosomes. 2N = 34; FN = 64. All autosomes are metacentric or submetacentric.

Comparisons. There is the possibility that moles of the genus *Condylura* (*Condylura cristata*) may occur in Illinois. *Scalopus* differs from *Condylura* in having a long, hairless snout rather than one with a ring of fleshy tentacles at the tip; tail about one-fourth the length of the body and nearly hairless rather than as long as the body, thick, black, and haired; teeth much heavier and first incisors much broader and longer; zygomatic arches stronger.

Secondary sexual variation. A sample of eight males and seven females from Vermilion and Champaign counties was analyzed for secondary sexual differences in the measurements given in Table 8.8. Males and females are compared separately. Males were found to be significantly larger than females in three of the four external measurements and six of the seven cranial measurements.

Aging. Animals that appeared to be of adult size externally—that is, larger than obvious nestlings—were used in comparative analyses.

Scalopus aquaticus, Eastern mole

Range. Throughout the state.

Diagnosis. *Scalopus* is a monotypic species; thus the diagnosis of the genus applies to *S. aquaticus*. Other diagnostic features are tail about ⅕ length of body; nostrils superior on long snout; forefeet handlike, broader than long, thick and well clawed; three pairs of mammae; braincase broad and flattened; auditory bullae complete.

Color. The dorsum and venter are of the same color and vary from blackish to grayish black and rusty black; the tops of the feet are whitish. One juvenile from 2 mi S Hartsburg, Logan County, is an albino. In a sample of 49 specimens from Illinois, only one had cream-colored

Table 8.7. External and cranial measurements (in mm), mean, minimum and maximum, and one standard deviation of *Scalopus aquaticus*. Males and females are treated separately, and localities are in general arranged from north to south. Superscripts indicate sample less than N.

Locality	Sex	N	Total length	Tail length	Body length	Hind foot length	Greatest length	Mastoid breadth	Least interorb. breadth	Post-palatal length	Length maxillary toothrow	Greatest br. across toothrows	Skull depth
Northern Ill.	♂	4	199.8	37.0	166.3	22.5	40.1	20.8	8.2	15.9	17.3	11.6	11.3
			195-205	33-43	158-170	21-24	39.5-40.5	20.5-21.6	7.9-8.7	15.7-16.1	17.1-17.5	11.3-11.8	11.1-11.5
			4.11	4.32	5.68	1.73	0.42	0.31	0.17	0.17	0.21	0.21	0.20
Central Ill.	♂	14	179.1	30.5[12]	148.5[12]	23.7	39.0	20.2	8.02	15.2	17.2	11.6	11.2
			161-198	25-36	129-170	20-38	37.0-40.8	19.3-21.4	7.5-8.6	14.0-15.9	16.4-18.1	10.7-12.5	10.7-11.7
			11.06	3.37	11.50	4.59	1.09	0.59	0.33	0.53	0.55	0.44	0.37
East central Ill.	♂	9	190.9	34.6	156.3	24.1	39.1	20.4	8.1	15.8	17.1	11.4	11.3
			173-201	27-40	138-167	23-25	38.2-39.7	19.6-20.9	7.7-8.6	15.0-16.3	16.6-17.5	10.9-11.8	10.9-11.7
			10.75	4.16	9.95	0.78	0.59	0.43	0.30	0.39	0.32	0.30	0.28
Southern Ill.	♂	6	181.0	28.7	152.3	21.9	38.3	19.7	8.0	14.7	16.7	11.0	11.1
			170-199	22-34	141-167	20-24	37.6-39.1	19.2-20.2	7.7-8.2	14.0-15.6	16.4-17.3	10.7-11.4	10.8-11.5
			10.30	4.72	10.73	1.80	0.59	0.34	0.20	0.53	0.32	0.24	0.28
Northern Ill.	♀	4	177.0	32.3	144.7	23.7	39.0	20.4	8.2	15.3	16.8	11.5	11.1
			170-190	26-36	136-154	22-25	37.4-40.9	19.1-21.6	7.9-8.5	14.5-16.5	16.3-17.5	10.9-12.0	10.9-11.4
			11.27	5.51	9.02	1.53	1.82	1.31	0.23	0.98	0.59	0.54	0.26
Central Ill.	♀	9	168.6	27.4	141.1	20.9[7]	37.8	19.6	7.87[8]	14.9[7]	16.6[8]	11.2[8]	11.0[8]
			148-191	23-37	124-166	19-25	37.2-39.0	18.7-20.4	7.6-8.2	14.4-15.5	16.0-17.1	10.8-11.8	10.5-11.6
			16.37	4.80	15.72	2.05	0.56	0.63	0.22	0.49	0.38	0.35	0.36
East central Ill.	♀	7	180.3	34.0	144.1	22.8	37.3	19.3	8.0	14.7	16.4	11.0	10.9
			164-192	31-39	131-157	22-23	36.3-38.0	18.7-19.8	7.6-8.6	14.5-15.2	15.8-16.9	10.2-11.5	10.6-11.1
			10.10	2.39	8.88	0.46	0.41	0.41	0.30	0.26	0.35	0.42	0.18
Southern Ill.	♀	7	167.4	27.0	140.4	21.3	36.4	18.9	7.7	14.0	15.9	10.6	10.6
			149-178	22-30	119-156	18-23	36.1-36.6	18.4-19.3	7.6-8.0	13.5-14.5	15.5-16.3	10.3-11.2	10.4-10.9
			10.26	3.06	11.62	1.38	0.20	0.37	0.16	0.32	0.26	0.31	0.18

spotting on the venter, but none on the dorsum. In Indiana, about 16 percent of the specimens had dorsal or ventral spotting, or both (Mumford and Whitaker, 1982:122).

Chromosomes. As given for the genus (p. 79).

Comparisons. Scalopus aquaticus cannot be confused with other Illinois mammals, with its combination of unique characters including no external eyes or ears; long naked snout; short, nearly hairless tail; blackish, velvetlike fur; and broad, thick paddlelike feet. Males appear superficially to have some features of the short-tailed shrew, *Blarina*.

The habitat of *S. aquaticus* is somewhat like that of the pocket gopher, *Geomys bursarius* but the mole differs in many morphological features, of which the most apparent are the absence or great reduction of eyes, broad forefeet with heavy nails on each toe rather than narrow feet with long claws on each toe, velvetlike fur, long snout, and conical skull with sharp-cusped teeth rather than prismatic grinding teeth.

Remarks. The presence of moles can be ascertained by the tunnels they make just below the surface of the ground. These tunnels cause the surface of the soil to be slightly mounded upward, resulting in numerous small tension cracks in the surface. These "mole runs" may be

seen in soft soil, leaf-mold, lawns, gardens, and a variety of other places. Moles may also push soil into mounds onto the surface of the ground. Such mounds may be confused with those of the pocket gophers, *Geomys bursarius*. However, pocket gophers and moles occur together in only a limited part of Illinois.

Although we have few records of *Scalopus aquaticus* from the northernmost counties in Illinois, the species is not uncommon in the Chicago area.

Habitat

Eastern moles are found in a great variety of habitats in Illinois as long as the soil is sufficiently friable to permit its being pushed upward or to the sides. In such soils, they are found in mature and second-growth woods, pasturelands, gardens, cemeteries, recently plowed fields, mowed lawns, and corn and soybean fields. They are commonly encountered in soils that contain much leaf mold, as found on forest floors, and in sandy soils. In places in central Illinois, east of the Illinois River, eastern moles and plains pocket gophers live in the same area, both building underground tunnel systems and throwing up surface mounds of extra soil. In most of the places where the two species occur together, moles have burrows near the ground surface, and pocket gopher's burrows are several inches deep. Usually the subterranean burrow of the mole is evident as a slight ridge (mole-run, but sometimes called molehill) running through the field or grassland, with the soil slightly cracked along the top of the ridge.

In the southernmost counties and near the Mississippi River, Klimstra (1969) found that moles were usually in the drier communities of the lowlands, in the recently disturbed fields, and in the more mature woodlands.

In the north central part of Illinois, moles are either absent or uncommon. Mohr (1946) thought that their absence might be correlated indirectly with the Iowan and early Wisconsin glaciation in this area.

Food

Eastern moles are mostly "insectivorous," feeding extensively on earthworms and a variety of ground dwelling adult and larval insects. In central Illinois, the stomachs of 56 moles were examined and reported on by James West (1914). He found that 53 specimens had eaten insects, amounting to 62 percent of the volume, 31 had eaten earthworms amounting to 26 percent, and vegetable matter was present in 28 stomachs, amounting to 11 percent. The remaining one percent consisted of one-time occurrence of hair, feather, myriapod, and spider (twice). Of the insect remains, larvae were present in 47 moles, adult remains in 42.

In an analysis of 90 stomachs of moles in Indiana, and mostly just across the Illinois line near Terre Haute, Whitaker and Schmeltz (1974) found that 43.7 percent of the volume of food was of insects, 26.8 of earthworms, and 14.6, vegetable matter.

Moles are opportunistic, preying upon those food items that are readily available. West (1914) pointed out that with Illinois moles, all that were taken in woodlands had fed on carpenter ants which nest in old logs and stumps in shady woods; those living in sodded areas fed extensively on May beetles in May and June, as well as sod webworms at other times. The only mole taken in winter had 150 ants in its stomach.

Frequently, moles will make a subterranean runway along a row of a newly planted field. I suspect that moles are seeking insects and earthworms in this freshly pulverized soil. By making tunnels immediately below the seeds or seedlings, they remove the rootlets from the soil and weaken or kill the plant. I also think that moles feed on newly planted corn seeds because these attracted insects. West (1914) found that the principal part of the stomach contents in some moles was corn, with one case in which 90 percent was corn. He concluded that "corn may form an important item of the food of moles; that recently planted corn is sometimes destroyed by them; and that if numerous in cornfields in spring, they are capable of doing considerable damage there." These seem

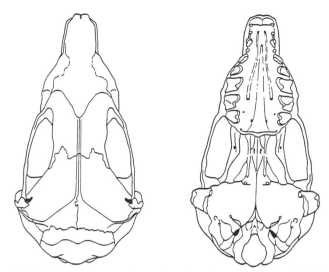

Fig. 8.19. *Scalopus aquaticus*, dorsal and ventral views of skull, 1 mi. NW Heringtown, Vermilion Co., Illinois, 59045 UI. Male, 40.1 mm greatest length.

to be overly strong conclusions; at any rate, with present-day agricultural practices in cultivation and in insect control, moles are of small economic importance in cornfields.

Reproduction

Details of many aspects of reproduction in the eastern mole are uncertain. The gestation period is reported to be anywhere between 28 and 48 days. Most authors say that there is only one litter annually. In Illinois, young are apparently born anytime between late February and June. One specimen from Pope County taken on April 8 contained four embryos, each with a crown-rump length of 16 mm. Another mole from the same locality, taken one day earlier, was lactating. Cory (1912) quoting Kennicott, says that a female from Winchester, Scott County, carried two full-term embryos the latter part of February.

Burrowing

Arlton (1936:352) observed that eastern moles burrow through the ground by putting their forefeet close to the snout and pushing the dirt aside, then finding a place with their snout for the next pushing aside of dirt with the forefeet. The mole "twists the anterior half of its body, turning on its side, and pushes the soil upward with its fore feet," not with its head. Burrows or tunnels just below the surface are at a uniform depth. Lowery (1974:91) found that when the soil is in good condition for tunneling—in his case, after a rain—a mole extended a subsurface tunnel at the rate of 18 feet in an hour. Also, deep burrows are dug; these serve as nest sites and retreats. They are dug out by the forefeet and when enough soil has been loosened, it is pushed to the surface

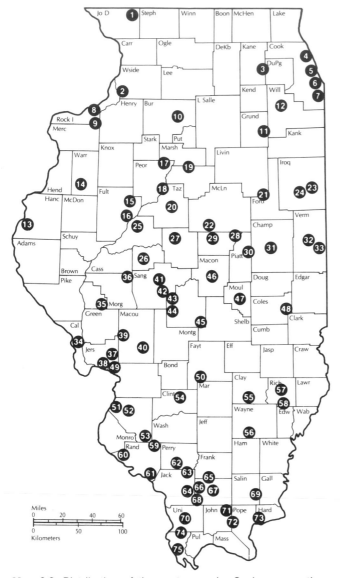

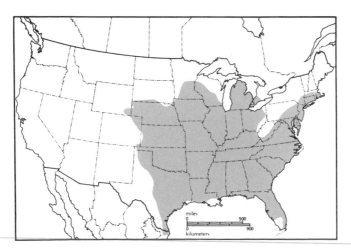

Map 8.8. Distribution of the eastern mole, *Scalopus aquaticus*. The subspecies is *S. a. machrinus*. Numbers are referenced in *Records of occurrence*. The distribution of the species in the United States is shaded.

with the forefeet. These piles of dirt form conspicuous mounds. Arlton (1936:353) found that a below-the-surface burrow of a mole near Iowa City, Iowa, was 91 meters (298.6 ft) long and a branched tunnel system covered about 3,540 sq m (11,614 sq ft). In Kentucky, Michael Harvey found that the runway of one mole extended along a fencerow for 275 m, with feeding runways branching off the main tunnel (in Barbour and Davis, 1974:49). Harvey found that the home range varied between 1,512 and 3,430 sq m for females and between 3,616 and 18,041 sq m for males.

When the subsurface runway becomes compressed, and if the runway is being used, it will be reopened by the occupant rather quickly. This behavior often provides a means of capturing moles, since when they push up the runway they can also trigger a device to trap them or to record their presence.

A mole can turn around in its narrow tunnel by placing its head under its abdomen and creeping under itself or turning a slow somersault.

Vision

Moles are said to be blind, or to have no eyes, or to have poor vision. The facts are that eastern moles do have eyes although they are degenerate and the eyelids are fused and thus the eyes are covered with an integument. The eye lacks or has a reduced aqueous and vitreous chamber. The eye is no longer confined to the bony socket as in other mammals, but instead is imbedded in the integument about 3.5 mm forward of a position in the socket. There is doubt that light ever enters the eye even though the retina is present. In the adult male, the position of the eye below the integument can be ascertained as a somewhat darker spot, although the integument over the eye is 0.3 mm or more thick. The eyeball is no more than 1.0 mm in diameter and the optic nerve is abnormally small.

James Slonaker (1902) did much of the research on the eyes of moles which was based mostly on moles from southern Indiana.

Variation

One subspecies, *Scalopus aquaticus machrinus*, has been ascribed as occurring in Illinois, but another, *S. a. machrinoides*, is ascribed as occurring in Iowa and Missouri.

Scalopus aquaticus machrinus (Rafinesque)

1832. *Talpa machrina* Rafinesque, Atlantic Jour., 1:61. Type locality near Lexington, Fayette Co., Kentucky.
1905. *Scalopus aquaticus machrinus*, Elliot, Field Columb. Mus. Publ. 105, zool. ser., 6:470.

1832. *Talpa sericea* Rafinesque, Atlantic Jour., 1:62. Type locality near Nicholasville, Jessamine Co., and Harrodsburg, Mercer Co., Kentucky.

1842. *Scalops argentatus* Audubon and Bachman, J. Acad. Nat. Sci., Phila., 8:292. Type locality in southern Michigan.

Range. Throughout the state (Map 8.8).

Diagnosis and Comparisons. A large subspecies of *S. aquaticus,* both externally and cranially. *S. a. machrinus* differs from *S. a. machrinoides,* to the west of Illinois, according to Jackson (1915:45) in larger size, less grayish color, and larger skull.

Remarks. Specimens of *Scalopus aquaticus* are progressively larger from southern to northern Illinois. This size change is readily apparent in Table 8.7. For example, males from southern Illinois have a skull length of 38.3 mm; central, 39.0 or 39.1; northern, 40.1 mm. If specimens from Reelfoot Lake, Tennessee, are included at the southern end of the cline, 37.2 mm. The clinal changes are just as impressive for females. In a shift of about 6° latitude, the skull is around 3.0 mm longer.

Records of occurrence. SPECIMENS EXAMINED, 158.
Jo Daviess Co.: [1] 3½ mi S, 2 mi E Apple River, 1 (UI). **Whiteside Co.:** [2] 5 mi W Erie, 1 (UI). **Kane Co.:** [3] Geneva, 1 (FM). **Cook Co.:** [5] Brookdale [now incorporated into Chicago], 1 (FM); [6a] Chicago, Jackson Park, 1 (US), 1 (FM); [6b] Oakwoods Cemetery, 6 (FM); [7a] Dolton, 2 (FM); [7b] Harvey, 1 (FM). **Rock Island Co.:** [8] Moline, 1 (NIU); [9] 12 mi S Moline, Johnson Farm, 1 (UI). **Bureau Co.:** [10] 4 mi NE Princeton, 1 (NIU). **Grundy Co.:** [11] Coal City, 1 (FM). **Will Co.:** [12] Joliet, 1 (FM). **Hancock Co.:** [13a] Hamilton*, 1 (US); [13b] Warsaw*, 9 (FM), 6 (US). **Warren Co.:** [14] 1 mi W Roseville, Tomlin Farm, 1 (UI). **Fulton Co.:** [15a] 2 mi NW Canton, 2 (UI); [15b] Canton, 3 (UI); [16a] Bryant, 1 (UI); [16b] 6 mi E Lewistown, 1 (ISM). **Peoria Co.:** [17] 18 mi N Peoria, 1 (UI); [18] Peoria, 1 (ISM); no specific locality [not plotted], 1 (ISM). **Woodford Co.:** [19] 15 mi N Eureka, 1 (UI). **Tazewell Co.:** [20] Tremont, [labelled Fremont], 1 (UI). **Livingston Co.:** [21] T25N, R8E, Sec. 15, 1 (UI). **McLean Co.:** [22] 1½ mi W Heyworth, 1 (UI); Ewing Farm [location?], 1 (ISU). **Iroquois Co.:** [23] ½ mi E Woodland, 2 (MSU); [24] 1½ mi N, 1 mi E Woodworth, 1 (UI). **Menard Co.:** [26] Lake Petersburg, 1 (ISM). **Logan Co.:** [27] 2 mi S Hartsburg, 1 (UI). **DeWitt Co.:** [28] 3 mi NW Farmer City, 1 (UI); [29] 2

mi N Wapella, 1 (UI). **Champaign Co.** [31a] 3 mi ENE Urbana, 1 (UI); [31b] Champaign, 1 (UI); [31c] Urbana, 1 (UI). **Vermilion Co.:** [32a] 1 mi S, 3 mi E Collison, 3 (UI); [32b] 2 mi N, 1½ mi E Newtown, 1 (UI); [32c] ½ mi S, 3 mi E Collison, 1 (UI); [33a] Danville, 9 (UI); [33b] 2 mi E Danville, 1 (UI). **Calhoun Co.:** [34] no specific locality, 1 (ISM). **Scott Co.:** [35] 2 mi W Manchester, 1 (ISM). **Morgan Co.:** [36] 3 mi S Ashland, 1 (UI). **Jersey Co.:** [37] 5 mi N, 2 mi W Godfrey [labelled Madison Co.], 1 (SIE); [38] Riehl Sta. [exact locality uncertain, may be Madison Co.], 1 (US). **Macoupin Co.:** [39] 1 mi W Chesterfield, 1 (UI); [40] 1 mi E, 5 mi N Wilsonville, 1 (SIE). **Sangamon Co.:** [41a] Springfield, 4 (ISM); [41b] 2 mi SE Springfield, 2 (ISM); [41c] 3 mi S Springfield, 1 (ISM); [42a] 6 mi S Springfield, 1 (ISM); [42b] 7 mi S Springfield, 1 (ISM); [42c] 2¼ mi NW New City, 1 (ISM). **Christian Co.:** [43] Sangchris State Park, 1 (ISM); [44] 6 mi N Morrisonville, 2 (UI); [45] Pana, 1 (ISU). **Macon Co.:** [46] Decatur, 1 (ISM). **Moultrie Co.:** [47] 2 mi N Sullivan, 1 (UI). **Coles Co.:** [48] ½ mi S Ashmore, 1 (UI). **Madison Co.:** [49a] Edwardsville, 1 (UI); [49b] Alton, 1 (USNM), 2 (SIE). **Fayette Co.:** [50] 7 mi S Vandalia, 1 (UI). **Saint Clair Co.:** [51] Cahokia, 1 (SIE); [52] Belleville, 2 (SIE); [53] ¼ mi W Marissa, 1 (UI). **Clinton Co.:** [54] 4 mi NNE Carlyle, Eldon Hazlet State Park, 1 (UI). **Wayne Co.:** [56] 3 mi E, 4 mi S Sims, Skillet Fork River, 2 (UI). **Richland Co.:** [57] Olney, 6 (US); [58b] Parkersburg, 2 (US); no specific locality [not plotted], 3 (US). **Randolph Co.:** [59] Tilden, 1 (SIC); [60] 2 mi N Modoc, 1 (ISM); [61] 6 mi SE Chester, 1 (UI). **Perry Co.:** [62] Pyatts Stripmines, 1 (SRL). **Jackson Co.:** [63] Elkville, 1 (SIC); [64a] 1 mi W Carbondale, 1 (SIC); [64b] Carbondale, 2 (SRL), 1 (FS), 3 (SIC); [64c] 2 mi E Carbondale, 1 (SIC); [64d] 4 mi E Carbondale, 1 (SIC); [64e] Old Crab Orchard Rd. [E of Carbondale], 2 (SIC); [64f] 3 mi S Carbondale, 1 (SIC). **Williamson Co.:** [65] Stiritz (near Herrin), 1 (KU); [66] Cambria, 1 (SIC); [67] Marion, 1 (SIC); [68] near Girl Scout Camp Rd., 1 (SRL). **Saline Co.:** [69a] 1½ mi W Horseshoe, 1 (UI); [69b] Horseshoe, 1 (SIC). **Union Co.:** [70] no specific locality but plotted in center of county, 1 (US). **Johnson Co.:** [71] Ozark, 1 (FM). **Pope Co.:** [72a] 1¾ mi W, ¾ mi S Glendale, 2 (UI); [72b] 1½ mi S Glendale, 1 (UI); [72c] Dixon Springs Experimental Station, 1 (UI). **Hardin Co.:** [73] Rosiclare, 1 (FM). **Alexander Co.:** [74] 1½ mi NW Elco, 1 (UI); [75a] Olive Branch, 1 (FM); [75b] 2 mi SE Olive Branch, Horseshoe Lake, 1 (FM); [75c] 3 mi S Olive Branch, 1 (UI).

Additional records. **Cook Co.:** [4] Evanston, 3 (UM). **Mason Co.:** [25] Topeka, (West, 1914:16). **Piatt Co.:** [30] White Heath, (West, 1914:16). **Clay Co.:** [55] Flora, (West, 1914:16). **Richland Co.:** [58a] Calhoun, 7 (UM).

* Worthen specimens.

Order Chiroptera, Bats

Flying mammals, with bones of fingers lengthened and connected with a patagial membrane, which is a nearly naked, double layer of skin forming a wing; membrane extends to legs and between legs, thus enclosing part or all of the tail; thumb reduced in size, free of wing membrane, and clawed; cartilaginous calcar on inner side of ankle usually present to support tail membrane; skull relatively small and teeth sharp-cusped; many species echolocate and hibernate. Order consists of two suborders and 17 families; two families are found in Illinois.

KEY TO CHIROPTERA (BATS) IN ILLINOIS AND ONE HYPOTHETICAL SPECIES (*Myotis leibii*)

1a. Tail contained in interfemoral (tail) membrane; ears not joined over forehead 2
1b. Tail at distal half free of interfemoral (tail) membrane; ears nearly joined over forehead ..... *Tadarida brasiliensis* p. 131
2a. Ears long, more than 30 mm and about ⅔ length of tail; glandular outgrowths or lumps on side of nose; first upper incisor with a secondary cusp ..... *Plecotus rafinesquii* p. 128
2b. Ears less than 23 mm and about ⅓ length of tail; no outgrowths or lumps on side of nose; large upper incisor without prominent secondary cusp 3
3a. Upper surface of tail membrane completely furred, underside of wing with patch of fur on distal part of forearm; one small premolar behind upper canine minute and squeezed lingually; ears small, rounded, and rimmed 4
3b. Upper surface of tail membrane appears bare or at least posterior third is bare, underside of wing naked; small premolar behind upper canine absent or, if present, not squeezed lingually; ears neither rounded nor rimmed 5
4a. Fur reddish, dusted with white; forearm length less than 45 mm; greatest length of skull less than 15.5 mm, braincase breadth less than 8.4 mm ..... *Lasiurus borealis* p. 117
4b. Fur a mixture of buff, yellow, and amber, heavily frosted with white; forearm length more than 45 mm; greatest length of skull more than 15.5 mm, braincase breadth more than 8.4 mm ..... *Lasiurus cinereus* p. 122
5a. Fur blackish, frosted with white; premolars-molars above 5, below 6 ..... *Lasionycteris noctivagans* p. 107
5b. Fur neither blackish nor frosted with white but rather brownish or yellowish brown; premolars-molars above and below never 5/6 but 4/5, 5/5, or 6/6 6

6a. Body length 65 mm or more, forearm 44 mm or more; two upper incisors but no small premolar behind canine ..... *Eptesicus fuscus* p. 113
6b. Body length less than 65 mm, forearm less than 44 mm; one upper incisor or, if two upper incisors, then one or two small premolars behind canine 7
7a. One upper incisor, no small premolar behind canine; tragus short, blunt, and slightly curved ..... *Nycticeius humeralis* p. 125
7b. Two upper incisors, one or two small premolars behind canine; tragus relatively long and not especially blunt 8
8a. Color yellowish brown to orangish brown, fur on dorsum tricolored (two color bands plus terminal tip); one small premolar behind upper canine ..... *Pipistrellus subflavus* p. 111
8b. Color brownish or grayish, fur not tricolored; two small premolars behind upper canine 9
9a. Wing membrane attached to ankles; base of hairs not black but almost uniformly gray from base to tip; forearm length more than 40 mm; skull large and with a sagittal crest ..... *Myotis grisescens* p. 103
9b. Wing membrane attached to side of foot; base of hairs black; forearm length 40 mm or less, greatest length of skull usually less than 15.5 mm and without a noticeable sagittal crest 10
10a. Fur on venter white or pale gray, fur on dorsum woolly and often mole-gray; skull deep (averaging 5.7 mm) ..... *Myotis austroriparius* p. 101
10b. Fur on venter brownish or buffy gray, fur on dorsum not woolly and brownish, skull shallow (depth averaging less than 5.7 mm) 11
11a. Ear long (15–18 mm) and tragus slender and pointed; toothrow C-M³ long (5.7 mm or more) ..... *Myotis keenii* p. 103
11b. Ear short, 15 mm or less, tragus not especially pointed; toothrow C-M³ short (5.7 mm or less) 12
12a. Forearm 33 mm or less in length; greatest length of skull less than 14 mm ..... [*Myotis leibii*] p. 43
12b. Forearm length more than 33 mm; greatest length of skull more than 14 mm 13
13a. Hairs on toes do not extend beyond claws, well-developed keel on calcar (rarely absent); palate narrow between M²s, braincase narrow ..... *Myotis sodalis* p. 95
13b. Some hairs on toes extend beyond claws, no keel on calcar; palate wide between M²s, braincase broad ..... *Myotis lucifugus* p. 90

Comparisons. Thirteen species of bats are found in Illinois, but one, *Tadarida brasiliensis,* has been taken only twice and is an accidental migrant. Two other species might be expected: *Myotis leibii* and *Plecotus townsendii.*

Table 8.8 gives some features that can be used in combination to help recognize and differentiate each of 13 species. Some species have one upper incisor in each jaw; others two. Some have one, two, or no small teeth (premolars) behind the upper canine. Six species have the forearm length short (40 mm or less): *Myotis lucifugus, M. sodalis, M. austroriparius, M. keenii, Pipistrellus subflavus,* and *Nycticeius humeralis.* Five have the forearm long (40 mm or more): *Myotis grisescens, Eptesicus fuscus, Lasiurus cinereus, Plecotus rafinesquii,* and *Tadarida brasiliensis.* Two species are intermediate in length of forearm: *Lasionycteris noctivagans* and *Lasiurus borealis.*

Some other diagnostic features include length and shape of ear, size of the tragus, color of the fur both dorsally and ventrally, hairiness of the tail membrane, length of hairs on the toes, and presence of a keel on the calcar.

Secondary sexual variation. Variation between males and females was checked in several species. Only *Lasiurus borealis* was significantly different in several measurements for males and females. The sexes were analyzed separately.

Aging. Animals were regarded as adults and used for comparisons where the epiphyses on the wings and legs were closed and no "suture" was visible near the end of the long bones.

Methods of taking measurements. Cranial measurements were taken as shown in Figure 8.23. For some species, some of these measurements were taken under magnification, using an ocular micrometer. The length of the forearm was taken from the dried, preserved specimen. Other external measurements are those recorded by the collector-preparator.

Hibernation. Illinois' bats are dependent upon insects as a source of food. In the summer there is an ample food supply but such is not the case in the winter. Either the bats in Illinois must migrate to a place where insects will be available during the winter or, in the face of a reduced food supply they must conserve their energy by going into a state of torpor or hibernation.

During hibernation, the bat reduces its metabolic activities; there is a reduction in body temperature, heart beat, and respiratory rate. The animal appears to be in a deep sleep. Since the body temperature is only a few degrees above environmental temperature, it is imperative that temperatures in hibernating chambers do not fall below freezing. Otherwise, ice crystals may form in the body and cause death. Thus, chambers suitable for hibernation for bats are sufficiently insulated to maintain

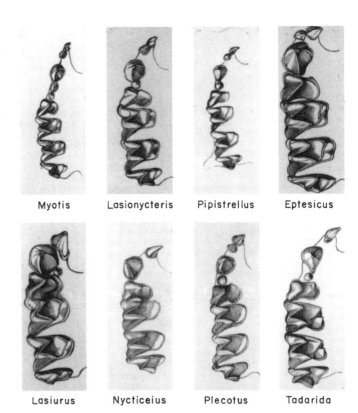

Myotis   Lasionycteris   Pipistrellus   Eptesicus

Lasiurus   Nycticeius   Plecotus   Tadarida

Fig. 8.20. Right upper toothrow of eight genera of bats found in Illinois. Note the number of incisors and the number and position of the small, unicuspid teeth behind the canine. (From Harrison Allen, 1893)

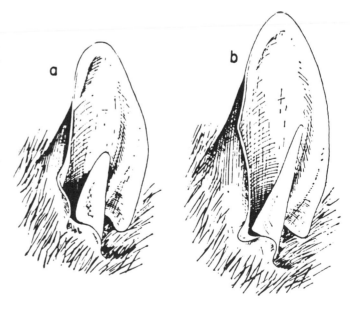

Fig. 8.21. Short, blunt tragus and small ear of *Myotis lucifugus* (a); slender, long tragus and long ear of *Myotis keenii* (b). (From Hoffmeister and Mohr, 1957)

the temperature above freezing in the coldest part of winter. Such chambers are also cool in the summer.

Bats that are known to hibernate in Illinois are:

Myotis lucifugus   *Myotis keenii*
Myotis sodalis   *Pipistrellus subflavus*
Myotis austroriparius   *Eptesicus fuscus*

Bats that may overwinter in Illinois, and some that may migrate south in winter:

Myotis grisescens   *Lasiurus borealis*
Lasionycteris noctivagans *Plecotus rafinesquii*

Bats that migrate south of Illinois in winter:

Lasiurus cinereus   *Tadarida brasiliensis*
Nycticeius humeralis

Dates of capture were recorded for some specimens of bats when they were examined. If the dates of capture are known, these are recorded under *"Specimens examined."* This is indicated as follows: Cave Spring Cave, 9 (UI), (Dec. 21, 1954). All nine specimens in this example were taken on this date. Cave Spring Cave, 14 (UI), (4, Nov. 21, 1922; 2, Dec. 17, 1956); six of the fourteen specimens were collected on dates as indicated, but dates for the remaining eight are unknown.

Migration. From the discussion above, it is obvious that some kinds of bats in Illinois are migratory and are most abundant when they are moving northward in the spring and southward in the fall.

Some overwintering bats may be "locally migratory," that is, move from wintering hibernacula to different summer roosts or maternity colonies. Some such movements may be for a distance of only a few miles; others, many miles.

Methods of studying bats. Bats may be taken alive, studied, banded, and released the same as other mammals. They can be caught in attics, mine shafts or caves, buildings (occupied or unoccupied), or hanging on foliage. They can be caught in special nets ("mist-nets") placed along flyways or near watering sources. To disturb them in their winter hibernacula is detrimental to the bats, for they are dormant and sluggish, cannot readily hang up again, and expend a large amount of energy when disturbed or alarmed.

Bands, somewhat like those used on small birds, can be affixed to the forearm of bats. When bats are hanging

Table 8.8. Features useful in distinguishing each of the 13 species of bats in Illinois. The characters must be used in combination in most cases.

Character	*Myotis lucifugus*	*Myotis sodalis*	*Myotis austroriparius*	*Myotis grisescens*	*Myotis keenii*	*Lasionycteris noctivagans*	*Pipistrellus subflavus*	*Eptesicus fuscus*
Number upper incisors	2	2	2	2	2	2	2	2
Number of small teeth behind upper canine	2	2	2	2	2	1	1	0
Length of forearm (in mm) Mean	36.6	37.7	38.1	43.6	34.7	41.0	33.5	46.5
(Min. and Max.)	(34-36)	(36-40)	(36-40)	(42-45)	(33-37.5)	(39-42.5)	(32-35)	(44-50)
Ear length: small or large (average not indicated)								
Hair on dorsal surface of tail membrane								
Unique features of dorsal coloration				Base of hairs not black		Silver gray to black		
Unique features of ventral coloration (otherwise, about same color as dorsum)			Whitish	Smoky or brownish-gray				
Tragus						Pointed	Blunt	
Other "unique" features		Hairs on toes not extending beyond claws		Wing attached to ankle rather than along side of foot				
		Well-developed keel on calcar						

* (but squeezed lingually)

in roosts either separately or in clusters, these bands can be detected. If all bats banded by a particular person in a particular roost have the same distinctive color bands, these bats can be recognized without disturbing the individual or cluster.

Ultrasonic sound detection equipment is available that will translate and even record the inaudible sounds produced by bats. It may be possible to recognize species by their distinctive ultrasonic sounds. "Snooper scopes" and infrared lights can be used with some degree of success in observing nighttime activities of bats.

Some caverns where bats are found in Illinois. Bats have been taken or are known to occur in various caves and mine shafts in Illinois. These are listed following, but do not necessarily include all caverns where bats occur in summer or winter, or both.

Jo Daviess Co.:
    Galena lead mine
    Little Princess Mine
Carroll Co.:
    Smith's Cave
La Salle Co.:
    Blackball Mine

Monroe Co.:
    Burksville Cave
    Eckhart Cave
Saline Co.:
    Cave Hill Cave
      (=Equality Cave)

Adams Co.:
    Burton Cave
    Marblehead Mine
Pike Co.:
    Twin Culvert Cave
    Limestone Mine (or Cave)
Jersey Co.:
    Grafton Cave
Madison Co.:
    Rock Ledge Cave
    Blue Pool Cave
Union Co.:
    Gurthrie Cave
    Rich's Cave
    Lilly Cave
    Silica mines
    Brasel's Cave

Jackson Co:
    Ava Cave
    Black Cave
    Sandstone Cave
    Toothless Cave
Hardin Co.:
    Cave Spring Cave
    Watter's Cave
    Griffith Cave
    Layoff Cave
    Fluorite mines
Alexander Co.:
    Various silica mines,
      near Elco
    Old Wagon Mine
    Silica mine near
      Olive Branch

We were told of bats in several caves in what we assume is Pope County: Buzzard's Roost, Fat-man's Squeeze, Devil's Smokehouse. In Carroll County, in Mississippi Palisades State Park, on the hillside there reportedly is a small hole that is an entrance and exit of a bat cave or chamber.

Echolocation. All species of bats in Illinois use echolocation to locate objects—those they seek as food and those they tend to avoid as they fly. Supersonic sounds of 25,000 to 100,000 cycles per second are emitted by the bat at the rate of up to 200 beeps per second. The bat modulates the frequency of these signals. As it zeros in on an insect, the sounds may be emitted at about 100,000 cycles per second and be quickly reduced to as low as 25,000. Direction to the object is judged by comparing the echo at one ear with that at the other and the distance is determined by the time delay between the outgoing sound and the returning echo.

Bats do have well-developed eyes and use them, as well as echolocation. In addition to supersonic sounds, they also make a variety of sounds that are audible to human ears.

Supersonic sounds emitted by bats do not travel great distances; usually the range is less than 15 feet. If an object is located and it is an insect suitable for eating, the insect may be caught in the mouth or in the tail or wing membrane and then transferred to the mouth. Normally each bat can recognize the echos from its own supersonic sounds, but when many bats in a small space are all echolocating, they may become confused by the array of returning signals and bump into objects that they normally would avoid. This is especially true when a large concentration of bats in a small attic is suddenly disturbed by several persons. They may fly into a person, which they normally would not do.

Rabies in Illinois bats. Since the early 1960's, the Illinois Department of Public Health has been checking

Lasiurus borealis	*Lasiurus cinereus*	*Nycticeius humeralis*	*Plecotus rafinesquii*	*Tadarida brasiliensis*
1	1	1	2	1
1*	1*	0	1	1
39.0	56.0	36.0	42.5	42.5
(37-42)	(54-58)	(34-38)	(40-45)	(40-45)
small, round	small, round		large	nearly joined over forehead
Yes	Yes			
Reddish	Silver-gray			
			Whitish	
		Short, broad	Long, pointed	Very short
Calcar keeled	Calcar keeled		Lumps on nose	Distal half of tail free of tail-membrane

bats that are sent to them for possible occurrence of rabies. These same specimens have then been sent to Dr. Glen C. Sanderson, Illinois Natural History Survey, and he in turn has placed the savable specimens in the collections of the Museum of Natural History.

A memorandum entitled "1966 Illinois Bat Rabies" from the Department of Public Health reports that in 1965, 13 of 210 bats examined by the Department were positive for rabies; in 1966, 6 of 247 were positive. I do not know how many positives were reported by the Illinois Department of Public Health for various years, but specimens obtained from them and in our collection are listed in Table 8.9. Only five species have been reported as rabid in Illinois and of these, red bats, hoary bats, and big brown bats are the most frequently encountered.

In the northeastern corner of Illinois (from Winnebago County on the west, Cook on the south), 42 bats have been reported as rabid; from the south (Randolph County and south), 22; from central Illinois, 13. One would suspect that the larger number of reports from the more populated northeastern corner indicates that more persons come into contact with bats which they submit to the public health authorities.

From 1965 through 1981, 369 specimens of *Lasiurus borealis* were sent to us and 25 of these were reported as rabid, or 6.8 percent; for *Lasiurus cinereus*, out of 134 sent, 20 were rabid, or 14.9 percent; for *Eptesicus fuscus*, of 355, 14 were rabid (3.9%); for *Lasionycteris noctivagans*, of 90, 3 were rabid (3.3%); for *Myotis lucifugus*, of 42, 3 were rabid (7.1%). It would be interesting to know if the percentage might have been less in *L. cinereus* if the sample had been smaller. It should be emphasized that these figures exaggerate on the high side the percentage of bats with rabies. Tests were done only on those bats that were suspected of being rabid.

Table 8.9. Bats from Illinois identified as rabid (first number) and total number (in parentheses) examined by the Illinois Department of Public Health, as turned over to the Illinois Natural History Survey and the Museum of Natural History, University of Illinois. The total number examined for 1982 is not available.

	Red bat (*Lasiurus borealis*)	Hoary bat (*Lasiurus cinereus*)	Big brown bat (*Eptesicus fuscus*)	Silver-haired bat (*Lasionycteris noctivagans*)	Little-brown myotis (*Myotis lucifugus*)
1965	0 (41)	3 (11)	1 (22)	0 (18)	0 (3)
1966	1 (50)	2 (4)	2 (15)	0 (6)	0 (1)
1967	1 (20)	0 (6)	0 (23)	0 (2)	0 (1)
1968	1 (3)	0 (9)	0 (9)	0 (0)	0 (0)
1969	0 (25)	0 (2)	0 (5)	1 (3)	0 (3)
1970	1 (19)	0 (5)	0 (8)	0 (2)	0 (1)
1971	5 (14)	4 (4)	0 (7)	0 (3)	0 (1)
1972	0 (24)	0 (5)	0 (10)	0 (10)	0 (3)
1973	1 (1)	1 (1)	0 (16)	0 (0)	1 (1)
1974	6 (6)	4 (5)	7 (41)	0 (0)	0 (0)
1975	2 (15)	0 (3)	2 (36)	0 (10)	0 (6)
1976	1 (25)	3 (19)	0 (39)	0 (10)	0 (4)
1977	1 (32)	2 (21)	0 (32)	1 (6)	0 (3)
1978	1 (25)	– (13)	2 (35)	1 (8)	2 (7)
1979	2 (24)	– (19)	0 (25)	0 (6)	0 (2)
1980	1 (25)	1 (5)	0 (13)	0 (3)	0 (4)
1981	1 (20)	– (2)	0 (19)	0 (3)	0 (2)
1982	9	–	1	1	1
Total	34	20	15	4	4

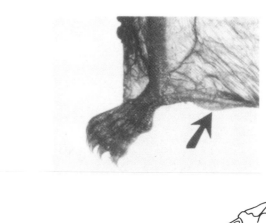

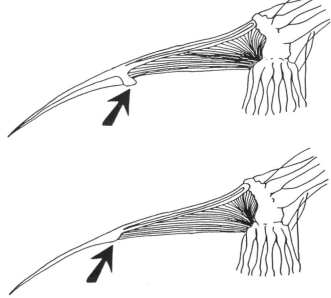

Fig. 8.22. Hind foot and attached tail membrane in *Myotis*. Arrow in top picture points to calcar; in middle picture, to the keel; lower, to the absence of a keel. (From Barbour and Davis, 1969, and J. S. Hall, 1962)

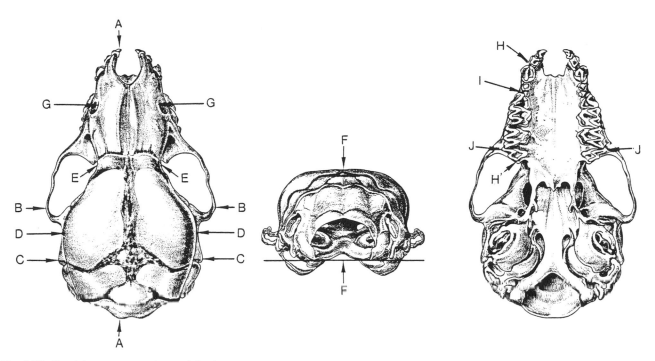

Fig. 8.23. Cranial measurements used for bats.

A-A	greatest length	D-D	greatest braincase	G-G	breadth between the	I-H'	molariform toothrow
B-B	greatest zygomatic		breadth		infraorbital canals		length (PM4 - M3)
	breadth	E-E	least interorbital breadth	H-H'	toothrow length (C - M3)	J-J	M3 - M3 breadth
C-C	greatest breadth across	F-F	skull depth				
	the mastoid processes						

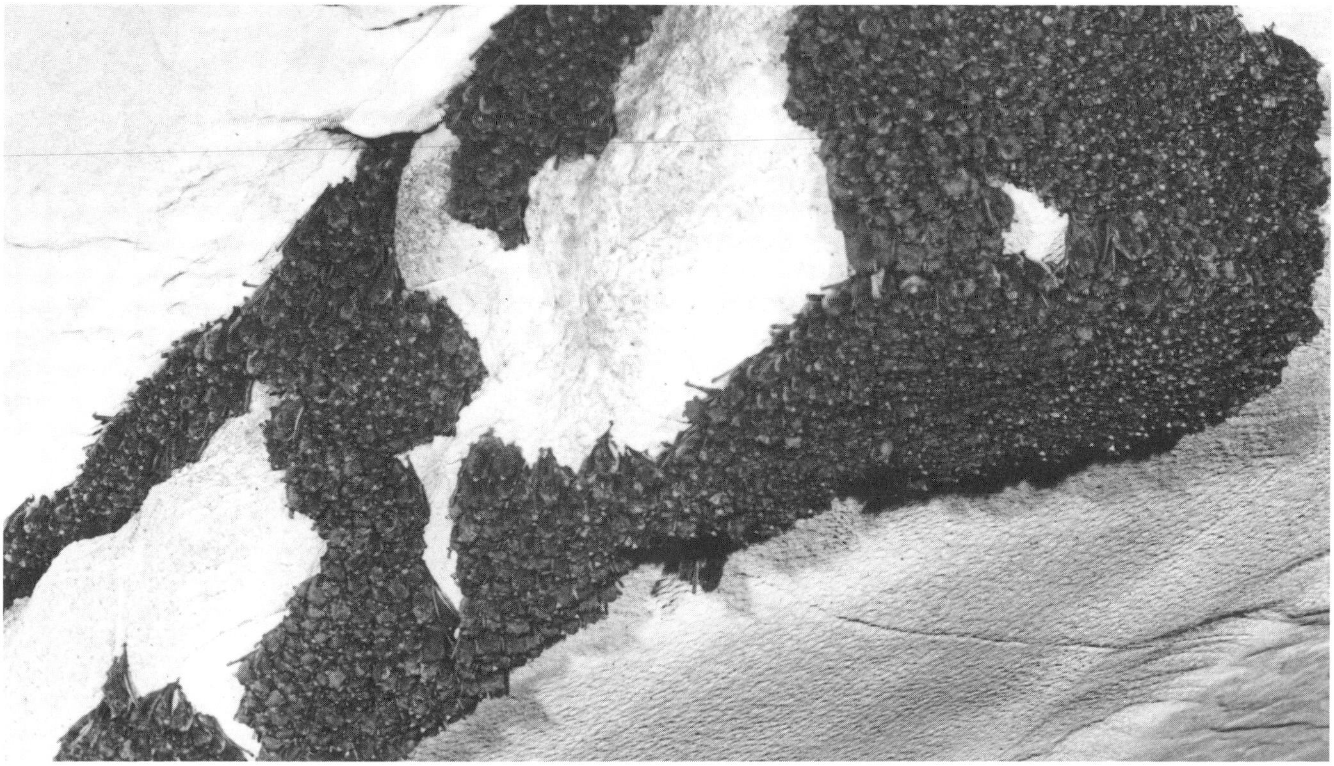

Fig. 8.24. Little brown bats frequently hang in dense clusters in mines or caves when in hibernation. Photograph by W. W. Goodpaster.

Family Vespertilionidae, Vespertilionid bats

No noseleaf; nostrils and lips simple, tragus well developed; tail not free of the uropatagial membrane; insectivorous. Seven genera are found in Illinois: *Myotis, Lasionycteris, Pipistrellus, Eptesicus, Lasiurus, Nycticeius, Plecotus.*

Myotis, Myotis bats

Diagnosis. Small-size, no noseleaf; tail extends to edge of wide interfemoral membrane, but not much beyond; no glandular lumps on muzzle; forearm length from 33 to 45 mm, hind foot 8 to 13 mm; two upper incisors with I^1 with two cusps, I^2 unicuspid, two small premolars behind upper canine; skull not deep, with height from bullae to top of skull usually less than 6.2 mm; skull short and narrow.

Dental formula. 2/3, 1/1, 3/3, 3/3. All *Myotis* in Illinois have two upper incisors and two small teeth (premolars) behind the upper canine.

Chromosomes. All *Myotis* in Illinois have a 2N=44, with four pairs as metacentrics or submetacentrics; 17 as acrocentrics, and X and Y submetacentric (Baker and Patton, 1967).

Comparisons. Myotis differs from *Pipistrellus* in Illinois in having darker coloration, forearms blackish rather than reddish; two small teeth instead of one behind upper incisor, three lower premolars instead of two; diploid number of chromosomes 44 rather than 30.

Myotis differs from *Eptesicus* in smaller size throughout, shorter forearm, two rather than no small teeth behind the upper incisor; diploid number of chromosomes 44 rather than 50.

Myotis differs from *Lasiurus* in not having the dorsal side of the tail membrane furred; ears relatively longer and less rounded; two upper incisors rather than one, two small teeth behind upper incisors; diploid number of chromosomes 44 rather than 28.

Myotis differs from *Plecotus* in having much smaller ears, no lumps on nose, two small teeth rather than one behind upper incisor. *Myotis* differs from *Tadarida* in not having tail free of the membrane; ears not nearly joined over the forehead, longer tragus; two upper incisors rather than one.

For a comparison with *Lasionycteris* and *Nycticeius,* see those accounts (pp. 107 and 125).

Remarks. Five species of *Myotis* are present in Illinois. Two are limited in their occurrences within the state — *M. austroriparius* and *M. grisescens. Myotis grisescens* is the most easily recognized species because of its large size, unique basal color of the dorsal fur, and wing attachment. *M. keenii* has long, pointed tragi, but this character is not always easy to recognize. *M. lucifugus*

and *M. sodalis* are the two species most alike. Further discussions on how to recognize the species are given in the account of each species and are summarized in Table 8.8 (p. 86).

Myotis lucifugus, Little brown myotis

Range. Throughout the state, but in winter in a limited number of hibernacula.

Diagnosis. A species of *Myotis* dark to medium in color, ears blackish to dark brown and not long; tragus of medium length but not pointed at tip; some hairs of the toes extending beyond tips of the claws; calcar without a well-developed keel (see Fig. 8.22); forearms short (34–39 mm); skull short, narrow, and not deep (or high).

Color. Upper parts are dark to medium brown, with considerable variation among individuals within a group, underparts lighter than back, ears slightly darker than back. Individuals with "white-spotting" or that are albinistic in Illinois are not represented in our collections. One specimen from Carter Caves, Carter Co., Kentucky, is a mutant pale tan, with no pigment in the ears or membranes. A piebald specimen from Blackball Mine, La Salle County, which was white on the venter and had a spot of white on the back, was reported by Walley (1971b:196).

Comparisons. M. lucifugus is most like *M. sodalis* in Illinois and can be told from that species as follows: some hairs on toes of hind foot extending beyond claws, rather than extending only to claws or not even that far; no well-developed keel on calcar rather than keeled (Fig. 8.22); fur often with a gloss or sheen rather than dull; broader braincase; palate wider between the M^2s, smaller in breadth of M^2, and smaller in lateral length of P^4.

M. lucifugus differs from *M. keenii*—with which it often hibernates in Illinois—in having shorter ears (usually 10 to 14 mm, rarely 15 mm, rather than 15 to 18 mm); tragus thick and rounded at tip rather than long, narrow, and pointed; fur of venter near tail membrane beige lightly tipped with cinnamon rather than heavily washed with orange; toothrow (C to M^3) shorter (5.5 mm or less rather than 5.7 and more).

M. lucifugus differs from *M. austroriparius* in having fur on venter brownish rather than whitish, fur of back glossy or with a sheen rather than dull and woolly; braincase not highly arched (as indicated in part by depth of skull, 5.2 mm rather than 5.7 mm).

M. lucifugus differs from *M. grisescens* in having a shorter forearm (less than 40 mm rather than more), wing membrane attached along side of foot rather than on ankle; base of hairs on back black rather than about

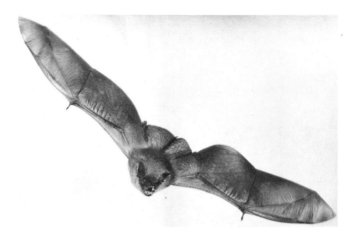

Fig. 8.25A. Little brown bat, *Myotis lucifugus*, in flight. (From Hoffmeister and Mohr, 1957. Photograph by Ernest P. Walker, Smithsonian Institution, Washington, D.C.)

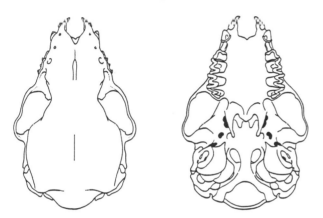

Fig. 8.25B. *Myotis lucifugus*, dorsal and ventral views of skull; 1¾ mi W Utica, La Salle Co., Illinois, 56507 UI. Female, 14.4 mm greatest length.

same color throughout; upper toothrow shorter; breadth across palate (as measured across M³s) less; skull shorter and narrower.

Remarks. M. lucifugus is an "average" kind of myotis in Illinois. It does not have the long ears and pointed tragi of *M. keenii*, not the whitish venter of *M. austroriparius,* and not the unicolored dorsal fur, long forearms, and attachment of the wing membrane to the ankles of *M. grisescens*. It is more difficult to distinguish from *M. sodalis,* but means of distinguishing these two species are discussed above and in the account of *M. sodalis.*

Habitat

In summer, little brown myotis are found in attics, steeples, under siding and shingles on buildings, on the ceilings of dilapidated buildings, and sometimes in mine shafts. During April, females move into summer quarters where they will establish maternity colonies. Males move later, in May or early June, into summer quarters. Many summer maternity colonies are located in attics with

high, beamed roofs that provided ideal places to hang and crevices in which to retreat.

Little brown myotis are said to congregate in tightly packed groups in night roosts after the initial feeding period (Fenton and Barclay, 1980). These night roosts may be in the same building as the day roosts, but not necessarily in the same locations.

When young leave the maternity colonies, the adults usually leave also and little brown myotis are found in a great variety of habitats from that time until they enter the winter hibernacula.

Suitable hibernacula for overwintering little brown myotis are deep caves or mines in which the temperature must remain above freezing on the coldest nights; usually some moisture or water is present. In Illinois, little brown myotis may hibernate in clusters of several to many individuals, or may be hanging individually in the hibernaculum.

When foraging for food, little brown myotis fly along the edges of forests and wooded areas, and probably into the woods although it is more difficult to see them there. Streams probably provide openings and flyways for the ready movements of these bats from one forage area to another.

Habits

Little brown myotis form colonies in the winter for purposes of hibernation; in the summer, females join together in nursery colonies. Apparently, males do not gather in large colonies during the summer. Sizeable winter colonies with both sexes are found at Blackball Mine, La Salle County; Rich's Cave, Union County, and Toothless Cave, Jackson County. One of the largest known maternity colonies formerly occupied the Old Main Building, Southern Illinois University, Carbondale, Jackson County. The destruction of that building has disrupted this maternity colony which had reportedly been in existence for 60 years or more.

In the summer colony at Carbondale, females moved away and down from the underside of the roof when the temperature was very high. During periods of extreme warmth in the colony, the number of ectoparasites increased and many bats suffered from this, including the loss of much hair. Individuals within the colony did not necessarily roost in the same place all of the time. Usually, little browns begin to forage after it is quite dark; this in contrast to the earlier foraging in red bats and pipistrelles.

In the winter colonies both males and females, adults and young of the year roost together. In most wintering hibernacula, little brown myotis are found in short rows or in small clumps and rarely are they in large clusters of overlapping individuals as may occur in large caves in Kentucky or Missouri. Although hibernating bats are in a torpor, they reportedly awaken every two or three

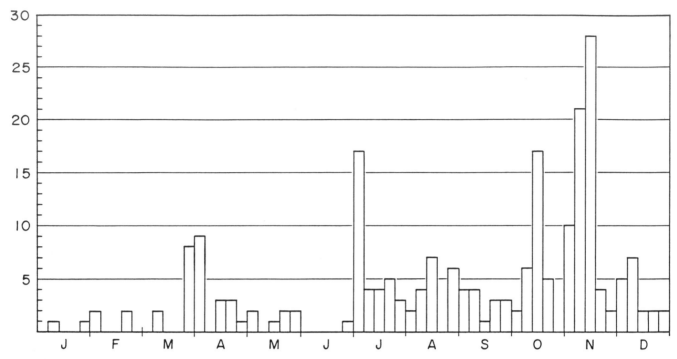

Fig. 8.26A. Known dates of capture of *Myotis lucifugus* in Illinois during each week of each month. This does not include animals that have been observed (but not collected) in summer and winter "colonies." Most bats taken between November and March were in hibernation. Numbers of animals are indicated to the left.

weeks, and fly from the cluster to another area of the hibernaculum to empty their bladder before returning.

Food

All myotis are insect-eaters. John Whitaker (1972a) examined the stomachs of 16 little brown myotis taken in Indiana and found that nearly 75 percent of the volume of food eaten was of moths, caddis flies, flies, leafhoppers, planthoppers, and coleopterous beetle larvae. The insects eaten were of small size, usually under 10 mm as reported in other feeding studies.

Dr. William Downes, when in the Department of Entomology at the University of Illinois, started to collect insects at different heights above the ground and at different time periods during the night, to learn whether the availability of food items was important in determining when and how different species of bats foraged. Although this work was prematurely terminated here, it perhaps has been conducted elsewhere. Whether a species of bat may be an early or late feeder, a high or low feeder, or an erratic feeder may be determined by food availability.

The ability of little brown myotis to catch a large number of insects in a short period of time, to chew rapidly, and to digest the food in less than an hour are specializations for feeding in this small volant animal.

Reproduction

Copulation in little brown myotis occurs in the fall, after the adult females and young-of-the-year females have left the maternity colony. The young bats may be only about four months old at this time. Additional copulations may occur in the winter or spring. Ovulation occurs in the females after they leave hibernation and an egg is fertilized by sperm that may have been stored over winter in the uterus of the female. The gestation is between 50 and 60 days. In the Old Main, Carbondale colony, most young were born from the latter part of May through the third week of June, although some carried over into July. It is thought that young can fly by three weeks of age; Cagle and Cockrum (1943) found that the young might be a month old when they first fly.

Usually each female has only one young which attaches itself to a nipple. The mother can fly with the young so attached up to the time they are ready to fly for themselves. For a period of up to a week after birth, females carry the young with them when they forage for food, but thereafter leave them in the maternity colony. Cagle and Cockrum (1943) found that three juveniles in mid-September, when they were probably three months old, had an average size that was greater than 29 adult females in the colony.

Fig. 8.26B. Hibernating little brown bats, *Myotis lucifugus*. Carter Caves, Kentucky. Photograph by W. W. Goodpaster.

Movements

Movements from winter to summer colonies, or vice versa, have been analyzed to some extent (Humphrey and Cope, 1976:7). Autumn movements ranged from 6.2 mi (10 km) to 282.1 mi (455 km) with an average of 100 km. Most migratory movements tend to be north to south.

Spring movements are less well known. Of nearly 8,700 little brown myotis banded in winter in Blackball Mine, La Salle County, only 36 were recovered during the summer (Walley, 1970:410). A few were taken in every month between late April and October.

Longevity

In reporting on some little brown myotis banded in Blackball Mine and subsequently recaptured, Walley (1971a:411) listed individual bats that had been banded for 11 and 10 years, and two that had been banded for six years. Some individuals have been reported as living in excess of 20 years.

Miscellaneous

Bats thought to be little brown myotis were caught by the burrs of burdock plants near the mill where they lived at Benham's Mill, Rock Island Arsenal (Lyon, 1925:280). Lyon said that on one occasion in 1892 he saw at least a dozen of these bats so entangled. They were all mummified at that time.

Variation

Methods of taking cranial measurements and remarks on secondary sexual variation and aging are found in the discussion of Chiroptera (p. 84).

Only one subspecies is known in Illinois.

Myotis lucifugus lucifugus (LeConte)

1831. V[*espertilio*]. *lucifugus* LeConte, in McMurtrie, The animal kingdom . . . 1:431. Type from Georgia: sometimes reported as LeConte Plantation, near Riceboro, Liberty Co., Georgia.
1897. *Myotis lucifugus*, Miller, N. Amer. Fauna, 13:59.

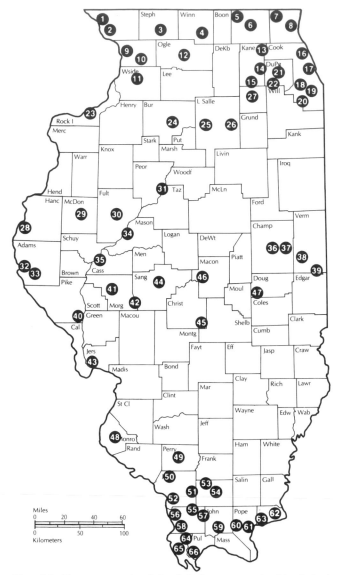

Map 8.9. Known records of the little brown myotis, *Myotis lucifugus*. The subspecies is *M. l. lucifugus*. Numbers are referenced in *Records of occurrence*. The distribution of the species in the United States is shaded.

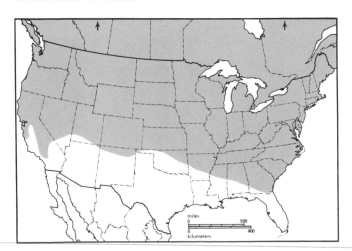

Range. As given for the species (p. 90 and Map 8.9).

Diagnosis and Comparisons. A subspecies of intermediate color, not so dark as *M. l. alascensis* but darker than *M. l. carissima*.

Remarks. Little brown myotis from southeastern Illinois are not well represented in collections. This may indicate that the species is uncommon or absent in many places or that there is a lack of collecting for these bats in these areas.

We have 34 records of these bats from northeastern Illinois: Cook, Du Page, Kane, Lake, McHenry, and Winnebago counties. Twenty-six of these were taken between May and September.

Records of occurrence. SPECIMENS EXAMINED, 363.
Jo Daviess Co.: [1a] Galena, 3 (UI); [1b] Little Princess Mine [SW of Galena], 1 (UI); [2a] 8 mi SE Galena, 1 (ISM), 1 (NHS); [2b] Lead Mine Caves, 9 mi SE Galena, 1 (UI); [2c] Elizabeth, 1 (UI); [2d] Hanover, 18 (UI). **Stephenson Co.:** [3] Freeport, 1 (UI). **Winnebago Co.:** [4] Rockford, 1 (UI). **McHenry Co.:** [5] Harvard, 1 (UI); [6] Woodstock, 2 (UI); no specific locality [not plotted], 1 (UI). **Lake Co.:** [7] Antioch, 1 (UI); [8a] Waukegan, 3 (UI), 2 (FM); [8b] Great Lakes, 1 (UI); no specific locality [not plotted], 11 (UI). **Carroll Co.:** [9a] near Savanna, 2 (FM); [9b] 2 mi W Mt. Carroll, 2 (NHS), 2 (SRL), 1 (UI); [10] Chadwick, 1 (UI). **Whiteside Co.:** [11] Morrison, 1 (UI). **Kane Co.:** [13] Dundee, 1 (UI); [14] Geneva, 1 (UI); [15] Sugar Grove, 5 (CAS); **Cook Co.:** [16a] Winnetka, 1 (UI); [16b] West Northfield, 1 (US); [16c] Evanston, 2 (UI); [17] Chicago, 1 (CAS), 6 (FMNH); [18a] Bridgeview, 1 (UI); [18b] Chicago Ridge, 1 (UI); [19] Blue Island, 1 (UI); [20] Tinley Park, 1 (UI). **Du Page Co.:** [21] Wheaton, 2 (UI); [22] Naperville, 1 (CAS); no specific locality [not plotted], 2 (UI). **Rock Island Co.:** [23] Rock Island, 1 (UI). **Bureau Co.:** [24] Princeton, 1 (UI). **La Salle Co.:** [25a] near La Salle, 16 (FM); [25b] Blackball Mine, 1¾ mi W North Utica, 82 (UI), 16 (NIU); [25c] 4½ mi E La Salle, 1 (NHS); [26] Marseilles, 1 (UI).

Kendall Co.: [27] Yorkville, 1 (UI). **Hancock Co.:** [28] Warsaw*, 11 (US). **McDonough Co.:** [29] Macomb, Western Ill. Univ., 1 (UI). **Fulton Co.:** [30] no specific locality, 1 (UI). **Peoria Co.:** [31] Peoria, 1 (UI). **Adams Co.:** [32] Quincy, 2 (UI); [33] 14 mi SE Quincy, Burton Cave, 1 (FM). **Mason Co.:** [34] Havana, 3 (FM). **Cass Co.:** [35] Beardstown, 2 (UI). **Champaign Co.:** [36b] Urbana, 2 (UI); [37] 1 mi N St. Joseph, 2 (UI). **Vermilion Co.:** [38] ½ mi SW Fairmount, 2 (NHS); [39] Ridge Farm, 1 (UI). **Pike Co.:** [40a] 3 mi W Pearl, 1 (NHS); [40b] 1 mi W Pearl, 1 (UI); [40c] Pearl, 1 (UI); [40d] 2 mi SW Pearl, Pearl Cave, 1 (ISM). **Morgan Co.:** [41] Jacksonville, 2 (UI); [42] Waverly, 1 (UI). **Jersey Co.:** [43a] Pere Marquette State Park, 1 (NHS); [43b] 1 mi W Grafton, 2 (UI); [43c] Grafton, 6 (NHS), 3 (UI). **Sangamon Co.:** [44] Springfield, 3 (UI). **Christian Co.:** [45] Pana, 2 (UI). **Macon Co.:** [46] Harristown, 3 (US), (July 1888). **Douglas Co.:** [47] Chesterville, 7 (NHS), 1 (UI). **Monroe Co.:** [48a] Burksville, 1 (UI); [48b] Eckhart Cave, 3 mi SE Burksville, 1 (NHS), 1 (ISM), 1 (UI). **Perry Co.:** [49] Pinckneyville, 1 (UI). **Jackson Co.:** [50] Ava, 1 (UI); [51] Carbondale, 9 (FM), 4 (NHS), 5 (SRL); 2 (SIC), 18 (UI); [52] 3 mi SSE Gorham, 1 (SRL). **Williamson Co.:** [53] Herrin, 1 (UI); [54] Marion, 2 (UI). **Union Co.:** [55c] Rich's Cave, 4 mi E Cobden, 1 (SRL), 3 (SIC); [56a] 1½ mi E Wolf Lake, 2 (SIC); [56b] T12S,

---

* Worthen specimens.

R3W, Sec. 2, 1 (SRL); [57] Lilly Cave, near Lick Creek, 2 (NHS); [58a] 3 mi SE Ware, 1 (UI); [58b] T13S, R2W, Sec. 27, 1 (SRL); Mine 15 [location uncertain, not plotted], 4 (SIC); Mine 3 [location uncertain, not plotted], 3 (SIC). **Johnson Co.:** [59] 2½ mi S Vienna, 1 (SIC). **Pope Co.:** [60] Lake Glendale, 1 (ISM); [61] Golconda, 3 (FM). **Hardin Co.:** [62] 2½ mi NW Cave in Rock, 1 (ISM); [63a] Cave Spring Cave, Eichorn, 3 (UI); [63b] 2¼ mi NW Elizabethtown, 1 (SRL); [63c] 4¼ mi NW Rosiclare, 3 (SIC), 2 (SRL); [63d] 5½ mi W, 1 mi N Elizabethtown, 1 (UI); [63f] ½ mi NE Rosiclare, 1 (NHS); Mine 5 [location uncertain, not plotted], 1 (SIC); Mine 8 [location uncertain, not plotted], 2 (SIC). **Alexander Co.:** [64] 2 mi W, ½ mi N Elco, 3 (UI); [65] 1 mi NNE Olive Branch, 1 (UI); Mine 5 [location uncertain, not plotted], 1 (SIC); Mine 6 [location uncertain, not plotted], 1 (SIC); Mine 7 [location uncertain, not plotted], 1 (SIC). **Pulaski Co.:** [66] Mounds, 1 (ISM).

Additional records. **Carroll Co.:** [9c] Smith's Cave, 2 mi W Mt. Carroll, 2 (FS). **Ogle Co.:** [12] no specific locality, (Miller & Allen, 1928:45). **Champaign Co.:** [36a] E edge Brownfield Woods (T20N, R9E, Sec. 31), (Koestner, 1942:227). **Jackson Co.:** [51] Carbondale, 29 (UM), 28 (FS). **Union Co.:** [55a] 4 mi E [=NE] Cobden, Guthrie Cave, 1 (FS); [55b] 3 mi E Cobden, (Layne, 1958a:224). **Hardin Co.:** [63c] 4¼ mi NW Rosiclare, 1 (FS); [63e] 2½ mi N Rosiclare (Layne, 1958a:224).

Myotis sodalis, Indiana myotis

Range. Summer range: southwestern and southern parts of state, with one early record (1928) from Chicago, with some straggler males in Blackball Mine, La Salle, Co., until April; winter range: La Salle Co., and various localities near the Mississippi and Ohio rivers (Map 8.10).

Diagnosis. A species of *Myotis* of small size; fur dark brown and dull in appearance, not especially glossy; calcar with a keel (although absent in a few individuals); tragus of medium length and not pointed; hairs of the toes not extending beyond tips of claws, forearms short; braincase not broad, premolar and molar teeth robust.

Color. Color of dorsum a dull grayish chestnut; basal two-thirds of hair fuscous black, terminal third with a grayish band tipped with cinnamon brown.

Comparisons. M. *sodalis* is most like M. *lucifugus* and these two can be readily confused. The correct identification of M. *sodalis* is needed since this is a federally designated endangered species. Therefore, a detailed comparison is given. M. *sodalis* usually has a keel on the calcar, whereas M. *lucifugus* lacks this; hairs on the toes and foot do not extend beyond the tips of the claws, whereas some do in *lucifugus;* the dorsal fur appears dull rather than glossy (but this is more evident in natural light in live or recently killed specimens); braincase narrower than in *lucifugus,* premolar and molar teeth larger.

In a few specimens, the keel on the calcar may be absent or not visible. In some specimens of M. *lucifugus* the hairs on the toes are sparse and it is difficult to ascertain if those present extend to and beyond the tips of the claws. Workers who have handled thousands of

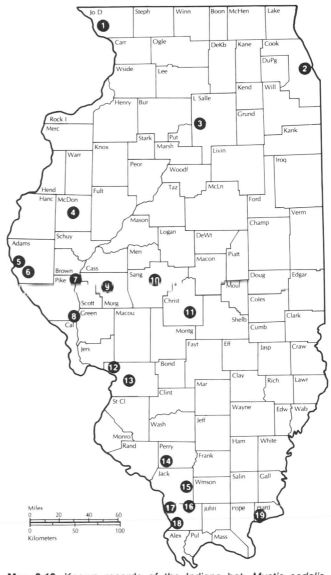

Map 8.10. Known records of the Indiana bat, *Myotis sodalis.* Numbers are referenced in *Records of occurrence.* For some specimens, dates of capture are also given there. The distribution of the species in the United States is shaded.

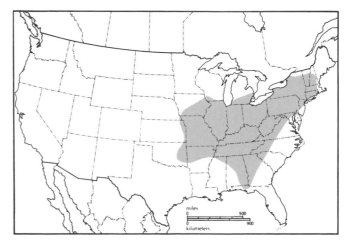

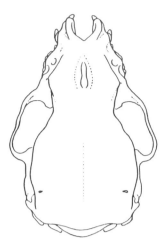

Fig. 8.27. *Myotis sodalis*, dorsal view of skull; 1¾ mi W Utica, La Salle Co., Illinois, 12055 UI. Female, 14.0 mm greatest length.

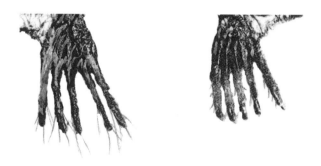

Fig. 8.28. Feet of *Myotis* to show hair, relative to toes. At left, *Myotis lucifugus* with some hairs extending to tip of claws or beyond; at right, *M. sodalis* with no hairs extending to tip of claws. (Adapted from Barbour and Davis, Mammals of Kentucky, Univ. Press of Kentucky, 1974)

live *M. sodalis* and *M. lucifugus* tell me that there are a few specimens for which a positive identification could not be made. Dr. Victor Diersing enlarged upon the cranial differences attributed to the two species. He summed the breadth of each M^2 and the lateral length of Pm^4 (as a measure of the robust teeth) and plotted this against the sum of the breadth of the braincase and the breadth between the M^2s. As shown in Fig. 8.29, there is no overlap in such a plotting with skulls of 107 *M. sodalis* and 74 *M. lucifugus*. If the braincase and interorbital breadth are summed and plotted against the length of $C-M^3$ toothrow for individuals of each species, I believe there would be little if any overlapping.

M. sodalis differs from *M. keeni, M. austroriparius,* and *M. grisescens* in much the same way that *Myotis lucifugus* differs from those species. See the Comparisons in the account of *M. lucifugus* (p. 90).

Remarks. *Myotis sodalis* is a species occurring mostly in mid-United States and in this area it is most numerous

in the winter in Missouri, Kentucky, and southern Indiana. Why there are not large concentrations of these bats in hibernacula in southern Illinois is not clear. Winter populations in Illinois have greatly decreased over the last 30 years: in Blackball Mine from 600 to about 27; in Cave Spring Cave from 83 to none. Less is known about this bat in the summer. A small number of breeding groups, consisting of only a few individuals, are known.

Habitat

The winter and summer habitats are quite different. In winter, Indiana myotis hibernate in caves and in mines. In most cases, large numbers constituting as much as 90 percent of the species population hibernate in a few caves or mines. In 11 winter colonies in Missouri, 350,000 individuals were present (LaVal et al., 1980). There are large hibernacula in Kentucky also. In Illinois, the hibernacula are small, with only about 600 bats (now considerably less) in one and a few individuals in others. Known hibernacula are: Blackball Mine, La Salle Co.; Twin Culvert Cave, Pike Co.; Blue Pool Cave, Madison Co.; Guthrie Cave and Rich's Cave, Union Co.; Cave Spring and Watter's Cave, Hardin Co.; lead mine, 8 mi SE Galena, Jo Daviess Co.

The largest wintering colony is in Blackball Mine. In 1953, there were approximately 600 individuals; 1956, 337; 1960, 120; 1983, 27. The latter figure was given me by Harlan Walley. In some years between 1960 and 1983, he has found no Indiana myotis in Blackball Mine. Blackball consists of two mining areas, separated by a stream, where ore for cement was extracted many years ago. The mineshafts are on several levels and include some 40 acres of underground rooms and passageways. Indiana myotis have been found in one or two rooms in a relatively dry part of the mine where there were some big brown bats. Little brown myotis were in adjacent areas but there were no pipistrelles or Keen's myotis. The mine is sufficiently insulated so that there is little fluctuation in temperature between summer and winter.

In west central Illinois, one specimen of *M. sodalis* was available from Twin Culvert Cave, Pike Co., taken on November 24, 1968, and Carol Mahan of the Department of Conservation reported six in Burton Cave, Adams Co., on October 19, 1982. Whether these bats would overwinter there is unknown. In southern Illinois, Cave Spring Cave, Hardin Co., had a wintering colony in 1953 of 83 Indiana myotis; 1954, 8; 1957, 0; 1958, 2; 1974, 0. One specimen was found in Guthrie Cave on December 31, 1954, and one in Rich's Cave on November 7, 1966, both in Union County.

Probably all of the wintering bats in Illinois represent colonizers from the larger wintering populations in Missouri and Kentucky. J. S. Hall (1962:45) thought that the hibernation sites required high humidity (85% or more) and an area of a cave, usually not far removed from an entrance, where the temperature may fluctuate from a high of 9° to 10°C to a minimum of 4° to 6°C.

Summer habitat of Indiana myotis was poorly known until recently because few individuals of the species were ever collected in the summer. Small colonies or groups of males were known from the summer, but these probably represent only a small fraction of the winter population. The number of females known from the summer was less than one percent and no maternity colonies were known until 1974 (Humphrey, Richter, and Cope, 1977). The requirements for nurseries for pregnant females appear to be dead trees with loose bark or living trees with shaggy bark under which the females can roost, parturate, and rear their offspring. Such trees have usually been found along or near waterways or ponds. Reproductive females and young have been reported as foraging along streams, edges of a lake, over floodplain trees, upland woods, and at edges of woodlots. Males tended to forage among trees more than over or along waterways.

In Illinois, Indiana myotis near Ware, Union Co., were mist-netted on August 7 and 9, 1979, along a ditch lined with a row of trees and bordered by swampland (Brack, 1979). Many of the trees in the swampland were silver maple and willow. Of seven specimens netted, four were post-lactating females and three were immature. Along Galum Creek, Perry Co., three adult females of *Myotis sodalis* were mist-netted on June 8 and June 9, 1979 (Sparling, Sponsler, and Hickman, 1979). The habitat was a mature riparian forest, including box elders, sycamores, and river birches, in a relatively closed canopy. In west central Illinois, along McKee Creek, Pike Co., Gardner and Gardner (1980) mist-netted 14 *M. sodalis* from July 14 to 17, 1980, in a riparian association of silver maples, cottonwoods, sycamores, and bur oaks. Ten of the 14 were immature (young of the year), three were post-lactating females, and one an adult male.

Habits

When returning to the winter hibernaculum, Indiana myotis go to the same spot in the same room to cluster, according to J. S. Hall (1962:37). Clusters do not necessarily contain the same individuals each year. Clusters do contain tightly packed individuals, each affixing its claws into irregularities on the rocky ceiling. There is only one tier of animals in a cluster.

Indiana myotis often, if not usually, awaken from hibernation during the winter (J. S. Hall, 1962:39). At this time, some fly to a different part of the hibernaculum. It is not known how long these individuals remain in a non-hibernating state or if they return to their original cluster.

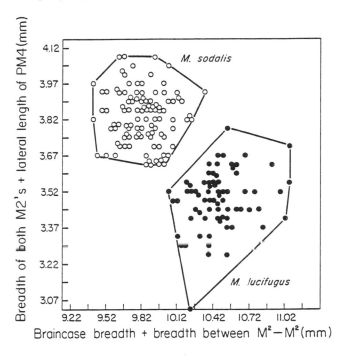

Fig. 8.29. A scattergram analysis comparing the cranial morphology of the 177 individuals of *M. sodalis* (open circles) and *M. lucifugus* (dots).

In summer foraging, a male Indiana myotis was observed for nearly one-half hour as it flew in an ellipitical pattern, rarely exceeding 100 m in length, along the edge of a small floodplain pasture and among adjacent trees. Another male foraged for 20 minutes in dense forest (LaVal et al., 1977). At a maternity colony, foraging "was confined to air space from two to 30 m high near the foliage of riparian and floodplain trees. The total foraging range of the population was a linear strip along 0.82 km of creek" (Humphrey, Richter, and Cope, 1977:341).

Along McKee Creek, Pike Co., Gardner and Gardner (1980) mist-netted one Indiana myotis at 80 min after sundown, two at 120 min, five at 302 min (now after midnight). Along Clear Creek, Union Co., Brack (1979) netted *M. sodalis* in August at 20:45 and 21:30.

Indiana myotis, like some other myotis, exhibit swarming behavior at the hibernating sites from mid-August until late October. This has been observed by numerous individuals and most recently reported upon by Cope and Humphrey (1977). By autumn, females have joined the males and great numbers of bats fly around and into the entrance chambers of the hibernaculum at this time. The peak of swarming is early September.

Reproduction

When the winter hibernacula break up, females segregate and move some distance. This usually occurs in April. Young are born between late June and early July. Of 43 females netted in Iowa in the summer of 1980,

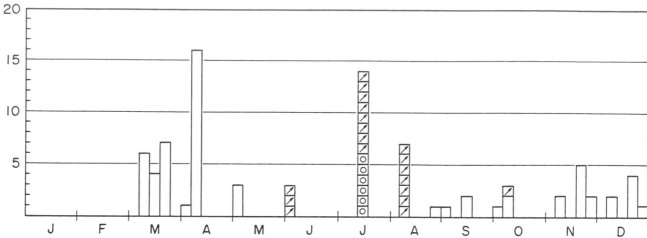

Fig. 8.30. Known dates of capture of *Myotis sodalis* in Illinois during each week of each month. Open areas are of specimens in collections; those with arrow, of male captured but released; with circle, of female captured but released. Between October 1 and May 6, all records are for captures in caves or mines except the October 8 capture. Males captured the third week of July are all young. Between May 15 and October 1, only one adult male was captured.

six were pregnant in June and July, 16 were lactating in June to August 9 (Bowles, 1980, personal communication).

Copulation occurs in the fall, and it may also occur during the winter and in April as the hibernacula disperse. Ovulation and fertilization probably do not occur until females leave hibernation, much the same as in *Myotis lucifugus*.

Nursery colonies

Nursery colonies have not been located in Illinois but the number of post-lactating females and young of the year caught in mid-summer in Union, Perry, and Pike counties in 1979 and 1980 (see under Habitat, p. 96) suggests that nursery colonies may be present in these parts of the state.

Food and feeding

Indiana myotis probably feed on many of the same kinds of insects as *Myotis lucifugus*. Thomson (1982) reports on the unpublished master's thesis of J. J. Belwood for this species in Indiana, apparently based upon fecal analysis. The diet consisted of 41.5 percent dipterans, 30.8 percent lepidopterans, and 17 percent trichopterans. During lactation, moths made up over 70 percent of the diet. Later in the summer, insects with harder bodies were taken to a greater extent.

Longevity

Indiana myotis are known to live more than 10 years. Some banded animals in excess of 13, 14, and 20 years of age have been taken.

Since this species occurs in large numbers in a few winter colonies, it is subject to rapid if not near-fatal depletion if these hibernacula are destroyed or disturbed.

Future work

Comprehensive studies need to be conducted in Illinois to (1) determine if there are maternity or nursery colonies of Indiana myotis in the state and where these are located, (2) recognize the habitat required by this species and plot its occurrence throughout the state, (3) sample bats at all potential hibernacula, either during fall swarming or after hibernation has started, to locate winter colonies, (4) enforce measures to prevent disturbance or destruction of winter and summer colonies.

Regulations should be enacted to enforce the protection of Indiana myotis on privately owned lands. One mine which currently houses these bats in winter is visited by large numbers of persons who are not supervised or controlled. Bats are frequently disturbed in this hibernaculum. In a cave in southern Illinois where Indiana myotis were known to be present at one time and where mining activities are going on now, the owner denied us entry to look for bats in April, 1981, and said he would "blow the cave in if it wasn't my water source."

Variation

Myotis sodalis is regarded as monotypic.

Myotis sodalis Miller and Allen

1928. *Myotis sodalis* Miller and Allen, Bull. U. S. Natl. Mus., 144:130. Type from Wyandotte Cave, Crawford, Co., Indiana.

Range. As given for the species.
Diagnosis and Comparisons. As given above.

Records of occurrence. SPECIMENS EXAMINED, 70.
Jo Daviess Co.: [1] 8 mi SE Galena, lead mine, 2 (ISM), 1 (NHS), (Dec. 9, 1953). **Cook Co.:** [2] Chicago, Field Museum Bldg., 1

(FM), (Sept. 18, 1928). **La Salle Co.:** [3] 1¾ mi W Utica, S Blackball Mine, 1 (US), 28 (UI), (Nov. through April; May 3, Sept. 1). **Adams Co.:** [5] Quincy, 1 (UI), (Aug. 25, 1980). **Pike Co.:** [8] 2½ mi SW Pearl, Twin Culvert Cave, 1 (SIE), (Nov. 24, 1968). **Morgan Co.:** [9] Jacksonville, 1 (UI), (Oct. 7, 1971). **Sangamon Co.:** [10] Springfield, 1 (ISM), (Sept. 1, 1970). **Christian Co.:** [11] Owaneco, 1 (UI), (April 27, 1972). **Madison Co.:** [12] Alton Bluff, Blue Pool Cave, 5 (SIC), (Nov. 20, 27, 1973); [13] Edwardsville, SIU campus, 1 (SIE), (Oct. 2, 1968). **Perry Co.:** [14] approx. 1 mi N Denmark, 1 (UI), (June 8, 1979). **Jackson Co.:** [15a] 3 mi W Carbondale, SIU airport, 1 (SIC); [15b] Carbondale, SIU campus, 1 (SIC); no specific locality [not plotted], 1 (SRL), (April 15, 1952). **Union Co.:** [16a] 4 mi E [=NE] Cobden, Guthrie Cave, 1 (FS), (Dec. 31, 1954); [16b] near Cobden, Rich's Cave, 1 (SRL), (Nov. 7, 1966). **Hardin Co.:** [19a] 4¼ mi NW Rosiclare, Watter's [=Cave Spring], 9 (SIC), 2 (FS), (4 taken Dec. 21, 1954); [19b] 2½ mi S Eichorn, Cave Spring Cave, 2 (UI), (Nov. 29, 1953); [19c] Rosiclare, 11 (FM), (April 8, 1907).

Additional records. **McDonough Co.:** [4a] Thompson Hall, Western Illinois Univ. [one female banded and released], (Oct. 8, 1980); [4b] Wagoner Hall, Western Illinois Univ. [sight record, John Warnock]. **Adams Co.:** [6] Burton Cave [sight record, 6 individuals, C. Mahan], (Oct. 19, 1982). **Pike Co.:** [7a] Chambersburg [8 individuals, captured and released], (Gardner and Gardner, 1980:9), (July 14, 1980); [7b] 1½ mi SE Chambersburg [3 individuals, captured and released] (Gardner and Gardner, 1980:9), (July 16, 1980); [7c] 2½ mi SE Chambersburg [2 individuals, captured and released] (Gardner and Gardner, 1980:9), (July 15, 1980); [7d] 3 mi SE Chambersburg [1 individual, captured and released] (Gardner and Gardner, 1980:9), (July 17, 1980). **Perry Co.:** [14] approx. 1 mi N Denmark, [2 individuals, captured and released], (Sparling et al., 1979), (June 9, 1979). **Union Co.:** [17a] T11S, R3W, Sec. 9 [=approx. 1½ mi NE Aldridge] (Klimstra, 1969:4); [17b] approx. 2½ mi WNW Wolf Lake [1 individual, captured and released], (Brack, 1979:21), (Aug. 7, 1979); [18] approx. 3 mi SE Ware [6 individuals, captured and released], (Brack, 1979:21), (Aug. 9, 1979).

Myotis austroriparius, Southeastern myotis

Range. Southernmost Illinois; recorded for winter and summer.

Diagnosis. A species of *Myotis* of medium size, underparts whitish or tan, upper parts not glossy but with a woolly appearance, calcar not keeled, hairs on toes extend beyond tips of claws, skull deep (or high).

Color. A unique feature of *M. austroriparius* is its light-colored venter. Frequently there is a frosting or wash of tan or light brown over the white. Elsewhere in the range of *M. austroriparius* the underparts are not so light. The dorsum appears, to my eye, as grayish with a slight purplish cast. The ears are the same color as the back.

Comparisons. M. austroriparius differs from *M. lucifugus* in lighter underparts, less bright brown fur on dorsum, more grayish ears, and greater depth of skull.

M. austroriparius differs from *M. sodalis* in much the same way it differs from *M. lucifugus*; in addition, the hairs on the toes extend beyond the claw tips and there is no keel on the calcar.

M. austroriparius differs from *M. keenii* in much the same way as *M. lucifugus* does and in having a shorter, less pointed, tragus and slightly shorter ear; it has a longer forearm.

M. austroriparius differs from *M. grisescens* in being of smaller size externally and cranially; having much shorter forearm, wing attached along side of foot; teeth are smaller.

Molt. La Val (1970:550) says there is a late summer molt following lactation by females. He found males already molting in late July.

Remarks. M. austroriparius is not well represented in Illinois. At an earlier time, Hoffmeister and Mohr (1957:71) thought the species might be present only in the winter. We now have records for eight months of the year (Fig. 8.34).

Three subspecies have been ascribed to *M. austroriparius*. See the discussion under *Variation* (p. 100).

Habitat

Southeastern myotis in Illinois occupy both caves and mines. In Indiana, Mumford and Whitaker (1982:146) found all were from caves except one southeastern myotis found in a building. Farther south, they also roost in hollow trees and in buildings. Summer roosts are usually close to water over which these bats forage. All of the sites of summer records in southern Illinois are close to water.

Winter colonies have been encountered just inside the entrance to a cave (Cave Spring Cave) and three clusters

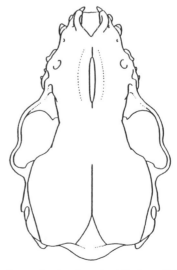

Fig. 8.31. *Myotis austroriparius,* dorsal view of skull; 1 mi NNE Rosiclare, Hardin Co., Illinois, 5893 UI. Female, 15.4 mm greatest length.

Map 8.11. Known records of the southeastern myotis, *Myotis austroriparius*. Numbers are referenced in *Records of occurrence*. For some specimens, dates of capture are given there. The distribution of the species in the United States is shaded.

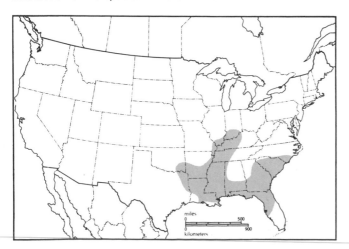

were in a bell-shaped cavity in a cave ceiling (probably Layoff Cave), according to Smith and Parmalee (1954:201).

Habits

Southeastern myotis are late flyers and they reportedly fly low, especially when feeding (Barbour and Davis, 1969). In the summer, females gather into maternity colonies for rearing young. I know of no maternity colonies in Illinois. Specimens in our collection for May 29 and August 6 are all males.

In winter, bats of both sexes form small tight clusters or hang in small groups for hibernating. The three clusters in Layoff Cave, Hardin Co., each had 30 to 40 bats. In Cave Spring Cave in 1953, Wayne Davis encountered 120 myotis hibernating in one tightly packed cluster. He estimated that 45 percent were females, 55 percent, males.

These bats occupy different roosts in summer and in winter in parts of their range. It is not certain that this is the case in southern Illinois. Although these bats at times have been known to hibernate in Cave Spring Cave, Whitaker (1977) netted seven at its entrance on August 28. These may have been bats in a swarming flight preparatory to occupying the cave during the winter, and this is not necessarily an indication that they were there during the summer.

Hibernating southeastern myotis readily and quickly respond to disturbances. Sometimes they take flight shortly after a light is shined on them, and Barbour and Davis (1969:60) say that "even in mid-winter the clusters were often composed of active individuals which flew when disturbed."

Reproduction

Maternity colonies of *Myotis austroriparius* in southern United States form in late March or early April. Young are born in late April or early May. Rice (1957) who studied these bats in Florida postulated that young are born in Illinois and Indiana in late June. Nearly all females produce two young in contrast to other species of *Myotis* that produce but one. The young, who are left in the cave while the mothers feed, are capable of flight by the fifth or sixth week.

Most breeding occurs in the fall, as in other species of *Myotis*.

Rice (1957) postulated that southeastern myotis in Illinois and Indiana might roost in buildings or houses as well as in caves in the summer. He thought that some caves might be too cold for summer colonies.

Variation

The subspecies *M. austroriparius mumfordi* has been ascribed to southern Indiana and Illinois, *M. a. gatesi* to southern Louisiana, and *M. a. austroriparius* for Florida.

La Val (1970) reviewed much of the available material and concluded that it was not desirable to recognize any subspecies. Nevertheless, specimens from southern Illinois and Indiana have lighter underparts than most other *M. austroriparius*.

Myotis austroriparius (Rhoads)

1897. *Vespertilio lucifugus austroriparius* Rhoads, Proc. Acad. Nat. Sci. Phila., 49:227. Type from Tarpon Springs, Pinellas Co., Florida.

1928. *Myotis austroriparius*, Miller and Allen, Bull. U. S. Nat. Mus., 144:76.

1943. *Myotis austroriparius gatesi* Lowery, Occas. Papers Mus. Zool., Louisiana State Univ., 13:219. Type from University Campus, near Baton Rouge, Louisiana.

1955. *Myotis austroriparius mumfordi* Rice, Quart. Jour. Florida Acad. Sci., 18:67. Type from Bronson's Cave, 3 mi E Mitchell, Lawrence Co., Indiana.

Range. Southernmost Illinois; recorded for winter and summer (Map 8.11).

Diagnosis and Comparisons. See p. 95.

Records of occurrence. SPECIMENS EXAMINED, 73. **Johnson Co.:** [3] Whitehill Quarry, 2 (UI), 20 (SIC), (2 taken Feb. 21, 1960). **Hardin Co.:** ([4a] 2½ mi NW Cave in Rock, fluorspar mine, 1 (NHS), (Oct. 28, 1953); [5a] Cave Spring Cave, 2½ mi E Eichorn, 4 (UI), (May 29, 1959); [5b] Cave, 7 mi E [probably should be (as plotted) W at Cave Spring Cave] Elizabethtown, 7 (UI), (Aug. 6, 1950); [5d] 5½ mi W, 1 mi N Elizabethtown, 2 (UI); [5f] 2½ mi NE Rosiclare, 1 (NHS); [5g] Layoff Cave, ½ mi NE Rosiclare, 2 (FMNH), 5 (NHS), 8 (ISM), 6 (SRL), 3 (SIC), 9 (UI), (mostly Nov. 29, 1953); [5i] ¼ mi NE Rosiclare, 1 (NHS); Mine 8 [location uncertain, not plotted], 1 (SIC). **Alexander Co.:** [6] ½ mi N Olive Branch, 1 (NHS), (April 7, 1954).

Additional records. **Union Co.:** [1a] Rich's Cave, [near] Cobden, 1 (FS), (Feb. 5, 1955); [1b] Rich's Cave, (Whitaker, 1977:304), (Feb. 26, 1974); [2] 4 mi NW Mill Creek, silica mine, (Whitaker, 1977:304). **Hardin Co.:** [4b] Crystal Mine, (Whitaker, 1977:304), (Aug. 27, 1974); [5c] Watter's [=Cave Spring] Cave, 4¼ mi NW Rosiclare, 1 (FS), (Dec. 21, 1955); [5e] Griffith Cave, (Rice, 1955:68); [5h] ½ mi NE Rosiclare, 4 (FS), (March 12, 1953, and Dec. 21, 1954).

Myotis grisescens, Gray myotis

Range. In summer, found in caves near the Ohio River, as in Hardin County; in winter or during migration, near the Mississippi River in west central Illinois and possibly a few in southern Illinois (see discussion under *Habitat*); one specimen taken in La Salle County in spring (see *Miscellaneous*).

Diagnosis. A species of *Myotis* of large size, with long forearm; wing membrane attached to foot at the ankle rather than side of foot; hairs of about the same color

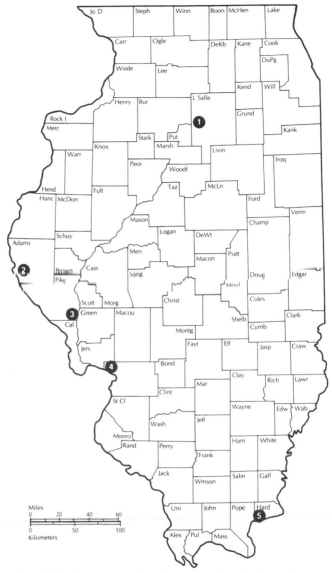

Map 8.12. Known records of gray myotis, *Myotis grisescens*. Dates of capture for most specimens are given in *Records of occurrence*. The distribution of the species in the United States is shaded.

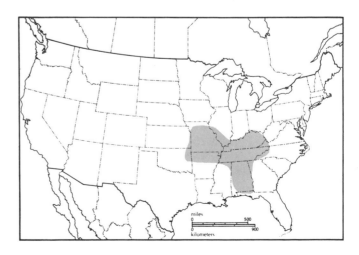

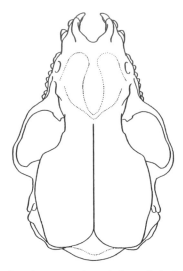

Fig. 8.32. *Myotis grisescens,* dorsal view of skull; 3 mi W Pearl, Pike Co., Illinois, 480 NHS. Female, 16.1 mm greatest length.

from the base to the tips, and grayish at base; calcar not keeled; skull long and broad; skull deep, in part because of a sagittal crest, palate broad.

Color. The fur when parted does not have a distinctive dark, basal band, but rather the color is nearly uniform throughout; the venter appears smoky or brownish gray.

Comparisons. M. grisescens has a long forearm (42 to 45 mm) and does not overlap in length with any other specimens of the other species. The grayish basal color band of the fur and the attachment of the wing membrane at the ankle instead of the side of the foot also set this species apart. Depth of skull (5.9 mm or more) separates nearly all specimens as does breadth of palate across M^3s (6.2 mm or more). *Myotis austroriparius* approaches *M. grisescens* in length of forearm and size of the skull, but differs in other features noted above.

Remarks. M. grisescens is the best differentiated species of *Myotis* in Illinois, with a combination of diagnostic features including large size, hairs nearly unicolor, sagittal crest, and attachment of wing membrane to ankle.

As will be pointed out, *M. grisescens* has a limited distribution in Illinois. One or a few summer colonies have been identified near the Ohio River; during the rest of the year a few migrating or wintering groups have been located near the Mississippi River in west central Illinois.

Habitat

Gray bats occupy different roosts in summer and winter. In the summer, females congregate in large maternity colonies, and a few males may be present also. These colonies are almost always in caves or mine shafts. Gray bats usually forage over water and adjacent riparian vegetation for insects (LaVal et al., 1977). The vegetative cover consists, in Missouri, of sycamores, willows, cot-

tonwoods, ash, elm, maples, and bitternut hickories. These bats have large foraging ranges in Missouri, according to LaVal et al. (1977). In Illinois, Cave Spring Cave, Hardin County, had large numbers of gray bats in the summer throughout the 1950's. In the summer of 1960, J. S. Hall and Wilson (1966) found a nursery colony of about 10,000 gray bats in this cave. In the summer of 1974 (August 28), Whitaker and Winter (1977) found one to two thousand gray bats in a compact cluster measuring one and one-half by five feet. If nursery or maternity colonies are still present in Illinois, Cave Spring Cave may be the only place in the state to house such a gathering.

In the winter, males and females are together in hibernating clusters. Apparently all or most gray bats present in summer in southern Illinois near the Ohio River move south into Kentucky to hibernate or to overwinter. There is one record for October 28, 1953, for a few of these bats in Layoff Cave, Hardin County. Near the Mississippi River in Adams, Pike, and Madison counties, however, there are several winter records of these bats. The caves involved are listed in the *Records of occurrence* section (p. 103). On October 1, 1953, the cave near Nebo had a gray bat cluster more than two feet in diameter, but most winter clusters in Illinois appear not to contain large numbers of *Myotis grisescens*. At a few sites in Missouri, these bats hibernate in large colonies of several thousands. Some caverns in western Illinois, such as Marblehead Mine, are used as refuges during migration—to a greater extent in the fall than in spring (Skaggs, 1973). Artificial caverns, other than mines, may be used by these bats. A few were taken by Harold Broadbooks from the Alton sewer system on October 11, 1968. Elder and Gunier (1978:463) referred to this record as a summer site, but it appears to me to be a fall migratory resting site. Even the cluster of bats in the cave near Nebo reported on by Smith and Parmalee (1954) may have been a migrating group since no bats were found there in December, and on October 1 they were not hibernating because they were quickly disturbed by a light and dispersed through the cave.

Habits

Gray bats forage among the trees—rarely feeding above the tree tops—and low over streams and bodies of water. They forage over small as well as large streams. LaVal et al. (1977) observed one female on May 19 in central Missouri forage continuously for 63 minutes above the Meramec River. It foraged only briefly in the adjacent trees but returned promptly to fly over the water. On another occasion they watched a female forage for 21 minutes over the river, always flying below two meters in height.

LaVal et al. (1977) found that gray bats have extensive

foraging beats and may cover up to 30 km a night. They can be rapid flyers when moving to the roosting site or migrating. Tuttle (1976) thought these bats migrated at average speeds of 20.3 km per hour. Gray bats that were removed as much as 38 miles southward or 75 miles northwestward returned to their summer roosts in central Missouri in about 25 percent of the cases (Gunier and Elder, 1971).

Reproduction

Adult females migrate from the hibernacula followed by males and yearling females, which do not bear young until their second year. Adult females establish nursery or maternity colonies that are usually large. A primary requisite for the site is that the cavern or building be sufficiently warm to conserve body heat. Parturition usually begins in late May. A single young is produced. After all of the young learn to fly, the maternity colony begins to break up; this happens usually in late July. The females and young remain in the general vicinity of the maternity colony through August and then migratory movement back to the wintering area begins. Copulation occurs before the animals enter the hibernaculum.

Miscellaneous

A gray bat banded at Marvel Cave, Stone Co., central Missouri, on March 23, 1970, was reportedly recovered at Blackball Mine, La Salle Co., Illinois, on September 8, 1973, according to a report of Ted Bulthaup (according to Harlan Walley, in litt.). Gunier (1971) reports movements of central Missouri bats of 637 miles in 35 days.

Growth in young gray bats is documented by Tuttle (1975, 1976b). Young weigh about 3 gm at birth and can fly at about four weeks (7 to 8 gms in weight).

Variation

As presently understood, the species is monotypic.

Myotis grisescens Howell

1909. *Myotis grisescens* A. H. Howell, Proc. Biol. Soc. Wash., 22:46. Type from Nickajack Cave, Marion Co., Tennessee.

Range. As given for the species (p. 101, and Map 8.12).
Diagnosis and Comparisons. As given for the species (p. 101-102).
Remarks. M. grisescens may be allied with *Myotis velifer* of southwestern United States, Mexico, and Central America.
Records of occurrence. SPECIMENS EXAMINED, 94.
Pike Co.: [3a] 4 mi W Pearl, 2 (UI), (May 20, 1950); [3b] 3 mi W Pearl [=4 mi E Nebo], 5 (NHS), (Oct. 1, 1953); [3c] 2.1 mi WSW Pearl, Limestone Cave, 18 (SIE), 1 (UI), (Oct. 17, 1964); [3d] 1½ mi S, 1.3 mi W Pearl, Twin Culvert Cave, 9 (SIE), 1

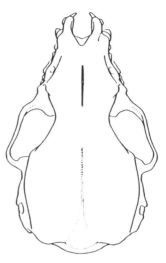

Fig. 8.33. *Myotis keenii,* dorsal view of skull; 1¾ mi W Utica, La Salle Co., Illinois, 26695 UI. Male, 15.4 mm greatest length.

(ISU), (Oct. 15, 1966). **Madison Co.:** [4a] 8 mi E Elsah, Rock Ledge Cave, 460 ft. [labelled Jersey Co.], 1 (SIE); [4b] Alton Sewer System, 1 (SIE), (Oct. 11, 1968). **Hardin Co.:** [5a] 7 mi E [probably W (as plotted) at Cave Spring Cave], Elizabethtown, 1 (UI), (Aug. 6, 1950); [5b] 4¼ mi NW Rosiclare, Watter's Cave [=Cave Spring Cave], 2 (SIC); [5c] 2¼ mi N Rosiclare, Griffith Cave, 2 (SIC); [5d] ½ mi NE Rosiclare, Layoff Cave, 2 (NHS), 2 (ISM), (Oct. 28, 1953); [5e] in caves near Rosiclare, 47 (FM), (April, July, 1907).
Additional records. **La Salle Co.:** [1] Blackball Mine [not seen, recapture & release of banded bat]. **Adams Co.:** [2a] Burton Cave [sight record], (Skaggs, 1973), (Oct. 12, 1970); [2b] Marblehead Mine [sight record, approx. 574 individuals and several small colonies], (Skaggs, 1973), (Sept. 14, Oct. 12). **Pike Co.:** [3e] Twin Culvert Cave [sight record, approx. 14 individuals and one small colony], (Skaggs, 1973), (Sept., Oct., 1971; March, April, 1972); [3f] Limestone Mine [sight record, approx. 106 individuals and one small colony], (Skaggs, 1973), (April, Oct., 1972).

Myotis keenii,* Keen's myotis

Range. Widely distributed throughout state in summer and winter.
Diagnosis. A small to medium-sized *Myotis* with long ears that extend slightly beyond tip of nose when laid forward; ears with long, pointed tragi; calcar not keeled; forearm short (usually 33 to 36.8 mm); toothrow relatively long and averaging longer than breadth across M^3s; no sagittal crest.

---

*After the text was completed, van Zyll de Jong (1985) divided the species previously called *M. keenii,* and the name for the species in Illinois would be *Myotis septentrionalis* according to him. The manuscript has not been altered to conform to this proposal. Further evidence corroborating this arrangement may be desirable.

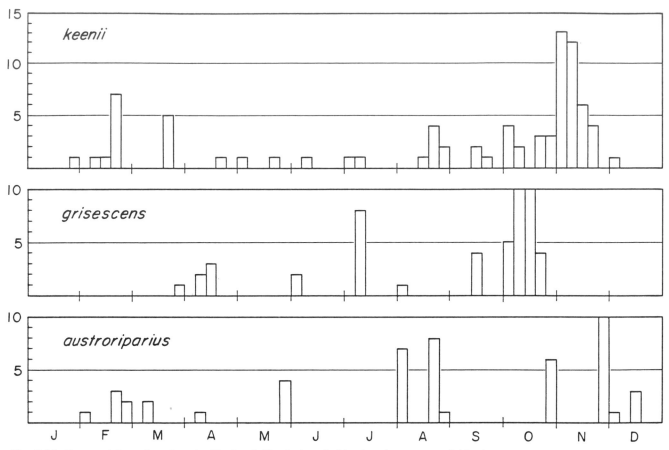

Fig. 8.34. Known dates of capture in Illinois of *Myotis keenii, Myotis grisescens,* and *Myotis austroriparius* during each week of each month.

Color. About the same as in *Myotis lucifugus* (p. 90).

Comparisons. M. keenii differs from *M. grisescens* in its smaller size, shorter forearm, attachment of wing membrane to side of the foot, blackish basal color of fur, and a smaller skull.

M. keenii differs from *M. lucifugus, M. sodalis,* and *M. austroriparius* in having longer ear that extends beyond tip of nose, longer and more pointed tragus, shorter forearm, and relatively longer toothrow.

M. keenii differs from other species of *Myotis* in Illinois in that the toothrow (canine to M³) is longer than the breadth of the palate across M³s.

Remarks. It may be difficult to determine if the ears in specimens of *M. keenii* extend beyond the tip of the nostrils. The height of the ear, measured from the notch, in fresh specimens is usually 15 mm or more and averages nearly 17 mm. In study skins, the ear measures 12.7 to 16.2 mm and all but one are 14 mm or more. In *M. lucifugus* the same measurements vary from 9.5 to 11.9 mm; in *M. sodalis,* 9.5 to 11.2 mm; in *M. grisescens,* 10.8 to 11.5 mm; in *M. austroriparius,* 10.0 to 11.1 mm.

The length of the tragus in study skins of *M. keenii* measures 7.3 to 9.0 mm, and all but one are 8.4 mm or more. The same measurement in *M. lucifugus* varies from

4.1 to 6.3 mm; *M. sodalis,* 5.5 to 7.5 mm; *M. grisescens,* 6.6 to 7.3 mm; *M. austroriparius,* 6.2 to 7.0 mm.

The toothrow in *M. keenii* averages longer (6.0 mm) than the palate is wide, as measured across the M³s (5.8 mm). These measurements of 6.0/5.8 mm compared with other species: *M. lucifugus,* 5.3/5.7 mm; *M. sodalis,* 5.6/5.7 mm; *M. grisescens,* 6.1/6.4 mm; *M. austroriparius,* 5.6/5.9 mm.

Habitat

Keen's myotis hibernate in Illinois in caves, mines, and sometimes buildings—for example, the specimen recorded as from Canton, Fulton County, taken on November 19. We also have numerous other winter records from places where there are no caves or mines (see *Records of occurrence*), but most of these records were received from the Illinois Department of Public Health and the locality may represent the place where they were examined by that department and not the exact spot where they were collected. The largest concentration of wintering Keen's myotis is in Blackball Mine, La Salle County. We have made no analysis of the numbers of individuals in this mine each winter, but I would estimate that spread throughout the various levels of the mine there are about 400 and 800 individuals. In southern Illinois 53 Keen's myotis were located in 13 mines at different times by E. W. Pearson (1962) and 12 specimens were found in mines in Alexander, Hardin, and Union counties by Whitaker and Winter (1977). During hibernation, this species does not form clusters or compact groups but instead tends to hang singly or in groups of only a few individuals. In Blackball Mine, Keen's myotis are commonly found in the same places as the little brown myotis. Usually they hang out in the open; occasionally they are tucked in crevices or drill holes.

In summer, Keen's myotis may roost in caves, mines, buildings, or under the bark on trees. One specimen was collected from a railroad bridge. Frequently these bats can be mist-netted at the entrances to caves and mines during the summer, although they may not be found within the chambers. In the fall, Keen's myotis may show a swarming behavior characteristic of preparation for hibernation. This occurs at the entrances to certain caves or mines.

Habits

Smith and Parmalee (1954:202) found that Keen's myotis did well in captivity and tamed sufficiently to crawl or fly onto the hand offering food. Some individuals are known to reach an age of 18½ years in the wild.

There is some evidence that lethargic and supposedly hibernating *Myotis keenii* arouse themselves more rapidly than other myotis. For example, Layne (1958a:225) noted that these bats in a mine in Alexander County on February 12, with a temperature in the hibernaculum of 35°F, became active immediately upon being touched. Pearson (1962:28) found that, in a hibernaculum in southern Illinois, bats thought to be *M. keenii* "became active and flew from their perches when approached."

Reproduction

Females gather in small maternity colonies shortly after leaving the hibernacula. Maternity colonies have been reported in Indiana, one consisting of about 30, another of about 24 females (Mumford and Cope, 1964), and one of about 50. Two adults and three young were found in a barn in New Hampshire (Barbour and Davis, 1969).

Copulation has occurred in the fall before hibernation and may occur again in the spring. Fertilization occurs in the late spring and parturition sometime in late June or early July. One female taken on June 8 at Aurora, Kane County, carried one embryo with a crown-rump length of 13 mm. There is some evidence that males may invade the maternity colony before the young have left.

Variation

For van Zyll de Jong's (1985) treatment of *Myotis keenii,* see the footnote to p. 103.

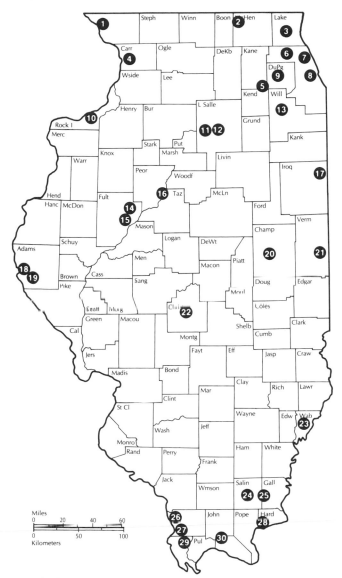

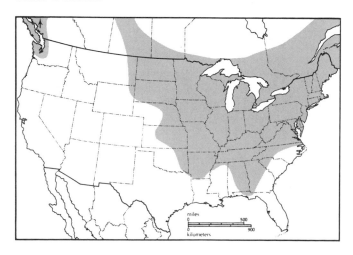

Map 8.13. Known records of the Keen's myotis, *Myotis keenii.* The subspecies is *M. k. septentrionalis.* Numbers are referenced in *Records of occurrence.* For some specimens, dates of capture are also given there. The distribution of the species in the United States is shaded.

Table 8.10. External and cranial measurements (in mm) of five species of *Myotis*. Mean, minimum and maximum, and one standard deviation are given for most species; for *M. grisescens*, individual measurements are given. Superscripts indicate sample less than N.

Species and subspecies	Locality	N	Total length	Tail length	Body length	Hind-foot length	Ear length
Myotis lucifugus	La Salle Co.	20	85.0 76-92 4.32	33.7 24-39 4.47	51.3	9.6 8-12 1.17	12.9 10-15 1.32
Myotis sodalis	La Salle Co.	20	89.6 83-96 3.33	37.9 35-44 2.05	51.7	8.9 8-10 0.60	13.9 13-15 0.67
Myotis austroriparius	Hardin Co.	21	89.1[13] 81-97 4.49	36.2[13] 32-41 2.73	52.9[13]	10.5[13] 9-13 0.84	14.0[13] 12-15.6 1.18
Myotis grisescens	2.1 mi WSW Pearl, Pike Co.	59497 UI	89	32	57	9	11
	4 mi W Pearl, Pike Co.	10266 UI	—	—	—	—	—
	" " "	10265 UI	—	—	—	—	—
	Alton, Madison Co.	256 SIE	89	36	53	12	13
	7 mi E Elizabethtown, Hardin Co.	3025 UI	—	—	—	—	—
	½ mi N Rosiclare, Hardin Co.	613752 ISM	95	35	60	10	16
	" " "	613753 ISM	99	38	61	10	16
Myotis keenii	La Salle Co.	28	88.0 75-97 5.22	37.9 27-46 4.79	50.1	9.1[27] 8-10 0.61	16.89 15-18 1.10
	Union and Alexander cos.	5	83.8 79-89 3.63	34.0 29-37 3.16	49.8	9.4 8-10 0.89	16.4 14-20 2.3

Myotis keenii septentrionalis (Trouessart)

1897. [*Vespertilio gryphus*] var. *septentrionalis* Trouessart, Catal. mamm . . . , fasc. 1, p. 131. Type locality, Halifax, Nova Scotia.

1928. *Myotis keenii septentrionalis*, Miller and Allen, Bull. U. S. Nat. Mus., 144:105.

Range. Widely distributed throughout the state in summer and winter (Map 8.12).

Diagnosis and Comparisons. A subspecies of *M. keenii*, with brown rather than dark brown fur (as in *M. keenii keenii*); ears brownish rather than blackish, skull longer and broader than in *M. k. keenii*.

Remarks. Specimens from north central Illinois are remarkably close to specimens from southern Illinois (Table 8.10).

Records of occurrence. SPECIMENS EXAMINED, 116.
Jo Daviess Co.: [1a] Cave, Galen, 1 (UI), (Oct. 4, 1968); [1b] Galena, 1 (UI), (Oct. 9, 1949). **McHenry Co.:** [2] Harvard, 1 (UI), (Sept. 4, 1968). **Lake Co.:** [3] no specific locality, 1 (UI), (Aug. 23, 1972). **Carroll Co.:** [4] Mt. Carroll Twp., 1 (NHS). **Kane Co.:** [5] Aurora, 2 (UI), (June 8, 1970, Aug. 31, 1977). **Cook Co.:** [6] Arlington Heights, 1 (UI), (Dec. 2, 1975); [7] Wilmette, 1 (UI), (May 1, 1975); [8] Chicago, 1 (US), 1 (FM); no specific locality [not plotted] 1 (UI), (Oct. 23, 1972). **Du Page Co.:** [9] Wheaton, 1 (UI), (Oct. 21, 1977). **Rock Island Co.:** [10] Rock Island, 3 (UI), (Sept. 16, 1976). **La Salle Co.:** [11a] Blackball Mine, 1¾ mi W Utica, 33 (UI); [11b] North Blackball Mine, 1¾ mi W Utica, 1 (NIU); [11c] near La Salle, 5 (FM); [12] 10 mi

E La Salle, 1 (ISU). **Will Co.:** [13] Joliet, 1 (UI), (Oct. 6, 1975). **Fulton Co.:** [14] Canton, 1 (UI), (Oct. 19, 1951); [15] Bryant, 1 (UI), (July 3, 1949). **Peoria Co.:** [16] Peoria, 2 (UI), (Aug. 13, 1965), Sept. 17, 1965). **Iroquois Co.:** [17] Donovan, 1 (UI), (May 22, 1971). **Adams Co.:** [18] Quincy, 3 (UI), (Aug. 20, 1971, Oct. 5, 1978); [19] Burton Cave, 14 mi SE Quincy, 1 (FM), 1 (ISM), (Sept. 7, 1979). **Champaign Co.:** [20] Champaign, 1 (UI), (Oct. 27, 1981). **Vermilion Co.:** [21] Danville, 2 (UI), (Aug. 29, 1976). **Christian Co.:** [22] Taylorville, 1 (UI), (April 23, 1974).

Wabash Co.: [23] no specific locality, 1 (US). **Saline Co.:** [24] Harrisburg, 1 (UI), (Aug. 24, 1976). **Union Co.:** [26] 1½ mi E Wolf Lake, 6 (SIC); [27a] 3 mi SE Ware, 1 (UI), (Nov. 4, 1972); [27b] 3 mi S Ware, 1 (UI), (Nov. 15, 1972); Mine 3 [location uncertain, not plotted], 3 (SIC); Mine 8 [location uncertain, not plotted], 1 (SIC); Mine 15 [location uncertain, not plotted], 3 (SIC). **Hardin Co.:** [28] 2¼ mi N Rosiclare, 1 (SIC), (Dec. 21, ?). **Alexander Co.:** [29a] 3½ mi NW Elco, 2 (NHS), (Nov. 15, 1953); [29b] 3 mi NW Elco, 1 (NHS), (Nov. 15, 1953); [29c] 2½ mi NW Elco, 6 (UI), (Sept. 27, 1975, Nov. 9, 1968, Nov. 20, 1968); [29d] 2 mi W, ½ mi N Elco, 2 (UI), (Nov. 4, and 16, 1972); [29e] 3 mi W Elco, 1 (UI), (Oct. 24, 1970); [29f] 2 mi W Elco, 1 (UI), (Oct. 24, 1972); [29g] 3 mi SW Elco, 1 (ISM), (Jan. 27, 1954); [29h] 4 mi SW Elco, 1 (SRL), 1 (FS), (Feb. 12, 1955); Mine 1 [location uncertain, not plotted], 1 (SIC); Mine 4 [location uncertain, not plotted], 1 (SIC); Mine 6 [location uncertain, not plotted], 5 (SIC); Mine 7 [location uncertain, not plotted], 1 (SIC). **Massac Co.:** [30] ½ mi SE Foreman, 1 (SRL), (July 8, 1960).

Additional records. **Gallatin Co.:** [25] Equality, (Necker and Hatfield, 1941:44). **Alexander Co.:** [29h] 4 mi SW Elco, 1 (FSM).

Forearm length	Greatest length	Zygomatic breadth	Mastoid breadth	Braincase breadth	Inter-orbital breadth	Depth skull	Rostral br. betw. infra-orbital f.	C-M³ length	Pm⁴-M³ length	Breadth across M³-M³
36.6	14.7	9.2	7.9	7.5	4.1	5.2	3.8	5.3	3.8	5.7
34.1-38.9	14.2-15.1	8.8-9.5	7.7-8.2	7.3-7.8	3.9-4.3	5.0-5.5	3.7-4.0	5.1-5.5	3.5-4.1	5.4-6.0
1.29	0.26	0.20	0.15	0.16	0.10	0.13	0.11	0.13	0.12	0.16
37.7	14.6	9.1	7.6	7.1	3.8	5.1	3.6	5.6	4.0	5.7
36.2-39.8	14.1-15.0	8.5-9.3	7.4-8.0	6.7-7.5	3.6-4.1	4.9-5.5	3.5-3.8	5.3-5.7	3.8-4.1	5.4-5.9
0.95	0.30	0.22	0.18	0.21	0.14	0.16	0.11	0.10	0.07	0.11
38.1[12]	15.1[19]	9.2	7.7	7.4	3.8	5.7	3.8	5.6	4.1	5.9
36.8-39.6	14.5-15.6	8.9-9.5	7.5-7.8	7.3-7.6	3.6-4.2	5.4-5.9	3.6-4.0	5.1-5.9	3.7-4.2	5.7-6.1
0.92	0.32	0.20	0.10	0.09	0.13	0.14	0.13	0.17	0.12	0.11
43.7	16.3	9.8	8.25	7.7	4.15	—	4.0	6.0	—	—
44.1	16.0	10.2	8.2	7.7	4.0	6.2	4.0	6.1	4.5	6.2
43.7	15.8	10.0	8.4	7.8	4.1	6.1	4.1	6.1	4.5	6.4
—	—	10.0	8.2	8.0	4.2	6.1	4.1	6.1	4.5	6.3
42.7	15.3	9.7	8.0	7.6	4.0	5.9	3.8	6.0	4.4	6.3
43.5	16.2	10.6	8.6	7.7	4.1	6.2	4.1	6.1	4.4	6.4
43.7	16.3	10.4	8.6	7.9	4.1	6.2	4.4	6.3	4.6	6.4
34.9	15.4[27]	9.3	8.0	7.4	3.7	5.3	3.6	6.0	4.1	5.8
33.1-37.3	14.7-15.9	9.0-9.8	7.6-8.3	6.9-7.7	3.5-3.9	4.9-5.7	3.4-3.9	5.7-6.3	3.8-4.3	5.4-6.0
1.04	0.28	0.20	0.17	0.20	0.13	0.15	0.12	0.15	0.11	0.14
34.5	15.4[4]	9.3	8.0	7.3	3.7	5.2	3.6	6.0	4.1	5.8
33.5-36.1	15.3-15.4	9.1-9.4	7.9-8.2	7.2-7.4	3.7-3.8	5.1-5.4	3.4-3.7	5.95-6.0	4.1-4.2	5.7-6.0
1.05	0.06	0.11	0.13	0.09	0.06	0.12	0.10	0.03	0.03	.10

Lasionycteris, Silver-haired bats

Diagnosis. Medium-sized bats that are blackish in color but with a conspicuous frosting or wash of white or silver on the back and usually on the venter; only two upper premolars; ear short and tragus blunt; interfemoral membrane lightly furred on dorsal surface part way toward edge; skull flattened.

Dental formula. 2/3, 1/1, 2/3, 3/3.

Chromosomes. Diploid number of 20, FN=28; four pairs of large metacentrics and submetacentrics, one pair of small metacentrics, four pairs of small acrocentrics, X a large submetacentric, Y a small acrocentric.

Comparisons. For comparisons, see account under the species (below).

Remarks. Lasionycteris is unique among Illinois bats because of its frosting of white on an otherwise blackish animal.

Lasionycteris noctivagans, Silver-haired bat

Range. Throughout the state except in July and early August and in the winter, when the species is probably restricted to a few of the southernmost counties.

Diagnosis. As given for the genus above.

Comparisons. L. noctivagans differs from species of *Myotis* in its conspicuous black color, with a frosting of white; only one small tooth behind upper incisor; some hairs on dorsum of tail membrane; rostrum broader as measured between infraorbital foramina (no overlap), and chromosomal differences (see preceding discussion).

L. noctivagans differs from *Lasiurus cinereus* in having a more blackish color, forearm much shorter, two upper incisors rather than one, hair less dense on dorsum of tail membrane, skull shorter and narrower.

L. noctivagans differs from *Tadarida brasiliensis* in having the tail enclosed within the tail membrane rather than the distal half free, two upper incisors rather than one, and in other features as pointed out in Table 8.8.

L. noctivagans differs from the other species in Illinois in blackish coloration with white frosting, in chromosomal numbers, and other features as given in Table 8.8.

Remarks. Lasionycteris noctivagans is present in Illinois in greatest numbers during spring and fall migrations, with some animals being summer residents. The species is a year-round resident in southernmost Illinois, with known winter records (January and February) for Alexander and Union counties.

There are a few winter records for northern Illinois: one from Blue Island, Cook County, on December 17, 1975; Elgin, Kane County, March 1, 1973; River Forest, Cook County, December 2, 1975; Field Museum, Chicago, February 5, 1910 and January 1977; Chicago State University, January 1977; Warsaw, Hancock County, November 4, 1972. These may represent bats that became ill while in migration and remained at these northern

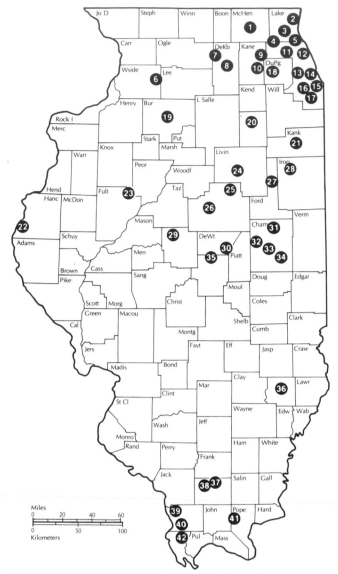

Map 8.14. Silver-haired bats, *Lasionycteris noctivagans,* occur statewide in the summer and in migration. Records of occurrence are numbered. Dates of capture of some specimens are given in *Records of occurrence.* The distribution of the species in the United States is shaded.

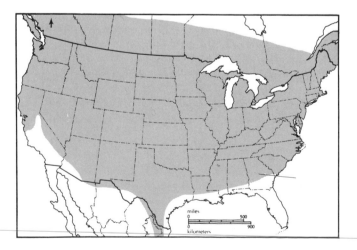

places, or they may be animals that were caught in the wild at an earlier time and were kept captive and killed on the dates recorded. Four of the six records are from specimens obtained from the Illinois Department of Public Health. Izor (1979:642) found that the bat captured at the Field Museum in January 1977 flew away after it was given food and water.

Habitat

Silver-haired bats inhabit mature woodlands, often those adjacent to streams, ponds, or lakes. The species is a tree-roosting bat, and frequently rests during the day behind the bark or within cavities of the trees. An adult male was collected under the loose bark of a dead poplar tree near Canton, Fulton County, on May 24 (Anderson, 1951:164). Klimstra (1969:4) found three silver-haired bats in hollow trees in Union County while checking for wood duck nests. During spring and fall migrations, silver-haired bats are often found in unlikely places: houses, stores, garages, large buildings, mines, and caves.

In the winter, silver-haired bats hibernate in small numbers in silica mines in southernmost Illinois, hanging separately on the walls. At a mine 3½ mi SW Elco, Alexander County, a few silver-haired bats were present on January 27 and February 2, 1954 (Smith and Parmalee, 1954:202). At other silica mines near Elco, Layne (1958a:227) found on February 12, 1955, one silver-haired bat in a vertical fissure and three wedged in cracks in the ceiling.

Habits

Silver-haired bats are relatively low flyers and exhibit a slow, erratic flight pattern. Sometimes they feed from 15 to 30 feet above ground; at other times above tree-top levels (Mumford and Whitaker, 1982). The flight may be erratic, and it is not especially fast.

These bats feed most intensively from two to four hours after sunset and again from six to nine hours after sunset in Iowa (Kunz, 1973). Mumford and Whitaker (1982:165) regard them as early flyers in Indiana since they are abroad at about the same times as red bats, eastern pipistrelles and evening bats. In contrast, Kunz (1982) says they are relatively late flyers, often appearing after other species have begun feeding. I do not know what the time of appearance of silver-haired bats is in Illinois.

It has been suggested that silver-haired bats may adjust some of their times of foraging so as not to conflict with those of red, hoary, or big brown bats (Kunz, 1973).

In early November 1972, numerous silver-haired bats reportedly migrating with various species of warblers flew into the McCormick Place building, Chicago, and 35 bats and several hundred warblers were killed. The bats were preserved by Harlan Walley, Northern Illinois University, and he informed us of this accident.

Fig. 8.35A. Silver-haired bat, *Lasionycteris noctivagans*. Note silvery tips of the hairs on the back and venter (From Hoffmeister and Mohr, 1957. Photograph by Ernest P. Walker, Smithsonian Institution, Washington, D.C.)

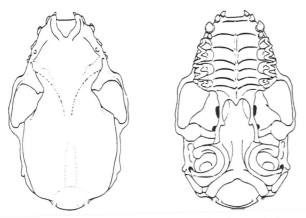

Fig. 8.35B. *Lasionycteris noctivagans,* dorsal and ventral views of skull. Vic. Camp Verde, Yavapai Co., Arizona, 31160 UI. Female, 16.2 mm greatest length.

Seasonal Distribution

Spring–Early Summer (mid-April to June). Females precede males in spring migration. Up to the end of May, only females (20) were collected; from June 1 to June 24, six adult females and nine males were collected.

Mid-summer (July to mid-August). Nearly absent according to available evidence, as only one specimen, a male, was taken. Young were reported to be flying as early as July 22 in central Iowa (Kunz, 1971).

Late Summer-Fall (mid-August to mid-October). During a 65-day span from August 20 through October 23, there have been 96 specimens of silver-haired bats collected in Illinois. During the first half of this period, 34 males and 16 females were collected; the second half, 19 males, 36 females. Probably most if not all of these specimens are migrants.

Winter (mid-October to mid-April). The northern Illinois winter records are discussed under *Remarks* (p. 107). There are reports of an occasional overwintering individual as far north as Ontario (Peterson, 1966), Minnesota (Beer, 1956), and Michigan (Gosling, 1977).

Reproduction

Females produce two young, rarely one, in late June or early July. No females taken in Illinois in May or early June are recorded as being pregnant. The gestation period is between 50 and 60 days and two newborn from central Iowa weighed 1.8 and 1.9 grams each. Lactation lasts slightly longer than a month. Young are flying by late July.

Variation

The genus and species are monotypic.

Lasionycteris noctivagans (Le Conte)

1831. *V[espertilio]. noctivagans* Le Conte, *in* McMurtrie, The animal kingdom . . . by the Baron Cuvier . . . 1:431. Type from eastern United States.

1894. *Lasionycteris noctivagans,* H. Allen, Bull. U. S. Nat. Mus., 43:105.

Range. As given for the species (p. 107 and Map 8.14).

Diagnosis and Comparisons. As given for the genus and species (p. 107).

Remarks. Some workers consider this species to be closely allied with certain species of *Myotis.*

Records of occurrence. SPECIMENS EXAMINED, 181.
Lake Co.: [2a] Zion, 1 (NHS), (Aug. 27, 1954); [2b] Beach, 2 (FM), (Aug. 23, 1900), [2c] Waukegan, 2 (UI), (June 26, 1979, Sept. 11, 1978); [2d] Downey, 1 (UI), (Sept. 19, 1975); [3] Mundelein, 1 (UI), (Sept. 1, 1962); [4] Barrington, 1 (UI), (May 25, 19—); [5a] Ft. Sheridan, 1 (UI), (April 25, 19—); [5b] Highland Park, 1 (UI), 1 (FM), (May 14, 1934, October 20, 1965); no specific locality [not plotted], 3 (UI). **De Kalb Co.:** [7] Esmond, 1 (UI), (Aug. 30, 1967); [8] De Kalb, 1 (UI), (Sept. 10, 1975). **Kane Co.:** [9] Elgin, 1 (UI), (March 1, 1973); [10a] St. Charles, 1 (NIU); [10b] Geneva, 2 (UI), (Oct. 12, 1974, May 14, 1975).

Cook Co.: [11a] Palatine, 1 (UI), (Aug. 29, 1972); [11b] Arlington Heights, 2 (UI), (Oct. 5, 1965); [11c] Hoffman Estates, 1 (UI), (May 10, 1979); [11d] Des Plaines, 2 (UI), (Oct. 7, 1971); [12a] Northbrook, 2 (UI), (Oct. 7, 1971); [12b] Winnetka, 1 (UI), (Oct. 3, 1967); [12c] Wilmette, 10 (UI), (Oct. 4, 1965, Aug. 30, 1966, June 30, 1967); [12d] Morton Grove, 1 (UI), (Oct. 3, 1974); [12e] Evanston, 25 (UI), (Sept. 3–26, 1965–66, Oct. 4–18, 1965, May 4, 1967, June 7, 1967, June 26, 1968, Oct. 7, 1971); [12f] Skokie, 10 (UI), (Oct. 5, 1965, August 26, 1966); [12g] Lincolnwood, 2 (UI), Sept. 11, 1979); [13a] Melrose Park, 1 (UI); [13b] River Forest, 3 (UI), (Jan. 2, 1975); [13c] Oak Park, 1 (UI), (Sept. 16, 1965); [14a] Chicago, 3 (UI), 4 (FM), (Sept. 20, 1941, Oct. 20, 1944, Aug. 20, 1946, Sept. 23, 1948, Dec. 11, 1969); [14b] Grant Park, 1 (FM), (Sept. 28, 1928); [14c] Shedd Aquarium, 1 (FM), (May 9, 1930); [14d] Field Museum Bldg., 10 (FM), Aug.

23, 1899, Feb. 5, 1910, Aug. 26, 1922, Sept. 1, 1922, Sept. 10, 1923); [14e] Chicago, McCormick Place, 6 (UI), (Aug. 28–29, 19—); [14f] Cicero, 1 (UI), (May 27, 1968); [15a] Jackson Park, 5 (FM), (Sept. 19, 1898, Sept. 13, 1902, Sept. 9, 1905, May 27, 1909, Sept. 28, 1922); [15b] Oakwoods Cemetery, 1 (FM), Sept. 19, 1902); [16] Chicago Ridge, 5 (UI), (Nov. 21, 1977); [17a] South Chicago, 1 (UI); [17b] Blue Island, 1 (UI); [17c] Midlothian, 2 (UI), (Oct. 5, 1965); [17d] Tinley Park, 1 (UI), (April 13, 1979); [17e] Homewood, 1 (UI), (Nov. 3, 1978); no specific locality [not plotted], 10 (UI).

Du Page Co.: [18a] West Chicago, 1 (UI), (Sept. 10, 1969); [18b] Glen Ellyn, 1 (FM), (May 30, 1903); [18c] Wheaton, 1 (UI), (May 21, 1979); no specific locality [not plotted], 1 (UI). **Bureau Co.:** [19] no specific locality, 1 (UI), (Oct. 6, 1965). **Grundy Co.:** [20] Morris, 2 (UI), (Sept. 25, 1975). **Kankakee Co.:** [21] no specific locality, 1 (UI), (Oct. 10, 1975). **Hancock Co.:** [22] Warsaw, 1 (UI), (Nov. 4, 1972). **Fulton Co.:** [23] 7 mi N Canton, 1 (UI), (May 24, 1951). **Livingston Co.:** [24] Pontiac, 1 (UI), (Sept. 3, 1965). **McLean Co.:** [25] 3 mi S Chenoa, 1 (ISU); [26] Normal, ISU campus, 1 (ISU). **Iroquois Co.:** [28] Ashkum, 1 (UI), (Sept. 18, 1972). **Logan Co.:** [29] Hartsburg, 1 (UI), (May 13, 1981). **De Witt Co.:** [30] Weldon, 1 (UI), (May 5, 1972). **Champaign Co.:** [31] Rantoul, 1 (UI), (May 17, 1972); [32a] Mahomet, 1 (UI); [32b] 1 mi SE Mahomet, 1 (UI), (Oct. 8, 1955); [33a] 3 mi ENE Urbana, Brownfield Woods, 2 (UI), (April 20, 1955); [33b] Champaign, 3 (UI), (Oct. 18, 1954, Oct. 1, 74, Sept. 15, 1981); [33c] Urbana, 4 (NHS), 2 (UI), (May 2 and 20, 1955, Oct. 11, 1955); [34] Sidney, 1 (NHS), (Oct. 5, 1953). **Macon Co.:** [35] Maroa, 1 (UI), (June 2, 1980). **Williamson Co.:** [37] Johnson City, 1 (UI), (April 2, 1981); [38] Herrin, 1 (UI), (Sept. 15, 1980). **Union Co.:** [39] T11S, R3W, Sec. 35, 3 (SRL), (Jan. 8, 19—); [40] T13S, R2W, Sec. 22, Mine 16, 1 (SRL), (Feb. 12, 19—); Mine 17 [location uncertain, not plotted], 1 (SIC). [41] Glendale, 1 (UI), (May 20, 1970). **Alexander Co.:** [42a] 4 mi W Elco, 1 (ISU); [42b] 3 mi W Elco, 1 (NHS), (Feb. 2, 1954); [42c] 2¾ mi SW Elco, 2 (SIC); [42d] 3 mi SW Elco, 1 (ISM), (Jan. 27, 1954); [42e] 4 mi SW Elco, 3 (FS), (Feb. 12, 1955); Mine 5 [location uncertain, not plotted], 1 (SIC).

Additional records. **McHenry Co.:** [1] Woodstock, (Harty, 1981 in litt.). **Whiteside Co.:** [6] Sterling, (Necker and Hatfield, 1941:44). **Cook Co.:** [14a] Chicago, 1 (UM). **Ford Co.:** [27] Piper City, T27N, R9E, Sec. 4, (Koestner, 1942:227). **Richland Co.:** [36] Olney, (Necker and Hatfield, 1941:44).

Pipistrellus, Pipistrelles

Diagnosis. A genus of vespertilionid bats of small size, with forearm short, ear short, tragus blunt but straight; each half of lower jaw with two premolars (three in *Myotis*) resulting in five teeth behind canine (six in *Myotis*), one small tooth behind upper canine; upper incisors of about equal size (second larger in *Myotis*).

Dentition. 2/3, 1/1, 2/2, 3/3.

Comparisons. For a comparison with *Myotis*, see account of that genus (p. 90). *Pipistrellus* differs from *Nycticeius* in having more orangish or yellowish coloration, smaller skull with two upper incisors rather than

Fig. 8.36A. Eastern pipistrelle, *Pipistrellus subflavus.* (From Hoffmeister and Mohr, 1957. Photograph by Ernest P. Mulch, Phoenix, Arizona)

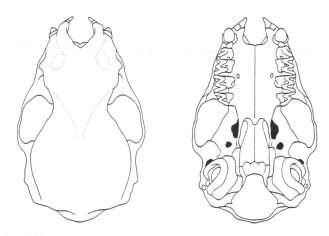

Fig. 8.36B. *Pipistrellus subflavus,* dorsal and ventral views of skull; 1¾ mi W Utica, La Salle Co., Illinois, 14403 UI. Male, 12.8 mm greatest length.

one; one small tooth behind each upper incisor rather than none.

Pipistrellus is smaller and differs in other ways from the other genera as pointed out in Tables 8.8 and 8.11.

Remarks. In North America, two species of *Pipistrellus* occur: *P. subflavus* and *P. hesperus.* The latter occurs farther west.

Pipistrellus subflavus, Eastern pipistrelle

Range. Throughout Illinois in both summer and winter, although uncommon to rare in some areas. Also, see *Remarks* (below).

Diagnosis. A species of *Pipistrellus* with coloration, in Illinois, that is usually orangish to pale yellow, with the fur having a tri-colored pattern; base of hair black, subterminal band light-colored, terminal band darker; hind foot more than half as long as tibia; P^1 when viewed labially is not concealed by canine; forearm reddish and contrasting sharply with black wing membrane.

Comparisons. *Pipistrellus subflavus* might be confused with certain species of *Myotis* (p. 90); also with *Nycticeius humeralis* (p. 125). See above under the genus *Pipistrellus* for comparisons.

Molt. Wayne Davis (1957) was of the opinion that in the northern part of the range of this species, young may go into hibernation before they have molted to adult pelage. Once molting has started, it occurs quite rapidly, in his estimation. There is no molt line present, but molting occurs over the entire body at about the same time.

Chromosomes. Diploid number, 30; FN=56; ten pairs of large metacentrics-submetacentrics, one small metacentric, three small subtelocentrics; X chromosome medium-sized metacentric; Y, small submetacentric.

Remarks. Eastern pipistrelles were unknown from collected specimens from northeastern Illinois until recently. In all of northern Illinois, there were records only for Jo Daviess, Carroll, and La Salle counties. We now have additional records from Rockford, Winnebago County, July 26, 1976, and Chicago, Cook County, September 15, 1977. The Rockford record and a male taken in La Salle County on June 5, 1964, are the only summer records from northern Illinois.

Habitat

During the summer, eastern pipistrelles may roost in caves, mine shafts, in attics of buildings (as in Randolph County), and possibly among clusters of leaves, under the bark of certain trees, or in cavities of trees. Even though these pipistrelles are commonly seen flying in the summer, their summer roosts are poorly known. Wayne Davis informs me that he has seen colonies in sheds and abandoned houses. He says that "colonies" are usually of less than a dozen individuals. Since they are not in large concentrations, eastern pipistrelles may be easily overlooked and since so few have been found in old structures, I have speculated that many are hanging in trees and other vegetation.

In winter, these pipistrelles hibernate in caves and mines from the northern part of the state (Jo Daviess County) to the southern part (Alexander County). They usually are hanging separately and fairly well spaced in the hibernaculum. We have found them hanging on the ceilings as well as the walls of the caves or mines. At one time, I thought that eastern pipistrelles sought the damper parts of the hibernaculum, but I am not certain of this. In northern Illinois, eastern pipistrelles are not the most common bat in hibernacula. In southern Illinois (Union and Alexander counties), however, E. W. Pearson (1962:29) reported them as being "encountered in larger numbers and in more mines than any of the other five species [Keen's myotis, little brown myotis, big brown bat, silver-haired bat, big-eared bat]."

Habits

Eastern pipistrelles are early flyers, being abroad almost as early as red bats. Long before dark, pipistrelles are usually feeding along the edge of wooded areas, over adjacent fields, and along streams. Gardner and Gardner (1980) took a lactating female on July 15 as early as 14 minutes after sundown in Pike County. On some occasions, these bats are flying even before sunset. Some pipistrelles evidently feed for a period of time early and then again at a later time. Flight is erratic as they maneuver for small insects.

Like most other winter-cave-dwelling bats, eastern pipistrelles swarm at cave entrances in the fall, supposedly at the caves where they will eventually hibernate. Barbour and Davis (1974:90) found that "it is not unusual to capture 100 or more pipistrelles at cave entrance in a single night" in the fall in Kentucky.

A pipistrelle kept captive by Smith and Parmalee (1954) for one month became quite tame and took food from the feeder's fingers with no adverse reactions. It would even fall asleep on his hand.

Reproduction

The solitary nature of eastern pipistrelles carries over to the reproductive period. Rarely do females congregate into what can be called maternity colonies. Wayne Davis tells me that the largest nursery colony he knows of was 30; most are less and with scattered individuals. Copulation apparently occurs in the fall as well as in the spring. Young are born in late June and early July. Lactating females were caught along McKee Creek, Pike County, on July 15, 1980, by Gardner and Gardner (1980). Two is the usual number of young: rarely one. In some years, adult females apparently do not produce offspring. Newborn can fly when they are one month old.

Sex Ratios of Wintering Pipistrelles

The ratio of males to females in hibernating eastern pipistrelles is greatly skewed toward males. In 95 specimens taken in Illinois between November and February,

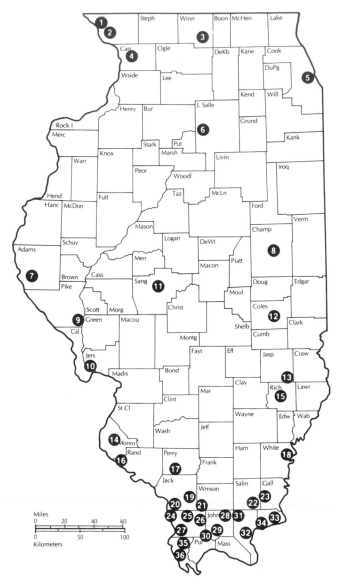

Map 8.15. Eastern pipistrelle, *Pipistrellus subflavus*, occurs state-wide. The subspecies is *P. s. subflavus*. Records of occurrence are numbered. Dates of capture of some specimens are given in *Records of occurrence*. The distribution of the species in the United States is shaded.

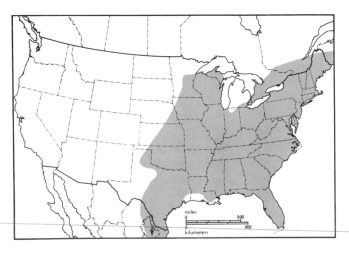

69.4 percent were males. In Missouri, of 431 bats handled in winter, 71 percent were males (Davis, 1957); in Kentucky, 69.5 to 85.1 percent (Davis, 1966); in Indiana, about 77 percent (Mumford and Whitaker, 1982). Wayne Davis (1959a) thought the severity of the winters in a region affected the sex ratio of eastern pipistrelles because the harsher the winter, the higher the percentage of males in the hibernaculum. More females may winter outside of caves. Also, there may be a difference in the survival rate of the sexes.

Movements

Eastern pipistrelles move between hibernacula and summer roosts. Barbour and Davis (1974) thought this movement was less than 80 km. If movements are no greater than this, the species is hardly migratory.

Longevity

A male eastern pipistrelle banded in Blackball Mine, La Salle County, on February 16, 1957, by Wayne Davis when he was a student at the University of Illinois, was recaptured at the same mine on February 25, 1971, by Harlan Walley (Walley and Jarvis, 1971:305). This bat was a minimum of 14.8 years old.

Variation

The study of Davis (1959b) indicated that there were four subspecies of *P. subflavus*, with the form *P. s. subflavus* in Illinois.

Pipistrellus subflavus subflavus (F. Cuvier)

1832. V[espertilio]. *subflavus* F. Cuvier, Nouv. Ann. Mus. Hist. Nat. Paris, 1:17. Type locality Le Conte Plantation, 3 mi SW Riceboro, Liberty Co., Georgia (Davis, 1959b:522).
1897. *Pipistrellus subflavus*, Miller, N. Amer. Fauna, 13:90.

Range. As given for the species (p. 110 and Map 8.15).
Diagnosis and Comparisons. A race of medium size and reddish coloration, but color is variable. Compared to *P. s. floridanus*, it is more reddish and slightly smaller.
Remarks. P. s. subflavus is a wide-ranging subspecies, with "peripheral races" in southeastern Georgia and Florida, and in southwestern Texas and eastern Mexico.

Records of occurrence. SPECIMENS EXAMINED, 253.
Jo Daviess Co.: [1] Galena, 1 (UI), (Nov. 12, 1947); [2a] 8 mi SE Galena, 2 (ISM), 3 (NHS), (Dec. 9, 1953); [2b] 9 mi SE Galena, lead mine, 1 (UI), (Oct. 10, 1949). **Winnebago Co.:** [3] Rockford, 1 (UI), (July 26, 1976). **Carroll Co.:** [4] 2 mi W Mt. Carroll, 2 (SRL), 1 (SIC), 3 (UI), (Nov. 28, 1953). **Cook Co.:** [5] Chicago, 1 (UI), (Sept. 15, 1977). **La Salle Co.:** [6a] 1¾ mi W North Utica, Blackball Mine, 1 (UI), 28 (UI), (Oct., Nov., Feb.); [6b] W side Utica, Pruce's Mine, 1 (UI), (April 13, 1957); [6c] 1 mi E La Salle, 2 (ISU); [6d] 4½ mi E La Salle, 3 (NHS), (Nov. 6, 1953; Feb. 19, 1954); [6e] near La Salle, 4 (FM). **Adams Co.:** [7] Burton

Cave, 2 mi SW Burton, 2 (FM), 4 (ISM), 3 (UI), (Nov. 10, 1946; Nov. 5, 1953). **Pike Co.:** [9a] 3 mi W Pearl, 1 (NHS), (Oct. 1, 1953); [9b] 2 mi SW Pearl, Pearl Cave, 3 (ISM), (Dec. 12, 1953); [9c] 4 mi S Pearl, 3 (UI), (March 4, 1948; May 20, 1950); [9d] between Pearl and Beecreek, 3 (ISM), (Feb. 16, 1972). **Jersey Co.:** [10a] Pere Marquette State Park, 1 (NHS), (Jan. 31, 1941); [10b] 1 mi W Grafton, in cave, 1 (UI); [10c] Grafton, 2 (NHS), (March, 1941). **Sangamon Co.:** [11] Springfield, 1 (UI), (May 13, 1977). **Jasper Co.:** [13a] Ste. Marie, 1 (UI), (May 29, 1954); [13b] 5 mi SE Ste. Marie, 1 (UI), (May 29, 1954). **Monroe Co.:** [14a] Burksville, 6 (UI), (Nov. 29, 1947); [14b] Burksville, Burksville Cave, 5 (NHS), 4 (UI), (Dec. 7, 1946; Jan. 23, 1947); [14c] 3 mi SE Burksville, Eckhart Cave, 2 (NHS), 4 (ISM), 8 (UI), (Jan., Nov., Dec., 1947). **Richland Co.:** [15] Olney, 1 (UI), (June 6, 1909). **Randolph Co.:** [16] Ft. Chartress State Park, 6 (NHS), (July 15, 1953). **Perry Co.:** [17] Pyatts Striplands, 3 (SRL). **White Co.:** [18] 2 mi S, 6 mi E Crossville, 1 (UI). **Jackson Co.:** [19] Carbondale, 1 (UI), (Oct. 24, 1968); [20a] 3 mi SSE Gorham, 1 (SRL), (Oct. 8, —); [20b] Pomona Natural Bridge, 1 (FS), (Aug. 5, 1954).

Williamson Co.: [21] W side Little Grassy Lake, 1 (UI), (May 6, 1955). **Saline Co.:** [22] 6 mi E, 3 mi S Harrisburg, Cave Hill Cave, 13 (UI), 1 (ISM), (Jan. 30, 1949; Dec. 26, 1949; Oct. 29, 1953). **Union Co.:** [24b] Pine Hills, near Wolf Lake, 1 (ISM), 2 (NHS), 1 (UI), (Oct. 9–10, 1953); [25a] 7 mi NE Cobden, 1 (NHS), (Nov. 14, 1953); [25b] 5 mi NE Cobden, Guthrie Cave, 3 (SRL), 2 (SIC), (Feb. 5, —, Aug. 8, —); [25c] Alto Pass, Cave, 1 (UI), (April, 1927); [25d] Rich's Cave, 3 mi E Cobden, 4 (SRL), 8 (SIC); [25e] SW Cobden, 1 (SRL); [25g] 3 mi SW Cobden, 1 (FS), (Aug. 17, 1954); [25h] Anna, 6 (FM); [26a] Lick Creek, 2 (US), (May 22, 1909); [26b] 14¼ mi SE Carbondale, Lilly Cave, 4 (NHS), 4 (SIC), (Nov. 14, 1953); [27a] 4 mi W Mill Creek, 1 (SRL); [27b] 3 mi W Mill Creek, 1 (SRL), (Jan. 30, —); Mine 1 [location uncertain, not plotted], 1 (SIC); Mine 3 [location uncertain, not plotted], 1 (SIC). **Johnson Co.:** [28] Ozark, 1 (FM), (April 21, 1897); [29a] 1 mi N Vienna, 1 (NHS), 1 (ISM), (Oct. 8, 1953); [29b] 2½ mi S Vienna, 6 (SIC); [30] 2½ mi SW Cypress, 1 (SRL), (Feb. 5, —). **Pope Co.:** [31a] Bell Smith Springs, 1 (FS), (June 16, 1957); [31b] 1 mi SE McCormick, 3 (SRL), (May 21, —); [32] Golconda, 10 (FM), (July 8, 1907). **Hardin Co.:** [33] 2½ mi NW Cave in Rock, 1 (NHS), (Oct. 29, 1953); [34a] 4½ mi NW Rosiclare, 1 (SRL), (Mar. 12, —); [34b] 4¼ mi NW Rosiclare, Watter's Cave [=Cave Spring Cave], 1 (UI), 1 (SIC), (Nov. 16, 1957); [34c] 5½ mi W, 1 mi N Elizabethtown, 2 (UI); [34d] 2¼ mi N Rosiclare, 1 (SRL), March 12, —; [34e] 2 mi N Rosiclare, Griffith Cave, 1 (ISM), (Oct. 28, 1953); [34f] Elizabethtown, 1 (SRL), (Dec. 21, —); [34h] Rosiclare, 17 (FMNH), (April 8, 1907; July 10–15, 1907). **Alexander Co.:** [35a] 3½ mi NW Elco, 3 (NHS), (Nov. 15, 1953); [35b] 2½ mi NW Elco, 2 (UI), 4 (SRL), (Nov. 9, 1968); [35c] 1½ mi W, 1 mi N Elco, 3 (UI), (Nov. 23, 1976); [35d] 1 mi E Elco, in mine, 2 (UI), (Oct. 5 and 19, 1942); [35e] 4 mi WSW Elco, 1 (SRL), Feb. 12, —; [35f] 4½ mi NW Tamms, 1 (UI), (Apr. 6, 1981); [36] Olive Branch, 8 (FM), 1 (US), (July 19–24, 1907, May 14, 1909); Mine 6 [location uncertain, not plotted], 2 (SIC).

Additional records. **Adams Co.:** [7] Burton Cave, 2 mi SW Burton, 2 (UM). **Champaign Co.:** [8] Brownfield Woods, (Koestner, 1942:227). **Coles Co.:** [12] Charleston, (Cory, 1912:467). **Jackson Co.:** [19] Carbondale, 1 (FS). **Gallatin Co.:** [23] Equality, (Necker and Hatfield, 1941:45). **Union Co.:** [24a] 2½ mi NE

Aldridge, 1 (FS); [25f] 3 mi SW Cobden, 1 (FS). **Hardin Co.:** [34d] 2¼ mi N Rosiclare, 1 (FS); [34g] ½ mi NE Rosiclare, 2 (FS), (Dec. 21, 1954). **Alexander Co.:** [35b] 2½ mi NW Elco, 6 (FS).

Eptesicus, Brown bats

Diagnosis. Vespertilionid bats of large size in Illinois; coloration usually dark brown; ears short; two upper incisors well developed, with the inner larger than the outer, no small teeth behind upper incisors, lower incisors crowded and imbricated; skull broad and flat.

Dental formula. 2/3, 1/1, 1/2, 3/3.

Secondary sexual variation. In an analysis for sex-related differences in six males and seven females from northern Illinois, no cranial measurements showed any significant differences, nor did length of forearm. Total, tail, and hind foot length did show significant differences. Burnett (1983) worked with much larger samples and found females significantly larger than males — by 1.3 to 3.8 percent in 12 cranial measurements.

Comparisons. Eptesicus in Illinois appears in many ways to be a large version of *Myotis* or *Nycticeius.* For a comparison with these, see accounts of those genera (pp. 90, 125, respectively).

Eptesicus differs from *Lasiurus* in having dark brown coloration, tail membrane not well furred on dorsal side; ears longer and less rounded; two upper incisors rather than one, one upper premolar instead of two.

Eptesicus differs from *Plecotus* in having much shorter ears; no lumps on muzzle; no small tooth behind upper incisors; auditory bullae smaller.

Eptesicus differs from *Lasionycteris* in being brownish rather than blackish in color; size larger both externally and cranially; no small tooth behind the upper incisor; dorsal surface of tail membrane not furred.

Eptesicus fuscus, Big brown bat

Range. Throughout the state.

Diagnosis. A species of large size, forearm in Illinois specimens between 44 and 50 mm in length; body length about 72 mm; no small tooth behind upper incisors (in this feature, similar to *Nycticeius*); calcar keeled; tragus broad, rounded.

Color. In Illinois specimens, dorsal coloration varies from chocolate brown to brown, with brownish-black ears and wing membranes, tail membrane usually brownish, underparts slightly lighter than dorsum.

Chromosomes. Diploid number for *E. fuscus* 50, FN = 48, all autosomes are acrocentric; X, submetacentric, Y, acrocentric.

Comparisons. E. fuscus may be confused with *Nycticeius humeralis* and species of *Myotis.* The coloration and broad head is much as in *Nycticeius humeralis* but *E. fuscus* has a much longer forearm (44 to 50 mm vs.

Fig. 8.37. Big brown bat, *Eptesicus fuscus,* in flight. The shiny object on the forearm is a bat band. Photograph by W. W. Goodpaster.

34 to 38 mm). Other differences are given in the account of *Nycticeius.*

E. fuscus differs from all species of *Myotis* in having no small teeth behind each upper incisor. It differs from most *Myotis* in having a keeled calcar, and differs from those *Myotis* with a keeled calcar in its larger size, longer forearm (44 mm or more, rather than 40 mm or less), larger skull. *Myotis grisescens* is the only species with forearm measurement approaching that of *E. fuscus,* and *M. grisescens* has the unique monocolored fur and the wing membrane attached to the ankle.

Growth. Kunz (1974) has analyzed growth of young *E. fuscus* in Kansas and found that adult size in both sexes was attained by about the 10th week, but females apparently develop faster than males. Growth of the wings is more rapid than other parts of the body (Davis, Barbour, and Hassell, 1968).

Remarks. Big brown bats are one of, if not the most conspicuous of, bats in Illinois because they are so widely distributed in the state and because they are closely associated with man by occupying some of the same buildings he does and by commonly foraging in yards and streets of urban areas. Big browns are more active during the cooler parts of the year than most other species and often are found hanging in conspicuous places in buildings in the middle of winter.

Habitat

Big brown bats in the summer roost in a great variety of places; attics of used and unused buildings—especially those with steeples or high lofts—barns, caves, mines, bridges, hollow trees. They forage nearly anywhere they can find a supply of insects: around outdoor lights, over ponds and streams, over and among wooded areas, over fields. During the daytime, big brown bats take refuge, perhaps only temporarily, in some unusual places—such as behind pictures hanging on walls, behind shutters, under leaves, in hollow walls. In the summer, big browns may roost individually, or in groups or colonies that may comprise several hundred individuals.

In winter, big brown bats occupy caves, mines, attics, and insulated or uninsulated buildings. Since these bats can withstand cold weather better than other Illinois bats, their places of overwintering are greatly increased. Big browns when hibernating do not usually hang in large clusters. For example, in Blackball Mine, La Salle County, these bats were hanging singly or in small groups of two to five, and often have crowded themselves into old drill holes or crevices. In this mine, big browns seem to prefer the drier parts even though these are not in the best insulated parts of the mine. If present in a cave or mine, they usually are near its entrances.

Habits

Big brown bats fly a steady, nearly straight course under usual conditions. They do not migrate great distances, but rather from winter roosts to summering quarters. This is only a few miles in most cases. Davis et al. (1968) in reviewing seasonal movements of these bats reported that most flights were less than 30 miles, although a few are more than this and can be up to nearly 150 miles.

Maternity or nursery colonies consisting of females and young may sometimes be invaded by a few adult

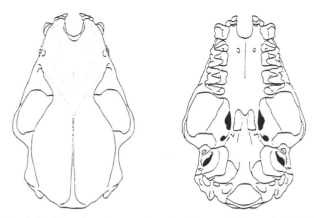

Fig. 8.38. *Eptesicus fuscus,* dorsal and ventral views of skull. Vic. Kingman, Mohave Co., Arizona, 33573 UI. Male, 18.5 mm greatest length.

males. As the young animals in the colony mature, more adult males may take up roosts near the group.

Because big brown bats can tolerate colder weather than other bats in Illinois, sizeable numbers of these hardy individuals have been found in buildings on the campus of the University of Illinois, Urbana-Champaign, during the coldest parts of the year. Some of these were hanging on walls, others were flying around. In 1963, a banded big brown escaped from a laboratory on the campus sometime between November 24 and December 1. On December 31, the bat was found alive about one-eighth mile away, under some four inches of leaves in temperatures of 3°F. During the night, the temperature had dropped to 0°F. The bat squeaked and moved as soon as it was uncovered.

Squeaking among young bats in a maternity colony is important because it gives a mother, returning to the colony, a chance to locate her young, even if they have fallen from their perch (Davis et al., 1968). Such squeaking can be heard for a distance of more than 300 feet and may aid a person in locating a maternity colony.

Food

Big brown bats feed on a variety of insects and they usually find enough to fill their stomachs within one hour (Davis et al., 1968). In Indiana, 56.5 percent of the diet of 184 big brown bats consisted of carabid beetles, scarab beetles, chrysomelids, stinkbugs, and ants. The remainder of the food was a great variety that included assassin bugs, leafhoppers, crane flies, and midges (Whitaker, 1972a). Of 178 stomachs of big brown bats taken November through March in Indiana, none contained food items although many of these bats had been flying around.

Reproduction

Copulation occurs in the fall, sometimes during the winter, and also in the spring. Ovulation occurs in early April. Newborn appear in late May and early June. In Kansas, the median parturition date was June 5 (Kunz, 1974), and two is the usual number of newborn. The young grow rapidly and Kunz (1974) showed that by two months of age they had attained 90 percent or more of adult size in nearly all measurements.

Lactation lasts for about 40 days. By late June and early July, young are beginning to fly. Fig. 8.39 graphically shows the relationships of pregnancy, parturition, and lactation in big brown bats in Kansas (Kunz, 1974).

Females congregate in maternity colonies two or three weeks before young are born. Many of these maternity colonies are in hot attics or lofts. Mothers leave their young hanging in the roost while they forage and then seek out their own when they return. Numerous maternity colonies are known throughout Illinois. Some colonies are shared with little brown myotis.

Miscellaneous

A big brown bat became entangled in the burrs of a burdock plant at the entrance to Blackball Mine, La Salle County. The bat was discovered alive on October 17 (Walley, Southern, and Zar, 1969). A big brown bat was entrapped in a cockroach trap consisting of a sticky material that was set on the floor in a laboratory of the Natural History Building, University of Illinois, on August 15, 1983. This bat must have crawled under the door or around some wall-pipes to get into the room. It may have become hungry, sought food on the floor, and been attracted by the roach trap. Once there, it became so stuck that it could not escape.

Variation

Several subspecies of *E. fuscus* are recognized, but all populations in Illinois are referred to as *E. f. fuscus.*

Eptesicus fuscus fuscus (Palisot de Beauvois)

1796. *Vespertilio fuscus* Palisot de Beauvois, Cat. Raisonné du mus de Mr. C. W. Peale, Phila., p. 18. Type from Philadelphia, Pennsylvania.
1900. *Eptesicus fuscus,* Mehely, Monogr. chiropterorum Hungariae, pp. 206, 338.

Range. Throughout the state (Map 8.16).
Diagnosis and Comparisons. A subspecies of *E. fuscus* of dark coloration and large size, externally and cranially. Long and Severson (1969) have reviewed the variation in color and length of the skull of eastern and mid–United States populations and have compared these with *E. f. pallidus* to the west.
Remarks. Specimens from northern and those from southern Illinois (Table 8.11) are inseparable on external and cranial measurements.

Records of occurrence. SPECIMENS EXAMINED, 520.
Jo Daviess Co.: [1] Little Princess Mine [SW of Galena], 1 (UI),

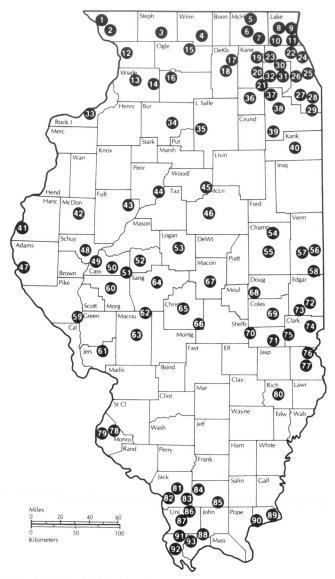

Map 8.16. Distribution of the big brown bat, *Eptesicus fuscus*. The subspecies is *E. f. fuscus*. The winter range is restricted to places of hibernation. Numbers are referenced in *Records of occurrence*. The distribution of the species in the United States is shaded.

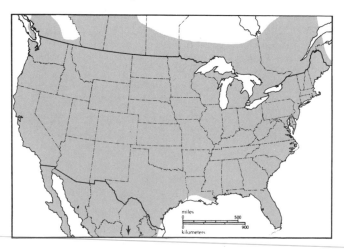

[2] 8 mi SE Galena, 3 (ISM), 2 (NHS). **Stephenson Co.:** [3] Freeport, 13 (UI). **Winnebago Co.:** [4] Rockford, 24 (UI). **McHenry Co.:** [5] Hebron, 1 (UI); [6] Woodstock, 8 (UI); [7] Crystal Lake, 1 (UI). **Lake Co.:** [8] Grayslake, 1 (UI); [9a] Waukegan, 5 (UI); [9b] North Chicago, 3 (UI); [9c] Downey, 1 (UI); [10] Lake Zurich, 1 (UI); [11a] Ft. Sheridan, 1 (UI); [11b] Lincolnshire, 2 (UI); no specific locality [not plotted], 11 (UI). **Carroll Co.:** [12a] Savanna, 1 (UI); [12b] 2 mi W Mt. Carroll, Smith's Cave, 2 (SRL), 1 (UI); [12c] Mt. Carroll Twp., 1 (NHS). **Whiteside Co.:** [13] Morrison, 1 (UI); [14a] Sterling, 3 (UI); [14b] Rock Falls, 1 (UI). **Ogle Co.:** [15] 15 mi SW Rockford, Byron, 1 (FM). **Lee Co.:** [16] Dixon, 1 (UI).. **De Kalb Co.:** [17] Sycamore, 3 (UI); [18] De Kalb, 1 (NIU), 6 (UI). **Kane Co.:** [19] Elgin, 4 (UI); [20a] St. Charles, 2 (UI); [20b] Geneva, 6 (UI); [21] Aurora, 1 (FM), 1 (UI). **Cook Co.:** [22a] Wheeling, 1 (UI); [22b] Des Plaines, 2 (UI); [23a] Elgin, 1 (UI); [23b] Streamwood, 1 (UI); [24a] Northfield, 2 (UI); [24b] Glenview, 1 (UI); [24c] Morton Grove, 1 (UI); [24d] Evanston, 22 (UI); [24e] Skokie, 9 (UI); [24f] Lincolnwood, 2 (UI); [24g] Norridge, 1 (UI); [25] Chicago, 2 (FM), 9 (UI); [26a] Elmwood Park, 1 (UI); [26b] River Forest, 2 (UI); [26c] Maywood, 2 (UI); [26d] Oak Park, 1 (FM), 10 (UI); [26e] Berwyn, 2 (UI); [26f] Riverside, 3 (UI); [26g] Brookfield, 1 (UI); [26h] La Grange, 3 (UI); [26i] Western Springs, 3 (UI); [27a] Oak Lawn, 1 (UI); [27b] Chicago Ridge, 5 (UI); [27c] Ridgeland, 1 (UI); [27d] Ridgeland Park, 1 (UI); [27e] Palos Park, 3 (UI); [27f] Alsip, 1 (UI); [27g] Orland Park, 5 (UI); [28a] Blue Island, 3 (UI); [28b] Harvey, 2 (UI); [29a] Homewood, 1 (UI); [29b] Chicago Heights, 2 (UI); [29c] Park Forest, 2 (UI); no specific locality, 13 (UI).

Du Page Co.: [30] Keeneyville, 1 (UI); [31] Lombard, 1 (UI); [32a] West Chicago, 1 (UI); [32b] Wheaton, 1 (UI); no specific locality [not plotted], 5 (UI). **Rock Island Co.:** [33a] Rock Island, 4 (UI); [33b] Milan, 1 (UI). **Bureau Co.:** [34] Princeton, 1 (UI). **La Salle Co.:** [35a] Peru, 6 (FM); [35b] La Salle, 1 (UI); [35c] near La Salle, 2 (FM); [35d] 2 mi E Peru, 1 (ISU); [35e] 1¾ mi W Utica, N Blackball Mine, 3 (NIU); [35f] Blackball Mine, 1¾ mi W Utica, 23 (UI); [35g] 4 mi E La Salle, 1 (NHS); [35h] Oglesby, 1 (UI). **Kendall Co.:** [36] Yorkville, 1 (UI). **Will Co.:** [37] Wheatland Twp., 2 (FM); [38] Joliet, 6 (UI); [39] Wilmington, 1 (UI). **Kankakee Co.:** [40a] Bradley, 1 (UI); [40b] Kankakee, 1 (UI). **McDonough Co.:** [42] Macomb, 1 (UI). **Fulton Co.:** [43] Canton, 15 (UI), 1 (NHS). **Peoria Co.:** [44] Peoria, 12 (UI). **Woodford Co.:** [45] El Paso, 1 (UI). **McLean Co.:** [46a] Normal, 1 (UI), 2 (ISU); [46b] Bloomington, 1 (UI). **Adams Co.:** [47] Quincy, 50 (UI), l (NHS), 1 (UI). **Schuyler Co.:** [48] Rushville, 1 (UI). **Cass Co.:** [49] Beardstown, 2 (UI); [50] Virginia, 1 (UI); [51] Ashland, 1 (UI). **Menard Co.:** [52] Petersburg, 1 (UI). **Logan Co.:** [53] Lincoln, 1 (UI). **Champaign Co.:** [54] Rantoul, Chanute AFB, 1 (UI); [55a] 2 mi NE Urbana, 2 (NHS); [55b] Champaign, 2 (UI), 3 (NHS); [55c] Urbana, 1 (US), 4 (UI), 3 (NHS). **Vermilion Co.:** [56] Danville, 11 (UI); [57] Oakwood, 1 (UI); [58] Ridge Farm, 1 (UI). **Pike Co.:** [59a] Pearl, 1 (UI); [59b] Limestone Mine, Pearl, 1 (UI); [59c] 2 mi SW Pearl, Pearl Cave, 1 (ISM). **Morgan Co.:** [60] Jacksonville, 1 (UI). **Jersey Co.:** [61] Jerseyville, 1 (UI). **Macoupin Co.:** [62] Virden, 1 (UI); [63] Carlinville, 1 (UI).

Sangamon Co.: [64a] 1 mi N Springfield, 1 (ISM); [64b] Springfield, 3 (UI), 3 (ISM). **Christian Co.:** [65] Taylorville, 1 (UI); [66] Pana, 2 (UI). **Macon Co.:** [67a] Decatur, 2 (UI); [67b] Wheatland Twp., 1 (UI). **Douglas Co.:** [68] Chesterville, 1 (NHS). **Coles Co.:** [69] Charleston, 1 (UI). **Cumberland Co.:** [70] Neoga,

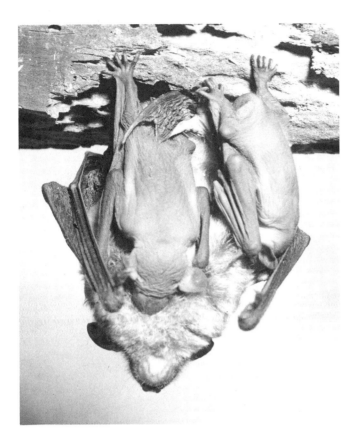

Fig. 8.39. Female big brown bat, *Eptesicus fuscus,* with two attached, nursing young. Note that the young are nearly hairless. Photograph by W. W. Goodpaster.

1 (NHS); [71] Greenup, 1 (UI). **Edgar Co.:** [72] Paris, 3 (UI); [73] Grandview Twp., 1 (UI). **Clark Co.:** [74] Marshall, 2 (UI); [75] Casey, 1 (UI). **Crawford Co.:** [76] Hutsonville, 1 (UI); [77] Robinson, 2 (UI). **Monroe Co.:** [78] Waterloo, 1 (UI); [79] 1 mi NE Valmeyer, 1 (NHS). **Jackson Co.:** [81] Murphysboro, 8 (UI); [82] 3 mi SSE Gorham, 1 (SRL); [83a] Carbondale, 7 (SRL), 3 (SIC), 19 (UI); [83b] Sandstone Cave, Giant City State Park, 1 (UI). **Williamson Co.:** [84] Carterville, 1 (UI); [85] Creal Springs, 1 (UI). **Union Co.:** [86a] 7 mi NE Cobden, 2 (NHS); [86b] Guthrie Cave, 2 (NHS); [86c] [near] Cobden, Rich's Cave, 1 (SRL); [87] Jonesboro, 3 (UI); Mine 7 [location uncertain, not plotted], 1 (SIC). **Johnson Co.:** [88] White Hill Rock Quarry, 1 (SIC). **Hardin Co.:** [89a] 2½ mi NW Cave in Rock, 2 (UI); [89b] Cave in Rock, 1 (ISM); [90b] 2¼ NE Rosiclare, Griffith Cave, 1 (SRL); [90c] ½ mi NE Rosiclare, 1 (SRL); [90d] Rosiclare, 1 (UI). **Alexander Co.:** [91a] 3½ mi NW Elco, 1 (NHS), 1 (ISM); [91b] 1½ mi NW Elco, 1 (SRL); [91d] 2½ mi WNW Elco, 1 (SRL); [91e] 4 mi W Elco, 1 (ISU); [91f] 2 mi W Elco, 2 (UI); [91g] abandoned mine nr. Elco, 1 (UI); Mine 5 [location uncertain, not plotted], 1 (SIC); Mine 4 [location uncertain, not plotted], 1 (SIC). **Pulaski Co.:** [93] Ullin, 1 (UI).

Additional records. **Hancock Co.:** [41] Warsaw, (Necker and Hatfield, 1941:45). **Richland Co.:** [80] no specific locality, (Necker and Hatfield, 1941:45). **Jackson Co.:** [83a] Carbondale, 13 (FS). **Hardin Co.:** [90a] 2½ mi N Rosiclare, 1 (FS). **Alexander Co.:** [91c] 1½ mi NW Elco, Old Wagon Mine, 1 (FS); [92] 1 mi NE Olive Branch, 1 (FS).

Lasiurus, Hairy-tailed bats

Diagnosis. Vespertilionid bats of medium to large size in which the tail membrane is well furred on the dorsal surface; ears are short and rounded; color of dorsum either reddish, yellowish, or a frosted brownish; skull relatively short and broad, single upper incisor of large size, first upper premolar absent or, if present, peg-like; width of palate at emarginations greater than length.

Dentition. 1/3, 1/1, 2/2, 3/3 in Illinois *Lasiurus.*

Comparison. Bats of the genus *Lasiurus* differ from all other Illinois genera in the well-furred, dorsal surface of the tail membrane, the short, rounded ears that barely stand above the fur; the single, small tooth, behind the upper canine, which is squeezed lingually.

Secondary sexual variation. In a sample of 19 *Lasiurus borealis* from east central Illinois (Table 8.11, p. 118), females average larger than males in 11 of 16 measurements but are significantly larger in only 6 measurements.

Remarks. Several species of *Lasiurus* are present in the New World. Recently, these bats have been referred to by the earlier name *Nycteris* (Hall, 1981:219). In 1913, the International Commission on Zoological Nomenclature took action requiring that the name *Lasiurus* be applied to these bats, but E. R. Hall believes that such action by the Commission will result in instability in nomenclature; others feel that making a change more than 70 years after the use of *Lasiurus* was approved would result in even greater instability. The name *Lasiurus* is employed here.

Lasiurus borealis, Red bat

Range. Throughout the state except during the winter; probably absent during winter, although some individuals may hibernate in central or southern Illinois.

Diagnosis. A lasiurine bat of reddish color, including reddish hairs on dorsum of tail membrane, anterior part of shoulder with buffy white patch, plus other external features of *Lasiurus;* skull weak and auditory bullae small, plus other cranial features as described under *Lasiurus.*

Color. Dorsum brick red to rusty red, but females less brightly colored than males; venter slightly lighter; underside of wing has patch of hair on forearm above wrist.

Comparisons. Lasiurus borealis differs from *L. cinereus* in being reddish in color and without a conspicuous frosting of white, and being smaller both externally and cranially; forearm length less than 45 mm rather than more than 50 mm; toothrow length (canine to M³) 5.0 mm or less, rather than 6.0 mm or more.

L. borealis differs from other species of Illinois bats as detailed in *Comparisons* under the genus *Lasiurus* above.

Chromosomes. Diploid number 28, FN = 50; seven pairs of large metacentrics-submetacentrics, three medium-sized metacentrics, two small metacentrics, one small acrocentric.

Habitat

Red bats are tree dwellers and rarely will be found in caves or attics. It has been said that if red bats enter caves, they have a good chance of getting lost therein. They not only rest and roost in trees, but also in shrubs, bushes, and weeds. They may hang from the petiole of a leaf or from a twig or branch. Often they are where the leaves and branches are thick and provide shelter and shade.

Red bats tend to use the same territory repeatedly, as evidenced by a few cases where individuals could be recognized night after night in the same area and flight pattern. These bats forage at different heights above the ground, probably depending on the availability of food and whether they are foraging or flying from one place to another irrespective of foraging.

At St. Joseph, Champaign County, during mid-August days red bats roosted on the underside of a large sunflower leaf about seven feet above ground. Although several sunflower plants were available and seemingly offered just as good retreats, the bats always hung under the same leaf. Two (an adult and juvenile male) were present on August 12, one female on August 14, none on August 15, one male on August 16, none on August 17, and one male on August 18 (Downes, 1964:143).

Red bats are probably the most common bat in many places in Illinois in the summer. In the southern part of the state, Layne (1958a) concluded it was the most common during the warmer months. In Pike County, west central Illinois, netting of bats by Gardner and Gardner (1980) showed that red bats were captured the most frequently.

We know of no records of capture of red bats in Illinois for December, January, and February. We have only four records after November 15 and two records

Table 8.11. External and cranial measurements (in mm) of eight species of bats in Illinois. Mean, minimum and maximum, and one standard deviation are given for most. Individual measurements are indicated where catalogue numbers are given. Superscripts indicate sample less than N.

Species and subspecies	Locality	N	Total length	Tail length	Body length	Hind-foot length	Ear length
Lasionycteris noctivagans	Champaign, Cook, Fulton cos.	10	107.5[6] 91-115 8.48	42.3 38-46 2.54	65.2	10.0[6] 9-11 0.63	16.3[6] 16-17 0.52
Pipistrellus subflavus subflavus	LaSalle Co.	17	88.2 83-92 2.73	40.1 38-42 1.43	48.1	9.9 9-10 0.24	13.7 13-15 0.69
" " "	Alexander, Hardin, Saline, Union, Williamson cos.	14	81.4 73-95 4.94	35.7 30-43 3.43	45.7	8.3 7-10 0.99	12.7 10-15 1.60
Eptesicus fuscus fuscus	LaSalle, Carroll, Champaign cos.	13	115.5 100-130 9.15	43.1 35-52 6.08	72.4	11.1[10] 9-13 1.45	16.4 14-19 1.80
" " "	Alexander, Hardin, Jackson cos.	8	115.8 107-122 5.34	43.6 39-50 4.10	72.2	10.4 8-12 1.51	17.1 16-18 0.83
Lasiurus borealis borealis	Champaign, Vermilion cos.	10 ♂	104.5 95-109 4.99	47.0 44-49 1.87	57.5	8.8 8-10 0.79	11.6 8-13 1.65
" " "	Champaign, Vermilion cos.	9 ♀	105.8 85-115 9.48	45.8 36-51 5.47	60.0	8.8 8-10 0.67	12.0 9-14 1.58
Lasiurus cinereus cinereus	Champaign Co.	839 ♀	135	61	74	11	17
	"	26298 ♀	140	63	77	12	19
	Douglas Co.	26784 ♀	142	60	82	12	17
Nycticeius humeralis humeralis	Bond, Champaign cos.	13 ♀	100.1 95-105 2.72	38.5 32-42 2.5	61.6	9.0 8.5-10 0.32	14.1 13-15 0.64
Plecotus rafinesquii rafinesquii	Alexander Co.	59008 ♂	99	50	45	11	31
	Johnson Co.	59252 ♂	—	—	—	—	—
Tadarida brasiliensis mexicana	DeKalb Co.	769 NIU	84	32.5	51.5	8	16

for March. Red bats are known in Illinois mainly from March until mid-November. Where they are during late November through March is unclear, although it is known that this species can withstand cold temperatures. *Lasiurus borealis* is better furred than most other species, especially on the tail membrane. Also, in subfreezing temperatures these bats raise their metabolic rate just enough to be above the critical lower limit, which is about 23°F (Reite and Davis, 1966). The presence of red bats during cold weather is documented by the records provided by Davis and Lidicker (1956). At a woods 3 mi ENE Urbana, Champaign County, six red bats were flying on October 22, although the temperature had been as low as 38°F four nights earlier; one red bat was flying on November 8, although seven days earlier the thermometer read 29°F.

The earliest spring record for Illinois is March 12 (southern Illinois, Layne, 1958a), and March 21 (Natural Bridge, near Pomona, Jackson County). In Indiana, Mumford and Whitaker (1982) reported that they have specimen records for every month except January and February, and sight records for those two months. In Iowa, Bowles (1975) noted that the earliest spring record was April 21 and the latest fall record was October 6.

We know of no hibernating red bats in Illinois, but records of occurrence suggest they may indeed winter over.

Habits

Red bats are solitary, although they may migrate in groups. Barbour and Davis (1969:132) describe their flight when they first emerge as "high in the air where they flutter in slow erratic flight as if in play." In less than a half hour this becomes a straight or widely arced flight, except when pursuit of an insect occasions a deviation in flight pattern.

Red bats are early flyers. In central Iowa, the peak of the foraging was the first hour after sunset, based on

Forearm length	Greatest length	Zygomatic breadth	Mastoid breadth	Braincase breadth	Inter-orbital breadth	Depth skull	Rostral br. betw. infra-orbital f.	C-M³ length	Pm⁴-M³ length	Breadth across M³-M³
41.0	16.6	10.2	8.8	7.8	4.2	6.8[7]	6.3	5.8	4.5	6.7
39.0-42.3	16.05-17.0	9.7-10.65	8.5-9.1	7.6-8.1	4.0-4.35	6.5-6.9	5.9-6.7	5.6-6.0	4.3-4.65	6.45-7.0
1.09	0.31	0.29	0.19	0.16	0.14	0.15	0.23	0.16	0.10	0.16
33.7	13.0	7.9	7.1	6.6	3.5	6.1	4.1	4.2	3.2	5.2
32.6-35.2	12.65-13.5	7.6-8.2	6.8-7.5	6.2-6.85	3.3-3.75	5.7-6.35	3.8-4.3	4.0-4.4	3.1-3.4	5.0-5.5
0.69	0.24	0.16	0.16	0.15	0.13	0.10	0.13	0.09	0.08	0.13
33.4	13.1	7.9	7.1	6.6	3.5	6.0	4.2	4.3	3.3	5.2
32.1-34.4	12.5-13.4	7.5-8.6	6.75-7.4	6.4-6.8	3.4-3.8	5.7-6.15	4.0-4.55	4.05-4.5	3.1-3.35	4.85-5.4
0.73	0.27	0.29	0.19	0.11	0.10	0.18	0.17	0.14	0.07	0.15
46.7	20.0	12.7	10.2	8.8	4.3	7.6	6.2	7.2	5.6	8.1
44.5-48.7	19.5-20.7	12.0-13.4	9.5-10.65	8.4-9.2	4.0-4.5	6.8-7.9	5.9-6.6	6.9-7.5	5.4-5.8	7.45-8.6
1.35	0.40	0.38	0.30	0.24	0.15	0.30	0.21	0.16	0.17	0.30
47.6	19.9	13.1	10.1	8.9	4.2	7.4	6.0	7.2	5.6	8.0
45.6-49.9	19.4-20.7	12.4-13.6	9.8-10.5	8.65-9.2	4.0-4.3	7.0-7.7	5.85-6.1	7.1-7.3	5.5-5.8	7.8-8.5
1.68	0.51	0.39	0.22	0.18	0.11	0.21	0.09	0.08	0.10	0.23
38.6	13.9	9.5	7.9	7.3	4.3	7.4	5.3	4.4	3.5	6.1
36.3-41.1	13.45-14.3	9.1-10.4	7.6-8.3	6.95-7.8	4.1-4.5	6.9-7.7	5.0-5.65	4.1-4.6	3.3-3.65	5.75-6.55
1.35	0.30	0.35	0.21	0.23	0.12	0.27	0.20	0.17	0.12	0.24
39.9	14.4	9.8	8.1	7.3	4.1	7.3	5.7	4.8	3.8	6.5
37.8-41.5	13.1-14.8	8.6-10.35	7.65-8.4	6.9-7.5	4.0-4.4	6.1-7.7	5.1-6.0	4.5-4.95	3.5-4.0	6.0-6.95
1.13	0.56	0.53	0.25	0.18	0.11	0.48	0.28	0.17	0.17	0.29
55.1	18.5	12.85	10.65	9.2	5.1	9.5	8.0	6.45	5.2	8.7
55.9	18.1	12.45	10.0	9.2	4.8	8.6	7.6	6.3	4.9	8.65
57.4	19.0	12.9	10.6	9.4	5.1	9.7	8.1	6.3	5.0	8.7
36.2	14.8	10.1	8.5	7.4	4.1	6.4[10]	5.1	5.3	4.1	6.5
34.8-37.4	14.4-15.1	9.8-10.4	8.1-9.6	7.2-7.7	3.9-4.5	6.2-6.6	4.8-5.35	5.15-5.4	3.95-4.3	6.2-6.85
0.73	0.24	0.18	0.39	0.14	0.17	0.14	0.17	0.08	0.10	0.22
42.8	16.7	—	19.5	7.3	3.65	7.8	4.8	5.45	4.1	6.2
—	17.3	—	—	7.7	3.7	7.45	4.8	5.25	3.95	6.1
—	—	10.0	9.5	8.3	4.0	6.1	4.2	6.1	4.9	6.9

Fig. 8.40A. Female and three young, nearly adult-size, red bats, *Lasiurus borealis,* hanging in a tree. (From Hoffmeister and Mohr, 1957. Photograph by J. C. Allen and Son, Lafayette, Indiana)

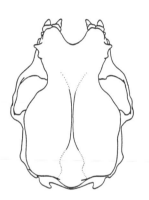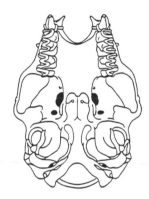

Fig. 8.40B. *Lasiurus borealis,* dorsal and ventral views of skull. Graham Mts., Graham Co., Arizona, 4842 UI. Female, 14.0 mm greatest length.

124 observations, and the next highest was the second hour after sunset (Kunz, 1973). On some occasions, red bats are flying in the afternoon before the sun has set. Either these bats are foraging early or they have been disturbed and have left their roosting place.

Nursing females that have been grounded with attached young frequently are unable to get airborne. This may be due in part to the combined weight of the young and an emaciated condition of the mother. The Museum of Natural History has received several adult females that have three or four young, all of which had been grounded and were discovered by persons. Sometimes the young collectively may weigh as much as nine grams, whereas the mother may weigh only 12 grams. Perhaps the almost pugnacious behavior of adult bats, in making much noise, threatening to attack, and trying to bite, is their attempt to protect themselves when they are grounded.

Food

Red bats feed extensively on moths, cercopids, flying ants, leafhoppers, and beetles. Probably many of the kinds of insects attracted by night-lights are preyed upon by red bats, which are ordinarily seen feeding at such sites. Red bats were attracted to corn cribs in Virginia to prey on emerging grain moths (Lewis, 1940). In 128 red bats in Indiana, Whitaker (1972a) found that the volume of food was 26.2 percent Lepidoptera (moths, butterflies), 28.1 percent Coleoptera (various beetles), and included leafhoppers, ants, various flies, and other insects in smaller numbers.

Reproduction

Red bats copulate in the fall and perhaps again in the spring. There is some evidence that bats may copulate while in flight (Murphy and Nichols, 1913). Fertilization occurs in the spring and the gestation period is thought to be 80 to 90 days. Females give birth to two, three, or four—rarely five—young. In Illinois, young are born in the last week of May or in June. In Indiana, Mumford and Whitaker (1982) examined 33 red bats with young, and the mean was 3.2 (1–4). Young are left at the roost site while the mother forages for food. During the day, the young support themselves by attaching to the mother and at the same time attaching to adjacent vegetation. Barbour and Davis (1969) think that those females flying with their young are most likely transporting them to a new place.

Miscellaneous

Red bats are preyed upon or harassed by blue jays. Two of these bats are known to have been attacked by these birds (Hoffmeister and Downes, 1964) and another was attached by its teeth to the head of a jay, perhaps in defense from an attack (Hoffmeister and Mohr, 1957). In Piper City, Ford County, 15 red bats were entrapped in a heavily oiled road (Koestner, 1942). Whether the bats mistook the oil for water or sought insects caught in the oil is not certain.

Variation

All red bats east of the Rocky Mountains are referred to the subspecies *L. b. borealis.*

Lasiurus borealis borealis (Muller)

1776. *Vespertilio borealis* Muller, Des Ritters Carl von Linne . . . , suppl. 20. Type from New York.
1897. *Lasiurus borealis,* Miller, N. Amer. Fauna, 13:105.

Range. As given for the species (p. 117 and Map 8.17).
Diagnosis and Comparison. A reddish subspecies that is washed with white; ears and membranes with reddish markings; lacrimal ridge developed. *L. b. borealis* differs

from the western subspecies *L. b. teliotis* in its larger size. These data are from Handley (1960:472).

Remarks. The eastern race is to be found from southern Canada to northeastern Mexico.

Records of occurrence. SPECIMENS EXAMINED, 610.
Winnebago Co.: [1] Rockford, 7 (UI). **McHenry Co.:** [2] Hebron, 1 (UI); [3] Spring Grove, 1 (UI); [4] McHenry, 1 (UI); [5] Woodstock, 3 (UI). **Lake Co.:** [6a] Waukegan, 13 (UI); [6b] Great Lakes, 2 (UI); [7] Wauconda, 1 (UI); [8a] Lake Forest, 1 (FM), 2 (UI); [8b] Ft. Sheridan, 1 (UI); [8c] Highland Park, 1 (FM), 2 (UI); [8d] Deerfield, 1 (UI); no specific locality [not plotted], 23 (UI). **Whiteside Co.:** [9] Sterling, 1 (UI). **Lee Co.:** [10] Sublette, 1 (FM). **De Kalb Co.:** [11] De Kalb, 3 (NIU), 1 (UI); [12] Sandwich, 5 (UI). **Kane Co.:** [13] Dundee, 2 (UI); [14] Elgin, 1 (US), 1 (UI); [15] Aurora, 1 (UI).

Cook Co.: [16a] Barrington, 1 (UI); [16b] Hoffman Estates, 1 (UI); [17a] Buffalo Grove, 1 (UI); [17b] Palatine, 2 (UI); [17c] Prospect Heights, 1 (UI); [17d] Arlington Heights, 7 (UI); [17e] Rolling Meadows, 1 (UI); [17f] Mt. Prospect, 7 (UI); [18a] Glencoe, 6 (UI); [18b] Northbrook, 4 (UI); [18c] Winnetka, 5 (UI); [18d] West Northfield, 1 (US); [18e] Northfield, 3 (UI); [18f] Kenilworth, 3 (UI); [18g] Wilmette, 30 (UI); [18h] Glenview, 6 (UI); [18i] Des Plaines, 3 (UI); [18j] Morton Grove, 5 (UI); [18k] Evanston, 1 (CAS), 87 (UI); [18l] Skokie, 7 (UI); [18m] Park Ridge, 2 (UI); [18n] Niles, 1 (FM), 1 (UI); [19a] Schiller Park, 1 (UI); [19b] Franklin Park, 1 (UI); [19c] Elmwood Park, 1 (UI); [19d] Stone Park, 1 (UI); [19e] River Forest, 3 (UI); [19f] Bellwood, 1 (UI); [19g] Maywood, 1 (FM), 5 (UI); [19h] Oak Park, 5 (UI); [19i] Broadview, 1 (UI); [19j] Berwyn, 1 (UI); [19k] Brookfield, 2 (UI); [19l] La Grange Park, 1 (UI); [20a] Chicago, 6 (CAS), 25 (FM), 4 (UI); [20b] McCormick Place, Chicago, 2 (UI); [21a] Forest View, 1 (UI); [21b] Stickney Twp., 1 (UI); [21c] Bridgeview, 1 (UI); [21d] Willow Springs, 1 (FM), 1 (UI); [21e] Oak Lawn, 5 (UI); [21f] Chicago Ridge, 10 (UI); [21g] Ridgeland Park, 1 (UI); [22] Lemont, 1 (UI); [23a] Alsip, 1 (UI); [23b] Blue Island, 1 (UI); [23c] Oak Forest, 1 (UI); [23d] Markham, 1 (UI); [23e] Tinley Park, 4 (UI); [24a] Calumet City, 1 (UI); [24b] Hazel Crest, 1 (UI); [24c] Lansing, 1 (UI); [24d] Glenwood, 1 (UI); Glendale Heights [location], 1 (UI); no specific locality [not plotted], 15 (UI).

Du Page Co.: [25a] Elmhurst, 1 (UI); [25b] Lombard, 1 (UI); [26a] West Chicago, 9 (UI); [26b] Wheaton, 3 (UI); [27] Hinsdale, 1 (UI); [28] Naperville, 1 (CAS); no specific locality [not plotted], 9 (UI). **La Salle Co.:** [29] Ottawa, 2 (UI). **Grundy Co.:** [30] Morris, 1 (UI). **Will Co.:** [31] Romeoville, 1 (UI); [32] Joliet, 2 (UI); [33] Peotone, 1 (UI). **Henderson Co.:** [34] opposite Burlington, Iowa, 3 (US). **Knox Co.:** [36] Maquon, 1 (UI). **Fulton Co.:** [37] Canton, 1 (UI); [38] Bryant, 2 (UI); no specific locality [not plotted], 1 (UI). **Peoria Co.:** [39] Peoria, 1 (UI). **Tazewell Co.:** [40] Pekin, 1 (UI). **McLean Co.:** [41a] Normal, 2 (ISU). **Adams Co.:** [43] Quincy, 23 (UI); no specific locality [not plotted], 1 (UI). **Mason Co.:** [44] Forest City, 1 (UI); [45] Havana, 1 (UI). **Logan Co.:** [46] Lincoln 2, (UI). **Champaign Co.:** [47] Rantoul, 2 (UI); [48a] 3 mi NE Mahomet, 1 (UI); [48b] Mahomet, 1 (NHS); [48c] 1 mi SE Mahomet, 5 (UI); [49a] 3 mi ENE Urbana, Brownfield Woods, 3 (UI); [49b] 5 mi ENE Urbana, Trelease Woods, 1 (UI); [49c] St. Joseph, 1 (NHS), 1 (UI); [50a] 2 mi NE Urbana, 1 (NHS); [50b] 3½ mi W Champaign, 1 (UI); [50c] Champaign, 1 (NHS), 9 (UI); [50d] Urbana, 4 (NHS), 13 (UI); [50e]

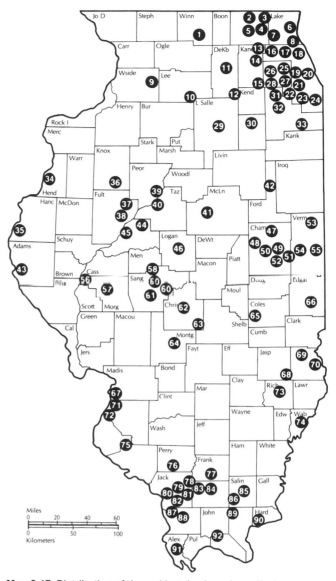

Map 8.17. Distribution of the red bat, *Lasiurus borealis,* in summer. Some may overwinter in southern Illinois. The subspecies is *L. b. borealis.* Numbers are referenced in *Records of occurrence.* The distribution of the species in the United States is shaded.

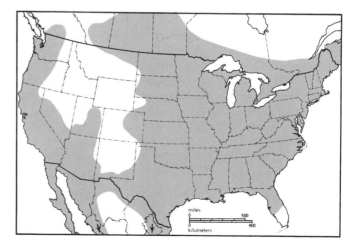

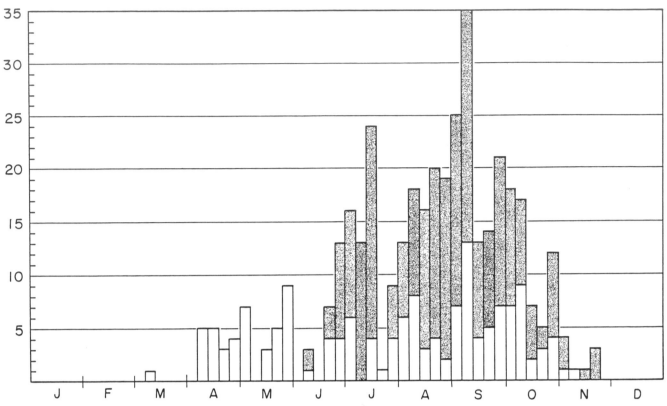

Fig. 8.41. Dates of capture of *Lasiurus borealis* in Illinois during each week of each month. Young of the year are represented by the shaded areas. Young first appear in the second week of June. *Lasiurus borealis* have not been captured between December 1 and April 1 except for one record in southern Illinois on March 12.

2 mi E Urbana, 1 (UI); [50f] UI campus, 1 (UI); [51] 1½ mi N Homer, Salt Fork River, 1 (UI); [52] Sidney, 2 (NHS); no specific locality [not plotted], 1 (UI).

Vermilion Co.: [53] Rossville, 1 (UI); [54] 1 mi E Muncie, 1 (UI); [55] Danville, 5 (UI). **Morgan Co.:** [56] Meredosia, 1 (UI); [57] Jacksonville, 4 (UI). **Sangamon Co.:** [58] Cantrall, 2 (UI); [59] Springfield, 3 (ISM), 17 (UI); [60] Rochester, 10 (ISM); [61] Chatham, 1 (UI). **Christian Co.:** [62] Taylorville, 2 (UI); [63] Pana, 2 (UI). **Montgomery Co.:** [64] Irving, 1 (UI). **Coles Co.:** [65] Mattoon, 1 (UI). **Edgar Co.:** [66] Paris, 1 (UI). **Madison Co.:** [67] Granite City, 1 (SIE). **Jasper Co.:** [68a] Ste. Marie, 1 (UI); [68b] 5 mi SE Ste. Marie, 1 (UI). **Crawford Co.:** [69] Eaton, 1 (UI); [70] Palestine, 2 (UI). **St. Clair Co.:** [71] East St. Louis, 2 (UI); [72] Dupo, 1 (UI). **Wabash Co.:** [74] Mt. Carmel, 1 (US). **Randolph Co.:** [75] Redbud, 1 (UI). **Perry Co.:** [76] Pyatts Striplands, 3 (SRL), 1 (NHS). **Franklin Co.:** [77] West Frankfort, 1 (UI). **Jackson Co.:** [79] Murphysboro, 2 (UI), 1 (SIC); [80] Gorham, 1 (UI); [81] Carbondale, 8 (UI), 3 (SIC), 7 (SRL); [82] Pomona Natural Bridge, 1 (SIC), 1 (SRL). **Williamson Co.:** [83a] Carterville, 1 (UI); [83b] Crab Orchard Lake at Pirate's Cove, 1 (UI); [84a] Johnston City, 1 (UI); [84b] Marion, 2 (UI). **Saline Co.:** [85] Harrisburg, 1 (UI); [86] Carrier Mills, 1 (UI). **Union Co.:** [87a] Pine Hills, near Wolf Lake, 1 (ISM), 1 (NHS), 1 (UI); [87d] Bald Knob, 1 (ISM); [88a] 3 mi SW Cobden, 1 (SIC), 1 (SRL); [88b] Anna, 5 (FM), 1 (UI). **Alexander Co.:** [91] Olive Branch, 1 (US), 3 (FM). **Massac Co.:** [92] 1½ mi SE Foreman, 2 (SRL).

Additional records. **Hancock Co.:** [35] Warsaw, (Necker and Hatfield, 1941:45). **McLean Co.:** [41b] Bloomington, 1 (UM).

Ford Co.: [42] Piper City, (Koestner, 1942:227). **Champaign Co.:** [50c] Champaign, 1 (UM). **Richland Co.:** [73] Olney, (Necker and Hatfield, 1941:45). **Jackson Co.:** [78] De Soto, 2 (FS); [81] Carbondale, 15 (FS); [82] Pomona Natural Bridge, 1 (FS). **Union Co.:** [87b] Pine Hills, 2 (FS); [87c] Aldridge, 2 (FS); [88a] 3 mi SW Cobden, 1 (FS). **Pope Co.:** [89] Bell Smith Springs, 1 (FS). **Hardin Co.:** [90] Rosiclare, (Necker and Hatfield, 1941:45).

Lasiurus cinereus, Hoary bat

Range. Primarily migratory through state in spring and fall, with some females oversummering; generally absent in winter (see discussion following).

Diagnosis. A large lasiurine bat of brownish and blackish color tipped with white producing a frosted or hoary effect, belly area not heavily frosted, plus other external features of *Lasiurus;* forearm long (54 to 60 mm); skull large and broad, auditory bullae large, lower premolar four single-rooted, plus other cranial features of *Lasiurus.*

Color. In addition to the frosted effect, brownish fur extends out on underside of wing nearly to wrist; light-colored fur at base of thumb. Juveniles appear nearly grayish, but still have a frosted appearance.

Comparisons. L. cinereus differs from all other bats in Illinois by characters given above and such other features as total length 130 mm or more, forearm length more than 50 mm; dorsum of tail membrane heavily furred

Fig. 8.42A. Hoary bat, *Lasiurus cinereus*. Note the white-tipped hair on the back and the well-furred tail membrane. (From Hoffmeister and Mohr, 1957. Photograph by Ernest P. Walker, Smithsonian Institution, Washington, D.C.)

and coloration silvery gray; height of skull more than 8.2 mm, rostral breadth 7.4 mm or more.

Chromosomes. Diploid number 28, FN = 50; seven pairs of large metacentrics-submetacentrics, three medium-sized metacentrics, two small metacentrics, one small acrocentric.

Remarks. This bat apparently does not stay year-round in Illinois, although some females are summer residents. Few if any adult males remain over the summer; they move farther northward in their spring migration and farther southward in the fall (see p. 124). We have not observed hoary bats to be abundant anywhere in Illinois during the summer.

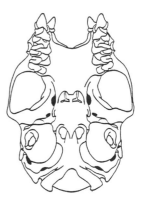

Fig. 8.42B. *Lasiurus cinereus*, dorsal and ventral views of skull. Vic. Portal, Cochise Co., Arizona, 16898 UI. Male, 17.7 mm greatest length.

Habitat

Hoary bats are solitary and usually roost in the foliage of trees or even in cavities in trees. They have been found beneath the eaves of a garage and on the trunk of a tree in Springfield, Sangamon County. Hoary bats will rest in nearly any kind of a tree that provides adequate cover during the daytime. A specimen was taken from a maple tree in a yard in Rantoul, Champaign County. Probably large-leaved trees provide the best shelter.

Habits

When moving from one place to another while not foraging, hoary bats are strong, fast flyers. This type of rapid flight in a relatively straight path is rather distinctive of hoary bats. When they are hunting for food, however, the flight is more leisurely, with soaring and gliding maneuvers.

Although some hoary bats may be flying two to three hours after sunset, the peak of activity is between four and five hours after sunset, according to the analysis of Thomas Kunz (1973) based on 26 observations in central Iowa. In Missouri, these bats were the last vespertilionids to fly (Shump and Shump, 1982).

Hoary bats may break their wings more frequently than other bats. Munyer (1967) says that a bat found on the sidewalk in Springfield on May 3 had a broken wing. One hanging in a tree at Arthur, Douglas County, on October 6 also had a broken wing; however, it may be that these bats, when they are unable to fly, are more conspicuous because of their large size.

Food

Hoary bats are thought to feed rather extensively on moths, but few stomachs have been examined. The largest numbers have been examined by Ross for 139 hoary bats from New Mexico, according to Mumford and Whitaker (1982), and, of these, 132 contained lepidopterans, quite a few ants, but relatively few beetles.

Reproduction

Copulation may occur in the fall, winter, or early spring. In Illinois, young, usually two, are born in late May and early June. A hoary bat taken in Springfield, Sangamon County, gave birth to two young on June 5 (Munyer, 1967). A lactating female was taken in Vermilion County on May 31 (Provost and Kirkpatrick, 1952). A female taken on June 24 in Urbana had two young thought to be two to three weeks old. When flying, females may carry the young until they are about a week old; subsequently they may be left hanging while the mothers forage for food. During the day, the mothers cover the young as they hang in the foliage.

Movements

From mid-April to May, hoary bats migrate northward through Illinois. Some females take up summer residency here, and adult females and their young (both juvenile males and females) are present. In the fall, hoary bats migrate south through Illinois and by November nearly all have moved out of the state. There are relatively few exceptions to this pattern. In Illinois, only four specimens have been recorded from April, the first being a female taken April 8 at Brownfield Woods, Champaign County. In November (14 and 21), only two adult females have been taken. There is also a juvenile male with a date of December 14. This is an Illinois Department of Public Health specimen which may have been taken alive several days or weeks before being killed. Also, this juvenile male may not have been in good physical condition for migrating.

Between May and October, we have records of 62 adult females (only nine adult males), 51 juvenile females, and 44 juvenile males. Thus, it seems that there are few adult males in Illinois during this six-month period.

Segregation of males and females occurs during spring migration. Females move into Illinois earliest. During April and May we have records of 16 adult females. Only one adult male is recorded as being taken in Illinois—on May 11 in Cook County. It should be pointed out, however, that we have only nine records of adult males for the spring, summer, and fall, and these were taken between May 11 and October 15.

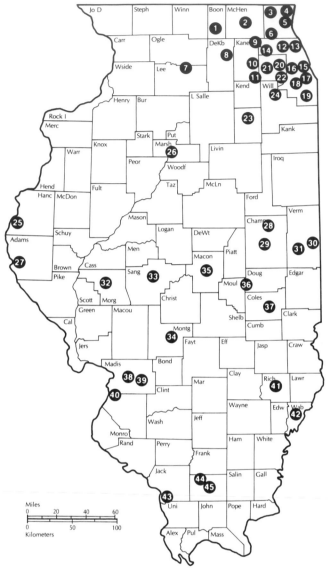

Map 8.18. Distribution of the hoary bat, *Lasiurus cinereus*. Most records are obtained during species migration. The subspecies is *L. c. cinereus*. Numbers are referenced in *Records of occurrence*. The distribution of the species in the United States is shaded.

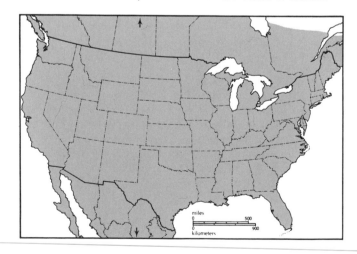

Variation

Three subspecies of *L. cinereus* are known: one in Hawaii, one in South America, and *L. c. cinereus* in much of North America.

Lasiurus cinereus cinereus (Palisot de Beauvois)

1796. *Vespertilio cinereus* (misspelled *linereus*) Palisot de Beauvois, Cat. . . . du mus. de Mr. C. W. Peale, Phila., p. 18. Type from Philadelphia, Pennsylvania.

Range. As given for the species (p. 122 and Map 8.18).

Diagnosis and Comparisons. L. c. cinereus in the United States needs no comparison with other subspecies.

Remarks. This subspecies is known from Keewatin at the north to Guatemala at the south, and from coast to coast.

Records of occurrence. SPECIMENS EXAMINED, 223. **Boone Co.:** [1] Belvidere, 1 (UI). **McHenry Co.:** [2] Woodstock, 2 (UI); no specific locality [not plotted], 2 (UI). **Lake Co.:** [3] Antioch, 2 (UI); [4a] Winthrop Harbor, 1 (UI); [4b] Zion, 8 (UI); [5a] Waukegan, 7 (UI); [5b] Lake Bluff, 1 (UI); [6] Lake Zurich, 1 (UI); no specific locality [not plotted], 7 (UI). **Lee Co.:** [7] Ashton, 1 (UI). **De Kalb Co.:** [8] Sycamore, 1 (UI). **Kane Co.:** [9] Dundee, 2 (UI); [10a] St. Charles, 1 (UI); [10b] Geneva, 8 (UI); [11] Aurora, 1 (UI). **Cook Co.:** [12a] Arlington Heights, 2 (UI); [12b] Rolling Meadows, 2 (UI); [12c] Mount Prospect, 1 (UI); [13a] Glencoe, 3 (UI); [13b] Northbrook, 1 (UI); [13c] Winnetka, 3 (UI); [13d] Northfield, 1 (UI); [13e] Wilmette, 1 (UI); [13f] Glenview, 4 (UI); [13g] Des Plaines, 3 (UI); [13h] Morton Grove, 1 (UI); [13i] Evanston, 18 (UI); [13j] Skokie, 8 (UI); [13k] Park Ridge, 1 (UI); [13l] Lincolnwood, 1 (UI); [14] Streamwood, 1 (UI); [15a] Chicago, 1 (FM), 1 (UI); [15b] Chicago, Field Museum Bldg., 1 (FM); [15c] Cicero, 1 (UI); [16a] River Forest, 1 (UI); [16b] Maywood, 3 (FM), 2 (UI); [16c] Oak Park, 1 (FM), 1 (UI); [16d] La Grange, 2 (UI); [16e] Stickney, 2 (UI); [16f] Western Springs, 1 (UI); [17a] Chicago, Jackson Park, 2 (FM); [17b] Chicago, Hyde Park, 1 (FM); [17c] Evergreen Park, 2 (UI); [18a] Chicago Ridge, 7 (UI); [18b] Ridgeland, 6 (UI); [19a] Harvey, 1 (UI); [19b] Oak Forest, 3 (UI); [19c] South Holland, 1 (UI); [19d] Homewood, 1 (UI); [19c] Flossmoor, 3 (FM); no specific locality [not plotted], 22 (UI).

Du Page Co.: [20a] Elmhurst, 1 (UI); [20b] Lombard, 1 (UI); [21a] West Chicago, 3 (UI); [21b] Wheaton, 1 (CAS), 2 (UI); [22] Hinsdale, 1 (UI). **Grundy Co.:** [23] Morris, 3 (UI). **Will Co.:** [24] Lockport, 1 (UI). **Marshall Co.:** [26] Lacon, 1 (ISU). **Adams Co.:** [27] Quincy, 4 (UI). **Champaign Co.:** [28] Rantoul, 1 (UI); [29b] Urbana, 3 (NHS), 3 (UI). **Vermilion Co.:** [30] Danville, 1 (UI); [31] 2½ mi NE Fairmount, 1 (NHS). **Morgan Co.:** [32] Jacksonville, 1 (UI). **Sangamon Co.:** [33] Springfield, 3 (ISM), 3 (UI); no specific locality [not plotted], 1 (UI). **Montgomery Co.:** [34] Irving, 1 (UI). **Macon Co.:** [35] no specific locality [not plotted], 1 (UI). **Douglas Co.:** [36] Arthur, 1 (UI). **Madison Co.:** [38] Edwardsville, 1 (SIE); [39] Marine, 1 (UI). **St. Clair Co.:** [40] 3 mi E St. Louis, 1 (SIE). **Wabash Co.:** [42] no specific locality, 1 (US). **Jackson Co.:** [43] Grand Tower, 1 (UI). **Williamson Co.:** [44] Herrin, 4 (UI); [45] Marion, 2 (UI).

Additional records. **McHenry Co.:** [2] Woodstock, (Harty, 1981 in litt.). **Cook Co.:** [15a] Chicago, 1 (UM). **Hancock Co.:** [25] Warsaw*, (Necker and Hatfield, 1941:45). **Champaign Co.:** [29a] Brownfield Woods, (Koestner, 1942:227). **Coles Co.:** [37] Charleston, (Cory, 1912:473). **Richland Co.:** [41] Olney, (Necker and Hatfield, 1941:45).

Nycticeius, Evening bats

Diagnosis. A vespertilionid bat of small to medium size, color brownish (like a miniature *Eptesicus*), tragus short, curved, and relatively broad; forearm length 34 to 38 mm; calcar not keeled; skull with no small teeth behind upper canine, skull small but broad and rugose.

Color. Dorsal coloration a dull umber brown, underparts lighter brown, ears and wings blackish.

Dental formula. 1/3, 1/1, 1/2, 3/3.

Comparisons. Nycticeius can be most easily confused with certain species of *Myotis* and with *Eptesicus. Nycticeius* differs from *Myotis* in having only one upper incisor rather than two; no small teeth behind the upper incisor rather than two; a short, curved, broad tragus; zygomatic breadth greater (9.8 mm or more usually) except for *Myotis grisescens;* skull (Fig. 8.43) broader across rostrum (rostral breadth between infraorbital foramina 4.8 mm or more, rather than 4.4 mm or less); diploid number of chromosomes 46 rather than 44.

Nycticeius differs from *Eptesicus* in a shorter forearm (38 mm or less, rather than 44 mm or more); one rather than two upper incisors; greatest length of skull less than 15.5 mm, rather than 19.0 mm or more; diploid number of chromosomes 46 rather than 50.

Remarks. The genus *Nycticeius* is represented by two species in North America, and 12 in the Old World, including Australia.

Nycticeius humeralis, Evening bat

Range. Throughout the state, except in winter when it seems to be absent from Illinois.

Diagnosis. As given for the genus, above.

Comparisons. As given for the genus, above.

Growth. Details of growth in young *Nycticeius humeralis* from Mississippi are given by Clyde Jones (1967). Total and tail lengths reach adult size at about 50 days of age, but the forearm—and probably all parts of the wing—attain this at 30 days. At four weeks of age, the permanent dentition is in place. Jones found that by the 15th day of age, these young bats, when released in the air, opened their wings and glided or parachuted to the floor. At the 19th day, they flew on their own.

Chromosomes. Diploid number, 46; FN = 48; two

---

* Worthen specimen.

pairs of large metacentrics; 20 pairs of medium to small acrocentrics.

Remarks. Nycticeius humeralis is not a common bat in Illinois.

Habitat

Evening bats inhabit buildings and trees and in all likelihood will not be found in caves or mines in Illinois. They are frequently found roosting in attics or in hollow walls. Sometimes they find their ways within the occupied parts of houses or buildings and thus attract attention and soon are collected. They forage among the nearby trees. For example, in Carbondale, they were observed flying along the edge of a mature woods or sometimes within clearings in the woods (Layne, 1958a). They also may have been foraging within the woods but could not be seen there. On August 9, a male was netted along a drainage ditch in Union County near riparian habitat consisting of cottonwoods, pin oaks, sycamores, and a variety of other trees (Brack, 1979). Along McKee Creek, Pike County, six evening bats were netted on July 18. Two were post-lactating females, three were juveniles, and one was an adult male (Gardner and Gardner, 1980). The most abundant tree along the creek is the silver maple, with cottonwoods, willows, and sycamores also present.

There are no known records of hibernating evening bats in Illinois.

Since evening bats often occupy attics of houses, one would guess that they frequently might come into contact with humans. If the bats were captured and killed, they might be submitted to the public health departments for checking for rabies. Of many hundreds of bats turned over to us by the Department of Public Health, only 21 were evening bats.

Habits

Evening bats are relatively slow flyers. In the earlier hours, they may forage at a higher level compared to later hours when they may fly below the treetops. Mumford and Whitaker (1982) found that when hovering, this bat holds the tip of the interfemoral membrane cupped forward, forming a deep pocket.

Evening bats are early flyers. In southern Illinois, these together with red bats made the earliest flights and were abroad when the light was still strong (Layne, 1958a). Much the same is true in central Illinois.

To my knowledge, the earliest records of evening bats in Illinois are specimens taken at Carbondale on March 27 and April 13; another record from Urbana is for April 21. The latest record is a specimen from Cook County provided with a date of October 8. The next late record is September 28 for Shelby County. I would think that most evening bats have migrated out of the state prior to September 15.

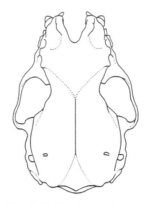
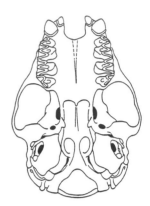

Fig. 8.43. *Nycticeius humeralis*, dorsal and ventral views of skull. Reno, Bond Co., Illinois, 11934 UI. Female, 14.4 mm greatest length.

Food

Nothing is known of the food of these bats in Illinois, nor is much known from other places. They apparently will do well in captivity on an improvised diet.

Reproduction

Several nursery or maternity colonies of evening bats have been reported for Illinois. One of these is in Reno, Bond County, near Greenup, Cumberland County; pregnant or lactating females have been encountered in Union, Pike, and Champaign counties.

On May 7, all eight females collected at Reno were pregnant, as were one female taken May 18 and two females taken on May 20, all in Champaign County.

In Illinois, young are born probably in early June. Most pregnant females have two young; a few, three. Newborn are nearly hairless. By about three weeks, young can fly for the first time. Juveniles collected on July 15 were approaching adult size and probably were six or seven weeks old.

Miscellaneous

It has been suggested that adult males may not be present, or may be rare, in the northern parts of the evening bat's range (Watkins, 1972). In southern Illinois (Carbondale, Jackson County), Layne (1958a) found that 9 of 11 that he shot between April 13 and June 20 were males. I assume that all of these were adults at this time of year. Of those netted on McKee Creek, Pike County, on July 18, one was an adult male. Of 31 adult animals taken at places other than maternity colonies, 27 were females, 4 were males. Of these four, one taken July 7 and one August 17 may have been young born in Illinois. The other two males were taken on March 27 and October 8, and may have been migrating individuals.

Variation

The subspecies in Illinois is *N. h. humeralis;* the other subspecies are from southernmost Florida and northeastern Mexico.

Nycticeius humeralis humeralis (Rafinesque)

1818. *Vespertilio humeralis* Rafinesque, Amer. Monthly Mag., 3:446. Type from Kentucky.
1819. *N[ycticeius]. humeralis,* Rafinesque, J. Phys. Chim. Hist. Nat. et Arts, Paris, 88:417.

Range. Throughout the state, except in winter, when it seems to be absent from Illinois (Map 8.19).

Diagnosis and Comparisons. N. h. humeralis is darker in color and has a slightly smaller skull than *N. h. mexicanus* from northeastern Mexico. *N. h. humeralis* is darker, less yellowish in color and has a broader and longer rostrum than *N. h. subtropicalis* from southern Florida.

Remarks. N. h. humeralis approaches its northern limits of distribution in Illinois.

Records of occurrence. SPECIMENS EXAMINED, 87
Winnebago Co.: [1] Rockford, 1 (UI), (June 10, 1975). **Lake Co.:** [2] no specific locality, 1 (UI), (May 28, 1976). **Cook Co.:** [3] Wilmette, 1 (UI), (June 20, 1968); [4] Maywood, 1 (UI), (May 25, —); [5] Oaklawn, 1 (UI), (June 13, 1967); no specific locality [not plotted], 1 (UI), (Oct. 8, 1975). **Will Co.:** [6] Joliet, 1 (UI), (May 29, 1975); [7] Frankfort, 1 (UI), (May 31, 1979). **Henderson Co.:** [8] no specific locality, 23 (US). **Fulton Co.:** [9] Fairview, 1 (UI), (May 10, 1949); [10] Liverpool, 1 (UI), (May 16, 1950). **Adams Co.:** [11] Mendon, 1 (UI), (June 7, 1967); [12] Quincy, 1 (UI), (May 17, 1975). **Champaign Co.:** [13] 1 mi SE Mahomet, 3 (UI), (Oct. 8, 1955; May 20, 1956); [14a] Brownfield Woods, 3 mi ENE Urbana, 2 (UI), (April 21, 1955; May 18, 1955); [14b] Champaign, 1 (UI), (May 22, 1947). **Pike Co.** [15] Pittsfield, 2 (UI), (July 10, 1971; July 25, 1981). **Green Co.:** [16] Greenfield, 1 (UI), (June 11, 1968). **Sangamon Co.:** [17] Springfield, 2 (UI), (July 7, 1977; May 29, 1978); [18a] 1 mi W Rochester, 1 (ISM); [18b] Rochester, 3 (ISM). **Christian Co.:** [19] Kincaid, 1 (UI), (May 21, 1974); [20] Pana, 1 (UI), (July 24, 1975). **Macon Co.:** [21] no specific locality, 3 (UI), (July 21, 1976; June 1, 1977; July 17, 1979). **Shelby Co.:** [22] no specific locality, 1 (UI), (Sept. 28, 1977). **Cumberland Co.:** [23] 3½ mi S Greenup, 4 (ISM). **Bond Co.:** [24] Reno, 14 (UI), 1 (ISU), (May 7, 1955; July 25, 1965). **Crawford Co.:** [25] 1½ mi NE Eaton, 2 (UI), (June 26, 27, 1958). **Jackson Co.:** [27] Carbondale, 2 (UI), 1 (SIC), 2 (SRL), (Oct. 15, 1974; March 27, 1976). **Saline Co.:** [28] Eldorado, 1 (UI), (Aug. 17, 1965). **Union Co.:** [29] Pine Hills Recreation Area, 1 (ISM). **Alexander Co.:** [30] Olive Branch, 2 (US). **Pulaski Co.:** [31] Ullin, 1 (UI), (July 7, 1974).

Additional records. **Du Page Co.:** Sugar Mound [location not found, not plotted], (Necker and Hatfield, 1941:46). **St. Clair Co.:** [26] Belleville, (Necker and Hatfield, 1941:46). **Jackson Co.:** [27] Carbondale, 3 (FS).

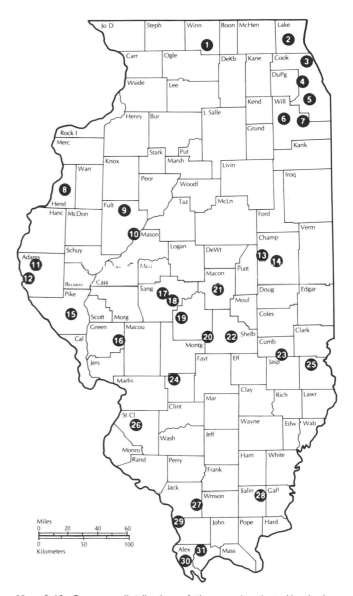

Map 8.19. Summer distribution of the evening bat, *Nycticeius humeralis.* The subspecies is *N. h. humeralis.* Dates of capture for most specimens are given in *Records of occurrence.* The distribution of the species in the United States is shaded.

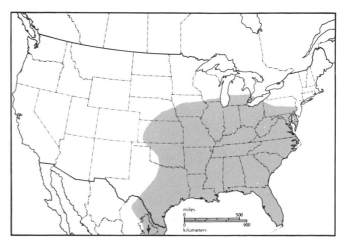

Fig. 8.44. Rafinesque's big-eared bat, *Plecotus rafinesquii,* in flight. Note the large ears with prominent tragi and the fleshy bumps on the nose. Photograph by W. W. Goodpaster.

Plecotus, Big-eared bats

Diagnosis. Vespertilionid bats with large ears, muzzle glands enlarged to form lumps on either side of muzzle; lower jaw with three premolars, first upper incisor larger than second; auditory bullae large and circular.

Dentition. 2/3, 1/1, 2/3, 3/3.

Comparisons. Plecotus is unique among all genera of Illinois bats in having large ears that, measured from the notch to the tip, are 27 mm or more, rather than 20 mm or less.

Plecotus rafinesquii (Lesson), Rafinesque's big-eared bat

Range. In southern Illinois, from Union, Johnson, and Alexander counties, and from Wabash County. Present in both winter and summer, but few records for summer.

Diagnosis. A long-eared bat in which the ears nearly join across the forehead; ear membranes thin so that they can be rolled up, tragus of ear long and pointed; muzzle with glandular masses between eye and nostril; color of venter conspicuously whitish; skull slender, highly arched, and not rugose; first upper incisor usually with a prominent secondary cusp.

Color. Dorsum brownish, with considerable blackish tinge; underparts appear whitish, with hairs blackish at base but tipped with white; tail membrane thin and translucent.

Comparisons. P. rafinesquii differs from all other Illinois bats with its large ears that are 27 mm and usually 30

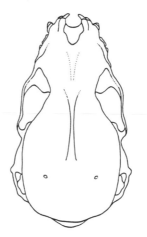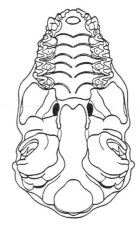

Fig. 8.45. *Plecotus rafinesquii,* dorsal and ventral views of skull; 1 mi NNE Olive Branch, Alexander Co., Illinois, 59008, UI. Male, 16.7 mm greatest length.

mm or more, measured from the notch to the tip (other species have ears less than 20 mm); glandular masses or lumps on side of muzzle (sometimes called lump-nosed bats), and in having a combination of other characters such as long tragi, whitish underparts, bifid first upper incisor, and a relatively high skull without a sagittal crest.

P. rafinesquii needs comparison with the related species *Plecotus townsendii,* known from Kentucky and Missouri but not from Illinois, as follows: venter with base of hairs blackish and tipped with white rather than bases gray and tipped with brownish or blackish, first upper incisor usually bifid rather than single-cusped, upper premolar four usually with an anterointernal cusp on cingulum rather than usually absent.

Chromosomes. Diploid number 32, FN = 50; 10 pairs of metacentrics and submetacentrics, 5 of acrocentrics; X and Y acrocentrics.

Secondary sexual variation. A sample of 28 adults from Reelfoot Lake, western Tennessee, consisting of 14 males and 14 females, were tested for differences between the sexes. There were no significant differences in six external measurements, including forearm and tragus length, and in eight of nine cranial measurements. Greatest length of the skull was significantly larger in females (16.35 mm vs. 16.14 mm) at the 0.02 level.

Habitats

Most of the information for Rafinesque's big-eared bats in Illinois is from specimens that were found hibernating in mines or caves. Andrew West of the Illinois Department of Conservation found a non-hibernating colony of some 30 of these bats on July 29, 1977, in a downstairs room of an old cabin on Boss Island, Little Black Slough, Johnson County. No young bats were reported to have been seen. There were said to be "a lot more bats in the attic," but how many and of what species is not certain. On August 5, the bats were still there in the same abundance. On September 9, only two remained. According to West, this cabin was occupied by some 30 *P. rafinesquii* each summer until about 1983. At that time, vultures began roosting in the structure and the bats moved out. On July 30, 1960, the attic of a house reportedly contained a colony of Rafinesque's big-eared bats at ½ mi N Forman, Johnson County. Elsewhere, these bats are reported to roost in unoccupied buildings and other man-made structures, as well as in trees and caves (Jones, 1977).

In winter, Rafinesque's big-eared bats are known in Illinois silica mines and caves in Alexander and Union counties. It is not certain where the specimen found in February at Mt. Carmel, Wabash County, was taken.

At a place less than 60 miles south of the area involved in our Illinois records, a small colony of Rafinesque's big-eared bats are known year-round, based on observations in February, March, April, May, and September. This colony is near Reelfoot Lake, Tennessee (Hoffmeister and Goodpaster, 1963) and may still be active. There may be fewer specimens present in September, although numbers seemed to be fluctuating continually.

Habits

In Illinois, colonies of big-eared bats in the summer must consist of about 30 individuals or less. In winter quarters they are in smaller groups or hang separately. In the colony near Reelfoot Lake, Tennessee, not far re-

Map 8.20. Known records of Rafinesque's big-eared bat, *Plecotus rafinesquii.* The subspecies is *P. r. rafinesquii.* Dates of capture for most records, summer and winter, are given in *Records of occurrence.* The distribution of the species in the United States is shaded.

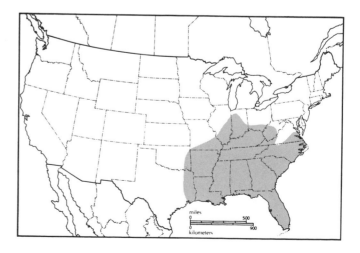

moved from those in Illinois, we (Hoffmeister and Good-paster, 1963) found the bats in winter in three clusters, each of about 20 individuals. This hibernaculum, how-ever, was an open cistern and it was probably colder than most silica mines at this time of the year. During the winter, the bats were nearly at the bottom of this 25-foot cistern, and only a few feet above the shallow water at the bottom. During the warmer periods, the bats hung higher up on the walls of the cistern.

The colony in the cistern in Tennessee was exposed to considerable light because the mouth of the structure was uncovered. We have noted Rafinesque's bats near the light zone in some silica mines in southern Illinois, and Mumford and Whitaker (1982) conjectured that they hibernate in the twilight zone near cave exits.

Rafinesque's bats must arouse from hibernation readily and even become active and fly outside the hibernaculum during the winter. We found this to be the case at the hibernaculum near Reelfoot Lake, Tennessee, and Hahn (1909) reported two of these bats flying out of their cave on February 22.

When resting or often when hibernating, big-eared bats curl their ears in such fashion that it is difficult to tell that they are truly big-eared bats. When awake, the ears are not only uncurled but moving to pick up sounds. Rafinesque's big-eared bats are late flyers and reportedly are fast flyers. When cornered, they are agile and difficult to bring down.

Reproduction

Copulation was observed at a hibernaculum in western Tennessee on February 14. The temperature outside the hibernaculum on that day rose to about 60°F. Copulation may also occur in the fall and spring. A single young is born in late May or early June, according to available information, but we do not have such data for Illinois. Young are nearly hairless at birth but develop rapidly and by about three weeks of age, can fly on their own. On September 2, six of 11 big-eared bats taken at the cistern near Reelfoot Lake, Tennessee, were young of the year but were sufficiently mature that the epiphyses of the long bones were almost entirely fused.

Variation

Two subspecies are presently referred to *P. rafinesquii*: *P. r. rafinesquii* and *P. r. macrotis*. The latter is reported to occur south of Tennessee; the former from Tennessee to central Indiana.

Plecotus rafinesquii rafinesquii Lesson

1818. *Vespertilio megalotis* Rafinesque, Amer. Monthly Mag., 3:466. Type locality restricted to Mt. Carmel, Wabash Co., Illinois (Handley, 1959). Not *Vespertilio megalotis* Bechstein, 1800.

1827. *Plecotus rafinesquii* Lesson, Manuel de mamm., 1827:96, a renaming of *Vespertilio megalotis* Rafinesque, 1818.

Range. As given for the species (p. 128 and Map 8.20).

Diagnosis and Comparisons. A subspecies of light color, underparts whitish, and mesopterygoid fossa and postdentary part of palate broad (Handley, 1959). *P. r. rafinesquii* compared with *P. r. macrotis* is lighter, underparts more whitish, and skull broader across palate.

Remarks. Nowhere within the range of this subspecies are large numbers of individuals encountered.

Records of occurrence. SPECIMENS EXAMINED, 27. **Union Co.:** [2] T11S, R3W, Sec. 35, 2 (SRL), (Jan. 8, 1959); [3a] 4 mi NW Mill Creek [abandoned silica mine], 1 (FS), [Jan. 30, —); [3b] 3 mi WSW Mill Creek [abandoned silica mine, may be Alexander Co.], 1 (SIC); Mine 2 [location uncertain, not plotted], 1 (SIC), (Feb. 7, 1960); Mine 3 [location uncertain, not plotted], 1 (SIC), (Feb. 7, 1960). **Johnson Co.:** [4b] ½ mi N Forman [attic of house], 13 (SRL), 1 (UI), (July 30, 1960). **Alexander Co.:** [5a] T14S, R2W, Sec. 1, Mine 14, 1 (SRL), (Feb. 12, 1959); [6a] 1 mi NNE Olive Branch, 1 (UI), (April 6, 1981); [6b] ½ mi N Olive Branch [abandoned silica mines], 3 (NHS), (Jan. 12, —; Feb. 1, —); Mine 1 [location uncertain, not plotted], 1 (SIC), (Jan. 23, 1960); Mine 5 [location uncertain, not plotted], 1 (SIC), (Jan. 23, 1960).

Additional records. **Wabash Co.:** [1] Mt. Carmel, 2 (US), (Feb., —). **Union Co.:** Mine 85 [location uncertain, not plotted, sight record, 1 individual], (Whitaker and Winter, 1977:309). **Johnson Co.:** [4a] Boss Island, Little Black Slough [sight record, K. Andrew West, several individuals in an old cabin]. **Alexander Co.:** [5b] Abandoned mine near Elco [sight record, 1 individual], (Elder, 1945:433).

Family Molossidae, Free-tailed bats

Tail projects conspicuously beyond free edge of tail membrane; nostrils usually open on a pad, the upper surface of which often has horny excrescenses; ears usually not long and tragus small; wings narrow; feet with long hairs extending well beyond toes. Represented in Illinois by the genus *Tadarida*.

Tadarida, Free-tailed bats

Diagnosis. A free-tailed (molossid) bat of medium to small size with vertical grooves or wrinkles on upper lip, two upper premolars, premaxillaries separate between upper incisors.

Dental formula. 1/3, 1/1, 2/2, 3/3.

Comparisons. Tadarida is unique among Illinois bats because of the "free-portion" of the tail extending beyond the membrane, the short monocolored fur, and short ears with practically no tragus. The skull of *Tadarida* in Illinois with a greatest length of less than 17.0 mm will have a canine-M³ toothrow length of 6.0 mm or more.

Chromosomes. See account of the species below.

Tadarida brasiliensis, American free-tailed bat

Range. Known only from two specimens, one at DeKalb, DeKalb County, and one at Carbondale, Jackson County. Probably wandering, fall migrants (Map 8.21).

Diagnosis. A small species of *Tadarida* which is unique among Illinois bats because of the tail which extends free of the tail membrane; short fur that is monocolor; ears short with exceedingly short tragi, ears nearly join over forehead; feet with long hairs protruding from toes; upper incisors converging strongly at their tips; braincase broad for the short skull.

Color. Dorsum dark gray, sometimes with a brownish cast; hairs nearly uniform in color from base to tips; if hairs are whitish at base, it is difficult to see with the eye; underparts only slightly paler; ears dark.

Chromosomes. Diploid number 48; FN = 56; one large metacentric, two submetacentrics, one medium-sized and one small subtelocentric, and 18 acrocentrics; X submetacentric; Y acrocentric.

Comparisons. The *Diagnosis* above gives characters for distinguishing *T. brasiliensis* from other species of bats known to be in Illinois.

There are no other free-tailed species of bats that

Map 8.21. Only two instances of capture of the American free-tailed bat, *Tadarida brasiliensis,* are recorded. The subspecies is *T. b. mexicana.* The United States distribution is shaded.

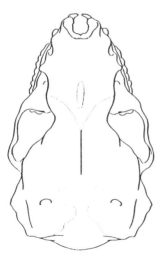

Fig. 8.46. *Tadarida brasiliensis,* dorsal view of skull. Vicinity of Aguila, Maricopa Co., Arizona, 25201, UI. Female, 16.7 mm greatest length.

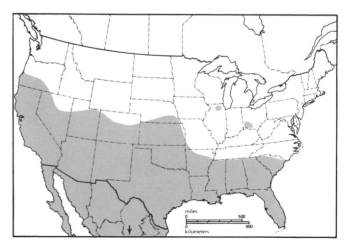

might possibly reach Illinois with which *T. brasiliensis* needs to be compared. At one time *T. cynocephala* was regarded as a distinct species, but it is not regarded as a subspecies of *T. brasiliensis*. Under the account of the subspecies there is a discussion on distinguishing *T. b. mexicana* and *T. b. cynocephala*.

Remarks. The presence of *Tadarida brasiliensis* in Illinois must be as an accidental migrant. The nearest record of *T. mexicana* from De Kalb is 400 miles to the west in Lincoln, Nebraska, and from Carbondale 260 miles to the south-southwest in Little Rock, Arkansas. Harlan Walley (1970) reported upon the specimen taken at De Kalb on October 17, 1969, and Feldhamer (1985) for the specimen taken at Carbondale on October 18, 1984.

Habitat and Habits

American free-tailed bats are cave- or building-inhabiting colonial animals. They usually hang in large clusters. They are rapid flyers, reportedly attaining speeds up to 60 miles per hour. The subspecies *Tadarida brasiliensis mexicana* is strongly migratory; *T. b. cynocephala* found in the southeast is apparently non-migratory (Barbour and Davis, 1969). Migration for *T. b. mexicana* may involve several hundreds of miles each spring and each fall. The specimen collected at De Kalb, Illinois, on October 17 was thought to be a young of the year, as was the one taken October 18 at Carbondale. These may have become disoriented in their migration pattern and moved northeast rather than southwest from a colony in another area—perhaps in Oklahoma or Kansas.

The long and narrow wings and rapid flight of free-tailed bats may be sufficient for recognition in flight.

Reproduction

American free-tailed bats may separate into maternity colonies for the birth of young, but this is not always the case. The single young is born in June, sometimes in July. Young can fly at about five weeks.

Variation

Two subspecies of *T. brasiliensis* are known from the United States: *T. b. mexicana* and *T. b. cynocephala*.

Tadarida brasiliensis mexicana (Saussure)

1860. *Molossus mexicanus* Saussure, Rev. et Mag. Zool., Paris, 12:283. Type from Cofre de Perote, 13,000 ft., Mexico.

1955. *Tadarida brasiliensis mexicana*, Schwartz, J. Mamm., 36:108.

Range. As given for the species (p. 131 and Map 8.21).

Diagnosis and Comparisons. A small subspecies of *T. brasiliensis,* averaging shorter in total and tail length than *T. b. cynocephala,* and with a narrower rostrum, and less elevated cranium.

Remarks. The specimen from De Kalb, De Kalb County, is referable to *T. b. mexicana.* A scattergram analysis using breadth between the upper canines and greatest breadth across the upper incisors separates most of the specimens of the two subspecies. The specimen from De Kalb falls with *T. b. mexicana.* Feldhamer (1985) thought the specimen from Carbondale was also referable to *T. b. mexicana.* I have not examined the specimen.

Records of occurrence. SPECIMENS EXAMINED, 1.
De Kalb Co.: [1] Northern Illinois University Campus, De Kalb, 1 (NIU).

Additional record. **Jackson Co.:** [2] Southern Illinois University Campus, Carbondale, 1 (Feldhamer, 1985).

Order Lagomorpha, Rabbits, hares, pikas

Small to medium-sized mammals, with short tails that are well furred; two pairs of upper incisors of unequal size, with the smaller pair behind the larger first pair, incisors ever-growing and with enamel all-around (extending onto posterior surface); rostrum fenestrated.

KEY TO LAGOMORPHA (RABBITS, COTTONTAILS, JACK RABBITS) IN ILLINOIS

1a. Size large; ear from notch more than 75 mm, hind foot more than 120 mm; color in winter white or grayish white; supraorbital process well separated from braincase, area of braincase anterior to bullae fenestrated, interparietal fused to parietals in adults *Lepus townsendii* p. 142

1b. Size medium; ear from notch less than 75 mm, hind foot less than 120 mm; color not whitish in winter; posterior extension of supraorbital process fused with braincase, area of braincase anterior to bullae not fenestrated; interparietal distinguishable from parietals 2

2a. Length of body less than 440 mm and hind foot less than 107 mm; anterior portion of supraorbital process extends forward free of braincase, posterior extension of supraorbital process fused to skull leaving a slitlike opening between supraorbital process and braincase; length of skull less than 80 mm; color of dorsum buffy or grayish brown *Sylvilagus floridanus* p. 134

2b. Length of body more than 440 mm and hind foot more than 107 mm, anterior portion of supraorbital process not separated but fused with braincase, posterior extension of supraorbital process fused with braincase with no slitlike opening; length of skull 84 mm or more; color of dorsum dark, with considerable reddish tinge *Sylvilagus aquaticus* p. 139

Family Leporidae, Rabbits and hares

Hind legs elongated for hopping, ears long, auditory bullae well inflated, frontal bone with a supraorbital process, nasal widest posteriorly. Two genera in Illinois: *Lepus,* which are hares; *Sylvilagus,* rabbits and cottontails. *Lepus* includes jack rabbits; young are precocial and at birth are fully haired, their eyes are open, and they are able to run. The species rest in the open. *Sylvilagus* young are helpless at birth and for a period of time they are naked, blind, unable to run, and remain in a fur-lined nest.

Cranial measurements. Measurements of the skull as given in Table 8.12 for various lagomorphs are taken as described in Diersing and Wilson (1980:2).

Sylvilagus Rabbits and cottontails

Diagnosis. Cottontails and rabbits are readily recognizable by their relatively large—not necessarily long—ears, white (cottony) underside of the short tail, and their hopping gait. A more detailed diagnosis would include: size medium for a lagomorph; hind feet large with fully haired soles; tail short; ears medium to long; upper parts brownish or grayish; underparts creamy white; tail white ventrally and either rufous or grayish dorsally; four pairs of mammae, one pectoral, two abdominal, and one inguinal; second upper incisors small and located directly behind the first pair; interparietal remains unfused to the

Fig. 8.47. Posterior views of skulls of *S. floridanus* from Iroquois Co., Illinois, to show condition of supraoccipital-exoccipital suture. In #1, suture is open; #2, beginning to fuse; #3 mostly fused; #4, obliterated. Animals with the conditions of #4 were regarded as adult. (From Hoffmeister and Zimmerman, 1967)

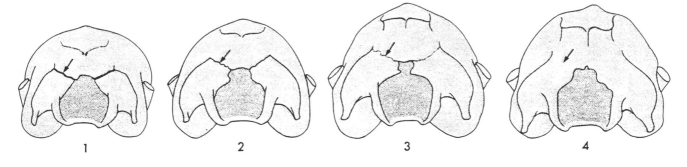

1 2 3 4

Table 8.12. External and cranial measurements (in mm) of *Sylvilagus floridanus, S. aquaticus* and *Lepus townsendii*. Mean, minimum and maximum, and one standard deviation are given. For comparison, measurements are included for *S. floridanus* in states near Illinois. Superscripts indicate sample less than N.

Species and subspecies	Locality	N	Total length	Body length	Tail length	Hind foot length	Greatest length	Basal length
S. floridanus mearnsi	NE Ill.	10	420.8[9] 355-460 36.70	363.4	57.4[9] 50-62 3.68	99.7 93-105 3.50	72.8 68.65-76.1 2.04	58.2[9] 53.45-63.2 2.62
" " "	East central Ill.	14	412.8[12] 354-537 48.50	364.4	48.4[11] 31-64 9.35	98.1[12] 90-107 5.95	74.2 68.8-78.35 2.34	59.3[13] 54.7-63.2 2.12
" " "	So. Ill.	11	453.0[10] 430-475 16.70	391.4	61.6 53-71 6.87	96.6 92-103 2.66	75.2 72.95-78.1 1.67	61.1 59.7-63.5 1.19
" " "	Ohio, Ontario	15	443.2[13] 401-492 31.15	397.5	45.7[8] 36-70 13.64	93.3[7] 86-102 5.91	75.1 71.5-78.0 1.91	60.9[14] 58.2-62.7 1.61
" " "	Wisconsin, Minn., Iowa	9	—	—	—	—	74.3 70.4-74.75 1.98	59.6 56.05-62.15 1.85
S. floridanus alacer	Eastern Missouri	3	414.7 386-442 28.02	366.0	48.7 47-51 2.08	97.7 93-103 5.03	73.2 71.85-74.5 1.33	58.3 57.2-59.15 1.00
S. aquaticus aquaticus	So. Ill.	6	521.5[4] 476-554 33.21	461.6[4]	59.8[4] 46-70 10.21	109.3 107-110 1.50	89.3 87.8-90.75 1.13	73.0[5] 70.05-75.4 1.95
Lepus townsendii campanius	Jo Daviess Co., Ill. Clark Co., Wisc. Wisconsin	3,540 ♂ 37,111 ♂ 3,539 ?	597 565 —	489 495 —	108 70 —	145 143 —	94.5 100.9 102.4	76.5 83.3 —

parietals in adults; bones of side of rostrum porous; postorbital processes extending posteriorly usually touching or fused to the braincase; tibia and fibula fused distally; radius and ulna separate; weight under four lbs or 1600 gms in Illinois. Newborn helpless or altricial.

Dental formula. 2/1, 0/0, 3/2, 3/3.

Comparisons. Sylvilagus, cottontails and rabbits, differ from *Lepus*—hares or jack rabbits—in the ear being shorter, hind foot shorter (less than 112 mm), young hairless and altricial at birth rather than furred and precocial; interparietal always distinguishable, rather than not, in skulls of adults; supraorbital processes more adpressed to frontals and less elevated; weight of nonpregnant adults under four lbs (1600 gms) rather than usually more.

Secondary sexual variation. A sample of 42 *S. floridanus* (19 males, 23 females) from north central Texas was examined by Diersing (1978) for sexual differences in 7 external and 26 cranial measurements. Females tend to be larger than males but they are significantly larger in only 3 of the 26 cranial measurements, and in total and body length, and in weight.

Data are not available for *S. aquaticus.*

Aging. A detailed method of determining the age of Illinois cottontails of the species *S. floridanus,* with use of weight of the lens of the eye, developed by Lord (1959), and closure or obliteration of certain sutures, was devised by Hoffmeister and Zimmerman (1967). A total of 125 cottontails of varying sizes were assigned ages following the data provided by Lord (1959, 1963) as based on lens weight. The obliteration of certain sutures correlates with cessation of growth of the lens. Specimens are considered as adult when both exoccipitals are fused to the supraoccipital and these sutures are obliterated. It is not known if the same criterion applies to adulthood in the skulls of *S. aquaticus.* See account of that species (p. 139).

At an earlier time, various workers had devised methods of aging cottontails based on the closure and obliteration of the epiphyses at the distal ends of the radius and ulna. This is shown in Fig. 8.48.

Sylvilagus floridanus, Eastern cottontail

Range. Throughout the state.

Diagnosis. A species of *Sylvilagus* of medium size in Illinois, with hind feet usually between 90–105 mm, length of body between 359–410 mm, greatest length of skull between 68–78 mm; supraorbital process with posterior part fused to braincase but leaving a distinct

Zygomatic breadth	Braincase breadth	Depth skull	Nasal length	Nasal breadth	Incisive for. length	Diastema length	Maxillary toothrow length	Palate length	Bulla length	Bulla breadth
36.0	27.0	32.3	32.5	14.7	18.1[9]	19.6	15.0	6.2[9]	10.6	24.9
33.85-37.25	25.7-28.3	30.85-33.75	30.4-34.3	13.25-16.95	16.65-19.15	17.65-21.5	13.8-15.9	5.6-6.8	9.95-11.35	23.3-26.45
1.13	0.97	0.84	1.39	1.16	0.80	1.09	0.62	0.44	0.49	1.13
36.4	27.2	31.9	32.7	15.1	18.3	19.8	15.1	6.5	10.6	25.0
34.25-37.4	25.05-28.9	30.65-33.55	29.7-35.85	13.05-16.9	17.3-19.45	18.45-21.45	13.05-16.9	5.8-7.5	9.7-11.35	23.1-26.6
0.90	0.87	0.77	1.72	1.14	0.75	0.82	1.14	0.50	0.43	1.02
36.6	27.1[10]	32.4[10]	33.5	15.2	18.6	20.6	15.3	6.6	11.0	25.6
35.8-38.1	26.3-28.2	31.5-33.6	32.3-34.75	14.1-16.65	17.4-19.45	19.7-22.1	14.75-15.9	5.9-7.35	10.45-11.35	24.05-26.35
0.88	0.72	0.74	0.80	0.83	0.72	0.73	0.35	0.50	0.32	0.73
37.0[14]	27.6[13]	32.0	32.2	15.0	18.8	20.7	15.0	6.5	10.9	25.6
35.15-39.2	25.8-29.1	30.6-33.05	28.9-35.0	13.8-15.95	17.85-20.1	19.0-21.6	14.5-15.75	5.5-7.5	10.35-11.5	23.85-27.35
1.18	0.96	0.69	1.41	0.74	0.76	0.82	0.34	0.64	0.40	0.95
36.9	27.6	31.9	32.5[8]	14.9	18.6	19.7	15.0	6.5	10.6	26.1[8]
35.95-38.65	26.15-28.75	31.0-33.5	30.0-34.8	13.6-15.7	17.65-19.4	18.4-20.85	13.8-15.6	5.6-7.9	9.8-11.35	24.95-26.7
0.98	0.99	0.88	1.84	0.64	0.61	0.80	0.60	0.70	0.46	0.55
35.4[2]	27.1	31.8	32.5	15.3	18.3	19.7	14.8	6.4	10.6	24.4
34.55-36.3	25.85-28.0	31.6-32.0	32.1-32.8	14.85-15.65	17.55-19.35	19.1-20.5	14.1-15.5	6.05-6.8	10.3-10.95	23.05-25.85
1.24	1.13	0.20	0.35	0.43	0.94	0.74	0.70	0.38	0.33	1.40
40.5	29.9	35.5	38.3	15.9	21.4	24.0	17.5	8.9	11.7	29.4
39.95-40.95	29.4-30.7	34.5-36.65	36.6-40.1	14.55-16.95	19.8-22.9	22.25-25.2	16.75-18.0	8.3-9.3	11.15-12.2	28.2-30.5
0.41	0.45	0.89	1.25	0.90	0.99	1.01	0.49	0.41	0.40	0.75
46.1	31.3	41.2	40.6	20.8	26.5	26.9	17.5	7.0	10.6	30.2
46.9	31.5	42.3	44.4	22.8	26.6	30.1	18.0	6.0	12.6	30.6
—	—	—	44.9	21.9	25.8	30.0	17.75	—	13.6	—

slitlike opening; anterior extension of supraorbital process present, and not fused to braincase; rostrum of skull relatively narrow.

Color. Dorsum buff or rusty brown; venter white, except throat is buffy. Ears are darker than the back, underside of the tail white, nape of the neck reddish.

Chromosomes. Diploid number 42. All autosomes are biarmed. X chromosome, metacentric; Y, acrocentric.

Comparisons. S. *floridanus* differs from S. *aquaticus* in being of smaller size; having a body length less than 440 mm rather than more, hind foot less than 107 mm rather than more; color of dorsum brownish or buffy rather than reddish with considerable black; skull smaller, with greatest length less than 80 mm rather than 84 mm or more (see Table 8.13 for other measurements); anterior part of supraorbital process extends forward free of braincase, posterior extension of supraorbital process fused to skull but a slitlike opening remains between process and braincase rather than being completely fused.

Growth. Growth in eastern cottontails was analyzed in 125 specimens from Iroquois and Champaign counties by Hoffmeister and Zimmerman (1967), who found that 90 percent of adult size is attained by 125 days of age; 96.5 percent by 170 days. At approximately 5½ months after birth, cottontails are at or near maximum size.

Length of the hind foot, breadth of the braincase, and the parietal breadth attain adult size before or by the 160th day. Nasal bones appear to increase in size for the longest period of time.

Growth in the lens of the eye is expressed by the change in weight with increasing age. Lord (1959) found that the lens weighed 6.6 to 8.4 milligrams at one day of age; 19.4 to 22.4 at two weeks; by the end of the second month, about 60 mg. At about a year of age, the lens weighs about 200 mg. The increase in weight after one year is greatly slowed.

Secondary sexual variation. See account of the genus *Sylvilagus* (p. 134).

Molt. Eastern cottontails have at least four distinct pelages—nestling, juvenile, subadult, and adult—judging from Negus' (1958) study in Ohio. Nestling fur is molted starting at the fifth week, juvenile at the tenth week, and subadult pelage is acquired by about the 15th week. Adults undergo two molts per year. The molt in the spring from winter to summer pelage extends for about five months. Summer pelage is retained for only a short time until the fall molt begins.

Remarks. Animals of the species S. *floridanus* are properly referred to as cottontails, and specifically as eastern cottontails. The name cottontail is given to certain species of rabbits and it is redundant to call these cottontail rabbits.

Habitat

Eastern cottontails prefer habitats which combine a variety of cover types. As a result, they are found in weeds, briars and brush piles, forest-edge, short grass (lawns), and ornamental shrubs. It would be easier to enumerate those habitats that are less preferred or avoided: marshes, deep woods, closely cropped grass with no cover nearby. A requisite for preferred habitats is the presence of adequate cover for hiding, resting, and nesting. Many things can provide such cover: brush piles, litter, unmowed railroad rights-of-way, thickets of ornamental shrubs and ground cover, multiflora rose thickets, fencerows, to mention a few.

The southern third and western parts of Illinois have the highest populations of cottontails. In the non-glaciated, rolling parts of the state there is less cultivation of land and more bushy ravines. This provides more suitable habitat for these animals.

Habits

Eastern cottontails are polygamous during the breeding season. A female will drive males away from her nest area after the young are born.

Attempts have been made to ascertain the home range of these cottontails. Schwartz (1941) in Missouri came up with a home range of 1.4 acres for adult males, 1.2 acres for adult females. In central Illinois (Allerton Park, Piatt County), Lord (1963) found a home range of 3.23 ± 1.84 acres each for 72 cottontails, with no differences between males and females.

The activities of eastern cottontails at the time of mating are complex and ritualistic. Dean Ecke and I had the opportunity to observe such behavior at a distance of about 50 ft about 6 a.m. on April 22, 1948. Four cottontails were present in a bluegrass pasture. The individual we designated as No. 3 was exceedingly restless and excited, did little feeding, and when it came across the track of the fourth rabbit, began following it around. Ecke (1948) recorded the ensuing behavior as follows:

> These rabbits acted very much the same as might two young roosters. Rabbit #3, always the aggressor, would approach rabbit #4 until the pair faced each other at close quarters. After a few minutes of looking each other in the face the "male" would advance and the "female" would issue a rapid series of blows at him with her front feet. A split second later, all in the same quick action, one or the other of the rabbits would jump about two feet into the air and the other would dash under the arc of the first one's jump. The jumper would twist in the air so as to land nearly facing the other animal. All of this took a matter of a few seconds, and was repeated over and over—first one rabbit doing the jumping and then the other—but rabbit #3 was always the

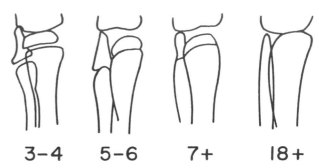

Fig. 8.48. Aging of eastern cottontails based upon closure of the epiphyses of the radius and ulna. Approximate age is given in months. (After Petrides, 1951)

aggressor until close contact was made. One got the impression by watching this that the animals were playing.

The "sparring" game continued for about 15 minutes before the female allowed the male to approach her rear. She turned from him once but the second time she allowed him to approach and mount. In mounting, the male grasped the female about her flanks with his front feet and held his head high. Contact was made very rapidly. He was not mounted longer than two or three seconds after which he backed off. If any pelvic thrusting was done the action was too fast to observe. The male did not fall off exhausted as is frequently the case among domestic rabbits. There was a time-lapse of 15 minutes between the moment when the male rabbit first discovered the female until coitus took place.

After copulation was completed the female leisurely hopped away, with the male staying close behind. Two or three more feints and jumps were made but with much less vigor than before. The two then remained together for a short while longer. Fifteen minutes after copulation—30 minutes

Table 8.13. Life-table for cottontails in Illinois, 1957 (from Lord, 1958:272).

Month	Adults at start of month	Juveniles at start of month	Births by end of month	Adult deaths by end of month	Juvenile deaths by end of month	Cotton-tails by end of month
January	233	2,626	0	76	853	1,930
February	157	1,773	0	77	853	1,000
March	1,000	0	1,486	76	853	1,557
April	924	633	638	77	852	1,266
May	847	419	2,665	77	853	3,001
June	770	2,231	2,028	77	853	4,099
July	693	3,406	1,463	76	853	4,633
August	617	4,016[1]	1,984	77	852	5,688
September	540	5,148[2]	889	77	853	5,647
October	463	5,184	0	77	853	4,717
November	386	4,331	0	76	853	3,788
December	310	3,478	0	77	852	2,859

[1] Since 55% of breeding females in August were juveniles, then 354 of these were breeding juveniles.
[2] Since 76% of breeding females in September were juveniles, then 795 of these were breeding juveniles.

after the first contact—the male and female parted ways having lost interest in each other.

Rabbit #3, the male, now acted very "normal." He ate a little grass and made one or two short, leisurely, runs. No longer did he display the excited temperament that he had before mating.

Food

In the spring and summer, eastern cottontails feed extensively on available succulent grasses, as well as clovers, alfalfa, plantain, dandelions, and other broadleafs. In late fall and winter, they supplement this with available foods such as seeds, buds, certain fruits, and the bark of various shrubs such as blackberries, roses, willows, and other smooth-barked trees.

Within the cities of Illinois, eastern cottontails commonly feed on white clover and dandelions in lawns. I have noted that if clover and dandelions are removed from a lawn, the cottontails will look elsewhere. It appears that clover is preferred over dandelions.

In Williamson County, southern Illinois, eastern cottontails throughout the year of 1952 fed almost entirely on herbaceous plants and few woody plants, as judged from analysis of fecal pellets (Klimstra and Corder, 1957). Since snowfall was light, and herbaceous material was available for much of that year, weather may have accounted for a cottontail diet of mostly herbaceous plants. Various grasses and crop plants accounted for much of the food eaten.

Cottontails are coprophagous in that they eat some of their dropping. They produce two kinds of fecal pellets: hard, brown pellets from which most of the nutritive material has been removed, and soft, greenish food pellets which still contain considerable nutritive material and large amounts of vitamin B. The latter pellets are reingested by the cottontails. This behavior permits them to ingest a considerable amount of food in a short time, perhaps when they are exposed to predators, and to digest it more completely in a safer situation when the fecal pellets are chewed for a second time.

Cottontails in the non-winter months feed from sunrise until two to three hours thereafter and again in the evening, from about sunset to one hour thereafter. This feeding time may fluctuate, however, and cottontails may be feeding in the mid-afternoon, several hours before sunset. In the winter, feeding usually occurs after dark.

Reproduction

Breeding of eastern cottontails in Illinois runs from February through September, although males may become reproductively active, with considerable fighting, in late January. Copulation is known to occur in February, and probably every month after that into early September. The length of gestation is somewhere between 28 and 30 days and females breed again almost immediately after bearing young (Casteel, 1967). The peak in mating is in April and May. An eastern cottontail usually breeds by six months of age, but reportedly some as young as two months may breed.

The number of young per litter usually ranges from four to six; however, the number of young per pregnancy varies from year to year and from locality to locality in Illinois. A female may produce about 20 to 25 young per breeding season.

Fig. 8.49A. Eastern cottontail, *Sylvilagus floridanus.* Photograph by W. W. Goodpaster.

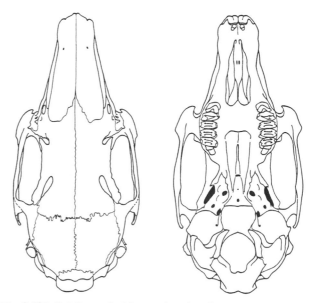

Fig. 8.49B. *Sylvilagus floridanus,* dorsal and ventral views of skull. Riverside, Cook Co., Illinois, 21778 UI. Female, 73.3 mm greatest length.

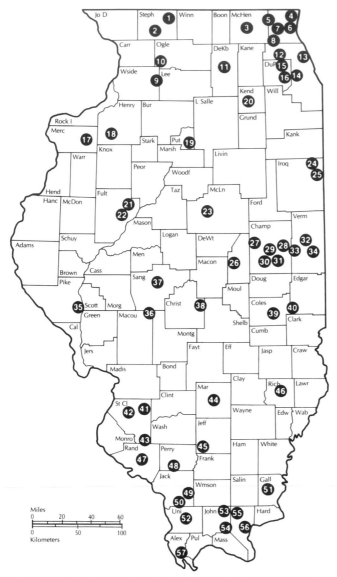

Map 8.22. Eastern cottontails, *Sylvilagus floridanus*, occur state-wide. The subspecies is *S. f. mearnsii*. Localities of occurrence as numbered are referenced in *Records of occurrence*. The range of the species in the United States is shaded.

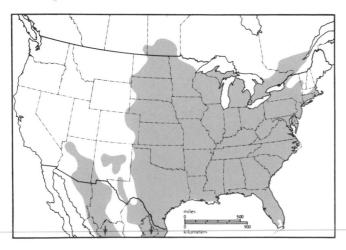

Young are helpless and blind at birth and are placed in a shallow depression or short burrow in the ground, dug by the female, or in a suitable natural hole. This is lined with hair from the female's throat and underparts and with grass or leaves. A plug of grasses or leaves seals the concavity when the mother is absent. The mother visits the nest to nurse the young only infrequently— perhaps only twice during a 24-hour period. Young are nursed for about two weeks.

Multiple use of a nest in east central Illinois was reported by Edwards (1963). At 4 p.m. on May 4, 1962, a female nursed young at a nest; at 7 p.m., a different female nursed the young at the same nest. On May 6, an examination of the nest revealed 15 young of at least two age groups, possibly three.

Cottontails born early in the season will mate the same year and contribute 12 to 23 percent of the cottontails present in the fall population. Lord (1958) prepared a life table for Illinois cottontails for the year 1957 (Table 8.13). It began with a theoretical population of 1,000 adults in March, peaked at 5,688 adults and young in August, and decreased back to 1,000 individuals by the end of the following February.

Ectoparasites

Eastern cottontails in Illinois are known to be infested in varying degrees with the bird and rabbit tick, *Haemaphysalis leporis-palustris;* eastern rabbit tick, *Ixodes dentatus;* wood tick, *Dermacentor variabilis; Ixodes sculptus;* many-spined rabbit flea, *Odontopsyllus multispinosus; Cediopsylla simplex;* chiggers, *Neotrombicula whartoni.* During parts of the winter, ticks go into hibernation and are absent from cottontails. Depending upon the weather and other conditions in Illinois, ticks may be absent from about October 20 to March 1.

Transplants

Eastern cottontails have been taken from Illinois and transplanted in western states. I do not know if any cottontails have been moved around (transplanted) within the state, but there is a good possibility this has happened several times.

Variation

In the taxonomic revision of the rabbits of North America, Nelson (1909) referred *S. floridanus* from southern Illinois to *S. f. alacer* and those from the remainder of the state to *S. f. mearnsii.* Nelson apparently examined no specimens from southern Illinois and had no basis for including *S. f. alacer* in the state. Other accounts of the mammals of Illinois have followed Nelson's reference of *alacer* to southern Illinois.

According to Nelson (1909:174), *S. f. alacer* is a small cottontail, *S. f. mearnsii* a large one. Table 8.12 (p. 134) shows that cottontails from southern Illinois are as large

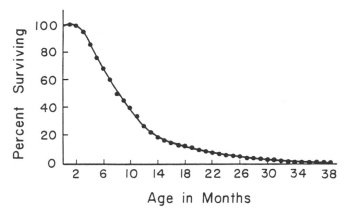

Fig. 8.50. Percentage of survival of eastern cottontails over a three-year span in Piatt County, Illinois. (From Lord, 1963)

or larger than *S. f. mearnsi* from east central or northeastern Illinois. Therefore, all cottontails in Illinois are here referred to *S. f. mearnsii*.

Sylvilagus floridanus mearnsii (Allen)

1894. *Lepus sylvaticus mearnsii* J. A. Allen, Bull. Amer. Mus. Nat. Hist., 6:171. Type from Fort Snelling, Hennepin Co., Minnesota.

1904. *Sylvilagus (Sylvilagus) floridanus mearnsi,* Lyon, Smithson. Misc. Coll., 45:336.

Range. Throughout the state (Map 8.22).

Diagnosis and Comparisons. A large subspecies of *S. floridanus* of variable color but darkish, with relatively long hind feet and short ears. *S. f. alacer* to the south and southwest is smaller and paler.

Remarks. See discussion above under *Variation* (p. 138) regarding *S. f. mearnsii* as the only subspecies in Illinois.

Records of occurrence. SPECIMENS EXAMINED, 372. **Stephenson Co.:** [1] 3 mi NE Rock Grove, 1 (UI); [2] 3 mi W Freeport, 1 (UI). **McHenry Co.:** [3] Woodstock, 3 (US). **Lake Co.:** [4] Camp Logan, 2 (FM); [5] Fox Lake, 2 (FM); [6] Waukegan, 1 (US); [7] 1½ mi S Ivanhoe, 21 (FM); [8] Barrington, 3 (FM). **Whiteside Co.:** [9] 2 km NE Sterling, 1 (NIU). **De Kalb Co.:** [11a] 3 mi N De Kalb, 1 (NIU); [11b] 4 mi W De Kalb, 1 (UI); [11c] De Kalb, 5 (NIU). **Cook Co.:** [12] Rohlwing Rd. & Rt. 53 [near Busse Wood Reservoir], 1 (NIU); [13] Evanston, 2 (FM); [14] Riverside, 1 (UI). **Du Page Co.:** [15a] ½ mi W Addison, 1 (UI); [15b] 1 mi W Oak Brook Terrace, 1 (UI); [16a] George Williams College, 2 (FM); [16b] ½ mi WNW Downers Grove, 1 (UI); [16c] Downers Grove, 1 (NIU). **Mercer Co.:** [17] 1 mi N Viola, 1 (UI). **Henry Co.:** [18] 2 mi S, 2½ mi E Andover, 1 (UI). **Putnam Co.:** [19] McNabb, 1 (FM). **Kendall Co.:** [20] 3 mi S Yorkville, 1 (UI). **Fulton Co.:** [21a] 1 mi W Canton, 1 (UI); [21b] 2 mi E Canton, 2 (UI); [21c] 3 mi E Canton, 1 (UI); [22] Bryant, 1 (UI). **McLean Co.:** [23] Normal, 4 (ISU). **Iroquois Co.:** [24] Beaverville, 56 (UI); [25a] Donovan, 48 (UI); [25b] Iroquois, 42 (UI); no specific locality [not plotted], 17 (UI). **Piatt Co.:** [26] Allerton Park, 5 mi W, 2½ mi S Monticello, 1 (UI). **Champaign Co.:** [27a] 3 mi NE Mahomet, 1 (UI); [27b] 1 mi S Mahomet, 1 (UI); [28] 3 mi N St. Joseph, 1 (UI); [29b] 1 mi W Champaign,

1 (UI); [29c] Champaign, 1 (UI); [29d] Urbana, 1 (UI); [29e] UI Farms, Urbana, 22 (UI); [29f] Urbana Wildlife Area [3½ mi SE Urbana], 1 (UI); [30a] 3 mi N Philo, 1 (UI); [30b] 2 mi N Philo, 1 (UI); [31a] Willard Airport, 1 (UI); [31b] 3 mi S Savoy, 1 (UI); [31c] 8 mi S Urbana, 1 (UI); [31d] 1 mi S Tolono, 1 (UI). **Vermilion Co.:** [32] 1 mi S, 3 mi E Collison, 4 (UI); [33] 1 mi W Fithian, 1 (UI); [34a] Danville, 4 (UI); [34b] Catlin, 5 (UI). **Pike Co.:** [35] Milton, 1 (UI). **Macoupin Co.:** [36] 2 mi E Virden, 1 (ISM). **Sangamon Co.:** [37] Springfield, 1 (ISM). **Christian Co.:** [38] 4½ mi SW Moweaqua, 1 (UI). **Coles Co.:** [39] Charleston, 2 (UI). **Edgar Co.:** [40] Kansas, 1 (US). **St. Clair Co.:** [41] 4 mi N Mascoutah on Rt. 43, 2 (UI); [42] Belleville, 1 (UI); [43] ½ mi W Marissa, 1 (UI). **Marion Co.:** [44] no specific locality, 2 (SRL). **Jefferson Co.:** [45] 6 mi N Sesser [labelled Franklin Co.], 1 (KU). **Richland Co.:** [46] Olney, 1 (FM). **Randolph Co.:** [47] no specific locality, 16 (SRL). **Perry Co.:** [48] Pyatts Striplands, 1 (SIC), 1 (SRL); no specific locality [not plotted], 3 (SRL). **Jackson Co.:** [49a] Carbondale, 1 (KU); [49b] 1 mi on Reservoir Road [=2 mi S, 1 mi W Carbondale], 1 (SIC); no specific locality [not plotted], 29 (SRL). **Gallatin Co.:** [51] 2 mi S Ridgeway, 1 (SIC); no specific locality [not plotted], 1 (SRL). **Union Co.:** [52] no specific locality, 7 (SRL). **Johnson Co.:** [53] Ozark, 2 (FM); [54] Reevesville, 3 (FM); no specific locality [not plotted], 1 (SRL). **Pope Co.:** [56] Golconda, 3 (FM); no specific locality [not plotted], 4 (SRL). **Alexander Co.:** [57a] Olive Branch, 2 (US), 3 (FM).

Additional records. **Ogle Co.:** [10] Polo, (Necker and Hatfield, 1941:56). **Champaign Co.:** [29a] 3 mi NE Urbana, 1 (UM). **Jackson Co.:** [50] Pomona, 1 (FS). **Pope Co.:** [55] 2 mi SE McCormick, 1 (FS). **Alexander Co.:** [57b] ¼ mi NW Cache on Illinois Rt. 3, 1 (FS).

Sylvilagus aquaticus, Swamp rabbit

Range. Southern third of state, mostly south of a line through Marion and Lawrence counties.

Diagnosis. A species of *Sylvilagus* of large size; adult males weigh about 4.9 lbs (2,235 gm), females, 4.75 lbs (2,161 gm); hind feet relatively narrow but long; ears relatively short; skull long and with anterior and posterior extensions of the supraorbital process fused with the braincase, breadth across auditory bullae great (28.0 mm or more), toothrow long (Fig. 8.51, p. 141).

Color. Dorsum dark, with a mixture of blacks and buffs, nape reddish and extending only slightly behind ears in most specimens, tops of feet tan, venter and underside of tail whitish except for area between forelegs which is orangish tan or cinnamon, eye ring prominent and orangish or cinnamon.

Chromosomes. Diploid number, 38; FN (=AN) 60 (Robinson, Elder, and Chapman, 1983).

Comparisons. *S. aquaticus* is the large cottontail of southern Illinois and needs comparison with *S. floridanus,* which is made in the account of the latter. Briefly, *S. aquaticus* is larger and heavier, darker in color, has different habitat preferences, and has certain distinctive cranial features such as the supraorbital process as well as overall larger size.

Map 8.23. Distribution of the swamp rabbit, *Sylvilagus aquaticus*. The subspecies is *S. a. aquaticus*. Localities of occurrence as numbered are referenced in *Records of occurrence*. The range of the species in the United States is shaded.

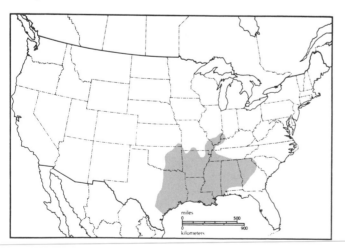

Aging. Specimens that have an eye lens-weight of 212.8 mg are adults according to Martinson et al. (1961:275); those less than this are juveniles and are first-year rabbits.

The epiphyses at the ends of the ulna and radius close between 10 to 13 months, and closure takes about two to three months longer than in eastern cottontails (Martinson et al., 1961).

Remarks. The swamp rabbit was present in Illinois in the early 1900's, for Arthur Howell (1910), when collecting in southern Illinois in 1909, found it to be "numerous" and ranging in the "narrow belt of swamps close to the Mississippi River, to within a few miles of Grand Tower" and in the Ohio River Valley to "about five miles below Golconda." When Parmalee (1967:144) analyzed the remains from Meyer Cave, Monroe County, which may date back to 4,000 B.C., he found no remains of *Sylvilagus aquaticus,* but at least 456 of *S. floridanus.* This leads me to suspect that swamp rabbits may have moved into southern Illinois not many centuries ago. Purdue and Styles (1986), however, report the occurrence, apparently based on one specimen, of the swamp rabbit from the Koster archeological site, Greene County, somewhere between 5,100 and 8,900 years before the present.

Habitat

Swamp rabbits in southern Illinois are found in cane thickets, in brush bordering swamps, or in dense woods. They are never far from water. The woods consist of sweet gum, oaks, hickories, pecan, box elder, silver maples, and sycamore with a variety of scattered ground-dwelling plants such as cane, sedges, nettle, poison ivy, morning glory, and greenbrier. They may inhabit forest floodplains. There needs to be some cover on the forest floor, but it can be widely dispersed because these rabbits can move rapidly through the forest to available cover.

The development of croplands from lowland forests and floodplains, with their rich soils, in southern Illinois has removed a considerable amount of ideal habitat of the swamp rabbit. In 1981, we were shown places in Alexander County near the Mississippi River where swamp rabbits formerly were present but the area had been logged and planted to crops. Levees usually keep these areas from flooding at this time. When this area was wooded and flooded, swamp rabbits had no difficulty swimming through the water to higher exposed land.

In Louisiana, swamp rabbits occur mainly in heavily wooded areas and coastal marshes and are replaced by eastern cottontails in dry, upland areas (Lowery, 1974). Swamp rabbits live here in dense stands of cane or bulrushes and on wooded ridges with abundant cover along canals.

Habits

Swamp rabbits have a habit of depositing their fecal pellets on raised logs or stumps, and this behavior together with the larger size of the dropping (in contrast to *S. floridanus*) serves to identify the presence of the species. Near Horseshoe Lake, Alexander County, 33 areas of pellets on logs were encountered in a one and one-half mile stretch of habitat (Carol Mahan, personal communication). Whether these platformlike defecating spots are a means of marking the rabbit's territory is not clear.

Male swamp rabbits have a social organization in which linear dominance is established among males (Marsden and Holler, 1964). Once dominance is established, it is maintained for a lifetime.

In southeastern Missouri, swamp rabbits become active in February shortly after sunset, in March at about sunset, and by May about an hour before sunset (Holler and Marsden, 1970). Lowery (1974) found that swamp rabbits in Louisiana usually feed at night, but frequently feed in the early morning or late afternoon; on rainy days they may feed at any time during daylight hours.

When pursued, swamp rabbits will readily take to available water, and they may go into water and swim even when not pursued. By tracking in the snow in southern Indiana, Terrell found that swamp rabbits initially walked into the water and then swam out from shore (Mumford and Whitaker, 1982). Frequently, they swam to patches of non-submerged land in the swamp where they rested and/or hid.

Swamp rabbits were reported to have home ranges averaging 4.6 acres for males and 5.9 acres for females in Missouri (Toll et al., 1960) and 10.3 to 15 acres in Indiana (Terrell, 1972). Home ranges probably are of different sizes in winter and summer, and the size is also dependent on the quality of the habitat.

Food

Swamp rabbits feed on herbaceous material including grasses, cane, sedges, and emergent aquatic vegetation. In southern Indiana, some of the known, commonly eaten plants (Terrell, 1972) were crossvine (*Bignonia capreolata*), gray sedge (*Carex grayii*), poison ivy (*Toxicodendron radicans*), wild rye (*Elymus virginicus*), greenbrier (*Smilax* sp.), and wahoo (*Euonymus atropurpureus*). Surprisingly, giant cane (*Arundinaria gigantea*) was plentiful but was hardly utilized. Perhaps in January, when these observations were made, it was not palatable to these rabbits.

A preferred food in Missouri is the sedge *Carex lupulina* during the period when it is green, which extends from spring into midwinter (Schwartz and Schwartz, 1981).

Like eastern cottontails, swamp rabbits are coprophagous (see also *Sylvilagus floridanus,* p. 137). Swamp rabbits indulge in coprophagy during the daytime after feeding during the night. Examination of 15 stomachs from rabbits taken in southern Illinois showed that all contained reingested pellets; one stomach held more than 200 (Layne, 1958a:235). The reingested pellets "soft and

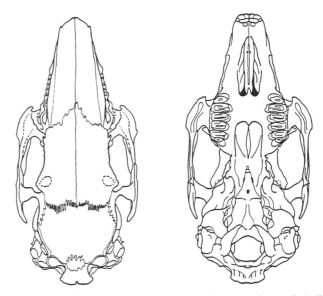

Fig. 8.51. *Sylvilagus aquaticus,* dorsal and ventral views of skull. Near Murphysboro, Jackson Co., Illinois, 3567 UI. Male, 92.2 mm greatest length.

putty-like ... 60 to 10 mm in greatest dimension ... occurred in the cardiac portion of the stomach."

Reproduction

Young are placed in a nest which usually is dug in the ground. The nest is not built sooner than three days before the young are born and sometimes only the night before parturition. The nest can be dug in a half-hour but numerous trips are needed to bring proper dry grasses and leaves for lining the cavity. The fur lining is added just before the young are born. The nests are usually dug in tall grass or in piles of fallen branches (Holler et al., 1963). The depression is four to seven cm deep. About two-thirds of the finished nest is above ground. In western Tennessee, Goodpaster and Hoffmeister (1952) found one nest entirely above ground with the stalks of dead weeds helping to support it. In an enclosed study area in Missouri containing active nests of swamp rabbits, 18 were in grass or other vegetation, and 29 were under or adjacent to logs, stumps, bases of trees, or man-made objects in the study area (Sorensen et al., 1972).

Trial nests or dummy nests are frequently built but not used. These are lined with vegetation, but usually not with fur.

The gestation period is about 38 (35–40) days. The breeding season extends from February into mid-summer. Some females probably produce young in the fall, for Layne (1958a) found a juvenile, weighing only two lbs two oz, in southern Illinois on January 1. The number of young average three per litter, but this is variable, with first litters being smaller. Also young females tend to have more litters per year (average of 3.5) than older females (average of 2.8) in Missouri (Sorensen et al., 1968).

Variation

Two subspecies are recognized by most workers: *S. a. littoralis*, from the Gulf coastal area and *S. a. aquaticus*, from the remainder of the range. Lowery (1974) proposes that *S. a. littoralis* be regarded as a synonym of *S. a. aquaticus* and thus the species would be monotypic. I follow his arrangement.

Sylvilagus aquaticus Bachman

1837. *Lepus aquaticus* Bachman, J. Acad. Nat. Sci. Phila., 7:319. Type locality, western Alabama.
1909. *Sylvilagus aquaticus,* Nelson, N. Amer. Fauna, 29:270.
1895. *Lepus aquaticus attwateri* J. A. Allen, Bull. Amer. Mus. Nat. Hist., 7:327. Type from Medina R., 18 mi S San Antonio, Bexar Co., Texas.
1899. *Lepus telmalemonus* Elliott, Field Columb. Mus., Publ. 38, zool. ser., 1:285. Type from Washita R., near Dougherty, Murray Co., Oklahoma.
1909. *Sylvilagus aquaticus littoralis* Nelson, N. Amer. Fauna, 29:273. Type from Houma, Terrebonne Parish, Louisiana.

Range. Southern third of state, mostly south of a line through Marion and Lawrence counties (Map 8.23).

Diagnosis and Comparisons. See p. 139.

Remarks. Since *S. aquaticus* is here regarded as monotypic, the diagnosis and comparison are as given in the earlier account of the species (p. 139).

Records of occurrence. SPECIMENS EXAMINED, 28. (Dates of capture, when recorded, are given by year in brackets.) **Marion Co.:** [2] 10 mi E Salem, Skillet Fork Bottoms, 1 (FS) [1955]. **Jefferson Co.:** [3b] 6 mi N Sesser [labelled Franklin Co.], 3 (KU) [1938]. **Wayne Co.:** [4] 2¾ mi NW Golden Gate, 2 (SRL). **Jackson Co.:** [10] 12 mi N Murphysboro, Beaucoup Creek, 1 (FS) [1955]. **Williamson Co.:** [11] 2½ mi N Herrin, 1 (KU); [12] 6 mi S Herrin, Crab Orchard Creek Bottoms, 2 (KU) [1938]; [13a] 1 mi S, 1 mi W New Dennison [labelled Franklin Co.], 1 (KU) [1938]. **Union Co.:** [15] 2 mi S Ware, Mississippi River Bottoms, 2 (SRL) [1955]. **Johnson Co.:** [17] West Vienna, 1 (SRL); [18] Reevesville, 1 (FM). **Alexander Co.:** [19a] Olive Branch, 1 (NHS), 3 (FM), 2 (US); [19b] ¼ mi SW Olive Branch, 1 (SIC); [19c] [near] Olive Branch, Horseshoe Lake, 1 (UI) [1954]; [19d] 2 mi NW Cache, 1 (ISU) [1955], 1 (FS) [1955]; [19e] ¼ mi NW Cache, 1 (SRL). **Massac Co.:** [20a] 7 mi NW Metropolis, 1 (SRL); [20b] Metropolis, 1 (NHS).

Additional records: **Washington Co.:** [1] no specific locality [sight record] (Klimstra and Roseberry, 1969:417). **Jefferson Co.:** [3a] near Waltonville [sight record] (Cockrum, 1949:428). **Lawrence Co.:** [5] near St. Francisville, Wabash River [sight record] (Terrel, 1969 in litt.). **Wabash Co.:** [6] Bonpas Creek, near Mt. Carmel [sight record] (Terrel, 1969 in litt.); [7] Beall Woods Cons. Area [sight record] (Terrel, 1969 in litt.). **Randolph Co.:** [8] Sparta [sight record] (Layne, 1958a:235). **Perry Co.:** [9] Du Quoin [sight record] (Layne, 1958a:235). **Williamson Co.:** [13b] Saline Creek, 3 to 4 mi S Marion [sight record] (Cockrum, 1949:428). **Gallatin Co.:** [14] no specific locality [sight record] (Klimstra and Roseberry, 1969:417). **Johnson Co.:** [16] Parker [sight record] (Cockrum, 1949:428). **Massac Co.:** [20] Metropolis [sight record], (Layne, 1958a:235.

Lepus, Hares and jack rabbits

Diagnosis. A large-sized leporid with ears long, hind feet long; auditory bullae inflated, interparietal fused to the parietals in adults, bones on sides of rostrum porous or fenestrated, supraorbital processes flared outward from braincase; tibia and fibula fused distally; newborn precocial.

Dental formula. 2/1, 0/0, 3/2, 3/3.

Comparisons. Lepus differs noticeably from *Sylvilagus* as pointed out in the account of that genus (p. 133).

Lepus townsendii, White-tailed jack rabbit

Range. Probably at one time from Whiteside and Lee counties northward; now probably mostly in western Jo Daviess County.

Diagnosis. A species of *Lepus* which in winter is white (except for certain black markings; see *Color,* following), tail white dorsally and ventrally, although there may be a few dark hairs dorsally; braincase relatively broad.

Color. In summer pelage, dorsum gray interspersed with some black and cinnamon, venter whitish except in the throat and neck area, which is the same color as dorsum, tops of hind feet white, tops of forefeet cinnamon. In full winter pelage, whitish except ears cinnamon-gray with black tips, and tops of forefeet cinnamon. In the fall and spring, there are transitional patterns of pelage as a result of molting from a summer to winter pelage, or vice versa.

Comparisons. L. townsendii is the only *Lepus* in Illinois.

Fig. 8.52A. White-tailed jack rabbit, *Lepus townsendii,* in winter pelage. (From Hoffmeister and Mohr, 1957. Photograph by U.S. Fish and Wildlife Service)

Least Shrew   *Cryptotis parva*

Virginia Opossum   *Didelphis virginiana*

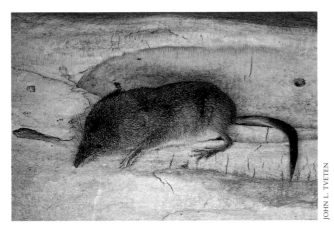

Masked Shrew   *Sorex cinereus*

Southern Short-tailed Shrew   *Blarina carolinensis*

Southeastern Myotis *Myotis austroriparius*

ROGER BARBOUR

Little Brown Myotis *Myotis lucifugus*

ROGER BARBOUR

Gray Myotis *Myotis grisescens*

ROGER BARBOUR

Keen's Myotis *Myotis keenii*

ROGER BARBOUR

Eastern Pipistrelle *Pipistrellus subflavus*

JOHN L. TVETEN

Silver-haired Bat *Lasionycteris noctivagans*

ROGER BARBOUR

Evening Bat *Nycticeius humeralis*

ROGER BARBOUR

Big Brown Bat *Eptesicus fuscus*

JOHN L. TVETEN

Red Bat *Lasiurus borealis*

American Free-tailed Bat *Tadarida brasiliensis*

Hoary Bat *Lasiurus cinereus*

Rafinesque's Big-eared Bat *Plecotus rafinesquii*

JOHN L. TVETEN

Swamp Rabbit *Sylvilagus aquaticus*

KARL H. MASLOWSKI

Eastern Cottontail *Sylvilagus floridanus*

KARL H. MASLOWSKI

Eastern Chipmunk *Tamias striatus*

ROGER BARBOUR

Franklin's Ground Squirrel   *Spermophilus franklinii*

JOHN L. TVETEN

Thirteen-lined Ground Squirrel
Spermophilus tridecemlineatus

ROGER BARBOUR

Red Squirrel   *Tamiasciurus hudsonicus*

ROGER BARBOUR

Woodchuck   *Marmota monax*

Eastern Gray Squirrel *Sciurus carolinensis*

Fox Squirrel *Sciurus niger*

Southern Flying Squirrel *Glaucomys volans*

Eastern Gray Squirrel (Albino) *Sciurus carolinensis*

KARL H. MASLOWSKI

Beaver   *Castor canadensis*

JOHN L. TVETEN

Marsh Rice Rat   *Oryzomys palustris*

JOHN L. TVETEN

Western Harvest Mouse   *Reithrodontomys megalotis*

Cotton Mouse   *Peromyscus gossypinus*

JOHN L. TVETEN

Golden Mouse   *Ochrotomys nuttalli*

JOHN L. TVETEN

White-footed Mouse   *Peromyscus leucopus*

KARL H. MASLOWSKI

Deer Mouse   *Peromyscus maniculatus*

ROGER BARBOUR

Eastern Wood Rat   *Neotoma floridana*

JOHN L. TVETEN

Plains Pocket Gopher (Illinois)   *Geomys bursarius illinoensis*

ILLINOIS NATURAL HISTORY SURVEY, MICHAEL JEFFORDS

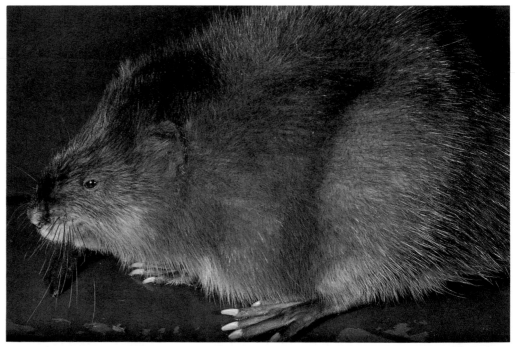

Muskrat   *Ondatra zibethicus*

ROGER BARBOUR

ROGER BARBOUR

Southern Bog Lemming *Synaptomys cooperi*

JOHN L. TVETEN

Prairie Vole *Microtus ochrogaster*

JOHN L. TVETEN

Pine Vole *Microtus pinetorum*

JOHN L. TVETEN

Meadow Vole *Microtus pennsylvanicus*

Norway Rat *Rattus norvegicus*

Meadow Jumping Mouse *Zapus hudsonius*

House Mouse *Mus musculus*

ROGER BARBOUR

Gray Fox   *Urocyon cinereoargenteus*

KARL H. MASLOWSKI

Red Fox   *Vulpes vulpes*

ROGER BARBOUR

Coyote   *Canis latrans*

Raccoon   *Procyon lotor*

Least Weasel   *Mustela nivalis*

Long-tailed Weasel   *Mustela frenata*

KARL H. MASLOWSKI

Mink *Mustela vison*

KARL H. MASLOWSKI

Mink *Mustela vison*

JOHN L. TVETEN

Striped Skunk *Mephitis mephitis*

JOHN L. TVETEN

Badger *Taxidea taxus*

White-tailed Deer *Odocoileus virginianus*

Bobcat *Felis rufus*

River Otter *Lutra canadensis*

Snowshoe rabbits, *Lepus americanus,* occur 100 miles to the north in Wisconsin; black-tailed jack rabbits, *Lepus californicus,* occur 100 miles to the southwest in Missouri. *L. townsendii* differs from *L. californicus* in having the top of the tail almost completely white, slightly shorter ears, more grayish and less blackish coloration of dorsum, and a white winter pelage.

L. townsendii differs from *L. americanus* in having longer ears, white winter pelage with tops of forefeet and most of ears with some cinnamon or gray rather than whitish; skull much larger.

Chromosomes. Diploid number of chromosomes, 2N = 48; 42 metacentrics and submetacentrics, 4 acrocentrics (Hsu and Benirschke, 1971a).

Secondary sexual variation. Orr (1940:20) reported that in California, females were 3.2 percent larger than males.

Molt. Adults have two molts each year. Summer pelage is acquired by March or April; winter pelage by November or December. Animals become physiologically "winter white" before the new white hair comes in. If a patch of gray hair is removed from a physiologically white animal, it will grow in as a white patch. The same is true for the physiologically "summer gray."

Remarks. White-tailed jack rabbits are truly hares, with all of the characteristics of *Lepus.* It would probably be better to call them white-tailed hares. These hares have a limited distribution in Illinois, being known only from the northwesternmost corner.

I have regarded *Lepus townsendii* as a "native" species of Illinois, although it probably reached here quite recently (80 to 120 years ago). For Wisconsin, however, Jackson (1961:106) concluded that it is not indigenous to the state. He wrote, "At one time, I too thought the

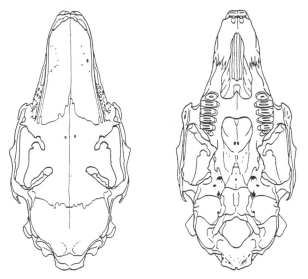

Fig. 8.52B. *Lepus townsendii,* dorsal and ventral views of skull. Near Hanover, Jo Daviess Co., Illinois, 3540 UI. Male, 91.0 mm greatest length.

white-tailed jack rabbit was native to western Wisconsin, but my travels and inquiries in that part of the state, and the history of the species in Iowa and Minnesota, convince me that it is not indigenous to Wisconsin." At an earlier time, Leopold (1947) thought that the white-tailed jack rabbit in Wisconsin was probably the result of a natural spread from the west, although there were some transplantings of these animals.

I have no reason to believe that white-tailed jack rabbits have been introduced by transplanting into northwestern Illinois. Rather, it would seem that this area in the sand prairie in and near the Savanna Ordinance Depot, Jo Daviess County, provides excellent habitat and they have moved, under natural population pressures, into this area, either from Wisconsin or Iowa.

We know that in 1892 white-tailed jack rabbits were established in Johnson County, Iowa, less than 80 miles south-southwest of Savanna Ordinance Depot (see Bowles, 1975:59). It would be no problem for these hares to move up to the Mississippi River and across it on winter ice to enter Illinois. Bowles (1975) pointed out that white-tailed jack rabbits were probably restricted to the northwestern part of Iowa prior to the cultivation of the tallgrass prairie by settlers. He thought that the white-tailed jack rabbits moved rapidly after the prairie cultivation and reached Muscatine County, Iowa, on the Mississippi River, by the late 1890's.

A perusal of the early literature on the histories of the counties in northwestern Illinois prior to 1900 gives no indication that white-tailed jack rabbits were present. Twelve county histories that give some information on the mammals of Jo Daviess, Stephenson, Carroll, Whiteside, Lee, and Ogle counties make no mention of large rabbits or rabbits that are white in winter. One account of 1877 for Whiteside County refers to a "Hare," but this could be a reference to *Sylvilagus.*

I suspect that white-tailed jack rabbits did not reach northwestern Illinois until the late 1800's or early 1900's. But it is not surprising, with the alteration of the original vegetation, that *Lepus* could and did voluntarily move into this area rather than being transplanted there. After all, western harvest mice, much less capable of moving great distances than hares, have moved across the state and into Indiana in less than 50 years.

Habitat

White-tailed jack rabbits throughout much of their range live in open country, often in grassland or sagelands, with relatively little cover. They are found in much the same habitat in the sand prairie country in northwestern Illinois. During the day, these hares rest in forms which are shallow depressions they dig among vegetation in which they can partially hide. In the winter, they may dig depressions or holes in the snow.

Map 8.24. Known records of occurrence of the white-tailed jack rabbit, *Lepus townsendii*. The subspecies is *L. t. campanius*. The range of the species in the United States is shaded.

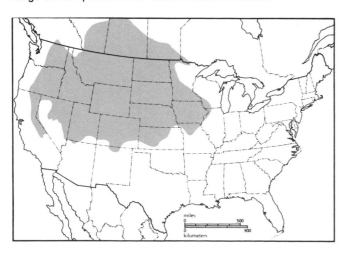

Habits

Whitetails are active primarily at night, but may also be active in the early morning and late evening. Thus, they often are not visible to casual observation. They are also well camouflaged when resting in their forms and are passed by without being seen. When they take flight, they can make long leaps, jumping high enough to keep an eye on any pursuer and to clear any ground vegetation.

Food

Nothing is known of the foods eaten by this species in Illinois. In Wisconsin, Jackson (1961) reported that in summer whitetails eat green vegetation of a variety of grasses, cultivated plants, and weeds. In winter, they eat buds and bark if green material is not available.

Reproduction

Mating is said to occur in April or later, with a gestation period of about one month, and with a litter size of two to six (Jackson, 1961). Young are precocial at birth, being well furred and with the eyes open. The young are brought forth in a form, not in specially prepared and lined nests. It is not certain if more than one litter may be produced in one year.

Remarks

Jackson (1961) indicated that the reported kill of white-tailed jack rabbits in 1951–1952 in Wisconsin was 19,383 and that the total population may have been between 50,000 and 75,000. If this is correct, it is surprising that the population of whitetails in northwestern Illinois has not increased more. However, it is not known how abundant the species is. Mohr (1941) considered the white-tailed jack rabbit to be "present in half a dozen counties in the northwest corner of Illinois." Yeager (1945) had one or two reports of whitetails from Winnebago County, but they were probably drifters. In 1955, the Rev. Mr. Paul Gordon of Dixon, Illinois, shot a white-tailed jack rabbit in the "Kingdom Area" located between Oregon and Dixon on the east side of the Rock River near the Ogle and Lee county line. A photograph of this hare and a cottontail appeared in the Dixon Evening Telegraph on December 22, 1955. The hare in this picture is undoubtedly a white-tailed jack rabbit in white pelage with black-tipped ears. On December 29, 1947 a specimen was collected 6 mi W, 1 mi N Hanover in Jo Daviess County. It is in the University of Illinois collection. Another specimen was collected on the Savanna Army Ordinance Depot on February 12, 1954, and is in the Illinois State Museum.

On February 2 and 3, 1983, numerous persons from the Illinois Department of Conservation made a survey in and around the Savanna Depot, searching especially for white-tailed jack rabbits. Although many miles of road were travelled and fields walked—and there was light snow and sleet at the time—only one jack rabbit was observed. At the Depot, however, workers said that they see white-tailed jack rabbits regularly and even put lettuce out for them.

Variation

Two subspecies have been ascribed to this wide-ranging species: *L. t. townsendii* to the west, and *L. t. campanius* to the east.

Lepus townsendii campanius Hollister

1915. *Lepus townsendii campanius* Hollister, Proc. Biol. Soc. Wash., 28:70, a renaming of *campestris* (following).

1837. *Lepus campestris* Bachman, J. Acad. Nat. Sci. Phila., 7:349, not *Lepus cuniculus campestris* Meyer, 1790. Type locality, plains of Saskatchewan, probably near Carlton House.

Range. As given for the species (p. 142 and Map 8.24).

Diagnosis and Comparisons. A subspecies of large size; dorsum with considerable buff color; skull larger with broader rostrum. See Table 8.12 (p. 134) for measurements.

Records of occurrence. SPECIMENS EXAMINED, 2. **Jo Daviess Co.:** [1a] 6 mi W, 1 mi N Hanover, 1 (UI); [1b] Savanna Army Ordinance Depot, 1 (ISM).

Additional records. [2] "The Kingdom Area" between Oregon and Dixon on east side of Rock River [photo of rabbit in Dixon Evening Telegraph, December 22, 1955].

Order Rodentia, Rodents

Rodents are gnawing mammals with a pair of ever-growing upper and lower incisors, specialized for cutting; anterior faces of incisors are enamel, remainder, dentine; diastema (gap) formed behind incisor by absence of other incisors and canine; maximum dental formula 1/1, 0/0, 2/1, 3/3, or 22 or less; interparietal bone present; incisive or palatine foramina large; females have duplex uterus, males an os penis or baculum; the masseter muscle and its attachment on the zygomatic arch results in three types of skulls: sciuromorph, myomorph, hystricomorph; size varies from as small as shrews (harvest mouse) to as large as pigs (beaver). Rodents occupy nearly every habitat from under the ground to the trees, water, and deserts; most have a high reproductive rate; some hibernate. In Illinois there are five families: Sciuridae, Geomyidae, Castoridae, Muridae, Zapodidae.

KEY TO RODENTIA IN ILLINOIS,
including *Reithrodontomys humilis* and
Sigmodon hispidus known from Kentucky

1a. Hairs at mid-length of tail longer than diameter of tail; frontal bones with well-developed postorbital process   SCIURIDAE   2

1b. Hairs at mid-length of tail shorter than diameter of tail or absent; frontal bones without well-developed postorbital processes   9

2a. Tail not more than one-fourth of total length, feet black, length of skull more than 70 mm, incisors whitish   *Marmota monax*   p. 154

2b. Tail more than one-fourth of total length, feet not black although may be grayish; length of skull less than 70 mm, incisors yellowish   3

3a. Large, loose fold of skin between front and hind legs, nocturnal in habits, interorbital region of skull deeply notched anterior to postorbital processes   *Glaucomys volans*   p. 181

3b. No loose fold of skin between legs, diurnal in habits, interorbital region not deeply notched anterior to postorbital processes   4

4a. Hairs at mid-length of tail less than 20 mm long (except in *Spermophilus franklinii* where nearly 35 mm), zygomata tend to converge anteriorly with the anterior part twisted toward a horizontal plane   5

4b. Hairs at mid-length of tail more than 35 mm long, zygomata nearly parallel   7

5a. Reddish on head, flanks, and rump, white stripe bordered with black on sides; one upper premolar (four cheek teeth)   *Tamias striatus*   p. 149

5b. No reddish (may be yellowish brown) on head, rump, and flanks, no solid white stripe on sides; two upper premolars (five cheek teeth)   6

6a. Numerous light stripes, some in the form of interrupted stripes, total length less than 320 mm, length of skull less than 45 mm   *Spermophilus tridecemlineatus*   p. 159

6b. No stripes on body, total length more than 320 mm, length of skull more than 45 mm   *Spermophilus franklinii*   p. 162

7a. Short black stripe on side between darker upper parts and lighter underparts, total length less than 350 mm, length of upper cheek teeth less than 10 mm   *Tamiasciurus hudsonicus*   p. 177

7b. No black stripe on sides, total length more than 350 mm, length of upper cheek teeth more than 10 mm   8

8a. Upper parts nearly uniformly gray, underparts gray or white, tail with white-tipped hairs, upper molariform teeth five, but anteriormost one rudimentary   *Sciurus carolinensis*   p. 166

8b. Upper parts dappled gray, underparts reddish, tail with red-tipped hairs, upper molariform teeth four   *Sciurus niger*   p. 171

9a. Claws on front feet three times as long as claws on hind feet, external cheek pouches present, color usually black, each upper incisor with two longitudinal grooves, but inner groove small   GEOMYIDAE *Geomys bursarius*   p. 185

9b. Claws on front and hind feet about equal in size, no external cheek pouches, color usually not black, each upper incisor without grooves or with only one   10

10a. Tail flattened dorsoventrally, size large (body length more than 400 mm), skull large (length more than 90 mm), incisive foramen (=palatine slit) shorter than grinding surface of first two upper cheek teeth   CASTORIDAE   *Castor canadensis*   p. 191

10b. Tail not flattened dorsoventrally, body length less than 400 mm, length of skull less than 75 mm, incisive foramen (=palatine slit) longer than grinding surface of first two upper cheek teeth   11

11a. Tail at least 1⅓ times the length of head and body, four upper cheek teeth, infraorbital foramen enlarged   *Zapus hudsonius*   p. 257

11b. Tail less than 1⅓ times the length of head and body, three upper cheek teeth, infraorbital foramen not enlarged but slitlike   12

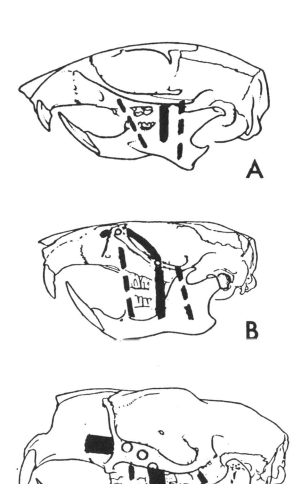

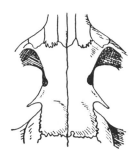

Fig. 8.55. *Glaucomys* with interorbital region deeply notched. (From Hoffmeister and Mohr, 1957. Charles A. McLaughlin)

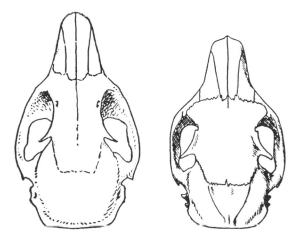

Fig. 8.53. Types of skulls in three groups of rodents. The heavy black line represents the path of the masseter medialis muscle. (A) Sᴄɪᴜʀᴏᴍᴏʀᴘʜ, with no part of the masseter medialis passing through the reduced infraorbital canal. (B) Mʏᴏᴍᴏʀᴘʜ, with a branch of the masseter medialis extending through infraorbital canal slightly onto rostrum. (C) Hʏsᴛʀɪᴄᴏᴍᴏʀᴘʜ, with greatly enlarged infraorbital canal with masseter medialis extending well onto side of rostrum. (From Hoffmeister, Mammals of Arizona, 1986)

Fig. 8.56. Zygomata of *Spermophilus* (left) converging anteriorly, as contrasted with *Sciurus* (right), nearly parallel. (From Hoffmeister and Mohr, 1957. Charles A. McLaughlin)

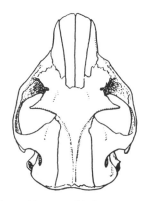

Fig. 8.54. Sciuridae with postorbital process. (From Hoffmeister and Mohr, 1957. Charles A. McLaughlin)

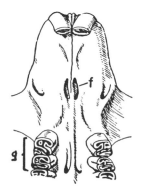

Fig. 8.57. *Castor canadensis* rostrum, ventral view, with palatine foramina (f) shorter than the grinding surface of first two molars (g). (From Hoffmeister and Mohr, 1957. Charles A. McLaughlin)

12a. Tail flattened laterally, front feet with five clawed toes, length of skull more than 60 mm
Ondatra zibethicus p. 241

12b. Tail not flattened, front feet with four clawed toes, length of skull less than 60 mm 13

13a. Tail less than ⅓ length of head and body, molariform teeth prismatic, consisting of enamel loops or triangles 14

13b. Tail more than ⅓ length of head and body, molariform teeth of cusps or lophs 17

14a. Fur long and fine; upper incisors broad, orange-colored, and grooved; tail short and usually equal to or shorter than hind foot
Synaptomys cooperi p. 247

14b. Fur not so long and fine; upper incisors ivory-colored, not broad, and ungrooved; tail usually longer than hind foot 15

15a. Tail less than 25 mm in length, hind foot less than 18 mm, interorbital region more than 4 mm wide *Microtus pinetorum* p. 238

15b. Tail more than 25 mm in length, hind foot more than 18 mm; interorbital region less than 4 mm wide 16

16a. Fur of underparts tipped with white, last upper molar with 5 or 6 enamel loops
Microtus pennsylvanicus p. 227

16b. Fur of underparts tipped with yellow or ochraceous (may be lacking in juveniles), last upper molar with 4 enamel loops
Microtus ochrogaster p. 234

17a. Length of body under 80 mm and each upper incisor with longitudinal groove 18

17b. Length of body more than 80 mm (except *Mus*), and upper incisors without longitudinal groove 19

18a. Upper parts grayish or light buff, top of head same color as back, nasals usually more than 7.0 mm *Reithrodontomys megalotis* p. 199

18b. Upper parts reddish or dark brown, top of head dark brown to blackish, nasals usually less than 7.0 mm *Reithrodontomys humulis* p. 44

19a. Total length more than 200 mm, hind foot 28 mm or more, greatest breadth of skull across zygomatic arches more than 15.0 mm 20

19b. Total length less than 200 mm, hind foot less than 28 mm; greatest breadth of skull across zygomatic arches less than 15.0 mm 24

20a. Cheek teeth without distinct cusp but lophs or connected triangles, tail sparsely haired 21

20b. Cheek teeth with distinctive cusps (unless teeth are badly worn), tail appears as hairless 22

21a. Hind feet white and more than 35 mm long, anterior edge of infraorbital plate of skull smooth, lateral edges of braincase smooth
Neotoma floridana p. 222

21b. Hind feet gray and 35 mm or less in length, anterior edge of infraorbital plate of skull with projecting spine, lateral edges of braincase beaded *Sigmodon hispidus* p. 44

Fig. 8.58. *Sigmodon hispidus*, side view of rostrum, showing projecting spine (arrow) on infraorbital plate. (From Severinghaus and Hoffmeister, 1978)

22a. Hind foot length 33 mm or less, upper cheek teeth with cusps in two rows, length of skull less than 35 mm *Oryzomys palustris* p. 196

22b. Hind foot length 34 mm or more, upper cheek teeth with extra cusp resulting in cusps in three rows, but with wear these fuse together, length of skull more than 35 mm 23

23a. Tail longer than head-body length, temporal ridges on sides of parietals bowed out with greatest distance between temporal ridges usually 13 mm or more *Rattus rattus* p. 251

23b. Tail shorter than head-body length, temporal ridges more or less parallel with greatest distance between temporal ridges usually less than 13 mm *Rattus norvegicus* p. 252

24a. Belly and feet dirty gray, tail sparsely haired, upper incisors when viewed from side with a pronounced terminal notch
Mus musculus p. 255

Fig. 8.59. *Mus musculus* with notched upper incisor. (From Hoffmeister and Mohr, 1957. Charles A. McLaughlin)

24b. Belly and feet whitish, tail haired, upper incisors without a pronounced terminal notch   25

25a. Upper parts reddish, anterior edge of infraorbital plate straight or even slightly concave   *Ochrotomys nuttalli*   p. 218

25b. Upper parts grayish brown or brownish, anterior edge of infraorbital plate bowed forward   26

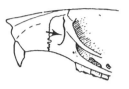 

Fig. 8.60. *Ochrotomys nuttalli* (left), lateral view of rostral region, showing a slightly concave infraorbital plate; this can be contrasted with plate in *Peromyscus* (right). (From Hoffmeister and Mohr, 1957. Charles A. McLaughlin)

26a. Hind foot length (if accurately measured) 18 mm or less, tail usually less than 60 mm, mid-dorsal dark stripe prominent, zygomatic width of skull anteriorly less than 12 mm   *Peromyscus maniculatus*   p. 202

26b. Hind foot length (in adults) more than 18 mm, tail usually more than 60 mm, mid-dorsal stripe may be suggested but not prominent, zygomatic width anteriorly more than 12 mm   27

27a. Hind foot length usually between 19 and 23 mm, crown length of upper toothrow 3.8 mm or less, lower molars usually without an entolophulid   *Peromyscus leucopus*   p. 206

27b. Hind foot length usually 23 mm or more, crown length of upper toothrow usually 3.8 mm or more, lower molars with entolophulids (see Fig. 8.88, p. 208)   *Peromyscus gossypinus*   p. 214

Family Sciuridae, Squirrels and allies

Squirrels, chipmunks, prairie dogs, marmots, and flying squirrels have a sciuromorph skull type with well-developed postorbital processes; four or five cheek teeth on each side of upper jaw; mostly diurnal except flying squirrels (nocturnal); some live in the ground, others in trees.

Tamias, Chipmunks

Diagnosis. A sciurid of small size with prominent stripes on back and face, tail about one-third of total length and bushy, hand with four fingers, internal cheek pouches, skull relatively long and narrow, infraorbital foramen round and situated in zygomatic plate, antorbital canal absent. The dark median dorsal stripes may extend from shoulders to rump with two shorter dark stripes on each side of lateral light stripe, less-well-defined stripes on face include one dark stripe through eye, one light one above and below eye, each bordered with a dark stripe.

Dental formula. 1/1, 0/0, 1/1, 3/3.

Chromosomes. 2N = 38; four pairs of large metacentrics, six large submetacentrics, one small metacentric, three large acrocentrics, four small acrocentrics, X, large submetacentric; Y, dotlike (D. P. Snyder, 1982).

Baculum. Straight-shafted with an upturned spoon-shaped tip.

Comparisons. Tamias can be distinguished from Franklin's ground squirrel, flying squirrels, and all tree squirrels in Illinois by its characteristic pattern of variously colored stripes and smaller size. *Tamias* differs from thirteen-lined ground squirrels, *Spermophilus tridecemlineatus,* in having white lateral stripes bordered with black, dark stripe through the eye, only four pairs of upper cheek teeth, and no antorbital canal.

Chipmunks of the genus *Eutamias (E. minimus)* occur less than 100 miles to the north of Illinois and differ from *Tamias* as follows: facial stripes more pronounced, dark stripes on dorsum more pronounced, five rather than four pairs of upper cheekteeth, baculum with a dorsal keel at tip.

Remarks. Some persons regard eastern chipmunks (*Tamias*) and other chipmunks (*Eutamias*) sufficiently similar and related to place them in the same genus. I have weighed the pros and cons for such an arrangement but at the present time still regard chipmunks as belonging to two genera, with *Tamias* being monotypic.

Tamias striatus, Eastern chipmunk

Range. Throughout the state, but not present in many habitats; may be absent in southeastern Illinois (Map 8.25).

Diagnosis. T. striatus is the only species of *Tamias,* and the *Diagnosis and Comparisons* given for the genus suffice for the species also (p. 152).

Fig. 8.61A. Eastern chipmunk, *Tamias striatus.* (From Hoffmeister and Mohr, 1957. Photograph by K. Maslowski)

Growth. Eastern chipmunks reach adult size in weight in about six months and the skull attains maximum size in four months or less in some measurements (Ellis, 1979).

Secondary sexual variation. Ellis (1979) found no consistent, significant differences in seven samples of *Tamias.*

Aging. Animals are considered as adult—that is, with little later increase in size—when the upper premolar has considerable wear.

Molt. In Illinois, adult males molt twice a year: in the spring in April or May and the fall, August or September. Adult females molt in June or July.

Habitat

Eastern chipmunks live on wooded bluffs or slopes, ravines, or in areas with much underbrush, all in or adjacent to deciduous forests. Primary needs are ample sites for perching and cover for burrow entrances, as well as places to dig burrows. Such areas often contain tree stumps, rocks or stones, and fallen timber. Chipmunks avoid areas that will flood, since their burrows would be endangered. Because these animals have limited digging ability, eastern chipmunks take advantage of natural crevices, cracks, and underground cavities. They often take refuge in rock fences and rock walls, along and under gravestones, and wood piles. Chipmunks are absent from low, flat lands that are without natural hiding places and are subject to periodic plowing. Thus, eastern chipmunks are absent from nearly all cultivated lands and from much of the bottomlands in Illinois.

Habits

Eastern chipmunks are diurnal. Activity and times of activity during the day are dependent upon many factors: time of year, weather conditions, breeding cycle, age and sex, and food availability. In general, much of the above-ground activity is spent in food hunting, food storage (hoarding), perching, vocalizing, and running (Yahner, 1978).

Food hunting goes on much of the time, but food hoarding intensifies in late summer and fall. Perch sites are selected to provide lookouts for possible predators and a place from which to give calls. All food items for storage are transported to the burrow in the mouth in internal cheek pouches; this activity requires much running. Running both to store and to search for food keeps chipmunks active during much of their above-ground time.

Burrow systems can be anywhere from simple to complex (Panuska and Wade, 1956). Those that are short and only slightly expanded at the end may be escape burrows. Others may be many feet (20±) long with laterals and storage chambers (Fig. 8.62). The same burrow system may or may not be used for the lifetime of the individual.

Eastern chipmunks are much less active above ground during the winter months but they do not hibernate in the true sense. Unlike hibernators, eastern chipmunks do not put on fat during the fall, do not reduce their metabolic rate for long periods of time, and are active at various if not all times during the winter. A state of

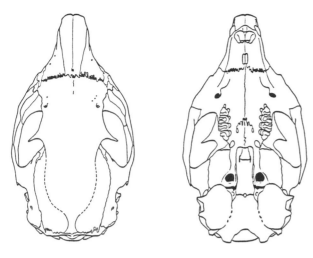

Fig. 8.61B. *Tamias striatus,* dorsal and ventral views of skull. Near Shelbyville, Shelby Co., Illinois, 41975 UI. Male, 43.9 mm greatest length.

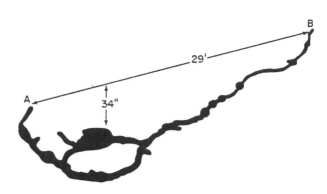

Fig. 8.61C. Burrow of *Tamias striatus* at Waupaca, Waupaca Co., Wisconsin. The burrow extended about 29 feet with one exit (B), but the burrow at the far left (A) is within a few inches of the surface. The large chamber is 34 inches deep. Numerous side passages of the burrow are not shown. From a photograph of a clay model reconstuction by Panuska and Wade (1956).

inactivity in chipmunks is best described as torpor, not hibernation, and this state of inactivity usually lasts for about 24 hours; in a few cases, for several days. It never lasts for several weeks or months as in Illinois ground squirrels and woodchucks. When in torpor, chipmunks gain more weight than non-torpid ones (Brenner, 1975). Bouts of torpor may be controlled endogenously (Scott and Fisher, 1972).

Eastern chipmunks show various agonistic behavioral characteristics: chasing, fighting, threatening. Threats include foot-stamping and tail-waving; chases may be associated with protection of territory, and fighting is mostly biting.

Food

Eastern chipmunks rely on nuts, seeds, fruits, fungi, flowers, and buds as staples for food. Their diet varies with the season and with availability. Chipmunks also take advantage of "unusual" food, such as snails, caterpillars, and frogs and of special handouts such as seeds from a bird feeder or leftovers at a picnic ground.

In Indiana, chipmunks feed extensively on nuts and acorns, which were the major items in their diet (61% by volume). Other items included blackberry (8%) and other vegetable material (nearly another 8%). A considerable number of invertebrates, such as beetles, grasshoppers, spiders, and others were eaten also, according to Mumford and Whitaker (1982).

In Ohio, a study was made of the fecal pellets to ascertain the food eaten (Wrazen and Svendsen, 1978). In May, root material made up 80 percent of the diet. From June to August, 46 percent of the diet was plant material, with a considerable number of insects and fungi also eaten. In the fall, consumption of acorns, nuts, and berries increased.

Reproduction

Mating occurs in late February and March and again in June and July. In central Illinois most young are born in April or May and in July or August. For example, females caught in March generally are pregnant; those caught in April and early May usually are lactating. Eight out of ten caught on August 7 were lactating; the other two were pregnant. On August 19, all six females caught were lactating.

The gestation period is 31 days. Our specimens had two to four embryos, although litter size may go to five or six. Young are hairless at birth and their eyes do not open until they are about one month of age. Mothers nurse young for about six weeks. By three months of age, young have nearly attained adult size. Young born during one year do not breed and produce young in the same year in Illinois (Ellis, 1979). Females that were born in the previous year commonly produce two litters the following year.

Populations

In Illinois, eastern chipmunks are abundant in some areas, so much so that they may become nuisances, in contrast with other localities where ecological conditions seem equally favorable, but no chipmunks are present. For example, in the Shawnee National Forest in parts of Massac, Johnson, Pope, Hardin, Saline, and Gallatin counties, chipmunks seem to be absent. What controlling factors are involved is not clear.

Scott Ellis (1979) captured 68 adult chipmunks in an 18-acre portion of a cemetery in Danville, Vermilion County, in 1975. Additionally, 86 juveniles were captured during the summer and the density increased to 8.6 animals per acre. Many other areas in east central Illinois that appear to be comparable ecologically have no chipmunks. In an area with more than eight chipmunks per acre, it is apparent that home ranges, if such exist, must overlap considerably and there must be constant competition to extend these areas.

Variation

Many workers have regarded two subspecies to be present in Illinois: *T. s. striatus* and *T. s. griseus*. The monographic and revisionary study by Ellis (1979) recognizes these two also, but for different reasons and with different distributions. I here follow Ellis.

Table 8.14. Summer foods of *Tamias striatus* in southeastern Ohio. Each value represents the percentage of the total number of fecal samples containing the items in a particular month. (After Wrazen and Svendsen, 1978)

	May	June	July	Aug.	Sept.	Oct.
Plant materials						
Acorns	12	8	2	21	57	85
Hickory nuts	44	25	9	0	21	15
Beechnuts	48	0	0	4	21	8
Small seeds	36	37	9	0	0	0
Fruit	24	12	9	36	43	31
Flowers	52	42	9	11	7	8
Leaves	32	21	20	14	14	38
Roots	80	33	15	46	0	0
Animal materials						
Lepidoptera	52	62	29	50	79	38
Coleoptera	32	67	31	57	36	23
Fungi						
Fungi	44	87	67	68	7	8

Tamias striatus striatus (Linnaeus)

1758. [*Sciurus*] *striatus* Linnaeus, Syst. Nat., 10 ed., 1:64. Type locality fixed as upper Savannah River, South Carolina (Howell, 1929).

1857. *Tamias striatus*, Baird, 11th Ann. Rept., Smiths. Inst. for 1856:55.

Range. Nearly all of Illinois except the northernmost counties (Map 8.25).

Diagnosis. A medium- to large-sized subspecies; color of dorsum usually dark with reddish or reddish-brown rump, underside of tail dark orange, nasals long, skull broad across zygomata.

Comparisons. T. s. striatus differs from T. s. griseus in having a slightly longer body, color darker with rump a darker reddish, underside of tail darker, nasals longer, skull broader. Table 8.15.

Records of occurrence. SPECIMENS EXAMINED, 263. **Bureau Co.:** [1a] 3 mi NE Princeton, 1 (NIU); [1b] 3 mi E Princeton, 1 (NIU). **La Salle Co.:** [2] 2 mi SE Utica, 1 (UI). **Hancock Co.:** [3] Warsaw*, 3 (US), 4 (AM). **Fulton Co.:** [4a] 7 mi N Canton, 2 (UI); [4b] 1 mi N Norris, 4 (UI); [5] 4 mi SW Canton, 1 (UI); [6] 5 mi W Bryant, 1 (UI). **McLean Co.:** [7a] 6 mi NW Hudson, 2 (ISU); [7b] 4 mi NW Hudson, 1 (ISU); [8a] 1 mi W Funks Grove, 1 (ISU); [8b] 13 mi SW Bloomington, 1 (ISU). **Piatt Co.:** [9] 7.1 mi W Bondville [maybe Champaign Co.], 1 (UI). **Champaign Co.:** [10a] 2 mi W Mahomet, 1 (UI); [10b] 1 mi E Mahomet, 3 (UI); [10c] 1 mi SE Mahomet, 6 (UI); [10d] Shady Rest, 1 (UI). **Vermilion Co.:** [11] 1 mi S, 3 mi E Collison, 1 (UI); [12] 5 mi NE Homer, 2 (UI); [13] 1 mi SE Oakwood, 1 (UI); [14a] Danville, 73 (UI); [14b] 4 mi SE Danville, 1 (UI); [14c] 4½ mi SE Danville, 12 (UI); [14d] 5 mi SE Danville, 35 (UI); [14e] 7 mi SE Danville, 1 (UI); [15] 5 mi SW Georgetown, 1 (UI). **Jersey Co.:** [16] 4 mi E, 1 mi S Elsah, 1 (SIE). **Macoupin Co.:** [17] 1 mi N White City, 1 (SIE). **Sangamon Co.:** [18]

*Worthen specimens.

Table 8.15. External and cranial measurements (in mm) of *Tamias striatus* in Illinois. Mean, minimum, and maximum, and one standard deviation are given.

	N	Total length	Tail length	Body length	Hind foot length	Greatest length	Palatilar length	Post-palatal length
T. s. griseus Lake Co.	13	251.7 234-275 10.2	91.4 82-100 5.9	160.8 150-180 7.8	35.3 33-37 1.4	41.03 40.1-42.4 0.62	18.24 17.5-19.3 0.51	14.25 13.6-14.6 0.33
T. s. striatus Vermilion Co.	84	255.8 236-278 8.4	92.6 80-103 4.9	163.6 146-180 6.7	36.7 34-40 1.3	42.89 40.3-44.9 1.03	19.34 17.9-20.7 0.61	14.81 13.6-15.9 0.51
Jersey, Macoupin, Madison, St. Clair cos.	19	263.8 250-279 10.5	95.9 86-102 6.0	167.2 151-178 6.1	35.3 32-38 1.6	42.63 40.7-43.9 0.78	19.13 18.0-20.1 0.50	14.91 14.0-15.6 0.41
Union Co.	7	261.4 248-270 10.6	95.6 83-110 9.7	166.0 153-187 10.9	35.7 34-37 1.1	42.30 41.2-42.8 0.59	19.29 18.7-20.0 0.41	14.32 13.8-14.7 0.33

Springfield, 5 (ISM). **Macon Co.:** [19] Decatur, 3 (UI). **Shelby Co.:** [20a] 3½ mi NE Shelbyville, 7 (UI); [20b] ½ mi N Shelbyville, 2 (UI). **Coles Co.:** [21a] 2 mi S Charleston, 1 (UI); [21b] Fox Ridge State Park, 1 (UI). **Clark Co.:** [22] 1 mi W Dolson, 1 (UI); [23] 2 mi S Marshall, Lincoln Trail State Park, 5 (UI).

Madison Co.: [24] 3 mi WSW Godfrey, 4 (SIE); [25a] 5 mi W Edwardsville, 1 (SIE); [25b] Edwardsville, 1 (SIE); [25c] 1 mi S Edwardsville, 1 (SIE); [25d] 2 mi SSW Edwardsville, 6 (SIE); [25e] 4 mi SW Edwardsville, 6 (SIE); [26] Highland, 1 (SIE). **Fayette Co.:** [27] 1 mi NW Vandalia, 1 (UI). **Effingham Co.:** [28] T7N, R6E, Sec. 12 [=5 mi SE Effingham], 1 (UI). **Jasper Co.:** [29] 3 mi NE Newton, Sam Parr State Park, 4 (UI). **St. Clair Co.:** [30] Belleville, 1 (SIE); [31] 2 mi E Marissa, 5 (UI). **Washington Co.:** [32] Posen, 1 (SIE). **Jefferson Co.:** [33] 8 mi SE Ashley, 1 (SIE). **Richland Co.:** [35] Olney, 1 (US). **Perry Co.:** [36a] Pinckneyville, 1 (SIC); [36b] near Pinckneyville, 1 (SRL); [37] Pyatt Stripmines, 2 (SRL). **Jackson Co.:** [38b] Carbondale, 2 (SIC); [38c] 1 mi S Carbondale, 7 (SIC); [39a] 7 mi SW Murphysboro, 1 (SRL); [39c] Hickory Ridge [labelled Union Co.], 1 (SRL); [39d] Pomona, 4 (SRL). **Williamson Co.:** [40] Herrin, 1 (KU); [41] Little Grassy Lake, 1 (SIC). **Union Co.:** [42b] Pine Hills Recreation Area, 2 (SIC), 1 (ISM), 3 (UI); [42c] 4 mi NW Wolf Lake, 1 (TU); [42d] Wolf Lake, Pine Hills, 1 (US); [3] (UI); [43a] 2 mi N Cobden, 1 (SRL); [43b] 1½ mi N Cobden, 1 (SRL); [43c] 2 mi W Cobden, 2 (SRL); [43d] Cobden, 1 (CU); [43e] 5 mi E Cobden, 1 (SRL); [44] 4 mi S Ware, 1 (UI). **Alexander Co.:** [45] 1½ mi NW Elco, 4 (UI); [46] 2½ mi SSW Olive Branch, 1 (UI).

Additional records. **Jefferson Co.:** [34] Woodlawn, (Cory, 1912:30). **Jackson Co.:** [38a] 3 mi N Carbondale, 1 (FS); [38a] 7 mi SW Murphysboro, Chalk Bluff, 1 (FS). **Union Co.:** [42a] Aldridge, Pine Hills, 1 (FS); [42e] ½ mi E Wolf Lake along bluffs, 1 (FS).

Tamias striatus griseus Mearns

1891. *Tamias striatus griseus* Mearns, Bull. Amer. Mus. Nat. Hist., 3:231. Type from Fort Snelling, Hennepin Co., Minnesota.

Range. Northern Illinois, from northern Will County northward.

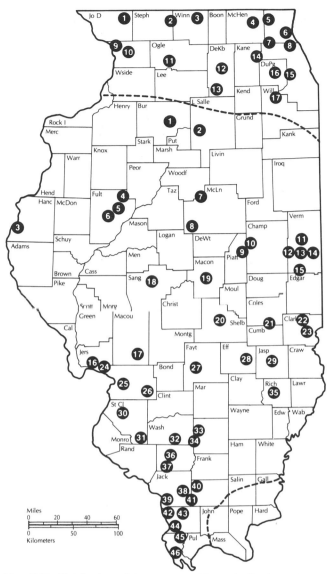

Map 8.25. Distribution of the eastern chipmunk, *Tamias striatus.* In northern Illinois, the subspecies is *T. s. griseus;* elsewhere, *T. s. striatus.* Localities of occurrence as numbered are referenced in *Records of occurrence.* The range of the species in the United States is shaded.

	Nasal length	Zygo-matic breadth	Inter-orbital breadth	Cranial breadth	Al. maxillary toothrow
	13.29	22.76	10.93	16.48	6.44
	12.9-14.1	21.5-23.5	10.1-11.3	15.7-16.9	6.2-6.8
	0.37	0.54	0.39	0.37	0.17
	14.58	23.70	11.43	16.79	6.57
	13.0-15.8	21.4-25.4	10.4-12.2	15.9-17.8	6.0-7.2
	0.67	0.75	0.41	0.35	0.23
	14,21	23.76	11.66	16.92	6.51
	13.1-15.2	22.7-25.1	10.4-12.7	16.9-17.5	5.9-7.3
	0.56	0.67	0.57	0.39	0.31
	13.96	23.40	11.50	16.77	6.60
	13.1-14.6	22.7-24.4	11.1-12.0	16.2-17.2	6.1-7.1
	0.56	0.68	0.37	0.35	0.40

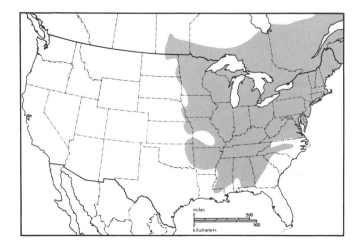

Diagnosis. A subspecies of *T. striatus* of medium size, color of dorsum with considerable gray and rump reddish orange, underside of tail orange, nasals short, skull narrow across zygomata.

Comparisons. For a comparison with *T. s. striatus,* see account of that subspecies (p. 152).

Records of occurrence. SPECIMENS EXAMINED, 35.
Jo Daviess Co.: [1] 3½ mi S, 2 mi E Apple River, 4 (UI). **Stephenson Co.:** [2] Rock Run Creek, 1½ mi SW Davis, 1 (UI). **Winnebago Co.:** [3a] 3 mi W South Beloit, 1 (SRL); [3b] 1 mi E, ½ mi S Rockton, 1 (UI); [3c] 1 mi S, ½ mi E Rockton, 1 (UI). **Lake Co.:** [5a] 2 mi W Antioch, Grass Lake Rd., Rt. 59, 1 (NIU); [5b] Fox Lake, 8 (FM); [5c] Pistakee Bay, 1 (FM); [6] Lake Forest, 4 (US); [7] Barrington, 2 (FM); [8] Highland Park, 8 (FM). **Carroll Co.:** [9] Mississippi Palisades State Park, 1 (NIU); [10] Mt. Carroll, 1 (US). **Ogle Co.:** [11a] 3 mi W Oregon, 1 (NIU); [11b] White Pines State Park, 1 (UI). **De Kalb Co.:** [12] De Kalb, 1 (NIU); [13] 4 mi SW Waterman, 1 (UI). **Kane Co.:** [14] 1 mi N Elgin, 1 (SIC). **Cook Co.:** [15] 1⅛ mi E US 45, ¼ mi S State Hwy. 55, 1 (UI). **Du Page Co.:** [16] Glen Ellyn, 1 (NIU). **Will Co.:** [17b] O'Hara Woods, Romeoville, 1 (UI).

Additional records: **McHenry Co.:** [4] Wonder Lake, 4 (FS). **Will Co.:** [17a] Romeoville, (Necker and Hatfield, 1941:49).

Marmota, Woodchucks, groundhogs

Diagnosis. A sciurid with relatively short legs and tail, size large (weight to 14 lbs); dorsum brownish to blackish with some reddish coloring; interorbital region of skull much wider than postorbital, skull heavy and cheek teeth high-crowned, cheek pouches rudimentary.

Dental formula. 1/1, 0/0, 2/1, 3/3.

Comparisons. *Marmota* is a ground squirrel, in contrast to tree or flying squirrels. It differs from *Spermophilus* as follows: tail short relative to length of body (usually 34% or less, rather than more), interorbital breadth of skull much greater than postorbital breadth, rostrum

nearly as large as cranium, paroccipital process projects ventrad well below level of tympanic bullae.

Marmota monax, Woodchuck

Range. Throughout the state.

Diagnosis. The only member of the genus *Marmota* east of the Mississippi River; body length usually more than 450 mm, hind foot more than 75 mm, color dark (see below), skull largest of the squirrels, mammary glands four pairs, hind feet black or dark brown.

Color. Dorsum reddish brown with black intermixed and entire dorsum grizzled or tipped with white, top of head orangish red in some, black in others and not grizzled; nose, lips, and chin whitish, hind feet and forelegs blackish. Albinism is not uncommon (one specimen from 2 mi SW Ipava, Fulton Co., Illinois; one from Catawba Island, Ottawa Co., Ohio, in University of Illinois Collection).

Chromosomes. 2N = 38; FN = 62; 26 metacentrics and submetacentrics, 10 acrocentrics, X metacentric, Y small acrocentric (Hoffmann and Nadler, 1968).

Growth. Woodchucks at birth usually weigh between 25 and 35 gms. At about six to eight weeks of age, males weigh about 600 gms, females about 690 gms (Snyder, Davis, and Christian, 1961). Snyder and Christian (1960) in another report indicated that woodchucks gain on the average 16 grams per day for the first 43 days. Young weigh about 3,000 gms prior to hibernation in south central Pennsylvania (Snyder et al., 1961).

Yearling animals, between 13 and 16 months old, weighed an average of 2,880.2 gms for 107 males and 2,703.2 gms for 117 females. Adult animals, 25 to 28 months old or older, averaged 3,915.5 gms for 150 males, and 3,560.0 gms for 129 females (Snyder et al., 1961).

Secondary sexual variation. On the evidence of the weights given by Snyder et al. (1961), adult males weigh more than females, and probably significantly more. Differences between the sexes for external and cranial measurements have not been reported.

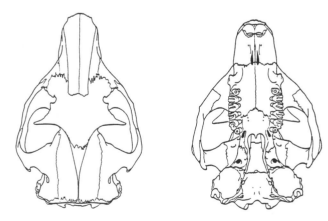

Fig. 8.62. *Marmota monax,* dorsal and ventral views of skull. Champaign, Champaign Co., Illinois 59827 UI. Male, 95.7 mm greatest length. Note that this specimen has a small, extra upper molar on each side behind the "normal" set (in ventral view).

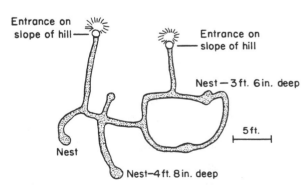

Fig. 8.63. Woodchuck burrow as diagrammed in a field at Lake Geneva, Wisconsin, by Cory (1912). Two entrances and three nests are indicated.

Molt. Howell (1915) stated that woodchucks have one molt a year, normally in August, but it may occur as early as June or July.

Remarks. Marmota monax is given a number of common names: woodchuck, groundhog, marmot. The "celebration" of Groundhog Day, February 2, is really Woodchuck Day! Tradition has it that if a hibernating woodchuck arouses from hibernation, comes above ground, and sees its shadow on this day, it will go back into hibernation for six weeks. If no shadow is seen, it follows that the weather is rainy or cloudy. The tale has it that spring is not far away, but this does not necessarily follow. The possibility that a healthy woodchuck in central and northern United States would rouse out of hibernation, open its plugged burrow, and go above ground on February 2 is unlikely but not impossible. The day continues to be celebrated, however, and probably more has been written about Groundhog Day than about groundhogs (=woodchucks).

Habitat

Woodchucks utilize a variety of habitats in Illinois. These include brushy or weedy areas on rocky or rolling land, timber-edges or along fencerows or earth-fills, railroad embankments, retaining walls, or dams. Such preferred habitat may be adjacent to grain fields, meadows, or other well-vegetated areas that provide a source of food. In Fulton County, Anderson (1951) found woodchucks most abundant on the wooded bluffs but they were also present along roadside banks and railroad rights-of-way. Woodchucks occupy much of the strip-mined lands in Illinois, as this provides rolling land with a grassy cover preferred by these animals. They avoid areas subject to periodic flooding.

In a report of 1857, Kennicott says that the woodchuck was exceedingly rare ten years earlier in northeastern Illinois, but was becoming quite common. Perhaps removal of much timber resulted in the increase.

Habits

Woodchucks live primarily on and under the ground. They dig extensive burrows with considerable branching, usually two or more entrances, and usually more than one nest. Parts of the burrow may be several feet deep, depending on the soil and other factors. Woodchucks are capable of digging through all soil types in Illinois, although the same apparently is not true for thirteen-lined and Franklin's ground squirrels. Cory (1912) gives the plan of a woodchuck burrow at Lake Geneva, Wisconsin (Fig. 8.63). Burrows are most often dug on ground with some slope.

Woodchucks have been known to climb trees, although this is not a common practice. Kennicott (1857) found that they will sometimes climb up the inside of a hollow tree.

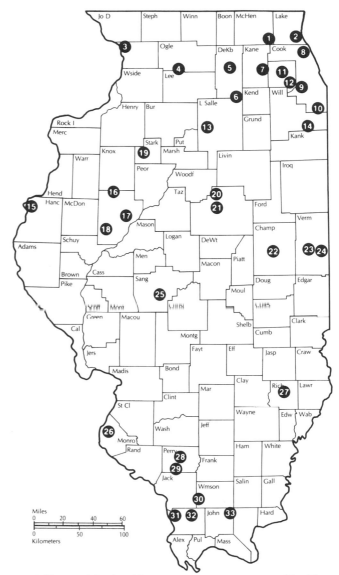

Map 8.26. Woodchucks, *Marmota monax*, occur statewide. The subspecies is *M. m. monax*. Localities of occurrence as numbered are referenced in *Records of occurrence*. The range of the species in the United States is shaded.

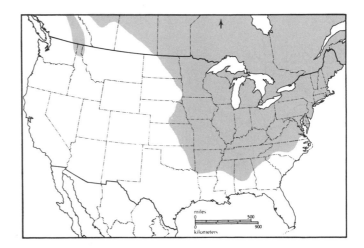

Table 8.16. Physiological differences between non-hibernating and hibernating woodchuck (from Benedict and Lee, 1938).

	Non-hibernator	Hibernator
Minimum heart rate/min.	80	4-5
Minimum average respiratory rate/min.	25-30	0.2
Rectal temp. C°	36±2	3 (low)
Minimum heat production/10w2/3[1] (in calories)	410	17-27

[1] Heat production per kilogram of body weight and per square meter of body surface.

Woodchucks may react to an adversary by chattering their incisors. Grizzell (1955) observed that an adult can defend itself successfully against a medium-sized dog, and this may be a frequent necessity since woodchucks are not especially fast runners. They may give a short, sharp whistle as a warning to other woodchucks.

Woodchucks normally feed and are active above ground only during the daylight hours. Usually they remain close to the burrow but radiate out to forage, often along established runways. In studying these animals in Maryland, Grizzell (1955) concluded that during the most active time of the year, they were above ground only one to two hours a day. Probably 80 to 90 percent of the woodchuck's life is spent in the burrows, resting, rearing young, or hibernating.

Food

Woodchucks feed extensively, if not exclusively, on plant material. They commonly feed in the early morning and late afternoon, but this varies with weather conditions, availability of food, and potential predators. They must harvest and eat material rapidly since they supposedly spend less than two hours above ground per day. They do not carry and store the plant materials below ground. They feed on clovers and grasses, but also on ferns, leaves of bushes and trees, fruits, and bark. They forage on garden and field crops when available, which may bring them into conflict with man and his interests.

Reproduction

In Illinois, breeding takes place in late February or in March, and young are born in April, as nearly as can be ascertained. The gestation period is 31 or 32 days. Woodchucks do not breed until the second year. Copulation must occur shortly after females emerge from hibernation.

In Maryland, 29 females had an average litter size of 4.6 young (Grizzell, 1955); in Indiana, it was 4.9 for 21 females (Mumford and Whitaker, 1982). Information on litter size in Illinois is not available. Only one litter is produced per summer, as would be expected in a hibernating animal of this size. It is necessary for young that are born in April and weigh about 30 gms each to attain a weight of some 3,000 gms before entering full hibernation.

Young are naked and helpless at birth, their eyes do not open until about one month of age, and they go above ground when they are around one and one-half months old.

Hibernation

Woodchucks in Illinois hibernate. Most adults go into hibernation in October, but juveniles and yearlings may

Table 8.17. External and cranial measurements (in mm) of *Marmota monax, Spermophilus tridecemlineatus,* and *S. franklinii.* Mean, minimum and maximum, and one standard deviation are given.

Species	Locality	Sex	No.	Total length	Tail length	Body length	Hind foot length
Marmota monax	Central Illinois; SW Ohio	♀	7	600.3 540-660 49.72	134.4 93-165 21.66	465.9 407-507 41.0	86.3 78-90 4.31
Spermophilus tridecemlineatus	Champaign Co., Ill.	♂	10	275.9 255-300 14.08	98.3 83-110 8.79	176.9 161-190 9.30	38.4 31-46 3.75
" "	" "	♀	10	276.6 250-291 15.45	94.7 80-115 12.12	182.4 170-196 7.75	37.9 35-40 1.52
Spermophilus franklinii	Champaign Co., Ill.	♂	9	392.0 368-425 23.76	134.8 113-156 19.2	249.4 205-276 22.08	52.1 47-58 3.72
" "	" "	♀	5	360.8 344-380 16.68	116.5 110-125 7.23	249.6 225-271 20.95	52.6 49-57 3.05

wait until mid-November. Some animals come out of hibernation as early as mid-February, and R. L. Snyder et al. (1961) reported that in Pennsylvania adult males emerge from hibernation about one month before females and yearling males.

Woodchucks begin to accumulate excess fat in August and September for utilization during hibernation; therefore, they spend more time feeding during these months. By October they begin to spend less time above ground. Eventually, the animal plugs the entrances to the burrow system and remains in a dormant state in one of the nests. Not all of the fat stored for hibernation will be used during this inactive period, and the remaining fat will be a source of energy if above-ground food is scarce in the spring. It will also supplement the energy requirements of females during gestation and lactation (Snyder et al., 1961).

The physiological differences between non-hibernating and hibernating woodchucks are summarized in Table 8.16.

Miscellaneous

In 1949, T. E. Musselman of Quincy wrote me that an increase in woodchucks in his area had resulted, in his estimation, in an increase in the number of burrowing owls, for these birds made use of the woodchuck's burrow entrances.

Some counties have paid bounties on the scalps of woodchucks, supposedly as a means of controlling their numbers. This gives an indirect measure of woodchuck abundance. For example, in a five-year period from March 1944 to March 1949, Fulton County paid bounties on 12,616 scalps or an average of 2,523 per year.

Fig. 8.64. Woodchucks infrequently climb trees. Photograph by K. Maslowski.

It is interesting that the written historical reports of conditions of the early settlers up to the 1840's made no mention of woodchucks. One gets the impression that they were not populous and not pests to garden plots. It well may be that the abundance of timberland together with prairie, especially tallgrass, was not conducive to large numbers of woodchucks, but as these prairies were plowed and the forests reduced, their population flourished.

Greatest length	Palatilar length	Zygomatic breadth	Cranial breadth	Least interorb. constr.	Postorbit. constr.	Nasal length	Maxillary toothrow (alveol.)	Bulla length
93.4	47.6	63.1	33.9	25.4	18.8	38.5	22.1	16.3
90.3-97.4	45.3-50.2	59.2-68.0	31.9-35.0	23.3-28.7	17.1-22.0	35.6-41.1	20.6-23.1	15.4-17.7
2.76	1.71	3.26	1.03	1.98	1.62	2.21	0.82	0.72
42.4	19.8	24.2	17.7	7.6	11.3	14.5	8.0	8.7
41.8-43.2	19.0-21.1	22.7-25.4	17.15-18.2	6.9-8.1	10.8-12.0	13.0-15.6	7.3-8.8	8.1-9.5
0.46	0.37	0.78	0.38	0.33	0.40	0.70	0.47	0.51
42.5	20.1	24.1	17.7	7.5	11.1	14.3	7.8	9.5
39.65-44.85	18.8-21.1	21.15-25.5	16.7-18.5	6.9-8.3	10.2-11.9	13.1-15.3	6.95-8.5	8.8-10.2
1.60	0.79	1.38	0.61	0.49	0.48	0.82	0.43	0.46
56.2	26.9	31.8	21.7	10.9	13.1	19.2	10.7	10.5
55.0-57.5	24.8-28.4	29.7-33.3	21.0-22.35	10.2-11.7	12.3-14.0	18.3-20.0	10.4-11.1	10.2-11.0
1.00	1.03	1.27	0.44	0.47	0.71	0.64	0.24	0.27
53.8	25.9	30.8	21.3	10.4	13.3	18.1	10.7	10.4
52.7-55.1	25.1-26.5	30.4-31.45	21.0-21.5	10.0-10.65	12.6-14.15	17.0-19.5	10.45-10.8	10.2-11.0
0.95	0.67	0.39	0.20	0.25	0.65	0.91	0.17	0.33

Variation

Although Howell (1915) in his revision of the wood-chucks indicated that the range of *Marmota monax rufescens* (type locality, Elk River, Minnesota) extended into Illinois, he ascribed all specimens from Illinois to *Marmota m. monax,* and this is followed here.

Marmota monax monax (Linnaeus)

1758. [*Mus*] *monax* Linnaeus, Syst. nat., ed. 10, 1:60. Type locality, Maryland.
1904. [*Marmota*] *monax,* Trouessart, Catal. Mann...., suppl., p. 344.

Range. As given for the species (Map 8.26).

Diagnosis and Comparisons. A subspecies of large size, less reddish on dorsum and venter than in *M. m. rufescens,* skull large and larger than in *M. m. rufescens.*

Cranial measurements. Cranial measurements are taken as described by Howell (1938:59). Cranial breadth is measured across points just dorsal to the base of the zygomatic arch and bulla length is taken on the ventral side.

Records of occurrence. SPECIMENS EXAMINED, 44. **McHenry Co.:** [1] Cary, 1 (FM). **Lake Co.:** [2] Lake Forest, 1 (FM). **Carroll Co.:** [3] Mississippi Palisades State Park, 1 (NIU). **Ogle Co.:** [4] Grand Detour, 1 (FM). **De Kalb Co.:** [5a] Rt. 64 and Glidden Rd., 1 (NIU); [5b] 2 mi N De Kalb, 2 (NIU); [6] Somonauk, 1 (CAS). **Kane Co.:** [7a] 1 mi W St. Charles, 1 (ISM); [7b] St. Charles, 1 (CAS). **Cook Co.:** [8] West Northfield, 1 (US); [9] Willow Springs, 1 (FM); [10] Chicago Heights, 1 (FM). **Du Page Co.:** [11] Glen Ellyn, Willowbrook, 1 (NIU); [12a] George Williams College, 2 (FM); [12b] Downers Grove, 1 (FM). **La Salle Co.:** [13] 2½ km W Utica, 1 (FM). **Will Co.:** [14] 2 mi E Peotone, 1 (UI). **Hancock Co.:** [15] Nauvoo, 1 (ISU). **Fulton Co.:** [16] London Mills, 1 (FM); [17] Bryant, 1 (UI); [18] 2 mi SW Ipava, 1 (UI). **Stark Co.:** [19] Toulon, 1 (US). **McLean Co.:** [20] 4 mi E Kappa, 1 (ISU); [21] 2 mi SE Towanda, 1 (SIU). **Champaign Co.:** [22a] Urbana, 1 (UI); [22b] 3 mi S Champaign, 1 (UI). **Vermilion Co.:** [23] 1¾ mi N, ¼ mi E Oakwood, 1 (UI); [24] near Danville, 1 (UI). **Sangamon Co.:** [25] 7½ mi S Springfield, 1 (ISM). **Monroe Co.:** [26] 4 mi NE Valmeyer, 1 (UI). **Richland Co.:** [27] Olney, 1 (US). **Perry Co.:** [28] near Pinckneyville, 2 (SRL); [29a] 5 mi W Pyatts, 1 (SIC); [29b] Pyatts Striplands, 2 (SRL). **Williamson Co.:** [30] 5 mi SE Carbondale, 1 (SIC). **Union Co.:** [31a] Pine Hills, near Wolf Lake, 1 (FM); [31b] Wolf Lake, 1 (UI); no specific locality [not plotted], 1 (SIC). **Johnson Co.:** [33] Ozark, 2 (FM).

Additional records: 2. **Perry Co.:** [29c] Pyatts Stripmine Research Area, 1 (FS). **Union Co.:** [32] 2 mi E Cobden, 1 (FS).

Spermophilus, Ground squirrels

Diagnosis. Size variable, from small to relatively large; tail medium to long; ears small; pelage of dorsum often mottled, spotted, or striped; dorsal outline of skull moderately convex, with a rapid slope from the highest

Fig. 8.65A. Thirteen-lined ground squirrel, *Spermophilus tridecem-lineatus.* Photograph by K. Maslowski and W. W. Goodpaster.

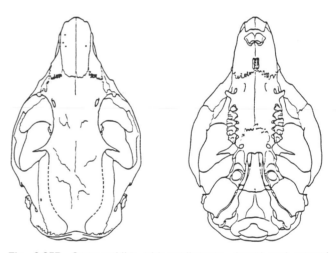

Fig. 8.65B. *Spermophilus tridecemlineatus,* dorsal and ventral views of skull. Near Morris, Grundy Co., Illinois, 59102 UI. Male, 43.1 mm greatest length.

point posteriorly to the lambdoidal crest; masseteric tubercle medium to large, mainly ventrolateral to infraorbital foramen; outer edge of infraorbital foramen slightly inclined ventrolaterally.

Dental formula. 1/1, 0/0, 2/1, 3/3.

Comparisons. For a comparison with *Marmota,* see account of that genus (p. 154).

Spermophilus differs from *Sciurus* in having a less bushy tail, relatively shorter feet; zygomata converge anteriorly with the anterior part twisted toward a horizontal plane rather than nearly parallel.

Spermophilus differs from *Tamias* as explained in the account of that genus (p. 149).

Measurements. Cranial measurements in Table 8.17 (p. 156) are as described by Howell (1938:59) and, in addition, cranial breadth was taken at a point just dorsal to the base of the zygomatic arch; bulla length was taken from the ventral side of the bulla.

Remarks. Two species of *Spermophilus* live in Illinois: *S. tridecemlineatus* and *S. franklinii.*

Spermophilus tridecemlineatus, Thirteen-lined ground squirrel

Range. Northern and central Illinois, north of a line extending from Madison County across to Clark County (Map 8.27).

Diagnosis. A species of *Spermophilus* of small size but with a unique color pattern with numerous stripes (Fig. 8.65A), tail approximately one-half length of head-body, hind foot between 35 and 42 mm, skull not especially broad at base of rostrum, supraorbital margins only slightly elevated, auditory bullae moderately inflated (Fig. 8.65B).

Color. Overall a light tan with a series of brownish black longitudinal stripes, each dark stripe with a series of squarish tan spots; in the area immediately behind the head the tan spots may be fused to form light-colored stripes; top and bottom of tail dark but bordered with ochraceous hair. It is difficult to ascertain that there are 13 lines or stripes on the sides and back.

Chromosomes. Diploid number=34; eight pairs of metacentrics, eight of submetacentrics, X submetacentric, Y medium-sized acrocentric (Nadler and Hughes, 1966).

Comparisons. S. tridecemlineatus differs from *Spermophilus franklinii* and *Tamias striatus* (p. 149) as pointed out in the accounts of those species. The unique pattern of stripes and tan spots should readily distinguish this ground squirrel.

Growth and Aging. In east central Illinois, the growth of *S. tridecemlineatus* has been reported on by Zimmerman (1972). By 75 days of age, 97 percent of adult body length has been achieved; by 69 days, the hind foot has achieved adult size; by the 75th day, most parts of the skull have reached adult size. Permanent premolars fully erupt by the 68th day. Thus, when teeth have reached the level of the molar teeth, the animals can be regarded as of adult age.

Remarks. Thirteen-lined ground squirrels and Franklin's ground squirrels have an unusual distribution in Illinois. They occur north of a line between Madison (on the west) and Clark counties and do not seem to be extending their ranges farther south. The southern limits of these

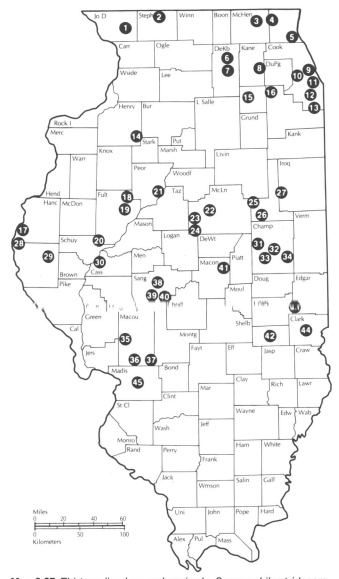

Map 8.27. Thirteen-lined ground squirrels, *Spermophilus tridecemlineatus,* occur in the northern two-thirds of Illinois. The subspecies is *S. t. tridecemlineatus.* Localities of occurrence as numbered are referenced in *Records of occurrence.* The range of the species in the United States is shaded.

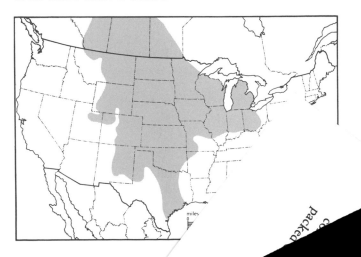

ground squirrels correspond in general with the Shelby-ville glacial moraine. Below this moraine the soil is shallow with an underlying hardpan. There is a distinct possibility that this hardpan prevents weaker diggers (such as thirteen-lined and Franklin ground squirrels) in contrast to stronger diggers (such as woodchucks) from reaching a depth below ground where they can safely hibernate. Or, this hardpan may result in slow run-off of water which in turn might result in the drowning of hibernating squirrels. Other factors also may be involved with this shallower soil south of the Shelbyville moraine.

Some ground squirrels find areas south of this moraine where they can successfully live. This may be in places where a greater quantity of workable soil has accumulated.

Habitat

Thirteen-lined ground squirrels live in short grasslands or in weedy areas where the weeds are short. When these squirrels sit up on their hind legs, the vegetation must be short enough that they can look over the top of it. Wherever they are found in taller grass or weeds, there are some parts of their home range that extend into shorter vegetation. If all of the vegetation becomes tall, these squirrels will move elsewhere.

Grassy areas that are kept cut—such as golf courses, cemeteries, parks, large lawns, roadside rights-of-way, and grassy landing strips—provide ideal habitat. Pastures that are closely cropped do also. Sometimes ground squirrels will be found living along railroad embankments, fence-rows, and the grassy floors of orchards. Wooded and marshy areas are avoided.

The draining of marshy areas of central Illinois by white settlers must have made available much more land for thirteen-lined ground squirrels.

Habits

Since thirteen-lined ground squirrels live in such conspicuous places and are diurnal as well as gregarious, they are seen by many people. From mid-November or December to late February or March, however, they are below ground and in hibernation.

These ground squirrels do not ordinarily produce whistles or calls, but an alarm call may be given by a female when her young are above ground. This call is heard as a high-pitched trill of short duration. Also, young may give a distress call (a *peep*) if they become too far separated from the mother (McCarley, 1966).

Burrows are dug by these squirrels, and are probably used, with alterations, for several generations. The entrances to burrows have no accumulation of soil. The digger effectively disperses this soil so as to leave no telltale mound. The dirt is scattered by the feet over a considerable area and the soil around the entrance is down, often using the top of the head. Burrows

are not much larger around than the bodies of the squirrels and the tunnels are usually only one to one and one half feet below ground, although hibernating chambers may be deeper. In southern Wisconsin, Rongstad (1965) found three kinds of burrows. Hiding burrows are short and shallow and probably are the most numerous. Nesting burrows have enlarged cavities for nests and some have areas for excrement. Hibernating burrows go sufficiently deep to get below the frost line. In central Illinois, the average frost depth in January is 10 in; in northern Illinois, 20 in, although depths of twice these values are common. Hibernation burrows contain a large nest and the entrance is tightly plugged during this phase. Sometimes an animal finds it easier to dig a new exit from the hibernaculum than to remove the plug. In describing a summer burrow in Illinois, Kennicott (1857) said several "were more than 20 feet in length, being simple galleries from six inches to a foot below the surface—deeper in sandy soil—opening at both ends, with the nest placed in a small side chamber; others were of much less extent, sometimes with but one entrance, and sometimes with a nest."

In the summer, squirrels make much use of the short "hiding" burrows. One summer, my son collected about 200 thirteen-lined ground squirrels in the Urbana-Champaign area by recovering them from their hiding burrows. When one ran down the burrow, he placed a live-trap made of hardware cloth over the hole and poured water through the trap into the burrow. The squirrel would shortly emerge and be caught in the trap. One five-gallon tank of water was sometimes enough for five or more burrows, so it was obvious that the burrow-system was not long.

Food

Thirteen-lined ground squirrels feed extensively on grasses, weeds, seeds, and sometimes cultivated plants. At an earlier time, there were numerous reports indicating that these squirrels were harmful to cornfields shortly after the seeds germinated, and sometimes to the seeds before they sprouted. Observations indicate that these squirrels also feed extensively on insects. The amounts and kinds that they eat may depend on the time of year.

In Indiana, these squirrels feed extensively upon the larvae of moths and butterflies (Whitaker, 1972b) and the same is true in Colorado (Streubel and Fitzgerald, 1978). In Iowa, 70 percent of the diet was insects in May, only 30 percent in June and July, and about 50 percent in August and September (Fitzpatrick, 1925). In Indiana, the plants commonly eaten (as represented by occurrence in gastric contents in 135 specimens) were clover, crab grass seeds, chickweed, and wood sorrel seeds (Whitaker, 1972b). Animal material in the stomachs of these 135 specimens were grasshoppers, beetles, ants, and earthworms. In Indiana chickweed was eaten only

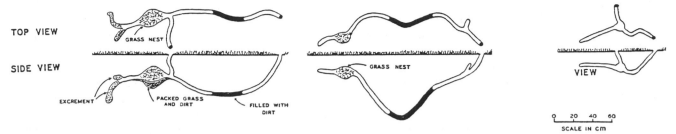

Fig. 8.66. Burrows of *Spermophilus tridecemlineatus* near Madison, Wisconsin. A and B are nesting burrows; C, hiding burrow. Burrow A has two surface openings; B, only one, although a lateral could be extended as an opening. (After Rongstad, 1965)

in June; mainly crab grass seeds and grasshoppers in September and October.

Food studies on Illinois thirteen-lined ground squirrels have not been made or reported.

Reproduction

Much has been written about the breeding activities and the rearing and growth of young in *Spermophilus tridecemlineatus*. In southern Wisconsin, breeding occurs between April 13 and May 4 as based upon the date of conception in 50 females (Rongstad, 1965). These dates probably vary with weather conditions. Males have enlarged testes when they emerge from hibernation and females begin estrus in April. It may be that females older than one year breed first. The gestation period is 27 or 28 days; most young are born between May 15 and June 7. Of 28 pregnant females captured in Champaign County and held in the laboratory, all gave birth to young between May 14 and May 28 (Zimmerman, 1972). Young are born in Illinois primarily in the last half of May.

The 22 pregnant females from Champaign County produced an average of 6.3 young. Litter sizes probably vary by the year and geographical area: Manitoba, an average of 8.1; Wisconsin, 8.7; Colorado, 8.7 and 6.2; Texas, 7.0 in older females, 4.9 in young females (as reviewed in Streubel and Fitzgerald, 1978).

At birth, young are hairless, their limbs are poorly developed, and they weigh between 2 and 3 gms. Stripes are visible around the eighth day; eyes open at about three weeks. Other details on development are reviewed under *Growth* (p. 159). Young are thought to spend approximately a month below ground before emerging. They attempt to establish territories fairly close to their place of birth. Rongstad (1965) found that in southern Wisconsin they were within 53.1 ± 4.7 m (= 174.2 ± 15.4 ft) of the natal burrow. Their establishment of territories evidently depends on the size of the area and population pressures.

Females in central Illinois have only one litter per year (Zimmerman, 1972). The same is probably true elsewhere in the state.

Hibernation

For thirteen-lined ground squirrels, one of the unique aspects of hibernation is the amount of time spent in this condition. In Texas, these animals reportedly are in hibernation for between 230 and 240 days (McCarley, 1966) and in Colorado possibly 210 to 250 days (Streubel and Fitzgerald, 1978). The long period of hibernation may be correlated with the early disappearance of green vegetation in the late summer in some regions. In Illinois, green vegetation is usually present throughout the summer and fall, in contrast to conditions in more xeric locations. Perhaps in Illinois, the hibernating period is shorter. Males emerge from hibernation first and adult males enter hibernation first. Adult females enter hibernation nearly a month later. Young may not enter hibernation until two months later than adults.

Before hibernation, these squirrels become increasingly more wary, spend less time above-ground, seemingly feed less often, and then disappear. Sometimes, thirteen-lined ground squirrels will come above ground in the middle of winter if the ground is not frozen so they can dig their way out of their hibernaculum (Wade, 1950). In Illinois, the earliest record that we have is of a specimen taken at Urbana, Champaign County, when it was above ground on February 20, 1940. There probably are several earlier records for the state. These squirrels, however, usually are not seen above ground until late March or April in central Illinois. We have numerous records of animals seen in October, presumably all young of the year, and one record each for November 3 and November 10. A specimen taken 3 mi E Gibson City, Ford County, on December 7, 1963, was either a young specimen that was insufficiently fat to hibernate sooner, or was unable to hibernate for some other reason.

Within the hibernaculum, the ground squirrels may awaken periodically. This behavior may be correlated with the physiology of the animal or possibly with decreasing temperature within the chamber.

Miscellaneous

Populations of thirteen-lined ground squirrels vary greatly from situation to situation and time of the year.

Certain cemeteries have great numbers whereas others, at the same time, have few. In southern Wisconsin, Rongstad (1965) cited evidence of the increase in numbers when young appear above ground. The numbers before and after, per hectare, were 2.5 to 5.0 versus 24.6.

Sometimes albino specimens are present, such as the one taken on July 4 at Urbana, Champaign County (Hoffmeister and Hensley, 1949). This specimen was a young animal with pink eyes, and one wonders how long it would have survived in the wild. Another albino squirrel from 2½ mi W Savoy, Champaign County, must have survived the summer for it was not taken until September 1. We also have a melanistic specimen in our collection; it is from 1 mi W Chillicothe, Ross County, Ohio. This ground squirrel is entirely black except for some buffy-colored hairs on the throat, toes, and inguinal area.

Because of the diurnal nature of these squirrels, they must rarely if ever be preyed upon by owls, foxes, or other nocturnal carnivores. Weasels and hawks may take them and badgers may dig them out of their burrows. Controlling factors must be food, flooding, too shallow a hibernaculum resulting in freezing, as well as death crossing roads, and predation by cats and dogs.

Variation

Ten subspecies of *S. tridecemlineatus* were recognized by Hall (1981). Only one subspecies, *S. t. tridecemlineatus*, is found in Illinois and all of north central United States.

Spermophilus tridecemlineatus tridecemlineatus (Mitchill)

1821. *Sciurus tridecem-lineatus* Mitchill, Med. Repos. 6(21):248. Type locality, central Minnesota (Allen, Bull. Amer. Mus. Nat. Hist., 7:338, 1895).

1849. *Spermophilus tridecem lineatus*, Audubon and Bachman, The vivip. quadrupeds No. America, 1:294.

Range. As given for the species (p. 159 and Map 8.27).

Diagnosis and Comparisons. A large subspecies with dark color, but variable; large skull.

Remarks. Specimens from east central Illinois appear to be slightly smaller, especially cranially, than specimens from Minnesota, on the basis of Howell's (1938) measurements of the latter populations.

Records of occurrence. SPECIMENS EXAMINED, 262. **Jo Daviess Co.:** [1] 4 mi WSW Stockton, 1 (UI). **Stephenson Co.:** [2] 2 mi S Orangeville, 1 (SRL). **Lake Co.:** [4] Fox Lake, 3 (FM): [5a] Lake Forest, 1 (US). **De Kalb Co.:** [6] 5 mi N De Kalb, 2 (NIU); [7] De Kalb, 3 (NIU). **Kane Co.:** [8] near St. Charles, 3 (ISM). **Cook Co.:** [9] Chicago, 10 (FM); [10b] La Grange, 4 (FM); [11] Chicago, Jackson Park, 13 (FM); [12a] Blue Island, 2 (US); [13] Chicago Heights, 1 (FM). **Henry Co.:** [14] Kewanee, 2 (FM). **Grundy Co.:** [15a] 6 mi W, ½ mi S Morris, 1 (UI); [15b] 1¼ mi W, ½ mi S Morris, 5 (UI). **Will Co.:** [16b]

Plainfield, 1 (NIU). **Hancock Co.:** [17] Warsaw*, 2 (US). **Fulton Co.:** [18a] 1 mi NW Norris, 1 (UI); [18b] 3 mi N Canton, 3 (UI); [18c] 4 mi NW Canton, 3 (UI); [19a] 3 mi W Canton, 1 (SIC); [19b] 4 mi SW Canton, 1 (UI); [20] 7 mi S Vermont, 1 (UI). **Peoria Co.:** [21] Peoria, 8 (FM). **McLean Co.:** [22a] 1 mi NE Normal, 2 (ISU); [22b] ½ mi NW Normal, 1 (ISU). **Ford Co.:** [25] 4 mi W Sibley, 1 (UI); [26] 3 mi E Gibson City, 1 (ISU). **Iroquois Co.:** [27] Thawville, 4 (UI). **Adams Co.:** [28] 4 mi NE Meyer [labelled Hancock Co.], 1 (ISM); [29] ½ mi E Camp Point, 2 (ISM). **Cass Co.:** [30] 1 mi E Beardstown, 1 (ISM). **Champaign Co.:** [31] 2 mi SE Mahomet, 1 (UI); [32a] Champaign, 68 (UI); [32b] Urbana, 65 (UI); [32c] Mt. Hope Cemetery, Urbana, 21 (UI); [32d] ½ mi W Mayview, 2 (UI); [32e] Mayview, 5 (UI); [33a] 3½ mi SW Champaign, 1 (UI); [33b] 2½ mi W Savoy, 1 (UI); [33c] Willard Airport, 1 (UI); [34] 3 mi W Homer [labelled Vermilion Co.], 1 (UI). **Macoupin Co.:** [35] ½ mi E Chesterfield, 1 (UI); [36] 1 mi NE Bunker Hill, 1 (SIC); [37] 2 mi S Mt. Olive, 1 (SIE). **Sangamon Co.:** [38] Springfield, 2 (ISM); [39] Chatham, 3 (UI); [40] 2 mi S New City, 1 (ISM). **Edgar Co.:** [43] Kansas, 1 (US).

Additional records. **McHenry Co.:** [3] Wonder Lake, 1 (FS). **Lake Co.:** [5b] Deerfield, 3 (UM). **Cook Co.:** [10a] north of Riverside, 1 (FS); [12b] Riverdale, 1 (UM). **Will Co.:** [16a] Wheatland Twp., 2 (UM). **McLean Co.:** [23] 2 mi E Stanford, 1 (FS); [24] McLean, 3 (FS). **Macon Co.:** [41] 10 mi NE Decatur, 1 (UM). **Cumberland Co.:** [42] no specific locality [sight record], (Mohr 1943:178). **Clark Co.:** [44] no specific locality [sight record], (Mohr 1943:178). **Madison Co.:** [45] no specific locality [sight record], (Mohr 1943:178).

Spermophilus franklinii, Franklin's ground squirrel

Range. Northern and central Illinois, possibly as far south as a line from Jersey County east through Clark County (Map 8.28, p. 164). See *Remarks* section (p. 163) for a discussion of a report from O'Fallon Depot, supposedly St. Clair County.

Diagnosis. A large ground squirrel, especially for Illinois, that resembles the gray squirrel, *Sciurus carolinensis;* ears low and rounded, tail slightly longer than half the head-body length; color dark and without stripes (see below); skull relatively long and narrow, rostrum not pinched in at base, interorbital region long, zygomata not greatly expanded.

Color. Dorsum tawny olive or clay-colored with black interspersed, venter buff or buffy white, head grayish and lightly tipped with white, tail above and below blackish mixed with buff and bordered with white, sides cinnamon buff mixed with grayish white.

Chromosomes. 2N=42; 10 metacentrics, 16 submetacentrics, 14 acrocentrics, X and Y submetacentrics (Nadler, 1966).

Comparisons. S. franklinii differs from the only other

---

* Worthen specimens.

Fig. 8.67A. Franklin's ground squirrel, *Spermophilus franklinii.* Photograph from Illinois Natural History Survey.

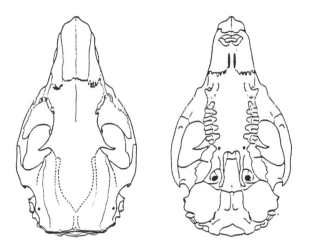

Fig. 8.67B. *Spermophilus franklinii,* dorsal and ventral views of skull. St. Joseph, Champaign Co., Illinois, 1368 UI. Female, 55.1 mm greatest length.

ground squirrel in Illinois, *S. tridecemlineatus,* in the absence of stripes, much darker color, bushier tail, and larger size both externally and cranially (Table 8.17, p. 156).

S. franklinii superficially looks much like *Sciurus carolinensis,* gray squirrel, but differs in having a tail only slightly longer than half of the head-body length rather than almost equal to the body length; hind foot if accurately measured probably always less than 59 mm rather than more; ears shorter and rounder; color of dorsum more mottled, lateral line tawny or grayish rather than reddish brown; skull narrower interorbitally and postorbitally, and third upper premolar (first tooth in molar series) less peglike.

Growth. *S. franklinii* is reported to grow more rapidly than other species of *Spermophilus.* Between 32 and 35 days of age, the hind foot has attained more than 75 percent of adult size; total and tail length 60 percent, but weight only 25 percent in laboratory-reared animals (Turner at al., 1976).

Molt. Evidently there is only one adult molt per year, in June, and juveniles molt into adult pelage in July.

Remarks. A pair of Franklin's ground squirrels captured somewhere in Illinois was the basis for this species becoming established in New Jersey. Sylvester Mathis took a pair to Tuckerton, New Jersey, in May, 1867, where they escaped, became established, and spread (Stone, 1908). Females taken in May probably were pregnant.

In an article on "prairie ground squirrels" in 1893, Vernon Bailey includes, as one of the southern limits of *S. franklinii,* O'Fallon Depot, Illinois. I assume that this is the depot in O'Fallon, St. Clair County. If so, this is some 47 miles south of the southernmost record based on a preserved specimen (1 mi N Carlinville, Macoupin County, locality No. 33). I do not know the basis for Vernon Bailey's records (1893:49) and have not included this on the map or in the *Range.*

The southern limits of the Franklin's ground squirrel in Illinois correspond rather closely with those of *Spermophilus tridecemlineatus.* The southern limits of both species of spermophiles may be delimited by the Shelbyville moraine, with soil depth and conditions north of the moraine more suitable for them.

Habitat

Franklin's ground squirrels live in Illinois in grasses of intermediate height—that is, taller than lawn and golf-course height preferred by thirteen-lined ground squirrels, but short enough so that when Franklin's ground squirrels stand upright on their hind legs, they can see over the grass. Often, they have runways through taller grasses but these lead to places where the grass is short enough to allow them to see above it. Because they live in such tall grasses, Franklin's ground squirrels are not often seen, and far less so than thirteen-lined ground squirrels. The whistle of a Franklin's ground squirrel—a trill or rapid chirp—may indicate the presence of these animals more easily than a sighting. Their presence may be detected also by following a runway through such grass and finding a burrow entrance with some dirt around it.

The availability of a place to construct an adequate burrow system is a limiting factor in this ground squirrel's distribution. The burrow must be sufficiently insulated (usually deep) to maintain temperatures above freezing in winter, cool in summer, and must remain drained and not subject to flooding. The elevated track bed of railroad rights-of-way often serve as ideal locations for such burrows. Ellis (1982) points out that such rights-of-way usually have a diversity of dicotyledonous plants and a mixture of weedy and native species. This mixture of plants may be an important part of the Franklin's ground squirrel habitat.

Franklin's ground squirrels were introduced and reportedly are doing well on an area restored as a tallgrass prairie at Knox College Biological Field Station, Knox

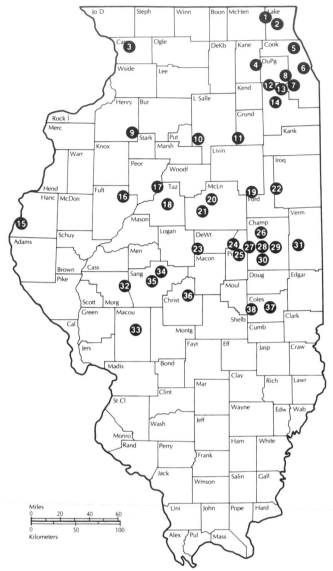

Map 8.28. Franklin's ground squirrels, *Spermophilus franklinii,* occur in the northern two-thirds of Illinois. Localities of occurrence as numbered are referenced in *Records of occurrence.* The range of the species in the United States is shaded.

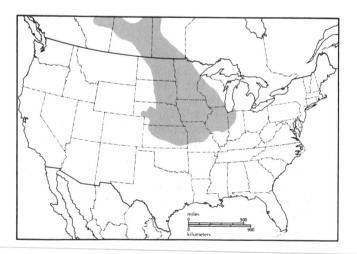

County. The area includes big and little bluestem, Indiangrass, switchgrass, dock, goldenrod, clover, foxtail, and other weeds. It is about 30 acres in size.

Kennicott (1857) stated that this species dug long burrows in banks of ditches and even in river banks where he encountered the species in Illinois. He reported that they also inhabited the thickets of low bushes and the edges of the timber.

Burrows

Burrows of Franklin's ground squirrels were reported by Kennicott (1857) as usually being deep but otherwise similar to that of thirteen-lined ground squirrels. In northeastern Missouri, Ellis (1982) found that tunnels averaged 8 to 10 cm in diameter and the enlarged parts of the underground system of chambers containing nests and/or food items were 12 to 20 inches below the surface. Burrows on the elevated portion of the bed of railroad tracks were simple in details in most cases. The burrows were often plugged.

Habits

Franklin's ground squirrels sometimes appear to be gregarious. It may be that several are sharing the only available habitat. For example, Kennicott (1857) says "twenty or thirty of these animals suddenly made their appearance and burrowed into an old enbankment, within three or four rods of my father's house." Sometimes these squirrels are seen along the edge of roads, often sitting upright. Here, the weeds usually are shorter and they can look around. Because they do not hesitate to eat carrion, they may dash onto the roadway to eat a recently killed mammal or insect.

These ground squirrels can and do climb trees. Sometimes this tree- and bush-climbing is to escape when too closely pursued; at other times their climbing appears to be without provocation.

These squirrels are diurnal and are most active above ground during the middle of the day. In Manitoba, Sowls (1948) estimated that these squirrels are above ground less than 10 percent of their lifetime (see also *Hibernation,* p. 165).

Krohne et al. (1973) concluded that the 13 adults at the Knox College Biological Station had considerable overlap in home ranges, and that the average home range of males was two to three times larger than that of females.

Food

Franklin's ground squirrels feed extensively on plant material, but they are actually omnivorous. They are known to feed on a variety of carrion, mammalian material, insects, bird eggs, and some ground-dwelling birds. Probably their food habits vary throughout the summer as the availability of different items changes. For example, in Manitoba in July there was an increase in seeds and fruits consumed, as well as mammalian matter and insects (Sowls, 1948). In 6 of 12 specimens in Minnesota (June 6–11), stomach contents consisted of 45 percent or more of animal matter (mostly insects), according to Vernon Bailey (1893).

These ground squirrels in Manitoba ate plant materials including sow thistle, chokecherries, elderberries, beach pea, and white clover (Sowls, 1948). Many species of plants were not identifiable. In northeastern Missouri, Ellis (1982) found that dicots were more prevalent than moncots in their diet.

Franklin's ground squirrels may have an adverse effect on ground-nesting birds because of their propensity to feed on eggs. These squirrels break an egg by wrapping the body around the egg and by using their teeth and feet in the breaking process. The squirrels reportedly actually kill small ground-dwelling birds.

Reproduction

Breeding occurs in Franklin's ground squirrels shortly after the females leave hibernation. Scott Ellis informs me that S. Haggarty's thesis research (MS, 1968) in Minnesota showed that parturition occurred early in June; breeding thus must have occurred early in May. The period of gestation is 26–28 days. In Manitoba, Sowls (1948) found that the peak of breeding was during the first week of May. I suspect that in Illinois most young are born during the last week of May and the first week of June. Only one litter per year is produced.

The number of embryos per female varies from 4 to 11 (Sowls, 1948). In Manitoba, the average number of embryos for 26 females was 7.5. At birth, the young are hairless; at three weeks the eyes and ears are open; young are weaned at about one month.

From July 26 to August 1, the young specimens in collections seem to be about half-grown. Young are at adult size by early October, and probably by late September.

Hibernation

The time when Franklin's ground squirrels emerge from and enter hibernation in Illinois is not certain. We have a male specimen taken on April 14. Our late fall records, based on collected specimens, were of adults taken September 9. Young of the year were taken as late as November 14.

Males probably emerge from hibernation in early April but the time and numbers may depend on weather conditions. In northeastern Missouri, Ellis (1982) also found they emerge in early April. We have females taken on April 25 and suspect they emerge nearly as early as males. Adult squirrels disappear early in September. In Missouri, Ellis (1982) found his last captures of adults were in late August.

It appears that adult squirrels in Illinois spend at least seven months in hibernation, and during the other five months spend two-thirds of the time within the burrow.

Variation

S. franklinii ranges from Alberta, Canada, southeastward to central Illinois and northwestern Indiana. Within this range, no geographic variants or subspecies have been described.

Spermophilus franklinii (Sabine)

1822. *Arctomys franklinii* Sabine, Trans. Linnean Soc. London, 13:587. Type from Carlton House, Saskatchewan.
1827. *Spermophilis Franklinii*, Lesson, Manuel de Mamm., p. 244.

Range. As given for the species (p. 162, and Map 8.28).
Diagnosis and Comparisons. As given for the species (p. 162 and 163).
Remarks. Our sample of adult specimens from one locality is not extensive, with nine males and five females. For these, the measurements indicate there may be significant differences between the sexes as follows: males larger in total length, greatest length of skull, palatilar length, and nasal length.

Records of occurrence. SPECIMENS EXAMINED, 86.
Lake Co.: [1] Fox Lake, 1 (FM); [2] Grayslake, 4 (CAS). **Carroll Co.:** [3] Mt. Carroll, 1 (US). **Kane Co.:** [4] near St. Charles, 5 (ISM). **Cook Co.:** [5] West Northfield, 2 (US); [6] Chicago, 1 (CAS); [7a] Maple Lake, 1 (SIC); [7b] Worth, 1 (FM). **La Salle Co.:** [10] Hwy 51 at McNabb-Lenore Rd., 1 (ISU). **Grundy Co.:** [11] ¼ mi W Kinsman, 1 (SIC). **Will Co.:** [12] 6 mi S Naperville [labelled Du Page Co.], 1 (FM); [13] near Lemont [may be Cook Co.], 1 (CAS). **Hancock Co.:** [15] Warsaw*, 1 (FM), 3 (US). **Fulton Co.:** [16a] 1 mi NW Norris, 2 (UI); [16b] 4 mi NW Canton, 1 (UI); [16c] 3 mi W Canton, 1 (UI). **Livingston Co.:** [19] 1 mi S Strawn, 1 (UI). **McLean Co.:** [20a] 7½ mi NE Normal, 2 (ISU); [20b] 6 mi NE Normal, 1 (ISU); [21a] 1 mi W, 1 mi S Bloomington, 1 (ISU); [21b] 4 mi SW Bloomington, 1 (ISU). **Iroquois Co.:** [22] Thawville, 2 (UI). **De Witt Co.:** [23] 3½ mi NE Chestnut, 1 (ISM). **Piatt Co.:** [24] 1 mi E Deland, 1 (ISM); [25] 1 mi N Monticello, 1 (UI).

Champaign Co.: [26] 10 mi N, 2 mi W Champaign, 1 (UI); [27] Seymour, 1 (UI); [28a] 3½ mi W Champaign, 1 (ISM); [28b] 1 mi W Champaign, Rt. 150, 1 (UI); [28c] Champaign, 1 (ISM); [28d] Urbana Twp., 1 (UI); [28e] 1 mi S Champaign, 1 (UI); [28f] 1½ mi S Champaign, 1 (UI); [28g] 3 mi S Champaign, 3 (UI); [29a] .4 mi W Mayview, 2 (UI); [29b] Mayview, 3 (UI); [29c] 1.2 mi E Mayview, 3 (UI); [29d] 1½ mi E Mayview, 1 (UI); [29e] 2 mi E Mayview, 3 (UI); [29f] 1½ mi W St. Joseph, 1 (UI); [29g] 1.2 mi W St. Joseph, 4 (UI); [30a] Willard Airport, 1 (UI); [30b] 2 mi S Savoy, 1 (UI). **Vermilion Co.:** [31] 10 mi W Danville, 1 (UI). **Morgan Co.:** [32] 5 mi W New Berlin, 1 (ISM). **Macoupin Co.:** [33] 1 mi N Carlinville, 1 (ISM). **Sangamon Co.:** [34] Bissell,

---

* Worthen specimens.

7 (ISM); [35a] Springfield, 1 (ISM); [35b] 1 mi E Springfield, 4 (ISM); [35c] 2 mi S Springfield, 1 (ISM). **Christian Co.:** [36] ½ mi E Stonington, 1 (UI). **Coles Co.:** [38] 1 mi N Mattoon, 1 (UI); No county named: Vermillion [*sic* Vermilion] River [not plotted], 1 (US).

Additional records. **Cook Co.:** [5] West Northfield, 1 (UM). **Du Page Co.:** [8] Hinsdale, (Necker and Hatfield, 1941:49). **Henry Co.:** [9] Kewanee, (Necker and Hatfield, 1941:49). **Will Co.:** [14] Joliet, 1 (UM). **Peoria Co.:** [17] Peoria, (Necker and Hatfield, 1941:49). **Tazewell Co.:** [18] Tremont, (Necker and Hatfield, 1941:49). **Coles Co.:** [37] 2 mi N Charleston, 3 (FS).

Sciurus, Tree squirrels

Diagnosis. A sciurid which in Illinois is of medium size, with tail long and bushy, ears prominent, hind feet relatively long; skull with infraorbital foramen forming a canal, braincase sloping downward posteriorly, coronoid process of mandibular ramus relatively weak and short, Pm^3 if present is peglike. All are diurnal and arboreal.

Dental formula. 1/1, 0/0, 1/1 or 2/1, 3/3.

Chromosomes. In the two species in Illinois, 2N=40; 14 metacentrics, 24 submetacentrics, X submetacentrics, Y acrocentric (Nadler and Sutton, 1967).

Comparison. For a comparison with *Spermophilus,* see account of that genus (p. 159).

Sciurus differs from *Tamiasciurus* in Illinois in its larger overall size, hind foot (if accurately measured) 54 mm or more, tail bushier and longer (usually 19.5 mm or more); there is no blackish stripe along side above white underparts; skull is larger; the baculum is well developed rather than vestigial.

Aging. Specimens are considered adult and used for comparative analyses when the permanent Pm^4 is fully erupted and in occluding position.

Sciurus carolinensis, Gray squirrel

Range. Formerly widespread throughout the state; still throughout Illinois but now occupying about half the area because of the reduction of much of the mature forest and woods; abundant in many cities (Map 8.29).

Diagnosis. A sciurid that is grayish in dorsal coloration, whitish on venter, with tail grayish above and below but bordered with white (see following for more details), head-body length usually less than 280 mm, length of hind foot less than 70 mm; five upper cheek teeth (Pm^3 peglike and occasionally absent).

Color. Dorsum grayish with the middle of back interspersed with buff or ochraceous hairs; along lateral line, a short to long stripe of dark orange or light chestnut; top of hind legs and feet often same color as lateral stripe; side of face and around eye cinnamon-rufous; underparts whitish although in a few animals the throat region or most of the underparts may be rufous; tail

Fig. 8.68A. Gray squirrel, *Sciurus carolinensis.* Photograph by W. W. Goodpaster.

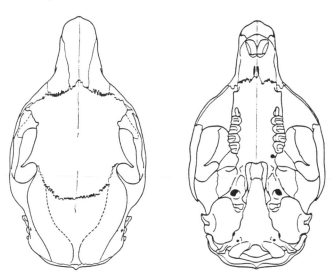

Fig. 8.68B. *Sciurus carolinensis,* dorsal and ventral views of skull. Urbana, Champaign Co., Illinois, 1508 UI. Male, 60.4 mm greatest length.

grayish above and below, with cinnamon-rufous intermixed; tail bordered with white on sides and at tip.

Color mutants are not uncommon, and include melanistic (black), albino, and, in Ohio, a tan-colored blond mutation. In the mid 1800's, large numbers of melanistic squirrels were present in several places in Illinois; in 1978, they were reported from 17 localities, all in the northern part of the state (Nixon et al., 1978). Albino gray squirrels are present in good numbers in Olney, Richland County. As many as 500 to a 1,000 may be present but the numbers vary from year to year.

Chromosomes. See account of the genus.

Comparisons. S. carolinensis differs from *S. niger* in

having underparts whitish in color rather than being mixed with rufous color, underside of the tail mostly grayish rather than rufous, tail when viewed from above bordered with white rather than with rufous; backs of ears whitish, dark gray, or blackish rather than reddish, tops of forefeet whitish mixed with gray rather than cinnamon-colored; head-body measurement usually less than 280 mm rather than more, hind foot less than 70 mm rather than usually more; five upper cheek teeth, with peglike Pm^3, rather than only four, and none is peglike.

S. carolinensis differs from *Tamiasciurus* as given in the *Comparison* for the genus *Sciurus*.

Secondary sexual variation. Havera and Nixon (1978) examined and measured over 100 gray squirrel skulls from Illinois and reported that there was no sexual dimorphism in cranial measurements (P < 0.49). In a sample of 11 males and 6 females from Champaign County, there was a slight but significant difference in greatest length and postorbital breadth. In another sample of 14 males and 9 females, there was a slight but significant difference in braincase breadth and postorbital breadth. In the analyses of populations, however, the sexes have been combined.

Molt. According to Brown and Yeager (1945), gray squirrels molt once a year. Males begin to molt in the spring and conclude the process in mid-summer; females molt between April and September, after their last young of the year are born. The process takes about a month.

Remarks. Gray squirrels have decreased in numbers in the "wild" over the years, as the forests have been reduced; those in the cities have held their own or increased in numbers. Gray and fox squirrels may occur together in some places in the wild; rarely do they occur together in cities. It is difficult to determine why gray squirrels occur in some cities, fox squirrels in others.

Habitat

Gray squirrels in non-urban situations inhabit the interior parts of extensive woods or forests, especially if there is some brushy understory. Ideally, the woods should have a large number of mature, over-mature, or nearly mature trees and should be ungrazed by livestock. It should have a closed canopy, should have trees that produce nuts, especially acorns and hickory nuts, and have cavities within some of the trees. Forests that lack an understory, especially as the result of heavy grazing by cattle, are less preferred. Although these squirrels build exterior leaf nests, the presence of cavities within trees is important because the holes provide refuges from predators and severe weather and nurseries for rearing young. Mature forests provide more cavities.

In Illinois, gray squirrels are usually found where there are black oaks, white oaks, northern red oaks, and sugar maples. In southern Illinois, these squirrels live most

often in upland forest, with the addition of beech, sweet gums, and pin oaks in their habitat. Since they do not develop cavities as readily as some other species of trees, hickories, cottonwoods, and Osage orange are less desirable for dens and nesting sites.

Gray squirrels occupy mature forests, and these forests have been extensively lumbered over the past years. For example, Nixon et al. (1978) stated that in 1800, gray squirrels made up an estimated 77.6 percent of the squirrels in the Lower Illinois River region (from Knox County south to the mouth of the Illinois River); only 22.4 percent were fox squirrels. By 1956–57, this was reduced to 16.6 percent for gray squirrels and is a reflection on the reduction of forest acreage (from 2½ million acres in 1800 to 670,000 acres in 1962). This has been the trend for the forests and the numbers of gray squirrels throughout the state. While their numbers have been decreasing in forested areas, they have greatly increased in many urban situations in the state.

The gray squirrel is the only species of tree squirrel in many cities in Illinois. In such situations, the habitat is very different from that in non-urban situations. Here, grays are found in open-forest conditions, without an extensive forest situation, often without much understory, and with conditions similar to hedgerows. For example, on the campus of the University of Illinois, with the lawns dotted by a variety of trees, gray squirrels are exceedingly abundant. A pair of mature oaks in one corner of the campus, representing an area slightly less than one-half acre, provides for five adults (although this number varies over the years). Some cities have only gray squirrels; others, seemingly with comparable vegetative conditions, only a few miles away have only fox squirrels.

Habits

One unique feature of gray squirrels is adapting quickly and thoroughly to urban conditions and situations. In cities, they lose their shyness and become almost tame. When Dutch elm disease killed all of the elms in towns where there were thousands of gray squirrels before, as in Champaign-Urbana, many naturalists thought that with the opening-up of these "urban woods" gray squirrels would decline if not disappear. Such was not the case.

Gray squirrels under urban conditions become proficient at moving along small wires and cables, climbing pipe-size poles, and ascending vertical brick walls. In such situations, they are to some an interesting part of the environment to be pampered and appreciated; to others, a pest to be eliminated.

In non-urban situations, gray squirrels are more active in the morning than in the afternoon between June and October and less active at midday (Brown and Yeager, 1945). They are most active when the incident light, measured six inches above the ground, is between 150 and 650 foot candles (Packard, 1956). During the time

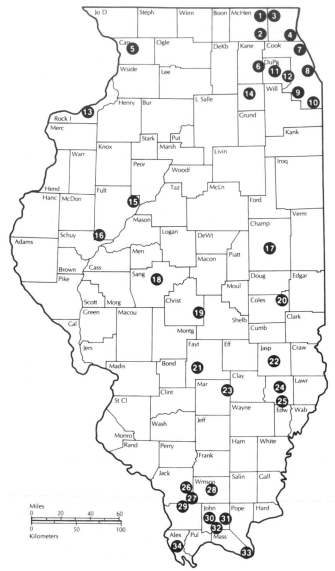

Map 8.29. Gray squirrels, *Sciurus carolinensis*, occur statewide. The subspecies is *S. c. carolinensis*. Localities of occurrence as numbered are referenced in *Records of occurrence*. The range of the species in the United States is shaded.

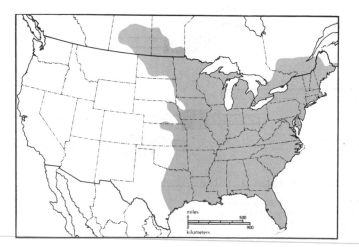

when the trees are producing a maximum amount of food, squirrels are active for longer periods of time.

During the winter, these squirrels do not hibernate but may sleep for extended periods of time, being lethargic. Brown and Yeager (1945) examined nest boxes during the winter and found that many squirrels were reluctant to leave the boxes when opened. Some of the squirrels were rolled up in a ball among the leaves within the box and in a deep sleep. Even then, when they were shaken, they would awaken slowly and hesitate to leave the nest.

There are several reports of squirrels entering water and swimming short distances of their own volition. During rainy days squirrels seem to avoid the water and are less active in feeding and foraging.

In the early literature on the gray squirrel in Illinois, the species was often referred to as the Migratory Squirrel. Kennicott (1857:64) observed that "the most interesting feature in the habits of this animal is the remarkable migration performed at times by large bodies of them. . . . Immense numbers congregate in autumn, and move off together, continuing their progress in the same general direction, whatever it may be, not even turning aside for large streams." Kennicott said that he had not observed such migrations in Illinois, but knew of such occurrences in Wisconsin and Michigan. There are numerous reports of movements of grays in Wisconsin. Jackson (1961) lists at least 21. At the present time, movements of squirrels for great distances are unknown in Illinois. Local movements are known to occur, however. In Illinois, Brown and Yeager (1945:66) reported that fox squirrels may in the course of a year move two or three miles and that gray squirrels "may travel equal if not greater distances." Squirrels shift their foraging to areas where food is most abundantly and readily available.

Leaf nests are built in crowns of trees. These serve mostly during the less severe climatic periods. These nests can be made entirely of leaves or with leaves and twigs interlaced. When nest boxes are used, the squirrels usually add a lining of leaves. In nests in cavities in trees, a lining of leaves may or may not be used. Brown and Yeager (1945) found that in Illinois these squirrels build leaf nests even when cavities are available.

Artificial den boxes can be built for gray squirrels. Such a box needs to have, near the top, an opening which is 2½ inches in diameter; the box needs to be about 1½ feet high, about one foot square, and the bottom can be of hardware cloth to allow dirt and moisture to escape. This can be attached to the trunk of a tree and placed as high as possible.

The home range of gray squirrels in Lawrence, Kansas, had mean distances between all location points for adult females of 145.3 ft (44.3 m); for adult males, 203.7 ft (62.1 m). For juveniles, the distances were less (Armitage and Harris, 1982). Within cities, gray squirrels usually have irregularly shaped home ranges. Wire and cables between utility poles, as well as the poles themselves, represent segments of their home range.

Food

Observations of foods eaten by gray squirrels in Illinois show that although a considerable variety of seeds and fruits are eaten, the mainstays are from oaks, hickories, walnuts, pecans, and elms. In Kansas, Packard (1956) analyzed foods by seasons. In the autumn, acorns, hickory nuts, and walnuts were utilized; in the winter, cached foods were recovered, and bark of oaks, currants, elms, hackberry, grapes, and other shrubs and trees also were eaten; in spring, buds and sprouting leaves of available trees and shrubs were used extensively; in summer, fruits, berries, and leaves were added to the diet.

Food caching by both gray and fox squirrels is a standard practice. If there is an abundance of nuts or acorns available at any time of the year, the surplus will be cached. Holes between one and two inches deep are dug in the ground, one or more items depending upon their size placed therein, and dirt tamped down over the cache. How effective squirrels are in recovering cached items is not fully known, but they do make use of some of these when other foods, or more desirable foods, are not available.

Reproduction

In Illinois, male gray squirrels may be in breeding condition continuously from late fall until midsummer. The peak of breeding occurs in January and again in June and July. In the southern part of Illinois, the first peak is January 1–10; in central Illinois, January 10–20; in northern Illinois, January 20–30. The peaks for the second breeding are for the south, June 15–25, central,

June 25–July 5, and northern, July 5–15, according to Brown and Yeager (1945). The gestation period is thought to be about 44 days.

Mating chases are indicative of the breeding season. Females usually bark at this time and are in turn pursued by several males any one of which may stop to challenge other males. Chases usually end, at least temporarily, with copulation or attempted copulation.

Young are cared for in a leaf nest, which can be in the branches of a tree, a cavity within the tree, or in an artificial squirrel or duck nest box. Litter size in Illinois averages 2.74 for the early breeding season and 2.43 for the second breeding season (Brown and Yeager, 1945). Young nurse for approximately eight weeks to a full two months.

Breeding and number of litters per year follow that of fox squirrels. Females two years or older produce two litters per year. Females from the first breeding period usually breed the next year during the first breeding season when they are about 11 months old. These females usually do not breed during the second breeding season.

Females born during the second breeding season usually do not breed until the following second breeding season. In all cases, breeding may be affected by the availability of food.

Miscellaneous

Melanistic gray squirrels at one time were abundant in several places in Illinois. Kennicott (1857) says that of some 50 gray squirrels shot near the Rock River, all were black. At the present time there may be a few "black" squirrels in this area, but nowhere near that high a percentage of the population. Nixon et al., in 1978, reviewed the known localities where melanistic grays are found: Jo Daviess County in East Dubuque and in

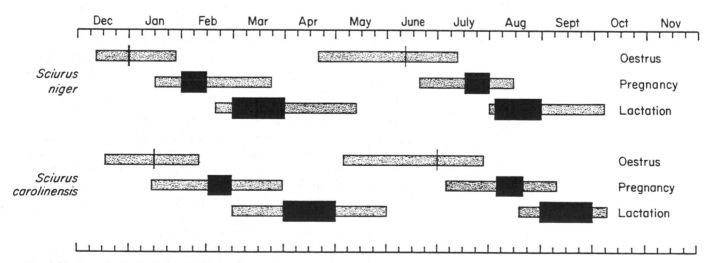

Fig. 8.69. Breeding periods for Illinois fox and gray squirrels that are old enough to produce two litters per year. The first litter is represented by events—oestrus, pregnancy, lactation—to the left. Earliest and latest times for each event provide the limits for the bars; the perpendicular, dark bar indicates the peak of the event. (Modified from Brown and Yeager, 1945)

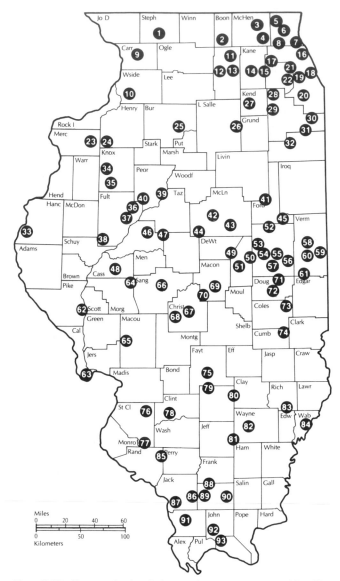

Map 8.30. Fox squirrels, *Sciurus niger*, occur statewide. The subspecies is *S. n. rufiventer.* Localities of occurrence as numbered are referenced in *Record of occurrence.* The range of the species in the United States is shaded.

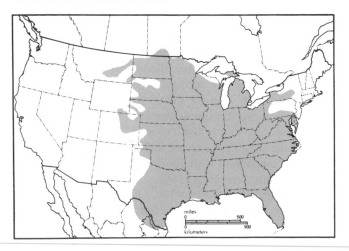

Hanover; Carroll County in Mt. Carroll; Cook County in Winnetka, Glencoe, Northbrook, Wilmette, and Evanston; Lake County in Highland Park, North Chicago (veterans hospital), Zion, Lake Forest, and Fort Sheridan; Rock Island County in Rock Island, Moline, Rock Island Arsenal, and Black Hawk State Park; Adams County in Quincy.

The area where most melanistic grays are found is along Lake Michigan from Evanston north to Zion. Melanistic squirrels now survive only where they are protected from being hunted, as in cities or preserves.

Albino gray squirrels have been established for at least 80 years in Olney, Richland County. There are various accounts of how and when this colony originated. This population of white squirrels has persisted there only because they have been protected, even from motorists. Supposedly a pair of albino squirrels captured near Sumner, Lawrence County, were purchased by a Mr. J. C. Banks and released in Olney in 1902. Another account has it that a local hunter captured a male and female white squirrel in 1902 and put them on display in an Olney saloon. Another citizen "rescued" the pair and released them within the city. In 1950, there were an estimated 650 white squirrels; in 1971, 1,000. On March 23, 1954, the Museum of Natural History, through arrangements with the Illinois Department of Conservation, was given a live female albino gray squirrel taken north of the city limits of Olney. During the night, this animal gave birth to two non-albino gray squirrels. It is obvious that many, if not all, gray squirrels in Olney are carrying genes resulting in albinism. However, these grays are not protected as are the whites.

Since European man has settled in Illinois, 75 percent of the forests have been depleted and removed. Some of the forests that persist have had the mature trees removed and in many places the understory is gone. All of this has resulted in a tremendous reduction of gray squirrels in the natural forests of Illinois. Probably the reduction of grays in the "wild" has been reduced much more than 75 percent.

Variation

E. R. Hall (1981) ascribes two subspecies to Illinois: a wide-ranging *Sciurus carolinensis pennsylvanicus* and in southernmost Illinois, *S. c. carolinensis.* He also shows the range of *S. c. hypophaeus* in northernmost Illinois but records no specimens. Havera and Nixon (1978) studied several hundred specimens from Illinois and concluded that those from north of a line through Rock Island, Livingston, and Kankakee counties are referable to *Sciurus carolinensis pennsylvanicus* (I suspect that they might have meant *S. c. hypophaeus*) and all south of this line to *S. c. carolinensis* (Map 8.29, p. 168).

To analyze the variation in Illinois and to determine what subspecific names should be used, I studied samples from northwestern Illinois, two populations in central Illinois, and one from southern Illinois, and compared these with samples from Minnesota-Wisconsin (*Sciurus c. hypophaeus*), northeastern United States and Canada (*S. c. pennsylvanicus*), southwestern Ohio (*S. c. carolinensis*), and from the Carolinas and Georgia (*S. c. carolinensis*). Measurements for these populations are given in Table 8.19 (p. 182) and they are presented in a more or less north-to-south sequence.

Specimens from Minnesota and Wisconsin are large; those from northeastern United States are nearly as large. Specimens from the Carolinas and Georgia are small and those from southwestern Ohio are nearly as small. From the northern populations through the populations in Illinois there is a clinal and gradual decrease in size. Specimens from Minnesota are appreciably larger than northern Illinois specimens. All Illinois specimens are much like specimens from northeastern United States. The greatest break in the cline comes between specimens of *S. c. carolinensis* from southeastern Ohio and the Carolinas-Georgia area. In my interpretation, no specimens from Illinois are referable to *S. c. carolinensis*. I am not certain that *S. c. hypophaeus* is a distinct subspecies but if it is, specimens from Illinois are not referable to it. All specimens in Illinois are regarded as *S. c. pennsylvanicus*.

Sciurus carolinensis pennsylvanicus Ord

1815. *Sciurus Pennsylvanicus* Ord, *in* Guthrie, A new geogr., hist.,... Phila., Amer. ed. 2:292. Type locality, Pennsylvania west of the Allegany Ridge.

1894. *Sciurus carolinensis pennsylvanicus*, Rhoades, App. of reprint of Ord, *in* Guthrie, A new geogr. hist., p. 19.

1815. *Sciurus hiemalis* Ord, in Guthrie, *op. cit.*, 2:292. Type locality near Tuckerton, near Little Egg Harbor, New Jersey.

1830. *Sciurus leucotis* Gapper, Zool. Jour., 5:206. Type from region between York and Lake Simcoe, Ontario.

1849. *Sciurus migratorius* Audubon and Bachman, The vivip. quad. No. Amer., 1:265. Based on *S. leucotis* Gapper, 1830.

Range. Throughout the state in forested areas and in some cities (Map 8.29, p. 168).

Diagnosis and Comparisons. A large-sized subspecies of *S. carolinensis*, slightly smaller than *S. c. hypophaeus* if that form is a recognizable subspecies; considerably larger than *S. c. carolinensis*.

Records of occurrence. SPECIMENS EXAMINED, 96. **McHenry Co.:** [1] Spring Grove, 1 (SIC); [2a] Crystal Lake, 1 (NIU); [2b] 1⅛ mi E Crystal Lake, 1 (NIU). **Lake Co.:** [3] Antioch, 1 (NIU); [4a] Lake Forest, 3 (FM), 1 (US); [4b] Highland Park, 1 (UI), 2 (FM); [4c] Deerfield, 1 (CAS). **Carroll Co.:** [5] 1 mi W Mt. Carroll, 1 (UI). **Kane Co.:** [6] St. Charles, 1 (NIU). **Cook Co.:**

[7a] Glencoe, 1 (CAS), [7b] West Northfield, 2 (US); [7c] Evanston, 6 (FM), 1 (UI); [8a] Chicago, 1 (UI), 4 (FM), 1 (CAS); [8b] Lincoln Park [Chicago], 1 (CAS); [9] Palos Park, 1 (CAS); [10] Glenwood, 1 (UI). **DuPage Co.:** [11] Glen Ellyn, 1 (FM), 1 (CAS); [12] Hinsdale, 2 (FM). **Kendall Co.:** [14] Yorkville, 1 (ISU). **Fulton Co.:** [15] 4 mi E Canton, 1 (UI); [16a] 2 mi S Vermont, 1 (UI); [16b] 2 mi W Astoria, 2 (UI).

Champaign Co.: [17a] ¼ mi W Champaign, 2 (UI); [17b] Champaign, 4 (UI); [17c] Urbana, 12 (UI); [17d] 2½ mi E Urbana, 1 (UI). **Sangamon Co.:** [18] Springfield, 4 (ISM). **Christian Co.:** [19] 6 mi N Pana, 1 (ISU). **Coles Co.:** [20] 2 mi E Rardin, 2 (UI). **Fayette Co.:** [21] 2½ mi SW Vandalia, 1 (UI). **Marion Co.:** [23] 4 mi ENE Omega, 2 (UI). **Richland Co.:** [24a] 1½ mi N Olney, 1 (UI); [24b] Olney, 1 (NIU); [25] Parkersburg, 9 (US). **Jackson Co.:** [26] Carbondale, 2 (SIC), 1 (SRL); [27] Giant City State Park, 1 (SIC). **Williamson Co.:** [28] Marion, 1 (SIC). **Union Co.:** [29a] 4 mi NW Cobden, 1 (SRL); [29b] Cobden [labelled Jackson Co.], 1 (SRL). **Johnson Co.:** [30] Cache River, 2 mi E Rt. 37, 1 (SIC); [31] between Cedar and Bay creeks, 2 (KU); [32] 2½ mi ENE Belknap, 1 (SIC). **Pope Co.:** [33] Black Bottoms, 8 mi SE Brookport [may be Massac Co.], 1 (SIC). **Alexander Co.:** [34] Olive Branch, 1 (FM), 1 (US).

Additional records. **Rock Island Co.:** [13] Milan, (Necker and Hatfield, 1941:50). **Jasper Co.:** [22] Newton, (Necker and Hatfield, 1941:50).

Sciurus niger, Fox squirrel

Range. Throughout the state in wooded areas; present in some cities.

Diagnosis. A sciurid of large size with the underparts reddish or washed with rufous color, edge of tail with rufous border, back of ears reddish; four upper cheek teeth; hind feet long, usually 70 mm or more; head-body measurement long, usually more than 280 mm.

Color. Dorsum blackish but heavily flecked with whites and buffs to give a salt-and-pepper effect, underparts including undersides of legs rufous or reddish, soles of hands and feet blackish, underside of tail rufous or reddish but with a narrow band of black submarginally, top of tail much the same color as the back, but fringed or bordered with rufous or red, tops of hands and feet reddish. In many winter specimens, the tips of the ears have long reddish hairs. I have not seen color mutants in Illinois specimens, but Kennicott (1857) reported that some specimens in northern Illinois had black underparts.

Chromosomes. See account of the genus (p. 166).

Comparisons. *S. niger* differs from *S. carolinensis* as described in the account of that species (p. 166). Obvious differences are the reddish color of the underparts, four rather than five upper cheek teeth, and larger size.

For a comparison with *Tamiasciurus,* see *Comparisons* for the genus *Sciurus* (p. 166).

Secondary sexual variation. Our data indicate that differences between males and females are not sufficiently great to consider them separately for geographical analyses.

Table 8.18. External and cranial measurements (in mm) of *Sciurus carolinensis* and *Sciurus niger*. Mean, minimum and maximum, and one standard deviation are given. Superscripts indicate sample less than N.

	N	Total length	Tail length	Body length	Hind foot length	Greatest length	Basal length
S. carolinensis hypophaeus Minnesota, Wisconsin	4	489.3 442-527 43.32	216.3 192-237 22.72	271.3 222-335 46.91	68.0 61-71 4.69	63.8 63.1-64.3 0.51	49.1 48.4-49.6 0.50
S. carolinensis pennsylvanicus NE U.S. and Canada Ontario, Maine, N.Y., Mass., Pa.	8	493.6[5] 457-520 23.37	220.3[6] 190-239 17.58	275.2[5] 264-310 19.54	67.0 63-71 2.76	62.1[7] 60.8-64.2 1.22	47.3[7] 45.3-35.6 0.75
NW Illinois: Jo Daviess, Carroll, Ogle, Boone cos.	22	485.6 450-522 22.93	220.0 192-242 16.53	263.6 245-280 12.12	68.4[21] 61-74 3.91	62.4[19] 60.2-65.5 1.38	47.6[18] 45.6-50.4 1.31
Central Illinois: Shelby, Fayette, Jasper cos.	23	477.2[16] 452-507 13.75	214.8[16] 200-232 9.27	262.4[16] 250-275 7.43	67.0[16] 63-70 2.31	61.7 59.65-63.5 1.07	46.8[20] 44.8-48.7 0.99
Central Illinois: Champaign County	17	468.8 433-520 26.46	214.0 180-270 21.01	249.0 222-290 21.88	63.4 57-77 4.83	61.0 59.6-63.6 1.05	46.35 45.1-49.8 1.13
Southern Illinois: Jackson, Union, Pope cos.	12	463.0 445-490 21.28	220.5 211-240 13.18	243.0 229-255 10.51	67.2 67-68 0.45	61.8 59.7-63.0 1.03	46.2 41.2-48.2 1.90
S. carolinensis carolinensis SW Ohio	8	454.0 395-483 30.17	212.6 192-235 17.01	241.4 205-263 19.15	63.7 61-67 2.14	59.6 59.1-60.7 0.55	45.6 44.5-46.6 0.73
No. Carolina, So. Carolina, Georgia	12	450.3 422-477 17.50	200.2 178-223 11.12	250.1 227-272 11.54	65.2 62-69 2.62	59.0 57.3-60.25 0.93	44.5 43.6-45.6 0.66
S. niger rufiventer N. Illinois	8	551.6 497-595 31.43	244.1 212-280 22.45	306.1 276-344 22.68	67.1 55-74 6.08	65.2 63.5-67.6 1.54	50.8 48.6-52.8 1.57
E. central Illinois	18	548.0 470-560 27.68	254.0 200-295 24.73	283.6 239-310 21.82	71.9 58-80 5.91	65.7 63.15-68.0 1.14	51.2 49.6-53.9 1.65
S. Illinois	9	528.3 500-564 23.8	238.5 215-295 32.64	289.8 269-315 16.77	68.8 61-75 5.04	65.8 63.5-68.0 1.49	51.5 49.05-54.0 1.51

Molt. The molt pattern is much the same as that described for gray squirrels. There is one molt per year, although Layne (1958a) thought there might be two. Males begin molting in early spring, females later, usually in April or after. The sequence takes about one month.

Remarks. Sciurus niger in Illinois is distinguishable from the other tree squirrel, *Sciurus carolinensis,* by differences of color, dental formula (upper cheekteeth), and habitat. The two species do not often occur together.

Habitat

The fox squirrel is an inhabitant of the forest edge, oak-covered ridges and oak openings, in the area between the prairie and the deciduous forest, in woodlots, and along hedgerows. In some places these squirrels occur with gray squirrels, but more frequently they are in the open forest, with relatively little understory. Kennicott

(1857) in reviewing the situation in Illinois says that the belts of timber that skirt the streams and the prairie groves or islands of trees within the prairie, with their pin oaks and other trees, provide the favorite habitat for fox squirrels. As the forests were thinned, the habitat for fox squirrels was improved. In southern Illinois, fox squirrels occupy bottomland forests, woodlots, fence-rows, and many urban situations (Layne, 1958a). Fox squirrels spend a considerable amount of time on the ground and when pursued, may run a considerable distance on the ground before taking to trees. In the fall, when many leaves have fallen, a single squirrel will make much noise as it runs across the forest floor.

Some towns are populated only by fox squirrels. A few towns may have both fox and gray, but these animals usually frequent different parts of the town. For example, at one time — and perhaps still — in Springfield fox squir-

Zygomatic breadth	Braincase breadth	Post-orbital breadth	Pre-maxillary breadth	Nasal length	Post-palatal length	Breadth across M-M	Maxillary toothrow (alv.)
35.7	24.8	19.65	15.0	21.1	20.5	14.4	11.4
34.9-37.2	24.25-25.2	19.2-19.9	14.5-15.35	20.55-21.5	20.2-20.8	14.0-14.9	11.35-11.55
1.02	0.46	0.31	0.35	0.40	0.31	0.39	0.09
34.6	24.4	19.3	14.9	20.8	19.9	14.4	11.2
33.6-35.6	23.9-24.75	18.65-19.6	13.9-16.6	19.8-22.5	18.9-20.65	14.0-15.15	10.6-11.9
0.75	0.31	0.37	0.78	0.94	0.64	0.40	0.45
35.0[18]	24.4[21]	19.4[22]	14.8[22]	20.3[22]	20.0[19]	14.3	11.3
33.9-36.5	23.1-25.9	18.7-20.5	14.0-15.7	18.3-22.0	19.0-21.1	13.3-15.3	10.5-11.8
0.76	0.68	0.48	0.52	0.87	19.00	0.51	0.32
34.75[19]	24.5	19.1	15.0	20.6	20.2	14.4	11.25
33.6-36.5	23.8-25.95	18.2-20.1	13.7-16.6	19.2-22.1	18.9-21.6	13.3-15.2	10.5-11.9
0.80	0.55	0.54	0.67	0.84	0.74	0.43	0.32
33.8	23.91	19.0	14.4	20.6	19.8	14.0	10.9
32.9-35.7	23.1-25.1	18.25-20.1	13.0-15.6	19.7-22.3	19.3-20.9	13.8-14.75	10.3-11.95
0.95	0.49	0.50	0.60	0.74	0.40	0.40	0.40
35.8	24.3	19.2	15.0	20.2	19.9	14.2	11.3
33.25-36.0	23.65-25.1	18.4-19.7	14.3-16.2	19.1-21.4	18.3-21.0	13.7-14.9	10.5-12.2
0.95	0.42	0.42	0.60	0.65	0.69	0.36	0.57
33.4	23.8	18.6	14.5	20.1	19.3	13.8	11.3
33.1-33.9	22.9-25.05	17.2-20.5	13.0-16.2	19.0-21.0	18.8-19.9	13.15-14.9	10.6-11.7
0.33	0.74	1.30	1.16	0.69	0.40	0.65	0.34
33.6	23.7	19.05	14.6	19.2	18.9	13.9	10.9
31.9-35.35	22.8-24.35	18.6-19.9	13.45-16.8	18.2-20.1	18.0-20.0	13.45-14.6	10.2-11.8
1.01	0.53	0.41	0.90	0.50	0.62	0.38	0.52
36.7	25.4	20.0	17.1	22.5	22.3	15.6	11.6
34.9-38.3	24.9-25.7	19.4-20.4	15.7-18.6	21.75-24.0	21.15-23.2	15.0-16.3	11.25-12.2
1.22	0.31	0.33	1.09	0.75	0.75	0.42	0.30
37.5	26.2	20.0	17.8	22.1	22.5	15.8	11.6
36.1-39.4	25.0-27.2	19.2-21.0	16.5-19.8	20.2-23.1	21.2-24.0	15.1-16.35	10.9-12.2
1.09	0.58	0.51	0.75	0.75	0.76	0.35	0.39
37.6	26.2	20.4	17.6	22.3	22.6	15.7	11.6
35.75-38.45	25.3-26.8	19.5-21.2	16.5-18.5	21.1-23.5	21.75-23.6	15.2-16.4	11.4-12.0
0.52	0.58	0.52	0.78	0.89	0.64	0.38	0.25

rels inhabited the central parts of town as in Washington Park and gray squirrels, the northern parts as in Carpenter Park, near the Sangamon River. Tappan Gregory (1936:53) commented, "When I first moved to Northfield Township, Illinois, there were no Gray Squirrels to be seen in our woods, only Fox Squirrels. Now, eight years later, the Gray probably outnumber the Fox, though both still occur on our property."

In 1966, Sharon Saari made a record of the presence or absence of gray and fox squirrels in towns of Champaign County that had a population of 150 people or more. Twenty-two towns were surveyed. Fox squirrels only were found in 16 towns; gray squirrels alone were found in only two towns, Champaign and Urbana—and they should be regarded biologically as one town. Three towns had both fox and gray squirrels. In two of these three towns—Philo and Ivesdale—both species could be found in the same tree at the same time. In the third town—Savoy—gray squirrels were in the center of town, fox squirrels in a woodlot on the edge of town.

Habits

Fox squirrels are most active in Illinois in the months of June through October between 5:00 and 9:00 a.m. (Brown and Yeager, 1945). In the afternoon, they are most active between 4:00 and 5:00 p.m., but not as active as during the morning span. In Iowa the morning peak of activity is between 8:00 and 10:00 and the afternoon between 1:00 and 2:00. In Indiana, a few squirrels are active as late as 10:00 p.m. in March on moonlight nights (Mumford and Whitaker, 1982). Diurnal activity is greatly curtailed by rain, snow, fog, high winds, and excessively high temperatures. During cold weather, fox squirrels become dormant and semilethargic for periods of several

Fig. 8.70A. Fox squirrel, *Sciurus niger*. Photograph by W. W. Goodpaster.

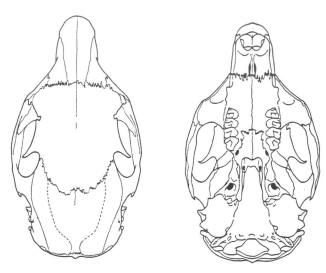

Fig. 8.70B. *Sciurus niger,* dorsal and ventral views of skull; 6 mi N Morrisonville, Christian Co., Illinois, 1534 UI. Male 65.7 mm greatest length.

days. They remain within the nest and curl up in a tight ball. Brown and Yeager (1945) found some nest boxes with two and one box with three dormant squirrels. They probably were taking advantage of the added heat produced by more bodies.

Fox squirrels are good swimmers and do not hesitate to enter the water. They swim usually with the head, back, and tail mostly out of the water, and we know of them jumping into water without provocation and swimming out to debris.

The habit of running on the ground, often in preference to going up into the trees, is a characteristic of fox squirrels. When closely pursued, they will run on the ground as long as possible before taking to the greater safety of trees.

Fox squirrels store excess foods at any time, although this activity increases in the fall when storable items become more available: acorns, hickory nuts, pecans. Storing occurs during the routine feeding activities of the squirrels.

In the forest-edge and black prairie in Illinois where many fox squirrels live, there are not enough tree cavities that can be used for nests. Therefore, leaf nests are important for this species. Nests are usually placed in larger trees about 30 feet above ground (D. L. Allen, 1943). Fox squirrels are said to build two types of leaf nests: a compact nest for rearing the young and a larger, more loosely constructed one. Actually, it is difficult to distinguish between the two types. The lining for the nest can be leaves more finely shredded, or the shredded bark of trees. Frequently in the fall, a squirrel will cut off a twig with three or four leaves attached. Often these will fall to the ground but the squirrel will quickly retrieve them and carry them to add to the nest. Not all

nests in a woodlot are necessarily occupied by squirrels; some may be old and unused, others may be temporary summer retreats. Dens in hollows within trees are also used when available. These cavity-nests are usually lined with leaves.

In Lawrence, Kansas, the mean distances between all location points of the home range for an individual male, adult fox squirrel was 255.6 ft (77.9 m); for an adult female, 204.4 ft (62.3 m), (Armitage and Harris, 1982).

In a study at Carbondale, Zelley (1971) analyzed the sounds made by fox squirrels. The most common sound is a bark, usually in a series of 6 to 10, with the barks decreasing in duration and intensity while the interval between the barks increased. The chatter-bark was given when the squirrel was suddenly startled, and grunts and squeals were emitted during chases. Tooth chatters and screams may be produced under stress. A high-pitched whine may be emitted during the mating chase.

Food

Food for fox squirrels varies with the seasons. When food items are stored, they may be available over several seasons. Fox squirrels are more tolerant of a limited variety of food items than are gray squirrels.

Winter. Food consists of cached materials, especially hickory nuts, acorns, and Osage orange fruits, and ears of corn that were dropped in the fields. Late in the winter, tree buds may be utilized and fruits that have hung on vines may be eaten. In southern Illinois, a fox squirrel was observed licking sap oozing from a broken limb of a sugar maple (Layne, 1958a). Bark may be eaten if necessary as a last resort.

Spring. Buds and flowers of trees and bushes are eaten extensively. Larvae of various insects wherever available may be eaten. Emerging leaves and parts of some fungi may be eaten and as seeds become available these are consumed.

Summer. A variety of fruits, fungi, seeds, and larvae of insects are eaten and as soon as acorns and nuts start to mature, fox squirrels turn to these. Green corn may be taken also.

Fall. During periods of good production, acorns and other nuts become available in far greater numbers than the squirrels can eat or store. Included are the masts of hickories, oaks, walnuts, butternuts, pignuts, hazelnuts, and Osage orange.

Reproduction

There are two breeding seasons. The first runs approximately from December 15 to 25, in southern Illinois; December 25–January 5, central; January 5–15, northern. The second breeding season runs approximately from May 25 to June 5 in southern Illinois; June 5–15, central; June 15–25, northern (Brown and Yeager, 1945). The gestation period is 45 days.

Females that are two years or more of age usually produce two litters per year, one litter at each breeding season. Females born in the first season of the previous year usually breed in the following first season but not in the second breeding season. Females born in the second breeding season rarely breed during the next first season, but breed in the second season. Breeding is negatively affected by inadequate food supply, adverse weather conditions, and probably other factors. In a population of fox squirrels in Carbondale, Jackson County, Harnishfeger et al. (1978) found that only 39 percent of the females more than one year old bred in the first breeding period and only 27 percent the second breeding season. Only two of 87 females reared two litters in the same year.

In the oak-hickory upland of Illinois 44 fox squirrels had an average of 2.63 embryos in 1941, and an average of 2.36 embryos in 1942 (Brown and Yeager, 1945). In the farmlands at the south edge of Urbana, Champaign County, the number of embryos was higher, 3.66 for six females in 1941, 3.75 for four females in 1942. The number of young in 30 litters just prior to weaning in Carbondale averaged 1.97. At birth they weigh between 14–18 gms, and they develop much as do gray squirrels. Young are nursed for about eight weeks.

Variation

In northern United States north of Mississippi and Alabama and west of the Alleghenies, specimens have been referred to the subspecies *Sciurus niger rufiventer*. I follow this arrangement.

Fig. 8.71. Ideal habitat for fox squirrels, with open woods that include hickory, black oak, white oak, walnut, and maple. Many of the trees are mature, with numerous cavities. (From Brown and Yeager, 1945)

Sciurus niger rufiventer E. G. St.-Hilaire

1803. *Sciurus rufiventer* E. Geoffroy St. Hilaire, Cat. des mamm. du Mus. Natl. d'Hist. Nat., Paris, p. 176. Type locality, Mississippi Valley, probably between southern Illinois and central Tennessee.

1907. *Sciurus niger rufiventer*, Osgood, Proc. Biol. Soc. Wash., 20:44.

1851. *Sciurus sayii* Audubon and Bachman, The vivip. quad. No. Amer., 2:pl. 89; 2:274. Type locality somewhere in bottomlands of Wabash, Illinois, or Missouri rivers, or in Michigan.

Range. Throughout the state in wooded areas; present in some cities (Map 8.30).

Diagnosis and Comparisons. A large subspecies of *S. niger*, both externally and cranially; it differs from the race to the south in these features and the skull is less angular.

Records of occurrence. SPECIMENS EXAMINED, 163.
Stephenson Co.: [1] 3 mi W Freeport, 1 (UI). **Boone Co.:** [2] Belvidere, 1 (NIU). **McHenry Co.:** [3] Greenwood, 1 (CAS); [4] 1 mi N Crystal Lake, 1 (NIU). **Lake Co.:** [5a] Antioch, 1 ((CAS); [5b] Fox Lake, 3 (FM); [6] Grayslake, 1 (CAS); [7a] Lake Forest, 2 (FM); [7b] Highland Park, 1 (CAS); [7c] Deerfield, 1 (CAS); [8] 1 mi W Lake Zurich, 1 (NIU). **Carroll Co.:** [9] Mt. Carroll, 1 (UI). **Whiteside Co.:** [10] 2 mi N Erie, 1 (NIU). **De Kalb Co.:** [11] 10 mi N De Kalb, 1 (NIU); [12] Malta, 1 (NIU); [13a] ¾ mi N De Kalb, 1 (NIU); [13b] De Kalb, 4 (NIU). **Kane Co.:** [14] 15 mi E De Kalb [labelled De Kalb Co], 1 (NIU); [15] St. Charles, 1 (ISM). **Cook Co.:** [16] West Northfield, 2 (US); [17] Bartlett, 1 (CAS); [18] Chicago, 2 (FM); [19a] Oak Park, 10 (FM); [19b] Berwyn, 1 (CAS); [19c] Riverside, 1 (UI); [19d] 1 mi S Cicero, 3 mi E Argo, 1 (UI); [20a] SW Chicago, 1 (UI); [20b] Palos Park, 1 (CAS). **Du Page Co.:** [21] 1 mi N, 1 mi W Bensenville, 1 (UI); [22a] 2 mi W, ½ mi N Oak Brook, 1 (UI); [22b] Downers Grove, 2 (UI). **Mercer Co.:** [23] 1 mi N Viola, 1 (UI). **Henry Co.:** [24] 1½ mi N Alpha, 1 (UI). **Bureau Co.:** [25a] 1 mi E Princeton, 1 (NIU); [25b] 4 mi E Princeton, 1 (UI). **La Salle Co.:** [26] 1½ mi N, 1½ mi E Marseiles, 1 (UI). **Kendall Co.:** [27] 2 mi S Fox, 1 (FM). **Will Co.:** [28] Wheatland Twp., 1 (FM); [29] 15 mi NE Morris [labelled Grundy Co.], 1 (ISU); [30] Park Forest, 1 (UI); [31] 2 mi S Peotone, 1 (UI). **Kankakee Co.:** [32] Rock Creek State Park, 1 (FM). **Hancock Co.:** [33] Warsaw*, 3 (US). **Knox Co.:** [34] Galesburg, 1 (UI); [35] ½ mi S, ½ mi W De Long, 2 (UI). **Fulton Co.:** [36] Canton, 1 (UI); [37] 1 mi N Bryant, 1 (UI); [38] 2 mi S Vermont, 1 (UI). **Peoria Co.:** [39] Peoria, 1 (US); [40] 4½ mi W, 2¼ mi S Hanna City, 1 (UI). **Livingston Co.:** [41] 4 mi N, 2 mi W Melvin [labelled Ford Co.], 1 (UI). **McLean Co.:** [42a] Normal, 8 (ISU); [42b] Bloomington, 1 (ISU); [43] 3½ mi N Le Roy, 1 (UI); [44a] 1½ mi N McLean, 1 (UI). **Ford Co.:** [45] Paxton, 1 (UI). **Mason Co.:** [46] 3 mi S Forest City, 1 (UI). **Cass Co.:** [48] no specific locality, 1 (UIS). **De Witt Co.:** [49] 1 mi E Weldon, 1 (UI). **Piatt Co.:** [50] White Heath, 1 (UI); [51] Allerton Park, 5 mi W, 2½ mi S Monticello, 3 (UI).
Champaign Co.: [52] 20 mi N, 3 mi W Urbana, 1 (UI); [53] 1 ½ mi ESE Mahomet, 1 (UI); [54] 1 mi W Bondville, 1 (UI);

[55a] 3½ mi N Urbana, 1 (UI); [55b] Urbana (collected 1932), 1 (UI); [55c] Univ. Illinois Woods, 1 (UI); [55d] Champaign, UI Woods, 1 (UI); [56] 2 mi SE Sidney, 2 (UI); [57] ½ mi S, 3 mi W Philo, 1 (UI). **Vermilion Co.:** [58a] Collison, 1 (UI); [58b] 1½ mi S, 3 mi E Collison, 2 (UI); [59] Danville, 1 (UI); [60a] 2 mi E Muncie, 1 (UI); [60b] 2 mi SE Oakwood, 1 (UI); [61] ½ mi N Sidell, 1 (UI). **Pike Co.:** [62] Milton, 1 (UI). **Calhoun Co.:** [63] near Golden Eagle, 1 (ISM). **Morgan Co.:** [64] 3 mi S Ashland, 1 (UI). **Macoupin Co.:** [65] 1½ mi W Chesterfield, 1 (UI). **Sangamon Co.:** [66a] Springfield, 2 (ISM), 1 (UI); [66b] on Sangamon River near Springfield, 2 (KU). **Christian Co.:** [67] Taylorville, 1 (ISU); [68] 6 mi N Morrisonville, 1 (UI). **Macon Co.:** [69] 3¼ mi S Decatur, 1 (UI); [70] 2 mi N, 1 mi W Blue Mound, 1 (UI). **Douglas Co.:** [71] 1 mi S Villa Grove, 1 (UI); [72] 3 mi S, 4 mi E Tuscola, 1 (UI). **Coles Co.:** [73] 2 mi E Radin, 3 (UI). **Cumberland Co.:** [74a] 10 mi S, 4 mi E Charleston [labelled Coles Co.], 1 (UI); [74b] 11 mi S, 5 mi E Charleston [labelled Coles Co.], 1 (UI). **Fayette Co.:** [75] 2 mi E Vandalia, 1 (UI). **St. Clair Co.:** [76] Bottomland of Silver Creek, 2 mi S Rt. 50, 1 (UI); [77] 5 mi W Marissa, 1 (UI). **Clinton Co.:** [78] ¼ mi E Germantown, 1 (UI). **Marion Co.:** [79] 11 mi S, 3 mi E Vandalia [labelled Fayette Co.], 1 (UI); [80] 4 mi ENE Omega, 4 (UI). **Jefferson Co.:** [81] 15 mi NE Ina, 1 (SIC). **Wayne Co.:** [82] Berry Twp., 1 (US). **Richland Co.:** [83] Parkersburg, 4 (US); no specific locality [not plotted], 1 (US). **Wabash Co.:** [84] Mt. Carmel, 3 (US). **Jackson Co.:** [86] Carbondale, 2 (SRL), 4 (SIC); [87] 10 mi SW Murphysboro, 2 (KU). **Williamson Co.:** [88] 3 mi N Herrin, 1 (KU); [89a] 1 mi W Carterville, 1 (SRL); [89b] 5 mi E, 1 mi N Carbondale, 1 (UI); [90] Crab Orchard, 2 (SRL). **Union Co.:** [91] 4 mi SW Cobden, 1 (SRL). **Johnson Co.:** [92] Cache River, 2 mi E Rt. 37, 1 (SIC). **Massac Co.:** [93] 2 mi SE Belknap, 1 (SRL).

Additional records: **Will Co.:** [28] Wheatland Twp., (UM). **McLean Co.:** [44b] 24 mi E San Jose [labelled Logan Co.], 1 (UM). **Mason Co.:** [47] San Jose, 1 (UM). **Randolph Co.:** [85] 5 mi W Sparta, 2 (FS).

Tamiasciurus, Red squirrels

Diagnosis. A tree squirrel of medium size, tail shorter (60–70%) than head-body length; color of dorsum dark — often reddish mixed with blackish or brownish; underparts white (species *T. hudsonicus*) or rusty (*T. douglasii*); notch in zygomatic plate as viewed ventrally opposite anterior margin of M^1 or more anteriorly as at posterior part of P^4; baculum vestigial and confined to glans penis.

Dental formula. 1/1, 0/0, 1/1 and rarely 2/1, 3/3.

Comparisons. *Tamiasciurus* was considered as synonymous with *Sciurus* for many years. *Tamiasciurus* differs from *Sciurus* in having a vestigial baculum, large fundamental number of chromosomes, minute Cowpers gland, notch in zygomatic plate nearly opposite P^4 rather than M^1, zygomata nearly parallel to long axis of skull.

Tamiasciurus differs markedly from *Glaucomys*. See account of the latter genus (p. 181).

Secondary sexual variation. Lindsay (1981) reported that his analysis of sexual dimorphism indicated that the sexes could be combined.

---

* Worthen specimens.

Aging. Specimens are considered adult and used for comparative analyses when the permanent Pm⁴ is fully erupted and in occluding position.

Remarks. The genus *Tamiasciurus* was long thought to consist of two species, *T. hudsonicus* and the western *T. douglasii.* Recently Lindsay (1981) has regarded the populations in Baja California as referable to a distinct species, *T. mearnsi.*

Tamiasciurus has been characterized as lacking an os penis. Layne (1952), however, concluded there was a minute os penis. In *Tamiasciurus,* the length of the os penis is less than 0.50 mm; in *Sciurus carolinensis* and *S. niger,* more than 3.00 mm.

Tamiasciurus hudsonicus, Red Squirrel

Range. In the 1800's, probably throughout northern Illinois; since about the 1960's, only along and near the Kankakee River, mostly from Kankakee eastward, north into eastern Will County and south along the Iroquois River (Map 8.31).

Diagnosis. A species of *Tamiasciurus* in which the underparts are whitish or grayish and without any ochraceous or orangish color, top of feet grayish and not extensively suffused or intermixed with reddish or ochraceous-colored hair (in central United States); dorsum in winter usually with a medial band of dark, orangish red fur down back and extending on top of tail, in summer, reddish band less noticeable.

Remarks. *T. hudsonicus* occurs in most forested areas of northern United States, and the other two species are found in the west coast states only.

Chromosomes. Diploid number, 46; FN = 84; 42 metacentrics, submetacentrics, subtelocentrics; 2 acrocentrics. X chromosome submetacentric; Y, metacentric (Hsu, 1966).

Molt. Molts occur twice annually; the tail molts once each year (Layne, 1954). The spring molt occurs from late March to early July. The fall molt extends from late August to December. Molting of the tail usually occurs in September during the fall body molt. According to Layne, spring molting occurs first on the feet, then on the head, and progresses toward the rump both dorsally and ventrally. Fall molting is the reverse of spring molting, with replacement occurring on the rump and moving forward.

History of Tamiasciurus hudsonicus in Illinois. It is not clear what the distribution of the red squirrel was in the 1800's in Illinois. It appears that Robert Kennicott was not familiar personally with this squirrel in the 1850's. He writes (1857:68): "In the interior [of the United States], it abounds in Ohio and Indiana, and is found sparingly in heavy timber in Illinois; but it is not common, if it occurs at all, in the southern parts of these

States." Further on the same page he writes "In parts of Northern Illinois, where it was not seen formerly, it is now occasionally found, and is increasing in numbers." Cyrus Thomas in his catalogue of Illinois mammals (1861) says nothing about their presence although he lists the species. However, being in southern Illinois, he may not have been familiar with the northern part of the state. Hoffmeister and Mohr (1957:143) said that there were four authentic records of this squirrel for Illinois taken before 1912. These were Lake County: Lake Forest and Fox Lake; Marshall County: Lawnridge; Putnam County: Hennepin. To my knowledge, there are no specimens now extant to verify these records. I once thought the Lake County records were based on specimens in the Field Museum, but none is present there now (1984), nor do I know of any specimens upon which J. A. Allen (1877) based his record for Lawnridge or Kennicott's record for Hennepin. In 1898, J. A. Allen (1898) lists no specimens of *T. hudsonicus* from Illinois in his revision of *Tamiasciurus.*

In 1910, F. E. Wood noted that the red squirrel "is said to occur at Onarga, in Iroquois County. It was probably introduced there, but is native in the northern part of the state" (1910:521). I do not know if the record for Onarga was authentic.

Despite the absence of preserved specimens from the 1800's, red squirrels probably were present in northern Illinois, although they must not have been abundant. It is believed that red squirrels disappeared from Illinois in the late 1800's and probably they were absent in the early 1900's. Perhaps this was the case until near the middle of this century. Jackson (1961) said they were scarce in southern Wisconsin, south of the Fox River before the twentieth century and disappeared from many parts of this region. If red squirrels persisted in Illinois,

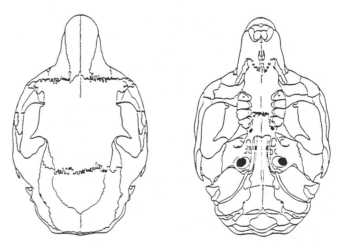

Fig. 8.72. *Tamiasciurus hudsonicus,* dorsal and ventral views of skull. Near Beaverville, Iroquois Co., Illinois, 55058 UI. Female, 47.8 mm greatest length.

Fig. 8.73. Red squirrel, *Tamiasciurus hudsonicus* photographed in the city park of Momence, Kankakee Co., Illinois, in October 1983. Photograph by Bruce Brown.

one would expect them to have persisted in the forest preserves in Lake, Cook, or Will counties; there are no records that they did.

Red squirrels were present in Newton and Lake counties, Indiana, adjacent to Cook, Will, Kankakee, and Iroquois counties, Illinois, in 1895 (Butler, 1895). In 1897, Blatchley (1898) observed that they were common in Lake County, Indiana. Hahn (1907) found some red squirrels in the Kankakee River valley at Aylesworth and Boone Grove, both in Porter County, Indiana, in 1905. Any of these populations of red squirrels might have moved into Illinois.

In the 1960's, red squirrels were present near the Kankakee River on the La Salle Fish and Wildlife Area, in both Lake and Newton counties, Indiana, according to information provided me by Russell Mumford in a letter of September 9, 1977. They may have been present there before the 1960's. In the early 1970's, these squirrels were present in Willow Slough Fish and Game Area, Newton County, Indiana. There was every reason to believe that red squirrels would be found near the Kankakee River in Kankakee County, Illinois.

In 1977, red squirrels were reported from several localities in Kankakee County, Illinois: Island in Kankakee River at Momence; Dudley Grove along Kankakee River; Spring Creek, 1½ mi E Aroma Park; Kankakee River State Park. The original verifications were made by Jack White and Kathryn Kerr of the Illinois Natural Areas Inventory. At these places in Kankakee County, they thought there might be a population in the low hundreds. Subsequently, the Illinois Department of Conservation has recovered red squirrels taken in the Iroquois County Conservation Area, where they were shot by persons hunting for fox squirrels. At least five have been so recovered and preserved but some are skins only, or skeletons only.

Although it would seem natural that red squirrels would move into these areas in Kankakee and Iroquois counties from the populations just across the state line in Indiana, there were several stories that persons had brought red squirrels from Minnesota and one or two releases of these were made in eastern Kankakee County. We may not ever know for certain whether such introductions were made. I believe that most of the squirrels that we know today in the Kankakee River area of northeastern Illinois are from animals that moved in from Indiana. This is discussed further in the account of *Tamiasciurus hudsonicus loquax* (p. 180).

Habitat

Red squirrels in Illinois prefer the plantations of red, white, jack, and Virginia pines, especially where these are in dense stands. Such stands of pines are found east of Aroma Park, Kankakee County, and in the Iroquois County Conservation Area, north of Beaverville, Iroquois County. In other places they live in hardwood forests containing oaks, maple, and hickories. Their needs require that these woods be dense with a dense understory. Often, pines are interspersed with hardwoods; both groups of trees are used by red squirrels, but pines are preferred. In one area of pines, a red squirrel had gone some distance to harvest oak leaves which had been used to build a nest. On the island in the Kankakee River at Momence, Kankakee County, where red squirrels are present, the woods consists largely of black walnut, red oak, and bur oak; there are no pines. All of the red squirrels here were living in nests in natural cavities in the trees. Dr. Bruce Brown who has studied red squirrels in Illinois has provided me with this information on red squirrels in northeastern Illinois.

In Wisconsin, red squirrels are found in coniferous forests or in mixed woods of deciduous and coniferous trees (Jackson, 1961). In central New York, the preferred habitat is ungrazed woods of mature beech, maple, hemlock, or stands of mixed hardwoods, predominantly oak-hickory (Layne, 1954). Red squirrels were also found in conifer plantations, parklike areas, and hedgerows. In central New York, Layne found that "there are too few extensive mature conifer plantations in the region to rank as an important habitat. . . . there is little evidence that many inhabit plantations exclusively" (1954:235).

In Indiana, red squirrels are found in hardwood stands along major streams, ungrazed wooded areas with good undergrowth, and in coniferous woods, all in the northern part of the state (Mumford and Whitaker, 1982).

Habits

Red squirrels are diurnal and are active throughout the year. They are most active for the three or four hours after sunrise and the two hours before sunset. They may be more active during the middle of the day in winter.

These squirrels are bothered by and thus less active during high winds, heavy rains, or heavy snowstorms.

Where these red squirrels now live in Illinois, they must come into contact with fox and gray squirrels. We have a report that persons at Momence, Kankakee County, saw two red squirrels kill a fox squirrel by biting it about the throat. Red squirrels are said to establish territories and defend them by chases and by various intimidating barks and vocalizations. The size of the territory must be dependent upon many factors, including availability of food, trees, and numbers of squirrels. Home ranges, or the area ranged over to gather food, carry on mating activities, establish nests, and rear young, are more easily observed than are territories. In central New York, Layne (1954) found the home range of adult males to average 6.0 acres; adult females, 4.7 acres.

Red squirrels build leaf nests in the crowns of trees or within cavities or holes in trees. In Indiana, nests are globular and are smaller and more compactly built than those of the fox squirrel or gray squirrel and contain more soft material such as shredded bark, grasses, or other soft vegetation (Mumford and Whitaker, 1982). Leaf nests may be near the trunk of the tree or some distance out on a sturdy limb. In New York, Layne (1954) found the diameter of four nests to be between 12 and 14 inches, the depth to be between 8 and 19 inches. For nests in holes, natural cavities or cavities made by woodpeckers are used. Sometimes underground nests are dug, especially in thick hedgerows, and used in winter. Bruce Brown saw red squirrels go into underground burrows in Illinois, but he was not certain that these were nesting chambers. Temporary summer nests may also be constructed and used. Red squirrels are not adverse to using attics of houses as places to build nests.

A variety of notes are sounded by these squirrels. One has been described as a rolling *tcher-r-r-r-r-r,* another as a *kak-kak-kak,* which is repeated. One call has been referred to as a whining *churr-churr.* Different descriptive terms can be given to each call, but the loud, scolding chatter of a red squirrel given with a flick of the tail with each utterance, is easy to recognize.

Red squirrels are good swimmers and it should be no trouble for them to reach islands in streams, as the island at Momence, in the Kankakee River. Jackson (1961) tells of a red squirrel in Wisconsin that was swimming across a lake where the nearest point of land was one-fourth mile away. When he intercepted the squirrel in open water, it hauled out onto his canoe and ran along the gunwale in the direction of the distant shore.

Food

Bruce Brown has provided me with feeding observations of red squirrels in Illinois. They eat acorns of all species of oaks, walnuts, hickory nuts, jack pines, Scotch pines, Virginia pines, and white pines. In Indiana, Mumford and Whitaker (1982) found that white pines were not preferred, and that also may be the case in Illinois. In one white pine, Bruce Brown found the cached cones of jack pines. In numerous places where squirrels are present, the telltale sign in the form of cone fragments at their feeding stations is evident.

In Indiana (Mumford and Whitaker, 1982) most of the food (79.5% by volume, 82.4% by frequency) is mast nuts of walnuts, butternuts, acorns, hickory, beech, cones of jack and Scotch pines. They also feed on berries, tubers, seeds of various kinds, and a limited quantity of insects. In New York, Layne (1954) found that mast was the staple food throughout the year, but was more important from fall to early spring. During the winter, these squirrels also ate the seeds and bark of sumac and the bark of several other shrubs as well, but especially sumac. Tree buds and flowers were eaten in the spring. Fruits, fungus, and a variety of seeds were added to the diet as they became available.

In feeding on hard-shelled nuts, such as walnuts and butternuts, red squirrels do not extensively gnaw the shell but instead make an irregular hole about one-half by three-quarters of an inch in size on either side of the shell and remove the meat (Mumford and Whitaker, 1982.) Fox and gray squirrels usually make larger openings.

Red squirrels frequently will cache nuts and surplus foods the same as other tree squirrels. However, they more frequently cache the items in small holes or cracks in the bark of trees, in crotches, and even in posts.

Red squirrels readily become accustomed to man and take advantage of food supplies offered them. At Momence, Kankakee County, numerous red squirrels live in the city park which is on an island in the Kankakee River. The caretaker of the park regularly feeds these animals, and five frequently come at one time. Two are sufficiently tame that they come in the office and sometimes take refuge behind filing cabinets.

Reproduction

Nothing is known about the reproductive behavior of red squirrels in Illinois. Elsewhere in the midwest and east, these squirrels are known to have two breeding seasons, late winter and midsummer. For example, in New York, Layne (1954) found a peak in pregnancies in March and in July, and a peak in lactation in April and May and in August and September. Apparently most females produce only one litter per year. The gestation period is about 38 days and litter size had a mean of 4.5 in New York.

Young are hairless at birth but shortly after the first week, hair becomes visible and eyes open at about one month. Around three months of age, red squirrels have nearly attained adult size.

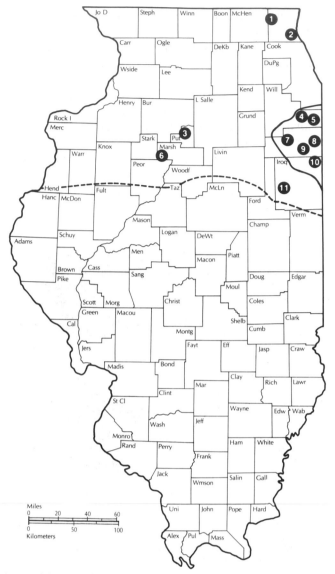

Map 8.31. The former range of red squirrels, *Tamiasciurus hudsonicus*, is thought to have been north of the broken line; the 1980's range is enclosed by the solid line. The subspecies is *T. h. loquax*. Localities of occurrence as numbered are referenced in *Records of occurrence*. The range of the species in the United States is shaded.

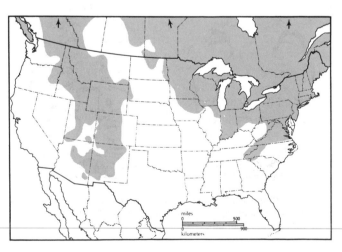

Variation

Tamiasciurus hudsonicus in Illinois has been referred in the past to *T. h. loquax,* but specimens have not been available to verify this allocation. In addition to *T. h. loquax* (type locality, Connecticut), *T. h. minnesota* has been described from Fort Snelling, Minnesota, and *T. h. hudsonicus* from Ontario, Canada, and specimens from Illinois might be referable to these subspecies.

Since there have been rumors that red squirrels have, within the last 25 to 30 years, been introduced into Kankakee County, Illinois, the few specimens from Illinois available with complete skulls were carefully examined to see if they might be *T. h. loquax, T. h. minnesota,* or *T. h. hudsonicus.*

Dr. Stephen Lindsay, while at Memphis State University, examined a specimen in the collection of the Museum of Natural History from 3 mi NNW Beaverville. He compared it with 40 adult *T. h. loquax,* 21 adult *T. h. minnesota,* and 21 adult *T. h. hudsonicus,* all females. He ran a discriminant analysis using nine variables and concluded: "I think there should be little doubt the specimen in your collection originated from an Indiana parental stock of the subspecies *T. h. loquax*" (letter of November 30, 1979).

Through the efforts of Dr. Brown, 10 specimens with skulls have been accumulated. These are now being studied by Drs. Stephen Lindsay and Bruce Brown. They find it difficult to differentiate the three subspecies (*loquax, minnesota, hudsonicus*) on a morphological basis in the central United States. Their preliminary findings suggest that some of the specimens are like *T. h. loquax* from Indiana, although the Aroma Park specimens may be closer to specimens from Minnesota (*T. h. minnesota*) and possible descendants of transplants. I suspect that Illinois may be an area of intergradation between *T. h. loquax* and *T. h. minnesota* and until more information is available, refer all Illinois specimens to *T. h. loquax.*

Tamiasciurus hudsonicus loquax (Bangs)

1896. *Sciurus hudsonicus loquax* Bangs, Proc. Biol. Soc. Wash., 10:161. Type from Liberty Hill, New London Co., Connecticut.
1936. *Tamiasciurus hudsonicus loquax,* A. H. Howell, Occas. Papers Mus. Zool., Univ. Mich., 338:1.

Range. As given for the species (p. 177 and Map 8.31).
Diagnosis and Comparisons. A large-sized subspecies of *T. hudsonicus,* with large hind feet; nasals not especially long, but broad, especially across base of rostrum.

T. h. loquax differs from red squirrels from Minnesota and northern Wisconsin in having larger hind feet, shorter nasals, and a broader rostrum.

Records of occurrence. SPECIMENS EXAMINED, 17.
Will Co.: [4] Monee Township, 1 (UI). [5] Will Township [near Goodenow], 1 (Gov. State Univ., specimen not seen by me,

but by Bruce Brown). **Kankakee Co.:** [8a] Momence, 1 (ISU). [9b] ½ mi NE Aroma Park, 4 (INHS); [9c] Aroma Park, 5 (UI); [9e] Otto Township, 1 (UI). **Iroquois Co.:** [10a] 3 mi NNW Beaverville, ½ mi NW of NW corner of Iroquois Co. Cons. Area, 1 (UI); [10b] Iroquois Co. Cons. Area, 1 (SIC), 1 (ISM); [10c] T29N, R11W, Sec. 22, Iroquois Co. Cons. Area, 2 mi N, 3 mi E Beaverville, 1 (IDC).

Additional records. **Lake Co.:** [1] Fox Lake, Cory (1912:126); [2] Lake Forest, Cory (1912:126). **Putnam Co.:** [3] Hennepin, Kennicott (1857). **Marshall Co.:** [6] Lawnridge, J. A. Allen (1877). **Kankakee Co.:** [7] Kankakee River State Park, sight record, Bob Fredericks, 1977; [8b] Island in Kankakee River at Rt. 1 bridge, in Momence, sight record, John White and Kathryn Kerr, 1977; [8c] T31N, R14E, Sec. 23, N ½, sight record, John White and Kathryn Kerr, 1977; [9a] Dudley Grove at route 17 bridge on Kankakee River, 3 mi NE Aroma Park, sight record, Kenney Young, 1977; [9d] ½ mi E Aroma Park, Spring Creek, sight record, John White and Kathryn Kerr, 1977. **Iroquois Co.:** [11] Onarga, F. E. Wood (1910).

Glaucomys, Flying squirrels

Diagnosis. Sciurid rodents that are morphologically modified to glide or volaplane; loose fold of furred skin stretches between fore and hind legs so that when limbs are stretched, a widened, flattened body can sail through the air; tail flattened and broad; skull lightly constructed, postorbital processes thin, nasals depressed anteriorly, infraorbital foramen oval and vertical, coronoid process of ramus relatively long; nocturnal.

Dental formula. 1/1, 0/0, 2/1, 3/3.

Comparisons. Glaucomys is unique among the sciurids in Illinois because of the fold of skin extending between the legs on each side, which folds—plus the flattened hairs on the tail—serve in gliding (not flying), active only at night; long coronoid process of ramus, narrow interorbital and postorbital regions.

Glaucomys volans, Southern flying squirrel

Range. In forested areas throughout the state (Map 8.32).

Diagnosis. A *Glaucomys* of small size, hind foot 33 mm or less, greatest length of skull less than 36.5 mm, hair on the venter white or creamy all the way to the base, underside of tail usually pinkish gray and darker than belly.

Color. Dorsum grayish, usually strongly suffused with ochraceous coloration, dorsum of tail same color as back, sides darker and with less ochraceous, venter and underside of legs and feet whitish, underside of tail pinkish or pinkish gray. Aberrant coloration of dorsum is sometimes encountered. A specimen from 3 mi N, ½ mi E Ingraham, Jasper County, is a light gray dorsally. White-spotting may be found, with usually only one spot, less

than 1 cm in circumference, appearing on the top of the head or back.

Chromosomes. 2N = 48; 30 biarmed and 16 acrocentric autosomes; X chromosome submetacentric; Y, acrocentric.

Baculum. A relatively long, slender bone with a slight twist and with a slight groove distally.

Comparisons. The northern flying squirrel, *Glaucomys sabrinus,* occurs in central Wisconsin and central Michigan. *Glaucomys volans* differs from *G. sabrinus* in smaller size, shorter hind feet (33 mm or less), shorter skull (greatest length less than 36.5 mm), hairs on venter white to bases rather than grayish, baculum relatively longer and thinner.

Fig. 8.74. Southern flying squirrel from central Illinois. Note the fold of skin along the lower side of the body. This is useful in gliding. Also note the bushy but flattened tail and the large eyes. Photograph by Patrick L. Shiels.

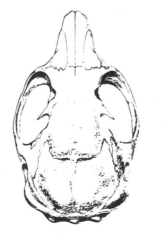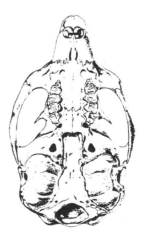

Fig. 8.75. *Glaucomys volans,* dorsal and ventral views of skull; 3 mi N, ½ mi E Ingraham, Jasper Co., Illinois, 52880 UI. Female, 34.5 mm greatest length.

Table 8.19. External and cranial measurements (in mm) of *Tamiasciurus hudsonicus, Glaucomys volans,* and *Geomys bursarius.* For Illinois *Tamiasciurus,* individual measurements are given for three specimens; for others, mean, minimum and maximum, and one standard deviation are given.

	N	Sex	Total lenght	Tail length	Body length	Hind foot length	Greatest length	Condylo-basal length	Zygomatic breadth	Braincase breadth	Mastoidal breadth
Tamiasciurus hudsonicus											
3 mi NNW Beaverville, Iroquois Co., III.	55058	UI	300+	106+	194	50	47.6	42.7	28.8	20.2	23.4
2 mi N, 3 mi E Beaverville, ″ ″		IDC	327	160	167	43	48.2	43.0	27.1	20.4	22.9
″ ″ ″ ″ ″	49	″	—	—	—	—	47.65	42.3	26.2	20.3	22.85
Indiana, Ohio	13		320.5	129.8	190.4	48.2	45.5	41.4	26.4	19.3	22.5
			300-344	119-136	170-205	42-51	44.1-48.25	39.8-45.0	25.1-27.8	18.35-20.25	21.2-23.9
			12.40	6.30	11.27	3.01	1.37	1.66	0.85	0.64	0.85
Minn., Wisc., Mich.	13		318.6	131.4	187.3	46.2	46.07	41.6	26.35	19.8	22.7
			300-343	106-160	167-231	33-51	45.4-47.15	40.65-42.45	25.35-28.2	19.15-20.95	21.7-22.9
			14.13	14.41	16.46	4.90	0.53	0.57	0.87	0.49	0.55
Glaucomys volans											
Central III.	9	♂	223.0	91.0	132.0	29.1	34.4	—	20.7	—	17.8
			201-245	70-105	119-148	26-34	33.4-35.8		19.95-21.95		16.75-18.6
			13.73	10.36	11.06	2.52	0.76		0.59		0.60
″ ″	9	♀	230.2	99.9	130.3	30.7	34.8	—	20.9	—	18.2
			205-246	83-112	116-147	26-33	33.95-35.7		19.7-21.55		17.3-18.6
			12.19	7.79	8.65	2,30	0.60		0.55		0.45
Geomys bursarius											
Central III.: McLean, Woodford cos.	18	♂	277.7	79.7	199.0	34.1	52.1	—	31.9	—	28.6
			237-345	59-98	160-242	31-37	44.6-59.5		26.8-37.25		25.4-32.0
			21.01	10.10	20.94	1.70	4.49		3.31		2.14
″ ″ ″ ″	18	♀	263.7	77.4	185.1	33.2	49.2	—	30.3[16]	—	27.7
			228-311	64-98	138-221	27-39	44.7-55.3		25.75-36.30		24.4-31.1
			25.25	9.59	21.63	2.76	2.46		2.39		1.43

Molt. Molting has not been studied in detail but there is thought to be only one adult molt per year, beginning in September or October. Molting occurs first on the sides, then to the dorsum and probably the venter, and on to the head. It supposedly is completed in November.

Secondary sexual variation. An analysis of 9 males and 9 females from central Illinois indicates that in 11 cranial measurements, females average larger than males in 9; in external measurements, larger in all except body length. However, there are no significant differences between males and females except for tail length (p= 0.05).

Habitat

Southern flying squirrels are inhabitants of hardwood forests, preferably those that have enough mature trees to provide holes for refuge and have sources of water not too far away. In central Illinois, southern flying squirrels are numerous in second-growth hardwoods such as those along and near the Sangamon River, Allerton Park, Piatt County. The squirrels live in the forests of white oaks, red oaks, and maples and usually avoid areas that have abundant shagbark hickories. Over a period of 23 years, we have annually censused by trapping the small mammals in one circular acre of oaks and maples, with a few shagbark hickories, and each time we have placed two to eight rat traps for three nights on trees to catch flying squirrels. In 12 of the 23 years, we have caught from one to three southern flying squirrels.

In southern Illinois, Layne (1958a) found flying squirrels in areas of oaks, hickory, beech, and hard maple and in typical swampy woodlands of black oak, sweet gum, and red maple.

In central Michigan, these squirrels live in much the same habitat as in central Illinois. Jordan (1948) found that in Michigan the average diameter breast-high of trees adjacent to traps set was 13 inches. He also found that some underbrush made the habitat more suitable for these flying squirrels. Since they frequently come to the ground, some cover may be advantageous. We found in central Illinois that we often took southern flying squirrels in traps set on the ground even though we had traps nailed to tree trunks. Also, the numerous flying squirrels taken by house cats probably were captured when they were on the ground.

Nasal length	Inter-orbital breadth	Post-orbital breadth	Palatal length	Post-palatal length	Toothrow length alv.	Bulla length	Skull depth	Gt. nasal breadth	Br. across premax-max sutures	Notch zyg. plate to front incisor
14.45	14.45	14.2	16.2	16.75	7.65	9,65	21.45	7.05	13.5	17.25
14.2	14.0	15.8	16.45	16.8	7.7	9.7	22.2	6.8	12.7	17.3
13.25	13.5	14.75	15.7	16.8	7.5	10.25	21.4	6.75	11.5	17.0
13.3	13.8	13.9	15.7	16.0	7.6	9.9	20.5	7.0	12.3	16.6
12.1-15.0	12.6-14.7	12.95-14.65	14.7-17.25	14.7-17.4	6.9-8.6	9.3-10.9	19.6-21.5	6.55-7.5	11.2-13.1	15.5-17.9
0.84	0.52	0.65	0.74	0.72	0.50	0.45	0.54	0.30	0.63	0.76
13.9	13.7	14.1	15.7	15.9	7.5	10.0	20.7	7.1	11.9	16.6
12.55-15.3	13.25-14.1	13.3-14.9	14.6-17.0	15.3-16.7	7.1-7.75	9.3-10.5	19.95-21.3	6.65-7.5	10.9-12.75	15.45-17.2
0.67	0.34	0.44	0.59	0.39	0.21	0.38	0.34	0.23	0.63	0.38
9.5	6.6	8.6	11.7	12.1	6.5	8.7	15.7	—	—	—
9.1-10.2	5.8-6.95	8.3-9.25	11.15-12.45	11.35-12.95	6.4-6.7	8.1-9.3	14.85-16.3			
0.36	0.36	0.29	0.38	0.49	0.11	0.37	0.51			
9.7	6.7	8.4	11.8	12.0	6.6	8.9	15.8	—	—	—
8.85-10.2	6.25-7.2	7.6-9.1	11.45-12.15	11.25-12.8	6.35-6.85	8.6-9.2	15.1-16.3			
0.41	0.28	0.49	0.24	0.42	0.16	0.19	0.36			
19.0	6.7	—	14.5	17.8	9.5	14.4	20.3	—	—	—
16.1-23.0	6.2-7.1		11.6-17.0	15.1-20.3	8.8-10.5	12.85-16.3	17.2-23.7			
2.12	0.28		1.38	1.44	0.45	0.89	1.76			
18.2	6.7	—	13.0	16.9	9.3	13.8	19.2	—	—	—
15.6-20.2	6.5-7.3		11.4-15.3	15.5-20.0	8.5-10.3	12.9-15.3	17.35-22.1			
1.12	0.23		1.03	1.07	0.54	0.65	0.94			

Habits

Southern flying squirrels are nocturnal. Rarely are they seen during the day unless they are routed out of their nest. These squirrels move from one place to another by gliding, landing on a tree trunk or some other object, such as a building, or by climbing up and down the trunks and branches of trees. Where flying squirrels glided from a woodlot onto the white side of a country church, they left a grayish mark. One of our students, equipped with a butterfly net, stationed himself near the landing spot and was successful in capturing the squirrels as they glided downward. Squirrels are able to make turns in mid-air while gliding. Most glides are less than 100 feet in distance and the squirrels always end up lower than the take-off spot.

Nests are usually situated in cavities relatively high in trees. These may be natural cavities or woodpecker holes and preferably are small enough to keep out other tree squirrels. Also, nests may be located in attics of buildings, in old bird nests, or in old leaf nests of fox or gray squirrels. In southern Illinois, a female and two young flying squirrels occupied a leaf nest about 10 inches in diameter located in a dense tangle of grapevines about 20 feet high (Layne, 1958a). A Mr. Brendel of Peoria informed Kennicott (1857) that a flying squirrel raised young in a deserted bird's nest.

Flying squirrels can be detected by a frequent birdlike chirping sound that has been called a chuck note and a high-pitched *tseet*. They may possibly produce high-frequency sounds for echolocating objects at night.

Southern flying squirrels may be communal during the winter, or perhaps the year around. Jackson (1961) says that in Wisconsin in the winter 8 to 15 animals may be in a single cavity and in one case there were 22. This is not unlike the groups of golden mice found in tree nests in the winter. The body temperature of these animals is depressed at time, and they are in a state of torpidity— but not hibernation—for short periods in the winter (Muul, 1968).

Food

Southern flying squirrels feed extensively on the nuts of trees in their immediate area: hickory nuts, acorns of all species of oaks and, in addition, seeds of maples, pignuts, fungi, berries, bark, and some invertebrates as

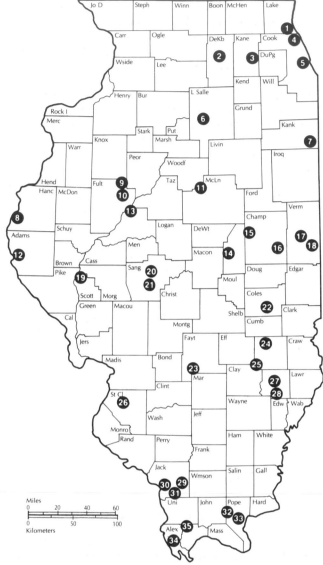

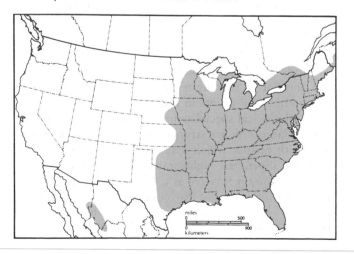

Map 8.32. Southern flying squirrels, *Glaucomys volans,* occur statewide. The subspecies is *G. v. volans.* Localities of occurrence as numbered are referenced in *Records of occurrence.* The range of the species in the United States is shaded.

well as bird eggs and reportedly even young birds. In October or whenever the hickory nuts and acorns are ready to harvest, flying squirrels gather these during the night. The nuts that fall to the ground may be retrieved.

Southern flying squirrels use special procedures for extracting meats from hard-shelled nuts—such as hickory nuts—since their teeth are not sufficiently strong to bite out pieces of the shell. On these nuts they start at one end, usually the peduncle end, and make a notch above and below the peduncle. These notches are used to grasp the nut with the teeth for carrying it. By much rasping with the teeth and turning, one notch is enlarged so that the meat can be extracted from the entire nut or one side of the septum. If only one-half is eaten, the nut may be set aside for future eating.

Water may be a critical item in the diet of these squirrels. If captive animals are deprived of water overnight, they will drink intensively when it is made available. In the wild, water is obtained from food (berries, fruits, and insects), from standing water, and moisture on foliage and in tree cavities.

Reproduction

Mating occurs in late February and in March, and again in July. Young are born from late March to May and in August and September. The gestation period is 40 days. It is not certain whether a female produces two litters per year or if the second breeding consists of females born late the previous year. A specimen in our collection that was taken on April 18 must be five weeks of age; three females taken in November were lactating. The number of young varies from two to seven. Eyes open at about four weeks and weaning occurs between the sixth and eighth weeks.

Miscellaneous

Southern flying squirrels have often been kept as pets, and rather successfully. Dorothy and the late Philip Smith of Champaign kept one for several years. By day, the squirrel was kept in a cage in the house; by night it was permitted to roam in parts of the house. It commonly climbed the drapes and then jumped and sailed to other places in the room.

Judging from our trapping experiences in hardwoods in central Illinois, those woods with mature or nearly mature trees that have woodpecker holes or other natural cavities and have species of trees that produce acorns and nuts that are not too thick-shelled should have about one flying squirrel per acre. If such a population holds for much of Illinois, the population in the state is sizable.

Variation

Southern flying squirrels in northern United States have been referred to *G. v. volans,* although a specimen in western Kentucky (Hickman) has been referred to *G. v. saturatus* (type locality, Dothan, Houston Co., Alabama) by A. H. Howell (1918).

Glaucomys volans volans (Linneaus)

1758. [*Mus*] *volans* Linnaeus, Syst. nat., 10th ed., 1:63. Type locality fixed as Virginia.

1915. [*Glaucomys*] *volans*, A. H. Howell, Proc. Biol. Soc. Wash., 28:109.

Range. In forested areas throughout the state (Map 8.32).

Diagnosis and Comparisons. A large subspecies, with those in western Illinois larger than those in eastern Illinois; color not especially dark, and less dark than *G. v. saturatus* and with toes more strongly marked with white.

Records of occurrence. SPECIMENS EXAMINED, 84. **Lake Co.:** [1a] Halfday, 2 (CAS); [1b] Highland Park, 1 (FM). **De Kalb Co.:** [2] Riverbed behind Taft Library on [NIU] campus, 1 (NIU). **Cook Co.:** [4b] 5 mi N Jct. 42A–58 on Rt. 58, 1 (UI); [5] Chicago, 2 (US). **Hancock Co.:** [8] Warsaw*, 6 (US), 1 (FM). **Fulton Co.:** [9] 7 mi N Canton, 1 (UI); [10a] 1 mi W Canton, 3 (UI); [10b] 3 mi E Canton, 1 (UI). **McLean Co.:** [11] 4 mi NW

---

* Worthen specimens.

Hudson, 1 (ISU). **Adams Co.:** [12] Quincy, South Park, 1 (UI). **Mason Co.:** [13] 7 mi NW Forest City, 1 (ISU). **Piatt Co.:** [14] Allerton Park, 5 mi W, 2½ mi S Monticello, 11 (UI). **Champaign Co.:** [15a] 3½ mi NE Mahomet, 1 (ISM), 2 (UI); [15b] Shady Rest [=1 mi S Mahomet], 1 (UI); [15c] Sangamon River, [near] Seymour, 1 (UI); [16a] 2 mi E, 2 mi N Sidney, 1 (UI); [16b] 2 mi E Sidney, 1 (UI). **Vermilion Co.:** [17] Kickapoo State Park, 1 (UI); [18a] Catlin, 1 (UI); [18b] 5 mi SE Danville, 6 (UI). **Scott Co.:** [19] near Bluffs, 1 (ISM). **Sangamon Co.:** [20] Springfield, 9 (ISM); [21] 2 mi E Chatham, 1 (ISM). **Coles Co.:** [22] 2 mi S Charleston, 1 (UI). **Fayette Co.:** [23] 7 mi S Vandalia, 1 (UI). **Jasper Co.:** [24] 3 mi W Rose Hill, 1 (UI); [25a] 3 mi N, ½ mi E Ingraham, 2 (UI); [25b] 2 mi N Ingraham, 1 (UI). **St. Clair Co.:** [26] Belleville, 1 (US). **Richland Co.:** [27] Olney, 4 (US); [28] Parkersburg, 1 (US). **Jackson Co.:** [29a] ½ mi W Carbondale, 1 (SIC); [29b] Carbondale, 2 (SIC), 2 (SRL); [30] 7 mi SW Murphysboro, 1 (SRL); [31] Pomona, 1 (SRL). **Pope Co.:** [32] 1½ mi S Glendale, 1 (UI); [33] Golconda, 1 (FM). **Alexander Co.:** [34b] Olive Branch, 1 (FM); [34c] 1½ mi NW Cache, 1 (SRL). **Pulaski Co.:** [35] Wetaug, 1 (CAS).

Additional records; **Kane Co.:** [3] St. Charles, (Necker and Hatfield, 1941:51). **Cook Co.:** [4a] West Northfield, 1 (UM). **La Salle Co.:** [6] Starved Rock State Park, (Necker and Hatfield, 1941:5). **Kankakee Co.:** [7] Pembroke Twp., (Necker and Hatfield, 1941:5). **Alexander Co.:** [34a] 2¾ mi NNW Olive Branch, 1 (FS).

Family Geomyidae, Pocket gophers

Pocket gophers of the family Geomyidae are sciuromorph rodents adapted for fossorial life; thick-bodied with strongly clawed forefeet, large fur-lined cheek pouches, a rugose skull with a small infraorbital foramen and no postorbital processes, and cheek teeth evergrowing and prismatic.

Geomys, Eastern pocket gopher

Diagnosis. A geomyid rodent with elongated claws on the forefeet; upper incisors bisulcate, resulting in the front surface of each upper incisor having a prominent groove near the middle with another small groove near the inner side (Fig. 8.78), premolars bicolumnar, M^1 and M^2 elliptical and each with anterior and posterior enamel plate.

Dentition. 1/1, 0/0, 1/1, 3/3.

Chromosomes. Variable between species and populations. See account of species (p. 186).

Comparisons. *Geomys* is the only gopher that lives anywhere near Illinois. Its unique geomyid characters and adaptations for fossorial life easily distinguish it.

Geomys bursarius, Plains pocket gopher

Range. Just east of the Mississippi River in St. Clair and Madison counties and then east and south of the Illinois River to its junction with the Kankakee River, and south of this river to the Indiana state line (Map 8.33). Records from Greene and Jersey counties are not known. See *Remarks* for comments about other reports of occurrence.

Diagnosis. A large species of *Geomys* with sagittal crest narrow and high, zygomatic arches widely divergent anteriorly in adults, frontal-premaxillary suture on dorsum anterior to or only reaching a line drawn between the anteriormost points in the orbits.

Morphological specializations for fossorial life include forefeet large with five strongly clawed toes, sides of toes lined with bristles which may assist in moving dirt, legs relatively short, tail highly tactile with a reduction of hairs near the tip to serve as a "feeler" when the animal backs up in the burrow; the mouth can be closed behind incisors so these teeth can be used in the digging process without getting dirt in the mouth; the narrowness of the pelvic girdle for life in a burrow results in too small a passage for young at parturition but this is compensated for by the resorption of the pubic symphysis when females reach sexual maturity (Hisaw, 1924, 1925).

Color. In Illinois specimens, the dorsum and sides coal black, underparts blackish but often with a light intermixing of buff, distal two-thirds of tail appears whitish or unpigmented, but mostly devoid of hair, tops of front and hind feet light with much white hair, spot on throat below chin often white.

A small percentage of the specimens are not coal black but much the same color as specimens in the St. Louis area, Missouri: dorsum chocolate brown with a dark middorsal stripe running from nose to base of tail, nearly all of tail light colored, forelegs as well as forefeet sometimes whitish, underparts slightly lighter brown than back. In our collection, 13 of 159 or eight percent of the specimens are dark brown rather than black, but the actual percentage must be much less because one has a habit of saving "unusually colored" individuals.

Chromosomes. 2N=72; FN=70; all autosomes are acrocentric, X a large acrocentric. Specimens from Wisconsin and Missouri are reported to have 2N=72, FN=72, with 68 acrocentrics and two biarmed autosomes (Hart, 1978).

Comparisons. G. bursarius was for many years regarded as the only species in middle United States. More recently, Heaney and Timm (1983) regarded specimens in parts of Nebraska south to Oklahoma and southeastern Missouri as referable to *G. lutescens*. *G. bursarius* differs from *G. lutescens* in having temporal ridges fused into a sagittal crest in females, rather than being separated; the rostrum is longer; frontal-premaxillary suture on dorsum usually anterior to or reaching a line drawn between anteriormost points in the orbits rather than exceeding the line; the

mastoid processes are longer and less closely appressed to skull.

In 1985, Burns et al. reviewed the status of *Geomys lutescens* using morphometric, bacular, karyotypic, and electrophoretic data. They concluded that *G. lutescens* was not a taxon distinct at the species level.

Secondary sexual variation. Males average larger than females, and this is shown in the external measurements and cranial measurements, except for interorbital breadth. In an analysis of 18 males and 18 females, however, tail length, zygomatic breadth, interorbital breadth, mastoidal breadth, maxillary toothrow, and nasal length are not significantly different.

Remarks. Pocket gophers in Illinois are unique among populations in middle United States, for they are black, with few exceptions. Also, in my interpretation, they are more like those in eastern Missouri—such as those around St. Louis—than those in Wisconsin.

Large waterways, such as the Mississippi and Illinois rivers, appear to be barriers in the distribution of plains pocket gophers. I suspect that these gophers most likely were isolated on the east side of the Mississippi River when the river changed course, probably in the late Pleistocene, at about the place where the Illinois River flows into the Mississippi River. Gophers were able to cross the dry river bed into Illinois, south of the Illinois River. Thence they moved northeastward along the east or south side of this river and the Kankakee River. This founding population fortuitously had a mutation for black color and this became established. This would appear to be a non-adaptive mutation, for these black gophers live in light-colored sandy soils and yellowish loam as well as in black prairie soils.

Pocket gophers have not occurred north or northwest of the Illinois or Kankakee rivers or east of the Mississippi

Fig. 8.76A. Plains pocket gopher, *Geomys bursarius*. Photograph by K. Maslowski and W. W. Goodpaster.

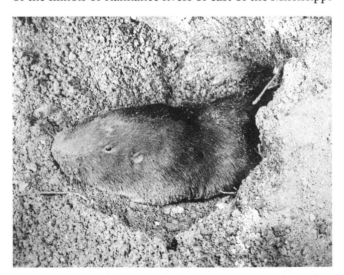

Fig. 8.76B. Plains pocket gopher, *Geomys bursarius*, pushing dirt out of its burrow. Note the blackish color of the fur and the conspicuous eyes and ears. Photograph by W. W. Goodpaster.

River north of its junction with the Illinois River. In Iowa, *Geomys bursarius* occurs in suitable habitat along the west side of the Mississippi. On January 7, 1949, Mr. T. E. Musselman of Quincy wrote me "had I known of your interest I should have sent you a single specimen of the pocket gopher which I found killed on the hard road between here and Payson [Adams County] last year." I do not regard this as an authentic record for no specimen is available. The likelihood of a gopher on a paved road is most unlikely.

Reports of pocket gophers—apparently based upon sightings of mounds since specimens are not available, at Odin, Marion County; near Olney, Richland County; and Woodlawn, Jefferson County—by A. H. Howell (1910) are here regarded as not authentic. Howell's record from Coulterville, Randolph County, could be valid. Parmalee and Hoffmeister (1957) reported remains of *Geomys* from an archeological site near Modoc, Randolph County. The report of a mounted specimen from Champaign County, Illinois, is an error (Komarek and Spencer, 1931).

In my estimation, the range of the pocket gopher is as indicated on the distribution map. We have no evidence that the range of this gopher has expanded eastward in the area from near Clinton, DeWitt County, and Bloomington, McLean County, in the last 40 years.

Habitat

Plains pocket gophers inhabit areas where the soil is well drained, not gummy or too hard-packed, and where there are tuberous-rooted plants that provide a ready source of food. In some places in Illinois they are found in areas of sand or sand loam, deep black soil, and where there is a mixture of black soil and heavy clay. Probably drainage is more important than the kind of soil, because these gophers are not found where there is water standing for prolonged periods of time. Also, fields that are deeply plowed once or twice a year are avoided, although burrow systems may extend part way into these fields. Fields that are not plowed annually—such as alfalfa fields—are often ideal habitats, for this leguminous plant also provides food with its tuberous roots.

Mounds of pocket gophers are most commonly seen along the shoulders of roads, and especially the embankments of such shoulders. Here, there is good drainage and less disturbance from plowing. However, pocket gopher mounds are also more obvious on the embankments of roads than they are in the level fields away from the road.

Burrows and Burrowing

Plains pocket gophers construct underground burrows in which they spend nearly all of their lives. At intervals, these burrows have laterals that come to the surface so that newly accumulated dirt, dug from the burrow system,

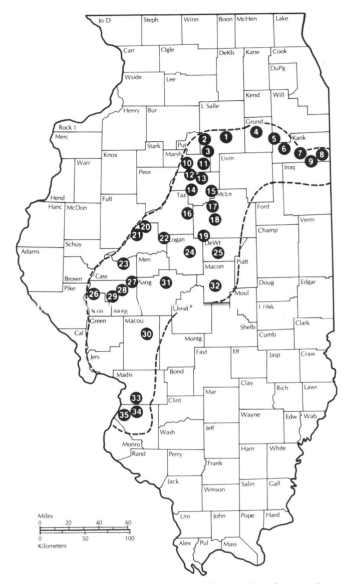

Map 8.33. The range of the plains pocket gopher, *Geomys bursarius,* is east and south of the Illinois and Kankakee rivers. The subspecies is *G. b. illinoensis.* Localities of occurrence as numbered are referenced in *Records of occurrence.* The range of the species in the United States is shaded.

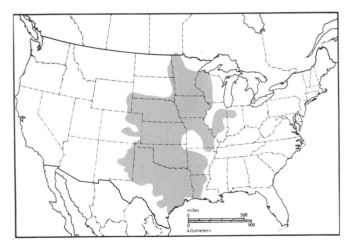

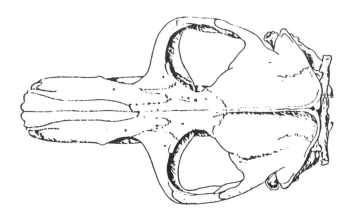

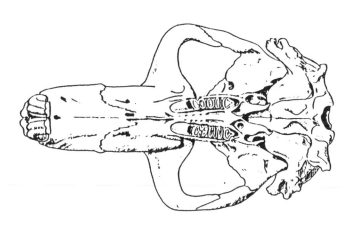

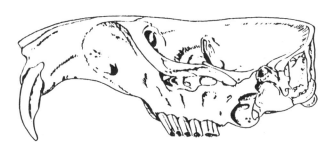

Fig. 8.77. *Geomys bursarius,* dorsal, ventral, and lateral views of skull; 4 mi W O'Fallon, St. Clair Co., Illinois, 1676 UI. Male, 51.7 mm greatest length. Charles A. McLaughlin.

can be discarded above ground. Also, these lateral passages serve as a means of access to preferred food items, either on or near the surface of the ground. The dirt thrown up results in "gopher mounds" and one individual is responsible for numerous mounds. Three gophers piled up 2.86 mounds per day for 12 days (B. Bailey, 1929). Mohr and Mohr (1936) found that seven gophers made 1.56 mounds each in five days. In Indiana, Mumford and Whitaker (1982) reported that C. H. Conaway found that a gopher, actively extending its burrow system into a field of winter wheat, made six mounds in seven days over a distance of 53 feet. It is obvious that one gopher can make numerous mounds.

When digging burrows, plains pocket gophers use their strongly clawed forefeet in rapid motion to bring dirt below the body. When enough has accumulated here, it is kicked backward by the hind feet. When enough dirt accumulates behind, the gopher turns around and with its front feet and head pushes this dirt down the burrow and out onto the ground. The animal turns around in its rather tightly fitting burrow by putting its head with the nose tucked down between the hind legs and doing a quick reversal. When the animal is finished removing dirt, the exit is plugged with tamped soil.

Dr. Charles McLaughlin examined the burrow system of a plains pocket gopher 1 mi N, 1 mi W Collinsville, Madison County, in October 1950 (McLaughlin, 1951). The system was more than 125 feet in length, with 57 recognizable mounds, and 14 more may have been associated also. At Manhattan, Kansas, a gopher had a burrow system 510 feet in length (Scheffer, 1940). The Collinsville burrow was situated in a five-year-old alfalfa field. The field was in the process of being plowed for replanting but only a few rows around its periphery had been turned. The most-used areas of the burrows were about four inches in diameter; less-used sections, about 3½ inches. Several feeding laterals came upward to or near the surface of the soil. Some were as close as three inches to the surface without an opening onto the surfaces; others had opened outward but were tightly plugged now. Most of the burrows were between two and three feet deep; the nest and burrows leading to it were about three feet deep. In one area, one burrow was above the deeper burrow and nest area, resulting in a two-level arrangement. This burrow system had only a small food storage chamber at the time McLaughlin examined it (Fig. 8.79, p. 190). Some others he examined had much larger food storage chambers.

Usually a burrow system is occupied by only one adult animal, and young animals probably are forced out of the system as soon as possible. Pocket gophers are solitary except during the breeding season, although there are occasions when more than one adult plains pocket gopher will be taken from a burrow system. If more than one

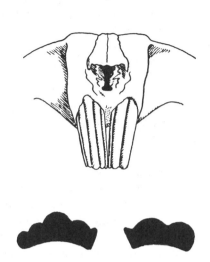

Fig. 8.78. Frontal view of rostrum of *Geomys bursarius* to show the abnormal grooving in the right (to the left, in this view) upper incisor. The lower sketches show a cross-sectional view of each incisor, with the abnormal one to the left. No. 52326, Field Museum specimen. Charles A. McLaughlin.

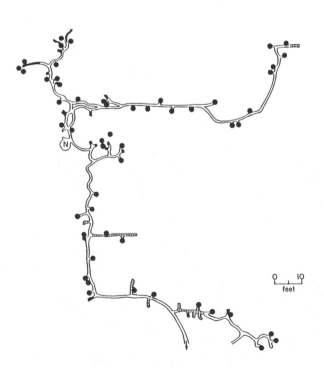

Fig. 8.79. Burrow system of pocket gopher at 1 mi N, 1 mi E Collinsville, Madison Co., Illinois, as excavated and sketched by Charles McLaughlin in October 1950. Total length of the burrow exceeded 425 feet. The burrow was located in a five-year-old alfalfa field. The burrow system was more complicated than can be accurately depicted here, and the below-ground depth is not shown. The nest (N) was about three feet below ground and was the deepest part of the system. Hatched areas are feeding runways; solid runways are plugged burrows; black dots are surface mounds of dirt.

newly captured gopher is placed in a holding container, fighting will immediately ensue, with resulting serious injury to the combatants.

A nest was located within the burrow system excavated by McLaughlin (1951) near Collinsville. It was about seven inches in diameter and was a hollow sphere of dry grass. The nest occupied nearly the entire chamber that had been enlarged in the burrow system to hold the nest. At one end of the nest there was a small cache of food, consisting of roots, stems, and leaves of dandelion and a few pieces of grass stems.

Pocket gopher mounds usually have a unique shape and design which distinguishes them from mole hills. Gophers push the dirt out of a burrow as it comes to the surface at an angle. Thus, most of the dirt is to one side of the hole. With moles, the burrow comes to the surface at more of a right angle and the dirt cascades down equally around the opening. However, in Illinois there are many places where it is impossible to distinguish between the mounds of pocket gophers and moles. This is especially true in sandy soil, such as in Mason County. In this soil, mole runs just below the surface are not very obvious and because of the looseness of the soil, both animals make especially large mounds. Many times I have selected mounds that seemed certain to be those of a gopher, but when the runway was opened it proved to be a mole run. Rarely do moles throw up mounds on embankments, so mounds found here are probably those of gophers. Mounds that are quite close together and near obvious mole runs are probably those of a mole. However, records of plains pocket gophers or of eastern moles in Illinois based solely on mounds of dirt are not sufficiently reliable in my estimation.

An animal collected at Lilly, Tazewell County, and held captive for about five months broke off an incisor on three different occasions (McLaughlin, 1951). This seemed to be no hindrance to the animal and the tooth grew to occluding length in 7 to 10 days. During such periods, McLaughlin could hear the gopher grinding its lower incisors against the one unbroken upper incisor as if the animal was trying to prevent abnormal growth of the teeth during this time.

Plains pocket gophers curl up into a ball when sleeping, with the nose tucked between the hind legs. Sometimes the entire weight of the animal is borne by the top of the head and the hind feet, or just the head alone, when sleeping.

Food

In Illinois, plains pocket gophers are known to feed on the roots of sweet clover, alfalfa, and dandelion. Stems and leaves of grasses, dandelions, clover, bluegrass, and alfalfa are also eaten. Probably nearly any available tuberous roots are taken, and these may be preferred to stems and leaves. Schwartz and Schwartz (1981) say that pocket gophers reingest their own droppings. I have seen no evidence to prove or disprove this. Pocket gophers may also feed on the roots of trees if necessary.

At a place ½ mi S, 1 mi E Clinton, DeWitt County, on February 9, McLaughlin (1951) uncovered a food storage chamber that contained a cache of sweet clover roots, amounting to 467 gm or about 1.2 liters. Most of the roots were about 1 cm in diameter and the average cut length was about five cm. The pocket gopher's well-developed cheek pouches are useful in transporting these pieces to the chamber.

McLaughlin (1951) kept a plains pocket gopher in an observation chamber for a short time. It soon started to rest on the surface of the ground rather than dig a burrow. When a carrot without green tops was inserted in the ground, the gopher would pull it completely to the surface if any part of the carrot was above ground. If the carrot was completely buried, a burrow was dug to the carrot, the part of the carrot uncovered in the burrow was cut off, and this was cut into pieces and stored. The remaining part of the carrot was pulled down into the burrow and harvested in the same manner. The forefeet are used dexterously in holding and manipulating food items and for inserting them in the cheek pouches.

Reproduction

On February 9, 1950, Charles McLaughlin caught two gophers—a male and a female—from the same burrow system, and he interpreted this as evidence that they were breeding. Bernard Bailey (1929) recorded embryos in plains pocket gophers taken in Minnesota between April 12 and May 22. Most of our trapping has been in the late fall. Of 68 females taken in September, October, and November, none is recorded as pregnant although one is recorded as lactating. The latter may be questionable. The breeding season in Illinois probably extends from late February until June. The gestation period is said to be about one month and the number of embryos varies from one to seven. Sudman et al. (1986) found that a female trapped in Kansas gave birth to one young 51 days after capture. Thus, the gestation period must be regarded as uncertain at this time. A cursory examination of our specimens indicates that young animals have attained adult size by October. Sudman et al. (1986) found that adult weight and total length were attained by about the hundredth day of age in two animals.

Collections of pocket gophers often show a preponderance of females. It may be that fewer males reach maturity. For example, of 121 gophers collected for and preserved at the Museum of Natural History for October through December, 61 percent are females. Since males are probably polygynous, the reduction in numbers of males may have little effect on the reproductive success of the population.

Variation

The pocket gophers in Illinois belong to the subspecies *G. b. illinoensis*. This subspecies extends into Indiana south of the Kankakee River.

Geomys bursarius illinoensis Komarek and Spencer

1931. *Geomys bursarius illinoensis* Komarek and Spencer, J. Mamm., 12:405. Type from 1 mi S Momence, Kankakee Co., Illinois.

Range. As given for the species (p. 185 and Map 8.33).

Diagnosis and Comparisons. A subspecies of *G. bursarius* characterized by and differing from other populations in its blackish coloration, larger size, long tail, and long rostrum.

Records of occurrence: SPECIMENS EXAMINED, 210. **La Salle Co.:** [1a] Ottawa (south side of river), 1 (CAS); [1b] 1 mi S, 3 mi E Ottawa, 1 (UI); [1c] 2½ mi S Ottawa, 1 (UI); [2a] Utica (south side of river), 1 (CAS); [2b] Oglesby, 1 (CAS); [2c] 3 mi E Oglesby, 1 (NIU); [2d] ¼ mi W Cedar Point, 2 (UI); [2e] 3 mi E Cedar Point, 1 (UI); [3] ⅘ mi S Lostant, 2 (UI). **Grundy Co.:** [4] Morris, 1 (UI). **Will Co.:** [5b] Custer Park, 2 (CAS). **Kankakee Co.:** [6a] Bonfield, [two are labelled Will Co.], 3 (FM); [6b] 5 mi W, 5 mi N Kankakee, 1 (UI); [7a] Kankakee, 1 (CAS); [7b] 1½ S, 1½ mi W Kankakee, 2 (UI); [7c] ½ mi S Aroma Park, 3 (UI); [7d] 4 mi N Chebanse, 1 (UI); [7e] 3 mi N Chebanse, 1 (UI); [8a] Momence, 2 (CAS); [8b] 1 mi S Momence [type locality], 1 (CAS); [8c] Pembroke, 3 (FM); [8d] Hopkins Park, 5 (CAS), 1 (FM); [9] St. Anne, 3 (CAS). **Marshall Co.:** [10] 2 mi E Lacon, 1 (UI); [11] 4 mi E Toluca, 3 (UI). **Woodford Co.:** [12] 15 mi N Eureka, 1 (UI); [13a] 7½ mi S Toluca, 1 (UI); [13b] 1 mi S, 8 mi W Minonk, 1 (UI); [13c] 1 mi W Benson, 1 (UI); [13d] 1 mi E Benson, 1 (UI); [14a] 6 mi N Eureka, 1 (UI);[14b] 2½ mi N Eureka, 1 (UI); [14c] 2 mi N Eureka, 1 (UI); [14d] Eureka, 1 (UI); [14e] 1 mi S, 1 mi W Eureka, 1 (UI); [15a] 4 mi N El Paso, 1 (UI); [15b] Panola, 2 (UI); [15c] 2½ mi N El Paso, 1 (UI); [15d] 1 mi S Panola, 5 (UI); [15e] 2 mi N El Paso, 4 (UI); [15f] 1½ N El Paso, 1 (UI); [15g] 1 mi N El Paso, 2 (UI); [15h] ¼ mi N El Paso, 2 (UI); [15i] 5 mi N Kappa [labelled McLean Co.], 1 (UI); [15j] 1 mi S El Paso, 2 (UI); [15k] 2 mi N Kappa, 1 (UI); [15l] 1 mi NW Kappa, 1 (UI); [15m] ½ mi N Kappa, 1 (UI); [15n] ½ W Kappa, 1 (UI); [15o] Kappa, 1 (UI).

Tazwell Co.: [16] Lilly, 1 (UI). **McLean Co.:** [17a] 10 mi N Normal, 1 (UI); [17b] 9 mi N Normal, 1 (UI); [17c] 3 mi NE Hudson, 1 (UI); [17d] 2 mi N, ½ mi W Hudson, 1 (UI); [17e] 2 mi N Hudson, 1 (ISU); [17f] 10 mi N Bloomington, 1 (UI); [17g] 4 mi W Hudson, 1 (UI); [17h] 2 mi W Hudson, 8 (UI); [17i] 1½ mi W Rt. 51 on Hudson Road, 1 (UI); [17j] 1 mi W Hudson, 1 (UI); [17k] 1 mi E Hudson, 1 (UI); [17l] 5½ mi N Normal, 1 (UI); [17m] 1 mi S, ½ mi W Hudson, 1 (UI); [17n] 2 mi SW Hudson, 1 (UI); [17o] 2½ mi SW Hudson, 2 (UI); [17p] 4½ mi W Normal, 1 (UI); [17q] 2 mi S Hudson, 6 (US); [17r] 1½ mi N Kerrick, 1 (UI); [17s] 3 mi N Normal, 1 (UI); [17t] 2.2 mi N Normal, 1 (UI); [18a] 1.4 mi N Normal, 1 (UI); [18b] 1 mi N Normal, 1 (UI); [18c] ½ mi NW Normal, 1 (ISU); [18d] 1 mi W Normal, 1 (ISU); [18e] Bloomington, 1 (UI); [18f] ½ mi S Bloomington, 1 (UI); [18g] 1 mi SE, 1 mi E Bloomington [*sic*],

1 (UI); [18h] 2 mi SE, 2 mi E Bloomington [*sic*], 1 (UI); [18i] 5 mi SE Bloomington, 1 (UI); [19a] 1 mi W McLean, 1 (UI); [19b] 2 mi E McLean, 1 (UI); [19c] 2½ mi E McLean, 3 (UI); [19d] 4 mi E McLean, 2 (UI); [19e] 5 mi E McLean, 1 (UI); [19f] 1 mi SW McLean, 1 (UI); [19g] 1 mi S McLean, 1 (UI). **Mason Co.:** [20] Mason State Forest, [=Sand Ridge State Forest], 1 (ISU); [21a] 6 mi W, 1 mi S Forest City, 1 (UI); [21b] 4 mi NNE Havana, 1 (UI); [21c] Havana, 5 (US); [22] San Jose, 1 (FM). **Cass Co.:** [23] Chandlerville, 1 (ISM). **Logan Co.:** [24a] 2 mi E Lincoln, 1 (UI); [24b] 5 mi E Lincoln, 1 (UI).

DeWitt Co.: [25a] 3 mi NE Clinton, 1 (UI); [25b] 1 mi N Clinton, 2 (ISM); [25c] 1⅓ mi NE Clinton, 1 (UI); [25d] 1 mi NE Clinton, 1 (UI); [25e] 1½ mi ENE Clinton, 1 (UI); [25f] 2 mi E, ½ mi N Clinton, 1 (UI); [25g] ½ mi N, 3 mi E Clinton, 1 (ISM); [25h] Clinton, 7 (US), 1 (UI); [25i] E Clinton, 1 (UI); [25j] 1 mi E Clinton, 2 (UI); [25k] 1½ mi E Clinton, 2 (UI); [25l] 2 mi E Clinton, 2 (UI); [25m] 3 mi E Clinton, 2 (UI); [25n] ½ mi SE Clinton, 1 (UI); [25o] 1 mi SE Clinton, 1 (UI); [25p] 1 mi SSE Clinton, 1 (UI); [25q] 1 mi E, 1 mi S Clinton, 6 (UI); [25r] 2 mi E, 1 mi S Clinton, 1 (UI); [25s] 3 mi S Clinton, 1 (UI). **Morgan Co.:** [27] Prentice, 1 (UI); [28] 5 mi NE Jacksonville, Strawn's Crossing, 2 (UI); [29] 1 mi W Jacksonville, 1 (ISM). **Sangamon Co.:** [31a] 3 mi N Springfield, 1 (UI); [31b] Bissell, 1 (UI). **Macon Co.:** [32] 3 mi S, 2 mi W Decatur, 1 (UI). **Madison Co.:** [33a] 7½ mi S SIU Edwardsville, 1 (SIE); [33b] 3 mi W, 1 mi N Collinsville, 4 (UI); [33c] ½ mi NW Collinsville, 1 (UI). **St. Clair Co.:** [34a] 2 mi W, 2 mi S Collinsville, 2 (UI); [34b] 3 mi S Collinsville, 4 (UI); [34c] 4 mi W O'Fallon, 2 (UI); [34d] Belleville, St. Henry's Seminary, 1 (SIE).

Additional records: **Will Co.:** [5a] 2 mi W Wilmington, 1 (UM). **Woodford Co.:** [15o] Kappa, 1 (FS). **McLean Co.:** [18e] Bloomington, 1 (UM). **Scott Co.:** [26] [near] Bluffs, (Mohr, 1946:390). **Macoupin Co.:** [30] Anderson, (Cory, 1912:243). **St. Clair Co.:** [35] [near] Centreville (Mohr, 1946:390).

Family Castoridae, Beavers

Sciuromorph rodents of large size and modified for aquatic life; broad, flattened paddlelike tail that is nearly hairless, hind feet webbed, ears and nose valvular, eyes with nictitating membrane; lips close behind incisors and incisors heavy and strong, cheek teeth high crowned but rooted; underfur dense; paired anal scent glands which are called castors and present in both sexes.

Some authors, such as Carleton (1984), have placed the Castoridae in a distinct infraorder, Castorimorpha.

Castor, Beavers

Diagnosis. As given for the family; skull massive, rostrum and zygomata heavy, infraorbital canal small and slitlike, basioccipital with a depression or pit; tubular extension of bulla encloses a long auditory meatus; coronoid process of mandible strong and projecting dorsally.

Dental formula. 1/1, 0/0, 1/1, 3/3.

Castor canadensis, Beaver

Range. Throughout the state, along most permanent larger streams and waterways.

Diagnosis. As given for the family and species above. Adults in Illinois average in total length about 1,000 mm (ca. 3 ft), weight under 60 pounds (dependent upon age) usually; skull about 120 mm long and two-thirds as wide across zygomatic arches.

Color. Brown on dorsum and venter, hairs on feet slightly darker brown, underfur brownish or brownish black but also with a lead color, guard hairs on venter less well developed; tail nearly hairless, scaly, and darker than body.

Chromosomes. 2N = 40. FN = 78. All autosomes biarmed. X chromosome a medium-sized submetacentric; Y, acrocentric.

Comparisons. The only beavers in North America are referable to this species.

Secondary sexual variation. An analysis of a large series of specimens from Vermont (Bond, 1956) revealed no differences in cranial measurements of males and females.

Aging. Bond (1956:510) found that two groups were readily discernible: immatures in which the occipital sutures were not obliterated and deciduous premolars were still present, and matures in which occipital sutures are obliterated and permanent premolars are in place. Bond points out that there is another group, based on cranial measurements, that falls between these two.

Baculum. A relatively straight bone with an enlarged base; greatest length in adults usually between 30 and 36 mm.

Remarks. As pointed out following, beaver were present in Illinois, then extirpated. The beaver now in Illinois are not native stock but transplants and emigrants, probably all from adjacent states.

The beaver is the largest rodent in Illinois, being larger than the porcupine that formerly lived in the state.

History of the beaver in Illinois. Beaver were present in Illinois up until the mid-1800's but they had mostly if not entirely disappeared by the end of that century. They had been present along major waterways, and the early literature referred to their presence and sometimes said they were common. Nowhere are there references that say they were abundant and extensively trapped for fur. Practically as soon as European man arrived in Illinois, the numbers of beaver began to decline.

Fig. 8.80A. Beaver, *Castor canadensis*. Photograph by W. W. Goodpaster.

Beaver had disappeared in much of Illinois by 1850. In his account of the mammals of Illinois, Cyrus Thomas (1861:657), writing of their scarcity, observed "that any individuals of this species now exist in this State is doubtful, yet possible. . . . one had been killed in Jackson County, so late as 1848." Thomas corrected this date to probably 1851.

Some of the dates when beaver were still known to be present in counties in Illinois are as follows:

Present to 1819 or 1820: Edwards, Alexander, Hancock, Jersey, Whiteside counties.

Present to 1830–1836: Peoria and Jasper counties.

Extirpated before 1835: Lee County and counties along Wabash River.

Present to 1855, Massac County; to 1882, Madison County; to 1900, Carroll County.

Beaver were restocked in Illinois as early as May 1929, when a male and female were released on the Savanna Army Depot (Proving Grounds), Carroll County, by the U.S. Fish and Wildlife Service. Between 1935 and 1938, eight more pairs of beaver were released in Carroll County, according to a report in Thiem (1968:283). Supposedly beavers produced by these individuals moved into other parts of Illinois and, also, many were live-trapped in Carroll County and transplanted elsewhere in the state.

Other releases of beaver were reviewed by Pietsch (1956) and Mohr (1943). Some of these include:

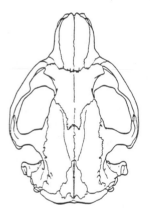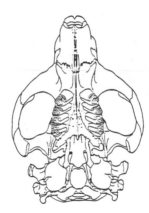

Fig. 8.80B. *Castor canadensis,* dorsal and ventral views of skull. "Central Illinois," 44914 UI. Sex unknown, 128.2 mm greatest length.

Pope County: Hunting Branch of Bay Creek, 6 mi SE Stonefort, 10, U.S. Forest Service, 1935; Grand Pierre Creek, 2 mi SE Herod, 9, U.S. Forest Service, 1935. All 19 of these beaver may have come from Wisconsin.

Union County: near Reynoldsville, 2, from Wisconsin, 1936; LaRue Swamp, 2 mi N Wolf Lake, 3.

Jersey County: Rosedale Township, 4, 1936, from Wisconsin.

Emigration of beaver from neighboring states undoubtedly occurred also. Beaver were stocked near the Mississippi River in Iowa in the 1940's, in Missouri in the 1930's, and, in Indiana, beaver were in the Kankakee River area and along the Wabash River in the 1930's.

By 1945, beaver in Illinois had become established widely; by 1954 beaver were reported in 55 of the 102 counties (Pietsch, 1956:196). As early as 1951, some 21 years after their release at the Savanna Army Depot, 149 beavers were trapped legally in Carroll and Jo Daviess counties. In 1951, just 15 years after the release of five animals in Union County, 59 were trapped legally (Pietsch, 1956:200).

At this time (1984), beaver are widespread and in many places are abundant. G. F. Hubert (1980) of the Illinois Department of Conservation estimated that the total trapper harvest for Illinois in 1979–1980 was 8,918 beaver. Forty-four percent of these came from a 31-county area in the central part of the Sangamon River Valley.

Habitat

Beavers live along large and small streams and rivers, ponds and lakes, drainage ditches and canals, and backwater embayments. There must be a source of food near the place where they live. They usually have homes in banks which are reached by a burrow which enters below water level. If the water is of the proper depth, they build a house in the form of a lodge within the pond or lake. Sometimes the lodge may be in the dam, if they build such a structure to increase the depth of the water.

Since beavers feed on the bark and twigs of trees, cornstalks, or even on water lilies and watercress, such items cannot be too distant from their homes. Trees should preferably be along the waterway where the animals have their dens.

The ponds and small lakes resulting from strip-mining and the successional growth of new, small trees around such ponds make an ideal habitat for beavers. Waterways in man-made parks and golf courses are attractive and used also.

Burrows and lodges

Burrows are dug into banks, and rest areas and nests are situated within these, above the water line. Banks must be sufficiently firm so that they will not cave in. Entrances to these burrows are below water level and are not much larger than the beaver. Fewer animals probably occupy a single burrow system than a lodge system. Most beaver in Illinois probably occupy bank burrows.

Lodges are sometimes built by beavers. They consist of small trees trunks, tree limbs, and sticks, often plastered with mud. Lodges may be situated along the bank, within the pond, or within the dam. Several beaver usually occupy a lodge. The entrances, one or more, into the lodge are below water level but the resting platform within the domed lodge is always above water level. The

tree parts making up the lodge or dam, especially those below water level, serve as a pantry where the beavers can go to obtain bark. Dams are built and maintained by the beaver to insure an adequate water level, especially to cover the below-water entrances, and for convenience in obtaining and storing food.

Habits

Beavers are aquatic animals and come on land mainly for resting, rearing young, and feeding. In some places, beaver even dig waterways to new sources of food so that they can swim back with the newly cut food to their lodge or storage area.

Beavers are colonial in that they remain together in what is called a colony, consisting of an adult male and female and sometimes with kits of the year and sometimes also with yearlings from the preceding breeding season. Usually lodges contain colonies of more than one animal and some may contain as many as 12 (Bradt, 1938). Bank burrows usually contain only one to two animals.

Beavers are well known for their tree-cutting abilities. Trees that they most easily fell are cottonwood, willow, and aspen, and tree trunks as much as two feet in diameter are successfully cut through. Harder woods such as oaks and maples will also be harvested. Trees are cut above ground at the level where a beaver sitting on its hind legs can conveniently gnaw with its incisors into the trunk. When the tree is felled, the branches and trunk are cut into appropriate lengths and transported and stored, either on a dam or lodge, or elsewhere.

Beavers are noted for their tail-slapping of the water. They usually do this just before they dive below the water surface, probably as a means of communicating with other beavers. They also make several kinds of vocal sounds: whine, cry, hiss, churr, and other sounds described by Leighton (1933).

Beavers are nocturnal animals, but sometimes may be seen in the twilight of late evening or early morning. In general, their nighttime activities include cutting and gathering food, strengthening dams, or adding to underwater caches of food.

Beavers are capable of moving considerable distances across land. They may be forced to move if the water supply is altered by man or by natural causes. This ability to move over land has been instrumental in the dispersal statewide of a relatively few transplanted beavers in Illinois.

Food

Beavers feed on plants, utilizing bark of many trees and shrubs, leaves, cornstalks, aquatic plants such as duckweed, water lilies (especially the roots), and grasses. They make use of many of the bushy plants and trees and aquatic vegetation where they live. In the summer, they eat more herbaceous material. Schwartz and Schwartz

(1981) pointed out that beaver eat the bark of the twigs and smaller branches, but they feed more extensively on the cambium layer of the trunk and larger branches.

Beavers cut down many trees and one wonders if they can eat all that they cut. Bradt (1938:154) noted that six captive beavers in Michigan consumed 180 trees, each one to three inches in diameter, in one month, or one tree per beaver, per day. These captive beavers, however, had no other foods available to supplement their diets.

Reproduction

Beavers breed only once during the year, with mating usually occurring in January or February, with the young born usually in May or June. The gestation period is around 107 days. Copulation usually occurs while the animals are in the water. It is thought that the young ordinarily do not breed until the second January or February after their birth. The number of young is usually three or four. At birth, the kits are fully furred and the eyes are beginning to open. The young are weaned by the end of two months.

Variation

According to some sources, the beavers in Illinois were supposedly referable to *C. c. carolinensis* Rhodes (type locality Dan River, North Carolina). Those in Wisconsin and northeastern Iowa were thought to be *C. c. canadensis* Kuhl (type locality Hudson Bay); those in Michigan, *C. c. michiganensis* Bailey (type locality Luce Co., Michigan). The native beavers as well as those introduced into Illinois could be any one of these three subspecies. No subspecific designation is suggested for the beavers in Illinois.

Castor canadensis, sp.

Range. Throughout the state, along most permanent larger streams and waterways; some lakes and marshes also.

Fig. 8.81A (above). Beaver house in northern Illinois. White hat on house gives a measure of the size. Photograph by Lyle Pietsch.

Fig. 8.81B (below). Beaver dam constructed in such a fashion that the water depth, upstream, is increased. The beaver lodge or house is usually located inside such a dam. Photograph by W. W. Goodpaster.

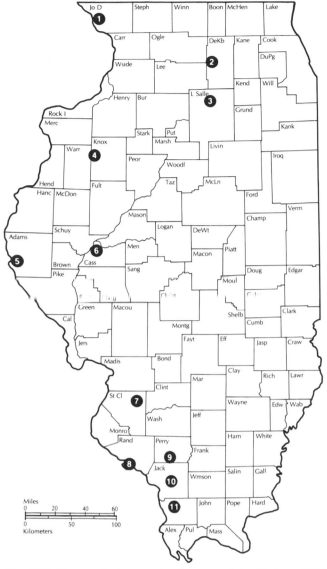

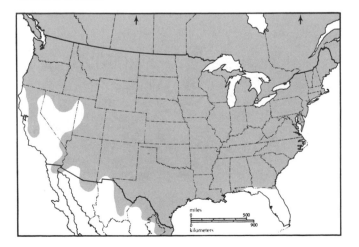

Diagnosis and Comparisons. Those animals in Illinois are large and dark colored, but the size and color are variable.

Records of occurrence. SPECIMENS EXAMINED, 13.
Jo Daviess.: [1] Mississippi River, 1 mi S ferry landing in Fish Trap Slough [location?], 1 (NIU), 1966. **De Kalb Co.:** [2] south of Malta, 1 (NIU), no date. **La Salle Co.:** [3] 4 mi W Jct Rt. 23 and Big India Creek, 2 (NIU), 1970. **Knox Co.:** [4] Lake Storey, 1 (UI), 1 (FM), 1949. **Cass Co.:** [6] Sangamon River bottoms, near Browning, 1 (ISM), 1956. **St. Clair Co.:** [7] Silver Creek bottomland, 2 mi S Rt. 50, 1 (UI), no date. **Randolph Co.:** [8] Kaskaskia Island, 2 (UI), 1982. **Perry Co.:** [9] Pyatts Striplands, 1 (SRL), 1 (SIC), no date. **Union Co.:** [11] Clear Creek, 1 (ISM), 1954.

Additional records. **Adams Co.:** [5] Quincy (migrated from Keokuk, Iowa?), (Musselman, 1949 in litt.). **Jackson Co.:** [10] no specific locality (Thomas, 1861:657–658).

Map 8.34. Beaver, *Castor canadensis,* occur statewide in suitable habitat. Because of various introductions, the subspecific status is uncertain. Localities of occurrence as numbered are referenced in *Records of occurrence.* The range of the species in the United States is shaded.

Family Muridae, Mice and Rats

Myomorph rodents characterized by having a medium-sized infraorbital canal, since only part of the masseter medialis muscle passes through it; zygomatic plate is nearly vertical, and cheek teeth are without premolars.

As defined here, the Muridae include the New World mice and rats, often referred to the family Cricetidae, and the Old World mice and rats. This family is here regarded as consisting of the subfamilies Cricetinae, Microtinae, and Murinae.

Subfamily Cricetinae, New World mice and rats

Murid rodents in which the molars, if cusped, have these cusps arranged in two longitudinal rows; tail usually partially to well haired and not conspicuously scaly. In Illinois, consists of the genera *Oryzomys, Reithrodontomys, Peromyscus, Ochrotomys,* and *Neotoma.*

Oryzomys, Rice rats

Diagnosis. A small-sized, ratlike murid with tail about equal to the head-body length, tail annulations prominent; teeth not hypsodont and relatively small, supraorbital bead or ridge on cranium; glans penis complex with several lobes on the glans, baculum with a trident-shaped cartilaginous cap.

Dental formula. 1/1, 0/0, 0/0, 3/3.

Comparisons. See account under the species (below).

Oryzomys palustris, Marsh rice rat

Range. Southernmost Illinois, from Franklin County south (Map 8.35).

Diagnosis. A species of *Oryzomys* of large size for the genus; head-body length usually 110 to 130 mm, and tail only slightly shorter than body; hind feet usually 24 to 30 mm in length; ears evident and fairly well haired, supraorbital ridges prominent in adults; incisive foramina long, extending posteriorly to plane of first molars; length of glans about 7.3 mm, bony baculum 3.9 mm; medial cartilaginous digit, 2.7 mm (Hooper and Musser, 1964:8).

Color. Dorsum a grizzled brownish with yellowish and blackish hairs intermixed, often darkest along the midline, underparts silvery but with much gray or plumbeous coloration and often with a slight frosting of yellow, feet whitish, tail on top about same color as dorsum and on bottom about same color as underparts.

Chromosomes. 2N = 56; FN = 56.

Comparisons. Oryzomys palustris might be confused with *Neotoma floridana* and *Rattus norvegicus* or *R. rattus* among Illinois mammals. Young specimens of *O. palustris* might be confused with some *Peromyscus,* especially *P. gossypinus.*

Oryzomys palustris differs from *Neotoma floridana* in its smaller size; hind foot (if accurately measured) less than 31 mm rather than more than 32 mm, tail less well-haired and ears less conspicuous, teeth with cusps rather than prisms and lophs, skull smaller, with noticeably smaller teeth, glans penis complex rather than simple, diploid number of chromosomes 56 rather than 52.

Oryzomys palustris differs from *Rattus* in having shorter hind feet, upper cheek teeth with two rows of cusps rather than three, skull smaller throughout, glans penis more complex.

Oryzomys palustris differs from *Peromyscus gossypinus* in having a longer tail (usually more than 100 mm, rather than less), supraorbital bead on brainbox rather than none, glans penis more complex, tail less distinctly bicolored.

Secondary sexual variation. The sexes are alike in size and color according to Lowery (1974:227).

Molt. Goldman (1918:6) stated that "there is no very definite period for molting, although the more northerly forms tend in winter to acquire a longer pelage, which becomes abraided in summer." Negus et al. (1961) indicate that juveniles molt to subadult pelage between the 30th and 80th days of age and begin to molt to adult pelage after the 150th day.

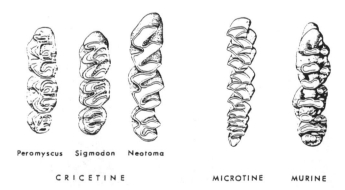

Peromyscus   Sigmodon   Neotoma

CRICETINE   MICROTINE   MURINE

Fig. 8.82. Upper cheek teeth in the three groups of murid rodents. Note the differences in the cusps and lophs. (From Hoffmeister, Mammals of Arizona, 1986)

Aging. Age classes can be established on the basis of size and weight, according to Negus et al. (1961). They regard animals as adult when the total length is more than 230 mm and the weight is 55 gms or more.

Remarks. Rice rats are now restricted to southernmost Illinois in the Shawnee Hills Section, the Mt. Vernon Hill Country, and near the Mississippi River and as far north as Franklin County (Klimstra and Scott, 1956). At an earlier time, however, they occurred as far north as Peoria County. This is verified by the remains of j*Oryzomys palustris* in the middens of Indians of Illinois. These remains are from the following archaeological or cave sites, arranged from north to south, in Illinois: Peoria County, 15 mi SE Peoria, Kingston site, Middle Mississippian, about 1200± 150 A.D., (F. C. Baker, 1936); Fulton County, 3¼ W Lewiston, Scovill site, Middle Woodland, 450 AD (Munson et al., 1971); Scott County, Smiling Dan Site, Middle Woodland; Greene County, 4 mi S Eldred, Schild Cemetary site, Late Woodland Early Mississippian, 1065± 60 A.D., (Parmalee, 1971); Cahokia Village site, Madison County (Parmalee, 1957); Meyer Cave fissure, Monroe County (Parmalee, 1967). Sometime within the last 1,000 years, rice rats must have been present along and near the Illinois River for some 200 miles north of where they are found today.

Habitat

Marsh rice rats live in the wet, swampy fields and marshes of southern Illinois, especially in areas of the Shawnee Hills or Ozark Uplift and to a lesser extent in the Mt. Vernon Hill country. We have taken these small rats from cypress swamps, from tall grasses adjacent to backwater lakes, and from brushy areas without much grass in swampy areas. The specimen from near Anna was taken on the dam of a three-acre farm pond (Klimstra and Scott, 1956) and specimens were taken in La Rue Swamp in a wet, woods-grass area (Klimstra and Roseberry, 1969). In western Tennessee, these rice rats were found in other habitats also: under clumps of soybean stubble near lakes, under boards and driftwood, in hollow stumps and logs, and under other debris (Goodpaster and Hoffmeister, 1952). In Kentucky, marsh rice rats are reported to be "fairly" common along roadside ditches and streams where there is sufficient cover of grasses and shrubs (Barbour and Davis, 1974).

Habits

Marsh rice rats are nocturnal. The best chance of seeing them in the daytime is by chasing them from their nests. Goodpaster and Hoffmeister (1952) found in Tennessee that rice rats when disturbed would frequently jump from their nests, and if these were over water the rats would jump and swim away. Esher et al. (1978) found that rice rats not only were good swimmers and divers, but floated well also. The pelage in rice rats is both water-repellent and insulative, which aids them in swimming. In drier situations, rice rats may make and use runways, but these are less distinct than those made by prairie voles.

Food

Marsh rice rats are opportunistic feeders and their diet varies with the seasons and the availability of foods. They are, however, more carnivorous than many rodents and will not hesitate to feed on turtles, fish, clams, snails, insects, bird eggs, and even small mammals. Their usual

Fig. 8.83A. Marsh rice rat, *Oryzomys palustris.* (From Hoffmeister and Mohr, 1957. Photograph by K. Maslowski and W. W. Goodpaster)

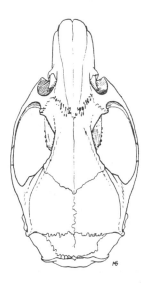
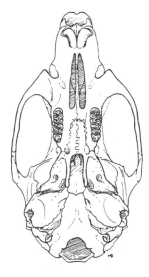

Fig. 8.83B. *Oryzomys palustris,* dorsal and ventral views of skull. Goose Creek, Charleston Co., South Carolina, 97182 Museum Vert. Zool. Male, 29.2 mm greatest length.

Map 8.35. Known records of occurrence of the marsh rice rat, *Oryzomys palustris*. The subspecies is *O. p. palustris*. Localities of occurrence as numbered are referenced in *Records of occurrence*. The range of the species in the United States is shaded.

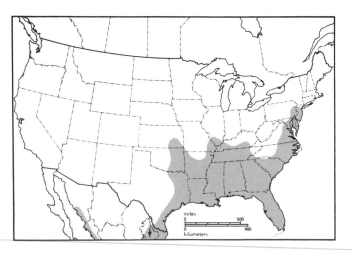

food includes the seeds and succulent parts of various grasses and water plants. Negus et al. (1961) found that stomach analyses showed a large amount of plant material, including seeds, with a large increase in insects in May and again in August.

In western Tennessee, marsh rice rats killed and fed on young turtles of the genera *Graptemys, Chrysemys,* and *Pseudemys.* Most of the fish and mammals that they feed on are probably carrion, but they probably take live minnows, crayfish, and clams if the opportunity arises.

Reproduction

Breeding in most places occurs throughout the year, but in the northern parts of its range, as in Illinois, breeding may be more seasonal. In Louisiana, most breeding occurs between January and March. Most of our specimens in Illinois were taken in the fall and, judging from their state of development, I would guess that all of the animals that are less than mature were born in September.

The gestation period is between three and four weeks and litter size, based on various sources, ordinarily is between three and five young. These reach puberty at between 50 and 60 days of age. At birth, hair on the body is discernible but with difficulty; at two days, hair is more readily seen. Eyes begin to open at about one week.

Young are reared in a dome-shaped nest built of grasses and vines loosely woven together. Nests are usually located above ground level and above flood level, and they may be located in thickets of vines, clumps of tall grasses or sedges, or in hollow logs. In Louisiana, Lowery (1974) found nests on the ground in slight depressions that were covered with tangles of vegetation.

Variation

In central United States, two subspecies of *Oryzomys palustris* are known: *O. p. palustris* (type locality Salem County, New Jersey) and *O. p. texensis* (Arkansas County, Texas). Specimens from Illinois have been referred to *O. p. palustris* but *O. p. texensis* reportedly occurs in the southeastern corner of Missouri (Goldman, 1918). Specimens from southern Illinois are here referred to *O. p. palustris*, but on a size basis show approach to the slightly smaller *O. p. texensis*.

Oryzomys palustris palustris (Harlan)

1837. *Mus palustris* Harlan, Amer. J. Sci., 31:385. Type locality, "Fast Land," near Salem, Salem Co., New Jersey.

1858. *Oryzomys palustris*, Baird, Mammals, *in* Repts. Expl. Surv. . . . , 8:459.

Range. As given for the species (Map 8.35).

Diagnosis and Comparisons. A medium-sized subspecies of grayish brown color, slightly darker than *O. p. texensis,* skull slightly broader than *O. p. texensis.*

Records of occurrence. SPECIMENS EXAMINED, 48.
Franklin Co.: [1] 3 mi NW Mulkeytown, 1 (SRL). **Jackson Co.:** [2] Murphysboro, 1 (SRL); [3] SIU Ag. Farm, 1 (SIC). **Williamson Co.:** [5] 5 mi ESE Crab Orchard, 1 (SRL), ditch E of Shellchers Woods [location?], 2 (SRL). **Union Co.:** [6a] 2 mi SE Aldridge, Pine Hills, 1 (UI); [6b] Pine Hills Recreation Area, 1 (ISM); [6c] "4 mi N and E" of Wolf Lake [assumed to be 4 mi NE], 5 (SIC); [7] 1 mi NE Anna, 1 (SIC). **Johnson Co.:** [8] ¼ mi E Grantsburg, 2 (UI). **Alexander Co.:** [9] Tammas, 6 (SRL); [10a] Olive Branch, 3 (US); [10b] Horseshoe Lake, 1 (NHS); [10c] Horseshoe Lake Island, 1 (UI); [10d] 2 mi S Olive Branch, 5 (UI); [10e] 2½ mi S Olive Branch, 1 (UI); [10f] 3 mi S Olive Branch, 7 (UI); [10g] ¼ mi N Miller City, 3 (UI); [10h] Miller City, 1 (UI); [10i] 1½ mi S Miller City, 2 (UI); [10j] ½ mi N Cairo, 1 (ISU). **Massac Co.:** [12] ½ mi E Metropolis, 1 (SIC).

Additional records: **Williamson Co.:** [4] 2 mi SW Cambria [may be same as Shellchers Woods] (Klimstra and Roseberry, 1969:416). **Alexander Co.:** [11a] Cache, (Necker and Hatfield, 1941:53).

Reithrodontomys, Harvest mice

Diagnosis. Small myomorph rodents in which each upper incisor has a median groove in its anterior face, no premolar teeth (in contrast with *Zapus* that has grooved upper incisors but a small upper premolar), the body is small (usually between 62 and 80 mm), tail usually from 15 percent shorter to 20 percent longer than body (depending upon the species), ears shorter than the hind feet; the skull has weak zygomatic arches, coronoid process of mandible relatively well developed.

Dental formula. 1/1, 0/0, 0/0, 3/3.

Comparisons. Reithrodontomys, especially the species *R. megalotis,* resembles *Mus,* house mice, but can be distinguished by the grooved upper incisors; tips of the upper incisors chisel-shaped rather than notched; tail more heavily haired and bicolored, with underparts whitish, upper parts yellowish brown or reddish brown rather than dark gray.

Reithrodontomys in Illinois can be distinguished from *Peromyscus,* white-footed mice, by the grooved upper incisors, weaker zygomatic arches, shorter toothrow, better-developed coronoid process on mandible, shorter baculum, and diploid number of chromosomes 42 (rather than 48). Young *Peromyscus* may be readily confused with *Reithrodontomys,* but the former are more grayish, and less reddish or yellowish brown.

Reithrodontomys differs from *Ochrotomys,* golden mouse (p. 217), in much the same way that it differs from *Peromyscus* (above), and has a diploid number of chromosomes 42 rather than 52; glans penis less complex.

For a comparison with *Zapus,* see account of that genus (p. 257).

Secondary sexual variation. Hoffmeister (1986:326) found that *Reithrodontomys megalotis* in Arizona showed no significant differences between the sexes in external or cranial measurements.

Aging. Specimens used in the table of measurements are considered as adults and include age-groups 3, 4, and 5 as determined by Hoffmeister (1986:326).

Reithrodontomys megalotis, Western harvest mouse

Range. Throughout much of the northern half of the state (Map 8.36). See *Remarks* (p. 200) for a discussion of the changes in the distribution.

Diagnosis. A species of *Reithrodontomys* which in Illinois has a tail shorter than the head-body (usually about 80%), tail scantily haired, ears prominent, length of hind foot 18 mm or less, skull small with weak zygomatic arches, greatest length of skull usually less than 21.5 mm. Other characters are given in the *Diagnosis* for the genus.

Color. Dorsum reddish with many black and brown hairs interspersed, venter grayish tipped with white, tail bicolored with dorsal color much as on back and ventral color as on underparts, feet whitish. *R. megalotis* in this part of its range may have a buffy pectoral spot. In an analysis of 31 specimens from Illinois in the University of Illinois Museum of Natural History collection, 22 have no pectoral spot, 8 have a weak spot, and one has a well-developed spot.

Chromosomes. 2N = 42; with 18 metacentrics, 16 submetacentrics, and 6 subtelocentrics; X-chromosome submetacentric, Y-chromosome subtelocentric (Shellhammer, 1967). Supernumerary chromosomes may be present.

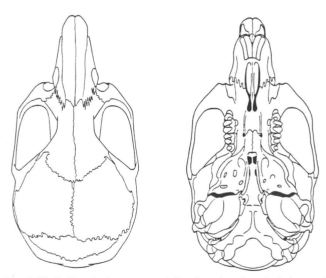

Fig. 8.84. *Reithrodontomys megalotis,* dorsal and ventral views of skull; 2 mi ESE Portal, Cochise Co., Arizona, 14905 UI. Female, 21.2 mm greatest length.

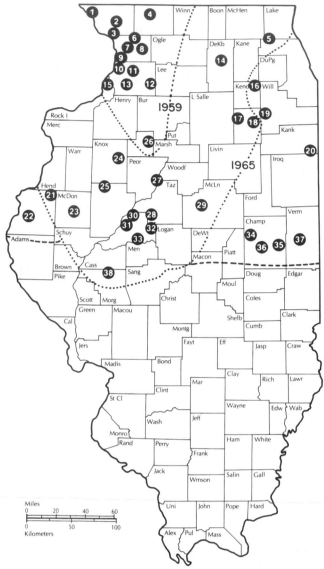

Map 8.36. Western harvest mice, *Reithrodontomys megalotis*, in Illinois. The probable extensions of the range of the species into the state by 1959 and by 1965 are indicated by dotted lines. The subspecies is *R. m. dychei*. Localities of occurrence as numbered are referenced in *Records of occurrence*. The range of the species in the United States is shaded.

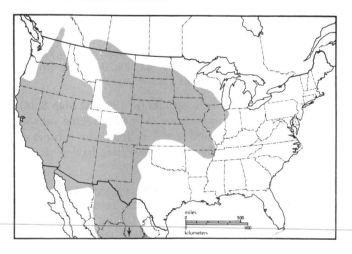

Comparisons. R. megalotis differs from *Mus musculus, Peromyscus* (species in Illinois), and *Ochrotomys nuttalli* as given under the genus (p. 199). For a comparison with *Zapus hudsonius,* see account of that species (p. 257).

Remarks. Some species of rodents in Illinois are represented in the numerous Indian sites, sinkholes, or natural traps that have been excavated and analyzed. These sites date from around 2,000 years before the present. In none of these sites have remains of *Reithrodontomys* been found. The first reported captures of *R. megalotis* in the state were specimens taken in November 1953 in the northwest corner in Carroll County (Hoffmeister and Warnock, 1955). Subsequently, a series of papers reported changes in the distribution of this species, and these indicated that the animals spread mostly eastward and southward.

On the distribution map (Map 8.36), localities of capture by certain dates, as can best be ascertained, are given. One line indicates the probable distribution by 1959; another, by 1965; the remainder as known by 1975 and later. Harvest mice have moved into Illinois relatively recently, probably within the last 100 years, and have spread across the state at a surprisingly rapid rate. By 1974, harvest mice had extended their range about 30 miles into northwestern Indiana, south of the Kankakee River.

It has been suggested by Birkenholz (1967) that western harvest mice in Illinois occupy an early seral stage which exists for only a short time and when other seral stages replace the first, harvest mice decrease or disappear. Harvest mice have been present in the Phillips and Trelease Research areas northeast of Urbana, Champaign County, since 1971, and possibly two or three years earlier. From 1971 until 1984, there seems to be no decline in the numbers of harvest mice in this area.

One may suspect that harvest mice have been present in northern Illinois for a much longer period than indicated here but were undiscovered because of little trapping or searching. Grasslands where harvest mice are found now in Champaign County have been trapped annually for about 50 years and harvest mice were not found there until 1969.

Habitat

Western harvest mice in Illinois live in grassy or weedy places with some taller weeds such as goldenrod or giant ragweed, and even scattered brush. Most of the localities where these mice have been taken have several of the following: brome grass, bluegrass, bluestem, foxtail, wild rye, panic grass, with the taller plants common ragweed, giant ragweed, asters, goldenrod, and smartweed.

A large population of harvest mice near Normal, McLean County, occupied an idle field and an unused railroad right-of-way where the average height of the vegetation was 18 inches (Birkenholz, 1967). The mice were living in burrows in the ground which was free of litter. The predominant plants were foxtail, ragweed, and aster.

In northwestern Illinois, harvest mice were taken in an orchard grown up with various tall plants, including blackberry and goldenrod, with a height between 4½ and 5½ feet; the understory was brome and bluegrass (Hoffmeister and Warnock, 1955). Verts (1960) found them to be most numerous in bluestem, bluegrass, oats, panic grass, ragweed and goldenrod. Klimstra (1957) took harvest mice from a railroad right-of-way that is burned each spring and from the edge of a dry marsh with sedges, cattails, and smartweed.

In northeastern Illinois, harvest mice at 3½ mi N Lorenzo, Will County, were taken in a marshy area not far from the Des Plaines River (Becker, 1975). The area contained prairie cordgrass, spotted smartweed, muhly, bugleweed, and cattail. Farther north, near Plainfield, Will County, harvest mice were taken in brome grass and Osage orange and near Barrington, Du Page County, in a "railroad prairie" (Stupka et al., 1972).

Western harvest mice in Illinois are usually found in early successional stages. As these areas pass through successional stages, harvest mice may not find the habitat as suitable, and the population then decreases. It is likely that areas that are occasionally burned may be more suitable for these mice.

Habits

Western harvest mice are nocturnal and rarely seen. They usually will not take up residency in old buildings as may house mice and white-footed mice. Harvest mice have the reputation of being belligerent and aggressive for their size, for they reputedly will attack and kill mice larger than they are when caged together.

In a 10-acre field at Normal, McLean County, the population in the fall of 1963 was estimated at 17 harvest mice per acre. Along an unused railroad right-of-way near the above locality, the population over a three-year period fluctuated between 4 to 12 per acre, depending on the season (Birkenholz, 1967).

Harvest mice in Illinois are usually associated with these species: *Blarina brevicauda*, *Peromyscus leucopus*, sometimes with *Peromyscus maniculatus*, *Microtus ochrogaster* and/or *M. pennsylvanicus*, and sometimes with feral *Mus musculus*.

Food

Little is known of the food habitats of harvest mice in Illinois, but they must feed extensively on the seeds of foxtail, bluestem, and all of the grasses where they live. In Indiana, these mice feed primarily on seeds but do take some lepidopterous larvae and other invertebrates including crickets, squash bugs, spiders, and leafhoppers (Whitaker and Mumford, 1972b).

Reproduction

Harvest mice at the Phillips Research Tract, east of Urbana, Champaign County, build small, round nests of grass that are placed above ground and among grasses and taller plants. The inner part of the nest is lined with milkweed down, according to Lowell Getz.

One specimen in our collection, according to the label, was pregnant with four embryos on April 14, and two harvest mice specimens were lactating in early November. Verts (1960) reported a pregnant female with six embryos on March 28 and another with two embryos and two partially resorbed on June 19. To judge from this evidence and from what Whitaker and Mumford (1972b) found in Indiana, harvest mice breed between March and November, but there may be some reduction in breeding during parts of the summer. Females become sexually mature when only slightly more than four months old. The gestation period is about 24 days. Newborn are hairless, and their eyes and ears are closed. At less than two weeks, the eyes and ears open, and the young are weaned at about three and one-half weeks. Bancroft (1967) found that a female under laboratory conditions could produce 14 litters in one year, each with a mean litter size of 4.1.

Variation

Present workers follow the conclusions of Hoffmeister and Warnock (1955) in regarding specimens of harvest mice in Illinois as referable to *R. m dychei*. These authors reviewed specimens from Wisconsin and Illinois as well as from Minnesota, Iowa, and Kansas, and concluded that *Reithrodontomys megalotis pectoralis* Hanson (type locality Westpoint, Columbia Co., Wisconsin) was not a recognizable subspecies. Additional material that has been seen tends to corroborate this earlier conclusion.

Reithrodontomys megalotis dychei Allen

1895. *Reithrodontomys dychei* J. A. Allen, Bull. Amer. Mus. Nat. Hist., 7:120. Type from Lawrence, Douglas Co., Kansas.
1914. *Reithrodontomys megalotis dychei*, Howell, N. Amer. Fauna, 36:30.
1944. *Reithrodontomys megalotis pectoralis* Hanson, Field Mus. Nat. Hist., publ. 564, 29:205. Type from Westpoint, Columbia Co., Wisconsin.

Range. As given for the species (p. 199 and Map 8.36).

Diagnosis and Comparisons. A medium-sized subspecies of *R. megalotis*, and it differs from the subspecies *R. m. aztecus* in being of smaller size, having darker upper parts, and ears slightly larger.

Records of occurrence. SPECIMENS EXAMINED, 65.
Jo Daviess Co.: [1a] T29N, R1E, Sec. 21, 1 (NHS). **Stephenson Co.**: [4] T28N, R7E, Sec. 16, 1 (NHS). **Carroll Co.**: [7a] ⅛ mi N Mt. Carroll, 2 (UI); [7b] Mt. Carroll, 2 (UI); [9] York Twp.,

5 (NHS). **Whiteside Co.:** [10] 4 mi N Fulton, 1 (UI); [11b] T21N, R8E, Sec. 22, 1 (NHS); [12] T20N, R7E, Sec. 15, 1 (NHS); [13] 1 mi W Denrock, 4 (SRL). **Kendall Co.:** [16] 10 mi NW Plainfield on RR tracks [labelled Will Co.], 1 (NIU). **Grundy Co.:** [17] 6 mi W Morris, 3 (UI); [18a] Goose Lake Prairie State Park, 1 (ISU), 2 (UI); [18b] 7 mi SE Morris, 1 (ISU). **Kankakee Co.:** [20] 6 mi E St. Anne, 1 (UI). **Hancock Co.:** [21] 1½ mi N La Harpe, 1 (ISU). **Knox Co.:** [24] 4 mi S Victoria, 2 (UI). **Fulton Co.:** [25] ½ mi W London Mills, 1 (UI). **Stark Co.:** [26] 2½ mi S Bradford, 2 (SRL). **Peoria Co.:** [27] Forest Park Wildlife Refuge, 4 (EU). **McLean Co.:** [29a] 2 mi N Normal, 1 (ISU); [29b] 1 mi N Normal, 1 (ISU); [29c] Normal, 3 (ISU); [29d] 2 mi E Normal, 1 (ISU). **Mason Co.:** [31a] 4 mi NNE Havana, 1 (UI); [31b] 3 mi NE Havana, 1 (UI); [32] 2½ mi W San Jose, 2 (ISU); [33] 4 mi S Easton, 2 (UI). **Champaign Co.:** [34] 3 mi NE Mahomet, 1 (UI); [35] 1 mi E St. Joseph, 1 (UI); [36a] 1⅛ mi N Urbana, 3 (UI); [36b] 2½ mi W Champaign, 1 (UI); [36c] 2 mi E Urbana, 1 (UI); [36d] 2 mi S Champaign, 1 (UI); [36e] 3 mi S Champaign, 2 (UI). **Vermilion Co.:** [37a] 1¼ mi W, ½ mi S Snider, 3 (UI); [37b] ½ mi S, ½ mi E Newton, 2 (UI).

Additional records: **Jo Daviess Co.:** [1b] T29N, R1W, Sec. 34, (Verts, 1960:2); [2] T27N, R3E, Sec. 15, (Verts, 1960:2); [3] T26N, R3E, Sec. 28, (Verts, 1960:2). **Lake Co.:** [5] Barrington [may be Cook Co., definitely not Du Page Co. as reported], (Stupka et al., 1972:112). **Carroll Co.:** [6] T25N, R5E, Sec. 10, (Verts, 1960:2); [7c] T24N, R4E, Sec. 24, (Verts, 1960:2); [8] T24N, R6E, Sec. 21, (Verts. 1960:2). **Whiteside Co.:** [11a] T22N, R5E, Sec. 15, (Verts, 1960:2). **De Kalb Co.:** [14] 2½ mi N De Kalb, (Stupka et al., 1972:112, from owl pellets). **Rock Island Co.:** [15] 2 mi N Cordova, 3 (MSU). **Will Co.:** [19] T34N, R9E, Sec. 29 [17 mi NNW Wilmington], (Becker, 1975:14). **Hancock Co.:** [22] ½ mi SW Elvaston, (John Warnock, pers. comm., 1968). **McDonough Co.:** [23] Macomb, (John Warnock pers. comm., 1968). **Tazewell Co.:** [28] 1 mi NW Green Valley, (Stains and Turner, 1963:274). **Mason Co.:** [30] Mason State Forest [=Sand Ridge State Forest], (Birkenholz, 1967:50). **Morgan Co.:** [38] 7 mi S Virginia, (Stains and Turner, 1963:274).

Peromyscus, White-footed mice

Diagnosis. Myomorph rodents in which the feet are usually white, ears conspicious, eyes large, tail about as long as head-body and haired but not bushy, underparts lighter colored than the dorsum, skull with long incisive (palatine) foramina, anterior border of infraorbital or zygomatic plate either convex or straight, coronoid process of mandible reduced.

Dental formula. 1/1, 0/0, 0/0, 3/3.

Chromosomes. 2N = 48; FN may vary among species.

Comparisons. Peromyscus differs from *Reithrodontomys* as specified in the account of that genus (p. 199). Critical features are the ungrooved upper incisors, reduced coronoid processes, and larger skull.

Peromyscus differs from *Ochrotomys* as given in the account of that genus (p. 217). Critical features are the grayish coloration of young animals (rather than reddish), convex or straight anterior border of infraorbital or zygomatic plate (rather than concave); glans penis less heavily spined and baculum relatively longer; chromosomes 2N, 48 (rather than 52).

Peromyscus differs from *Mus* (p. 255) in having lighter-colored underparts, more densely haired tail, tail bicolored; upper incisors chisel-shaped at tip rather than notched, upper teeth with two rows of cusps; chromosomes 2N, 48 (rather than 40); only two or three pairs of mammae (rather than five).

Peromyscus differs from *Zapus* as given in the account of that genus (p. 257).

Aging. It is important to compare animals of the same age. Therefore, specimens were put into five age groups based on tooth wear, as given by Hoffmeister (1951:1). Group 1, M^3 just erupting; Group 2, M^3 worn smooth; Group 3, M^1 and M^2 with lingual cusps not quite worn smooth and labial cusps with little wear; Group 4, lingual cusps worn smooth and labial cusps showing considerable wear; Group 5, all cusps worn smooth.

Secondary sexual variation. For the species found in Illinois, there are no significant differences between males and females of age group 3 or older.

Molt. Molting occurs in a sequence as described by Collins (1918, 1923) and Hoffmeister (1951). Molt from a juvenile to postjuvenile pelage occurs at about one month of age.

Peromyscus maniculatus, Deer mouse

Range. Throughout the state in prairie or grassland habitat; seemingly not abundant.

Diagnosis. A species of *Peromyscus* in which the hind foot is small, 18 mm or less if accurately measured from heel to tip of claws and not only short but narrow also; tail usually less than 65 mm, and always shorter than the head-body length; animals appear dark in color, especially down middle of back; skull with toothrow less than 3.3 mm crown length and 3.5 mm alveolar length, greatest skull length usually less than 24.0 mm, zygomatic arches pinched in anteriorly, with the width across the zygomatic arches just behind the infraorbital plate less than 12 mm.

Color. Dorsum dark; most specimens have a broad dark band extending from the top of the head to the rump, underparts whitish and never with a yellowish pectoral spot, tail blackish above and whitish below, hind feet whitish above but, on some, darkish fur may extend to the base of the toes, ears are blackish with a narrow rim of white.

Chromosomes. 2N = 48; biarmed chromosomes are reported as 34, 36, and 38; acrocentrics usually 10 but as many as 18 (Bradshaw and Hsu, 1972; Singh and McMillan, 1966; Sparkes and Arakai, 1966).

Comparisons. P. maniculatus is often confused with *P. leucopus* in Illinois. For comparisons, it is important that animals of comparable age are used. Those *P. leucopus*

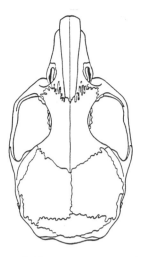

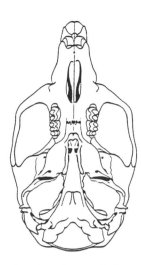

Fig. 8.85. Deer mouse, *Peromyscus maniculatus,* from near Urbana, Champaign Co., Illinois. Note the white rim on the tip of the ears and short tail with its narrow dorsal dark stripe. Photograph by Illinois Natural History Survey.

Fig. 8.86. *Peromyscus maniculatus,* dorsal and ventral views of skull. Dixon Springs, Lake Glendale, Pope Co., Illinois, 57851 UI. Male, 23.0 mm greatest length.

that are grayish in color are juveniles and should be compared with juvenile *P. maniculatus.* However, some adult *P. maniculatus* are dark, and might be regarded as grayish juveniles. The sides of these animals should be checked to determine if there is brownish fur in this area. Also see Table 8.20 (p. 205).

Adult and juvenile *P. maniculatus* differ from adult *P. leucopus* in having shorter hind feet (15 to 18 mm rather than 18 mm or more), overall smaller hind feet, tail shorter (40 mm to 65 mm, rather than usually 70 mm or more), skull smaller throughout and this is exemplified by the product of greatest length of skull multiplied by crown length of maxillary toothrow (usually 65 to 80 rather than 82.0 or more), zygomatic arches compressed anteriorly with the width across them just behind the zygomatic plate usually less than 12 mm rather than more, maxillary toothrow shorter (crown length usually 2.9–3.3 mm instead of 3.3 mm or more).

When juvenile mice—that is, those in all grayish pelage—are compared, *P. maniculatus* differs from *P. leucopus* in shorter hind foot and shorter toothrows (see paragraph preceding); the length of tail is usually less than 55 mm rather than 60 mm or more; the product of the greatest length of skull multiplied by crown length of maxillary toothrow is usually less than 76 rather than more; the width across the zygomatic arches just behind the zygomatic plate is usually 10.9 mm or more.

P. maniculatus differs from *P. gossypinus* in having much shorter and smaller hind feet, a shorter tail, much smaller skull in length and breadth, toothrow shorter (see Table 8.20).

P. maniculatus differs from *Reithrodontomys megalotis, Ochrotomys nuttalli,* and *Mus musculus* as mentioned above under the genus *Peromyscus* (p. 202).

P. maniculatus differs from *Zapus hudsonius* in having ungrooved upper incisors, no upper premolars, tail and hind feet much shorter, skull without greatly enlarged infraorbital foramen. See Table (p. 260) and *Diagnosis* of *Zapus* (p. 257).

Remarks. Peromyscus maniculatus is often confused with *Peromyscus leucopus.* On the basis of various morphological features used in combination, together with the ecological separation of the two species, all individuals, but especially adults, should be told apart readily. In most places in Illinois, *P. maniculatus* is not as abundant within its preferred habitat as *P. leucopus* is within its habitat.

Habitat

Deer mice in Illinois are inhabitants of the grasslands and prairies. They do not live in forests or wooded areas and as soon as shrubs and trees invade prairies, the mice disappear from this habitat. They do often live along railroad rights-of-way if they are grassy and not bordered with trees, as well as in barren fields that have been plowed for overwintering, pastures, stubble fields, and lawnlike grassy situations.

In plowed fields, the burrow openings of deer mice frequently can be found in the soft ground. I know of no investigation of these burrow systems in Illinois, but in Indiana Houtcooper (1972) found that the burrows averaged about 16 feet in length and were 1 to 12 inches below the surface. One suspects that these deer mice can dig such burrows only when the ground is soft, usually after it has been fall-plowed.

In an ungrazed bluegrass field at the edge of a mixed forest at Allerton Park, near Monticello, Piatt County, in once-a-year trapping between November 1946 and

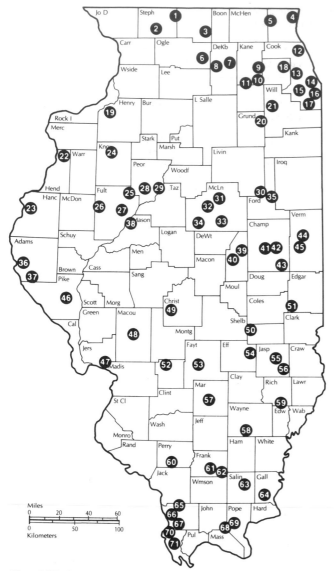

Map 8.37. Deer mice, *Peromyscus maniculatus*, occur statewide. The subspecies is *P. m. bairdii*. Localities of occurrence as numbered are referenced in *Records of occurrence*. The range of the species in the United States is shaded.

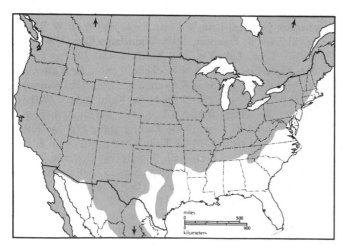

November 1969, we took only one deer mouse and this was in the eighth year of trapping. We suspect that the bluegrass was much too thick, tall, and matted for deer mice. By the 11th year, small trees and bushes had invaded the trapping site to the extent that we did not expect to take deer mice.

The early successional stages following strip-mining provide ideal habitat for deer mice. For example, in Perry County, Verts (1959:136) found these to be the "predominate species of *Peromyscus* and attained highest population levels in more recently strip-mined areas. . . . Four hundred twenty-seven taken in 6,221 trap-nights from August, 1954, to May, 1955."

In Fulton County at a site ½ mi N Norris, Elsie P. Anderson investigated a prairie area through which the railroad right-of-way for the Chicago, Burlington, and Quincy line and the abandoned Illinois Central Electric Railway ran. She described the area as consisting of prairie plants, rosin weeds, sunflowers, blackberries, and a few cherry saplings. Three nights of snap-trapping in a circular acre with 200 traps in October 1949 produced 15 deer mice; four months later in February 1950 the same type of trapping produced 32 deer mice. The only other species caught in numbers was the prairie vole. Other species caught were the meadow vole, least shrew, short-tailed shrew, white-footed mouse, and bog lemming.

Habits

Deer mice usually leave little evidence of their presence. They do not make above-ground food caches or runways. On fall-plowed fields, however, the tracks of deer mice are quite visible—especially if there is shallow snow—as they radiate out from their burrow entrances.

Deer mice are not climbers. When placed in an enclosure with numerous branches, deer mice do not make use of these as avenues of travel. Goodpaster and Hoffmeister (1954:24) give an account of the hesitancy of a deer mouse to use such branches.

> On one occasion, a deer mouse, *Peromyscus maniculatus bairdii*, was introduced into a large cage with four established golden mice. The *Peromyscus maniculatus* was never accepted. The deer mouse remained at the bottom of the cage and made little attempt to run the branches in the cage. Within ten minutes after the introduction two golden mice were out of their nest and another in the nest's entrance. The two *Peromyscus nuttalli* began shortly to chase the *P. maniculatus*. The golden mice were so much more adept at running the branches and wire of the cage that they repeatedly overhauled and nipped at the deer mouse. Within minutes the deer mouse was bleeding from the nose and very slightly from the base of the ear. The pursuit ended shortly thereafter. The deer mouse made one or two convulsive kicks, and was dead.

In Illinois, deer mice rarely build nests in bushes or trees, although Mumford and Whitaker (1982) found nests in

Table 8.20. Characters useful in distinguishing the three species of *Peromyscus* in Illinois. In some cases, age classes are important considerations. There may be some overlap in characters. Length measurements are in millimeters.

Character	Age-class	*P. maniculatus*	*P. leucopus*	*P. gossypinus*
Hind foot length	2 to 5	16-18	18-22	22-25
Tail length	3 to 5	40-65	70-85	77-88
Crown length of maxillary toothrow	2 to 5	2.9-3.3	3.3-3.7	3.7-4.1
Product of greatest length of skull × crown length of maxillary toothrow	3 to 5	65.0-80.0	82.0-97.8	97.9+
Entolophulid in M_1 and/or M_2		Absent usually	Absent usually	Present usually
Mesolophid in M_1 and/or M_2		Absent usually	Absent usually	Present usually

hollow fenceposts and bushes in Indiana. In Michigan, Howard (1949a) was able to study these mice by placing nest boxes in the ground which they frequently occupied.

Howard (1949a) found that burrow systems usually are simple and shallow, especially if the deer mice dig them. They may use burrows abandoned by other mammals. He found that deer mice lived in small social groups, usually the male, female, and young. In winter, the groups were larger and often not related.

Food

Deer mice are opportunistic omnivores. If they are in or near cultivated fields, they will feed on seeds of soybeans, wheat, oats, or sometimes on corn. In prairie situations, they will feed on the seeds of plants in the area. When available, insects, especially larvae, are extensively eaten as food.

The foods eaten by several hundred wild-taken deer mice in Indiana have been summarized by Whitaker (1966) and Mumford and Whitaker (1982). They report that in winter the diet is predominantly seeds of grasses, shrubs, and available leftover field crops. From spring until fall, more herbaceous material and insects are eaten.

Reproduction

According to our data, deer mice in Illinois give birth to young in each month of the year. The gestation period is about 23 to 25 days. Although a female may give birth to several litters in a year, the life expectancy is so short that a female rarely gives birth to more than two or three litters in her lifetime. Howard (1949a) found that females born between late March and middle May may breed as soon as they are sexually mature; if born in late September and October, they breed in the spring.

Litter size varies from one to nine. The mean for specimens in Illinois is 4.7. Litter size may be correlated with the size and weight of the mother (Myers and Master, 1983). Eyes open at about two weeks of age; young are weaned at about one month. Howard (1949a) found that many deer mice moved away for their places of birth just prior to becoming sexually active for the

first time. He found that of more than 1,200 deer mice that he followed, less than one-fifth reached sexual maturity, but eight did live for more than 73 weeks.

Variation

All of the deer mice in Illinois are referable to the subspecies *P. m. bairdii*.

Peromyscus maniculatus bairdii (Hoy and Kennicott)

1857. *Mus bairdii* Hoy and Kennicott, *in* Kennicott, Agric. Rept., U. S. Comm. Patents, 1856, p. 92. Type from Bloomington, McLean Co., Illinois.

1909. *Peromyscus maniculatus bairdii*, Osgood, N. Amer. Fauna, 28:79.

Range. Throughout the state in prairie or grassland habitat; seemingly not abundant (Map 8.37).

Diagnosis and Comparisons. A subspecies of *P. maniculatus* with a short tail (less than 65 mm usually), small hind feet, and dark coloration of dorsum and top of the tail. *P. m. bairdii* differs from *P. maniculatus gracilis* (type locality, Michigan) in having a much shorter tail (usually less than 65 mm rather than usually more than 75 mm), hind feet shorter, color darker.

Records of occurrence. SPECIMENS EXAMINED, 372. **Stephenson Co.:** [1a] 1 mi W Davis, 2 (UI); [1b] ½ mi W Davis, 2 (UI); [2] 3 mi W Freeport, 2 (UI). **Winnebago Co.:** [3] 4 mi E Rockford, 1 (UI). **Lake Co.:** [4a] Beach, 1 (FM); [5] Fox Lake, 17 (FM). **Ogle Co.:** [6] 6 mi N Rochelle, 1 (NIU). **De Kalb Co.:** [7a] 5.7 mi N De Kalb, 5 mi W Sycamore, 1 (NIU); [7b] Mayfield Twp., Sec. 28, 6 (NIU); [7c] 5 mi N De Kalb, 2 (NIU); [7d] ½ mi S of Jct. Rt. 64 & Glidden Rd., 2 (NIU); [7e] De Kalb Twp., Sec. 4, 8 (NIU); [7f] 2 mi N De Kalb, 1 (NIU); [7g] De Kalb Twp., Sec. 14, 5 (NIU); [7h] De Kalb, 1 (NIU); [7i] ¼ mi E De Kalb, 1 (NIU); [7j] 3 mi E De Kalb, 1 (NIU); [7k] Cortland Twp., Sec. 28, 34, 9 (NIU); [8a] Malta Twp., Sec. 19, 5 (NIU); [8b] De Kalb Twp., Sec. 19, 6 (NIU). **Kane Co.:** [9a] ½ mi W St. Charles, 2 (ISM); [9b] St. Charles, 1 (ISM); [10] 2 mi W, 1 mi N Aurora, 1 (UI). **Cook Co.:** [12b] 1 mi E Des Plaines, 1 (UI); [12c] Morton Grove, 1 (UI); [13] 1.3 mi E US 45 on state hwy. 55, 2 (UI); [14a] Kocour Co. yard [4800 S] Chicago, 2 (NIU); [14b] Chicago,

Jackson Park, 4 (FM); [14c] N Ford City, Chicago [=E edge Bedford Park], 2 (UI); [14d] SW Chicago, 4 (UI); [15] Palos Park, 1 (UI); [16] Calumet Lake, 1 (FM); [17a] SW Hazelcrest, 4 (UI); [17b] Homewood, 1 (FM). **Du Page Co.:** pb18] 1 mi N Rt 64, 2 mi E Rt 53, 3 (UI). **Henry Co.:** [19] T17N, R2E, Sec. 30 [=9 mi N, 6 mi W Cambridge], 5 (KU). **Grundy Co.:** [20] Goose Lake Prairie State Park, 4 (UI). **Will Co.:** [21] 4.1 mi W Joliet (Black Road), 2 (KU). **Henderson Co.:** [22] 1½ mi E, 6 mi N Oquawka, 8 (UI). **Hancock Co.:** [23] Camp Eastman, 5 mi N Hamilton, 1 (UI). **Knox Co.:** [24] 1.3 mi NE Wataga, 1 (UI).

Fulton Co.: [25] ½ mi N Norris, 18 (UI); [26] 2 mi W Marietta, 1 (UI); [27] 1 mi E Bryant, 1 (UI). **Peoria Co.:** [28a] 12 mi W Peoria, 1 (UI); [28b] 2¼ mi S, 1 mi W Hanna City, 1 (UI); [29] 1 mi E Peoria, 2 (UI). **Livingston Co.:** [30a] 7 mi E, 1 mi S Strawn, 4 (UI); [30b] 8 mi E, 2 mi S Strawn, 3 (UI). **McLean Co.:** [31] 12 mi NE Normal, 2 (ISU); [32a] 2 mi N Normal, 3 (ISU); [32b] 1 mi N Normal, 2 (ISU); [33a] 3½ mi N, 3 mi W Le Roy, 1 (UI); [33b] 3 mi NW Le Roy, 2 (UI); [33c] 2 mi E Le Roy, 1 (UI); [34] ½ mi S Funks Grove, 1 (ISU). **Ford Co.:** [35] 1 mi N, 1 mi W Roberts, 1 (UI). **Adams Co.:** [36] South Park, Quincy, 3 (UI); [37] 3 mi W Plainville, 2 (UI). **Mason Co.:** [38] 3½ mi N, 2 mi E Havana, 1 (UI). **Piatt Co.:** [39a] 1¼ mi NW White Heath, 1 (UI); [39b] 1 mi NW White Heath, 2 (UI); [40a] 1½ mi ENE Cisco, 3 (UI); [40b] Allerton Park, 5 mi W, 2½ mi S Monticello, 1 (UI). **Champaign Co.:** [41a] 1 mi N Champaign Airport, 2 (UI); [41b] Champaign Airport, 2 (UI); [41c] 2 mi N Urbana, 2 (UI); [41d] 1½ mi N Urbana, 3 (UI); [41e] Busey Woods, 1 (UI); [41f] 1⅛ mi N Urbana, 3 (UI); [41g] Champaign, 8 (UI); [41h] ½ mi W Staley, 1 (UI); [41i] Urbana, 12 (UI); [41j] 1 mi S Champaign, 5 (UI); [41k] S campus, UI, 2 (UI); [41l] 1 mi S Urbana, 2 (UI); [41m] 2 mi SW Champaign, 3 (UI); [41n] St. Mary's Cem., ICRR [=1½ mi S Champaign], 6 (UI); [41o] 2 mi S Urbana, 1 (UI); [41p] 2½ mi S Champaign, 6 (UI); [41q] 2 mi S UI campus, 1 (UI); [41r] 3 mi S Champaign, 1 (UI); [41s] 4½ mi SW Urbana, 1 (UI); [42a] Brownfield Woods [3 mi NE Urbana], 4 (UI); [42b] 4½ mi NE [3 mi E, 1¼ mi N] Urbana, Phillips Tract, 3 (UI); [42c] Trelease Woods, 3 mi E, 1 mi N Urbana, 1 (UI); [42d] 5 mi E Champaign, 2 (UI); [42e] 2 mi E Urbana, 2 (UI); [42f] 3 mi E Urbana, Mayview Prairie, 2 (UI); [42g] 4 mi E Urbana, Mayview Prairie, 3 (UI); [42h] 5 mi E Urbana, Mayview, 8 (UI); [42i] Mayview Prairie, 4 (UI); [42j] Myra [=Mira], 1 (UI); [42k] Urbana Twp. Wildlife Area, 2½ mi E, 2½ mi S Urbana, 18 (UI); [43] 7 mi SE Philo, 2 (UI). **Vermilion Co.:** [44] 1 mi W Higginsville, 14 (UI); [45] 1 mi NE Muncie, 1 (UI). **Pike Co.:** [46] Pittsfield, 3 (UI). **Jersey Co.:** [47] Riehl Station [may be Madison Co.], 1 (US). **Macoupin Co.:** [48] 3 mi NE Beaver Dam State Park, 1 (UI). **Christian Co.:** [49] 6 mi N Morrisonville, 1 (UI). **Cumberland Co.:** [50] Neoga, 1 (UI). **Bond Co.:** [52] ½ mi E Reno, 1 (UI). **Fayette Co.:** [53a] 2 mi NE Vandalia, 1 (UI); [53b] 1 mi NW Vandalia, 2 (UI); [53c] 1 mi W Vandalia, 1 (UI). **Effingham Co.:** [54] T8N, R7E, Sec. 32, 2 (UI). **Jasper Co.:** [55] 3 mi NE Newton, Sam Parr State Park, 1 (UI); [56] Ste. Marie, 1 (UI). **Wayne Co.:** [58] 3 mi S, 3 mi E Sims, 1 (UI). **Richland Co.:** [59] Parkersburg, 4 (US). **Perry Co.:** [60] Pyatts Striplands, 2 (SRL). **Franklin Co.:** [61] 4 mi S Benton, 1 (UI). [62] ½ mi S Thompsonville, 1 (UI). **Saline Co.:** [63] 1 mi E Raleigh, 1 (UI). **Gallatin Co.:** [64] 3 mi SE Equality, 1 (UI). **Union Co.:** [65] 4 mi NW Cobden, 1 (SRL); [66] Pine Hills,

near Wolf Lake, 1 (UI); [67] 3 mi S, 1 mi E Ware, 1 (UI). **Johnson Co.:** [68] Reevesville, 3 (FM). **Pope Co.:** [69a] 1½ mi S Glendale, 21 (UI); [69b] 2½ mi S, ½ mi E Glendale, 1 (UI); [69c] Dixon Springs, Lake Glendale, 1 (UI); [69d] 2 mi WSW Dixon Springs, 1 (UI). **Alexander Co.:** [70] McClure, 1 (US); [71d] Olive Branch, 6 (FM), 1 (US); [71c] 2¼ mi NW Miller City, 2 (UI).

Additional records. **Lake Co.:** [4b] Illinois Dunes State Park, 11 (FS). **Kane Co.:** [11] 2 mi W Sugar Grove, 1 (UM). **Cook Co.:** [12a] West Northfield, 1 (UM). **Piatt Co.:** [40b] Allerton Park, 5 mi W, 2½ mi S Monticello, 1 (FM). **Champaign Co.:** [41i] Urbana, 1 (UM). **Edgar Co.:** [51] Kansas, (Necker and Hatfield, 1941:52). **Marion Co.:** [57] Salem, (Necker and Hatfield, 1941:52). **Jackson Co.:** [65] Carbondale, 1 (FS). **Alexander Co.:** [71a] 2 mi NE Olive Branch, 1 (FS).

Peromyscus leucopus, White-footed mouse

Range. Throughout the state; found in nearly every habitat.

Diagnosis. A medium-sized species of *Peromyscus* in which the tail is longer than the head-body, hind foot in subadults and adults between 18 and 22 mm (if accurately measured), tail length usually between 70 and 85 mm, skull of medium length with a toothrow length (measured at the crown) between 3.3 and 3.7 mm; product of greatest length of skull by crown length of maxillary toothrow usually between 82.0 and 97.8; lower molars usually without a mesolophid or entolophulid (*see* Fig. 8.88).

Color. Dorsum, in adults, dark reddish brown usually with a band of darker hair along midline, sides usually ochraceous with less mixture of dark hairs, upper half of tail about same color as back, underparts whitish with considerable grayish coloration showing, underside of tail slightly darker than venter. Juveniles lead gray in color with some whitish on venter; older juveniles may have reddish brown on sides.

Chromosomes. 2N = 48; usually with 6 pairs of large metacentrics, 2 to 13 pairs of acrocentrics, and the remainder medium to small-sized biarmed pairs (Hsu and Arrighi, 1968b); Singh and McMillan (1966) report 6 pairs of submetacentrics, 13 pairs of acrocentrics, and 4 pairs of metacentrics.

Comparisons. *P. leucopus* can be confused with *P. maniculatus* and *P. gossypinus.* *P. leucopus* is compared with *P. maniculatus* in the account of the latter species (p. 202). Trenchant differences are the longer hind feet (18+ mm), longer tail (70+ mm), and larger skull in *P. leucopus.*

P. leucopus differs from *P. gossypinus* in having shorter hind feet (usually 22 mm or less), lower first two molars usually without mesolophids or entolophulids; skull shorter and toothrow shorter, with the product of the greatest length multiplied by the crown length of the maxillary toothrow between 82 and 97.8 instead of 97.9 or more. Hoffmeister (1977:222) pointed out differences useful in comparing animals of comparable ages: *P. leucopus* of age group 3 or older (as defined on p. 205) and *P. gossypinus* of age group 3: hind foot, 19–21 vs. 22–25; greatest length of skull, 25.5–27.4 vs. 26.9–29.6; crown length maxillary toothrow, 3.3–3.8 vs. 3.7–4.1; total external length, mean 168 mm vs. 185 mm. For animals age group 2, hind feet 18–22 vs. 22–25; greatest length of skull, 24.9–26.5 vs. 26.1–29.9; crown length of maxillary toothrow, 3.2–3.65 vs. 3.7–4.1.

For a comparison with *Reithrodontomys megalotis, Ochrotomys nuttalli, Mus musculus, Zapus hudsonius,* and *Oryzomys palustris,* see *Peromyscus* (p. 202) or under the respective accounts.

Remarks. Peromyscus leucopus must be the most ubiquitous native species in Illinois. It is found in nearly every habitat, and sometimes invades occupied dwellings.

In Illinois, most specimens of this species have been referred to *P. l. noveboracensis;* those in southern Illinois to *P. l. leucopus.* Under *Variation,* (p. 209) reasons are given for referring all specimens in Illinois to *P. leucopus leucopus.*

Habitat

White-footed mice live in nearly every available habitat in Illinois, but they prefer wooded or brushy areas. They are found in hardwood forests, mixed woodlots, forest edge, river bottoms, swampy woodland, in caves and mine tunnels, in abandoned (and sometimes occupied) buildings, and even in grasslands, especially if there is some brush nearby. They live in woods that normally flood once a year. A railroad right-of-way through the prairie country east of Urbana was an ideal place for deer mice, but as soon as preventive spraying and cutting was stopped, thus allowing growth of shrubs and trees, white-footed mice moved in and deer mice disappeared. The same is true in strip-mined areas. With the invasion of shrubs onto the land laid barren by stripping, white-footed mice appear.

In the upland forests of Allerton Park, Piatt County, in a woods consisting primarily of white and red oaks, maple, and some hickory, fall snap-trapping commonly will produce 15 to 39 white-footed mice per acre. In southern Illinois in upland hardwoods of oaks (black, post, and blackjack), black walnut, and some yellow pine (*Pinus echinata*), Krull and Bryant (1972) found that white-footed mice made up 100 percent of their catch. Also in southern Illinois, white-footed mice are commonly found in tangles of honeysuckle and greenbrier, in habitats where one might expect golden mice. White-footed mice in southern Illinois live in the limestone bluffs, in crevices, and in rocky litter at the bottom of the bluffs, all in places where eastern woodrats are found.

Floodplain forests have their own populations of white-footed mice, independent of those in the adjacent uplands

Fig. 8.87A. White-footed mouse, *Peromyscus leucopus.* (From Hoffmeister and Mohr, 1957. Photograph by K. Maslowski)

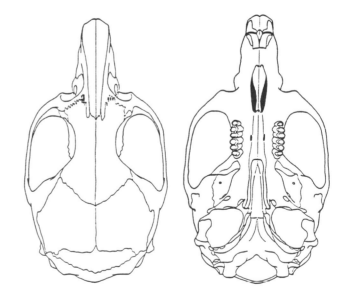

Fig. 8.87B. *Peromyscus leucopus,* dorsal and ventral views of skull; 2¼ mi NW Miller City, Alexander Co., Illinois, 59014 UI. Male, 25.4 mm greatest length.

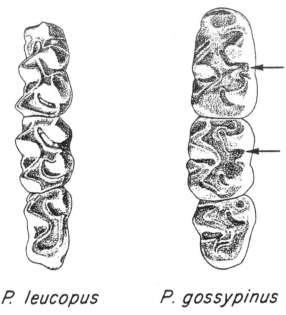

P. leucopus   P. gossypinus

Fig. 8.88. Left lower molar teeth of *Peromyscus leucopus* and *Peromyscus gossypinus*. Note the presence of entolophulids (sometimes called mesostylids) as indicated by arrows in *P. gossypinus*.

(Batzli, 1977). Here there are oaks, maple, hickory, ash, sycamore, and hackberry and an understory of nettles, poison ivy, clearweed, coneflower, and marsh buttercups.

White-footed mice are reported to move from forested areas into grasslands to forage at night. Animals caught in the grassland may give the impression that they are grassland inhabitants, but in our experience, this is not the usual or preferred habitat.

Habits

White-footed mice live mostly on or above the ground, in hollow logs, holes in stumps or higher in trees, in abandoned bird nests, or in nests placed in thickets of bushes and grasses. They less frequently occupy underground burrows as deer mice often do. White-footed mice are excellent climbers and this permits them to occupy nests well up in trees and not only along the trunk but out on the smaller branches where old bird nests are used. Bird nests are added to and domed over by these white-footed mice. Bird-boxes that were placed on the trunks of trees, three to five feet above ground, in Brownfield Woods, Champaign County, were nearly all taken over by white-footed mice. Available cavities and holes on or above the ground are also used. In the laboratory, Kantak (1983) found that when offered a choice, white-footed mice nest as high above ground as possible.

Nests are made of materials available, with the innermost part of the nest lined with finely shredded plant fibers or down. Openings are usually not discernible in an occupied nest.

We have never caught white-footed mice in traps set during the daytime for they normally are entirely nocturnal, although they will exit from a nest during the day if disturbed. It is not clear how communication occurs for they make no audible sounds.

The ability of these mice to move through trees and shrubs is indicated in part by a white-footed mouse in the flooded area of the Sangamon River bottoms, Piatt County, that moved 70 m (230 ft) through the forest canopy over the floodwaters (Batzli, 1977:23).

Populations

Numbers of white-footed mice per acre vary seasonally as well as between different habitats. Stickel (1946) found near the Patuxent River, Maryland, in bottomland forest, six to seven white-footed mice per acre by live-trapping. She points out that snap-trapping makes the number of these mice per acre appear to be more than three times as much as this figure. In a one-acre plot at Allerton Park, snap-trapping for a three-day period produced one to 39 *Peromyscus leucopus* per acre over a 23-year period (see p. 22). Batzli (1977) studied populations in the same general area and found that populations increase most during the autumn but decline in the winter, with a smaller increase in late spring. At the beginning of summer and of winter, 40 to 50 percent of the population was composed of juveniles and subadults. By the end of winter, however, the populations contained almost all adults. Batzli (1977) found that the numbers per hectare by live-trapping in upland woods in November 1972, reached 11; in November 1973, 16; in September 1972, they were at a low of 3; in September, 1973, 9. In the floodplain area of Champaign County, Blem and Blem (1975) found populations of white-footed mice in June to be about 8.6 per hectare; in October, 48.7 per hectare.

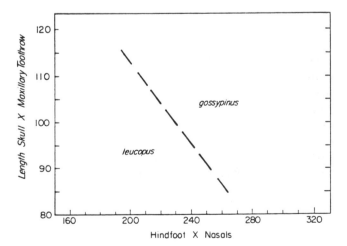

Fig. 8.89. Ratio of hind foot × nasals and skull length × crown length of maxillary toothrow, useful in separating *Peromyscus gossypinus* and *P. leucopus*. (After Hoffmeister, 1977)

They found the populations in the uplands in October to be 23.2 per hectare.

A detailed analysis of white-footed mice in forested areas of floodplains and of adjacent uplands has been made by Batzli (1977). He found that each area had separate, resident populations and the floodplain population did not depend upon recruitment from the uplands. During times of flooding, the white-footed mice moved into the trees but not out of the floodplain. The density of mice in the floodplains lags only slightly behind that of the uplands. Batzli (1977:28) summarized the problems of whitefooted mice on the floodplains by stating that

> flooding influences the resources available to white-footed mice in several ways: (1) during a flood the forest floor is not available for foraging or nesting; (2) floods wash away organic material, rearrange it into scattered piles on the forest floor and deposit silt which covers it, and (3) flooding causes dramatic differences in the flora and, therefore, seed production, compared to that found on the upland. Furthermore, flooding on the Sangamon floodplain appeared to be unpredictable; it occurred at any time of the year and at different times in different years. Thus, the floodplain appeared to be a more severe and less predictable habitat for mice than upland, and yet *Peromyscus* was more productive there than on the upland.

Food

White-footed mice are primarily seed-eaters but are opportunistic and may feed extensively on insects and other animal matter, as well as green vegetation. The diet, by necessity, varies with the availability of food items.

An analysis of 67 stomachs of mice from Piatt County was made by Batzli (1977). In spring and autumn, the major part of the diet was seeds; in summer and winter, arthropods were more important and, together with seeds, made up the bulk of the diet. Batzli found that over 90 percent of the stomachs of these mice contained seeds and arthropods, no matter when or where the samples were taken. Foods most commonly consumed were the seeds of oaks and hickories, beetles, moth larvae, and spiders. Mumford and Whitaker (1982) in Indiana found that white-footed mice fed extensively on cockleburs when available and the same was true for beechnuts and seeds of black cherry and ash. They were able to store these items. They do not make extensive use of seeds from cultivated fields, such as corn or wheat. Mumford and Whitaker (1982) give a long list of foods consumed by mice in Indiana, including foods eaten in different habitats and at different times of the year.

Bird nests that the mice have not modified for their own nesting purposes may be used as feeding platforms. In southern Illinois, golden mice may use these feeding platforms also.

Reproduction

In our collection, 59 specimens of white-footed mice taken in Illinois are recorded as containing embryos and these pregnant females were captured in every month except January, February, and July. In April, 31 females were pregnant, and this was 52 percent of the females preserved in our collection for that month. In September, 18 percent, and in May and October, 8.4 percent of the females were pregnant. In the other five months, only five percent or less of the females had embryos in each month. In March, one specimen was pregnant and three were lactating out of a total of five females. Some mice collected the last week of January appear to be about eight weeks old and were probably born in early December. Some specimens collected in September may have been born in July. Thus it appears that white-footed mice may be born in each month of the year in Illinois, but there is no proof for January and early February, and only speculation about July. In 1976, Hansen (1977) found individuals breeding in mid or late February in Champaign County and correlated this with the mild February weather that year.

The number of embryos in females in our collection had a mean of 4.25 (2–6). The gestation period is 21 to 23 days, but may be extended to more than 30 days. Young are hairless and pink at birth. The eyes open in about two weeks and the young are weaned at between three and four weeks of age. Before the young are weaned, they hang tightly to the mother's teats and, while so attached, are often dragged from place to place by the mother if she happens to be frightened from the nest.

Variation

Two subspecies of *Peromyscus leucopus* have been ascribed to Illinois: *P. l. leucopus* (type locality the pine barrens of Kentucky) from the southern part of the state and *P. l. noveboracensis* (type locality New York) from the central and northern parts of the state. It was thought by many workers that *P. l. leucopus* was a shorter-tailed, slightly smaller subspecies than *P. l. noveboracensis*. The boundaries between the two subspecies were even more indefinite than the characters separating the two.

For a better understanding of the variation in Illinois and its relationship to the two subspecies, 276 adults from Illinois, 17 specimens from western Kentucky (*P. l. leucopus*), and 15 from New York, Connecticut, Massachusetts, and Vermont (*P. l. noveboracensis*) were analyzed. Three external measurements and seven cranial measurements were used (Table 8.21). The Illinois specimens were placed in 15 samples, each with 10 to 39 individuals, representing geographical areas throughout the state. These 15 samples in Illinois are all listed in

Table 8.21. Means (in mm) and one standard deviation of 17 samples of *Peromyscus leucopus* for selected external and cranial measurements. Locality numbers refer to the Illinois map of *P. leucopus* with the locality numbers for each sample.

Locality	Locality Nos.	N	Head-body length	Tail length	Hind foot length	Greatest length	Post-palatal l.	Crown l. maxillary toothrow
New York & vicinity		15	96.07 6.98	76.80 4.68	21.33 0.62	26.18 0.65	9.54 0.30	3.47 0.08
Illinois:								
Cook	22, 23, 25-31, 42-44	16	91.94 7.39	74.63 5.55	20.25 1.06	26.11 0.59	9.37 0.33	3.39 0.13
Carroll	1-5, 12-14, 34	15	96.93 7.41	78.27 5.36	20.47 1.25	26.22 0.63	9.55 0.41	3.47 0.12
Grundy	36-38, 40, 41, 45, 46	15	98.53 4.42	75.93 4.13	22.20 0.94	26.29 0.54	9.54 0.37	3.53 0.09
Pike	48, 68-70, 91-96	23	95.43 5.19	75.26 5.62	21.48 0.90	26.56 0.81	9.68 0.37	3.54 0.12
Peoria	51-62, 71, 72	14	96.86 7.58	77.64 6.85	20.43 1.16	26.45 0.57	9.56 0.43	3.54 0.12
Piatt	64-67, 75-80	12	93.00 5.03	79.25 5.72	21.33 0.78	26.37 0.59	9.48 0.33	3.46 0.33
Champaign	81-83	22	92.36 5.87	80.14 6.84	20.82 1.14	26.06 0.69	9.45 0.40	3.40 0.14
Vermilion	85-90	14	95.29 5.80	81.50 4.29	20.29 0.61	26.24 0.51	9.47 0.23	3.38 0.17
Madison	2, 3, 14	16	96.81 4.17	80.81 5.68	20.69 0.70	26.36 0.56	9.48 0.26	3.48 0.11
Fayette	9-11, 19-23	10	92.70 4.79	74.90 4.01	20.20 0.92	25.73 0.67	9.21 0.36	3.39 0.11
Williamson	25, 29-35, 37-47	21	89.52 6.04	74.48 5.85	20.10 0.89	25.91 0.59	9.31 0.39	3.45 0.11
Union	48-50	17	92.18 6.63	73.65 4.94	19.76 1.30	25.99 0.68	9.36 0.44	3.47 0.13
Alexander	62-65	39	90.44 6.43	72.79 6.63	20.10 1.07	26.09 0.63	9.26 0.58	3.52 0.14
Johnson	51-54	20	91.45 5.80	72.65 4.26	20.30 0.86	25.79 0.64	9.27 0.40	3.51 0.12
Pope	56-60	22	91.00 5.67	73.73 4.51	21.27 0.77	25.69 0.68	9.32 0.36	3.47 0.13
Kentucky, western		17	95.24 3.96	72.00 5.61	19.65 0.93	25.72 0.71	9.24 0.45	3.35 0.11

Table 8.21 and are arranged, as far as possible, in a north to south sequence.

Specimens comprising these samples were compared in a canonical variate analysis to each other and to the population from western Kentucky and from northeastern United States by Victor Diersing. The sample labeled as "Grundy County" does not fit in well with the others because the measurement of the hind foot appears out of line, and nearly all of the specimens were measured by one collector.

In the canonical analysis, all geographically adjacent samples in Illinois have overlapping ellipses at the one standard deviation level (except for the Grundy County population). The ellipse of the Kentucky population (*P. l. leucopus*) overlaps the ellipses of 10 of the Illinois samples, including two that are the northernmost in Illinois (Cook and Carroll counties). The ellipse of the sample from Pope County does not overlap that of Kentucky. The ellipse of the sample from northeastern United States (*P. l. noveboracensis*) overlaps the ellipse of all of the 15 Illinois samples at the one standard deviation level.

The series from Kentucky (*P. l. leucopus*) and northeastern United States (*P. l. noveborancensis*) are separated at the one standard deviation level but would overlap at approximately the 69 percent level.

All of this overlap suggests that the populations in Illinois are all sufficiently similar to be of a single subspecies and they are like both *P. l. leucopus* and *P. l. noveboracensis*. Furthermore, the subspecies *leucopus* and *noveboracensis* when compared, one with the other, are

so much alike that they could well be considered a single subspecies. There is slight clinal variation from the northeastern United States population through northern to southern populations in Illinois, to Kentucky (Table 8.21). When individual populations are compared from Illinois, as the population from Champaign-Urbana with that from Pope County, there are significant differences (T. 8.21). In a clinal analysis, however, it would be difficult to determine where there was a break in the variation.

I would interpret the data to indicate that there is only one subspecies in Illinois and regard this as *Peromyscus leucopus leucopus*. Furthermore, I am not certain that *Peromyscus leucopus noveboracensis* is a valid subspecies; it may be inseparable from *P. l. leucopus*. In any event, all populations in Illinois are here referred to *P. l. leucopus* and populations in adjacent states should be reexamined to determine their subspecific status.

Peromyscus leucopus leucopus (Rafinesque)

1818. *Musculus leucopus* Rafinesque, Amer. Month. Mag., 3:446. Type locality, pine barrens of Kentucky.
1895. *Peromyscus leucopus*, Thomas, Ann. Mag. Nat. Hist., ser. 6:15.

Range. Throughout the state; found in nearly every habitat.

Diagnosis and Comparisons. A subspecies of medium-size, tail averaging 75 to 90 percent of the head-body length, hind foot usually 18 to 22 mm, skull medium to large. For a comparison with *P. l. noveboracensis*, see account above under *Variation* (p. 209).

Zygomatic breadth	Braincase breadth	Bullae breadth	Skull depth	Tail-body %
13.49 0.33	11.38 0.25	8.29 0.28	9.38 0.21	80
13.43 0.37	11.39 0.23	8.37 0.21	9.35 0.24	81
13.48 0.40	11.45 0.25	8.28 0.25	9.37 0.23	81
13.67 0.38	11.48 0.28	8.37 0.25	9.45 0.32	77
13.83 0.48	11.60 0.26	8.53 0.31	9.57 0.25	79
13.74 0.39	11.45 0.23	8.48 0.33	9.52 0.21	80
13.59 0.34	11.51 0.29	8.42 0.33	9.44 0.33	85
13.55 0.40	11.35 0.40	8.30 0.23	9.35 0.25	87
13.35 0.19	11.47 0.27	8.26 0.20	9.46 0.25	86
13.58 0.39	11.46 0.25	8.23 0.31	9.45 0.20	83
13.35 0.46	11.37 0.45	8.18 0.31	9.30 0.24	81
13.36 0.38	11.48 0.32	8.26 0.29	9.40 0.33	83
13.48 0.46	11.72 0.32	8.16 0.34	9.52 0.24	80
13.42 0.35	11.62 0.28	8.35 0.30	9.44 0.27	80
13.50 0.41	11.59 0.41	8.36 0.24	9.42 0.25	79
10.07 0.07	11.44 0.34	0.00 0.00	9.57 0.10	81
13.37 0.43	11.26 0.45	8.16 0.29	9.17 0.27	76

Records of occurrence. SPECIMENS EXAMINED, 1,417.
Jo Daviess Co.: [1a] 3½ mi S, 2 mi E Apple River, 8 (UI); [1b] Apple River Canyon State Park, 5 mi SW Warren, 2 (UI); [2] near Galena, 9 (FM). **Stephenson Co.**: [3a] 2 mi N Rock Grove, 2 (UI); [3b] 2 mi NE Rock Grove, 2 (UI); [3c] Rock Run Creek, 1 mi W Davis, 6 (UI); [3d] Rock Run Creek, 1½ mi SW Davis, 1 (UI); [4a] 3 mi W Freeport, 5 (UI); [4b] ½ mi SW Freeport, 2 (UI). **Winnebago Co.**: [5a] 1 mi S, ½ mi E Rockton, 7 (UI); [5b] 2 mi E Roscoe, 2 (UI); [5c] Kilbuck Park, 10 mi N Rockford, 1 (UI). **McHenry Co.**: [7] 2 mi E Union, 2 (UI). **Lake Co.**: [8a] Camp Logan, 7 (FM); [9a] Fox Lake, 31 (FM); [9b] Pistakee Bay, 8 (FM); [9c] Volo Bog Nature Preserve, T45N, R9E, Sec. 28, 2 (ISM); [10a] 1 mi N Lake Zurich, 2 (NIU); [10b] Lake Zurich, 2 (UI); [11a] Highland Park, 2 (FM); [11b] Deerfield, 1 (FM). **Carroll Co.**: [12] Mississippi Palisades State Park, 1 (FM), 1 (UI), 2 (NIU); [13a] ½ mi W Mt. Carroll, 1 (UI); [13b] Mt. Carroll, 2 (UI); [13c] 2 mi S, 2 mi E Mt. Carroll, 1 (UI). **Whiteside Co.**: [14a] 5 mi W Erie, 3 (UI); [14b] ¼ mi W Erie, 3 (NIU); [14c] 2 mi S Erie, 2 (NIU). **Ogle Co.**: [15] Loredo Taft campus, 3 mi N Oregon, 5 (NIU); [16] White Pines State Park, 3 (UI). **De Kalb Co.**: [17a] ½ mi N Rt 72 on Glidden Rd., 1 (NIU); [17b] ¼ mi NE Genoa, 2 (UI); [18a] 6 mi N De Kalb, Wilkerson's Marsh, 1 (NIU); [18b] 1 mi N Rt 64 on Glidden Rd., 1 (NIU); [18c] 1 mi NW Jct. Rt 64 and Glidden Rd., 9 (NIU); [18d] 5.7 mi N De Kalb, 5 mi W Sycamore, 15 (NIU); [18e] ½ mi E Glidden Rd. on Rt 64, 1 (NIU); [18f] Rt 64 and Kishwaukee River, 1 (NIU); [18g] 2 mi N De Kalb, 1 (NIU); [18h] ¼ mi N De Kalb, 1 (NIU); [18i] Kishwaukee River S of Lincoln Hwy., 1 (NIU); [18j] De Kalb, 10 (NIU); [18k] ¼ mi S De Kalb, 1 (NIU); [18l] De Kalb Twp., 1 (NIU); [19a] Malta Twp., Sec. 19, 1 (NIU); [19b] De Kalb Twp., Sec. 19, 1 (NIU); [19c] 2.5 mi W De Kalb, 0.4 mi S Rt 38, 3 (NIU); no specific locality [not plotted], 1 (NIU). **Kane Co.**: [20] 7.3 mi W, 4.8 mi N Elgin, 3 (UI); [21] ⅛ mi W Virgil, 1 (NIU); [22a] near St. Charles, 1 (ISM); [22b] Wheeler Park, 4 (UI); [23] 2 mi W, 1 mi N Aurora, 2 (UI). **Cook Co.**: [25a] Des Plaines River, 4 mi NE [=N] Des Plaines, 3 (UI); [25b] West Northfield, 2 (US); [25c] 3 mi N Des Plaines, Dam No. 2, 3 (UI); [25d] 1 mi E Golf, 1 (UI); [25e] Rt 58, 5 mi W Jct. Rt 58 and Rt 42A, 1 (UI); [25f] Des Plaines, 3 (UI); [25g] 1 mi W Park Ridge, 2 (UI); [25h] ½ mi W Park Ridge, 2 (UI); [25i] ¼ W Park Ridge, 3 (UI); [26a] River Forest, Thatcher Woods, 2 (UI); [26b] Riverside, Forest Preserve, 1 (UI); [26c] Hollywood [=Brookfield], Forest Preserve, 1 (UI); [26d] Lyons, 1 (UI); [27a] Hodgkins, Sun Meadow Forest Preserve, 2 (UI); [27b] 1⅛ mi E Rt 45, ¼ mi S Rt 55, 1 (UI); [27c] ½ mi NE Jct. Rt 45 and Rt 4A, 1 (UI); [27d] ½ mi W Hickory Hills, 1 (UI); [27e] ¼ mi E Hickory Hills, 1 (UI); [27f] 95th St. and Willow Springs Rd. [=1 mi S Willow Springs], 1 (UI); [27g] Maple Lake, 1 (FM); [29] Chicago Heights, Thorn Creek, Wilson Woods, 1 (UI); Sokol Camp, Forest Preserve [location?], 1 (UI). **Du Page Co.**: [30] Wood Dale, 4 (NIU); [31a] 2 mi W Lombard, 1 (UI); [31b] Lombard, 3 (UI); [31c] 3 mi S Villa Park, 1 (UI); [31d] 1 mi W Lisle, 7 (UI); [31e] Lisle, 2 (UI); [31f] Downers Grove, 2 (FM), 2 (UI). **Rock Island Co.**: [32 Loud Thunder Forest Preserve, 1 (NIU); [33] 1½ mi E Moline, 1 (UI). **Henry Co.**: [34a] 5 mi E Colona, 3 (UI); [34b] 9 mi N, 6 mi W Cambridge, 6 (KU). **Bureau Co.**: [35a] 3 mi N Bureau, 1 (UI); [35b] 3 mi NW Bureau, 1 (UI). **La Salle Co.**: [36a] Blackball Mine, 1¾ mi W Utica, 2 (UI); [36b] Starved Rock State Park, 2 mi SE Utica, 1 (UI); [37] N Bluff, Ottawa, 3 (UI). **Kendall Co.**: [39] Yorkville, 2 (UI). **Grundy Co.**: [40a] 6 mi W Morris, 14 (UI); [40b] Morris, 9 (UI); [40c] 6 mi W, ½ mi S Morris, 7 (UI); [41] Goose Lake Prairie State Park, 1 (NIU), 3 (ISU), 8 (UI). **Will Co.**: [42] O'Hara Woods, Romeoville, 1 (UI); [43] Plainfield, 3 (NIU); [44] New Lennox, 4 (UI). **Kankakee Co.**: [45a] Aroma Park, 1 (UI); [45b] 5 mi S, ½ mi E Kankakee, 12 (FM); [45c] St. Anne, 1 (UI); [46a] 6 mi E St. Anne, 3 (UI); [46b] 9 mi E St. Anne, 1 (UI). **Henderson Co.**: [47] 1½ mi E, 6 mi N Oquawka, 2 (UI); no specific locality [not plotted], 2 (US). **Hancock Co.**: [48a] 2 mi E, 1 mi N Warsaw, 11 (UI); [48b] Warsaw 2 (US), 1 (FM). **Warren Co.**: [49a] 2 mi S Smithshire, 2 (UI); [49b] 1 mi N, ½ mi E Roseville, 1 (UI). **Fulton Co.**: [50] ½ mi W London Mills, 1 (UI); [51a] 10 mi NW Canton, 1 (UI); [51b] ½ mi N Norris, 5 (UI); [52] 1 mi W Canton, 3 (UI); [53] 9 mi E Canton, 1 (UI); [54] Duck Island, 5 (UI); [55] 6 mi W Lewistown, 1 (UI); [56] Dickson Mounds, 1 (ISM); no specific locality [not plotted], 3 (UI). **Peoria Co.**: [57] 3 mi N Dunlap, 5 (UI); [58] 10 mi N Peoria, 4 (UI); [59a] 2 mi W Edwards, 1 (UI); [59b] 1 mi NW Hanna City, 1 (UI); [59c] 12 mi W Peoria, 1 (UI); [59d] 10 mi W Peoria, 6 (UI); [59e] 2¼ mi S, 1 mi W Hanna City, 1 (UI); [59f] 2⅛ mi S, 3 mi W Hanna City, 1 (UI); [60a] 4 mi W Peoria, 4 (UI); [60b] Peoria, 6 (UI). **Tazewell Co.**: [61a] Sunnyland, 1 (UI); [61b] 1 mi N Morton, 1 (UI); [62] 7 mi E Forest City [labeled Mason Co.], 1 (ISU). **McLean Co.**: [63a] 1 mi NE Lexington, 1 (UI); [63b] 12 mi NE Normal, 1 (ISU); [64a] 2 mi N Normal, 1 (ISU); [64b] Normal, 1 (ISU); [64c] 2 mi W, 1 mi S Bloomington, 3 (UI): [65] 3½ mi N, 3 mi W Le Roy, 1 (UI); [66] 5 mi ENE Le Roy, 1 (UI); [67] Funk's Forest, 1½ mi N McLean, 3 (UI). **Adams Co.**: [68] 10 mi NE Quincy, 6 (UI); [69] Quincy, South Park, 2 (UI); [70a] 2 mi W Plainville, 1 (UI); [70b] 3¼ mi S Payson, 3 (UI). **Mason Co.**: [71a] 7 mi W, 1 mi S Forest City, 1 (UI); [71b] 3½ mi N, 2 mi E Havana, 5 (UI); [71c] 5 mi NE Havana, 3 (UI); [72] Havana, 1 (FM); [73] 13½ mi SW Havana, 4 (UI). **Cass Co.**: [74] 7½ mi SW Virginia, 3 (UI). **De Witt Co.**: [75] ½ mi S Farmer

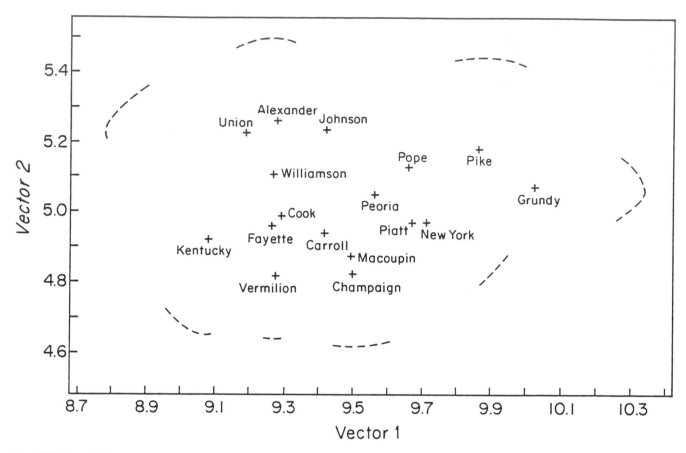

Fig. 8.90. Canonical variate analysis of 15 populations of *Peromyscus leucopus* from various counties in Illinois as indicated, one population from Kentucky (*P. l. leucopus*), and one from New England (labeled as New York and representing *P. l. noveboracensis*). Sample means are indicated by a cross; the periphery of ellipses representing one standard deviation is indicated by the broken line for peripheral samples. All ellipses for the 17 populations greatly overlap.

City, 1 (UI); [76] ½ mi S Clinton, 1 (UI). **Piatt Co.:** [77a] 3½ mi N White Heath, 1 (UI); [77b] 2 mi N White Heath, 1 (UI); [77c] 3 mi E Lodge, 4 (UI); [77d] 1¼ mi NW White Heath, 2 (UI); [77e] 1 mi NW White Heath, 10 (UI); [78] Monticello, 4 (UI); [79a] 1 mi NW Cisco, 2 (UI); [79b] 1½ mi ENE Cisco, 4 (UI); [79c] Allerton Park, 11 (UI).

Champaign Co.: [80a] ½ mi W Mahomet, 4 (UI); [80b] Mahomet, 3 (FM), 1 (UI); [80c] ½ mi E Mahomet, 4 (UI); [81a] 6 mi NE Urbana, 2 (UI); [81b] Yearsly Cemetery [4 mi N, 2½ mi E Urbana], 2 (UI); [81c] 3½ mi N Urbana, 3 (UI); [81d] Brownfield Woods [=3 mi NE Urbana], 8 (UI); [81e] 3 mi NE Urbana, 3 (UI); [81f] 2 mi N Urbana, 10 (UI); [81g] 2 mi NE Urbana, 5 (UI); [81h] Woodlawn Cemetery, Urbana, 1 (UI); [81i] Trelease Woods [=3½ mi E, 1⅓ mi N Urbana], 5 (UI); [81j] NW Champaign, along RR tracks, 1 (UI); [81k] 1⅛ mi N Urbana, 3 (UI); [81l] 1 mi N, 1 mi W Urbana, 1 (UI); [81m] Busey Woods, 1 (UI); [81n] Champaign, 4 (UI); [81o] 3 mi E Champaign, 2 (UI); [81p] ¼ mi S Champaign, 2 (UI); [81q] Urbana, 3 (FM), 24 (UI); [81r] 2 mi E Urbana, Mayview Prairie, 2 (UI); [81s] 2⅛ mi E Urbana, 1 (UI); [81t] 2½ mi E Urbana, 3 (UI); [81u] 3 mi E Urbana, Mayview Prairie, 3 (UI); [81v] 4 mi E Urbana, Mayview Prairie, 12 (UI); [81w] 4½ mi E Urbana, Mayview Prairie, 1 (UI); [81x] 5 mi E Urbana, Mayview Prairie,

3 (UI); [81y] Natural Prairie, Mayview, 1 (UI); [81z] Rt 150, near Mayview, 1 (UI); [81aa] 6 mi E Urbana, Mayview Prairie, 2 (UI); [81bb] Natural Prairie, 1 mi E Mayview, 2 (UI); [81cc] ½ mi S Urbana, 4 (UI); [81dd] 1 mi S Champaign, 7 (UI); [81ee] Cemetery, 1 mi S UI campus [Mt. Hope Cemetery], 1 (UI); [81ff] SE Champaign, along ICRR tracks [=1½ mi S Champaign], 3 (UI); [81gg] St. Mary's Cemetery [=1¾ mi S Champaign], 5 (UI); [81hh] 2 mi SE Urbana, 1 (UI); [81ii] 2 mi E, 1½ mi S Urbana, 1 (UI); [81jj] 2 mi S Champaign, 6 (UI); [81kk] 2 mi S Urbana, 3 (UI); [81ll] 2½ mi S Champaign, 4 (UI); [81mm] 3 mi SE Urbana, 1 (UI); [81nn] 2 mi S UI campus, 1 (UI); [81oo] Urbana Twp Wildlife Area, 2½ mi E, 2½ mi S Urbana, 10 (UI); [81pp] 3 mi S, 3 mi E Urbana, 8 (UI); [82] ½ mi W St. Joseph, Salt Fork River, 3 (UI); [83a] 3½ mi W Champaign, 3 (UI); [83b] 1 mi E Bondville, Kaskaskia River, 4 (UI); [83c] 4½ mi SW Urbana, 1 (UI); [83d] 1 mi S Savoy, 2 (UI); [83e] 9½ mi SW Champaign, 1 (UI); [84] 7 mi SE Philo, 2 (UI); no specific locality [not plotted], 4 (UI).

Vermilion Co.: [85] Potomac, Middle Fork Vermilion River, 3 (UI); [86] 6 mi N Danville, 1 (UI); [87a] 1 mi W Higginsville, 1 (UI); [87b] 1 mi S, 3 mi E Collison, 3 (UI); [87c] 2½ mi N, 1¾ mi E Newtown, 4 (UI); [87d] 1¼ mi W, ½ mi S Snider, 3 (UI); [87e] ½ mi S, ½ mi E Newtown, 3 (UI); [88a] 1½ mi NE

Danville, 1 (UI); [88b] ½ mi NE Danville, 1 (UI); [89a] 1 mi NE
Muncie, 2 (UI); [89b] Salt Fork, Vermilion River, 4 mi S
Oakwood, 1 (UI); [89c] 3 mi NE Fairmount, 1 (UI); [90a] 4½
mi E, 2 ¼ mi S Westville, 2 (UI); [90b] 3⅘ mi E, 2⅗ mi S
Westville, 1 (UI). **Pike Co.:** [91a] 1 mi S Griggsville, 5 (UI); [91b]
4 mi N, 1 1¼ mi E Pittsfield, 4 (UI); [91c] 3 mi N, 1 mi E
Pittsfield, 1 (UI); [92] 6 mi SW Hull [plotted 6 mi S Hull], 1
(ISM); [93a] Pittsfield, 1 (UI); [93b] 3½ mi S Pittsfield, 19 (UI);
[94] 2 mi W Nebo, 10 (UI). **Calhoun Co.:** [95] 3 mi N Hardin,
3 (UI). **Jersey Co.:** [96] 11 mi NW Grafton, 1 (ISU); [97] Riehl
Station [may be Madison Co.], 1 (US).

Macoupin Co.: [1] Virden, 8 (UI); [2a] 1½ mi NW Chesterfield,
8 (UI); [2b] 1½ mi W Chesterfield, 27 (UI); [2c] 1½ mi Sw
Chesterfield, 2 (UI); [3a] 3 mi NE Beaver Dam State Park, 9
(UI); [3b] 3 mi NE Beaver Dam State Park, 8 (UI); [3c] 1 mi N
Beaver Dam, 2 (UI); [3d] Beaver Dam Lake, 7 mi SW Carlinville,
2 (UI). **Sangamon Co.:** [4] Springfield, 1 (ISM); [5a] 3 mi W, 2
mi N Chatham, 3 (UI); [5b] Chatham, 1 (ISM); [6a] 1½ mi W
Auburn, 1 (UI); [6b] 1½ mi E Auburn, 1 (UI). **Christian Co.:** [7]
Taylorville, 1 (UI); [8] 6 mi N Morrisonville, 2 (UI). **Moultrie
Co.:** [9a] 2 mi N Sullivan, 3 (UI); [9b] Sullivan, 1 (UI), [9c] 3 mi
E Sullivan, 1 (UI). **Shelby Co.:** [10] 2 mi S Cowden, 1 (UI).
Douglas Co.: [11] 2 mi SW Camargo, Embarrass River, 5 (UI).
Edgar Co.: [12a] 1 mi E Grandview, 2 (UI); [12b] 8 mi SW
Paris, 1 (UI). **Clark Co.:** [13] 4 mi N, 8½ mi E Marshall, Clear
Creek, 8 (UI). **Madison Co.:** [14a] ¼ mi E Fosterburg, 2 (UI);
[15] 3½ mi WSW Grantfork, 1 (UI); [16] 1½ mi SE Kuhn, 1
(UI); [17] 1½ mi E Collinsville, 1 (UI). **Bond Co.:** [18] ½ mi SE
Reno, 2 (UI). **Fayette Co.:** [19a] 3 mi N Vandalia, 3 (UI); [19b]
2 mi NE Vandalia, 4 (UI); [19c] 1 mi NW Vandalia, 1 (UI); [19d]
2½ mi SW Vandalia, 3 (UI); [20] 3 mi S Brownstown, 2 (UI);
[21] 3 mi NE Pittsburgh, 3 (UI). **Effingham Co.:** [22a] T8N,
R6E, Sec. 1, 1 (UI); [22b] T8N, R7E, Sec. 32, 1 (UI). **Jasper Co.:**
[23] Sam Parr State Park, 3 mi NE Newton, 4 (UI). **Crawford
Co.:** [24] Flat Rock, 12 (CAS). **Monroe Co.:** [25a] 2½ mi N
Fountain, 4 (UI); [25b] 1 mi E, 2 mi N Fountain, 3 (UI); [25c] 1
mi E, ¼ mi N Fountain, 8 (UI). **Jefferson Co.:** [26a] 4 mi E
Ashley [labelled Washington Co.], 1 (SIC); [26b] Woodlawn,
[labelled Madison Co.], 1 (UI).

Richland Co.: [27] Olney, 2 (US); [28] Parkersburg, 8 (US).
Randolph Co.; [29] 6 mi E Redbud, 4 (UI). **Perry Co.:** [30] 6
mi NW Pinckneyville, 2 (KU); [32] 2 mi W Du Quoin, 2 (SIC).
Franklin Co. [33] 4 mi S Benton, 1 (UI); [34] ½ mi S Thomp-
sonville, 5 (UI). **Hamilton Co.:** [35a] 6 mi E McLeansboro, 7
(UI); [35b] 8 mi ESE McLeansboro, 2 (UI). **White Co.:** [36] 2 mi
S, 6 mi E Crossville, 9 (UI). **Jackson Co.:** [37] Murphysboro, 2
(SRL); [38a] Carbondale, 2 (SRL), 1 (SIC); [38b] Thompson Woods,
Carbondale, 4 (SIC); [38c] 2 mi E Boskydell, 3 (UI); [39a] 7 mi
SW Murphysboro, 1 (SRL); [39b] 10 mi SW Murphysboro, 1
(UI); [39c] 12 mi SW Murphysboro, 2 (UI); [40] 3 mi N Pomona,
1 (SRL). **Williamson Co.:** [41a] 3 mi N Johnston City, 1 (UI);
[41b] 2 mi N Marion, 1 (KU); [42] 6 mi S Marion, 3 (KU); [43]
W side Little Grassy Lake, 1 (UI). **Saline Co.:** [44a] 1 mi E
Raleigh, 1 (UI); [44b] 3 mi WNW Eldorado, 2 (UI); [45] 1.4 mi
N Harrisburg, 4 (UI). **Gallatin Co.:** [46] Shawneetown, 1 (US);
[47a] Old Salt Well, 4 mi SE Equality, 3 (UI); [47b] slough, 4⅓
mi SE Equality, 3 (UI); [47c] 3 mi N Karbers Ridge [labeled
Hardin Co.], 1 (UI). **Union Co.:** [48f] 1½ mi ESE Aldridge, 2
(SRL); [48g] 3 mi N Wolf Lake, 12 (UI); [48i] N end Wolf Lake,

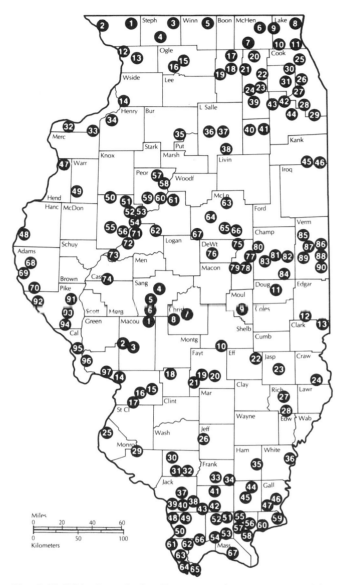

Map 8.38. White-footed mice, *Peromyscus leucopus,* occur statewide. The subspecies throughout Illinois is *P. l. leucopus.* Localities
of occurrence as numbered are referenced in *Records of occurrence.* The range of the species in the United States is shaded.

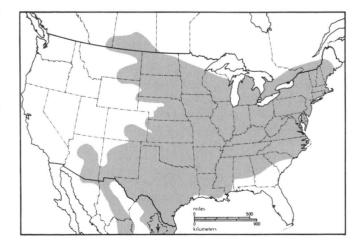

2 (UI); [48j] Wolf Lake, 4 (CAS), 1 (NIU), 1 (ISU), 8 (US); [48k] Pine Hills, near Wolf Lake, 14 (UI); [48m] 8 mi S, 3 mi W Alto Pass, Union County Tree Nursery, 4 (SIC); [49d] Alto Pass, 1 (SRL); [49e] 3 mi W Cobden, 1 (SIC); [50a] 2½ mi SW Ware, 5 (SRL); [50b] Union County Conservation Area, 1 (UI); [50c] Union County Conservation Area, S boundary, 1 (UI); [50d] 6 mi S, 2 mi E Ware, 8 (UI).

Johnson Co.: [51] Ozark, 20 (FM); [52] 7 mi N Vienna, 1 (UI); [53a] 2 mi E Vienna, 2 (UI); [53b] ⅓ mi NE Grantsburg, 10 (UI); [53c] Grantsburg, Bay Creek, 8 (UI); [53d] ¼ mi E Grantsburg, 3 (UI); [53e] ½ mi E Grantsburg, 5 (UI); [53f] Reevesville, 14 (FM), 2 (US); [54] 1 mi S Foreman, 3 (UI). **Pope Co.:** [55b] 1¾ mi NE McCormick, 1 (SRL); [56a] 3 mi E Eddyville, 1 (UI); [56b] 4 mi SE Eddyville, 9 (UI); [57a] 1 mi S Robbs, 1 (UI); [57b] 3¾ mi N Dixon Springs, 5 (UI); [57c] 1½ mi S Glendale, 2 (UI); [57d] 2½ mi S, ½ mi E Glendale, 2 (UI); [57e] Dixon Springs, Glendale Lake, 10 (UI); [57f] 2 mi S, ½ mi E Rock, 7 (UI); [57g] 2 mi S, ½ mi E Rock, 7 (UI); [58a] 3.8 mi W Golconda, 6 (UI); [58b] Golconda, 7 (UI), 4 (US), 7 (FM). **Hardin Co.:** [59] 3 mi E Lamb, 8 (UI); [60] 1 mi S Eichorn, 4 (UI). **Alexander Co.:** [61a] McClure, 3 (US); [61b] Cypress Junction [=McClure], 1 (US); [62a] 1½ mi NW Elco, 5 (UI); [62b] 3 mi W Tamms, 3 (UI); [62c] ½ mi W Tamms, 13 (UI); [62d] Tamms, 2 (SRL); [63a] ½ mi NNW Olive Branch, 5 (SRL); [63b] Olive Branch, 2 (UI), 1 (SRL), 9 (FM), 11 (US); [63c] 2¼ mi NW Miller City, 4 (UI); [63d] 2 mi NW Miller City, 7 (UI); [63e] 2½ mi S Olive Branch, 26 (UI); [63f] Horseshoe Lake, 6 (UI); [63g] 3 mi S Olive Branch, 16 (UI); [63h] SE edge Horseshoe Lake, 1 (SIC); [63i] 1½ mi NW Cache, 9 (SRL); [63j] Miller City, 4 (UI); [63k] 1½ mi E, ½ mi S Miller City, 48 (UI); [64] 5¼ mi S, 2 mi E Willard, 8 (UI); [65a] ½ mi N Cairo, 1 (ISU). **Pulaski Co.:** [66] Wetaug, 8 (CAS). **Massac Co.:** [67a] 2 mi N Metropolis, 2 (SIU); [67b] 1½ mi N Metropolis, 3 (SRL), 2 (SIC); [67c] Metropolis, 4 (CAS).

Additional records: **McHenry Co.:** [6] Wonder Lake, 1 (FS). **Lake Co.:** [8b] Illinois Dunes State Park, 4 (FS); [11a] Highland Park, 3 (FS). **Kane Co.:** [24] 2 mi W Sugar Grove, 7 (UM). **Cook Co.:** [28] Tinley Park Forest Preserve, 1 (UM). **LaSalle Co.:** [38] 4 mi N, 2 mi E Streator, 32 (UM). **Piatt Co.:** [77f] White Heath, 1 (FS). **Champaign Co.:** [81q] Urbana, 1 (UM). **Madison Co.:** [14b] Alton, 3 (UM). **Perry Co.:** [31] Pyatts Striplands Project, 1 (FS). **Jackson Co.:** [38d] Giant City State Park, 1 (FS). **Union Co.:** [48a] Government Rock, 6.6 mi WNW Alto Pass, 1 (FS); [48b] 1¾ mi NE Aldridge, 1 (FS); [48c] Aldridge, 4 (FS); [48d] 1⅓ mi E Aldridge, 1 (FS); [48e] 1¾ mi E Aldridge, 2 (FS); [48h] 2 mi S Aldridge, 2 (FS); [48j] Wolf Lake, 3 (FS); [48l] ½ mi E Wolf Lake, 3 (FS); [49a] 4 mi N Cobden, 1 (FS); [49b] 5 mi NW Cobden, 1 (FS); [49c] 3 mi N Cobden, 3 (FS); [49f] Cobden, 2 (FS); [50a] 2½ mi SW Ware, 8 (FS). **Pope Co.:** [55a] Burden Falls, 3 (FS); [55c] 2 mi SE McCormick, 2 (FS). **Alexander Co.:** [62d] Tamms, 2 (FS); [63a] ½ mi NNW Olive Branch, 2 (FS); [63i] 1½ mi NW Cache, 2 (FS); [65b] 2½ mi SE Cairo, 1 (FS).

Peromyscus gossypinus, Cotton mouse

Range. Southernmost Illinois, only in Alexander, Johnson, Pope, Pulaski, and Union counties (Map 8.39). Not known to have been captured in Illinois since 1909.

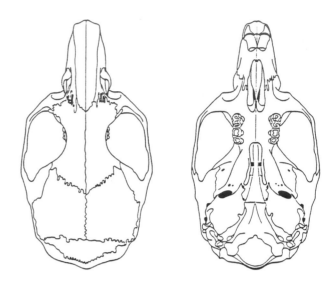

Fig. 8.91. *Peromyscus gossypinus,* dorsal and ventral views of skull; 4¼ mi ESE Tiptonville, Obion Co., Tennessee, 36965 UI. Male, 28.9 mm greatest length.

Diagnosis. A species of *Peromyscus* with a large-sized body (usually more than 100 mm in adults), hind foot usually more than 22 mm long; greatest length of the skull in adults usually more tnan 28.0 mm; crown length of maxillary toothrow usually 3.7 or more, M_1 and M_2 usually with a mesostylid and/or an entolophulid (Fig. 8.91).

Color. Dorsum brownish with a heavy admixture of black; midline darker than sides, top of tail about same color as back, venter whitish with much gray showing, underside of tail whitish, tops of feet white. Juveniles are lead- or gray-colored on dorsum. Coloration almost the same as in *P. leucopus.*

Chromosomes. 2N = 48; autosomes of five pairs of large or medium-sized biarmed, three small biarmed, and 15 acrocentrics; X a large subtelocentric; Y a small metacentric (Hsu and Arrighi, 1968b).

Comparisons. For a comparison with *P. maniculatus* (p. 202) and *P. leucopus* (p. 206) see accounts of those species. For a comparison with other cricetines, see account of the genus *Peromyscus* (p. 202).

P. leucopus is the species most readily confused with *P. gossypinus.* Fig. 8.89 shows another means of differentiating the species, and the mesolophid and entolophulid in lower molars is shown in Fig. 8.88.

Growth. Cotton mice in Florida, according to the study of Pournelle (1952), by the 30th day of age have acquired 83 percent of their adult total length and tail length, and the hind foot has reached adult length. Only 62 percent of adult weight is attained by the 30th day.

Remarks. Early collectors caught specimens of *P. gossypinus* in southern Illinonis in 1906, 1907, and 1909. Subsequent collecting in southern Illinois, at or near the same places, has produced no known *P. gossypinus.* Some may have been taken and not preserved; others may be collections but unknown to us.

In 1906, Edward Heller visited Olive Branch, Alexander County, and on November 26 collected one *P. gossypinus,* one *P. maniculatus,* and two *P. leucopus.* In 1907, Heller collected at Golconda, Pope County, and on April 12–13 took two *P. gossypinus* and eight *P. leucopus.* On April 20–22, he collected seven *P. gossypinus* and 15 *P. leucopus* at Ozark, Johnson County.

In 1909, Arthur H. Howell collected in parts of Illinois. On May 16, at Olive Branch he took *P. gossypinus, P. leucopus,* and *Blarina carolinensis.* On May 25, he collected at Wolf Lake, Union County, and obtained *P. gossypinus.* On June 20–21, at Golconda, Pope County, he caught both *P. gossypinus* and *P. leucopus.*

What has happened to *P. gossypinus* in southern Illinois remains a mystery. Ample search within the last 30 years has been made specifically for these mice. Trapping has been done in habitat that should be suitable for the species but no specimens of *P. gossypinus* have been found. Seemingly there is still suitable habitat for the species.

Habitat

Nothing is known about the ecology and life history of cotton mice in Illinois. In Kentucky, these mice live along the wooded streambanks, swampy woods, and brushland (Barbour and Davis, 1974). Nests are located on higher ground, often above ground level and in hollow stumps or trees.

In western Tennessee, these mice occupy much the same habitat as white-footed mice, but—in particular—swampy woodlands (Goodpaster and Hoffmeister, 1952). Nests were found both in and under fallen logs, but in other sites where cotton mice were abundant (34 caught in 70 traps), no nests were found under logs.

Cotton mice sometimes live on rocky bluffs, often in areas of annual flooding, and infrequently in upland timber.

Habits

Near Reelfoot Lake, western Tennessee, Goodpaster and Hoffmeister (1952) found cotton mice nesting beneath the moss on floating logs in the sloughs. When these nests were disturbed, the mice readily dived into the water and swam away. Pournelle (1950) found that these mice could swim almost constantly for an hour when placed in a jar of water.

Cotton mice are good climbers and do not hesitate to climb. Pournelle (1950) released an animal eight feet up in a tree and it immediately climbed to the top, going around the trunk in a circular fashion. When released from traps they will sometimes take refuge in bushes and small trees. Several were taken in an abandoned gray squirrel nest some 20 feet up in an oak (Wolfe and

Map 8.39. Known records of occurrence of cotton mice, *Peromyscus gossypinus,* in southern Illinois as numbered are referenced in *Records of occurrence.* The subspecies is *P. g. megacephalus.* The range of the species in the United States is shaded.

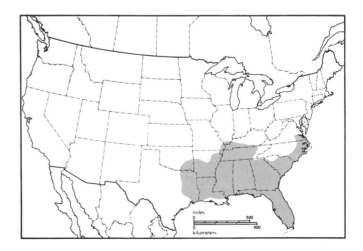

Table 8.22. External and cranial measurements of *Oryzomys, Reithrodontomys, Peromyscus,* and *Ochrotomys* in Illinois. Mean, minimum-maximum, and one standard deviation are given. Measurements (in mm) are given for adult and subadult *Peromyscus gossypinus.* If there are only two measurements available, both are given, one below the other. Superscripts indicate sample less than N.

Species, subspecies, and locality	N	Total length	Tail length	Body length	Hind foot length	Ear length	Greatest length
Oryzomys palustris palustris Alexander and Jackson cos.	8	243.57[7] 225-270 13.91	118.14[7] 112-133 7.38	123.63 110-137 10.82	29.0 25-31 1.93	16.29[7] 14-18 1.50	30.58 28.9-33.2 1.44
Reithrodontomys megalotis dychei Grundy, Champaign, Vermilion cos.	13	131.5 121-142 6.70	60.9 54-69 4.60	70.6 65-79 4.07	16.4 14-18 1.26	12.3 10-14 1.38	20.48 19.7-21.25 0.47
Peromyscus maniculatus bairdii Champaign Co.	19	134.1 115-147 11.56	53.7 42-65 5.96	80.0 69-95 7.16	16.6 15-19 3.09	13.4 11-15 1.34	23.20 22.0-24.1 0.58
S. Ill.: Alexander, Pope, Union cos.	8	137.5 123-167 13.20	53.5 48-70 7.69	84.0 74-97 7.63	18.25 17-20 0.89	13.4 12-16 1.51	23.19 22.05-23.9 0.54
Peromyscus leucopus leucopus Champaign-Urbana	19	173.3 158-191 8.52	78.5 66-95 7.51	94.7 84-103 4.86	20.3 18-22 1.23	15.9 13-19 1.62	26.30 25.2-28.0 0.75
Pope Co.	17	163.1 150-176 8.81	73.4 64-81 5.88	89.6 80-100 5.17	21.0 20-22 0.71	15.6 14-17 0.94	25.69 24.75-26.7 0.59
Peromyscus gossypinus megacephalus Alexander, Johnson, Pope cos.	4 ad	191.5 187-196 3.87	83.5 78-88 4.43	108.0 104-111 2.94	23.1 22-24 0.85	17.5 19	29.73 29.3-30.4 0.59
" " "	4 subad	179.0 172-188 7.79	77,8 73-83 4.11	101.3 95-106 5.11	24.1 24-24.5 0.25	18.5 18-19 0.50	28.58 28.05-28.9 0.46
Ochrotomys nuttalli lisae Johnson, Pope, Union cos.	11	160.7 152-179 8.08	74.5 68-81 3.45	86.3 80.98 6.17	18.0 15-20 1.48	16.1 15-19 1.37	25.56 24.4-26.6 0.60

Linzey, 1977). In an outdoor laboratory setting, Taylor and McCarley (1963) found that cotton mice showed a 93 percent preference for elevated nest sites. When cotton mice were competing with white-footed mice for the elevated nests, cotton mice more frequently (75%) were in the ground-level nests.

Food

Cotton mice are omnivorous and their diet reflects their living area. At Reelfoot Lake, Calhoun (1941) found these mice feeding extensively on the readily available slug *Derocerus agreste;* analysis showed that 68 percent of their food was animal matter. Other such material included beetles, spiders, and moth larvae. The plant material was primarily spores of Endogone. Pournelle (1950) found that Florida cotton mice while in captivity ate grasshoppers, roaches, spiders, meat, bread, and crackers.

Reproduction

Studies on reproduction and postnatal development are few, but Pournelle (1952) has done a detailed study of these mice in Florida. The gestation period is about 23 days in non-lactating females. Litter size averaged 3.7 (1–7). The embryo count in 32 females was 3.9 (2–6). In the southern states, cotton mice are thought to breed throughout the year. At birth the young are hairless but are well covered with hair by the 10th day. Eyes open around two weeks of age. The young remain firmly attached to the mother's teats during much of the pre-weaning period. Young in the wild are weaned probably between the third and fourth weeks. They can be removed from the mother at this age in the laboratory. Animals are sexually mature probably around 70 days of age.

Variation

The subspecies ascribed to the central United States has long been regarded as *P. g. megacephalus* and the

Basilar length	Braincase breadth	Inter-orbital breadth	Nasal length	Shelf bony palate	Length incisive foramen	Length diastema	Post-palatal length	Alv. l. maxillary toothrow	Crown l. maxillary toothrow
23.75[6]	12.53	4.89	12.08	5.51	6.59	7.69[6]	10.25	4.73[6]	
22.9-25.2	12.0-12.8	4.65-5.25	11.0-14.05	5.2-6.05	5.4-7.35	7.2-8.15	9.45-11.25	4.4-5.1	
0.87	0.28	0.22	0.90	0.32	0.64	0.37	0.63	0.26	
15.22	9.77	3.10	7.85	3.34	4.38	4.82	6.88	3.12	
14.8-15.7	9.5-10.1	2.95-3.25	7.6-8.3	3.15-3.45	4.2-4.7	4.6-5.1	6.5-7.2	3.0-3.2	
0.29	0.21	0.10	0.24	0.07	0.14	0.16	0.26	0.06	
18.02	10.75	3.73	9.12	3.60	4.77	6.13	8.33	3.33	3.05
16.85-18.85	10.0-11.2	3.4-3.9	8.45-9.8	3.05-4.2	4.35-5.15	5.7-6.5	7.6-8.9	3.1-3.5	2.9-3.3
0.58	0.28	0.13	0.41	0.27	0.23	0.23	0.33	0.13	0.14
17.9	10.77	3.76	8.99	3.77	4.59	5.93	8.29	3.39	3.07
17.0-18.5	10.4-11.1	3.5-4.05	8.1-9.9	3.2-4.2	4.05-4.8	5.5-6.3	7.8-8.6	3.3-3.5	3.0-3.15
0.50	0.23	0.18	0.66	0.33	0.25	0.29	0.32	0.06	0.06
20.1	11.73	4.18	9.96	4.21	5.01	6.97	9.43	3.70	3.45
19.0-21.8	11.3-12.7	3.9-4.4	9.3-10.55	3.7-4.6	5.0-5.7	6.5-7.6	8.8-10.3	3.5-4.05	3.1-3.7
0.63	0.38	0.16	0.40	0.26	0.18	0.23	0.37	0.15	0.15
19.38	11.88	4.11	9.71	4.14	5.06	6.73	9.06	3.69	3.47
18.3-20.45	11.3-12.3	3.85-4.3	9.0-10.5	3.7-4.55	4.7-5.55	6.3-7.2	8.3-9.7	3.40-3.9	3.2-3.8
0.66	0.31	0.13	0.40	0.21	0.21	0.25	0.46	0.16	0.16
22.8[1]	12.70	4.50	11.83	4.6[1]	6.25	8.0	—	—	3.8
	12.35-13.1	4.5-4.5	11.15-12.35		6.15	7.4			3.85
	0.38	0.0	0.57						
21.6[1]	12.47	4.39	11.33	4.8[1]	5.65[1]	7.5[1]	9.95[1]	4.5[1]	3.8
	12.2-12.7	4.3-4.55	10.65-11.85						3.7-4.0
	0.25	0.11	0.50						0.17
19.64	11.6	4.11	9.41	3.75	5.12	6.92	9.11	3.9	3.7
18.4-20.3	11.25-12.0	3.95-4.3	8.9-10.3	3.5-3.9	4.7-5.7	6.4-7.3	8.45-9.5	3.65-4.1	3.5-3.8
0.55	0.27	0.10	0.37	0.12	0.26	0.28	0.33	0.14	0.13

named population from Reelfoot Lake, northwestern Tennessee (*Peromyscus gossypinus mississippiensis*, type locality Samburg, Obion Co., Tennessee) regarded as a synonym.

Peromyscus gossypinus megacephalus (Rhoads)

1894. *Sitomys megacephalus* Rhoads, Proc. Acad. Nat. Sci. Phila., 46:254. Type from Woodville, Jackson Co., Alabama.

1909. *Peromyscus gossypinus megacephalus*, Osgood, N. Amer. Fauna, 28:138.

Range. As given for the species (p. 214 and Map 8.39).

Diagnosis and Comparison. A large subspecies of *P. gossypinus* that differs from adjoining subspecies in slightly paler coloration and larger size.

Records of occurrence. SPECIMENS EXAMINED, 16. **Union Co.:** [1] Wolf Lake, 1 (US). **Johnson Co.:** [2] Ozark, 7 (FM). **Pope Co.:** [3] Golconda, 3 (US), 2 (FM). **Alexander Co.:** [4] Olive Branch, 2 (US), 1 (FM).

Additional records. **Pulaski Co.:** [5] Wetaug, (Necker and Hatfield, 1941:53).

Ochrotomys, Golden mouse

Diagnosis. A cricetine rodent of the proportions of a medium-sized peromyscus (long regarded as a subgenus of *Peromyscus*), color of dorsum and sides reddish or golden in color, venter creamy with an ochraceous wash, juveniles with reddish color of upper parts also; tail equal to or slightly longer than head-body; hind feet with seven plantar tubercles, but one rudimentary and adjacent to large tubercles at base of fifth digit; anterior edge of zygomatic plate convex, molars with well-developed lophs and styles (Fig. 8.88); posterior palatine foramina are nearer to interpterygoid fossa than to posterior edge of anterior palatine foramina; baculum small and short in proportion to the width of the base, and capped with a cartilaginous cone; glans penis urn-shaped and with large spines. Some other characters are the presence of a

Map 8.40. Golden mice, *Ochrotomys nuttalli*, in southern Illinois as numbered are referenced in *Records of occurrence*. The subspecies is *O. n. lisae*. The range of the species in the United States is shaded.

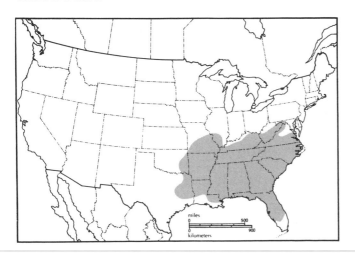

urethral process, lack of an entepicondylar foramen, lack of a gall bladder, and large preputial glands but no ampullary glands.

Dental formula. 1/1, 0/0, 0/0, 3/3.

Chromosomes. 2N = 52; 22 metacentrics and submetacentrics, 28 acrocentrics; X a large submetacentric, Y a small acrocentric (Patton and Hsu, 1967).

Comparisons. Ochrotomys differs from *Peromyscus* as pointed out in the account of the latter genus (p. 202). It differs from *Reithrodontomys* (p. 199) and *Mus* (p. 255) in much the same way that *Peromyscus* differs from them.

Secondary sexual variation. Skulls of females average slightly longer and broader but the differences are not significant (Packard, 1969).

Ochrotomys nuttalli, Golden mouse

Range. Southern Illinois, probably from Perry County southward; records are available from Jackson County southward (Map 8.40). See *Remarks* below for the reported occurrence in Marion County.

Diagnosis. Since the genus is monotypic, the characters given for the genus are those of the species.

Color. Dorsum and sides reddish or orangish and only slightly intermixed with black, underparts with ochraceous or light buff wash, tops of feet whitish, face and ears same color as dorsum; dorsum of tail darker than back. Specimens in juvenile pelage are dark but not as gray or lead-colored on the dorsum as are *Peromyscus* in comparable juvenile pelage, and the ears are more reddish.

Comparisons. In Illinois, *O. nuttalli* is most readily confused with *Peromyscus leucopus.* Some of the key diagnostic features for separating the two are as follows: *O. nuttalli* has more golden or reddish upperparts (but some aged *P. leucopus* may be quite reddish), underparts are more creamy colored and with an ochraceous wash, ears more reddish, including hairs on the inside of the ears; hind foot shorter (usually 19 mm or less), tail less distinctly bicolored, baculum smaller, anterior edge of zygomatic (or infraorbital) plate convex rather than concave, posterior palatine foramina nearer pterygoid fossa than to anterior palatine foramina, chromosomes with 2N of 52 rather than 48.

O. nuttalli differs from *P. maniculatus* (p. 202) in much the same way it differs from *P. leucopus* (p. 206).

Remarks. Voucher specimens of *Ochrotomys nuttalli* are available from as far north as two miles east of Murphysboro, Jackson County; Klimstra and Roseberry (1969:416) stated that "our collections contribute Pope and Perry counties," with Perry County being farther north. We know of no specific locality and have not seen a specimen from Perry County.

Kennicott (see Cory, 1912:201) said that these animals, known locally as red mice, are "not very uncommon near Salem, in Marion County." There is no way to know if Kennicott really did refer to *Ochrotomys* at this locality. However, Kennicott's description of the habitat is not typical for that of *Ochrotomys nuttalli*, for he said the farmers informed him that they "frequented clumps of hazel bushes at the edges of the prairies" and that several nests were found in "the tops of hazel bushes, and built neatly, somewhat like a bird's nest, but covered at top with a small opening on the side." The location of the nest, the type of bush, and the opening into the nest do not seem typical of *Ochrotomys* but more nearly that of *Peromyscus*.

Golden mice prepare rather characteristic and distinctive nests in vines, bushes, and trees. We have additional reports based largely on the presence of these nests. At a site 3.8 mi W Golconda, Pope County, Woodrow Goodpaster found two old nests and one fresh nest on April 16, 1980. In June or July, 1975, Stanley Sipp reported seeing a golden mouse and a nest near the Old Iron Furnace, 4 mi N, 1 mi E Rosiclare, Hardin County. On April 8, 1981, our field party found an old nest of *Ochrotomys nuttalli* in an old pine plantation grown up with much honeysuckle ¾ mi S Temple Hill, Pope County. These three localities are not plotted on the map but probably represent authentic records for the species.

Habitat

Golden mice in Illinois are inhabitants of thickets of honeysuckle and greenbrier, especially where there are some conifers, or they may be in thickets of sumac and cane where there is greenbrier and honeysuckle. Probably the most important elements are greenbrier and honeysuckle although cedars are usually present also. The thickets of vines serve as avenues of movement from trees to trees and trees to ground. Although mice may short-circuit the vines by jumping directly to the ground when disturbed, we think that in their normal activities they make great use of runways over the vines.

As forests mature, there is the likelihood that the shrubby habitat preferred by golden mice may disappear. The partial lumbering of such forests or woods may be beneficial to these mice.

In Kentucky, Barbour and Davis (1974) regarded this mouse as an inhabitant of greenbrier thickets, with an overstory of hardwoods, pines, and cedars. In eastern Kentucky, Goodpaster and Hoffmeister (1954) found that in the valleys where these mice lived, the greenbrier and honeysuckle were intermixed with spice bush, water beech, dogwood, wild grape, and blackberry. At or near the tops of ridges, there are greater numbers of pines and hardwoods.

Habits

Golden mice are nocturnal. When they are forced out of their nests in the daytime, they move with great

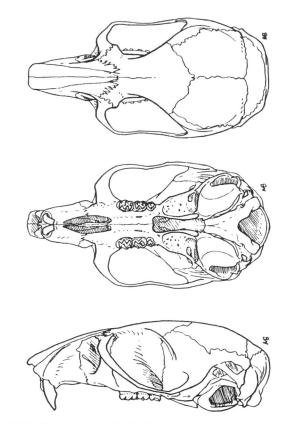

Fig. 8.92. *Ochrotomys nuttalli*, dorsal, ventral, and lateral views of skull. Chapanoke, Perquimans Co., North Carolina, 54089 Museum Vert. Zool. Male, 25.3 mm greatest length.

facility. They are excellent climbers on relatively small branches and vines. In a cage where numerous branches were fixed in place, golden mice soon were using certain paths or routes over these branches. At times they moved along these branches so rapidly that the eye could hardly follow them (Goodpaster and Hoffmeister, 1954). The tail is employed in climbing not only as a balancing organ, but as a semiprehensile structure which is wrapped partially around vines and branches or as a support used in conjunction with the hind feet to free up the front feet. I placed a golden mouse in an empty two-foot high wooden nail keg. It did not have any trouble climbing to the top of the keg; apparently the inner surfaces were rough enough to give it footing to reach the top.

These mice are most docile. Usually within a day after removal from the wild and being placed in a cage, they can be handled with no reaction or biting. When picked up by the base of the tail, an animal holds its body still but rigid.

Golden mice are communal and sociable animals. One nest may contain numerous adults, especially in the winter. Barbour (1942) reported eight adult males in one nest; it is not uncommon to find two to six adults in a nest. In Kentucky, Goodpaster and Hoffmeister (1954) found the mean number of animals in 17 nests to be 2.94.

Fig. 8.93. Golden mouse, *Ochrotomys nuttalli*, on grapevine adjacent to nest. Photograph by W. W. Goodpaster.

When one or more golden mice are established in a cage and a new individual is introduced, there usually is no resulting fighting or chasing. When an adult was introduced into a cage with a family group of five established mice, "the new mouse did very little moving about for almost two hours.... Gradually... so slow were its actions that it took nearly four minutes to move ten inches.... it reached the edge of the nest, it slowly and easily slipped past the waiting mouse at the entrance and joined the others" (Goodpaster and Hoffmeister (1954:23).

Golden mice are capable swimmers. Mice that have been frightened from nests have jumped into an adjacent stream and have quickly swum to the shore and run off. Also, when they have been disturbed they may either jump to the ground, run through the adjacent vines, or quickly climb to the top of the nearest tree.

Nests

Golden mice are unique in that they often build above-ground nests in vines, bushes, or trees. Many times these are located where they can be reached only by traversing small branchlets or vines. These nests, especially in winter,

can be conspicuous. White-footed mice may also inhabit nests in branches of trees or bushes, but these are bird nests which the mice have domed over for their use. Golden mice ordinarily build their own nests completely. If they do use an old bird nest, it serves only as the platform on which they build.

The nest is a resting and rearing place for one or several mice, and is not to be confused with a feeding platform (see p. 221). Nests in southern Illinois average 5.8 in. in diameter and are globular (Blus, 1966); in Kentucky, about 4.9 in. The height above ground for the nests in Illinois varied from 8 in to 20 ft, 10 in with a mean of 7 ft, 2 in. The inner layers of the nest consist of shredded parts of grasses and bark, and milkweed down, feathers, and fur. The nest itself is capped with a covering of leaves, unshredded grasses, and stems. During the daytime, openings into the nest are non-existent. If, however, an individual wants to leave the nest—as, for example, when disturbed—it exits through the nest wall with seemingly little difficulty.

In southern Illinois, Blus (1966) found 81 of 87 nests well above ground. Most were supported by cane, honeysuckle, greenbrier, and/or grape. A few were in the forks of trees and one was in a cluster of thorns on the trunk of a honey locust. In Kentucky, Goodpaster and Hoffmeister (1954) found only one in a cavity of a hollow tree. Of the six nests that Blus (1966) found in Illinois that were not above ground, four were at the bases of spice bush clumps, one was under a log, and one was on some cane and about one inch above the ground.

Goodpaster and I were of the opinion that golden mice may, during the warmer months, spend their resting time in shelters on or near the ground, or under logs and debris on the ground. We thought that there was a slightly better chance of catching them in traps set on the ground in the summertime. Blus (1966), however, found no evidence to suggest a greater degree of use of ground nests at a particular period of the year.

A second type of nestlike structures is utilized by golden mice. These are feeding platforms which may be modified old nests, modified bird nests, or specially constructed platforms where the mice bring, and often store, their seeds, open them, and eat their contents. The empty hulls are left on the platform and they soon form a thick flooring mat. Sometimes feeding platforms are covered; sometimes unroofed. In one feeding platform near Vanceburg, Kentucky, Goodpaster and Hoffmeister (1954) estimated there were the hulls of 10,000 seeds. In southern Illinois, Blus (1966) found two nestlike structures that had the hulls of 100 and 2,000 seeds, respectively. In Kentucky, we thought that feeding platforms were about six times as numerous as nests. In southern Illinois, we have never found feeding platforms, and Blus (1966) found only two, if those truly were feeding platforms.

Food

In southern Illinois, Blus (1966) found food items (seeds) in nearly all nests examined, together with a large number of seeds in two structures that may have been either feeding platforms or nests. The principal foods were seeds of oaks (small acorns), poison ivy, bedstraw, blackberry, and grape. Other seeds were sassafras, bindweed, pokeberry, and hackberry. He found no greenbrier.

In Kentucky, the remnants of seeds most numerous in feeding platforms were sumac, wild cherry, dogwood, and greenbrier. Less abundant were acorns, bindweed, peppervine, pokeweed, and tick clover.

We suspect that golden mice at certain times of the year feed on the soft parts of fruits and berries and possibly on some seeds that are never taken to the feeding platform or nest.

Reproduction

Golden mice probably produce two sets of young per year in Illinois. Blus (1966) found nests with suckling young on April 6 and subadults in a nest in November. These were probably born in late March and late Sep-

tember, respectively. Young specimens taken in Illinois in our collection were probably born, judging from their stage of development, between September 25 and October 10. In Kentucky, we found golden mice pregnant in the months of March, April, July, and October. In Tennessee, the peaks of breeding are said to be in late spring and early autumn although breeding extended from mid-March through early October (Linzey and Packard, 1977).

The gestation period is around 28 days, but varies. None of our specimens of golden mice from Illinois was carrying embryos. In Tennessee, Linzey and Linzey (1967) found the litter size for 85 mice to be 2.65 (1–4).

At birth, the young are essentially hairless, with the eyes and ears closed. At one week, the body is furred, with a coat of reddish-brown fine hair on the dorsum. At about one and a half weeks, the ears open and shortly thereafter the eyes open. Young can stand on all fours at eight days; by two weeks they can walk and jump readily. Young are weaned by the age of three weeks.

Variation

At an earlier time, golden mice appeared in the literature under the genus *Peromyscus*. In the late 1950's and 1960's, the subgenus *Ochrotomys*, to which golden mice were referred, was elevated to generic rank by various workers. Packard (1969) revised *O. nuttalli* and referred specimens from the Mississippi River Valley and much of the adjacent area to a new subspecies, *O. n. lisae*.

Ochrotomys nuttalli lisae Packard

1969. *Ochrotomys nuttalli lisae* Packard, Univ. Kansas Mus. Nat. Hist. Misc. Publ., 51:398. Type from La Nana Creek bottoms, Nacogdoches, Nacogdoches Co., Texas.

Range. As given for the species (p. 218 and Map 8.40).
Diagnosis and Comparisons. A medium- to small-sized subspecies of *O. nuttalli*, small in head-body and tail lengths; skull of average size. Differs from *O. n. flammeus* in being more yellowish red rather than orangish red in color of dorsum, and of smaller size. Differs from *O. n. aureolus* in having a paler color, a tail more distinctly bicolored, and a slightly smaller skull (after Packard, 1969).

Remarks. Packard (1969) regards this as a "yellowish-washed, small subspecies."

Records of occurrence: SPECIMENS EXAMINED, 32. **Jackson Co.:** [3] 2 mi E Murphysboro, 1 (SRL). **Union Co.:** [5b] Pine Hills, 2 mi SE Alridge, 3 (UI); [5c] 3 mi N Wolf Lake, 2 (ISU); [5d] Wolf Lake, 1 (ISU); [6] 6 mi S, 2 mi E Ware, 1 (UI). **Johnson Co.:** [7] 1 mi S Foreman, 3 (UI). **Pope Co.:** [8a] T12S, R5E, Sec. 28, 6 (UI); [8b] 3¾ mi N Dixon Springs, 4 (UI); [8c] 1½ mi S Glendale, 3 (UI); [8d] 2½ mi S Glendale, 1 (UI); [8e] 2½ mi S, ½ mi E Glendale, 2 (UI). **Alexander Co.:** [9b] ½ mi N Olive Branch, 1 (NHS); [9d] Olive Branch, 3 (NHS); [10] Cairo, 1 (CAS).

Additional records: **Marion Co.:** [1] Salem (Kennicott in Cory, 1912:201, see text (pp. 218–219) for comments on this record). **Perry Co.:** [2] no specific locality (Klimstra and Roseberry, 1969:416). **Union Co.:** [4] 5½ mi NE Cobden (Layne, 1958a:242); [5a] 1¾ mi E Aldridge, 2 (FS). **Alexander Co.:** [9a] 3 mi NNW Olive Branch (Layne, 1958a:242); [9c] ½ mi NNW Olive Branch (Layne, 1958a:242); [9d] Olive Branch (Cory, 1912:201).

Neotoma, Wood rats

Diagnosis. A large-bodied, long-tailed rat with the tail relatively well-haired and bicolored (dark above, light below), underparts whitish, tops of feet light colored or whitish; females with only two pairs of inguinally situated mammae; cheek teeth high-crowned but rooted, prismatic, and folded; rostrum relatively slender; large intestine much longer than small intestine; glans penis with deep terminal crater.

Dental formula. 1/1, 0/0, 0/0, 3/3.

Comparisons. Neotoma differs from *Rattus* in having a more heavily haired tail with the annulations and scales on the tail less apparent, tops of feet lighter in color, underparts whitish; cranium without prominent lateral fronto-parietal ridges; teeth higher crowned and prismatic; hard palate does not extend beyond the last upper molar rather than extending well beyond; mammary glands absent in pectoral region.

Neotoma differs from *Oryzomys* in its larger size (in Illinois, hind foot 35 mm or more, rather than less; head-body length more than 150 mm, rather than less), tail more heavily haired dorsally, teeth higher crowned and prismatic, skull larger and without a supraorbital bead, and bullae more inflated.

Neotoma floridana, Eastern wood rat

Range. In southernmost Illinois near the Mississippi River from southern Jackson County southward (Map 8.41). For other distributional records, see *Remarks.*

Diagnosis. A species of *Neotoma* of large size, tail haired but not bushy, length of hind foot (in Illinois) 35–41 mm, dorsum dark gray to blackish interspersed with brown, venter creamy or whitish, ears nearly naked and conspicuous, feet whitish, skull with narrow, elongate rostrum, anterior palatal spine, which extends part way between the anterior palatine slits, forked at tip; premaxillary tongues project posterior to nasals; hard palate does not extend beyond the last upper molar.

Color. Dorsum a mixture of grays and blacks interspersed with browns and ochraceous, with this color extending down top of tail and legs nearly to wrist and ankle; sides more ochraceous than back, underparts whitish or creamy, often with a slight overlay of buff, face and top of head often more grayish than back.

Chromosomes. 2N = 52; FN = 56; autosomal pairs are one large biarmed, two small biarmed, and the remainder acrocentrics. X, a large submetacentric; Y, a medium-sized subtelocentric (Baker and Mascarello, 1969).

Comparisons. Neotoma floridana might be confused with *Rattus* or *Oryzomys.* It is much larger than all other cricetine and microtine rodents. For a comparison with these two genera, see *Neotoma.*

Molt. Wood rats have a postjuvenile molt, then acquire subadult pelage and undergo another molt into adult pelage. After this, there is one obvious molt in the autumn of each year.

Growth. Weight increases rapidly until the end of the third month; adult weight is reached at about eight months (Rainey, 1956).

Aging. Specimens were considered adult and used in the table of measurements if the length of the back (posterior) lingual groove of M¹ was 40 mm or less in length. As animals mature, this groove becomes shorter.

Secondary sexual variation. In some species of *Neotoma,* there are significant differences in external size and in many skull measurements between males and females. In others, there is none. In this study, males and females were treated separately.

Remarks. Remains of *Neotoma floridana* have been taken in Illinois from as far north as 10 mi S Belleville at Meyer Cave, Monroe County. Wood rats were present here around 8,000 years ago and in great numbers. Fragments of skulls or skeletons numbering 6,053 items and representing a minimum of 535 individuals were recovered (Parmalee, 1967). Only two cranial elements of this wood rat were found near Modoc, Randolph County.

Table 8.23. External and cranial measurements (in mm) of *Neotoma floridana,* with mean, minimum-maximum, and standard deviation.

		Total lenght	Tail length	Body length	Hind foot length	Ear length	Condylo-basal length	Zygo-matic breadth	Braincase breadth
Neotoma floridana Union County	11♂	387.8 360-408 16.12	178.2 150-195 14.47	208.4 192-219 9.76	38.9 36-41 1.62	29.3 28-31 0.87	48.60 46.5-50.3 1.23	25.62 23.3-26.9 1.11	18.18 17.55-18.85 0.39

Fig. 8.94. Eastern wood rat, *Neotoma floridana*. Photograph by K. Maslowski and W. W. Goodpaster.

Throughout the Shawnee Hills region, from near the Mississippi River east to near the Ohio River, Nawrot and Klimstra (1976) found 24 sites of past wood rat occupancy based mostly on abandoned houses. These are listed at the end of *Records of occurrence* (p. 227).

In 1972 and 1973, wood rats were present in reduced numbers only in the limestone bluffs of the Pine Hills, Union County, and in Fountain Bluff, Jackson County, with probably less than six here (Nawrot and Klimstra, 1976). In 1982-1983, Michael Sweet of the Illinois Department of Conservation estimated the total population to be between 25 and 35 and restricted to the Pine Hills.

It is uncertain to me whether the name *N. floridana illinoensis* or *N. floridana magister* is the proper one to use for the wood rats in Illinois. See the discussion under *Variation* (p. 225).

Habitat

In Illinois, eastern wood rats are inhabitants of the crevices, rock piles, ledges, overhangs, and caverns of the

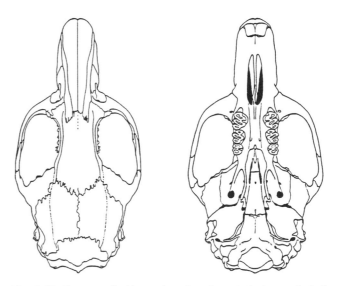

Fig. 8.95. *Neotoma floridana*, dorsal and ventral views of skull. Pine Hills, near Wolf Lake, Union Co., Illinois, 7082 UI. Male, 52.1 mm greatest length.

Mastoidal breadth	Length nasals	Greatest breadth nasals	Inter-orbital breadth	Incisive for. length	Diastema length	Post-palatal length	Crown l. max. toothrow	Bulla length	Skull depth
19.10	19.88	5.78	6.53	10.36	14.45	20.28	9.32	5.29	17.51
18.15-19.9	18.8-21.0	5.4-6.1	6.25-6.95	9.65-11.05	13.6-15.35	18.9-21.5	9.1-9.9	4.6-5.6	16.2-18.2
0.58	0.61	0.22	0.24	0.45	0.53	0.98	0.22	0.27	0.57

bluffs of the Pine Hills, Fountain Bluff, and Horseshoe Bluff, and at an earlier time in similar situations throughout much of the Shawnee Hills terrain. Probably the availability of food close to the area of occupancy has been one critical factor.

The presence of these wood rats usually can be detected by their characteristic houses consisting of a pile of sticks, leaves, and debris such as paper, cloth, cans, and almost anything else that is available and of a size that can be carried to the house. In the cliffs near the Mississippi River, as in the Pine Hills, houses are sometimes back in crevices or within piles of boulders and the accumulated materials may not be readily evident. Also, eastern wood rats may repeatedly use areas for defecation and urination, and the resulting accumulations are characteristic of these rats.

Trees that are near the areas where wood rats live in Illinois are oaks, hickories, elm, hackberry, sassafras, and pawpaw, and in addition there are the various plants that are a part of the white oak-hickory community.

Our experiences with wood rats in Illinois and those of Layne (1958a) and Nawrot and Klimstra (1976) indicate that they build their houses in the cliffs, or in boulders at the base of cliffs, or in caves in rocky areas. Nawrot and Klimstra, however, report on a thesis by J. Crim, who found 10 wood rats that had built houses in the trees of the bottomlands adjacent to the bluffs of the Pine Hills. These may have been so situated because of population pressure (in 1960), and nests so built and situated have not been seen subsequently.

In other places in the Mississippi River Valley, eastern wood rats build nests in trees, bushes, attics of old buildings, and in hollow, fallen logs, as in western Tennessee, around Reelfoot Lake (Goodpaster and Hoffmeister, 1952). In Louisiana, these rats often build nests around the base of trees or part way up in a tree (Lowery, 1974).

By contrast, the eastern wood rats in Indiana are "apparently restricted to caves and limestone escarpments in the heavily forested hills" (Mumford and Whitaker, 1982). In central and eastern Kentucky, they are in cliffs with deep crevices, caves, and piles of large boulders (Barbour and Davis, 1974). They occur in much the same habitat in Ohio.

The nesting behavior and habits of eastern wood rats in Illinois are much more like the behavior of wood rats in Indiana, Ohio, and eastern Kentucky (subspecies *Neotoma floridana magister*) than they are like the behavior of eastern wood rats in western Tennessee and Louisiana. Also, nearly throughout the range of *N. f. magister,* these wood rats are uncommon or rare, and not unlike the status of the wood rats in southern Illinois. Ecologically, the Illinois wood rats may best be referred to *N. f. magister.*

Habits

Wood rats are nocturnal, although those living in deep, dark caves may be active during parts of the day. In our experience, rats living in caves do not bother to roof or dome over their open nests.

These wood rats individually are docile animals in the wild or in captivity, but when they encounter another wood rat, they usually become belligerent and combative. Individuals that have well-established territories are the most belligerent.

Wood rats transport a wide variety of items to build or to add to their nest or house. As a result of this habit they are frequently called pack rats. In one house in southern Illinois, Nawrot and Klimstra (1976) found in the upper part of a wood rat house a matchbox that was about 25 to 30 years old and at a lower level in the same house, an Indian artifact judged to be between 1,000 and 1,300 years old. It is not clear whether this house had been in existence all of this time.

Within the bulky house, one or several areas may be used to store food for later use. These stores can include such seeds as honey locust, beechnuts, and acorns, and also green leaves.

Young adhere tightly to the teats of their mother and are frequently dragged or led around while so attached. Although it may be difficult for a person to remove the young, the mother releases herself from a young one by placing a foot on it and turning repeatedly in a circle.

Food

Little is known of the food habits of the eastern wood rat in Illinois. Stomachs from 13 specimens from southern Illinois obtained in June, July, and August contained fleshy fruits, leaves, herbaceous stems, seed pods, and other plant material, traces of insects, and several small feathers (Layne, 1958a). Two stomachs, from specimens collected in January that Layne examined, contained mast with a trace of green vegetation. These wood rats are primarily vegetarians and rarely eat animal matter. Barbour and Davis (1974), however, found that they were fond of sardine oil.

In eastern Kansas, Rainey (1956) found that these rats fed extensively on seeds, fruits, and leaves of Osage orange; in western Tennessee, they fed on honey locust, acorns, beechnuts, and in one place, mint (Goodpaster and Hoffmeister, 1952).

Reproduction

We have no records of any of our specimens in Illinois containing embryos. One animal, however, taken July 23 is probably only one month old and one taken October 27 two months old. This would place the birth dates in mid-June and late August. Three juveniles from western

Tennessee in our collection were probably born in early June; two from Ohio in mid-June; one from Kentucky, late October. There appears to be considerable variation in the breeding seasons, probably dependent to some degree upon the locality: February through August in Kansas, March through October in Oklahoma, perhaps throughout the year in the south. In Illinois, young are probably born in June and August.

The gestation period is between 33 and 35 days with an average litter size of about three (1 to 7). Young are darkly pigmented dorsally at birth. Ears open at about nine days, eyes at 15 to 21 days. The young are reared in a nest within the larger bulkier house. More than one nest may be present within the house. The nest is usually spherical and consists of finely shredded bark, leaves, grasses, or other available materials. Exits from the nests follow established pathways through the sticks and debris making up the house and to pathways that are often imperceptible beyond the house.

It is thought that early-born animals may breed the same year, but since puberty is not reached until the fifth or sixth month, probably animals born in Illinois in June, or even in May, do not produce young in the year in which they were born.

Variation

Eastern wood rats in Illinois have been referred to the subspecies *N. floridana illinoensis* based on specimens in southern Illinois near the Mississippi River. At an earlier time it was not suspected that eastern wood rats in southern Illinois might intergrade with *N. floridana magister* in southern Indiana. Instead, they were thought to intergrade in the Mississippi Valley to the south. Although the habitat occupied by, and habits of, wood rats in Illinois are more like those of *N. f. magister* to the east than those to the south, the Illinois population appears to be morphologically distinct from *N. f. magister*.

Neotoma floridana illinoensis Howell

1910. *Neotoma floridana illinoensis* A. H. Howell, Proc. Biol. Soc. Wash., 23:28. Type from Wolf Lake, Union Co., Illinois.

Range. As given for the species (p. 222 and Map 8.41).
Diagnosis and Comparisons. A medium-sized subspecies of *Neotoma floridana* with a bicolored tail; zygomatic arches tend to be squared anteriorly. Markedly smaller than *N. f. magister* to the east, being smaller externally and cranially.

Records of occurrence. SPECIMENS EXAMINED, 81.
Jackson Co.: [1a] N end Fountain Bluff, 1 (SRL). **Union Co.:** [2a] 6½ mi WNW Alto Pass, Pine Hills, 1 (SRL); [2b] Pine Hills, WNW Alto Pass, 1 (SIC); [2c] 6 mi N Wolf Lake, 1 (UI); 3 (SRL); [2d] Pine Hills, 3 (FM), 2 (ISU); 5 (ISM), 6 (UI), 5 (SRL), 2 (SIC); [2e]

Map 8.41. Known records of occurrence of the eastern woodrat, *Neotoma floridana*. The subspecies is *N. f. illinoensis*. Numbered localities are referenced in *Records of occurrence*. The range of the species in the United States is shaded.

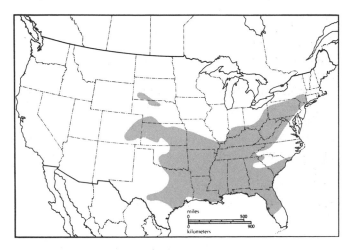

Fig. 8.96. Habitat of the eastern wood rat, *Neotoma floridana,* in crevices and debris of the rocky bluffs along the Mississippi River floodplain near Wolf Lake, Union Co., Illinois. (From Hoffmeister and Mohr, 1957. Photograph by Illinois Natural History Survey)

1½ mi ENE Aldridge, 1 (SRL); [2f] 4 mi N, 1 mi E Wolf Lake, 3 (KU); [2g] Aldridge, Pine Hills, 4 (SRL), 1 (FS); [2h] 2 mi E Aldridge, 1 (FS); [2i] 3 mi N Wolf Lake, 1 (ISU); [2k] Pine Hills E of Larue, 1 (UI); [2l] 4 mi N and E Wolf Lake [assumed to be 4 mi NE], 7 (SIC); [2m] 2 mi SE Aldridge, 3 (FS); [2n] 2 mi S Aldridge, 2 (SRL); [2o] Wolf Lake [*N. f. illinoensis* type locality], 1 (CAS), 16 (US), 6 (FM); [2p] Pine Hills near Wolf Lake, 2 (UI); [2q] ½ mi E Wolf Lake, 1 (SRL). **Alexander Co.:** [3b] Miller City, 1 (UI).

Additional records. **Jackson Co.:** [1b] Horseshoe Bluff, (Crim, unpublished master's thesis SIC, *in* Nawrot and Klimstra, 1976). **Union Co.:** [2j] 1.5 mi SE Aldridge, 1 (UM); [2m] 2 mi SE Aldridge, 1 (UM). **Alexander Co.:** [3a] Olive Branch, (Wetzel, 1947:232).

Historical records (from Nawrot and Klimstra, 1976, unless otherwise specified, and within the last 100 years unless otherwise indicated). **Monroe Co.:** Meyer Cave fissure, 4 mi SSW Columbia, 2,000 to 8,000 B.P. (Parmalee, 1967). **Randolph Co.:** Modoc Rock Shelter, 4,000 to 10,000 B.P. (Parmalee, 1959). **Jackson Co.:** Kincaid Lake, Cedar Creek, Rocky Hollow, Poplar Camp Creek, Cave Valley, Cedar Creek Bluffs, Cove Hollow. **Gallatin Co.:** Garden of the Gods, Pounds Escarpment. **Union Co.:** Cliff View Park, Giant City State Park, East Cobden Ridge, Kerr Canyon, Lick Creek. **Johnson Co.:** Ferne Clyffe State Park, Ozard Creek. **Pope Co.:** Burden Falls, Jackson Hollow, Bell Smith Springs, Indian Kitchen, One Horse Gap, Avery Hollow, Brownfield Bluff. **Hardin Co.:** Griffith Cave.

Subfamily Microtinae, Voles and lemmings

Myomorph rodents, here regarded as of the family Muridae, with cheek teeth that are prismatic, long-crowned and, in most species, persistently growing; tail shorter than head-body length; body relatively heavy and well furred, including tail (except in *Ondatra*). In Illinois, consists of the genera *Microtus* (including the pine voles formerly in the genus *Pitymys*), *Ondatra*, and *Synaptomys*.

Methods of taking cranial measurements for certain microtines: Cranial measurements for *Microtus* and *Synaptomys* were taken as follows: *greatest length* was taken from the front surface of the incisors to the condyles, but if the nasals protruded beyond the plane of the incisors, the measurement was still taken from the incisor; *condylozygomatic length* from the anterior edge of the ramus of the zygoma to the condyle; *zygomatic breadth*, taken as greatest; *cranial breadth*, the least distance between the prelambdoidal fenestra; *interorbital* breadth, least; *nasal length*, greatest of one nasal bone; *incisive foramen length*, greatest of longest foramen; *diastema length*, between alveoli; *maxillary toothrow*, measured at base of teeth and same as alveolar; *cranial height*, greatest when sitting on a plate or slide; *auditory meatus*, horizontal inside diameter.

Microtus, Voles

Diagnosis. Short-furred, short-tailed microtines with grizzled or reddish brown fur, rounded ears that are almost concealed by the fur; molars with inner and outer re-entrant angles approximately equal, and always with two or more triangles.

Dental formula. 1/1, 0/0, 0/0, 3/3.

Chromosomes. See under the species accounts.

Comparisons. *Microtus* differs from *Synaptomys* (p. 247), the only other small microtine genus in Illinois, in having ungrooved upper incisors that are whitish in color rather than grooved and orangish-colored, molar teeth with re-entrant angles on each side almost equal, rather than re-entrant angles excessively deep on buccal side; tail longer than hind foot; fur not especially long.

Microtus differs noticeably from *Peromyscus*, especially in having a shorter tail, less conspicuous ears, ever-growing molar teeth that consist of triangles and loops, heavier skull with stronger zygomatic arches, and in numerous other features.

Aging. The basioccipital-exoccipital suture becomes completely fused and obliterated at six weeks of age in *Microtus ochrogaster* (Hoffmeister and Getz, 1968). The obliteration of this suture probably occurs at a comparable age in other microtines in Illinois. If this suture is obliterated, the animals are considered adult for comparative purposes.

Remarks. Some authors would place the three species of *Microtus* in Illinois in three separate subgenera: *M. (Microtus) pennsylvanicus*, *M. (Pedomys) ochrogaster*, and *M. (Pitymys) pinetorum*.

Microtus pennsylvanicus, Meadow vole

Range. Northern Illinois south to a line through southern Fulton County to southern Champaign and Vermilion counties; also in easternmost Clark County (see Map 8.42, p. 230).

Diagnosis. A species of *Microtus* which in Illinois is blackish with some reddish hairs interspersed, underparts are blackish and often tipped with white but not yellow; tail long (in adults, usually 36 to 49 mm); upper M^3 with four triangles between the anterior loop and the posterior loop, upper M^2 has a small triangle attached posteriorly and directed lingually; six plantar tubercles; eight mammary glands.

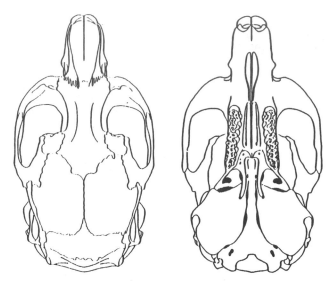

Fig. 8.97. *Microtus pennsylvanicus*, dorsal and ventral views of skull; 1 mi NW Lombard, Du Page Co., Illinois, 40746 UI. Female, 26.9 mm greatest length.

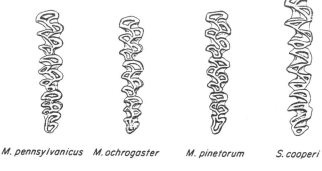

M. pennsylvanicus   *M. ochrogaster*   *M. pinetorum*   *S. cooperi*

Fig. 8.98. Upper right molar teeth in four species of microtines. Note that M^3 in *Microtus pennsylvanicus* has 5 enamel loops or 3 loops between the first and last loops; *Microtus ochrogaster* and *Microtus pinetorum* have 4 loops (only 2 between the first and last). M^2 in *Microtus pennsylvanicus* has 5 loops. In *Synaptomys cooperi* the loops or prisms are more acute.

Color. Dorsal coloration is variable but mostly blackish with a mixture of reddish or dark brown hairs, sides slightly less blackish, top of tail blackish, underside of tail varying from lead-colored to cream-colored, top of feet dusky or blackish, venter blackish with varying degrees of tipping of hairs with cream or white. Juveniles are noticeably darker than adults.

Chromosomes. 2N-46; FN-50. Autosomes: two pairs of large subtelocentrics, one pair of large metacentrics, 19 pairs of small to large acrocentrics; X, large subtelocentric; Y, small acrocentric.

Comparisons. Microtus pennsylvanicus may be confused with *M. ochrogaster*, *M. pinetorum*, or *Synaptomys cooperi*. It differs from *Synaptomys cooperi* as pointed

Table 8.24. Trenchant features for identifying four species of microtines in Illinois.

CHARACTER	Microtus pennsylvanicus	Microtus ochrogaster	Microtus pinetorum	Synaptomys cooperi
Upper M³ (see Fig. 8.98)	3 or 4 triangles in addition to anterior and posterior loop	2 triangles in addition to anterior and posterior loop	2 triangles; with posterior loop simple	1 triangle in addition to anterior and posterior loops. Triangle prismatic.
Upper incisor	Ungrooved Bone-colored	Ungrooved Bone-colored	Ungrooved Bone-colored	Grooved Orange-colored
Length of tail	36-49 mm	29-39 mm	18-24 mm	15-21 mm
Tail relative to hind foot (with a few exceptions)	Longer	Longer	Longer	Same, or only 1 mm longer or shorter
Interorbital breadth usually	Under 4.3 mm	Under 4.3 mm	4.3 mm or more	Under 4.3 mm
Color of dorsum	Brownish black	Dark with light hairs interspersed, giving a hispid or salt-and-pepper effect	Uniformly reddish black	Dark with considerable reddish interspersed
Color of venter	Blackish, usually with a frosting of white	Blackish with a frosting of yellow or reddish tan	Blackish with a light frosting of reddish brown	Whitish with a small amount of blackish visible
Number of mammary glands	8	6	4	6
Upper M² (see Fig. 8.98)	Small triangle attached posteriorly and directed lingually	No small posterior triangle	No small posterior triangle	No small posterior triangle

Table 8.25. Foods eaten by meadow voles in east central Illinois in a bluegrass oldfield and a tallgrass prairie, as determined by stomach analysis (number of stomachs in parentheses), for different seasons. The percentage given is by volume. (After Lindroth and Batzli, 1984:603)

Plant species and part	Apr-May	June-July	Sept-Oct	Jan
Bluegrass oldfield	(11)	(15)	(13)	(11)
Monocotyledons				
Shoots				
Brome grass, *Bromus inermis*	8.7	3.7	0.0	0.0
Timothy, *Phleum pratense*	3.5	0.5	0.9	0.0
Bluegrass, *Poa pratensis*	28.9	19.7	7.9	39.5
Other/unknown	8.4	1.8	0.3	0.2
Seed heads	0.7	8.7	0.9	12.7
Roots	0.1	1.1	11.2	23.8
Dicotyledons				
Shoots				
Giant ragweed, *Ambrosia trifida*	17.5	5.5	2.9	0.0
Alfalfa, *Medicago sativa*	4.0	0.0	0.0	0.0
Dandelion, *Taraxacum officinale*	6.7	17.5	45.4	0.0
Red clover, *Trifolium pratense*	0.2	27.2	10.6	0.0
Other/unknown	13.0	9.7	6.6	11.5
Seed heads	0.0	0.0	0.8	0.0
Roots	0.0	0.0	0.0	0.0
Prairie	(12)	(25)	(17)	(11)
Monocotyledons				
Shoots				
Wild rye, *Elymus canadensis*	0.3	2.7	0.6	0.0
Bluestem, *Andropogon gerardii*	11.8	20.0	9.4	1.6
Bluegrass, *Poa pratensis*	0.0	0.0	0.0	2.9
Other/unknown	10.7	5.8	1.9	0.4
Seed heads	3.2	0.0	3.1	14.6
Roots	2.3	0.0	4.7	14.2
Dicotyledons				
Shoots				
Bush-clover, *Lespedeza cuneata*	23.7	27.9	26.1	10.6
Foxglove penstemon, *Penstemon digitalis*	12.0	16.1	9.3	22.6
Goldenrod, *Solidago canadensis*	6.8	14.9	3.0	2.2
Other/unknown	10.8	5.8	3.0	5.6
Seed heads	3.5	0.5	13.3	21.3
Roots	1.7	0.3	1.7	2.6

out in the *Comparisons* for the genus *Microtus* (p. 227, and Table 8.25).

M. pennsylvanicus is most readily confused with *M. ochrogaster* from which it differs as follows: fur of venter white- or cream-tipped rather than yellow- or ochraceous-tipped, underside of tail dusky or sometimes blackish rather than cream or tan; tail longer, usually more than 36 mm, rather than usually 37 mm or less; six plantar tubercles rather than five; eight mammary glands rather than six; M³ with three or four closed triangles between the anterior and posterior lophs, rather than two.

For a comparison with *Microtus pinetorum*, see account of that species (p. 238).

Molt. Summer pelage is sparser and coarser than winter pelage and the molt of adult pelage is of the underfur or underhairs with little change in the guard hairs, according to Reich (1981) in reporting on material from the thesis of A. Starrett.

Remarks. Microtus pennsylvanicus was for a long time regarded as a mammal of northern Illinois. In 1957,

Hoffmeister and Mohr said the species was known to occur as far south as an imaginary line drawn between Kankakee and Havana. Certain specimens from south of this line that had been reported as *M. pennsylvanicus* were regarded as *Microtus ochrogaster*. For example, an albino, skin-only, taken in Cass County in 1904 and referred to *M. pennsylvanicus* by Necker and Hatfield (1941) was regarded as *Microtus ochrogaster* by Hoffmeister (1954). A skin-only from Arcola, Douglas County, referred to by Wetzel (1947) as *M. pennsylvanicus* was also assigned to *M. ochrogaster* (Hoffmeister, 1954). In a report for 1915, Hankinson considered *M. pennsylvanicus* to be present at Charleston, but this was not based upon the collection and comparison of actual specimens.

The southern limits of *M. pennsylvanicus* in Illinois have moved further south since the report of Hoffmeister and Mohr (1957). This is indicated by those dates when specimens were preserved in collections: 2 mi N Normal, McLean County, locality 52 on Map 8.42, 1964; 8 mi

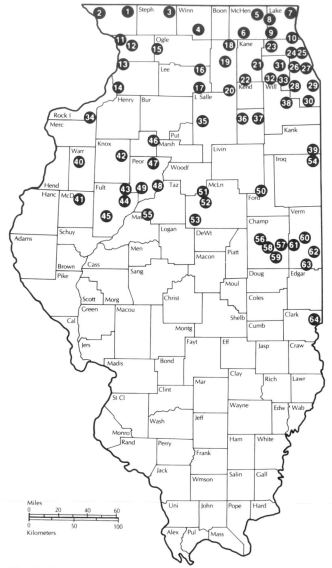

Map 8.42. Meadow voles, *Microtus pennsylvanicus,* as known in Illinois from the early 1980's. Localities of occurrence as numbered are referenced in *Records of occurrence.* The range of the species in the United States is shaded.

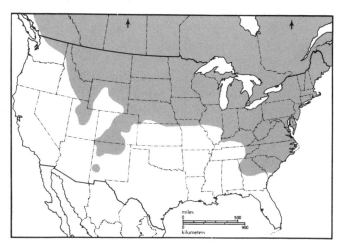

E, 2 mi S Strawn, Livingston County, locality 50, 1967; 3 mi E Urbana, Champaign County, locality 58, 1967; 4 mi SE Danville, Vermilion County, locality 62, 1969. These dates do not necessarily represent the earliest dates of the presence of meadow voles at these localities. It does show that by these dates they were already present this far south.

Getz et al. (1978) found *M. pennsylvanicus* along Interstate 74 in small numbers 12½ km east of Urbana in 1970, and by 1975 they were along nearly all parts of the interstates in Champaign County.

Microtus pennsylvanicus is taking advantage of habitat conditions along interstates to extend its range southward in Illinois. These voles occur near the interstate west of Terre Haute, Vigo Co., Indiana, at 6 mi E Marshall, Clark County (locality 64). Whether these voles have moved southwest in Illinois is not certain. Also, *M. pennsylvanicus* is known from the Indiana side of the Wabash River in Gibson County. There is no apparent reason why these voles should not become established in Wabash County, Illinois, and they may have already.

Habitat

In Illinois, meadow voles are inhabitants of moist areas with grasses or sedges, especially where ample cover is provided by the grasses. The species also occurs in marshy areas, damp fields, along lake shores and streams, and sometimes in gardens. In places where meadow voles are living in or near areas occupied by prairie voles, the meadow voles prefer dense, unmowed grass and a deeper litter layer. The taller, thicker grass can provide more protection from predators and thus make it possible for meadow voles to forage along runways during the day as well as at night. The taller grass also provides a greater source of food and may keep the runways damper and cooler.

In southern Wisconsin, Getz (1970) found that a cattail marsh was preferred by these voles over areas of grass and forbs. In Indiana, meadow voles were taken in grassy fields around Terre Haute, in marshes in the north, and even in the beachgrass growing in the sand dunes near Lake Michigan (Mumford and Whitaker, 1982). In another study in Indiana, Zimmerman (1965) found that in contrast to prairie voles, meadow voles preferred grassy fields that had bluegrass (*Poa compressa*) and muhly (*Muhlenbergia sobolifera*), but lacked foxtail (*Setaria faberi*), and a greater percentage of the cover was made up of grasses.

The habitat of meadow voles, in contrast to that of prairie voles, in Illinois, is in thick grasses that are several inches tall and soil that is damp or moist.

Habits

Because of the protected runways in which meadow voles forage, they may be active throughout the day as well as the night, but they are usually more active at night. When it is warmer (above 20°C), these voles are more nocturnal (Getz, 1961b). Adult males get along less well with other adult males than they do with females. Females show less antagonism to either sex than do males. Aggression is correlated with population density and other factors.

Meadow voles construct and occupy underground burrows. One burrow system usually has several entrances. These burrows may be anywhere from one to eight inches below ground level, and may go to greater depths for the nest chamber; however, in some places in Illinois nests are placed above ground. This is in contrast to prairie voles, whose nests are almost always below ground in the burrow system.

Foods

Meadow voles feed extensively on grasses and other green plants such as clover and plantain. They often leave cut sections of these grasses in their runways. Some of these cuttings represent the removal of grasses from the runway, for these passages are kept free of vegetation when in active use. Most of the caches of cuttings must represent a source of food.

In the vicinity of Urbana, Champaign County, meadow voles fed mainly on green shoots, with increasing amounts of dicots and decreasing amounts of monocots from winter to autumn (Lindroth and Batzli, 1984). Roots and seeds were taken more often in the autumn and winter. These authors found that voles living in bluegrass fields ate more monocots whereas those in prairie situations ate more dicots. Meadow voles took advantage of what was available and fed extensively on *Poa, Bromus, Taraxacum, Trifolium, Andropogon, Lespedeza, Penstemon,* and *Solidago* (Table 8.25, p. 229).

In west central Indiana, Zimmerman (1965) found that 71 percent of the volume in the stomachs of 43 meadow voles consisted of bluegrass, tumblegrass (*Panicum*), and muhly. The most commonly eaten grass was bluegrass. The remains of very few insects but some *Endogone* were found in the stomachs.

Meadow voles will eat grains and seeds and even bulbs if given the opportunity. When other foods are not available, the voles will eat the bark from trees and shrubs. This is done usually under the protection of a mantle of snow. At this time, dependent upon the depth of the snow, they may be able to reach bark several inches up the trunks.

Reproduction

Breeding is said to occur primarily in the spring and the fall. We have records of pregnant females in Illinois in April and from August to November. However, under laboratory conditions and with proper diet, meadow voles may breed the year around. Seventeen litters of young were reportedly produced by one female in one year. The young in turn could produce many offspring, since a female less than a month old may breed, become pregnant, and produce young when about one and one-half months old. The amount of breeding and number of litters may be dependent upon the physiological condition of the population, especially with regard to the stage in any cyclical fluctuation.

The gestation period is 21 days, but varies depending on whether the female is lactating and other factors. The number of young is variable. Only 18 specimens from Illinois in our collection are recorded as with embryos and these had a mean of 5.8 (3–9). In Indiana, Mumford and Whitaker (1982) report the findings of Corthum for 153 females with a mean of 4.46 (1–9), Keller and Krebs for 152 with a mean of 4.54, and their own study on 48 with a mean of 4.81 (2–8).

At birth, young are hairless. Eyes and ears open around day eight. Young are reared in a nest which is globular in shape and consists of dry, shredded grass. They are weaned at about two weeks of age. Young attain adult weight by the third month, but young females may be sexually mature at less than one month.

There is about 88 percent mortality during the first month of life, according to Getz (1960). He also found that the approximate maximum age in the wild was 11 to 12 months. Only 25 percent of the adults survive the three months between the spring and fall breeding seasons and only six percent survive the five months following the end of fall breeding.

Populations

Meadow voles have the ability to move into a new area and become abundant in a short period of time. This is true in Champaign County in east central Illinois. Meadow voles probably did not reach the county until the late 1960's. Getz et al. (1979) thought they did not become well established in Trelease Prairie near Urbana until November 1973. By late 1975, they had become far more abundant than prairie voles in this area. They also found that there was no evidence of population synchrony between these voles and prairie voles. Refer also to the section, "Numbers, populations, and fluctuations of Illinois mammals" (p. 21).

In most places, meadow voles exhibit cyclical fluctuations in the population density. Such cycles are variable in length, but usually are between two and five years. Thus, population numbers and size of home range is dependent upon the stage of the cyclical variation.

Variation

There are numerous subspecies of *M. pennsylvanicus,* but most populations in central and eastern United States are referred to *M. p. pennsylvanicus.*

Table 8.26. External and cranial measurements (in mm) of microtines *Microtus pennsylvanicus*, *Microtus ochrogaster*, *Microtus pinetorum*, and *Synaptomys cooperi*, with mean, minimum-maximum, and standard deviation. Superscripts indicate sample less than N.

Species & Subspecies	Locality	N	Total length	Tail length	Body length	Hind foot length	Greatest length	Condylo-zygomatic length
M. pennsylvanicus pennsylvanicus	Champaign Co.	64	147.9 128-173 10.62	40.3 33-53 4.45	107.8 91-127 0.62	20.0 17-23 1.02	25.83 23.8-27.8 1.00	20.31 18.9-22.2 0.78
M. ochrogaster ochrogaster	Grundy, Livingston, LaSalle cos.	12	144.1 129-160 10.01	33.2 29-39 3.21	111.8 94-122 9.14	19.3 18-21 0.86	25.77 23.7-27.9 1.18	20.18 18.4-22.0 0.98
" " "	Pike Co.	34	141.1 121-162 9.69	30.25 27-36 2.25	110.8 94-130 8.28	18.8 17-21 1.00	25.56 23.15-27.8 1.00	20.04 18.3-20.9 0.65
" " "	Pope Co.	29	141.4 134-158 6.31	30.1 24-37 2.91	111.1 101-126 5.75	18.6 17-20 0.87	25.71 23.1-27.0 0.87	19.98 18.0-21.3 0.66
M. pinetorum scalopsoides	Piatt, Champaign, Fulton cos.	14	118.1 110-128 5.32	19.3 14-24 2.84	98.9 90-111 5.75	16.5 13-18 1.40	24.86[12] 23.9-25.75 0.59	19.08 18.4-19.8[5] 0.46
M. pinetorum auricularis	Alexander, Johnson, Pope, Hardin cos.	11	118.8 108-128 7.18	19.8 15-23 2.32	98.7 90-107 6.33	16.4 15-17 0.90	24.71[9] 23.2-26.45 1.10	18.91 17.2-20.7 1.01
Synaptomys cooperi gossii	McLean, Piatt, Champaign, Vermillion cos.	17	123.4 110-139 8.15	17.3 11-21 3.06	106.1 95-118 6.97	18.6 13-20 1.73	27.03 25.3-29.25 0.89	—
Synaptomys cooperi gossii	Fulton, Mason, Pike cos.	8	123.0 117-129 4.17	17.5 14-21 2.07	105.5 99-111 4.57	19.0 18-21 1.20	27.08 26.2-27.8[5] 0.55	—
" " "	Pope, Alexander, Hardin cos.	20	126.9 119-134 3.73	18.4 14-21 1.63	108.6 100-117 4.05	18.6 17-20 0.94	27.79 25.95-29.2 0.75	—

The population from Champaign County, regarded as recent immigrants, was compared with populations in northern Illinois (Bergstrom, 1984). No significant differences in the population means or in the degree of variation were found.

Microtus pennsylvanicus pennsylvanicus (Ord)

1815. *Mus Pennsylvanicus* Ord, *in* Guthrie, A new geog...., Phila., Second Amer. ed., 2:292. Type from meadows below Philadelphia, Pennsylvania.

1895. *M[icrotus]. pennsylvanicus*, Rhodes, Amer. Nat., 29:940.

1854. *Arvicola dekayi* Anderson and Bachman, The viv. quadrupeds..., 3:287. Type from New York or Illinois.

1858. [*Arvicola riparia*] var. *longipilis* Baird, Mammals, *in* Rept. Expl. Surv...., 8:524. Type from West Northfield, Cook Co., Illinois, or Racine, Wisconsin.

Range. As given for the species (p. 227 and Map 8.42).

Diagnosis and Comparisons. A relatively large, dark subspecies.

Records of occurrence. SPECIMENS EXAMINED, 312.

Jo Daviess Co.: [1] Apple River Canyon State Park, 1 (UI); [2] Galena, 2 (FM). **Stephenson Co.:** [3a] 2 mi N Rock Grove, 1 (UI); [3b] 1½ mi SW Davis, Rock Run Creek, 1 (UI). **Winnebago Co.:** [4] Rockford, Pierce Lake, 1 (NIU). **McHenry Co.:** [5a] 1 mi NW Solon Mills, (SRL); [6] 2 mi E Union, 3 (UI). **Lake Co.:** [7a] Camp Logan, 1 (FM); [8a] Fox Lake, 10 (FM); [8b] Volo Bay Nature Preserve, 5 (ISM); [9a] 3 mi W Wauconda, 1 (UI); [9b] Lake Zurich, 1 (UI). **Carroll Co.:** [11] Mississippi Palisades State Park, 1 (UI); [12] Mt. Carroll, 3 (UI). **Whiteside Co.:** [13] 4 mi N Fulton, 1 (UI); [14] 5 mi W Erie, 2 (UI). **Ogle Co.:** [15] Brookville Twp., Sec. 23, 1 (NIU). **Lee Co.:** [16] 5 mi S Rochelle, Kyte River, 2 (SRL); [17] Brooklawn Twp., 1½ mi SW Compton, 1 (NIU). **De Kalb Co.:** [18] ¾ mi NNE Genoa, 2 (UI); [19a] 3 mi N De Kalb, 1 (NIU); [19b] ⅛ mi E De Kalb, 1 (NIU); [20] Somonauk, 1 (CAS). **Kane Co.:** [21a] near St. Charles, 3 (ISM); [21b] Wheeler Park, 1 (UI). **Cook Co.:** [23] Barrington, 2 (CAS); [24a] 3 mi N Des Plaines, 3 (UI); [24b] 1 mi N Des Plaines, 1 (UI); [24c] 1 mi W Park Ridge, 5 (UI); [24d] ¼ mi W Park Ridge, 2 (UI); [24e] Park Ridge, 1 (UI); [24f] ½ mi E O'Hare Airport, 1 (UI); [24g] 1½ mi E O'Hare Airport, 3 (UI); [25] Evanston, 2 (CAS); [26a] Elmwood Park, 1 (CAS); [26b] River Forest Jct., 1 (CAS); [26c] 1.3 mi E US Jct 45, State Hwy 55, 1 (UI); [26d] Lyons, White Eagle Woods, 1 (UI); [27] Chicago, 1 (UI), 6 (FM); [28a] 95th and Willow Springs Road [=1 mi S Willow Springs], 3 (UI); [28b] 1 mi W Hickory Hills, 1 (UI); [28c] Hidden Lake Woods, 9 mi W Chicago on 95th, 2 (UI); [28d] Palos Park, ¾ mi W Rt 45, 1 (UI); [29] Chicago, Calumet River Preserve, 2

Zygomatic breadth	Cranial breadth	Inter-orbital breadth	Nasal length	Incisive foramen length	Diastema length	Max. toothrow at base	Cranial height	Auditory meatus
14.15	—	3.79	7.28	5.48	9.02	6.35	9.52	2.98
12.5-15.9		3.4-4.15	6.3-8.4	4.6-6.3	7.7-10.1	5.9-6.8	8.7-10.3	2.5-3.8
0.76		0.18	0.46	0.36	0.52	0.20	0.20	0.21
14.32	10.24	4.04	7.32	4.90	8.69	5.83	9.81	2.63
13.0-15.7	9.15-11.0	3.7-4.3	6.85-8.5	4.45-5.4	7.8-9.5	5.35-6.35	9.3-10.4	2.35-2.85
0.84	0.49	0.15	0.48	0.34	0.48	0.31	0.40	0.14
14.76	10.69	4.21	7.16	5.03	8.58	5.94	9.86	2.68
12.7-16.3	9.8-11.55	3.8-4.65	6.35-8.2	4.05-5.7	7.65-9.45	5.4-6.4	9.05-11.95	2.4-3.1
0.79	0.41	0.17	0.50	0.37	0.44	0.28	0.48	0.18
14.89	10.53	4.17	7.31	4.76	8.47	6.08	9.75	2.67
12.9-16.4	9.5-11.25	3.9-4.7	6.45-8.00	4.05-5.45	7.45-9.0	5.4-6.75	9.05-10.65	2.25-3.0
0.68	0.37	0.16	0.34	0.31	0.41	0.30	0.41	0.19
14.06[12]	9.92	4.42	7.40	4.31	7.29	5.93	9.69[12]	2.28
13.6-15.8	9.5-10.5	4.1-4.6	6.76-7.95	4.0-4.66	6.8-7.8	5.7-6.2	9.3-10.0	1.8-2.6
0.70	0.40	0.14	0.33	0.24	0.22	0.17	0.30	0.18
14.90	9.98	4.25	7.26[9]	4.38	7.21	6.00	9.68[9]	2.31
13.5-16.4	9.5-10.95	3.95-4.5	7.0-7.55	3.9-4.9	6.6-7.85	5.45-6.6	9.5-10.2	2.15-2.6
0.79	0.49	0.17	0.19	0.33	0.36	0.37	0.27	0.15
16.54	8.81	3.28	7.38	5.14	—	7.31	10.55	—
15.5-18.2	8.1-9.2	2.85-3.6	6.85-8.25	4.65-6.65		7.0-7.55	9.65-11.7	
0.70	0.33	0.20	0.40	0.27		0.17	0.49	
16.22	8.98	3.34	7.31	4.93	—	7.16	10.57	—
15.4-16.8	8.5-9.2	2.95-3.55	6.9-7.9	4.55-5.45		6.9-7.6	10.1-11.1	
0.51	0.20	0.23	0.40	0.29		0.29	0.36	
16.89	9.08	3.40	7.36	5.35	—	7.19	10.74	—
15.5-17.9	8.65-9.8	3.0-3.7	6.7-8.2	4.55-6.1		6.9-7.6	10.0-11.55	
0.62	0.31	0.23	0.40	0.35		0.23	0.42	

(UI); [30a] Hazel Crest, 1 (UI); [30b] ½ mi N, ½ mi W Flossmoor, 1 (UI); [30c] Chicago Heights, 2 (UI).

Du Page Co.: [31a] 1 mi N Rt 64, 2 mi E Rt 53, 3 (UI); [31b] 1 mi NW Lombard, 1 (UI); [32] Naperville, 1 (UI); [33] 4 mi SSE Downers Grove, 2 (UI). **Rock Island Co.:** [34] 12 mi S Moline, 3 (UI). **La Salle Co.:** [35] 1 mi W Utica, 1 (UI). **Grundy Co.:** [36a] 6 mi W Morris, 11 (UI); [36b] 5 mi W Morris, 1 (UI); [36c] 6 mi W, ½ mi S Morris, 12 (UI); [37] Goose Lake Prairie State Park, 9 (UI). **Will Co.:** [38a] 8 mi E Joliet, 1 (UI); [38b] New Lenox, 1 (CAS). **Kankakee Co.:** [39] 6 mi E St. Anne, 5 (UI). **Knox Co.:** [42] 4 mi S Victoria, 2 (UI). **Fulton Co.:** [43] ½ mi N Norris, 2 (UI); [44a] 1 mi W Canton, 3 (UI); [45] 6 mi W Lewistown, 2 (UI). **Stark Co.:** [46] 2½ mi S Bradford, 1 (SRL). **Peoria Co.:** [47] 3 mi N Dunlap, 1 (UI); [48] 1 mi E Peoria, 1 (UI); [49] 2¼ mi S, 1 mi W Hanna City, 1 (UI). **Livingston Co.:** [50a] 7 mi E, 1 mi S Strawn, 37 (UI); [50b] 8 mi E, 2 mi S Strawn, 18 (UI). **McLean Co.:** [51] 4 mi NW Hudson, 1 (ISU); [52a] 4 mi N Normal, 1 (ISU); [52b] 2 mi N Normal, 1 (ISU); [52c] 1 mi N Normal, 1 (ISU); [52d] ½ mi N Normal, 1 (ISU); [52e] Normal, 3 (NHS); [53] ½ mi N Funks Grove, 1 (ISU). **Iroquois Co.:** [54] T29N, R11W, Sec. 22, 2 (UI).

Champaign Co.: [56a] 5 mi N Champaign, 1 (UI); [56b] 5 mi N Urbana, 1 (UI); [56c] 5¾ mi NW Champaign, 11 (UI); [56d] 1 mi S Rt 150 on Hwy 57, 1 (UI); [56e] 4 mi W Champaign, 6 (UI); [56f] 2½ mi W Champaign, 1 (UI); [56g] 2 mi W Champaign, 2 (UI); [56h] Champaign, 4 (UI); [57a] 8 mi E, ½ mi N Urbana, 2 (UI); [57b] 1 mi W St. Joseph, 1 (UI); [57c] ½ mi W St. Joseph, 1 (UI); [57d] ½ mi E St. Joseph, 1 (UI); [57e] Ogden, 1 (UI); [58a] 2 mi E, 3 mi N Urbana, 1 (UI); [58b] 1 mi E, 1¾ mi N Urbana, 1 (UI); [58c] ½ mi N Urbana, 1 (UI); [58d] 2 mi E, ½ mi N Urbana, 2 (UI); [58e] 4 mi E, ½ mi N Urbana, 1 (UI); [58f] ¼ mi N Mayview, 2 (UI); [58g] Urbana, 2 (UI); [58h] 3 mi E Urbana, 3 (UI); [58i] 1 mi W Mayview, 1 (UI); [58j] 1 mi S Champaign, 1 (UI); [58k] 1 mi S Urbana, 2 (UI); [58l] 2 mi S Champaign, 1 (UI); [58m] 3 mi SE Urbana, 1 (UI); [58n] 2½ mi SE Urbana, 5 (UI); [58o] 3 mi S Champaign, 2 (UI); [58p] 3 mi S Urbana, 11 (UI); [58q] 4 mi S Champaign, 1 (UI); [58r] 5 mi S Urbana, 1 (UI); [59a] 1 mi S, ½ mi E Sidney, 1 (UI); [59b] 2 mi S, 2 mi W Sidney, 1 (UI). **Vermilion Co.:** [60a] 1¼ mi W, ½ mi S Snider, 2 (UI); [60b] 3.6 mi N, 1½ mi W Hillery, 1 (UI); [61a] 3 mi W, 1 mi N Fithian, 2 (UI); [61b] 2 mi W, 1 mi N Fithian, 3 (UI); [62a] 4 mi SE Danville, 3 (UI); [62b] 3⅘ mi E, 2⅖ mi S Westville, 4 (UI); [63] 5 mi SW Georgetown, 1 (UI). **Clark Co.:** [64] 6 mi E Marshall, 1 (UI).

Additional records. **McHenry Co.:** [5b] Wonder Lake, 1 (FSM). **Lake Co.:** [7b] Illinois Dunes State Park, 2 (FSM); [10] Highland Park, 1 (FSM). **Kane Co.:** [22] 2 mi W Sugar Grove, 2 (UM). **Warren Co.:** [40] Monmouth (Wetzel, 1947:230). **McDonough Co.:** [41] 2 mi SE Good Hope (Wetzel, 1947:230). **Fulton Co.:** [44b] ½ mi W Canton, 1 (FSM). **Mason Co.:** [55] Green Valley Junction [may be Tazewell Co.], 1 (FSM).

Fig. 8.99. Prairie vole, *Microtus ochrogaster.* Photograph by K. Maslowski and W. W. Goodpaster.

Microtus ochrogaster, Prairie vole

Range. Throughout the state (Map 8.43).

Diagnosis. A species of *Microtus* which in Illinois is characterized by underparts with ochraceous, yellow, or reddish-tan wash, upper parts dark but interspersed with hairs tipped with tan or silver, giving a salt-and-pepper appearance; M^3 with two closed triangles between the anterior and posterior loops, M^2 with no small posterior triangle; six mammary glands; five plantar tubercles.

Color. Dorsum blackish or brownish, with numerous yellow-tipped hairs interspersed; top of tail about same color as back; ears partly haired on inside near tip but not conspicuous; venter with conspicuous ochraceous, yellow, or reddish-tan wash, with few exceptions; underside of tail noticeably lighter than belly; juveniles darker than adults, especially on venter, and with a less conspicuous ochraceous wash.

Numerous color-mutants are known. Two specimens from Illinois (4½ mi N Kewanee and Danville) are honey-colored or light pinkish on the dorsum, slightly lighter on the venter, and this includes the tail and feet. On one specimen it has been noted that the eyes were pigmented (black).

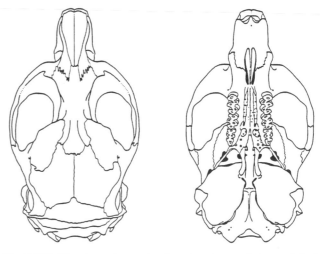

Fig. 8.100. *Microtus ochrogaster,* dorsal and ventral views of skull; 1½ mi S. Glendale, Pope Co., Illinois, 45020 UI. Male, 27.2 mm greatest length.

Chromosomes. 2N = 54; FN = 64; 20 pairs of acrocentrics, 6 of submetacentrics (Hsu and Benirschke, 1971b).

Comparisons. M. ochrogaster differs from *M. pennsyl-*

vanicus as pointed out in the account of the latter species (p. 227). Also see Table 8.26, p. 232.

M. ochrogaster differs from *Microtus pinetorum* (p. 238) in having a longer tail (27 mm or more, rather than less); dorsum dark, with a grizzled or salt-and-pepper rather than reddish-black coloration; six mammary glands rather than four; skull narrower through interorbital region (less than 4.3 mm in adults rather than 4.3 mm or more); M_1 with anterior enamel border of fourth triangle forming an angle of 60° or greater with the anteroposterior midline of the tooth rather than 50° or less (Smolen, 1981).

For a comparison with *Synaptomys cooperi*, see *Comparisons* in the account of the genus *Microtus* (p. 227).

Growth. Prairie voles mature rapidly. Hoffmeister and Getz (1968) found that the hind foot attains adult size by the 21st day and length of ear even before this time; body length and tail length continue to increase slightly after two months of age. In most cranial features, as determined by 18 cranial measurements, 95 percent of adult size is attained in 7 measurements by 45 days of age; in 8 other measurements, 90 percent of adult size, in this same time. The rostral area of the skull continues to lengthen until nine months of age (reflected in the measurements of the nasals and diastema) and the zygomatic arches continue to spread laterally until the eighth month of age.

Secondary sexual variation. Hoffmeister and Getz (1968) found that males usually are slightly larger, on the average, than females but they are not significantly larger to a degree that would justify treating the sexes separately.

Remarks. The most widely distributed vole in Illinois is *Microtus ochrogaster*. It occurs throughout the state and is frequently taken in the same trapline with *Microtus pennsylvanicus* and *Synaptomys cooperi*.

Habitat

Prairie voles in Illinois usually are found in grassy fields that are not too wet or damp. They may live in ungrazed, bluegrass pastures, in abandoned fields, such as alfalfa fields, if the alfalfa is not too tall, in tallgrass prairies with big bluestem (*Andropogon*), Indian grass (*Sorgastrum*), switchgrass (*Panicum*), and bluegrass (*Poa*), and in weedy lots. These voles can be found along the shoulders of roads in abandoned or set-aside fields, pastures, lawns, golf courses, grassy fencerows, and vacant lots within towns. Mowing of the grasses or burning of the above-ground grasses does not adversely effect the presence of prairie voles, and in the long run may be beneficial to their continued presence.

In southernmost Illinois, Layne (1958a:246) found that prairie voles were sometimes "caught in traps set on bare earth in sparsely vegetated sites as well as in well-defined trails in areas of thick cover." He caught them in broom-sedge and in weedy fields with many small trees, brambles, and greenbrier.

Prairie voles generally are less abundant or absent in places where the bluegrass is tall and dense. In the grasslands of Allerton Park, Piatt County, however, we found prairie voles to be present and often abundant in bluegrass that was as much as one foot tall and so thick that it was difficult to separate the grass to place a trap. Meadow voles did not occur in Piatt County at the time of our study and their absence may have made it possible for prairie voles to occupy such habitat. We think that if meadow voles had been present, they would have occupied this niche, perhaps to the exclusion of prairie voles.

The presence of voles can be told by surface runways that are found by parting the grass. Prairie voles "build" and maintain an intricate network of runways that are used to get from one burrow entrance to another, or from a burrow to a food source, under the protection of a canopy of grass. Classes in mammalogy have frequently investigated these surface runways and subsurface tunnels in 16-foot square plots (256 sq ft) near Urbana, Champaign County. Most of these studies were done in apple orchards where bluegrass and some mix of weeds were permitted to grow, with only infrequent cutting. Runways average about two inches wide. Several plots of 256 sq ft had between 70 and 80 linear feet of runways; one had 172 feet. Some randomly selected plots had no underground burrows; others had as much as 25 linear feet. In parts of the burrow systems, there were enlarged areas for nests, for storage of food, and sumps that apparently were used as latrines.

In any given area where prairie voles are present, they remove a considerable quantity of grasses in the construction and maintenance of runways, move considerable soil to the surface in the digging of burrows, and store considerable grass below ground in the form of nests or in food chambers.

Behavior and Habits

Prairie voles, like meadow voles, exhibit a variety of agonistic behaviors and postures. Some of these are: *threat,* with the forefeet raised, head extended, and teeth chattering; *upright stand,* on the hind legs and closely facing the adversary; *lunge* or jump, leaving the surface in the process; *boxing,* in which the voles strike with their forefeet at the head and shoulders of their adversary; *wrestle* with two voles rolling and tumbling while locked together; *chase* involving one pursuing another and often attacking; and *retreat* (Hofmann et al., 1982).

Prairie voles may be active throughout a 24-hour period, but they are more likely to be active during the twilight and dark hours. In Kansas, Martin (1956) found that these voles in the summer were active mainly between dawn and 8:00 a.m. and between sunset and dark.

Getz and Hofmann (1986) found that a male and a female, regarded as constituting a breeding unit, remained together for an average of 42 days. More than 50 percent of all vole breeding units were monogamous and this was the case regardless of the time of year or the density of the population.

Food

In central Illinois, Cole (1977) found that prairie voles fed more extensively on dicotyledonous plants than monocots. The dicots most commonly eaten were clovers (*Trifolium*), dandelions (*Taraxacum*), alfalfa (*Medicago*), *Penstemon, Ambrosia,* and goldenrod (*Solidago*). Of the monocots, bluegrass (*Poa pratensis*), was most frequently eaten, but also brome grass (*Bromus*), timothy (*Phleum pratense*), and big bluestem (*Andropogon*).

During the growing season, dicots are consumed more heavily; during the winter, grasses are used more frequently but as the stems become older and drier they are used less often. Cole (1977) also found that seeds were eaten at all times of the year and wondered if they were cached for use during winter months. Roots and mosses were also eaten in winter and spring as were some fruits in the fall.

In west central Indiana, the most important foods of prairie voles were bluegrass, red clover, lespedeza, tumble-grass, and roots (Zimmerman, 1965).

Reproduction

In some parts of their range, prairie voles may breed throughout the year. Our data for Illinois—based primarily on specimens recorded as being pregnant, but also on the size of juveniles—showed that voles can have embryos every month of the year, although none had embryos in January and August. Females are most likely to have embryos in April, May, October, and December. In central Illinois, Cole (1977) found that breeding decreased drastically in winter but, in summer, declines occurred only in some populations. Nevertheless, breeding did not cease altogether in the winter, and when the season was less severe than usual, breeding increased.

In 330 adult females taken in Illinois, 94 contained embryos with a mean of 3.67 (1–8). In central Illinois, Cole (1977) found that 56 females in a bluegrass habitat in the spring had a mean of 3.68 embryos; in summer, 19 females had a mean of 3.68; in autumn, 9 had 3.67. In an alfalfa habitat adjacent to the bluegrass, 30 females in spring had a mean of 5.03 embryos; in autumn, 21 females had a mean of 5.19 embryos.

The gestation period is about 21 days. Young are hairless at birth but are already capable of making faint squeals. Eyes open at 9 or 10 days of age. At 17 days, young can forage for themselves.

Nests in which to rear the young are usually located below ground in an enlarged part of the burrow system. This is in contrast to the meadow vole in Illinois which usually builds its nest above ground. Underground nests of prairie voles are usually of large size, requiring extensive underground excavation of soil. The removed soil is often placed above ground in a pile, resulting in a noticeable mound. These voles in the summer may build surface nests consisting entirely of dried grasses, with the center part that is lived in consisting of finely shredded grasses. In one plot we examined, three nests were each about 15 cm below the ground surface. In two old nests, no longer in use, we found 22 fleas, numerous flea larvae, and a large number of small white mites. The fleas were identified as *Diamanus montanus* (Baker).

Getz et al. (1979) analyzed the average life expectancy for prairie voles in east central Illinois. Animals were taken in fields of alfalfa, in bluegrass, and in a prairie of bluegrass and a mixture of other plants. In the alfalfa, expectancy was 4.3 weeks for males and 4.5 weeks for females beyond their first capture as juveniles, which was estimated at three weeks. In the bluegrass, this was 3.3 weeks for males, 3.6 for females; in the prairie, 2.2 weeks and 2.3 weeks, respectively. It should be pointed out that survival or life expectancy is correlated with the cyclical condition of the population and other factors. Judged from Getz et al. figures, however, life expectancy at that time (1972–1976) was between 5.3 weeks and 7.5 weeks.

Populations

Numerous accounts detail the populations of prairie voles and the changes in the numbers of individuals within a population throughout the year and from year to year (cyclical). For example, in southern Indiana, approximately 8 voles were caught in the grassland in 1966 in 100 trap-nights the first third of the year, 18 in the second third, and 3 in the last third. In 1967, only one, one, and less than one were caught in 100 trap-nights in the same three periods (Keller and Krebs, 1970).

In Champaign County, Illinois, Getz et al. (1979) found peak densities of prairie voles in alfalfa mixed with bluegrass, goldenrod, and other grasses of 240 per hectare in November 1972 and 110 per hectare in July 1976; in 1974 there were less than 10 per hectare. Populations in bluegrass fields at the same times did not reach such high peaks, for they were 125 in 1972 and 60 in 1976. Refer also to the section "Numbers, populations, and fluctuations of Illinois mammals," page 21.

Variation

Within the range of *M. ochrogaster*, five subspecies are currently recognized. Within and surrounding Illinois, specimens are referred to *M. o. ochrogaster,* with the subspecies *M. o. ohionensis* occurring no closer than eastern Indiana.

Microtus ochrogaster ochrogaster (Wagner)

1842. *Hypudaeus ochrogaster* Wagner, *in* Schreber, Die
Saugthiere . . ., suppl., 3:592. Type from America,
but probably New Harmony, Posey Co., Indiana.

1898. *Microtus (Pedomys) ochrogaster*, J. A. Allen, Bull.
Amer. Mus. Nat. Hist., 10:459.

Range. Throughout the state (Map 8.43).

Diagnosis and Comparisons. A subspecies of medium
size; hind foot usually between 18 and 20 mm; dorsum
dark brownish-black with blond-tipped hairs interspersed, resulting in a grizzled effect; venter with an
ochraceous wash. Differs from *M. o. ohioensis* in that
the venter has an ochraceous rather than a silvery to gray
wash; total length averaging greater, hind foot longer.

Records of occurrence. SPECIMENS EXAMINED, 1,105.
Jo Daviess Co.: [1] near Galena, 2 (FM). **Lake Co.:** [2] Beach,
1 (FM); [3] Fox Lake, 6 (FM). **Carroll Co.:** [4] Mississippi Palisades
State Park, 3 (UI). **Lee Co.:** [5] 5 mi N Meriden [labeled La
Salle Co.], 1 (NIU). **Cook Co.:** [7] Des Plaines, 4 (UI); [8] Chicago,
1 (UI); [9a] ⅔ mi W McCook, 1 (UI); [9b] Hodgkins, 2 (UI); [9c]
Justice, 1 (UI); [9d] ½ mi W Hickory Hills, 3 (UI); [10] Chicago
Heights, 1 (NIU); Sokol Camp, Cook Co. Forest Preserve
[location uncertain], 3 (UI). **Rock Island Co.:** [13] 12 mi S
Moline, 2 (UI). **Henry Co.:** [14] 4½ mi N Kewanee, 1 (UI). **La
Salle Co.:** [15] ½ mi S, 2 mi W Marseilles, 9 (UI). **Grundy Co.:**
[16a] 6 mi W Morris, 8 (UI); [16b] 6 mi W, ½ mi S Morris, 3
(UI); [17a] Morris, 5 (UI); [17b] Goose Lake Prairie State Park,
10 (UI). **Will Co.:** [18] Wheatland Twp., 1 (FM). **Kankakee Co.:**
[19] 6 mi E St. Anne, 1 (UI). **Warren Co.:** [20] 2 mi S Smithshire,
4 (UI). **McDonough Co.:** [21] Macomb, 1 (ISM). **Knox Co.:** [22]
4 mi S Victoria, 1 (UI). **Fulton Co.:** [23a] ½ mi N Norris, 3 (UI);
[23b] 2 mi NW Canton, 2 (UI); [23c] 1 mi W Canton, 7 (UI);
[24a] Bryant, 1 (UI); [24b] 1 mi E Bryant, 2 (UI); [25] 6 mi W
Lewistown, 1 (UI). **Peoria Co.:** [26a] 2 mi N Edwards, 1 (UI);
[26b] 12 mi W Peoria, 3 (UI); [26c] 10 mi W Peoria, 1 (UI); [27]
4 mi W Peoria, 2 (UI). **Woodford Co.:** [28a] 1 mi S, 1¼ mi W
Eureka, 1 (UI); [28b] 1 mi S, 1 mi W Eureka, 1 (UI); [28c] 1¼
mi S, 1 mi W Eureka, 1 (UI). **Tazewell Co.:** [29] 3 mi N, 4 mi
W Washington, 1 (UI); [30] 1 mi N Morton, 1 (UI); [31] ½ mi
E Green Valley, 3 (UI). **Livingston Co.:** [32] 8 mi E, 2 mi S
Strawn, 2 (UI). **McLean Co.:** [33a] 2 mi W Normal, 1 (ISU); [33b]
Bloomington, 3 (UI); [34a] 3½ mi SE Bloomington, 1 (UI); [34b]
5 mi SE Bloomington, 2 (UI); [35] 1 mi SW Funks Grove, 1
(ISU); [36a] 3 mi NW Leroy, 1 (UI); [36b] 2 mi N, 1½ mi W
Leroy, 1 (UI); [36c] 1 mi N, ½ mi W Leroy, 4 (UI); [36d] Leroy,
1 (UI). **Iroquois Co.:** [37] 1 mi W Donovan, 2 (UI); [38] 1 mi W
Loda, 1 (UI). **Adams Co.:** [39] 10 mi NE Quincy, 1 (UI); [40] ½
mi W Camp Point, 2 (ISM). **Mason Co.:** [41a] 3½ mi N, 2 mi
E Havana, 2 (UI); [41b] 5 mi NE Havana, 2 (UI); [42] 2½ mi W
San Jose, 1 (ISU). **Cass Co.:** [43] 1 mi NW Virginia, 1 (UI). **Logan
Co.:** [44] 1 ½ mi S Latham, 1 (UI). **De Witt Co.:** [45] ½ mi S
Farmer City, 1 (UI); [46] 1 mi W Clinton, 1 (UI); [47] 1 mi SE
Lane, 1 (UI). **Piatt Co.:** [48] 2½ mi W Mansfield, 1 (UI); [49a] 2
mi N White Heath, 1 (UI); [49b] Sangamon River, 1¼ mi N
White Heath, 2 (UI); [49c] ½ mi N Monticello, 1 (UI); [49d]
Monticello, 2 (UI); [50a] 1 ½ mi ENE Cisco, 4 (UI); [50d] Allerton
Park, 6 (UI).

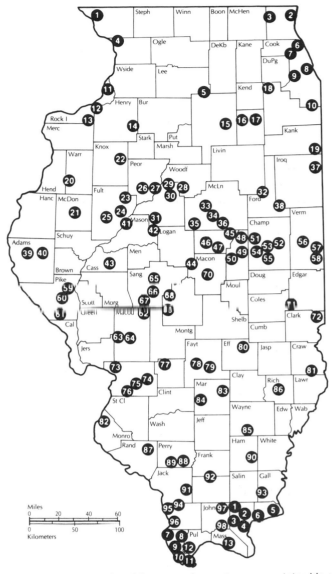

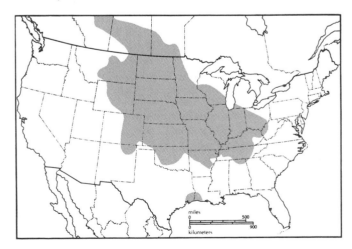

Map 8.43. Prairie voles, *Microtus ochrogaster,* occur statewide.
The subspecies is *M. o. ochrogaster.* Numbered localities of
occurrence are referenced in *Records of occurrence.* The range
of the species in the United States is shaded.

Champaign Co.: [51a] 2 mi NE Mahomet, 1 (UI); [51b] 1½ mi NE Mahomet, 1 (UI); [51c] 1 mi W Mahomet, 1 (UI); [51d] ½ mi W Mahomet, 4 (UI); [51e] Mahomet, Sangamon River, 2 (UI); [52a] 6 mi NE Urbana, 1 (UI); [52b] 5 mi E Urbana, 6 (UI); [52c] 1 mi E Mayview, 1 (UI); [53a] 4 mi N, 1½ mi E Urbana, 5 (UI); [53b] 2 mi N Urbana, 4 (UI); [53c] 2 mi E, 2 mi N Urbana, 2 (UI); [53d] 1⅛ mi N Urbana, 6 (UI); [53e] 1 mi W, 1 mi N Urbana, 2 (UI); [53f] 1 mi N Urbana, 1 (UI); [53g] 3 mi E, 1 mi N Urbana, 6 (UI); [53h] ¾ mi N, 3 mi E Urbana, 2 (UI); [53i] 1½ mi W Champaign, 2 (UI); [53j] 1 mi W Champaign 2 (UI); [53k] Champaign, 36 (UI); [53l] Urbana, 39 (UI); [53m] ⅕ mi S Urbana, 2 (UI); [53n] ½ mi S Champaign, 1 (UI); [53o] 1 mi S Champaign, 6 (UI); [53p] ½ mi SW UI, 1 (UI); [53q] 1 mi S, ½ mi W Urbana, 1 (UI); [53r] 1 mi S Urbana, 4 (UI); [53s] 1 ½ mi S Champaign, 1 (UI); [53t] 1 mi S UI, 1 (UI); [53u] 2 mi S Champaign, 7 (UI); [53v] 1½ mi SW UI, 4 (UI); [53w] 2 mi S Urbana, 1 (UI); [53x] 2½ mi S Champaign, 6 (UI); [53y] 2½ mi S Urbana, 4 (UI); [53z] 3 mi S Champaign, 3 (UI); [53aa] 3 mi S, 3 mi E Urbana, 1 (UI); [54a] 1 mi E Bondville, Kaskaskia River, 3 (UI); [54b] 9 mi SW Champaign, 1 (UI); [55] 6 mi S Urbana, 5 (UI); no specific locality [not plotted], 4 (UI).

Vermilion Co.: [56a] 1 mi W Higginsville, 2 (UI); [56b] 2½ mi N, 1¾ mi E Newtown, 1 (UI); [56c] 2 mi N, 1½ mi E Newtown, 1 (UI); [56d] 1¼ mi W, ½ mi S Snider, 1 (UI); [56e] ½ mi S, ½ mi E Newtown, 3 (UI); [56f] 1 mi WSW Oakwood, 1 (UI); [57a] 1½ mi NE Danville, 1 (UI); [57b] ½ mi NE Danville, 1 (UI); [57c] Danville, 1 (UI); [57d] 4 mi SE Danville, 1 (UI); [58] 3 ⅘ mi E, 2⅖ mi S Westville, 3 (UI). **Pike Co.:** [59] 1 mi S Griggsville, 17 (UI); [60a] 3 mi N, 1 mi E Pittsfield, 13 (UI); [60b] Pittsfield, 2 (UI); [60c] 3½ mi S Pittsfield, 13 (UI); [61] 2 mi W Nebo, 15 (UI). **Macoupin Co.:** [62] Virden, 1 (UI); [63] 1½ mi S Chesterfield, 190 (UI); [64a] 3 mi NE Beaver Dam State Park, 1 (UI); [64b] 2 mi NE Beaver Dam State Park, 15 (UI); [64c] 1 mi N Beaver Dam, 1 (UI). **Sangamon Co.:** [65a] 2 mi N Springfield, 1 (ISM); [65b] ½ mi S Springfield, 4 (UI); [66a] 1 mi E Chatham, 1 (ISM); [66b] Old Chatham Rd. near Arnold School, 1 (ISM); [66c] 2 mi N Glenarm, 1 (ISM); [67] Auburn, 1 (UI). **Christian Co.:** [68] 4 mi WSW Edinburg, 1 (UI); [69] 6 mi N Morrisonville, 3 (UI). **Macon Co.:** [70a] 2.3 mi W Decatur, 3 (UI); [70b] Decatur, 2 (UI). **Edgar Co.:** [71] Kansas, 2 (US). **Clark Co.:** [72] 4 mi N, 8½ mi E Marshall, Clear Creek, 9 (UI). **Madison Co.:** [73a] ¼ mi E Fosterburg, 1 (UI); [73b] 1 mi N Alton, 1 (UI); [74] 3½ mi WSW Grantfork, 1 (UI); [75] 1½ mi SE Kuhn, 3 (UI); [76a] 2 mi NE Glen Carbon, 1 (UI); [76b] 1½ mi SE Glen Carbon, 1 (UI); [76c] 2 mi E Collinsville, 1 (UI). **Bond Co.:** [77a] ½ mi E Reno, 1 (UI); [77b] 1 mi E Reno, 2 (UI). **Fayette Co.:** [78] 1 mi NW Vandalia, 1 (UI); [79] 3 mi S Brownstown, 5 (UI). **Effingham Co.:** [80] 1½ mi N Effingham, 1 (UI). **Crawford Co.:** [81] Flat Rock, 2 (CAS). **Monroe Co.:** [82] 2½ mi N Fountain, 6 (UI). **Marion Co.:** [83] ½ mi N Omega, 1 (UI); [84] Odin, 2 (US). **Wayne Co.:** [85a] 3 mi S, 3 mi E Sims, 2 (UI); [85b] 4 mi S, 3 mi E Sims, 3 (UI). **Richland Co.:** [86] Olney, 2 (US). **Randolph Co.:** [87] near Sparta, 1 (UI). **Perry Co.:** [88] 2 mi W DuQuoin, 13 (SIC); [89] Pyatts striplands, 2 (SRL). **Hamilton Co.:** [90] ½ mi W Hamilton County Conservation Area, 1 (UI). **Jackson Co.:** [91a] Carbondale, 4 (SRL), 4 (SIC); [91b] ½ mi S Carbondale, 1 (SRL). **Williamson Co.:** [92] 3 mi N Johnston City, 2 (UI). **Gallatin Co.:** [93] 3 mi SE Equality, 2 (UI). **Union Co.:** [94] 4 mi NW Cobden, 1 (SRL); [95a] Pine Hills Rec. Area, 3 (UI), 1 (ISM); [95b] Wolf Lake, 1 (US); [96a] 1.9 mi E Ware, 1 (UI); [96b] 3 mi SE Ware, 4 (UI); [96c] 3 mi S Ware, 1 (UI); [96d] 4 mi S Ware, Union County Conservation Area, 1 (UI); [96e] 6 mi S, 2 mi E Ware, 1 (UI). **Johnson Co.:** [97] Ozark, 1 (FM); [98a] ⅓ mi NE Grantsburg, 7 (UI); [98b] Reevesville, 2 (FM).

Pope Co.: [1] ½ mi E McCormick, 2 (SRL); [2a] 3 mi E Eddyville, 1 (UI); [2b] 4 mi SE Eddyville, 2 (UI); [3a] 1½ mi S Glendale, 136 (UI); [3b] 3¾ mi N Dixon Springs, 2 (UI); [3c] 2½ mi S Glendale, 1 (UI); [3d] 2½ mi S, ½ mi E Glendale, 2 (UI); [3e] Dixon Springs, Glendale Lake, 15 (UI); [3f] 2 mi E, ½ mi S Dixon Springs, 6 (UI); [4a] 3.8 mi W Golconda, 12 (UI); [4b] Golconda, 1 (UI). **Hardin Co.:** [5] 3 mi E Lamb, 1 (UI); [6a] 1 mi S Eichorn, 6 (UI); [6b] Rosiclare, 15 (FM). **Alexander Co.:** [7] McClure, 1 (US); [8] Tamms, 9 (SRL); [9a] 3¼ mi NNW Olive Branch, 4 (SRL); [9b] Olive Branch, 21 (FM), 3 (US); [9c] Horseshoe Lake, 10 (UI); [9d] Horseshoe Lake Island, 1 (UI); [9e] 2½ mi S Olive Branch, 31 (UI); [9f] 3 mi S Olive Branch, 4 (UI); [9g] 2 ¼ mi NW Miller City, 23 (UI); [9h] 2 mi NW Miller City, 14 (UI); [9i] ¼ mi N Miller City, 1 (UI); [9j] 1½ mi E Miller City, 36 (UI); [9k] 1½ mi E, 1½ mi S Miller City, 2 (UI); [10a] 1½ mi NW Cache, 1 (SRL); [10b] Cache, 6 (SRL); [10c] 5¼ mi S, 2 mi E Willard, 1 (UI); [11] ½ mi N Cairo, 1 (ISU). **Pulaski Co.:** [12] 2 mi W Mounds, 1 (UI). **Massac Co.:** [13a] 4 mi NE Metropolis, 1 (SIC); [13b] 1½ mi N Metropolis, 2 (SRL); [13c] 3 mi E Metropolis, 1 (SIC).

Additional records. **Cook Co.:** [6] West Northfield, 1 (UM). **Rock Island Co.:** [11] Cordova (Severinghaus, 1976:125); [12] 5 mi E, 2 mi S Moline, (Severinghaus, 1976:125). **Piatt Co.:** [50c] Allerton Park, 5 mi W, 2½ mi S Monticello, 1 (FSM). **Champaign Co.:** [53l] Urbana, 2 (UM). **Macoupin Co.:** [63] 1 ½ mi S Chesterfield, 11 (UM). **Alexander Co.:** [8] Tamms, 3 (FSM); [9b] Olive Branch, 2 (FSM).

Microtus pinetorum, Woodland vole

Range. Throughout the state.

Diagnosis. Regarded as a species of *Microtus* but formerly placed in the genus *Pitymys,* characterized in Illinois by short tail (less than 25 mm), color of dorsum uniformly reddish black or chestnut with venter with a frosting of reddish brown; skull broad interorbitally (usually 4.3 mm or more), M^3 with two closed triangles in addition to an anterior and posterior loop, posterior loop simple; number of mammary glands four; plantar tubercles five. Other characters include relatively small eyes, fore claws larger than hind claws, M_1 with anterior border of fourth triangle slopes posteriorly at an angle of 50° or less to the anteroposterior midline of the tooth.

Color. Dorsum a dark chestnut or reddish black, sides more reddish, venter dark and lightly washed throughout with reddish brown. Juveniles appear more blackish than adults, with less reddish or chestnut. On a color basis, juveniles of all three species of *Microtus* are difficult to distinguish.

Chromosomes. 2N = 62; FN = 62; all autosomes acrocentric except one pair of small metacentrics; X

Fig. 8.101A. Pine vole, *Microtus pinetorum*. (From Hoffmeister and Mohr, 1957. Photograph from U.S. Fish and Wildlife Service)

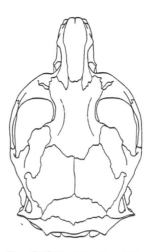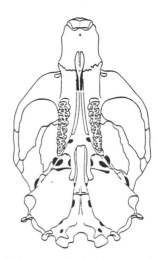

Fig. 8.101B. *Microtus (Pitymys) pinetorum*, dorsal and ventral views of skull; 5 mi W, 2½ mi S Monticello, Piatt Co., Illinois, 7524 UI. Male, 25.7 mm greatest length.

submetacentric, 'Y' small acrocentric (Beck and Mahan, 1978).

Comparisons. Microtus pinetorum differs from *M. pennsylvanicus* in having a much shorter tail (usually less than 25 mm rather than more than 36 mm), dorsum with fur more or less uniformly dark reddish brown or chestnut rather than blackish interspersed with browns and reds, venter with a heavy ochraceous wash rather than silver or cream; four mammary glands rather than eight; five plantar tubercles rather than six; M^3 with two closed triangles between the anterior and posterior loop and the posterior loop is simple, M^2 without a small triangle attached posteriorly; all autosomal chromosomes are acrocentrics except for one pair.

For a comparison with *Microtus ochrogaster,* see account of that species (p. 234).

For a comparison with *Synaptomys cooperi,* see *Comparisons* in the account of the genus *Microtus* (p. 228).

Remarks. In the earlier literature, these voles were referred to usually under the name *Pitymys pinetorum* and as pine voles. Since they no longer are regarded as distinct from voles of the genus *Microtus,* they are now placed in this genus. Because these animals live in a variety of habitats, but especially in wooded areas (although not necessarily in pine forests), they have been given the name woodland voles. Frequently the name pine voles still appears, and this refers to *Microtus pinetorum.*

Habitat

In central Illinois, woodland voles occur in the forest floor of those woods where there are oaks, maples, and hickories, with considerable decayed or decaying branches and trunks on the ground, and with leaf mold and humus. Here in the soft terrain they make use of the numerous burrows, some of which have been made by woodland voles, but others made by moles and short-tailed shrews. In southern Illinois, the voles may occur in bottom woodlands, grassy shoulders of roads, or in grassy fields beginning to grow up with brambles and honeysuckle (Layne, 1958a).

In western Tennessee, these voles were found in grassy patches within or adjacent to woods (Goodpaster and Hoffmeister, 1952). In Indiana, they have been taken in orchards, old corn stubble, pastures, railroad embankments, and cultivated fields, as well as the more expected places such as deciduous or mixed coniferous woods (Mumford and Whitaker, 1982).

Habits

Woodland voles dig shallow burrows in the friable soil or just under the leaf mold where they live. They also make use of runways made by other mammals. It is not unusual to trap these voles in the runways made by eastern moles. When woodland voles dig their own burrows, they use their forefeet, pushing the dirt under the body, and kicking it further back with their hind legs. When enough dirt has accumulated behind them, they turn around and push the dirt out, using their head, but leave the dirt under the leaf litter (Benton, 1955).

Nests may be placed in the burrow system or under a rotted log or stump which is reached by an underground burrow. Within a burrow or nest system, woodland voles may be colonial. Under decayed logs or stumps we have found several adult woodland voles together, four in one case and more than four in another case when they moved out so rapidly they could not all be counted.

Woodland voles are active during the day as well as at night, but may not be seen because they usually are moving under a leaf litter or a canopy of grasses. In Connecticut, 54 percent of 221 captures of the voles

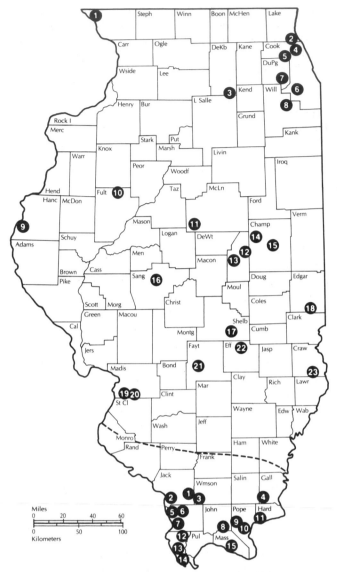

Map 8.44. Pine voles, *Microtus pinetorum*, occur statewide. Two subspecies are found in Illinois: *M. p. scalopsoides* north of the broken line; *M. p. auricularis*, south. Numbered localities of occurrence are referenced in *Records of occurrence*. The range of the species in the United States is shaded.

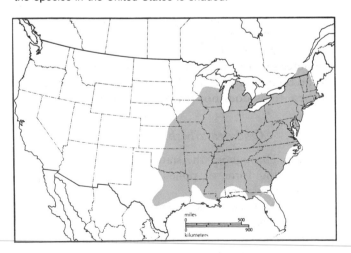

was made between 8:00 p.m. and 9:00 a.m.; 46 percent between 9:00 a.m. and 8:00 p.m.

Food

Nothing is known of the food habits of woodland voles in Illinois. In Indiana, of 25 animals taken throughout the year, but with 13 taken in the fall, the stomach contents consisted of roots, green vegetation, and mast in 63 percent of the volume and 96 percent of the frequency. There was a small amount of *Endogone* and insects.

In New York and Pennsylvania, woodland voles are said to feed on grass roots and stems in summer, fruits and seeds in the fall, bark and roots in the winter (Benton, 1955).

One gets the impression that woodland voles may be more opportunistic feeders than other microtines in Illinois. They may feed on grasses when these are available and the same for such fruits and bulbs as poke berries, wild onions, roots of various grasses and weeds, acorns, and various bulbs.

Reproduction

In northeastern United States, the breeding season is reported to extend from January through November. In Illinois, we have females carrying embryos in April, July, August, and October. Judging from young animals in the collection, it appears that young are born in Illinois in March and April, and in August through November. Whether they are born in other months is not certain.

The gestation period is about three weeks (20 to 24 days). The number of young for seven females in Illinois is 2.3 (2–3). In eastern United States, means for litter size (probably embryo-numbers) varies from means of 2.0 to 3.1.

Young have the eyes open at seven to nine days of age and are weaned at three weeks. Females are sexually mature at about two and a half months of age.

Variation

Three subspecies of *Microtus pinetorum* may occur in Illinois, judging from the current literature: *M. p. scalopsoides* (type locality, Long Island, New York) with a synonym of *Microtus pinetorum kennicottii* (type locality, Illinois), *M. p. auricularis* (type locality, Adams County, Mississippi), *M. p. nemoralis* (type locality, Adair County, Oklahoma).

It is apparent from available material that specimens from southern Illinois have longer skulls that are broader across the zygomatic arches. These specimens are here referred to *M. p. auricularis* (p. 241), but others might argue that they are referable to *M. p. nemoralis*. Specimens from central and northern Illinois are referred to *M. p. scalopsoides*.

Microtus pinetorum scalopsoides (Audubon and Bachman)

1841. *Arvicola scalopsoides* Audubon and Bachman, Proc. Acad. Nat. Sci. Phila., 1:97. Type from Long Island, New York.

1896. *Microtus pinetorum scalopsoides*, Batchelder, Proc. Boston Soc. Nat. Hist., 27:187.

1858. *Arvicola kennicottii* Baird, Mammals, *in* Repts. Expl. Surv. . . . , 8:547. Type from Illinois.

Range. Northern and central Illinois, mostly north of the Mt. Vernon Hill Country (Map 8.44).

Diagnosis and Comparisons. A subspecies of *M. pinetorum* with a short, narrow skull (in Illinois), lateral pits of palatines not especially shallow; externally small.

In Illinois, *M. p. scalopsoides* differs from *M. p. auricularis* in having a shorter, narrower skull, slightly shorter feet and total length, and shallower lateral pits of the palatines.

Records of occurrence. SPECIMENS EXAMINED, 46. **Jo Daviess Co.:** [1] 1 mi W, ½ mi S Menominee, 1 (SRL). **Lake Co.:** [2] Highland Park, 2 (FM). **De Kalb Co.:** [3] Somonauk, 2 (CAS). **Cook Co.:** [4] West Northfield, 1 (US); [5] Elk Grove, 1 (CAS); [6] Palos Park, 1 (CAS). **Du Page Co.:** [7] Downers Grove, 1 (FM). **Hancock Co.:** [9] Warsaw*, 1 (US). **Fulton Co.:** [10] 10 mi NW Canton, 4 (UI). **McLean Co.:** [11] 1 mi SW Funks Grove, 1 (ISU). **Piatt Co.:** [12] White Heath, 1 (UI); [13] Allerton Park, 5 mi W, 2½ mi S Monticello, 15 (UI). **Champaign Co.:** [14] 3½ mi NE Mahomet, 1 (UI); [15a] Brownfield Woods, 1 (FM); [15b] Trelease Woods, 1 (UI). **Sangamon Co.:** [16] Springfield, 1 (ISM). **Edgar Co.:** [18] 6 mi S Paris, 1 (UI). **Madison Co.:** [19] 3 mi W, 1 mi N Collinsville, 3 (UI); [20] 1½ mi E Collinsville, 1 (UI). **Fayette Co.:** [21a] 2 mi NE Vandalia, 1 (UI); [21b] 1 mi NW Vandalia, 1 (UI); [21c] 1 mi W Vandalia, 2 (UI). **Effingham Co.:** [22] 3 mi NW Effingham, 1 (UI). **Crawford Co.:** [23] Flat Rock, 1 (CAS).

Additional records. **Will Co.:** [8] New Lenox, (Necker and Hatfield, 1941:55). **Shelby Co.:** [17] Hidden Springs State Forest, Report, Ill. Dept. Conserv.

Microtus pinetorum auricularis Bailey

1898. *Microtus pinetorum auricularis* V. Bailey, Proc. Biol. Soc. Wash., 12:90. Type from Washington, Adams Co., Mississippi.

Range. Southern Illinois, mostly in the Shawnee Hills and southward (Map 8.44).

Diagnosis and Comparisons. A subspecies of *M. pinetorum* with a fairly long and broad skull, lateral pits of the palatines shallow; total length and hind feet long. For a comparison with *M. p. scalopsoides*, see account of that subspecies, above.

Records of occurrence. SPECIMENS EXAMINED, 46. **Jackson Co.:** [1a] Carbondale, 2 (FS), 5 (SRL), 1 (SIC), 1 (US); [1b]

---
* Worthen specimen.

Drury Creek, 1 (SRL); [2] Fountain Bluff, 1 (NHS). **Williamson Co.:** [3] W side Little Grassy Lake, 2 (UI). **Gallatin Co.:** [4a] 3 mi SE Equality, 2 (UI); [4b] 3 mi N Karbers Ridge [labelled Hardin Co.], 1 (UI). **Union Co.:** [5a] Aldridge, Pine Hills, 1 (FS); [5b] Pine Hills near Wolf Lake, 1 (SIC), 1 (UI); [6] 3 mi W Cobden, 1 (SIC); [7] 5 mi S Ware, 1 (UI). **Johnson Co.:** [8] Reevesville, 2 (FM); no specific locality [not plotted], 1 (UI). **Pope Co.:** [9] Dixon Springs, 1 (NHS); [10] Golconda, 1 (UI). **Hardin Co.:** [11] Rosiclare, 1 (FM). **Alexander Co.:** [12] 1½ mi NW Elco, 1 (UI); [13a] Olive Branch, 14 (FM); [13b] 2½ mi S Olive Branch, 1 (UI); [14] 5¼ mi S, 2 mi E Willard, 1 (UI). **Massac Co.:** [15] Metropolis, 1 (CAS); no specific locality [not plotted], 1 (UI).

Ondatra, Muskrats

Diagnosis. A large microtine or vole that is highly specialized for living in the water, tail elongated, nearly hairless, and compressed laterally; hind feet elongated, toes with a fringe of hairs which extends to heel; fur thick, long, and lax; skull vole-like but larger and heavier, cheek teeth prismatic; mammary glands, three pairs.

Dental formula. 1/1, 0/0, 0/0, 3/3.

Chromosomes. 2N = 54, FN = 54; autosomes are acrocentric except for one pair of submetacentrics; X acrocentric; Y acrocentric (Hsu and Benirschke, 1971b).

Comparisons. Ondatra differs from *Microtus* and *Synaptomys* and all other Illinois murid rodents in its large size, tail compressed laterally, hind feet elongate (usually more than 75 mm) and partly webbed, toes with a well-developed fringe of hairs; underfur on dorsum and venter well developed and thick; alveolar length of upper molar toothrow exceeding 12 mm, jugal portion of zygomatic arches deep dorsoventrally, skull relatively narrow interorbitally.

Aging. Various methods of placing muskrats in broad age categories have been proposed. In animals between five and eight months, the distal processes of the baculum are entirely cartilaginous or centers of calcification have only just started (Elder and Shanks, 1962). Animals with testes less than 7/16 in. long, turgid, and cream colored have not reached their first breeding season (Schwartz and Schwartz, 1981).

In young muskrat, the re-entrant folds (or grooves) on the outer side of the first upper molar extend all the way to the bony alveolus. In adult animals, the anteriormost of these folds does not reach the alveolus.

Ondatra zibethicus, Muskrat

Range. Throughout the state where there is sufficient water in the form of ponds, lakes, streams, drainage ditches, or swamps.

Diagnosis. Characters as given for the genus since it is now considered as monotypic; additional characters for Illinois *O. zibethicus* include: total length in excess of 475 mm, hind foot more than 60 mm; tail not

Fig. 8.102. Muskrat, *Ondatra zibethicus.* Photograph from Illinois Natural History Survey.

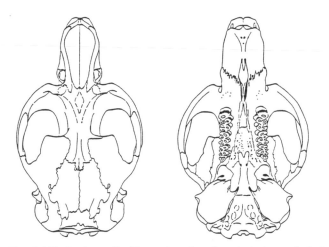

Fig. 8.103. *Ondatra zibethicus,* dorsal and ventral views of skull; 2 mi S Peotone, Will Co., Illinois, 31054 UI. Female, 66.5 mm greatest length.

only compressed and nearly as long as the body but nearly hairless; ears small and nearly lost in fur; incisor broad and orangish-colored, M^3 with two closed triangles between anterior loop and complicated posterior loop; interorbital region exceedingly narrow relative to size of skull and this is indicated by least interorbital breadth

usually being less than 16 percent of zygomatic breadth whereas in other murids, it is usually more than 20 percent.

Color. Dorsum dark or reddish brown with guard hairs blackish, venter chestnut or tawny, underfur more grayish, tops of feet about same color as back, bottoms of feet blackish, tail slightly darker than back. Juveniles darker than adults.

Comparisons. For a comparison with other microtines as well as other murids, see account for the genus *Ondatra* (p. 241).

Remarks. Muskrats are abundant in Illinois, judged from the fact that over many years the annual harvest of these animals for fur is among the top 10 states in the nation. The many miles of man-made drainage ditches, ideal soil conditions, and suitably vegetated banks provide excellent habitat for these rats.

Habitat

Muskrats in Illinois may be house builders or bank dwellers. House builders live in conspicuous cone-shaped or mounded houses built of bulrushes, cattail, smartweed, or similar material in a marsh, shallow lake, embayment, or shallow pond. The house always protrudes above the water level and the nest, situated within the house, is

Fig. 8.104. Marshy area of Chautauqua Lake, Mason Co., Illinois, with numerous muskrat houses. Entrances to the houses are below the water line. Photograph by James Ayers, 1945.

above the high-water line. In such situations, these animals are often referred to as marsh muskrats. They require that water levels should be relatively stable in places where they live. If the water is shallow and the level stable enough in stripmined ponds, the animals may build houses.

Other muskrats in Illinois are bank dwellers and dig burrows back into the banks where they rest and rear young. There are probably more bank-inhabiting than house-dwelling muskrats in Illinois. Between 6,000 and 7,000 miles of ditches and small stream banks in Illinois, or about one mile of ditch for every two and one-half square miles of land, make this possible. There may be several entrances to such bank nests, but all access is intended to be below the water level. Reduction in the water level may cause some entrances to be above the water. Bank muskrats live along drainage ditches, creeks, streams, and ponds. The many hundreds of miles of drainage ditches together with small streams and ponds provide ideal habitat for bank muskrats.

Strip-mining in Illinois, as in Perry County, resulted in new habitat for muskrats. Verts (1959) found that they soon occupied almost every pond that was sufficiently deep to retain water throughout the year, but were more abundant in the smaller ponds. Also, he found that they

were less numerous in ponds with banks that were rocky or with much shale.

The numerous bottomland lakes that occur in the valleys of the Illinois and Mississippi rivers provide habitat for house-building muskrats. Nevertheless, the fluctuation of water in such lakes may be considerable, and the drying up as well as the flooding of such lakes, together with fluctuations between these extremes, is critical to muskrat occupation and even more important than the kinds and availability of food. Food and these fluctuations, however, are correlated. Bottomland lakes with limited water fluctuation usually provide good stands of cattails, smartweed, duck potato (*Sagittaria*), and black willow.

Burrows and Houses

In strip-mine ponds in southern Illinois, Arata (1959) found that the burrows or tunnels in six dens averaged 18 (12–24) ft. The amount of burrowing was dependent upon the kinds of substrate and obstacles in the way. Burrows averaged six inches in diameter and sloped upward just beyond the entrance at about a 45° angle. At about five feet into the bank, they widened to form a chamber or den. Such chambers were about 24 by 36 inches, with a height of eight inches. Entrances were

Fig. 8.105. Bank burrow entrance, indicated by arrow, to a muskrat den. The paths that lead to the entrance are in an accentuated black. (From Hoffmeister and Mohr, 1957)

frequently lined with cattail or sweet clover. As many as three muskrats were found in one system that had a large chamber and numerous interconnecting burrows. Arata (1959) thought there were, on the average, two entrances per animal. Thus a den area with four entrances might have two muskrats. If the water level dropped to the point of exposing the main entrance, Arata said that some muskrats established new dens. He did not indicate that they dug a deeper burrow but one would expect that they would.

Bank-dwelling muskrats may construct feeding platforms which consist of accumulated vegetation placed on rocks or logs in the pond.

Houses in lakes or marshes are built so as to extend above the water level. They consist of cut vegetation which a muskrat has hauled to the house site. Nests are built within and near the top of the house. In central Illinois near the Illinois River, dwelling houses varied from 20 to 46 inches above ice-level and measured between four and six feet in longest diameter (Bellrose, 1950). Several underwater tunnels or burrows lead through the house to the nest chamber. In most places, muskrats build two types of houses: dwelling house and feeding houses. Feeding houses are smaller than dwelling houses. Bellrose (1950) found they extended only 6 to 18 inches above the ice and had a diameter between 1½ and 2 feet. Feeding houses have no nest chamber and usually only one entrance hole.

Habits

Muskrats are nocturnal, but they may also be active on cloudy, dark days. In the winter, they are active under the ice but also surface at holes in the ice. Muskrats produce some sounds that have been likened to a squeak, a high-pitched *n-n-n-n*, and a chattering, produced by clicking the incisors (Willner, et al., 1980).

Muskrats do considerable fighting, especially during the breeding seasons and at times of territorial expansion.

Muskrats are well equipped for aquatic life. They swim well, both forward and backward. They can remain submerged with only their eyes and tips of the nose above water.

During the breeding period, a secretion with a musky odor exudes from the paired perineal musk glands at the ventral base of the tail of both males and females.

Food

In central Illinois, Bellrose (1950) found the food preference of marsh muskrats to be the following plants, in descending order of importance:

1. Cattails
2. Pickerelweed
3. Hard- and softstem bulrush
4. River bulrush
5. Marsh smartweed
6. White waterlily
7. Sedges
8. American lotus
9. Black willow
10. Duck potato
11. Reed cane
12. Wild rice
13. Water milfoil
14. Coontail

He found that the overall population value — that is, the muskrat-house density relative to a species of plant — was as follows:

1. River bulrush
2. Cattails
3. Marsh smartweed
4. Hardstem bulrush
5. Reed cane
6. Sedges
7. American lotus
8. Wild rice
9. Duck potato

In winter, bank muskrats in southern Illinois feed most extensively on cattail and narrow-leaved pondweed, with lesser amounts of stonewort, willow, sweet clover, and broomsedge (Arata, 1959). Throughout the rest of the year, bank muskrats feed on any of the available vegetative items that are listed above for marsh muskrats. For example, Arata (1959) found that when cattails were present, about 50 percent of the diet was of this plant. When cattail was absent, sweet clover was high in the diet. Other foods commonly eaten in summer were broomsedge, goldenrod, and willow, as well as various rushes, sedges, manna grass, rose, and nightshade.

Although muskrats are principally herbivorous, they are known at times to eat crayfish, clams, parts of fishes, and turtles. They are opportunistic feeders primarily, depending upon kinds of plants and the other food items available, the density, and water levels.

Reproduction

In Illinois, muskrats usually have young in April through June and in the fall. Arata (1959) after analyzing the reproductive tracts of females in southern Illinois concluded that two litters a year were generally produced. He found the average litter size to be 3.4. Other workers have found the mean litter size to be higher, some as high as eight. At Willow Slough, Indiana, almost adjacent to the Illinois line, the mean was 6.9.

The gestation period is between 25 and 30 days. Young are nearly hairless at birth and are reared in the nest within the burrow or house. Eyes open at about two weeks; the young can swim at three weeks, and are weaned at four weeks.

Populations

In central Illinois near the Illinois River, Rice Lake contains about 1,034 acres of water and marsh, with an average depth of two feet. The take of muskrats in 11 years between 1932 and 1943, as given by Bellrose (1945), is shown in Figure 8.107. Variation in numbers of muskrats in any given place may be caused by several factors, including food, water depth and fluctuation, and flooding. Bellrose (1950) made a survey of muskrat houses by different types of vegetation in shallow lakes and marshes adjacent to the Illinois River. In one 11-acre cattail-reed situation, there were 75 houses one year; in areas that were predominantly sedges (*Carex*), there were 8 to 38 percent fewer houses. Places of extensive growths of lotus or duck potato were also low in the number of houses.

Fig. 8.106. Two man-made drainage ditches in Champaign County showing well-vegetated banks that are ideal for bank-dwelling muskrats. Photographs by Charles Hume, 1949.

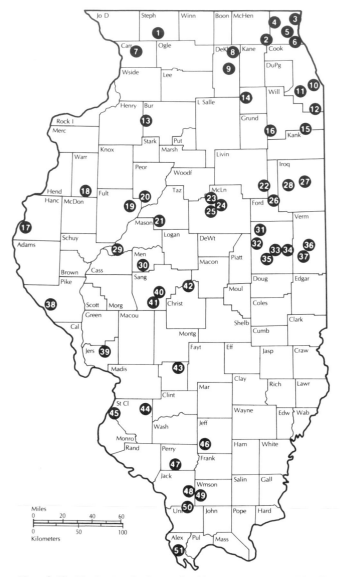

Map 8.45. Muskrats, *Ondatra zibethicus,* occur statewide. The subspecies is *O. z. zibethicus.* Numbered localities of occurrence are referenced in *Records of occurrence.* The range of the species in the United States is shaded.

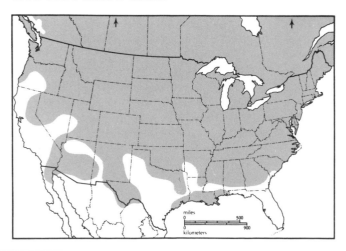

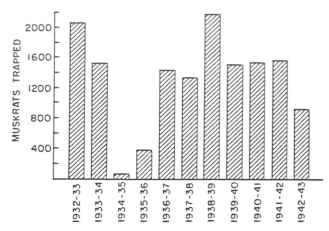

Fig. 8.107. Numbers of muskrat harvested, by years, at Rice Lake, Fulton Co., Illinois, an area of approximately 1,034 acres with an average depth of two feet. (Modified from Bellrose, 1945)

In the late 1940's, Hume (1949) studied the habits and numbers of muskrat along drainage ditches in Champaign County, with special attention to the variation caused by differing bank conditions: bare bank, sparsely vegetated bank, thickly grown bank, over-grown bank. He found that the type of soil composing the banks and bottom were probably more important than the amount of vegetation. Recently dredged ditches have few rats as do those with steep banks, chiefly because vegetation cannot grow on them. Also, if the banks and bottom are of a dense clay, the muskrats cannot burrow into them. Hume found that if food plants were not sufficiently abundant on or along the banks, but cultivated fields were adjacent, muskrats made use of some of the vegetation in the fields. In central Illinois, drainage ditches with bare banks are uncommon unless recently dredged, however. Hume found that ditches with well-vegetated banks supported approximately 60 muskrats per mile.

Variation

Nearly all populations of muskrats in eastern United States are referred to *Ondatra z. zibethicus.*

Ondatra zibethicus zibethicus (Linnaeus)

1766. [*Castor*] *zibethicus* Linnaeus, Syst. nat., 12, 1:79. Type from eastern Canada.
1795. [*Ondatra*] *zibethicus,* Link, Beytrage zur Natur-gesch., 1 (2):76.

Range. As given for the species (p. 241).

Diagnosis and Comparisons. A subspecies of large size, long tail, dark color; skull large but not especially broad across zygomata.

Records of occurrence. SPECIMENS EXAMINED, 116.
Stevenson Co.: [1] 3 mi W Freeport, 1 (UI). **Lake Co.:** [3] Beach, 1 (FM); [4] Fox Lake, 7 (FM); [5] Libertyville, 1 (FM); [6a] Prairie

Table 8.27. External and cranial measurements (in mm) of *Ondatra zibethicus*: mean, minimum-maximum, and standard deviation.

Species & Subspecies	Locality	N	Total length	Tail length	Head-body length	Hind foot length	Condylo-basal length	Zygomatic breadth	Cranial breadth	Inter-orbital breadth	Nasal length	Alveolar maxillary toothrow
Ondatra zibethicus	Northeastern Illinois	12	558.2 471-595 37.17	248.4 213-263 14.79	309.6 258-342 29.41	77.3 70-83 3.58	64.75 59.8-67.6 2.22	40.48 37.6-42.6 1.61	18.93 17.5-20.8 0.99	6.60 5.9-7.0 0.38	21.13 19.0-22.9 1.05	16.31 15.6-17.2 0.44

View, 1 (UI); [6b] Highland Park, 5 (FM). **Carroll Co.:** [7] Mt. Carroll, 1 (UI). **De Kalb Co.:** [8a] ¾ mi NNE Genoa, 1 (UI); [8b] 1 mi W Genoa, 1 (NIU); [9] De Kalb, 2 (NIU). **Cook Co.:** [10a] Chicago, Jackson Park, 3 (FM); [10b] Chicago, Oakwoods Cemetery, 2 (FM); [11] Palos Hills, 1 (FM); [12] Chicago Heights, 1 (FM). **Bureau Co.:** [13] 1 mi NW Mineral, 1 (UI). **Kendall Co.:** [14] 2 mi S Plano, 1 (NIU). **Will Co.:** [15a] 2 mi E Peotone, 1 (UI); [15b] 2 mi S Peotone, 2 (UI); [16] 2 mi E, 1 mi N Diamond [labelled Grundy Co.], 1 (UI). **Hancock Co.:** [17] Warsaw* 1 (FM). **Warren Co.:** [18a] 2 mi E Roseville, 1 (UI); [18b] 1¼ mi S Youngstown, 1 (UI). **Fulton Co.:** [19a] 1 mi W Canton, 1 (UI); [19b] 3 mi S Canton, 1 (UI); no specific locality [not plotted], 1 (UI). **Peoria Co.:** [20] 3½ mi S, 2 mi W Hanna City, 1 (UI). **Tazewell Co.:** [21] near Green Valley, 1 (UI). **Livingston Co.:** [22] Chatsworth, 1 (UI). **McLean Co.:** [23] 10 mi N Normal, 2 (ISU); [24] 2 mi SE Towanda, 2 (ISU); [25] Normal, 3 (ISU). **Ford Co.:** [26] Roberts, 2 (UI). **Iroquois Co.:** [27] 1 mi N, 2 mi W Watseka, 1 (UI); [28] Gilman, 1 (ISU). **Mason Co.:** [29] 13½ mi SW Havana, 1 (UI). **Menard Co.:** [30] 3 mi S Petersburg, 1 (UI). **Champaign Co.:** [31] 3 mi N Fisher, Sangamon River, 1 (UI); [32] near Seymour, Sangamon River, 1 (UI); [33a] Urbana, 11 (UI); [33b] 1 mi S Urbana, 1 (UI); [33c] 3 mi SE Urbana, 2 (UI); [33d] within 25 mi radius of Urbana [plotted as Urbana], 8 (UI); [34] ½ mi N St. Joseph, I-74, 1 (UI); [35] Savoy, 2 (UI). **Vermilion Co.:** [36] Kickapoo State Park, 1 (UI); [37a] ¼ mi E, ¾ mi S Oakwood, 1 (UI); [37b] Fairmount, 1 (UI). **Pike Co.:** [38] 2 mi NW Rockport, 1 (UI). **Jersey Co.:** [39] Jerseyville, 1 (SRL). **Sangamon Co.:** [40a] 6 mi S Springfield, 1 (ISM); [40b] Lake Springfield, 1 (ISM); [41] 2½ mi ENE Auburn, 1 (UI); no specific locality [not plotted], 1 (UI). **Christian Co.:** [42] Mt. Auburn, 1 (UI). **Bond Co.:** [43] 7 mi E Reno, 2 (UI). **St. Clair Co.:** [44] 4 mi N Mascoutah, on Rt. 43, 1 (UI); [45] 1 mi S Dupo, 1 (UI). **Jefferson Co.:** [46] Waltonville, 2 (SIC). **Perry Co.:** [47b] Pyatts Striplands, 1 (SRL). **Jackson Co.:** [48a] Crab Orchard Creek, 1 (SRL); [48b] 1 mi W Carbondale, 2 (SIC); [48c] 1 mi W SIU campus, Carbondale, 1 (SIC). **Williamson Co.:** [49a] Crab Orchard Lake, 1 (SIC); [49b] 5 mi SE Carbondale, 1 (SRL). **Union Co.:** [50] 4 mi N Cobden, 2 (SRL). **Alexander Co.:** [51a] Olive Branch, 7 (US); [51b] 2½ mi S Olive Branch, 1 (UI).

Additional records. **McHenry Co.:** [2] near Cary, (Necker and Hatfield, 1941:55). **Perry Co.:** [47a] 3 mi W Pyatts Striplands, 1 (FS).

Synaptomys, Bog lemmings

Diagnosis. A microtine with long, silky pelage, short tail which is about the same length as the hind foot;

upper incisors grooved, molars with prismatic triangles, M^3 with one closed triangle between anterior and posterior loops (see Fig. 8.98); six plantar tubercles; rostrum short (see Table 8.25).

Dental formula. 1/1, 0/0, 0/0, 3/3.

Comparisons. For a comparison with *Microtus,* see account of that genus (p. 227).

Synaptomys can readily be told from *Peromyscus, Reithrodontomys,* and *Oryzomys* by its shorter tail, grooved upper incisors, and all the features of the Microtinae (p. 227 and Table 8.24, p. 228).

Synaptomys cooperi, Southern bog lemming

Range. Throughout most of Illinois, but no records are available for the northeastern counties (Map 8.46).

Diagnosis. A species of *Synaptomys* with the characteristics given for the genus, plus orangish-colored anterior face of incisors, palate with broad, blunt median projection, lower molars with closed triangles on labial side; six mammary glands.

Color. Dorsum dark with considerable reddish and chestnut interspersed, venter dark but usually washed with silvery-tipped hairs, tail dark above and light below, juveniles blackish, with little or no reddish interspersed and underparts less heavily washed with silver or white.

Chromosomes. 2N = 50; FN = 48; autosomes acrocentric, with two pairs considerably larger than others; X submetacentric; Y, small acrocentric (Hoffmann and Nadler, 1976).

Comparisons. Synaptomys cooperi differs from *Microtus pennsylvanicus, M. ochrogaster,* and *M. pinetorum* in the features given under *Microtus.* The most obvious characters are the broad, grooved, orange-colored upper incisors, short tail, long fur, and unique arrangement of the triangles in the molar teeth.

Growth. On the basis of data presented by Connor (1959), it is assumed that animals in captivity attained nearly adult weight by about 40 days of age. Animals in the wild do not grow this rapidly, but one would surmise that animals two months of age have nearly reached adult size.

Secondary sexual variation. There apparently are no significant differences in cranial and external measurements between adult males and females.

* Worthen specimen.

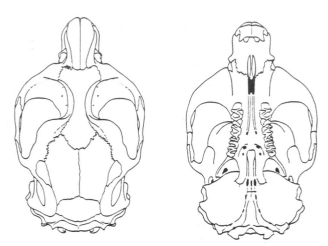

Fig. 8.108. *Synaptomys cooperi,* dorsal and ventral views of skull; 5 mi W, 2½ mi S Monticello, Piatt Co., Illinois, 2390 UI. Female, 27.8 mm greatest length.

Molt. Hayase (1949) has studied molt in Illinois specimens. Nestlings have a short, light brown coat of hair. Any light-colored tips of the hair soon become broken off and this results in a more blackish color. The post-juvenile molt begins along the sides and moves both ventrally and dorsally as well as anteriorly and posteriorly. Parts of the face molt last. It was impossible for Hayase to be certain whether one or two adult molts occurred annually, but she thought there were two: one in the fall (September to November) and one in the spring (May to June).

Remarks. Southern bog lemmings are relatives of the lemmings of arctic regions. The species reaches its southern limits not much farther south than a line drawn through the southern tip of Illinois.

Populations of these mice are not well enough known in Illinois to determine if they have pronounced and regular cyclical variations.

Habitat

Southern bog lemmings occur sporadically in Illinois. Some years they are common to abundant at a given place, but then may disappear or become scarce. For example, in November 1946 at Allerton Park, Piatt County, we took 35 lemmings in three nights' trapping in a circular acre; in February 1947, we took 20, and in April 1947, 22. Thus, in five months we took 77 animals. Our trapping in a circular acre each year for the next 21 produced a total of only 78 lemmings. We have similar experiences in other places in the state.

In central Illinois, these bog lemmings prefer a moist or damp habitat with almost pure stands of dense bluegrass. For example, at Allerton Park the bluegrass had not been grazed or cut for many years and the plots investigated were within 50 yards of the bottomlands of the Sangamon River. Depressions in parts of the area resulted in the accumulation of moisture making the area boggy at times. Also, the heavy matting of grasses retained the water. In addition to bluegrass, some of the common plants were sumac, evening campion (*Lychnis alba*), and late goldenrod (*Solidago serotina*).

The habitat occupied by southern bog lemmings in Illinois may be more like that used by meadow voles than by prairie voles. In much of Illinois where bog lemmings are present there are no meadow voles, however. Getz (1961b) concluded that meadow voles avoided grassy fields with considerable woody vegetation whereas bog lemmings tolerated such vegetation.

Near Eddyville, Pope County, Woodrow Goodpaster found these bog lemmings to be abundant in a heavy stand of fescue grass growing in a young pine plantation. Runways in this grass were present but not definite or distinct.

In Kansas, Linsdale (1927) found these lemmings in thick growths of tall, native prairie grasses and also in seepy places in bluegrass pastures. In Connecticut, Goodwin (1932) found them in forested areas with dense growths of ferns.

Southern bog lemmings build and maintain surface runways and underground burrows in much the same way as do *Microtus*. Most places where we have collected bog lemmings we have also taken voles. Sometimes it was impossible to determine which species had built the runways. Runways which Hayase (1949) regarded as built and maintained by bog lemmings were of three kinds: *old runways* sunk about one inch into the soil and with sides of soil and grass roots, the surface of the runway frequently moldy and without droppings; *actively used runways* with the surface paved with grass cuttings and with considerable amounts of characteristically grass-green or bright green droppings; *inaugural runways* which may be exploratory and often without heavy canopy of grass but with green droppings.

Green feces in runways are most indicative of bog lemmings. When populations are high, runways are seemingly paved with green droppings, some of which have been flattened by having been run over so often.

In any network of surface runways, some entrances to burrows are present. Hayase (1949) found these runways entered burrows that were about 1½ in. in diameter and soon enlarged slightly in diameter. At no time did she find underground chambers, and no nests. Some other workers have found some nests below ground; others on the surface. The underground nests, however, could have been made and used by *Microtus* since animals were not found therein.

Habits

In central Illinois, we have found southern bog lemmings to be active both day and night when the populations are high. At other times, they seem to be more crepuscular and nocturnal. Connor (1959) found that captive animals made a variety of sounds that he felt were either quarrelsome and threatening, courting, or maternal.

Bog lemmings are good swimmers, keeping their bodies high in the water (Connor, 1959).

In Pope County, Illinois, Beasley (1978) recorded some exceedingly high population densities of bog lemmings in 1973–1974. For several months, his censuses were more than 100 animals per hectare. During 1972, the populations were mostly less than 10 animals per hectare. Beasley prebaited his traps, leaving the traps open and baited. There is a good possibility that this may have accounted for the large population in 1973 and 1974 since there was a ready source of food and additional refuge chambers in the form of live-traps.

Food

Food studies for southern bog lemmings in Illinois have not been made, but food caches and food left in runways would suggest that lemmings feed extensively on bluegrass. In New Jersey, Connor (1959) found that in 86 lemming stomachs, green vegetation made up 85 percent of the frequency of occurrence and 66 percent of the volume; berries made up 23 and 14 percent, respectively. In Kentucky, Knopf (according to the report of Linzey, 1983) found that during the winter and spring months bluegrass, fescue, panic grass, and manna grass (*Glyceria striata*) were eaten.

Reproduction

In specimens from Illinois, the presence of female lemmings with embryos and juveniles estimated to be one month old indicated that pregnancies or births of young occurred in April, May, July, October, and November. Other reports indicate that these bog lemmings breed throughout the year. In Pope County, Illinois, 13 of 20 females we took between April 18 and 30, 1980, were pregnant. The studies of Beasley (1978) in Pope County recorded that breeding occurs between March and June, and remains relatively inactive during the summer; breeding activity is greatest in the fall. Beasley also found that during the peak months of the breeding season, 50 to 85 percent of the mature females were "reproductively active."

In 19 specimens from Illinois recorded as pregnant, the mean number of embryos is 3.58 (2–6). Linzey (1983) reviewed the records of litter size (=number of embryos) and found the mode was 3 (1–8). The gestation period is between 23 and 26 days. At birth the young have a thin coat of short hair on the dorsum. Eyes open at 10 to 12 days. Weaning occurs shortly after two weeks and the young are very active at three weeks.

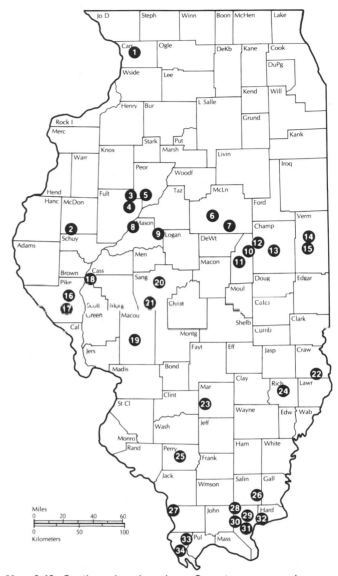

Map 8.46. Southern bog lemmings, *Synaptomys cooperi,* may occur statewide but records are not available for much of northern Illinois. The subspecies is *S. c. gossii.* Numbered localities of occurrence are referenced in *Records of occurrence.* The range of the species in the United States is shaded.

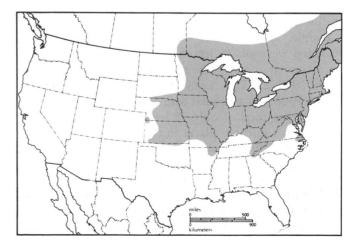

Fig. 8.109. Habitat of the southern bog lemming at Allerton Park, Piatt Co., Illinois, in 1948. Note the heavy matting of tall bluegrass. Relatively few other grasses were intermixed. The thickness of the grass and the slight depressions in the ground allowed surface water to be retained longer than elsewhere, resulting in boggy conditions. Photograph by S. Hayase.

Variation

Specimens of *Synaptomys cooperi* are currently referred to *S. c. gossii* (type locality, Woodson Co., Kansas). In 1942, a population at Bloomington, McLean Co., Illinois, was described (*Synaptomys cooperi saturatus* Bole and Moulthrop). Subsequent workers have suggested that the rich chestnut or "saturate" color and features of the skull are not sufficiently distinctive to recognize this subspecies (Wetzel, 1955).

A large sample of *S. cooperi* from northwestern Illinois might indicate that these are referable to *Synaptomys cooperi cooperi*. Such a sample is not available, however, and a decision cannot be reached.

Synaptomys cooperi gossii (Coues)

1877. *Arvicola (Synaptomys) gossii* Coues, *in* Coues and Allen, Monogr. N. Amer. Rodentia, p. 235. Type from Neosho Falls, Woodson Co., Kansas.

1897. *Synaptomys cooperi gossii*, Rhoads and Young, Proc. Acad. Nat. Sci. Phila., 49:307.

1942. *Synaptomys cooperi saturatus* Bole and Moulthrop, Sci. Publ. Cleveland Mus. Nat. Hist., 5:149. Type from Bloomington, McLean Co., Illinois.

Range. As given for the species (p. 247 and Map 8.46, p. 249).

Diagnosis and Comparisons. A subspecies of *S. cooperi* of large size, darkish color, long and broad skull, and wide upper incisors. These characters are useful in distinguishing the species from *S. c. cooperi*. For measurements, see Table 8.26 (p. 232).

Records of occurrence. SPECIMENS EXAMINED, 185. **McDonough Co.:** [2] Bethel Township, Sec. 17, 2½ mi S Fandon, 5 (UI). **Fulton Co.:** [3a] 1 mi N Norris, 3 (UI); [3b] ½ mi N Norris, 3 (UI); [4a] 1 mi W Canton, 4 (UI); [4b] ½ mi W Canton, 1 (UI); [4c] Canton, 1 (UI). **Peoria Co.:** [5] 2¼ mi S, 1 mi W Hanna City, 1 (UI). **McLean Co.:** [6a] Bloomington, 2 (UI); [6b] 3½ mi SE Bloomington, 1 (UI); [6c] 5 mi SE Bloomington, 1 (UI); [7a] 3 mi NW Le Roy, 2 (UI); [7b] 2 mi N, 1¼ mi W Le Roy, 1 (UI); [7c] 1 mi N, ½ mi W Le Roy, 1 (UI). **Mason Co.:** [8] 5 mi NE Havana, 1 (UI); [9] 2 ½ mi W San Jose, 1 (ISU). **Piatt Co.:** [10] Grassland, 2 mi N White Heath, 1 (UI); [11a] 5½ mi W, 1½ mi S Monticello, 1 (UI); [11b] 5 mi W, 1½ mi S Monticello, 1 (UI); [11c] 2½ mi SW Monticello, 1 (UI); [11d] 5 mi W, 2 mi S Monticello, 1 (UI); [11e] 5 mi W, 2 mi S Monticello, 32 (UI); [11f] Allerton Park Grassland, Monticello, 5 (UI); [11g] 5½ mi SW Monticello, 1 (UI). **Champaign Co.:** [12] Mahomet grassland, 1 (UI); [13a] 3 mi E, 1 mi N Urbana, 1 (UI); [13b] Urbana, 1 (NHS); [13c] 1½ mi S Champaign, 1 (UI).

Vermilion Co.: [14a] ½ mi S, 3 mi E Collison, 1 (UI); [14b] 2½ mi N, 1¾ mi E Newtown, 1 (UI); [14c] 2 mi N, 1½ mi E Newtown, 1 (UI); [15a] 1¼ mi W, ½ mi S Snider, 2 (UI); [15b] ½ mi S, ½ mi E Newton, 1 (UI); [15c] Kickapoo State Park, 1 (UI), 2 (FM). **Pike Co.:** [16] 3 mi N, 1 mi E Pittsfield, 2 (UI); [17] 3½ mi S Pittsfield, 4 (UI). **Morgan Co.:** [18] Meredosia, 1 (NHS). **Macoupin Co.:** [19] 2 mi NE Beaver Dam State Park, 4 (UI). **Sangamon Co.:** [20] Springfield, 3 (ISM); [21] ½ mi N Auburn, Panther Creek, 1 (UI). **Crawford Co.:** [22] Flat Rock, 3 (CAS). **Marion Co.:** [23] Odin, 1 (US). **Richland Co.:** [24] Olney, 1 (FM). **Perry Co.:** [25] no specific locality, 2 (SIC). **Saline Co.:** [26] 1½ mi W Horseshoe, 1 (UI). **Union Co.:** 1½ mi NE Aldridge, 1 (NHS). **Pope Co.:** [29] 4 mi SE Eddyville, 19 (UI); [30a] ½ mi S, ½ mi E Glendale, 1 (UI); [30b] 1 mi S, ½ mi E Glendale, 1 (UI); [30c] 1½ mi SW Glendale, 12 (UI); [30d] 2 mi SW Glendale, 1 (UI); [30e] 1½ mi S Glendale, 3 (UI); [30f] Dixon Springs, Glendale Lake, 25 (UI); [31a] 3.8 mi W Golconda, 3 (UI); [31b] Golconda, 1 (UI). **Hardin Co.:** [32a] 1 mi S Eichorn, 1 (UI); [32b] Rosiclare, 10 (FM). **Alexander Co.:** [34] 2¼ mi NW Miller City, 1 (UI).

Additional records. **Carroll Co.:** [1] Mt. Carroll and vicinity, (Hoffmeister and Warnock, 1955:161). **McLean Co.:** [6a] Bloomington, 2 (UM). **Piatt Co.:** [11g] Allerton Park, 5 mi W, 2½ mi S Monticello, 3 (FS). **Union Co.:** [27b] Aldridge, Pine Hills, 2 (FS). **Pope Co.:** [28] 1 mi E McCormick, 1 (FS). **Alexander Co.:** [33] Tamms, 1 (FS).

Subfamily Murinae, Old World rats and mice

Old World murines in Illinois include *Rattus* and *Mus* which were introduced, directly or indirectly, by European man. They differ from native cricetine and microtine rodents in that the upper molars have three longitudinally arranged rows of cusps and the tail is sparsely haired, scaly, and annulated.

Rattus, Old World rats

Diagnosis. A large-sized murine rodent having upper molars with three longitudinally arranged rows of cusps; hard palate extends posteriorly beyond plane of last molar; tail sparsely haired and with prominent annulations; hind foot usually 35 mm or more; total length usually 375 mm or more; five pairs of mammary glands.

Dental formula. 1/1, 0/0, 0/0, 3/3.

Comparisons. Rattus differs from other myomorph rodents in Illinois except *Neotoma* and *Ondatra* by its larger size with a total length usually in excess of 375 mm, hind foot of 35 mm or more, and a large skull. It differs from *Neotoma* in having the three rows of cusps in the upper molars, a nearly hairless tail, five rather than two pairs of mammary glands, teeth cuspidate rather than with lophs, and hard palate extending farther posteriorly. *Rattus* differs from *Ondatra* in having a rounded tail, non-webbed hind feet, more conspicuous ears, and the dental features given above.

Remarks. Two species of *Rattus* are found in Illinois: *R. norvegicus,* Norway rat, and *R. rattus,* black rat. *R. norvegicus* is the more commonly encountered, both in cities and in the wild.

Rattus rattus, Black rat; also called Roof rat

Range. Known only from Chicago, Cook County, and Urbana, Champaign County.

Diagnosis. A species of *Rattus* in which the tail is longer than the head-body length; temporal ridges are bowed outward, length of parietal measured along temporal ridge less than greatest distance between ridges, anterior edge of infraorbital plate gradually sloping posteriorly along its upper part. These and other features are given in Table 8.28.

Color. Variable; dorsum brownish intermixed with grays and blacks or blackish with a small amount of light-colored hairs intermixed; tail both above and below about same color as dorsum; venter usually cream-colored in specimens with more brownish dorsum, smoke-colored with a light wash of buff in those with blackish dorsum; tops of hind feet about same color as dorsum.

Chromosomes. 2N = 38, with 22 metacentrics or submetacentrics, 14 acrocentrics; X and Y acrocentric (Hsu and Benirschke, 1973) or 2N = 42, with 18 metacentrics or submetacentrics, 22 acrocentrics; X and Y acrocentric (Hsu and Benirschke, 1971c).

Comparisons. R. rattus differs from *R. norvegicus* as indicated in the account of that species and the features given in Table 8.28.

R. rattus differs from the large myomorph rodents as described above under the genus *Rattus.*

Remarks. Black rats or roof rats are known from only two localities in Illinois. The date of capture for Urbana is January 31, 1948; for Chicago, March 10, 1972. Black rats may have been more widely distributed in the Chicago area at an earlier time. The comments about the life history of these rats is based on information other than in Illinois.

Black rats are thinner bodied than Norway rats and less aggressive.

Habitat and Habits

Black rats are excellent climbers: they can scale the sides of brick and stucco buildings, traverse ropes and cables, and climb trees. They apparently cannot tolerate cold as well as Norway rats. Black rats are established in the wild in southern states where the weather is milder and fruits and nuts are available for food throughout much of the year. Many of these rats build nests high in trees, including palm trees.

The rats that infested sea-going ships at an early time were nearly all black rats. As the ships tied up in American ports, some black rats were able to come ashore and establish themselves. Since sea-going vessels often docked in the Chicago area, it is possible that at an earlier time black rats may have inhabited the docks and areas adjacent to Lake Michigan. Nonetheless, I know of no early records of *Rattus rattus* from Chicago. The one specimen from Chicago, now preserved in the Field Museum, was taken in a railroad car in 1972. It may have come into the city in this car from another locality. The specimen from Urbana was taken in 1948 from within a block of the University of Illinois campus and made into a study skin by a student in a class in mammalogy. There is a remote possibility that this was an escaped animal from a university laboratory; but it is most unusual to use black rats, *Rattus rattus,* experimentally.

Some persons may claim that *Rattus rattus* should not be considered a resident species of Illinois, and indeed such may be the case. I suspect, however, that the species has been established for short periods of time within the state, and I have included it as a one-time resident species.

Black rats are less aggressive and vicious than Norway rats. The latter have driven black rats out of most areas in the United States where they formerly were quite abundant. Frequently, Norway rats by persistent aggressiveness have driven black rats to the very tops of buildings and there eventually eradicated them.

Food

Although they are omnivorous much the same as Norway rats, black rats may maintain themselves for long periods of time on fruits.

Reproduction

Black rats are prolific breeders but less so than Norway rats. They have fewer and smaller litters, with an average of about six embryos per pregnancy. In the wild in Louisiana, they breed throughout the year, but most breeding occurs in early spring and in early summer (Lowery, 1974).

Variation

Since innumerable introductions into North America of *Rattus rattus* from various parts of the Old World have occurred, it is impossible to assign a subspecific name to specimens from Illinois. At least three subspecies have been recognized in the United States: *R. r. rattus* (Linnaeus), *R. r. alexandrinus* (Desmarest), and *R. r. frugivorus* (Rafinesque).

Rattus rattus (Linnaeus) subsp.?

1758. [*Mus*] *rattus* Linnaeus, Syst. nat., 10:1–61. Type locality Uppsala, Sweden.
1916. *Rattus rattus*, Hollister, Proc. Biol. Soc. Wash., 29:126.

Range. Known only from Chicago, Cook County, and Urbana, Champaign County.

Diagnosis. As given for the species (p. 251).

Records of occurrence. SPECIMENS EXAMINED, 2. **Cook Co.:** [1] Chicago, 1 (FM). **Champaign Co.:** [2] Urbana, 1 (UI).

Rattus norvegicus, Norway rat

Range. Throughout the state.

Diagnosis. A species of *Rattus* in which the tail is shorter than the head-body; the body is heavy, and hind feet usually are 39 mm or more; temporal ridges are nearly parallel and the greatest distance between them is usually less than 13 mm, length of parietal measured along the temporal ridge approximately equal to greatest distance between ridges; anterior edge of infraorbital plate often projecting slightly forward (Fig. 8.110).

Color. Dorsum has a grizzled appearance, with a mixture of brown, ochraceous, and black coloring; often slightly darker down midline of back; tops of feet whitish and much lighter than back; venter may be grayish or cream-colored; tail unicolored and about same color as dorsum.

Chromosomes. 2N = 42; 22 metacentrics, submetacentrics, or subtelocentrics; 18 acrocentrics; X and Y acrocentric (Hsu and Benirschke, 1967b).

Comparisons. *R. norvegicus* differs from *R. rattus* (Table 8.28) in having the tail shorter than head-body (Fig. 8.112), hind feet averaging longer; temporal ridges more or less parallel, with the distance between the ridges usually less than 13 mm; length of parietal measured along temporal ridge is about equal to greatest distance

Table 8.28. Characters helpful in distinguishing *Rattus rattus* and *Rattus norvegicus*

Rattus rattus	Rattus norvegicus
Tail longer than head and body	Tail shorter than head and body
Temporal ridges on each side of the parietals bowed outward	Temporal ridges more or less parallel
Greatest distance between temporal ridges usually 13 mm or more	Greatest distance between temporal ridges usually less than 13 mm
Length of parietal, measured along the temporal ridge, decidedly less than greatest distance between ridges	Length of parietal, measured along the temporal ridge, approximately equal to greatest distance between ridges
M¹ usually with distinct notch on first row of cusps	M¹ often without a distinct notch on first row of cusps
Anterior edge of infraorbital plate usually slopes posteriorly	Anterior edge of infraorbital plate often projects anteriorly (Fig. 8.110)

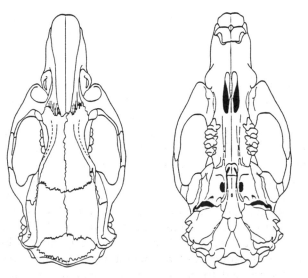

Fig. 8.110. *Rattus norvegicus*, dorsal and ventral views of skull. Urbana, Champaign Co., Illinois, 3456 UI. Male, 49.4 mm greatest length.

between ridges and not appreciably less; anterior edge of infraorbital plate projects slightly forward rather than sloping posteriorly; M^1 with a distinct notch at anterior end.

R. norvegicus differs from other large myomorph rodents as described in the account of the genus *Rattus* (p. 252).

Remarks. Norway rats are non-native mammals but now found throughout the state and together with house mice have caused large sums of money to be spent in trying to prevent them from spoiling man's food and from spreading diseases. Rats have been vectors of murine typhus fever and plague.

The albino rat, often cherished as a pet or used widely in laboratory research, is a non-color mutant of the Norway rat.

Habitat

Norway rats live in a variety of habitats in Illinois but are mainly associated with man and his dwellings: houses, buildings, barns, or any outbuildings, dumpsites, and picnic grounds. They rarely are found living solely in native or cultivated vegetation far-removed from man.

Norway rats find ideal conditions in places that have poor sanitary standards such as may occur at some food-handling establishments and food warehouses, and among garbage and refuse improperly disposed of or excessive litter. Many large and small livestock-raisers may inadvertently provide ample food and hiding areas for rats from the excess livestock feed. If such food becomes unavailable, the rats may turn to feeding on nearby crops.

If necessary, Norway rats will dig burrows as, for example, under a foundation to get to food or to provide a nesting-site. Burrows are usually less than 18 inches deep. The rats will gnaw through wooden barriers. In most places they continually use the same routes, making well-defined runs. Often these runs show discoloration from dirt on the rats' bodies as well as from droppings.

Habits

Norway rats are primarily nocturnal, although on occasion they may be active at dawn and dusk. They are good to excellent climbers, but less agile than are black (roof) rats. Norway rats can shinny up steel bars and wires, walk along cables and ropes, crawl for short distances on vertical brick walls, as well as other equally difficult situations. They are excellent and persistent gnawers and often gnaw through lead cables and pipes.

Rats may produce several sounds: a weak clicking of the teeth to show contentment; a strong clicking for anger; a clucking by a female with young; single chirp for surprise; squeaks of varying loudness to express pain.

Rats are said to be able to do a standing high-jump of nearly two feet and, when in motion, they can jump even higher. They require one-half to one ounce of water daily, although on some days they may go without water.

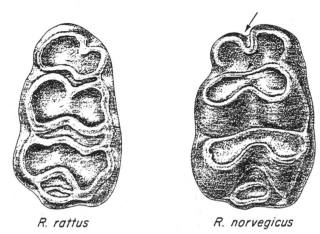

Fig. 8.111. Lower first molar of *Rattus rattus* and *R. norvegicus*. *R. norvegicus* often has a deeper notch at the front of the tooth and a less distinct notch at the front edge of the second series of cusps. Drawing of *R. rattus* is of the right first molar; of *R. norvegicus*, of the left first molar.

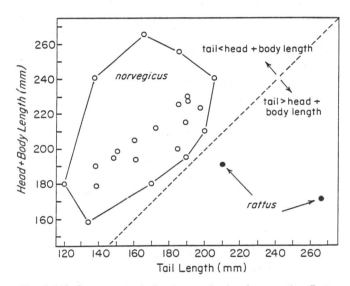

Fig. 8.112. Scattergram indicating methods of separating *Rattus rattus* and *R. norvegicus* in Illinois on the basis of head and body length versus tail length.

Norway rats often live in what might be called colonies. In one city block, all of the rats may be living within a circumscribed area that may be only 100 or 200 feet in diameter.

Food

Norway rats will eat anything that man will and in the process of doing this, they contaminate much of the food. They also live readily on the food that man discards. One of the best ways to discourage rats is to keep food away from them.

Rats normally do not eat the food at the spot where they have found it, but carry it—a mouthful at a time—to the vicinity of the nest site.

Map 8.47. Black rats, *Rattus rattus,* are rare or absent now in Illinois.

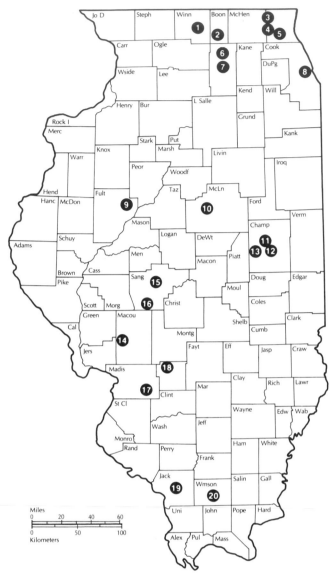

Map 8.48. Norway rats, *Rattus norvegicus,* occur statewide, as shown by the numbered locations keyed to *Records of occurrence* in the text.

Reproduction

Under good conditions, such as living within winter-warm buildings, Norway rats may breed and produce young any time during the year. In rural areas and around cold farm buildings, young may be produced more seasonally. The average number of young is seven, with extremes of two and fifteen. The gestation is between 21 and 23 days, but longer if the female is nursing. Young are weaned at three to four weeks and females rarely breed before they are three months old. A female may produce a litter practically every month if the living conditions and food supply are good. Experimentally, one female can produce directly or indirectly (through her offspring) more than 1,500 rats during one year.

Young are helpless at birth. Eyes open at about two weeks. The life span is probably less than 18 months on the average.

Variation

Although there are several subspecies of *R. norvegicus* in the world, E. R. Hall (1981) regards all of the introduced Norway rats as referable to *R. n. norvegicus.*

Rattus norvegicus norvegicus (Berkenhout)

1769. *Mus norvegicus* Berkenhout, Outlines of the nat. hist. . . . , 1:5. Type locality, England.
1916. *Rattus norvegicus,* Hollister, Proc. Biol. Soc. Wash., 29:126.

Range. Throughout the state.

Diagnosis and Comparisons. As given for the species (p. 252).

Records of occurrence. SPECIMENS EXAMINED, 33. **Winnebago Co.:** [1] 4 mi N Rockford, 1 (NIU). **Boone Co.:** [2] Belvidere, 1 (NIU). **Lake Co.:** [3] Fox Lake, 1 (FM); [4] Volo [labelled McHenry Co.], 1 (NIU); [5] Diamond Lake, 2 (UI). **De Kalb Co.:** [6] 10 mi N De Kalb, 1 (NIU); [7] De Kalb, 1 (NIU). **Cook Co.:** [8a] Chicago, 1 (CAS), 1 (FM); [8b] Cicero, 1 (UI). **Fulton Co.:** [9] Canton, 2 (UI). **McLean Co.:** [10a] 4 mi N Normal, 3 (ISU); [10b] 2 mi N Normal, 2 (ISU); [10c] Normal, 1 (ISU); [10d] Bloomington, 2 (ISU). **Champaign Co.:** [11] 6 mi N Champaign, 1 (UI); [12a] Urbana, 1 (UI); [12b] 3 mi SE Urbana, 1 (UI); [13] 1½ mi S Staley, 1 (UI). **Macoupin Co.:** [14] 1 mi S Chesterfield, 1 (UI). **Sangamon Co.:** [15] Springfield, 2 (ISM); [16] Auburn, 1 (UI). **Madison Co.:** [17] 5 mi W, 1 mi N Highland, 1 (UI). **Bond Co.:** [18] ½ mi E Reno, 1 (UI). **Jackson Co.:** [19] no specific locality, 1 (SRL). **Williamson Co.:** [20] 3 mi S Marion, 1 (SRL).

Mus, House mouse and relatives

Diagnosis. A murine rodent characterized by body and tail of roughly the same length, tail usually unicolor, upper incisors with distinct notch at the tips when viewed laterally (see Fig. 8.59), skull relatively broad interorbitally, rostrum relatively short; cusps of upper molars in three longitudinal rows, but one row small.

Dental formula. 1/1, 0/0, 0/0, 3/3.

Comparisons. Mus needs comparison with the genera *Peromyscus, Reithrodontomys, Ochrotomys,* and *Zapus,* and differs from these in having a unicolored tail rather than bicolored; notch at the tip of the upper incisors rather than no notch, upper molars with three rather than two longitudinal rows of cusps; interorbital region relatively broader; incisive foramina relatively longer and extending farther posteriorly relative to M^1; underparts usually nearly as dark as the dorsum, rather than whitish.

Mus differs markedly from the microtines in having a longer, naked tail, shorter fur, conspicuous ears, notched upper incisors, cuspidate rather than prismatic molars, and other features separating the murines and microtines.

Mus musculus, House mouse

Range. Throughout the state.

Diagnosis. A species of *Mus* with the additional features: total length in Illinois usually between 145 and 180 mm, hind foot usually 17 to 20 mm; fur short, tops of feet dusky, ears conspicuous and nearly naked; five pairs of mammary glands.

Color. Variable; in Illinois specimens the dorsum is blackish or dark gray with a light ochraceous infusion; venter usually plumbeous with an ochraceous wash, but sometimes whitish; tail blackish or dark gray above and

Fig. 8.113A. House mouse, *Mus musculus.* (From Hoffmeister and Mohr, 1957. Photograph by Ernest P. Walker, Smithsonian Institution, Washington, D.C.)

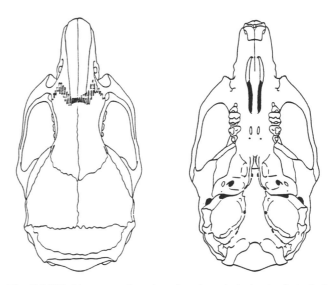

Fig. 8.113B. *Mus musculus,* dorsal and ventral views of skull; 1 mi NE Florence, Pinal Co., Arizona, 14285 UI. Female, 22.5 mm greatest length.

below, feet dusky. Numerous color variants are known—from solid black to white (albino).

Chromosomes. 2N = 40 with 38 acrocentrics or telocentrics; X and Y acrocentric (Hsu and Benirschke, 1967a).

Comparisons. Mus musculus differs from various comparably sized mice in Illinois as described under *Mus.*

Habitat

House mice live in a variety of habitats in Illinois. Many of these are associated with man's houses, commercial buildings, farm structures, and warehouses. They also commonly live in natural settings where there is adequate food, cover, and some protection from the most severe winter weather. We have taken them in grassy and cultivated fields close to human habitation and at distances of one-half mile. For example, in southern

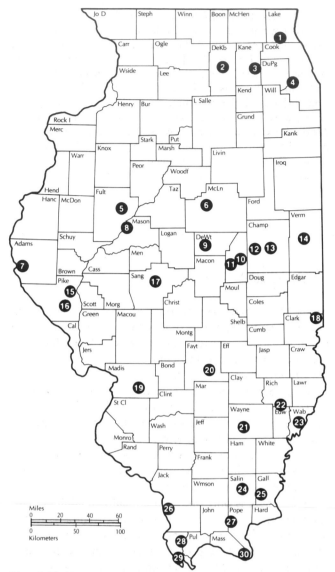

Map 8.49. House mice, *Mus musculus*, occur statewide, as indicated by the numbered locations keyed to *Records of occurrence* in the text.

Illinois house mice were trapped in grassy or weedy fields with scattered brush, swampy woodlands, dense stands of grape, thickets with willow, mulberry, and sycamore, and ditch banks (Layne, 1958a). In a dense bluegrass field at Allerton Park, Piatt County, where we trapped from 1946 to 1969, house mice appeared in 1949, and were taken usually in small numbers in 1950, 1951, 1956, 1957, 1960–1968. In 1957, the predominant species caught was the house mouse with 16 taken in three days in a circular acre. Nine prairie voles, six southern bog lemmings, five white-footed mice, and one least shrew were taken during the same trapping.

House mice are common to abundant around man's structures nearly everyplace in Illinois where they are not discouraged by proper sanitation and mouse-proofing. They do not hesitate to take up residence in used as well as unused buildings.

Habits

House mice have good senses of smell and hearing. They climb and swim well and they can be deprived of food and water for longer periods of time with less ill effect than most native mice.

House mice are principally nocturnal but under pressure for food or under partial cover may be active during parts of the daytime.

They produce a characteristic odor, somewhat musky in nature, that may be a clue to their presence.

Food

House mice eat any available items of food for human consumption or that have been discarded by man, as well as eating feed for livestock, and seeds and fruit of native vegetation.

In Indiana, Whitaker (1966) examined the stomachs of 478 wild-taken house mice. The more important food items were foxtail, seeds of various grasses, seeds of cultivated plants including corn, wheat, sorghum, and soybeans, and the larvae of certain insects.

Reproduction

Under ideal conditions, house mice will probably breed throughout the year. In much of Illinois, breeding probably does not occur in midwinter. However, in west central Indiana, pregnant house mice were taken from November through February (Mumford and Whitaker, 1982).

The gestation period is 21 to 24 days. The number of young varies between two and 10. A female frequently has five or six litters per year. Young are hairless and blind at birth. They grow rapidly and by 43 days of age females are sexually mature and may breed.

Variation

There are innumerable named forms that are referable to *Mus musculus* and probably several different subspecies have been introduced into North America. No subspecific designation is given for the house mice in Illinois.

Mus musculus Linnaeus subsp.?

1758. *Mus musculus* Linnaeus, Syst. Nat., 10th ed., 1:62. Type locality, Uppsala, Sweden.

Range. Throughout the state.
Diagnosis and Comparisons. As given for the species (p. 255).

Records of occurrence. SPECIMENS EXAMINED, 87.
Lake Co.: [1] 20 mi NW Chicago, 1 (UI). **De Kalb Co.:** [2] De Kalb, 1 (NIU), 1 (UI). **Kane Co.:** [3a] ¼ mi W St. Charles, 1 (ISM); [3b] near St. Charles, 1 (ISM). **Cook Co.:** [4] 1.3 mi E Jct. US 45 and Ill. 55, 3 (UI). **Fulton Co.:** [5] 5 mi SE Canton, 1 (UI). **McLean Co.:** [6a] 4 mi N Normal, 1 (ISU); [6b] 2 mi N Normal, 1 (ISU). **Adams Co.:** [7] Quincy, 1 (UI). **Mason Co.:** [8] 5 mi NE

Havana, 1 (UI). **De Witt Co.:** [9] 1 mi W Clifton, 1 (UI). **Piatt Co.:** [10] Monticello, 3 (UI); [11] Allerton Park, 1 (UI). **Champaign Co.:** [12] 1 mi E Bondville, Kaskaskia River, 1 (UI); [13a] 3½ mi N Urbana, 2 (UI); [13b] 1 mi N Urbana, 1 (UI); [13c] Champaign, 11 (UI); [13d] 3 mi E Champaign, 1 (UI); [13e] 5 mi E Champaign, 1 (UI); [13f] Urbana, 8 (UI); [13g] 1½ mi E Urbana, 1 (UI); [13h] 2½ mi E Urbana, 3 (UI); [13i] 3 mi E Urbana, 2 (UI); [13j] 4 mi E Urbana, 5 (UI); [13k] 5 mi E Urbana, 2 (UI); [13l] Mayview, 1 (UI); [13m] 1 mi E Mayview, 1 (UI); [13n] ½ mi S Champaign, 1 (UI); [13o] 1 mi S Champaign, 1 (UI); [13p] 1 mi S UI campus, 2 (UI); [13q] 2 mi S Champaign, 1 (UI); [13r] 4½ mi SW Urbana, 1 (UI). **Vermilion Co.:** [14] ½ mi S, 3 mi E Collison, 2 (UI); Crystal Springs [location?], 1 (UI). **Pike Co.:** [15] 1 mi S Griggsville, 1 (UI); [16] 3½ mi S Pittsfield, 1 (UI). **Sangamon Co.:** [17] Springfield, 2 (ISM). **Clark Co.:** [18] 4 mi N, 8½ mi E Marshall, Clear Creek, 3 (UI). **Madison Co.:** [19] 1½ mi SE Kuhn, 1 (UI). **Fayette Co.:** [20] 3 mi S Brownstown, 1 (UI). **Wayne Co.:** [21] 2 mi ENE Sims, 1 (UI). **Richland Co.:** [22] Parkersburg, 1 (US). **Wabash Co.:** [23] Mt. Carmel, 1 (US). **Saline Co.:** [24] 1.4 mi N Harrisburg, 1 (UI). **Gallatin Co.:** [25] 3 mi SE Equality, 1 (UI). **Pope Co.:** [27] 1½ mi S Glendale, 1 (UI). **Alexander Co.:** [29a] 2 mi NW Miller City, 2 (UI); [29b] 1½ mi E Miller City, 1 (UI); [29c] 5¼ mi S, 2 mi E Willard, 1 (UI). **Massac Co.:** [30] 5 mi SE Unionville, 1 (ISM).

Additional records. **Union Co.:** [26] Pine Hills, Aldridge, 1 (FS). **Alexander Co.:** [28] Tamms, 3 (FS).

Family Zapodidae, Jumping mice

Mice with the infraorbital canal large, the zygoma depressed, the jugal prolonged and forming a suture with the lacrimal, upper incisors grooved, coronoid process of lower jaw well developed and projecting far posteriorly; the infraorbital region has two openings — one large and one small — when viewed from the front; the tail is long. Jumping mice are myomorphs, but some features of the zygomasseteric structure are the same as in hystricomorphs.

Zapus, Jumping mice

Diagnosis. A zapodid with four upper cheek teeth, second molar no smaller than first molar; upper incisors deep orange or yellow and strongly grooved; tail without a distinct white tip; hind feet long; eight mammary glands.

Dental formula. 1/1, 0/0, 1/0, 3/3.

Comparisons. Zapus differs from Illinois *Peromyscus* and *Ochrotomys* in having grooved upper incisors, a small upper premolar, and the infraorbital foramen greatly enlarged; tail usually longer than 110 mm.

Zapus differs from *Reithrodontomys* in its large size, in having much longer hind feet (26 mm or more, usually), a much longer tail; small premolars, and the infraorbital foramen greatly enlarged.

Zapus hudsonius, Meadow jumping mouse

Range. Throughout most of the state (map 8.50).

Diagnosis. A species of *Zapus* with additional characters of an ochraceous or dark brown back that contrasts with sides to appear as a broad, dark band down back; baculum small and with lanceolate tip; M^1 short, usually 0.35 mm or less, coronoid process of mandible short and broad.

Color. In Illinois, dorsum dark brown as the result of many ochraceous hairs interspersed, sides more ochraceous than back; narrow orangish stripe along lateral line; venter white, tail bicolor with top almost the same color as back, underside whitish; tops of feet whitish or cream-colored; ears with ochraceous fringe.

Chromosomes. 2N = 72.

Aging. Specimens were considered as adult, for purposes of analyses and comparisons, when there was at least some wear on all cusps of M^1 and M^2, even through Pm^4 had only slight wear (Krutzsch, 1954).

Secondary sexual variation. Krutzsch (1954) found that the differences in measurements between the sexes was no greater than individual variation.

Molt. There is only one molt annually in adults in late summer (Krutzsch, 1954). Animals less than a year old molt shortly before going into hibernation. In molt, new hair appears on the top of the rostrum and on the back between the shoulders. The molt continues posteriorly from the nose and anteriorly and posteriorly from the back between the shoulders.

Remarks. Zapus hudsonius is more widespread in Illinois than earlier workers believed. Furthermore, these mice continue to be found in new places. For example, the habitats where jumping mice might be found east of Urbana, Champaign County, have been extensively and intensively trapped for many years; however, on June 6, 1984, the first *Zapus hudsonius* was caught in this area.

Napaeozapus insignis, the woodland jumping mouse, was reported to occur at Turkey Run State Park, Indiana, less than 20 miles from the Illinois state line. The specimen upon which this record is based is at the University of Michigan Museum. Mumford and Whitaker (1982:5) extensively trapped for this species without success and concluded: "Possibly the species no longer occurs in Indiana. Another possibility is that the specimen may have been incorrectly labeled as to locality. For these reasons, we have not included the woodland jumping mouse on our current list [of Indiana mammals]." Features

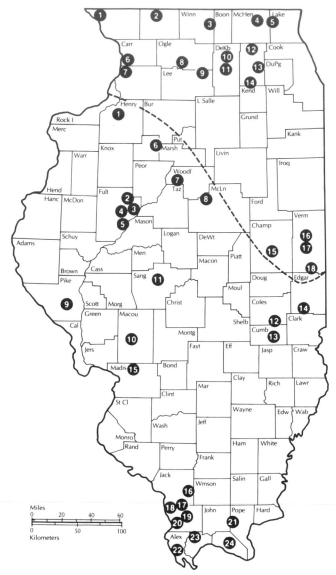

useful in distinguishing *Napaeozapus* from *Zapus* are the conspicuous white tip of the tail, absence of the small upper premolar, the longer baculum; sides of the body are more brightly colored in *Napaeozapus*.

Habitat

Meadow jumping mice often live in moist areas, but the vegetative cover may be variable: thick grassy fields, dense weeds and grasses along streams, ponds, and marshes, and damp grassy areas within or adjacent to woods. Some habitats where they have been taken in Illinois follow: Hancock County, in an upland field grown up with big bluestem, Indian grass, and switch grass. This area had been cleared of forest and had not been farmed for about 20 years, although it had been burned, prior to the presence of jumping mice. Henry County, near Cambridge, along an interstate shoulder that had not been mowed for at least two years and was grown up with bluegrass and brome, with a few scattered herbaceous plants. Union County in a tile partially filled with water at a spring at the foot of a limestone bluff. In Vermilion County along Jordan Creek numerous meadow jumping mice were seen and caught in the marshy, thick vegetation along or near the creek banks and adjacent to or part way into the adjacent dense woods. These were observed by persons searching with lanterns for reptiles and amphibians during the middle of the night on May 21, June 11, July 29, and October 13, all in 1952. Several of the jumping mice were caught after they jumped into the water and began to swim away or while they were in the vegetation. In Champaign County, one was taken three miles northeast of Urbana in an abandoned alfalfa field.

Habits

The jumping behavior of these mice was described in the field notes of herpetologists working along Jordan Creek, east central Illinois. Lester Burger's field notes indicate that "jumping mice appear to always take off in a series of jumps when disturbed. Some of the jumps surely approach a yard. Between jumps when crouching in the apparent security of shadows [from their lanterns] they shuffle about a bit but never seem to run." Again Burger's notes, taken at a pond near Jordan Creek, likened the jumping as follows: "it proceeded by its peculiar grasshopper-style gait to a cluster of bushes. Cornered there it crouched in a shadow but jumped before it could be grabbed. I followed it closely to the water's edge and saw it dive into the water. It must have remained submerged for a full minute. Waiting where I last saw it, I was rewarded when its head reappeared above water near the edge of the pond. When I made a grab for it, it headed back out into the pond, swimming on the surface."

Map 8.50. Meadow jumping mice, *Zapus hudsonius*, are distributed statewide. Two subspecies occur in Illinois: *Z. h. intermedius* north of the broken line; *Z. h. americanus*, south. Numbered localities are referenced in *Records of occurrence*. The range of the species in the United States is shaded.

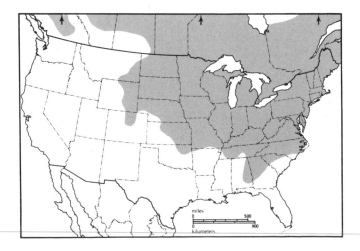

Fig. 8.114A. Meadow jumping mouse, *Zapus hudsonius*. (From Hoffmeister and Mohr, 1957. Photograph by Ernest P. Walker, Smithsonian Institution, Washington, D.C.)

We have kept a meadow jumping mouse from Champaign County in captivity for one year. Its nesting chamber, a wide-mouthed glass bottle, is buried in the substrate. Never have we seen this mouse above ground during the daytime even though at times it may be quite dark in the area where the cage is housed. Each night, after retiring to the nest-bottle, the opening is tightly packed with dry grass and other materials to close it. Never was the nest open during the daytime. However, Whitaker (1972c) caught 2 animals out of 31 in Indiana in the daytime.

Meadow jumping mice tolerate others of their own species better than some other myomorphs do (Whitaker, 1972c).

Hibernation

Meadow jumping mice hibernate, usually entering hibernation between mid-September and the end of October. They emerge from hibernation around the last week of April or the first week of May. Whitaker (1972c) summarizes much of the hibernating information. The meadow jumping mouse we held in captivity from June 6, 1983, until June 10, 1984, and beyond, apparently did not hibernate or did not go into a typical hibernating behavior. It was usually active to some degree every night during the winter. For example, every night during the winter it drank some water from an open dish and then kicked dirt and seeds into the dish. The cage was kept in a room where the temperature rarely dropped below 60°F. Animals in Illinois may not hibernate for so long as they do elsewhere. For example, we have late fall trapping records as follows: adults, October 7, November 2, and November 4; subadults, October 1, October 7,

October 13, and November 11. The earliest record we have in the spring is April 30.

I suspect that many or all of the subadults listed above would not have enough accumulated fat for them to go into hibernation at the time they were collected.

Food

Food habits of jumping mice in Illinois have not been reported. Data are available for Indiana where Whitaker and Mumford (1971) examined 131 stomachs. By percentage of frequency, *Endogone* was the highest; by volume, *Impatiens* (or Touch-me-not) seeds were 21.4

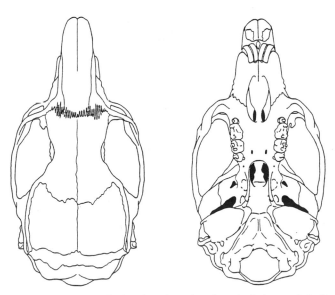

Fig. 8.114B. *Zapus hudsonius,* dorsal and ventral views of skull; 3½ mi S Pittsfield, Pike Co., Illinois, 58162. Male, 22.5 mm greatest length.

Table 8.29. External and cranial measurements of *Zapus hudsonius,* with mean, minimum-maximum, and standard deviation. Superscripts indicate samples less than N.

Subspecies and Locality	N	Total length	Tail length	Head-body length	Hind foot length	Ear length	Greatest length	Zygomatic breadth
Z.h. americanus								
Union and Alexander cos.	9	195.6[5]	119.2[5]	76.6[7]	27.4[7]	12.3[6]	21.66	10.39
		184-210	105-130	65-84	25-30	11-15	20.75-22.6	9.9-10.9
		9.34	9.78	5.86	1.80	1.47	0.59	0.44
Fulton Co.	8	206.0	118.8	86.5	28.3	12.3	21.88	10.53
		184-235	108-133	76-107	27-30	8-14	21.15-22.7	10.1-11.2
		15.04	9.16	9.77	1.04	2.05	0.61	0.39
Z.h. intermedius								
Vermilion Co.	8	203.0	118.9	83.1	28.4	11.6	22.73	11.01
		185-220	108-131	72-99	26-31	10-13	21.9-23.75	10.55-11.6
		13.94	7.97	8.53	1.51	0.92	0.72	0.42
Stephenson, Carroll, Whiteside, Ogle cos.	4	212.3[3]	127.3[3]	85.0[3]	29.0[3]	10.3[3]	22.65	10.61
		205-218	123-133	82-88	27-30	9-12	21.75-23.45	10.25-11.1
		6.66	5.13	3.00	1.73	1.53	0.73	0.43

percent, *Endogone* 15.6 percent, a variety of small seeds made up 46.1 percent. Few insect remains were found.

The animal we have kept in captivity has thrived on a diet of small birdseeds—including sunflower—and rat biscuits. When unhulled sunflower seeds were buried, the mouse quickly dug them up. Ample water was provided continuously. When we have placed the flower-heads of dandelions and clover in the cage, they have been ignored.

Reproduction

In Illinois there appear to be at least two breeding seasons a year—one in June and another in the latter part of August and in early September. We base this on two jumping mice specimens that were pregnant on June 11 and a young animal that was born probably in mid-June. As for the fall breeding season, we have several young animals that we think were born between August 15 and September 15; a female lactating on October 7 may have given birth to young in mid-September.

The gestation period is about 18 days, longer if the female is lactating. The number of embryos per litter was 5.7 (4–7) in Minnesota and 5.5 (2–9) in New York (according to Whitaker's 1972c review). Only two of our specimens in Illinois are recorded as with embryos: five and six. Young at birth are hairless. Eyes open at about 25 days. By the fourth week the young are nearly on their own.

Variation

Three subspecies of *Zapus hudsonius* may occur in Illinois: *Z. h. americanus* (type locality considered as near Philadelphia, Pennsylvania), *Z. h. intermedius* (type lo-

cality Ridgeway, Iowa), *Z. h. pallidus* (type locality near Lawrence, Kansas).

According to the revisionary study of Krutzsch (1954) *Z. h. pallidus* and *Z. h. americanus* are smaller than *Z. h. intermedius.* In our interpretation, specimens from southern and western Illinois are small, like those from Ohio, Indiana, Michigan, and Kansas. These specimens are referred to *Z. h. americanus* and I am not certain how *Z. h. pallidus* differs from *Z. h. americanus.*

Specimens from eastern and northern Illinois, Wisconsin, and Minnesota, are similar to those from Iowa and are here referred to *Z. h. intermedius.*

Eleven populations of *Zapus hudsonius* from central United States were examined, especially the cranial measurements. These are listed in Table 8.29. These measurements were tested with a canonical variate analysis in which the centroids and ellipses connecting one standard deviation around the centroid were plotted. These indicate that populations regarded as *Z. h. intermedius* group together as do those of *Z. h. americanus-pallidus.*

Skulls of *Z. h. intermedius* average longer, broader, and deeper (Table 8.29). As we interpret it, specimens are referable to *Z. h. intermedius* north of a line drawn between southern Whiteside County and northern Edgar County; south of this line, specimens are referred to *Z. h. americanus.*

Zapus hudsonius intermedius Krutzsch

1954. *Zapus hudsonius intermedius* Krutzsch, Univ. Kansas Publ., Mus. Nat. Hist., 7:447. Type from Ridgeway, Winneschick Co., Iowa.

Range. Northern and northeastern Illinois, north of a line extending from southern Whiteside County to northern Edgar County (Map 8.50, p. 258).

Inter-orbital breadth	Nasal length	Length palatal slits	Maxillary toothrow length	Post-palatal length	Mastoid breadth	Height cranium	Gt. breadth across incisive for.	Length bulla	Least pterygoid breadth
3.97	8.38	4.16	3.44	7.17	9.67	8.48	2.06	3.77	1.51
3.7-4.25	8.0-8.95	4.0-4.6	3.3-3.6	6.7-7.6	9.3-10.0	8.0-8.7	1.95-2.15	3.6-3.95	1.4-1.65
0.19	0.29	0.21	0.10	0.31	0.23	0.21	0.08	0.14	0.09
4.10	8.47	4.12	3.63	7.28	9.71	8.64	2.14	3.68	1.51
3.9-4.3	8.2-9.2	3.95-4.35	3.5-3.85	6.9-7.5	9.1-10.15	8.35-8.9	2.05-2.3	3.3-3.9	1.3-1.7
0.17	0.33	0.16	0.12	0.26	0.35	0.19	0.09	0.18	0.16
4.14	8.90	4.43	3.61	7.68	10.23	8.56	2.25	3.98	1.73
3.9-4.45	8.3-9.9	4.1-4.8	3.4-3.9	6.7-8.4	9.8-10.75	7.3-9.4	1.9-2.4	3.7-4.35	1.6-1.9
0.20	0.57	0.21	0.15	0.48	0.35	0.62	0.19	0.20	0.10
4.14	8.73	4.28	3.58	7.94	10.04	8.88	2.19	3.92	1.55[3]
3.85-4.4	8.45-9.3	4.05-4.4	3.3-3.8	7.5-8.25	9.65-10.25	8.55-9.2	2.1-2.35	3.6-4.05	1.45-1.7
0.24	0.39	0.16	0.22	0.34	0.27	0.28	0.12	0.22	0.13

Diagnosis and Comparisons. A subspecies of *Zapus hudsonius* of medium size both externally and cranially. Differs from *Z. h. americanus* in having a larger skull, on the average, in nearly all characters.

Records of occurrence. SPECIMENS EXAMINED, 42.
Jo Daviess Co.: [1a] 1 mi W, ½ mi S Menominee, 1 (SRL); [1b] near Galena, 3 (FM). **Stephenson Co.:** [2] 2 mi E McConnell, 1 (SRL). **Winnebago Co.:** [3] Rock Cut State Park, Harlem Twp., 1 (UI). **Lake Co.:** [5a] Fox Lake, 4 (FM); [5b] Pistakee Bay, 1 (FM); [5c] 3 mi NW Volo, 1 (ISU). **Carroll Co.:** [6] T23N, R4E, Sec. 25, 1 (SRL). **Whiteside Co.:** [7] 6 mi NE Fulton, 3 (UI). **Ogle Co.:** [8] 3 mi S Oregon, 1 (ISU). **Lee Co.:** [9] 5 mi S Rochelle, Kyte River, 1 (SIU). **De Kalb Co.:** [10a] ½ mi S Glidden Rd. and Rt 64., 1 (NIU); [10b] Wilkinson's Marsh, near De Kalb, 1 (UI); [11a] 2 mi W De Kalb, 1 (NIU); [11b] De Kalb, 1 (UI), 1 (NIU). **Kane Co.:** [12] 7.3 mi W, 4.8 mi N Elgin, 2 (UI); [13] near St. Charles, 1 (ISM); [14] Sugar Grove, 1 (CAS). **Champaign Co.:** [15] 3 mi NE Urbana, 1 (UI). **Vermilion Co.:** [16] 1 mi S, 3 mi E Collison, 1 (UI); [17a] 3.6 mi N, 1½ mi W Hillery, 3 (UI); [17b] ½ mi S, ½ mi E Newtown, 1 (UI); [17c] Kickapoo State Park, 1 (UI); [17d] Kickapoo Park stripmines, 1 (UI); [17e] 3 mi NE Fairmount, Jordan Creek, 5 (UI); [18] 5 mi SW Georgetown, 2 (UI).
Additional records. **McHenry Co.:** [4] Wonder Lake, 2 (FS).

Zapus hudsonius americanus (Barton)

1799. *Dipus americanus* Barton, Trans. Amer. Philos. Soc., 4:115. Type locality near Schuylkill R., near Philadelphia, Pennsylvania.
1899. *Zapus hudsonius americanus*, Batchelder, Proc. New England Zool. Club, 1:6.

Range. Central, southern, and parts of western Illinois south of a line extending from southern Whiteside County to northern Edgar County (Map 8.50, p. 258).

Diagnosis and Comparisons. A subspecies of *Zapus hudsonius* of small size both externally and cranially. For differences from *Z. h. intermedius*, see that account and Table 8.29.

Records of occurrence. SPECIMENS EXAMINED, 50.
Fulton Co.: [2a] ½ mi N Norris, 6 (UI); [2b] 3 mi N Canton, 1 (UI); [2c] 2½ mi N Canton, 2 (UI); [2d] 2 mi NW Canton, 3 (UI); [2e] 2 mi W Canton, 3 (UI); [3] 3 mi SW Monterey, 1 (UI); [4] Bryant, 1 (UI); [5] Dickson Mounds, 2 (ISM). **Stark Co.:** [6] 2½ mi S Bradford, 1 (SRL). **Woodford Co.:** [7] 2 mi W Metamora, 1 (ISU). **McLean Co.:** [8] 2 mi WNW Hudson, 5 (ISU). **Pike Co.:** [9] 3½ mi S Pittsfield, 1 (UI). **Macoupin Co.:** [10a] 2 mi NE Beaver Dam State Park, 1 (UI); [10b] 1 mi N Beaver Dam, 1 (UI). **Sangamon Co.:** [11] Springfield, 1 (ISM). **Coles Co.:** [12] Fox Ridge State Park, 1 (UI). **Edgar Co.:** [14] 8 mi SW Paris, 1 (UI). **Madison Co.:** [15] 3½ mi E Moro, 1 (SIU). **Union Co.:** [17] 5½ mi NW Cobden, 1 (SRL); [18b] Pine Hills, 1 (UI); [18c] 4 mi N and E Wolf Lake [assumed to be 4 mi NE Wolf Lake], 1 (SIC); [18d] 4 mi SE Aldridge, 1 (UI); [18e] 7 mi W Cobden, 1 (SIC); [19] 1 mi NE Anna, 1 (SRL); [20a] 2 mi SW Ware, 2 (SRL); [20b] Union County Game Refuge, 1 (UI). **Pope Co.:** [21] 2½ mi S, ½ mi E Glendale, 1 (UI). **Alexander Co.:** [22a] Horseshoe Lake, 1 (UI); [22b] 2½ mi S Olive Branch, 1 (UI); [22c] 3 mi S Olive Branch, 3 (UI); [22d] 3 mi SW Horseshoe Lake, 1 (SRL). **Pulaski Co.:** [23] 3 mi E Ullin, 1 (SRL).
Additional records.: **Henry Co.:** [1] 9 mi N Cambridge, 1 (KU). **Cumberland Co.:** [13] Greenup [sight record, two individuals, Philip Smith]. **Jackson Co.:** [16] Carbondale, (Necker and Hatfield, 1941:56). **Union Co.:** [18a] Pine Hills, 1½ mi ESE Aldridge, 1 (FS). **Massac Co.:** [24] no specific locality (Klimstra and Roseberry, 1969:417).

Order Carnivora, Carnivores

Mostly medium to large-sized mammals with clawed toes, usually with shearing carnassial teeth (Pm^4, M$_1$), canine teeth well-developed and conical, postorbital processes distinct, stomach simple. Of the seven families of fissiped carnivores, four are found in Illinois. If the seals (Pinnipedia) are included in this order, there are three additional families, none of which is in Illinois.

KEY TO CARNIVORA IN ILLINOIS

1a. Claws retractile; muzzle short and broad; premolars and molar in each lower jaw three, tail short   FELIDAE, *Felis rufus,*   p. 310

1b. Claws not retractile; muzzle long and often pointed; premolars and molars in each lower jaw five or more   2

2a. Hind feet with five toes; premolars and molars in each lower jaw seven   CANIDAE   4

2b. Hind feet with four toes; premolars and molars in each lower jaw five or six   3

3a. Tail with rings; no anal scent glands; six premolars and molars in each upper and each lower jaw   PROCYONIDAE, *Procyon lotor,*   p. 282

3b. Tail without rings; anal scent glands present (but better developed in skunks); five premolars and molars in each lower jaw and usually less than six premolars and molars in each upper jaw (*Taxidea* has six)   MUSTELIDAE   6

CANIDAE

4a. Adults weigh more than 16 lbs.; postorbital processes thick and convex above; greatest length of skull 165 mm or more   *Canis latrans,**   p. 270

4b. Adults weigh less than 16 lbs.; postorbital processes thin and concave dorsally; greatest length of skull less than 140 mm   5

5a. Tail with dark stripe all the way down upper side; backs of ears red; cranium with raised, lyrate ridges (U-shaped); posterior end of mandible appears to have three notches
          Urocyon cinereoargenteus,   p. 278

5b. Tail without dark stripe; backs of ears black or brown; cranium without beaded or raised lyrate ridges; posterior end of mandible with two notches   *Vulpes vulpes,*   p. 275

---

* This keys out *Canis familiaris,* dog, also. See p. 270 for means of distinguishing *C. latrans* and *C. familiaris.*

Fig. 8.115. The third notch in the lower jaw of *Urocyon* (left) is indicated with an arrow; the third notch is absent in *Vulpes* (right). (From Hoffmeister and Mohr, 1957. Charles A. McLaughlin)

MUSTELIDAE

6a. Color black and white (in various combinations); posterior border of hard palate not extending appreciably beyond last molars
          Mephitis mephitis,   p. 302

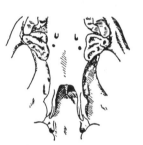

Fig. 8.116. Hard palate in *Mephitis* (left) does not extend appreciably beyond last molars; in other mustelids, as in *Taxidea* (right), it does. (From Hoffmeister and Mohr, 1957. Charles A. McLaughlin)

6b. Color other than black and white; posterior border of hard palate extending markedly beyond last molars   7

7a. Toes extensively webbed; total length more than 800 mm, five teeth behind canine in each upper jaw   *Lutra canadensis,*   p. 305

7b. Toes not noticeably webbed; total length less than 800 mm; four (or sometimes three) teeth behind canine in each upper jaw   8

8a. White stripe on head continuing posteriorly on back between the shoulders; zygomatic breadth greater than 50 mm   *Taxidea taxus*   p. 299

8b. No white stripe on head continuing posteriorly part way down back; zygomatic breadth less than 50 mm   9

9a. Head-body length more than 300 mm, upper toothrow length from canine to last molar than 16 mm, underparts without white, except in throat area and possibly a small spot on belly
          Mustela vison   p. 295

Fig. 8.117A. Coyote, *Canis latrans*. (From Hoffmeister and Mohr, 1957. Photographs by U.S. Fish and Wildlife Service)

9b. Head-body length less than 300 mm, upper toothrow length from canine to last molar less than 16 mm, underparts entirely white or white from throat extending down over chest   10

10a. Tail long and with a conspicuous black tip, head-body length more than 200 mm, hind foot length more than 32 mm   *Mustela frenata*   p. 291

10b. Tail short and without an obvious black tip, head and body less than 200 mm, hind foot length 32 mm or less   *Mustela nivalis*   p. 288

Family Canidae, Doglike and Foxlike Mammals

Long-legged carnivores with ears prominent, five toes on forefoot, four on hind foot, tail long and bushy, carnassial teeth well developed, rostrum of skull elongate. Most dig dens, and vocalize with barks and howls. Van Gelder (1978) would regard all species in Illinois as belonging to the genus *Canis;* for now, I regard these as three genera: *Canis, Vulpes,* and *Urocyon.*

Canis, Wolves, Coyotes, Dogs

Diagnosis. Medium to large size, tail bushy, legs long, ears prominent; skull massive with heavy rostrum, teeth large, usually with sagittal crest, postorbital processes thickened and convex dorsally.

Dental formula. 3/3, 1/1, 4/4, 2/3.

Comparisons. Canis differs from *Vulpes* in Illinois in having a larger external size, greater body weight, larger skull, being longer and broader, with teeth larger, rostrum heavier, postorbital processes thickened and convex dorsally, and upper incisors lobed.

Canis differs from *Urocyon* in Illinois in being larger in size, both externally and cranially, having the ventral border of the lower jaw without a prominent step (Fig. 8.115), crests on brainbox usually present and near

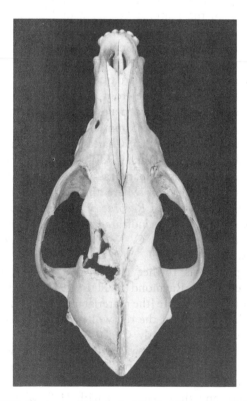

Fig. 8.117B. Photograph of skull of *Canis latrans* from Galesburg, Knox Co., Illinois. Specimen in collection of Illinois Natural History Survey.

midline rather than widely spaced; temporal ridges which unite posteriorly on top of skull; teeth are larger, upper incisors lobed.

Remarks. In the past, three species of *Canis* have been present in Illinois. *Canis lupus,* wolf, was exterminated in Illinois many years ago. This species is discussed in the section on Extirpated Species (p. 47) and in the historical section on mammals in Illinois (p. 27).

Canis latrans, coyote, has been present since and before European man arrived in Illinois. It has profited by the removal of forests and woods and is more abundant now than ever.

Canis familiaris, dog, was a domesticated member of many villages of early Illinois Indians. More recently, domestic dogs have gone feral (wild) in Illinois, becoming independent of humans. They have also interbred with coyotes extensively. This is discussed in the section on *Canis latrans.*

Status of the red wolf, Canis rufus, *in Illinois*

The red wolf, *Canis rufus,* has been ascribed as occurring in Illinois (Goldman, 1944; Miller and Kellog, 1955). This was based upon a skin and skull labelled as if it had been collected at Warsaw, Hancock Co., Illinois, February 7, 1893, with the name of C(harles) K. Worthen on the label. This specimen, if taken at Warsaw, is removed from other known records by 240 miles to the southeast (New Harmony, Posey Co., Indiana. Mumford, 1969, Lyon, 1936) and 200 miles to the south (Cooks Station, Crawford Co., Missouri. Goldman, 1944).

When Goldman (1944) reviewed the taxonomy of the red wolves, he believed that there was an authentic record of this species from Wabash, Wabash Co., Indiana. This would have placed the species in northern Indiana and slightly north of the record at Warsaw, Illinois. This may have influenced Goldman to regard the specimen from Warsaw as an authentic record. Mumford (1969) and Lyon (1936) point out that the Indiana record, which is a skull-only, was preserved by Maximilian, Prince of Wied, in 1832. The prince spent from the fall of 1832 until the spring of 1833 along the Wabash River at New Harmony, and did not visit Wabash, Wabash County. Mumford and Lyon regard the Indiana specimen as from the vicinity of New Harmony, which is almost due east of the northern record in Missouri. The red wolf was an inhabitant of the Ozark Hills of southern Missouri, probably occurred in the Ozark Hill country of southern Illinois (see Map 2.2), and extended eastward to southern Indiana near New Harmony.

The person who preserved the specimen from Warsaw, Illinois, Charles K. Worthen, can best be characterized as a professional taxidermist and preparator in his later

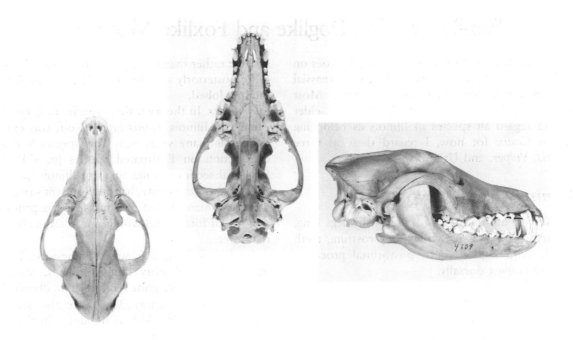

Fig. 8.118. Skull, dorsal, ventral, and lateral aspects, of *Canis* sp. from Warsaw, Hancock Co., Illinois, taken February 7, 1893. Prepared by C. K. Worthen. No. 4609, Male. American Museum Natural History. See text for a discussion of this specimen.

years. His letterhead says "Chas. K. Worthen, Naturalist & Taxidermist, also dealer in Bird & Mammal Skins, Warsaw, Illinois." Born September 6, 1850, he was the son of Amos H. Worthen, who for many years was the Illinois State Geologist. Part of Charles's early life was spent as a delineator, doing art work for his father's geological reports and for the reports of Wheeler's expedition to the West, and drawings for Agassiz's fishes. While working at the Museum of Comparative Zoology, Harvard, Charles must have become sufficiently interested in animal life to develop his skills as a preparator of study specimens and of taxidermy mounts. When he returned to Warsaw, he must have set himself up as a taxidermist and preparator. He sent specimens that he had prepared, mostly birds, to museums throughout the world, according to newspaper accounts and a report in the *Oologist* (23 [1911]:112). He sent several shipments to the British Museum, including nearly 400 skins of birds "taken by his collector from Guadoloupe [*sic*], San Benito and Clarion islands"; to the Imperial University of Moscow ("rare raptores . . . from Greenland, Iceland, and Arctic regions"); numerous birds to the Zoological Museum (Rothschild Collection) of Tring, England; to several museums in Scotland; to the New York Zoological Society, through its director William T. Hornaday (29 lots of bird specimens, apparently all mounts); and other museums.

All specimens of Illinois mammals with C. K. Worthen's labels thereon, which are in several museums in the United States, are labelled as "Warsaw," as far as I can ascertain. Perhaps Worthen did not collect or obtain specimens from anywhere in Illinois except Warsaw. However, five specimens of eastern moles, *Scalopus aquaticus,* in the National Museum of Natural History with C. K. Worthen's labels and a Warsaw locality are interesting. Dr. Victor Diersing examined these specimens and pointed out to me that the five, all adults, show such a great degree of variation that it is difficult to believe that they all came from one place. The greatest length of the skull in two males is 35.3 mm and 39.45 mm; in two females, 36.85 mm and 38.9 mm.

I have a suspicion that Charles Worthen may have attached his name and Warsaw address to many specimens of Illinois mammals prepared as mounts or as research specimens regardless of where they came from in the state. In the sections of *Records of occurrence* under the various species, I have indicated with a footnote those specimens labelled by C. K. Worthen. All are from Warsaw.

The picture is further complicated by a statement attributed to E. Raymond Hall. In 1972 Paradiso and Nowak (1972:8) wrote [the material in brackets is added]: "The Illinois skull [of the red wolf] was possessed by an animal dealer [apparently C. K. Worthen] in Hancock County and apparently was from a captive wolf (E. Raymond Hall, pers. comm.)." The basis for this statement is not known to me but Nowak was at the University of Kansas, and thus associated with Hall, when he co-authored this article and apparently reported something told him by Hall.

Table 8.30. Ratios and measurements useful in separating coyotes and dogs.*

		Coyote	Ratio		Dog	Ratio
Rostral breadth	=	61 to 69			62 to 72	
Rostral breadth × 2	=	58 to 66	0.915 to 0.990		62 to 82	1.085 to 1.290
Breadth across upper incisors		18.9 to 21.9			22.4 to 27.5	
Mastoidal breadth		57.9 to 65.3			65.0 to 72.9	

* Ratios for coyotes are usually less than 1.000. The measurement for rostral breadth has been multiplied by 2. For example, the "58" for coyote is an actual measurement of 29 mm × 2 = 58.

Table 8.31. Ratios of various measurements to basilar length for separating coyotes and dogs or coyote-dog hybrids.

Coyote less than	Ratio	Dog and hybrid more than
.371	$\dfrac{\text{Mastoidal breadth}}{\text{Basilar length}}$	.372
.281	$\dfrac{\text{Postorbital breadth}}{\text{Basilar length}}$	.282
.184	$\dfrac{\text{Rostrum width}}{\text{Basilar length}}$	.185
.122	$\dfrac{\text{Breadth upper incisors}}{\text{Basilar length}}$	.123
.195	$\dfrac{\text{Width between Pm}^4\text{s}}{\text{Basilar length}}$	.196
.168	$\dfrac{\text{Width between M}^2\text{s}}{\text{Basilar length}}$	.169

Table 8.32. Features suggested by Hoffmeister and Mohr (1957) for separating coyotes, hybrids, and dogs.

Formula		Coyote	Hybrid	Dog
$\dfrac{\text{Palatal width between inner margins of alveoli of upper first premolars}}{\text{Alveolar length of upper premolars and molars}}$ × 100		25-32	32-38	32-52
$\dfrac{\text{Width of basioccipital bone}}{\text{Width of braincase}}$ × 100		23.3-28.1	28.0-29.1	29.1-34.3
$\dfrac{\text{Depth of lower jaw below second molar}}{\text{Length of lower jaw}}$ × 100		12.2-14.1	14.2-14.7	14.0-17.8

In 1986, Dr. John Warnock of Western Illinois University, sought information for me about Charles Worthen. Warnock found the following article dated February 10, 1893, in "The Warsaw Bulletin." The specimen of "red wolf" which is the source of concern for this report is labelled as having been collected on February 7, 1893, three days before this news report. The Marsh farm mentioned in the article was located about 4 miles east of Warsaw, according to an early map of Wilcox Township, Hancock County. The article reads:

Recently Col. Marsh lost two horses and their carcasses were dragged to a hollow on the extreme south of his farm. Within a day or two thereafter a pack of wolves scented the dead animals, and they made the night hideous with their howling. Gus Brault and a couple of companions set to work to capture one or more of them and they succeeded in killing two last Monday [February 6, 1893] night. They are large, fine specimens of grey or timber wolf, one especially being a rarity hereabouts. His fur was as red as that of a fox. Chas. K. Worthen purchased both and will mount their skins.

The specimen referred to as a grey or timber wolf with fur as red as that of a fox may very well be the specimen now preserved in the American Museum of Natural History, No. 5450/4609, consisting of a skull and a nearly flat, but partially stuffed, skin. The skin is not now a mount, in the sense of a taxidermist's type of mount, and probably never was. The skull is that of a not fully mature animal, less than a year old judging from comparisons with other skulls. The skull is photographed in Fig. 8.118. The skin is reddish in color, more so on the sides than on the dorsum, but it is not as reddish as some coyote x dog hybrids in Illinois. The feet look large in the preparation, but probably no larger than some dogs. Measurements that are available from the label are "body 3 ft., 8½ inches" (=1,130 mm); "tail 1 ft., 8 inches" (= 508 mm); "ear 4⅞ inches" (= 124 mm).

The specimen has been lent to us by the American Museum through the help of Dr. Sydney Anderson. He has also provided copies of some letters on file in the American Museum written by Worthen to Dr. J. A. Allen of that museum which pertain to this specimen. On February 7, 1893, the day the specimen was said to have been collected, Worthen wrote Allen that "I have just had brought to me two more Timber wolves, killed last night by poison. . . ." The poisoning mentioned is not consistent with the newspaper account. His letter reiterates that one of the wolves "is an iron gray, and the other is *red*, all over, almost the color of a red fox!"

Worthen in a follow-up letter of February 15, 1893, to Allen says of the so-called wolves that "I had promised Ward [Natural History Establishment?] one of them, but I kept the big red one for you, although Ward & F. W. True wanted it, and I was offered $20.00 cash for it by two parties. I have held him for you & made a nice skin of him; he is fine and will please you. Shall I send him *now* or hold until he is dry? There are several more [wolves?] in the gang, and I have parties out after them. . . ." In a letter of March 27, Worthen says he is sending the specimen to J. A. Allen.

On April 15, 1893, Worthen replied to a letter received from and written by Allen apparently as soon as the specimen was received at the American Museum. Worthen's reply was delayed by illness in his family. Worthen wrote

I was awfully sorry to hear that you were somewhat disappointed in the wolf, and especially so when I had refused it *entire* [unskinned?] to two other parties at same price and took upon myself the extra work of skinning & making skin etc. in order to *save it for you!* I never dreamed of such a thing as it being a hybrid, but considered it an extra fine and interesting specimen on *account of the color* as I wrote you. It was the only reddish one in the "gang" of seven—and I have not been able to get any more of them since.

This last letter indicates that J. A. Allen regarded the specimen as a hybrid, but it is not clear as to what kind of hybrid. Also, there is a reference by Worthen that the entire gang of seven animals had been seen, although until now there is no indication that this was the case.

Assuming that this specimen did come from Illinois and the vicinity of Warsaw, Mr. David Nelson and I set about to determine if it was a (1) red wolf, *Canis rufus*, (2) coyote, *Canis latrans*, (3) dog, *Canis familiaris*, (4) wolf, *Canis lupus*, (5) hybrid coyote x dog, (6) hybrid red wolf x dog, or (7) hybrid red wolf x coyote. In an earlier account (p. 33), I stated that I thought wolves, *Canis lupus*, were gone from Illinois sometime before 1860. Employing features and measurements of the skull, we reached the following conclusions. It should be pointed out that in our estimation the reddish color of the pelt does not in itself indicate that this is a red wolf for we have seen pelts of hybrids of coyote x dog that are more reddish.

The skull of the "Warsaw" specimen probably is not a dog, for the rostrum is long for its breadth (twice the rostral width is not greater than its rostral length); the toothrows are long; the skull is narrow across the postorbital processes for its length.

The skull probably is not a coyote because of its large size, both in length and breadth; the rostral region is longer, as measured by rostral, palatilar, and nasal lengths; the palate is wide relative to the width between the incisors.

Table 8.33. Winter foods of coyotes in southeastern Illinois as determined by analysis of 89 stomachs collected from 29 November 1977 through 28 February 1978 (from Phillips and Hubert, 1980).

Food Item	Frequency of occurrence (%)	Aggregate volume (%)
MAMMALS	98.0	87.7
Rabbits		
Cottontail, *Sylvilagus* sp.	51.6	49.7
Deer		
White-tailed deer, *Odocoileus virginianus*	6.7	7.0
Rodents		
Woodchuck, *Marmota monax*	1.1	1.5
Prairie vole, *Microtus ochrogaster*	3.3	tr.[a]
White-footed mouse, *Peromyscus leucopus*	15.7	5.4
Deer mouse, *Peromyscus maniculatus*	8.9	1.8
House mouse, *Mus musculus*	7.8	2.2
Undetermined mouse	17.8	1.7
Livestock		
Pig, *Sus scrofa*	22.4	13.9
Sheep, *Ovis aries*	1.2	tr.
Other mammals		
Racoon, *Procyon lotor*	4.4	3.3
Striped skunk, *Mephitis mephitis*	5.6	0.8
BIRDS	24.7	3.4
Poultry	10.1	2.9
Game birds		
Bobwhite	11.2	tr.
Non–game birds		
Redwinged blackbird, *Agelaius phoniceus*	1.0	tr.
Bluejay, *Cyanocitta cristata*	1.0	tr.
Eastern meadowlark, *Sturnella magna*	2.2	tr.
Swamp sparrow, *Melospiza georgiana*	1.0	tr.
Tufted titmouse, *Parus bicolor*	1.0	tr.
INVERTEBRATES	2.2	tr.
Crustaceans		
Crayfish, *Cambaridae* spp.	1.0	tr.
Insects		
Grasshopper, *Acrididae* sp.	1.0	tr.
UNDETERMINED ANIMAL MATTER	20.2	8.0
PLANT FOODS	92.6	1.2
Persimmon, *Diospyros virginiana*	5.6	tr.
Grass, *Graminae* spp.	71.9	0.5
Corn	11.2	tr.
Potato	1.0	tr.
Soybean	1.0	tr.
Goosefoot, *Chenopodium hybridum*	1.0	tr.
MISCELLANEOUS	7.8	tr.
Paper	5.6	tr.
Leather	1.0	tr.
Rubber	2.2	tr.
Plastic	1.0	tr.[a]

[a] tr. = trace (less tran 0.5%)

The skull has many features that fall within the range of variation for hybrids of *C. latrans* x *C. familiaris*. The skull is only 0.3 mm larger in basilar length than the largest hybrid we have examined (Table 8.32); it (as marked with an asterisk) falls well within the range of hybrids on the three scattergrams (Figs. 8.119–8.121). When a principal component analysis was run, with principal component one giving an indication of size and principal component two giving an indication of shape, the Warsaw skull (marked with a star) falls with the hybrids (Fig. 8.122).

The skull of the "Warsaw" specimen has been compared with that of red wolves only on the basis of measurements published by Nowak (1979). Measurements of 11 male red wolves taken before 1919 indicate that the "Warsaw" specimen is only slightly less in greatest length. Comparisons of a larger sample of 63 male red wolves taken between 1919 and 1929 indicate that the "Warsaw" specimen is within the range of variation.

A discriminant function analysis was performed to differentiate red wolves and hybrid dog x coyotes. Three measurements taken by Nowak (1979)—zygomatic breadth, postorbital processes breadth, canine breadth—were compared with similar measurements taken by David Nelson for hybrids with a basilar length greater than 162 mm. The 11 male red wolves taken before 1919 were compared with 12 dog x coyote hybrids from Illinois. The linear discriminant function is successful in differentiating between the two groups as indicated by its 100 percent correct classification of the knowns and an estimated, apparent error rate of 4.3 percent. This linear function classified the "Warsaw" specimen as a red wolf, and based upon squared distances, the probability that it is a red wolf rather than a hybrid is 0.993. It should be pointed out that we have not measured any skulls of red wolves and the measurements taken by others may not be made in precisely the same fashion as we took ours. However, the three that we have used should be easy to duplicate.

From all of the information reviewed above, the "Warsaw" specimen seems to be either a hybrid of a dog x coyote or a red wolf. I prefer to regard it as a dog x coyote hybrid. Our principal component analysis indicated that it is such. A visual examination of the skull implies this also. The preceding discriminant function analysis may indicate otherwise, but this analysis is based on red wolves taken from a large geographical area. Someone else's examination may indicate that indeed this specimen is a red wolf and if it truly came from Warsaw, Illinois, then it will be the first record for the state and the species *Canis rufus* must be regarded as a member of the Illinois fauna up to 1893. Red wolves had a good chance of living in the Ozark or Shawnee hills of southern Illinois at an early time, but there are no known specimens to verify this.

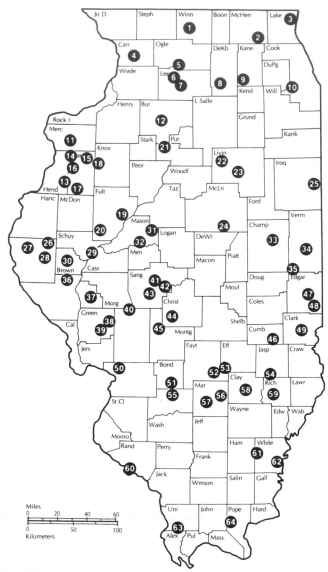

Map 8.51. Coyotes, *Canis latrans*, occur statewide. The subspecies is *C. l. thamnos*. Numbered localities are referenced in *Records of occurrence*. The range of the species in the United States is shaded.

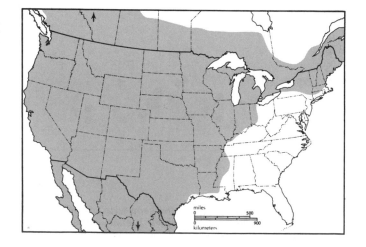

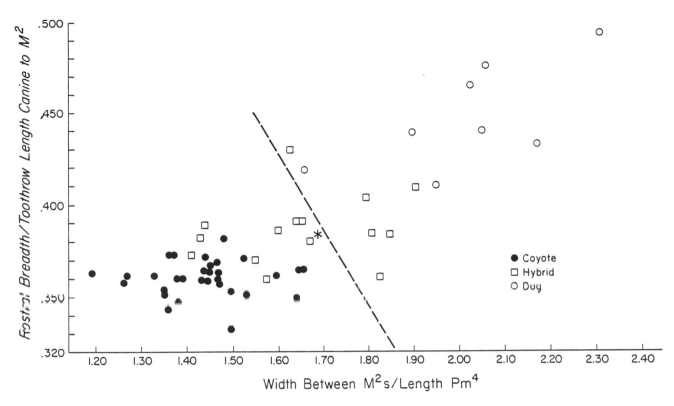

Fig. 8.119. Scattergram based on a ratio of rostral breadth divided by the length of the canine—M² toothrow and the palatal width as based on width between M²s divided by length of Pm⁴. The asterisk is for the specimen from Warsaw, Illinois.

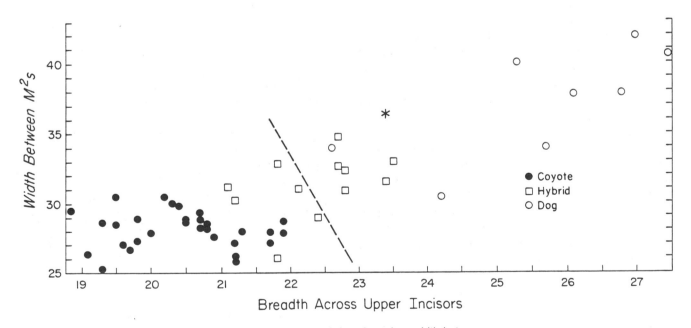

Fig. 8.120. Scattergram showing the separation of coyotes and dogs based on width between the upper second (last) molars and the breadth across the upper incisors. The rostral portion of the skull from the last molar forward is narrower in coyotes than in dogs. The asterisk is for the specimen from Warsaw, Illinois.

Canis latrans, Coyote

Range. Throughout the state, but avoiding urban areas.

Diagnosis. A medium-sized canid with pointed ears, nose pad usually 25 mm or less in width, heel pad of forefoot usually less than 32 mm in width, tail tipped with black; anteroposterior diameter of upper canine tooth at base less than 11.0 mm; upper canine tooth usually extends to middle or below plane of anterior mental foramen when lower jaw is articulated and in closed position; premolars widely spaced and relatively narrow; narrow across upper incisors (alveolar breadth usually 21 mm or less), narrow between upper M²s (alveolar breadth across innermost parts of each alveolus usually 30 mm or less). *C. latrans* in Illinois is exceedingly large, with weights to 40 lbs and reports of weights up to 50 lbs. This large size has caused many who know the small coyote in the West to call this animal in Illinois a wolf.

Color. Variable; dorsum with incomplete dark stripe down midline, which in some is blackish, and about three cm wide; in others, much of the dorsum darkened; sides lighter with less blackish; venter variable, being creamy-colored or grayish with varying mixtures of ochraceous tint; tail with black color of back usually extending onto top of tail, tip black; underside often mostly same color as abdomen; backs of ears reddish or ochraceous intermixed with black; snout, anterior to eyes, reddish.

A specimen from Richland County, Illinois, represents a reddish phase occasionally encountered; back and sides are nearly as reddish as in *Vulpes vulpes;* hairs are darker red along the midline; tail with some black on the top and at the tip; venter cream-colored.

Chromosomes. 2N = 78. All autosomes acrocentric. X chromosome submetacentric; Y, minute.

Comparisons. C. latrans needs detailed comparisons with the dog, *Canis familiaris,* with which it is known to hybridize in Illinois.

To more easily separate *C. latrans* and *C. familiaris,* animals of about the same external size and build as well as age should be compared. Furthermore, when one compares Illinois coyotes with dogs, it is best that the sample of coyotes had been collected before 1940. Up to that time there was not a great deal of hybridization in coyotes and dogs. Now, we are of the opinion that a great deal of hybridization is occurring and it may be difficult to find a "full-blooded" coyote.

Canis latrans in comparison with *C. familiaris* has a relatively longer, narrower snout or rostrum. This is indicated (Table 8.30) in the narrowness across the upper

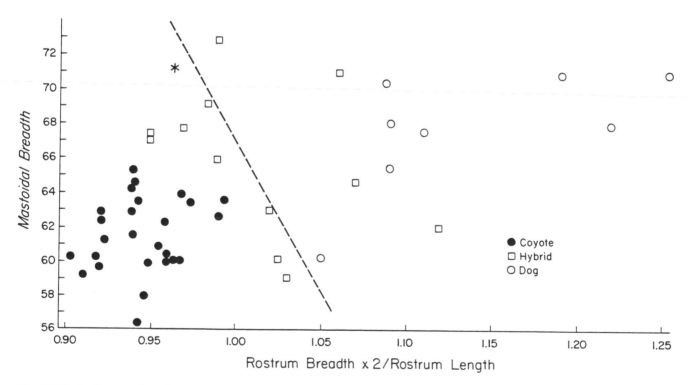

Fig. 8.121. Scattergram based on mastoidal breadth of the skull and a ratio of double the rostral breadth divided by the rostral length. Note in coyotes that double the rostral breadth is less than the rostral length (less than 1.00); in dogs, double the rostral breadth is usually more than the rostral length. Hybrids tend to group around the line separating the two species. The asterisk is for the specimen from Warsaw, Illinois.

incisors, the rostrum breadth, the width between M²s, and the narrowness across the postorbital processes. In *C. latrans,* the rostrum breadth doubled is usually less than the rostral length; in *C. familiaris,* more. *C. latrans* is narrower across the brainbox and this is indicated by the mastoidal breadth. This is shown in part in scattergrams (Figs. 8.119–8.121). Using the characters or ratios given in these figures, all specimens can be separated as coyotes or dogs. The differences between the two might be even greater if the samples of coyotes were pre-1940 or before a time when hybridization between coyotes and dogs was as general or great as it is in the 1980's.

In Illinois, coyote and dog skulls can usually be separated on the basis of these measurements or ratios. Skulls that have a basilar length of 160 mm or more have been used (Table 8.30, p. 266).

When various ratios are made to basilar length, there is usually a separation of *C. latrans* and *C. familiaris.* Six of these ratios are especially useful. If four or more of these ratios for a particular specimen fall with one species, the chances are good that it is that species. These ratios are recorded in Table 8.31 (p. 266).

Other combinations of characters have been suggested for separating *C. latrans* and *C. familiaris.* Hoffmeister and Mohr (1957:11) proposed the formula in Table 8.32.

Howard (1949b) proposed to use the ratio of the palatal width between the first upper premolars and the upper premolar-molar toothrow length. Lawrence and Bossert (1967, 1969) and Elder and Hayden (1977) employed 15 cranial measurements in multiple character analyses and obtained separation between dogs and coyotes (as well as between *Canis lupus* and *Canis niger*).

In our examination of 228 coyotelike skulls from Illinois, we think that 34, or 15 percent, are hybrids. We are not certain, however, that some of the remaining 194 specimens, especially those more recently collected, do not show some influence of *C. familiaris* characters.

C. latrans differs from the wolf *C. lupus* in having more pointed ears, narrower nose pad, narrower heel pad on forefoot, upper canine at base narrower and tips of canines extending below level of anterior mental foramina, teeth less massive, skull smaller, tympanic bullae more inflated, mandible thinner, lower toothrow less bowed outward, Pm⁴ and M¹ differing in cusp arrangement.

Aging. Most *C. latrans* in Illinois are born in April. Thus, animals taken in winter, as in January or February, are about 10 months old or a year and 10 months, or a progression based on this birthdate.

Cranial measurements. Methods of taking cranial measurements are shown in Figure 8.123 (p. 274).

Secondary sexual variation. The measurements of skulls of 15 males and 7 females from southern Illinois were analyzed for difference between the sexes. In 17 measurements there were no significant differences; in 6 there were. Males, however, averaged slightly larger than females in all measurements except width of Pm⁴, and the differences in this case were not significant.

Molt. There is only one molt each year, according to Young and Jackson (1951:247). They stated that this may be irregular but that it usually starts in the summer and continues over a rather long period, ordinarily being completed in early autumn. They said the pelage "is at its prime usually from the last of November until well into February."

Remarks. The increase in the number of coyotes in Illinois in the last 40 years is phenomenal in my estimation. In 1950, if one shot or trapped a coyote, it was sufficiently newsworthy for one's picture or story to appear in the local paper. In 1950, I know of eight accounts, and undoubtedly there were others. Between 1950 and 1969, at the cooperative wildlife research laboratory at Southern Illinois University, only nine coyotes were brought in and identified.

In the mid-1970's, about 3,000 coyotes were taken annually for their pelts; by the early 1980's, more than 10,000 were reportedly taken annually and the resident population was supposed to be between 20,000 and 30,000. It is not certain what proportion of this population is coydogs but if the percentage is 15, as suggested by 15 percent of the skulls being those of hybrids, then between 3,000 and 4,500 coydogs are present in the state.

With this population explosion and the possible pres-

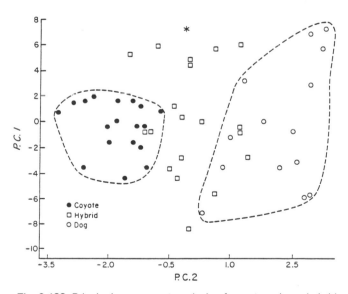

Fig. 8.122. Principal component analysis of coyotes, dogs, hybrid coyote × dog, and the specimen from Warsaw, Illinois (indicated by asterisk), based on three cranial measurements. P.C.1 is a measure of shape as based on width measurements vs. length.

Table 8.34. Cranial measurements (in mm) of *Canis latrans, Canis familiaris,* and hybrid *C. latrans* × *C. familiaris* taken in Illinois. Mean, minimum-maximum, and one standard deviation are given. Measurements are taken as shown in Fig. 8.123. Note that the standard deviations are higher for the dogs and hybrids. The individual measurements for the specimen from Warsaw, Hancock Co., Illinois, discussed in the text, are given last.

	Sex	N	Basilar length	Zygomatic breadth	Brain case breadth	Inter-orbital breadth	Mastoidal breadth	Post-orbital processes breadth	Nasal length	Nasal width	Infra-orbital foramina width	Palatilar length
Canis latrans* Fur-buyer in Richland Co. (15) and through-out state (6).	♂	21	173.24 164.7-181.0 4.50	101.29 94.9-106.4 3.35	60.69 58.1-63.8 1.45	33.46 29.6-37.0 1.75	61.56 56.1-65.3 2.43	47.82 43.4-51.8 2.38	74.77 68.1-82.0 3.43	16.80 13.9-19.4 1.43	43.26 38.6-47.6 2.22	92.55 84.7-97.9 2.92
Fur-buyer in Richland Co.	♀	7	170.67 167.7-173.9 2.06	98.79 96.3-104.0 2.86	59.53 58.7-60.8 0.73	32.37 30.1-33.5 1.29	61.01 59.8-62.6 1.14	47.36 43.2-50.1 2.17	75.24 72.2-79.4 2.19	16.01 14.4-18.4 1.17	42.64 40.2-44.2 1.23	92.94 91.0-94.9 1.52
Canis familiaris* various localities in Illinois	♂, ♀	9	178.66 160.7-189.0 10.25	108.67 99.7-116.0 5.58	64.84 61.2-69.3 2.52	39.51 35.6-42.0 2.34	68.07 60.1-72.9 3.81	56.42 49.9-62.0 4.44	77.01 70.7-81.7 3.79	18.84 16.6-21.1 1.76	48.58 42.7-53.0 3.22	98.37 92.6-103.2 3.84
Canis latrans × *C. familiaris** various localities in Illinois	♂, ♀	14	173.32 168.8-192.9 10.07	101.48 92.4-111.2 5.50	60.77 52.4-66.0 3.46	34.85 31.5-38.4 2.41	64.34 59.0-70.6 3.71	50.93 45.6-59.0 4.43	76.34 68.6-86.8 5.79	17.24 14.2-22.2 1.94	44.38 40.2-49.9 2.79	94.77 85.8-106.2 6.72
Warsaw, Hancock Co. AMNH possibly *Canis rufus*	♂	4609	193.2	115.3	65.9	38.3	71.4	54.2	84.5	18.5	49.0	104.1

* Specimens with a basilar length of 160 mm or more.

ence of so many hybrids, many detailed studies on the behavior, food habits, ecology, and population dynamics of these canids are needed now.

Habitat

Coyotes live in a variety of habitats in Illinois—the brushy country at the edge of woodlands, the rolling landscape of southern Illinois, wooded bluffs of the Mississippi River, strip-mined spoil-lands, and the prairie lands in the areas where the prairie chickens do their courtship dances. The early settlers in Illinois referred to these animals as prairie wolves to contrast their habitat with that of the timber wolf. Also, they were frequently called gray wolves. The wolf bounties paid in Illinois for the last 50 years have been for coyotes, whether or not one prefers to call coyotes by the name prairie or gray wolves. The name "wolf," however, should be reserved for *Canis lupus* and *Canis niger.*

Present-day information on the habitat of coyotes in Illinois may actually refer to hybrids or coydogs, whose habitat may be different from than of pure-bred coyotes.

Habits

Only recently, in Illinois, have the howls of coyotes become noticeable. In many counties, their characteristically quavering *yip-yap* that often ends in a prolonged howl can be heard at certain times of the year. Probably the howls of the coyote are heard more frequently in Illinois now than at any time since their existence here. Their calls can be heard not far distant from larger downstate towns. Near Mahomet, about 10 miles NW Champaign, one can frequently hear coyotes howling.

A mated pair may breed together more than once during their lifetime. The male usually brings food to the nursing female and for the pups. When the young reach the weaning stage, both adults may regurgitate semisolid food for the young.

Whether coyotes form packs in Illinois is not known. Usually there is a complicated social organization within such packs.

It is interesting to note that nearly 96 percent of the coyotes in Illinois are taken by hunters; only four percent by trappers (Hubert, 1979a). In many states nearly the reverse of this would be true.

Food

In southern Illinois, coyotes during the winter feed extensively (87.7 percent) on mammals (Phillips and Hubert, 1980 and Table 8.33). Cottontails, pigs, mice (various species), deer, and raccoon make up the principal components of their mammalian diet. Poultry made up 2.9 percent of the volume. Otherwise, there were only traces or a small percentage of various birds, crayfish, and grasshoppers; 8 percent of the animal matter was not determinable. In winter, only traces of plant material were found in analyzed stomach contents.

In Missouri, Korschgen (1957) found that 79 percent by volume of the food eaten by 770 coyotes consisted of mammals, most of these being cottontails (52%); other food items included livestock (9%), mice (9%), raccoon

Rostrum length	Rostrum breadth	Breadth across incisors	Canine breadth	Width between Pm⁴'s	Width between M²'s	Length C-M²	Length C-Pm⁴	Length Pm⁴	Width Pm⁴	Length lower C-M₃	Length M₁	Breadth M₁
65.00	30.66	20.60	11.06	33.10	28.20	85.64	69.43	19.86	9.16	97.54	21.86	7.97
60.5-69.8	28.3-33.2	19.3-21.3	10.1-12.1	29.7-36.1	25.2-30.5	80.1-90.5	64.7-73.8	18.3-22.0	8.0-10.5	92.1-101.2	20.2-23.8	6.9-9.4
2.55	1.20	0.84	0.50	1.84	1.43	2.60	2.54	0.99	0.66	2.79	0.97	0.58
63.73	30.34	20.00	10.31	31.31	28.06	83.81	67.40	19.17	9.50	96.33	21.36	7.53
62.5-65.0	29.2-31.2	18.8-21.2	9.4-11.0	29.4-32.9	26.3-29.6	82.3-85.1	66.2-68.6	18.0-20.6	8.8-10.1	95.0-97.6	20.2-23.2	7.0-8.2
0.94	0.73	0.96	0.51	1.31	1.18	1.05	0.72	0.97	0.51	1.06	1.03	0.50
66.00	36.96	25.30	12.22	39.28	36.21	83.67	67.91	18.59	10.22	96.00	21.47	7.87
60.8-71.2	31.9-42.1	22.4-27.6	10.5-13.8	32.7-47.0	28.9-41.9	77.8-89.7	62.1-71.7	17.4-20.1	8.9-11.5	90.5-102.3	19.9-22.5	6.8-8.4
3.25	3.29	1.88	1.03	4.84	4.64	3.75	3.12	0.91	0.81	4.36	0.92	0.59
64.19	32.48	21.86	11.22	34.88	30.77	84.25	67.49	18.51	9.56	95.22	20.92	7.44
57.4-71.8	30.2-35.7	19.8-23.5	9.5-12.2	30.8-41.2	25.1-34.8	78.5-92.2	62.1-73.6	16.3-20.9	8.6-12.2	88.9-103.7	19.1-23.0	6.8-8.0
4.68	1.87	1.08	0.91	3.13	2.62	4.56	3.81	1.24	0.90	5.05	1.17	0.40
71.6	04.0	23.7	11.2	39.5	36.1	90.7	73.7	21.2	9.9	103.3	22.4	8.3

(2%), and deer (1.6%). Poultry made up 11 percent; quail, only 0.2 percent of their diet. There is the probability that some food items, especially livestock and deer, were from carrion or previously dead animals.

Cottontails serve as food more extensively in winter than during other parts of the year. Phillips and Hubert's study in southern Illinois showed that sheep and cattle are insignificant in the diet.

There are many feral (wild-living) dogs in Illinois, and since many of them are exceedingly large and capable of killing prey that coyotes could not, it is possible that reported kills of large animals, allegedly by coyotes, may actually have been by feral dogs.

Reproduction

In Illinois, George Hubert of the Illinois Department of Conservation informs me that breeding occurs most often in February and young are born usually in April. The gestation period is about two months (58 to 65 days). The average litter size is not well known in Illinois. In seven female coyote specimens, Hubert (1979a) found the mean number of placental scars was 6.9 (4–9). Elsewhere the mean is about six, but variable. Most females have eight mammary glands. Hubert (1979a) thought that some females may breed and bear young before they are two years old.

Young are cared for in a burrow or den. Near Greenville, Bond County, a den had been dug between the roots of a dead tree stump. The eight pups were in an area that was within arm's reach of the surface. Eyes open at about two weeks. The young are fed solid or semisolid food at about three weeks and are entirely weaned around 1.5 months of age.

Hybrids or coydogs may have a reproductive cycle slightly different from coyotes. Mengel (1971) had evidence that mating occurs in December and thus young would be born in February. If such is the case, the offspring would have the disadvantage of being reared during the coldest part of the year. In Arkansas, Gipson et al. (1975) found that there was overlap between the breeding cycles of coyote and coydogs although there may be decreased fecundity among coydogs.

Variation

In 1949, Jackson described a large-sized coyote from Wisconsin that fit the description of coyotes in Illinois. I regard all coyotes in Illinois as referable to his *C. l. thamnos* although there is the possibility that some specimens from southernmost Illinois may be referable to *C. l. frustror* (type locality near Perkins, Payne Co., Oklahoma).

Canis latrans thamnos Jackson

1949. *Canis latrans thamnos* Jackson, Proc. Biol. Soc. Wash., 62:31. Type from Basswood Island, Apostle Islands, Ashland Co., Wisconsin.

Range. Throughout the state, but avoiding urban areas.
Diagnosis and Comparisons. A large-sized subspecies of *Canis latrans,* skull broad.

Fig. 8.123. Dorsal, ventral, and lateral views of coyote, *Canis latrans*. Cranial measurements used in the text, as indicated below, were taken as illustrated.

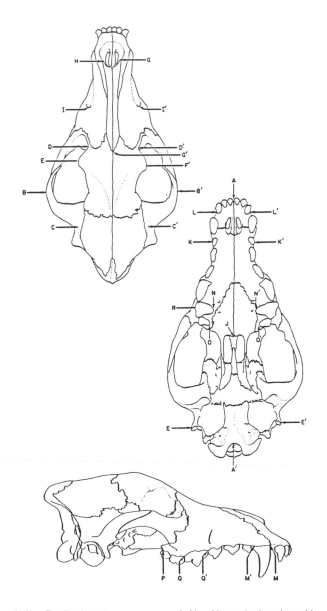

A-A'	Basilar length
B-B'	Zygomatic breadth
C-C'	Braincase breadth
D-D'	Interorbital breadth
E-E'	Mastoidal breadth
F-F'	Greatest breadth-postorbital processes
G-G'	Nasal length
G-H	Nasal width—greatest near tips
I-I'	Infraorbital breadth across infraorbital foramina
A-J	Palatilar length
A-I	Rostrum length
K-K'	Rostrum breadth (Pm¹)

L-L'	Upper incisor breadth (alveolar)
M-M'	Upper canine breadth (at alveolus)
N-N'	Width between Pm⁴s (at alveolus)
O-O'	Width between M²s (at alveolus)
M-P	Length C to M² (at alveolus)
M-Q	Length C to Pm⁴ (at alveolus)
Q-Q	Length Pm⁴ (at alveolus)
R-N	Width Pm⁴ (at alveolus)
	*Length lower C to M₃ (at alveolus)
	*Length M₁ (at alveolus)
	*Breadth M₁ (at alveolus)

*Not illustrated

Records of occurrence. SPECIMENS EXAMINED, 194. **Winnebago Co.:** [1] Wempleton, 1 (NHS). **McHenry Co.:** [2] near Crystal Lake, 1 (ISM). **Lake Co.:** [3] Camp Logan, 1 (FM). **Carroll Co.:** [4] no specific locality, 1 (UI). **Ogle Co.:** [5] 10 mi NE Dixon, 2 (ISM); no specific locality [not plotted], 1 (UI). **Lee Co.:** [6] 8 mi NE Dixon, 1 (ISM); [7] no precise locality, 1 (Hubert Collection). **De Kalb Co.:** [8] near Hickley, 3 (Hubert Collection). **Kane Co.:** [9] near Sugar Grove, 1 (Hubert Coll.). **Cook Co.:** [10] Willow Springs, 1 (NHS); Cook Co. Forest Preserve [location uncertain, not plotted], 1 (NHS). **Mercer Co.:** [11] no precise locality, 1 (Hubert Coll.). **Bureau Co.:** [12] no precise locality, 2 (Hubert Coll.). **Henderson Co.:** [13] 3 mi from Media [plotted as Media], 1 (ISM). **Warren Co.:** [14] near Little York, 1 (ISM); [15a] near Alexis, 1 (ISM); [15b] Kelly Twp., 1 (NHS); [15c] ½ mi N Gerlaw, 1 (ISM); [16] 4 mi W Monmouth, 1 (ISM); [17a] Swan Twp., Sec. 4, 1 (ISM); [17b] 2 mi S, 1 mi E Roseville, 2 (ISM); no specific locality [not plotted], 1 (ISM), 1 (Hubert Coll.). **Knox Co.:** [18] Galesburg, 1 (NHS). **Fulton Co.:** [19a] 6 mi NW Lewistown, 1 (UI); [19b] 2½ mi S St. David, 1 (ISM); [20a] 3½ mi SE Ipava, 1 (UI); [20b] 5½ mi SE Ipava, 1 (UI); no specific locality, 1 (ISM). **Marshall Co.:** [21] 9 mi W Henry, 1 (US). **Livingston Co.:** [22] near Cornell, 2 (Hubert Coll.); [23] no specific locality, 1 (ISM). **McLean Co.:** [24] Le Roy, 1 (NHS), 1 (US). **Iroquois Co.:** [25] 2 mi E Sheldon, 1 (UI). **Adams Co.:** [26] NW area of NE Twp., 1 (ISM); [27] near Mendon, 2 (ISM); [28] 2 mi S Camp Point, 2 (ISM). **Schuyler Co.:** [29] Frederick, 1 (NHS). **Brown Co.:** [30] Mt. Sterling, 2 (ISM). **Mason Co.:** [31a] W of San Jose, 1 (ISM); [31b] 1 mi W, 2 mi N Mason City, 1 (ISM); [32] 8 mi NW Greenview, 1 (ISM). **Champaign Co.:** [33] 9 mi NE Champaign, 1 (ISM). **Vermilion Co.:** [34] 1 mi E Kickapoo State Park, (¼ mi N Rt. 150), 1 (ISM); [35] 2 mi S, 3 mi E Allerton, 1 (ISM); no specific locality [not plotted] 1 (ISM) **Pike Co.:** [36a] 2 mi W Perry, 1 (ISM); [36b] near Perry, 8 (ISM). **Scott Co.:** [37] Winchester, 1 (ISM). **Greene Co.:** [38] 3 mi N Greenfield, 1 (UI); [39] 5 mi E Carrollton, 1 (ISM). **Macoupin Co.:** [40] near Waverly [may be Morgan Co.], 1 (ISM). **Sangamon Co.:** [41] Springfield, 1 (ISM); [42] 1½ mi E Rochester, 1 (ISM); [43] near Chatham, 1 (ISM). **Christian Co.:** [44] Palmer, 1 (ISM). **Montgomery Co.:** [45] Raymond, 1 (ISM). **Cumberland Co.:** [46] 10 mi NW Yale [labelled Jasper Co.], 1 (UI). **Edgar Co.:** [47a] 5 mi N, ¼ mi W Paris, 1 (ISM); [47b] 5 mi N Paris, 1 (ISM); [48a] Paris, R. R. #2, 1 (ISM); [48b] near Paris, T13N, R11W, Sec. 9, 1 (UI); [48c] Vermilion, 1 (ISM); no specific locality [not plotted], 14 (ISM). **Clark Co.:** [49] no specific locality, 5 (ISM). **Madison Co.:** [50] between Alton and Fosterburg, 1 (ISM). **Bond Co.:** [51] 6 mi S Greenville, 1 (ISM). **Fayette Co.:** [52] 1½ mi NW Loogootee, 1 (UI). **Effingham Co.:** [53] 10 mi S Altamont, 1 (ISM). **Jasper Co.:** [54] T5N, R9E, Sec. 11, 2 (ISM). **Clinton Co.:** [55] 6 mi N, 2 mi W Carlyle, 1 (UI); no specific locality [not plotted], 1 (UI). **Marion Co.:** [56] 1½ mi S, 1 mi W Omega, 1 (ISM); [57a] 3 mi W Salem, 1 (ISM); [57b] Salem, 1 (SRL). **Clay Co.:** [58] probably from county, from fur buyer, 17 (Hubert Coll.). **Richland Co.:** [59] 4 mi SW Olney, 1 (ISM); probably from county, from fur buyer, [not plotted], 4 (Hubert Coll.). **Randolph Co.:** [60] Kaskaskia Island, 6 (UI). **White Co.:** [61] near Enfield, 1 (ISM); [62] near Maunie, 1 (ISM). **Union Co.:** [63] 3 mi W Mill Creek, 1 (ISM). **Pope Co.:** [64a] Dixon Springs, 8 (UI), 3 (ISM); [64b] 2 mi SW Glendale, 1 (ISM).

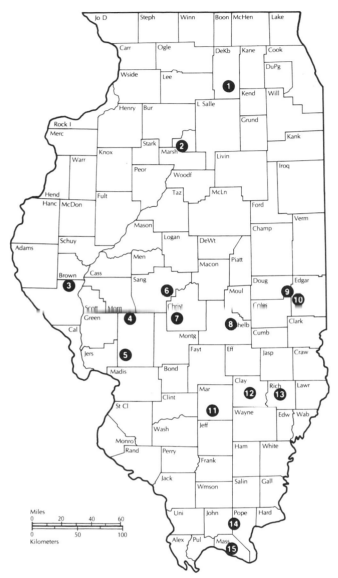

Map 8.52. Known hybrids of coyotes × dogs are indicated by numbered localities keyed to *Records of occurrence* under *Canis latrans × Canis familiaris.*

Canis latrans X Canis familiaris, Coydog

Range. See Map 8.52.

Remarks. Hybridization between coyotes and dogs is discussed in the account of *Canis latrans* (p. 270 and Tables 8.30–8.32).

As pointed out in that account, many *C. latrans* in Illinois may have some introgression with *C. familiaris.* Therefore, the differences between those animals regarded as *C. latrans* and those regarded as *C. familiaris* may be less apparent than is truly the case.

Skulls of hybrids average in measurements between *C. familaris* and *C. latrans,* but they are much nearer the latter (Table 8.32). The rostral proportions, however, are

intermediate. For example, the ratio of rostral length/ rostral breadth × 2 is below 0.990 in *C. latrans,* above 1.085 in *C. familaris.* Of the 14 hybrids, 7 fall between the two species, one falls with *C. familiaris,* 6 with *C. latrans.* In breadth across the complement of upper incisors, 8 hybrids fall within the range of *C. latrans,* 6 within *C. familiaris.*

Records of occurrence. SPECIMENS EXAMINED, 34.
De Kalb Co.: [1] near Hinckley, 1 (Hubert Coll.). **Putnam Co.:** [2] along Illinois River, S of Hennepin, 1 (UI). **Pike Co.:** [3a] near Perry, 1 (ISM); [3b] 2 mi W Perry, 1 (ISM). **Macoupin Co.:** [4] Modesto, 1 (ISM); [5] Shipman [labelled Jersey Co.], 1 (NHS). **Sangamon Co.:** [6] Rochester, 1 (ISM). **Christian Co.:** [7] between Palmer and Clarksdale, 1 (ISM). **Shelby Co.:** [8] 7 mi NW Strasburg, 1 (ISM). **Douglas Co.:** [9] 4½ mi S Newman, 1 (ISM); no specific locality [not plotted], 1 (ISM). **Edgar Co.:** [10] 1½ mi NW Redmon, 6 (ISM); no specific locality [not plotted], 1 (ISM). **Marion Co.:** [11] S of Salem [melanistic pelage], 1 (ISM). **Clay Co.:** [12] exact locality unknown, plotted in center of county, 3 (Hubert Coll.). **Richland Co.:** [13] probably collected in county by fur buyer, plotted in center of county, 5 (Hubert Coll.). **Pope Co.:** [14a] 1 mi W Robbs [may be Johnson Co.], 1 (ISM); [14b] E of Lake Glendale, 1 (ISM). **Massac Co.:** [15] near Metropolis, 1 (UI); no specific locality [not plotted], 2 (KU).

Vulpes, Red and Kit Foxes

Diagnosis. Doglike carnivores, with relatively long legs, ears prominent and pointed, muzzle elongate, tail bushy, rostrum of skull delicate; teeth widely spaced and not massive.

Dental formula. 3/3, 1/1, 4/4, 2/3.

Comparisons. Vulpes differ from gray foxes, *Urocyon,* in the absence of a median dorsal line of stiff black hairs on the tail; back of ears are black or grayish brown rather than red; temporal ridges of skull are not prominent but are V-shaped rather than heavy and forming a lyrate-shaped figure on dorsum of braincase; ramus of lower jaw without a notch below angular process rather than having a prominent notch—thus forming three, rather than two, notches at rear of ramus (Fig. 8.124, p. 276).

For a comparison with *Canis,* see that account (p. 263).

Remarks. One species of *Vulpes* is found in Illinois, *V. vulpes.* At an earlier time, red foxes in North America were referred to the species *Vulpes fulva.* Churcher (1959) pointed out that Old and New World red foxes were of the same species, *Vulpes vulpes* Linnaeus.

Vulpes vulpes, Red Fox

Range. Throughout the state.

Diagnosis. A species of *Vulpes;* mandible without a notch or step on the inferior margin; tail white at tip, ears black externally; skull large; ridges on top of skull, extending from postorbital processes, weak and coalescing far posteriorly; weight of adults usually between 8 and 14 pounds.

Color. Dorsum reddish, being purest red behind the ears and across the shoulders; remainder of back and forehead intermixed with white hairs; venter with narrow band of dark hairs intermixed with white and ochraceous hairs extending from chin to base of tail; tops of feet black; tail black near end and just anterior to terminal white tip.

Several color variations are known: Silver fox is a melanistic phase with white hairs intermixed with the black. Black fox is entirely melanistic. Cross fox has part of the fur black and part red, with the black along the midline of the back and over the shoulders forming more or less a cross when viewed from above.

Secondary sexual variation. Males average larger than females in external measurements, except for postorbital breadth. From our small sample size, however, it does not appear that the differences are significant.

Comparisons. Vulpes vulpes differs from the gray fox, *Urocyon cinereoargenteus,* as described under the genus *Vulpes* (p. 275). Critical features are the white tip of the tail, no dark stripe on top of tail, overall color more reddish, no prominent lyrate ridges on top of braincase, mandible without a prominent notch below angular process.

Chromosomes. Diploid number, 34. Autosomes metacentric or submetacentric; variable number of micro-chromosomes. X chromosome submetacentric; Y, submetacentric.

Remarks. Red foxes continue to do well in Illinois despite the precariousness of their existence, which was intensified by the payment of bounties for dead foxes. For many years, an act of the Illinois legislature authorized counties in their discretion to allow a bounty on fox scalps. Also, the northern two-thirds of the state had a year-round open season on foxes; in the southern third there was a short season when they could be taken. In 1948, the Illinois legislative council determined that 62 counties were currently paying, or had sometime during the year indicated they would pay, bounties on foxes. These bounties ranged from one to seven dollars with a mean of $3.50. Of these 62 counties, 44 reported that they paid bounties on 18,295 foxes during 1947. Most of the bounties were on red foxes, according to the counties reporting. Also see comments under *Urocyon cinereoargenteus* for additional bounties (p. 279).

The plight of this species is well stated by Seagers (1944).

> The red fox is the best-loved and most hated, praised and berated, wisest, smelliest, daintiest, thinnest, sleekest, most flea-bitten and most controversial creature to occupy the ardent attentions of hound, hunter and hennery owner in the nation.... There are many houndsmen who hunt him but won't shoot him. Small game hunters by the thousands believe there should be a bounty on his neck. Orchard owners, plagued by mice, want a bounty on those who want a bounty.

Despite the persecution of the red fox in Illinois, its numbers have been sustained remarkably well. In many areas, these foxes are more abundant now than previously and this is the result of more suitable habitat available rather than because they are hunted and trapped less.

The number of red foxes taken in Illinois for the two seasons of 1929–1931 was estimated at 16,000; for the two seasons 1938–1940 at 17,400. Forty years later, the number estimated to be taken for the two seasons of 1978–1980 was 27,700.

Habitat

Red foxes in Illinois inhabit the open grasslands, ditch banks, unmowed field-edges, and brushland adjacent to wooded areas. They are not inhabitants of forests or dense woods. The removal of forests and the creation of much more forest-edge has increased the amount of available habitat. In southern Illinois, red foxes frequently live in the open bottomlands while the more abundant gray foxes live in the hilly, wooded uplands (Layne, 1958b).

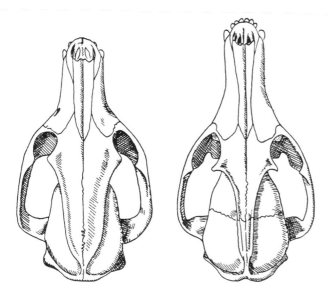

Fig. 8.124. Dorsal views of skull of red fox, *Vulpes vulpes,* left, and gray fox, *Urocyon cinereoargenteus.* (From Hoffmeister and Mohr, 1957. Charles A. McLaughlin)

Habits

Red foxes are oriented to raising a family and much of their activity centers around the den. Dens are underground burrows, either dug by foxes or by other mammals and taken over by red foxes. After the young are born, the adults do not range so far distant from the den site. Animals are more gregarious and more intraspecifically tolerant during the denning period with pups. If necessary a female may move the young, either to an unused den or even into a used den where there already is a litter of young.

When the pups have matured sufficiently, the family unit leaves the den and moves to another location that provides a food source as well as sufficient cover. The family tends to stay together until fall. At that time the unit begins to break up and the young disperse. They will then become vulnerable to the elements of approaching winter, conflicts with man, the search for den sites, and the establishment of a territory.

When not occupying dens, red foxes will bed down during the day in a weedy patch, uncut fencerow, brush pile, or similar place. These animals are active primarily at night.

Food

Although red foxes are termed carnivorous, they eat a considerable quantity of plant material as well as insects. Seasonal changes influence the kind of food consumed. In winter and spring, mammals were the main sources of food for foxes in central Iowa, according to T. G. Scott (1943); in summer and fall, plants and insects superseded mammals in the red fox diet.

In southern Illinois, the stomachs of 180 foxes collected over an 11-year period were studied by Knable (1970). Animal remains were found in 98.8 percent of the stomachs, plant remains in 97.1 percent. The volume of animal material in the stomachs was 81.2 percent; of plant material, 18.6 percent. Mammals most frequently present were cottontails, prairie voles, and white-footed mice. Birds made up about 10.3 percent of the volume, with domestic chicken represented by 8.9 percent. Although grass, leaves, stems, and bark were frequently present, the amount was not great. Persimmons and apples, the latter available from numerous orchards, were frequently eaten.

Similar studies on red foxes in the northern part of Illinois are not known to me. In Indiana, a study (Kase, 1946) that for the most part involved the northern area of the state and another study of Tippecanoe County (Mangus, 1950), as reported in Mumford and Whitaker, 1982) showed that the preferred food was cottontail, followed by microtines and *Peromyscus*. Among birds, domestic chicken was dominant in Kase's study but not in Mangus's.

Table 8.35. Foods eaten by red foxes in Union County, Illinois, as based on analysis of 170 stomachs collected between 1956 and 1967. Only those with a percentage by volume of 5% or more and frequency of occurrence of 10% or more are included. (Modified from Knable, 1970).

	Percentage of volume	Percentage of volume (5% or more)	Percentage of frequency (10% or more)
Mammals	67.1		
Eastern cottontail		25	32
Prairie vole		15	21
Peromyscus		6	15
Raccoon		6	10
Red fox			28
Birds	10.3		
Chicken		9	
Undetermined			15
Reptiles	0.3		
Invertebrates	2.9		
Short-horned grasshopper			12
Plants	18.6		
Persimmon		10	
Stems, bark, grasses			16
Miscellaneous	0.8		83
	100.0		

Reproduction

According to information in Illinois and adjacent states, red foxes probably breed in late January and in February. They are monoestrous, and the gestation period is about 51 days. Young are born in late March or in April. Dens in which young are reared usually are deeper than those used as temporary retreats. If the rearing den proves unsatisfactory for various reasons, the young may be moved to a new den. Sometimes two litters occupy the same den. This probably was the case in a den near Ursa, Adams County, where 14 young pups were found at one time.

In Indiana, 31 females had 6.8 (4–12) embryos or uterine enlargements.

Variation

East of the Mississippi River and except at its headwaters, red foxes are referred to *Vulpes vulpes fulva*. When more specimens become available from the northwestern corner of Illinois, they will need to be compared with *Vulpes vulpes regalis* (type locality Elk River, Sherburne Co., Minnesota).

Vulpes vulpes fulva (Desmarest)

1820. *Canis fulvus* (Desmarest, Mammalogie . . . Pt. 1, p. 203. Type locality, Virginia.
1960. *V[ulpes]. v[ulpes]. fulva,* Churcher, J. Mamm., 41:359.

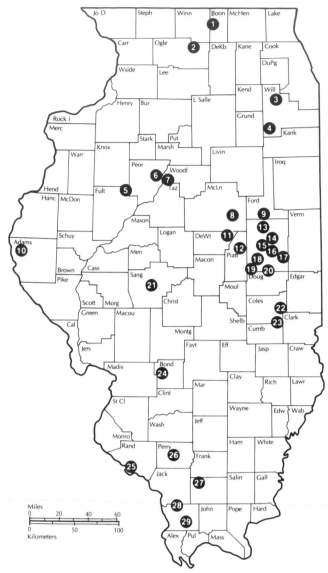

Map 8.53. Red foxes, *Vulpes vulpes*, occur statewide. The subspecies is *V. v. fulva*. Localities of occurrence as numbered are referenced in *Records of occurrence*. The range of the species in the United States is shaded.

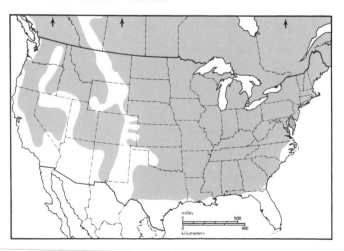

Range. Throughout the state.

Diagnosis and Comparison. A medium-sized, bright-colored subspecies.

Records of occurrence. SPECIMENS EXAMINED, 48.
Boone Co.: [1] [Jct.] Argyle & Harlem Roads, 1 (NIU). **Ogle Co.:** [2] 5 mi W Rt. 51 on Rt. 72, N ½ mi, 1 (NIU). **Will Co.:** [3] Joliet, 1 (FM); [4] Wilmington, 1 (FM). **Fulton Co.:** [5] 1 mi NE Farmington, 1 (UI). **Peoria Co.:** [6] Mossville, 1 (ISM). **Woodford Co.:** [7a] 6 mi W Metamora, 1 (ISU); [7b] 5 mi W Metamora, 1 (ISU). **McLean Co.:** [8] Arrowsmith, 1 (ISU). **Ford Co.:** [9] 6 mi W, 3 mi N Ludlow [labelled Champaign Co.], 1 (UI). **Adams Co.:** [10] ½ mi SW Ursa, 1 (UI). **De Witt Co.:** [11] 3 mi W Farmer city [labelled Piatt Co.], 1 (UI). **Piatt Co.:** [12] 1 mi N, 1 mi E Lodge, 1 (UI). **Champaign Co.:** [13a] 3½ mi N, 1½ mi E Tomlinson, 1 (UI); [13b] 3½ mi N, ½ mi W Dewey, 2 (UI); [13c] 3 mi N Tomlinson, 2 (UI); [13d] 2½ mi N, ½ mi E Dewey, 1 (UI); [14] 4 mi E, ¼ mi N Leverett, 2 (UI); [15] 2 mi N Champaign, 1 (UI); [16] 4 mi E Urbana, 1 (UI); [17] 3 mi W, ½ mi S Homer, 1 (UI); [18] 2 mi N, 3 mi W Tolono, 1 (UI); [19] 3 mi W, 4 mi S Sadorus, 1 (UI); [20] 1½ mi N Douglas Co. line on Embarrass River, 1 (UI); no specific locality [not plotted], 4 (UI). **Sangamon Co.:** [21] no specific locality, 1 (UI). **Coles Co.:** [22] Ashmore, 1 (KU); [23] 10 mi SE Charleston, 1 (UI). **Bond Co.:** [24] 6 mi W Greenville, 2 (UI). **Randolph Co.:** [25] Kaskaskia Island, 1 (UI). **Perry Co.:** [26] no specific locality, 1 (SIU). **Williamson Co.:** [27] N of Herrin, 1 (KU); no specific locality [not plotted], 1 (SRL). **Union Co.:** [28] Alto Pass, 8 (SRL).

Additional records. **Union Co.:** [29] between Anna and Dongola, 1 (UM).

Urocyon, Gray fox

Diagnosis. Doglike carnivores that are grayish and grizzled in color with median line of black hairs on dorsum of the tail, tip of tail black, back of ears reddish; top of skull with pronounced temporal ridges that are widely separated except where they join near back of skull, forming lyre-shaped ridges; ventral border of lower jaw with a "step" at the rear, resulting in three "notches" at the rear of the jaw (in contrast with *Vulpes*) (Fig. 8.115); rostrum relatively heavy and short.

Dental formula. 3/3, 1/1, 4/4, 2/3.

Comparison. For a comparison with *Vulpes*, see account of that genus (p. 275).

Remarks. One species, *Urocyon cinereoargenteus*, is widespread throughout the United States and ranges southward into South America. Another species, *U. littoralis*, is present on several Pacific islands off the coast of California.

Urocyon cinereoargenteus, Gray fox

Range. Throughout the state, but less abundant in the northern third and more abundant in the southern part and in wooded areas near the Mississippi and Illinois rivers.

Fig. 8.125. Gray fox, *Urocyon cinereoargenteus*. (From Hoffmeister and Mohr, 1957. Photograph by Charles and Elizabeth Schwartz)

Diagnosis and Comparison. A species of *Urocyon* which is characterized as given for the genus, lyre-shaped ridges on top of cranium prominent; rostrum broad at base, not pinched in; weight of adults usually between five-and-one-half and nine pounds.

Color. Dorsum with an overall grayish effect as a result of a mixture of hairs that are cream-colored and tipped with black, or with black tip missing; underfur light tan, and some hairs with long orangish tips; sides and underparts reddish except for a narrow and irregular whitish band extending from throat to tail; tops of feet reddish brown; tail same color on top as dorsum but with a medial dark stripe extending to tip, underside of tail reddish; nose, lips, and chin blackish.

Chromosomes. 2N = 66, FN = 66; autosomes of 31 pair of acrocentrics, one pair of medium-sized metacentrics; X a submetacentric, Y a metacentric (Fritzell and Haroldson, 1982).

Comparisons. For a comparison with *Vulpes vulpes*, see account of that species (p. 275).

Secondary sexual variation. In Arizona, Hoffmeister (1986) found a significant difference between the males and females in certain cranial measurements: greatest length, condylobasal length, greatest zygomatic width,

width of rostrum, least interorbital width, and palatal length. In all measurements, however, males averaged larger than females.

Remarks. Whereas red foxes may have benefited by man's activities in reducing the forest and creating more forest-edge in Illinois, the gray fox has suffered through the same activities. The removal of timber, both in riverbottoms and uplands, continues in Illinois.

Furthermore, at an earlier time when bounties were paid on foxes, no distinction was made between gray and red foxes and many grays were taken. In Pike County, there probably were as many foxes as any place in central Illinois in mid-1900's. However, between September 1, 1949, and January 21, 1950, bounties were paid on 608 foxes in Pike County. I would think that well over half of these were gray foxes.

For a variety of reasons, some of which were just mentioned, gray foxes may not be present in parts of Illinois where they were found at an earlier time.

In the 1800's a Gordon Hubbard reportedly captured foxes in the woods to release them on a sand bar in the [Chicago?] river for sport hunting (Goodspeed and Healy, 1909:91). One suspects that these may have been gray foxes if they were taken in the woods.

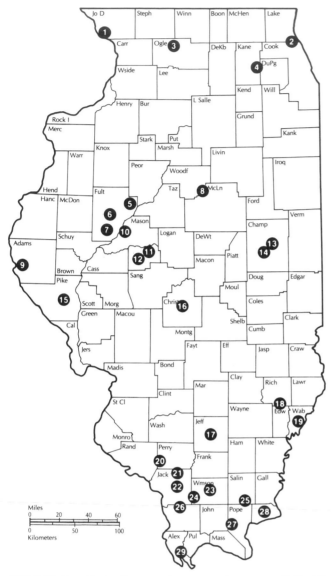

Map 8.54. Gray foxes, *Urocyon cinereoargenteus*, occur statewide. The subspecies is *U. c. cinereoargenteus*. Localities of occurrence as numbered are referenced in *Records of occurrence*. The range of the species in the United States is shaded.

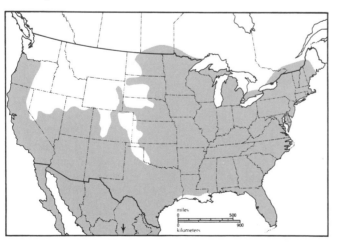

Habitat

Gray foxes are inhabitants of the deciduous forest or woods of Illinois. They stray from woods into brush or wooded pastures, but more often they remain in forested areas regardless of whether these are on rolling hills or river bottoms or levels in between. In southern Illinois, Layne (1958a) found gray foxes abundant in bottomlands and in hilly uplands. In the Pine Hills and adjacent swamplands, Klimstra (1969) found them more abundant in the uplands.

In central Illinois in an opening in the forested part of Allerton Park, Piatt County, a gray fox had a den on the flat terrain above the nearby Sangamon River. Gray foxes are also known to den in hollow trees or logs, in piles of brush, or in piles of rocks.

Habits

Gray foxes are good tree-climbers. Often they will climb a tree for refuge during the night and may still be in the tree at daylight. If the tree is devoid of leaves, the fox becomes most obvious and often attracts onlookers. Gray foxes in climbing grasp the trunk with their forelegs and push with their hind legs.

Layne (1958a) found that gray foxes could be easily decoyed by giving a call that supposedly sounded like an injured cottontail. His account (1958a:250) of the behavior of these foxes responding to such calls in southern Illinois follows:

A stand would be taken in an open spot affording a clear view for a hundred or so yards around the hunter but located in proximity to suitable cover. The hunters usually worked in pairs or groups of three or four, the individuals standing closely back to back and each covering a given sector. Head lamps were used and these were kept on with the beam directed upwards at about a 45° angle. All parts of the gun and body were kept behind the beam. Moonless nights were considered most favorable for this activity, since on bright nights it was claimed that an approaching fox could perceive the hunters behind the lights. The most satisfactory method of calling appeared to be a sequence of several calls given in rapid succession, alternating with a short pause. Foxes responding at a given stand would usually appear within five or ten minutes and often much sooner. The shine of the eyes in the side beams of the head lamps was usually visible while the animal was still at a considerable distance. When the fox had been lured within shot-gun range, the light was directed full upon it. Usually the animal remained motionless for a few moments, thus offering a comparatively easy target. Gray foxes were easily attracted to within 25 or 30 yards and not infrequently came much closer. Occasionally an individual would bark or growl as it approached the sound, and often two more more animals would appear simultaneously.

Red foxes, although also attracted to the call, appeared much more cautious than gray foxes. They usually remained well out of the gun range while investigating the situation and then quietly disappeared. An indication of the difference in response of the two species to this kind of hunting is obvious from the fact that in a sample 216 foxes taken by this method only one was a red fox. The effectiveness of the technique in hunting gray foxes is well illustrated by the fact that one group of hunters, concentrating their activities within a radius of a few miles of one town, was known to have killed 187 foxes in the interval from late December through June.

Food

Gray foxes are quite omnivorous and probably eat a diet as varied as that of domestic dogs. They commonly feed on cottontails and a variety of mice, a variety of birds, including domestic chickens, insects, various nuts, fruits, apples, persimmons, dry corn, roots, even breads if they are available.

The stomachs and digestive tracts of 169 gray foxes collected in southern Illinois in October, November, and December were studied by Pils and Klimstra (1975). In October, the percentage, by volume, of plants in the contents was high (88.5%); of mammals, only 11.5 percent. For the next two months, volume of consumed plants was still substantial (69.5% in November, 57.1% in December) (Fig. 8.126). The plants most commonly found were persimmon, wild grape, and corn; for mammals, *Sylvilagus* species, *Peromyscus* species, prairie vole, gray fox, and house mice were known to be included. "Clusters" of the instar stage of periodical cicadas were present in the digestive tract. It is not clear how the foxes obtained these at this time of year unless they dug them up. When available, persimmons may also be eaten in large quantities.

Reproduction

In southern Illinois, breeding occurs between the last week in January and the end of February (Layne, 1958b). In the northern part of the state it may extend into March. Examination of the testes of 130 gray foxes from southern Illinois (Follmann, 1978) showed that spermatozoa were present in abundance only from December through March. The gestation period is probably somewhere between 53 and 63 days (see Fritzell and Haroldson, 1982). Thus young are born from sometime in April to the end of May. Lactating females were encountered by Layne (1958b) in April, May, and June. He thought that weaning probably occurred toward the end of June.

The mean litter size in southern Illinois was 3.8 (2–6) based on embryos, placental scars, and uterine swellings. Throughout most of the range of the species, the mean litter size was also 3.8, based on 304 samples (Fritzell and Haroldson, 1982). Young are usually on their own by four months of age. At less than seven months of age, females have attained adult size, and they are usually sexually mature by ten months of age.

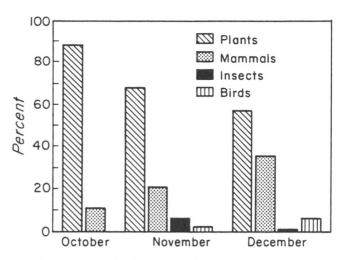

Fig. 8.126. Various foods consumed by gray foxes in southern Illinois in October, November, and December from 1954 to 1963. The results are given in percentage of volume. (Based on Pils and Klimstra, 1975: 256)

Variation

Specimens in Illinois have been referred to the nominotypical subspecies, *U. c. cinereoargenteus*. Jackson (1961) regards specimens from all of Wisconsin as referable to *U. c. ocythous* (type locality Platterville, Grant Co., Wisconsin). It may be that all specimens or those from the northern counties in Illinois are referable to this subspecies. Until we have a better understanding as to how these subspecies differ, all specimens are referred to *U. c. cinereoargenteus*.

Urocyon cinereoargenteus cinereoargenteus (Schreber)

1775. *Canis cinereo argenteus* Schreber, Die Saugthiere . . . , 2(13):pl. 92. Type locality, eastern North America.
1894. *Urocyon cinereo-argenteus*, Rhoads, Amer. Nat., 28:524.

Range. As given for the species (p. 278).
Diagnosis and Comparisons. A subspecies of medium to large size and dark color.
Records of occurrence. SPECIMENS EXAMINED, 38. **Jo Daviess Co.:** [1] Savanna Ordinance Depot, 1 (UI). **Kane Co.:** [4] near St. Charles, 1 (ISM). **Fulton Co.:** [5] 3 mi E Canton, 1 (UI); [6] 6 mi NW Lewistown, 1 (UI); [7a] 4 mi SE Ipava, 1 (UI); [7b] 5 mi SE Ipava, 4 (UI). **Woodford Co.:** [8] ¾ mi E Kappa, 1 (UI). **Adams Co.:** [9] 3 mi E Quincy, 1 (ISM). **Mason Co.:** [10] Havana, 1 (UI). **Menard Co.:** [11] Greenview, 1 (ISM); [12] near Petersburg, 1 (FM). **Champaign Co.:** [13] 4 mi NE Urbana, 1 (UI); [14a] Champaign, 1 (UI); [14b] 2 mi S Urbana, 1 (UI). **Pike Co.:** [15a] Pittsfield, 1 (UI); [15b] near Pittsfield, 1 (ISM). **Jefferson Co.:** [17] no specific locality, 1 (SRL). **Richland Co.:** [18] Parkersburg, 1 (US). **Perry Co.:** [20] Cutler (albino), 1 (SRL). **Jackson Co.:** [22] Murphysboro, 1 (SRL); no specific locality [not plotted],

1 (SRL). **Williamson Co.**: [23] Marion, 1 (SIC); [24] 6 mi SE Carbondale, 1 (SIC). **Saline Co.**: [25] 1 mi S Rudement, 1 (UI). **Union Co.**: [26a] Alto Pass, 2 (ISM), 5 (SRL); [26b] 2 mi NW Cobden, 1 (SRL); no specific locality [not plotted], 2 (SRL). **Pope Co.**: [27] 2 mi S Dixon Springs Exp. Station, 1 (UI).

Additional records. **Lake Co.**: [2] Deerfield, (Gregory, 1936:45).

Ogle Co.: [3] Leaf River, 1 (UM). **Christian Co.**: [16] no specific locality, (Cory, 1912:301). **Wabash Co.**: [19] Mt. Carmel, (Necker and Hatfield, 1941:48). **Jackson Co.**: [21] Vergennes, 1 (FS); [22] Murphysboro, 2 (FS). **Union Co.**: [26a] Alto Pass, 1 (FS); [26c] Cobden, 1 (FS). **Hardin Co.**: [28] no specific locality, (Cory, 1912:301). **Alexander Co.**: [29] 2 mi NW Cache, 1 (FS).

Family Procyonidae, Raccoons and relatives

Medium size, with a long tail that is banded with alternating dark and light rings, although indistinct in *Nasua* and *Potos;* carnassials weakly developed; five elongate toes on each foot; semiplantigrade to plantigrade; mostly omnivorous. There are five genera in the family: *Procyon, Bassariscus, Nasua, Potos, Bassaricyon.*

Procyon, Raccoons

Diagnosis. A relatively long-legged, ring-tailed, medium-sized carnivore with a black facial mask, head broad, soles of feet naked, digits free and elongate, ears only slightly conspicuous above the fur. Skull with well-developed postorbital processes on frontals and zygoma, bony palate extends well posterior to plane to last molar, teeth relatively heavy and not sharply cusped. Mammae include two pairs pectoral, two abdominal, two inguinal.

Dental formula. 3/3, 1/1, 4/4, 2/2.

Chromosomes. See *P. lotor.*

Comparisons. Procyon is the only member of the family in Illinois. It differs from all other Illinois carnivores in being ring-tailed, having a black facial mask and crushing rather than shearing carnassial teeth (Pm^4, M_1), and being plantigrade (flat-footed).

Remarks. Procyon is exclusively a New World genus and consists of two groups of raccoons: crab-eating

Table 8.36. Measurements of various carnivores in Illinois. Mean, minimum-maximum, and one standard deviation are given. The sexes are treated separately. Superscript figures indicate sample less than N.

	Sex	N	Total length	Tail length	Hind foot length	Ear length	Condylo-basal length	Zygomatic breadth
Vulpes vulpes Various localities in Illinois	♂	8	1034.5 954-1114 52.17	389.1 342-426 27.79	162.6 156-175 6.55	94.0 80-102 7.27	138.82[6] 132.65-146.8 5.72	75.99[6] 70.2-78.95 3.15
	♀	7	961.6[5] 925-1002 33.13	343.8[5] 306-365 22.60	151.8[5] 149-154 2.17	88.4[5] 84-95 4.34	134.54[5] 128.8-139.1 3.91	72.19 69.3-75.2 2.03
Urocyon cinereoargenteus Various localities in Illinois	♂	5	1050.2 981-1130 71.52	367.2 345-381 13.75	132.0 120-146 11.64	67.0 60-82 8.83	120.22 114.3-126.0 4.40	69.43 66.3-70.7 1.86
	♀	7	962.5[4] 920-1030 47.87	330.3[4] 310-356 20.01	127.0[4] 110-140 13.39	69.0[3] 67-70 1.73	120.58 115.9-126.8 3.69	67.43 63.1-72.6 3.86
Procyon lotor hirtus Central and No. Illinois 21 months or more of age	♂	11	845.3[3] 775-911 66.12	266.3[3] 240-280 22.81	106.3[3] 89-120 15.82	60** 61**	113.19 103.2-119.0 4.56	77.13 73.75-81.55 2.68
21 months or more of age	♀	5	740** 800**	200** 240**	110** 110**	60** 60**	112.22 105.2-118.5 4.73	74.22 69.7-79.5 3.84
11 months or less of age	♂	7	736.4	218.7	106.0	55.1		
11 months or less of age	♀	5	719.4	246.4	101.4	52.2		

* To anterior edge of alveolus of anteriormost incisor. ** Individual measurements for each of two specimens.

raccoons, *P. cancrivorus,* and a group of closely related forms including *P. lotor.* Crab-eating raccoons occur no closer than Costa Rica.

Procyon lotor, Raccoon

Range. Throughout the state.

Diagnosis. A species of *Procyon* with characters as given for the genus; pelage long, hair of neck directed posteriorly, bony palate extending posterior to plane of last molars a distance of more than one-fourth the length of the palate; baculum elongate, bilobed anteriorly and strongly bowed and recurved at distal end.

Color. In addition to five to seven brownish black rings alternating with light areas on the tail and a blackish facial mask extending through the area of the eyes, the dorsum is greyish black and grizzled; a band as much as 50 mm wide down the back is more blackish; venter with most hairs tan- or ochraceous-tipped, top of feet essentially same color as underparts, ears tipped with conspicuous white hairs.

Chromosomes. 2N = 38, FN = 66; 6 acrocentrics and 30 metacentrics, submetacentrics, or subtelocentrics; X, submetacentric; Y, submetacentric or subtelocentric.

Inter-orbital breadth	Post-orbital breadth	Palatal* length	Maxillary toothrow length
27.08[6]	23.26[6]	70.86	62.85
25.5-28.25	21.0-25.65	67.3-76.8	60.3-66.35
0.96	1.90	3.47	2.51
25.74	23.55	69.41	61.54
23.8-26.5	21.0-25.5	65.2-72.9	58.8-63.7
0.96	1.35	3.09	1.78
25.71	28.38	58.76	50.27
25.0-26.5	26.8-30.8	55.1-62.1	47.6-52.7
0.80	1.76	2.64	2.12
24.16	26.64	58.46	51.30
22.55-26.5	24.6-29.3	56.1-61.3	49.75-53.45
1.49	1.45	1.67	1.14
24.21	22.13	68.90	43.03
20.6-27.5	20.0-25.7	63.2-73.1	41.1-45.5
2.01	1.75	3.12	1.48
25.33	24.40	69.26	42.85
22.5-29.0	22.2-27.3	64.9-72.5	41.4-44.3
2.42	1.93	2.83	1.30

Comparisons. For a comparison with other Illinois carnivores, see above account of the family and the species.

Aging. Skulls can be placed in age categories for two-month periods—starting at two months, up to two years and with some degree of accuracy, up to four years—on the basis of the obliteration of certain cranial sutures which can be used in combination as explained by Junge and Hoffmeister (1980). Eighteen sutures are used. The first to become obliterated (at two months of age) are the exoccipital-basioccipital and exoccipital-supraoccipital sutures. At one year, the maxillary-premaxillary and interparietal sutures first become obliterated. At two years, the squamosal-mastoid suture is becoming obliterated. Various other combinations of obliteration can be used at other intervals. Toothwear, as described by Grau et al. (1970), can be used to place skulls in five age categories, but the youngest categories extend to 14 months of age. Montgomery (1964) found that the deciduous I^{1-3} erupt at one month, deciduous Pm^{2-4} erupt at 1½ months, deciduous Pm^1 and permanent I^1 erupt at two months, and permanent canines at 3½ months.

By the time they are nine months old, as determined by suture obliteration, raccoons have attained nearly full growth externally and cranially, although probably not in weight; but they can be considered as adults for purposes of comparison.

Features other than those of the skull have been used in calculating ages of raccoons. These include closure of the epiphyses of the radius and ulna of the hand and the ossification of the baculum.

Molt. Adults have one annual molt and this may occur from spring well into summer.

Secondary sexual variation. Differences in the limited cranial measurements that we have taken do not appear to be significant between the sexes.

Remarks. Raccoons are widespread and abundant in much of Illinois. They seemingly have not suffered as much as many other forest-associated mammals with the removal of much wooded lands in the state.

Habitat

Raccoons will live in a variety of habitats if certain requirements are met—principally, a permanent source or supply of water, places to den, and available food. Raccoons apparently never den more than 1,200 feet from a water source and usually make little use of uplands that are more than one mile from a floodplain. Dens are often situated in hollow trees and require that the cavity in the tree be large and dry. Raccoons may be unique among Illinois carnivores in not building or digging nest sites or altering a site; neither do they add any nest material to the den. Raccoons may choose the hay pile

Fig. 8.127. Raccoon, *Procyon lotor*. Photograph by K. Maslowski and W. W. Goodpaster.

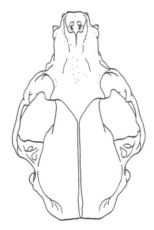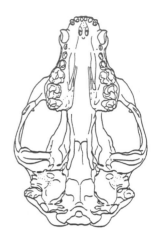

Fig. 8.128. *Procyon lotor,* dorsal and ventral views of skull; 3 mi W Canton, Fulton Co., Illinois, 914 UI. Male, 118.4 mm greatest length. Age of animal estimated to be between 30 and 45 months.

Table 8.37. Foods consumed by raccoons before and after the hunting season at Horseshoe Lake Game Refuge, Illinois (modified from Yeager and Elder, 1945). Note the great increase in birds which were chiefly Canada geese.

	Percentage of bulk	
	Pre-hunt (116 scats)	Post-hunt (107 scats)
Insects	30.3	5.9
Crayfish, snails, mussels	0.2	tr
Fishes	tr	0.6
Birds (chiefly *Branta*)	3.2	65.1
Mammals	0.1	0.5
Corn	21.0	8.2
Greenbrier	—	2.6
Pecan	7.2	0.5
Grape	19.2	0.1
Acorns	8.4	1.3
Hazelnut	tr	7.6
Miscellaneous plants	7.7	2.5
Detritus (inert)	2.1	4.3

in a barn loft, a dry brush pile, or den under a fallen log, or in a rocky crevice. Attics and chimneys of abandoned farm houses, as well as of occupied homes in both country and town, are favorite sites. Artificial dens, similar to wood duck houses, but larger and with the opening on the side but nearer the top, will often be used.

Food must also be available, but since these animals are so omnivorous, this is probably the least important requirement of the habitat.

Raccoons have adjusted and adapted to urban conditions in Illinois, feeding on garbage scraps and dog and cat foods, and finding suitable denning sites. They have for several years lived successfully within the city limits of Champaign and Urbana, and probably most other towns of the state, especially where there are leash laws to prevent dogs from roaming widely.

Habits

Raccoons are excellent climbers and swimmers. They descend a tree either head-first or tail-first. They walk with a flat-footed gait and because they make such frequent use of water-edges and mudholes, their tracks — consisting of the complete foot print — are often visible.

Raccoons are often said to wash their food before eating it. More likely, this is a carry-over of the habit of reaching in the water and feeling for food items. The front feet are effectively used in obtaining, holding, and manipulating food.

Food

Raccoons are omnivorous but they do eat large numbers of aquatic animals, such as crayfish, fish, and turtles, in addition to cottontails, voles, and white-footed mice, and a wide variety of plant materials, such as nuts, berries, grains, especially corn, and other seeds. Being opportunistic feeders, raccoons rely primarily on food items that are readily available. Nearly mature sweet corn is a favored item, and many fields have been devastated at picking time because of their feeding activities.

In southern Illinois near Horseshoe Lake, 116 scats of raccoons were collected on October 16, 1942, the second day of waterfowl hunting, but before many crippled or dead birds were lost by hunters. On January 14, 1943, 107 scats were collected, three weeks after the close of hunting season and when there were ample dead and crippled geese. Results of the analyses of these scats are shown in Table 8.37. Raccoons fed extensively on waterfowl left crippled by hunters, or on the unrecovered kills.

In western Illinois at Pere Marquette Wildlife Area, just north of the confluence of the Illinois River with the Mississippi River, Calhoun County, the fall foods of raccoons were analyzed on the basis of 419 scats (Yeager and Rennels, 1943). Vegetable material made up 72.4 percent of the bulk, animal food 27.6 percent. Persimmons, pecans, wild grapes, pokeweed berries, fox squirrels, ducks, and numerous insects made up the bulk of the items. Tables 8.37 and 8.38 give the details of the items eaten.

Reproduction

Mating in Illinois may occur between December and May. Young are born between early March and June, with a mean of April 18 (Sanderson and Nalbandov, 1973). The gestation period is approximately 63 days. The mean litter size over three years from three regions in Illinois consisting of 439 females is given in Table 8.39. The mean of the entire 439 is 3.36, but regionally there is considerable variation, with those in the south having significantly smaller litters.

Young are weaned at any time between two and four months of age. Females born in April or thereabouts may breed in their first winter-spring when other females wait until the following year when they are almost two years old (Sanderson and Nalbandov, 1973).

Populations

Numbers of raccoon vary over periods of time. However, since the 1930's, numbers of raccoon in Illinois have increased, but with some ups and downs. In the mid-1930's, the annual take of raccoons by hunters was about 10,000; in the early 1950's, 80,000; in the late 1970's, over 300,000 (Table 8.40). This in part indicates the increase in numbers although demand for pelts may figure in the totals. How abundant raccoons may become when they are not hunted is indicated by the fact that in 1948, over a five-day period 100 were collected in 100 acres at Swan Lake National Wildlife Refuge, Chariton Co., Missouri (Twichell and Dill, 1949).

Table 8.38. Fall (October-November) foods of raccoons as based upon 419 scats at Pere Marquette Wildlife Area, Illinois (modified from Yeager and Rennels, 1943).

Food	Total bulk 1939-40	Oct. 1939	Nov. 1939	Oct. 1940	Nov. 1940
Mammals	0.70				
Fox squirrel		100	65	53	tr
Muskrat		—	—	—	62
Eastern cottontail		—	—	tr	34
Mice, shrews		tr	tr	47	tr
Miscellaneous		—	35	—	4
		100	100	100	100
Birds	5.6				
Various ducks		—	89	—	76
Cormorant		—	7	—	—
Chicken		—	—	85	—
Miscellaneous		100	4	15	24
			100	100	100
Fishes (various)	1.2				
Snails (*Physa, Stagnicola, Helisoma*)	3.4				
Insects	8.0				
Hornets		46	34	—	—
Water bugs, beetles		44	53	78	76
Miscellaneous		10	13	22	24
		100	100	100	100
Crayfishes	8.6				
Plant Materials	72.1				
Persimmon		29	27	43	50
Pecan		23	37	6	31
Wild grapes		30	29	23	14.5
Pokeweed		15	7	12	3
Miscellaneous		4	0.7	16	1.5

Table 8.39. Litter size for raccoons from various parts of Illinois as based on specimens at three furhouses. The mean and standard error is followed by the sample size. (Based on Sanderson and Hubert, 1981:495)

Section of state	Litter size
North central Illinois	
Maier and Tompkins Furhouse	
1977-78	3.73 ± 0.24 (37)
1978-79	3.32 ± 0.16 (34)
1979-80	3.75 ± 0.16 (51)
Total mean	3.62 ± 0.11 (122)
West central Illinois	
Perardi Bros. Furhouse	
1977-78	3.51 ± 0.16 (49)
1978-79	3.57 ± 0.16 (60)
1979-80	3.47 ± 0.12 (73)
Total mean	3.51 ± 0.08 (182)
Southeastern Illinois	
Hasler Furhouse	
1977-78	2.85 + 0.14 (41)
1978-79	2.96 ± 0.14 (52)
1979-80	2.93 ± 0.17 (42)
Total mean	2.92 + 0.09 (135)

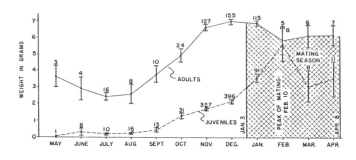

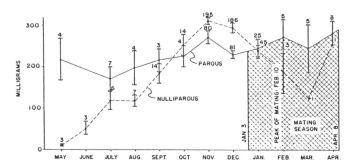

Fig. 8.129. Seasonal variations in the weight of one testes in adult and juvenile Illinois raccoons (upper) and of both ovaries of parous and nulliparous female raccoons (lower). With each mean the sample size is indicated and one standard error above and below the mean. (From Sanderson and Nalbandov, 1973:36,44)

Variation

In his revision of *Procyon lotor*, Goldman (1950) regarded two subspecies as present in Illinois: *P. l. lotor* and *P. l. hirtus*. He referred two specimens from Belleville, St. Clair County, to *P. l. lotor* and we regard specimens from the southern third of Illinois as referable to this subspecies.

Procyon lotor lotor (Linnaeus)

1758. [*Ursus*] *lotor* Linnaeus, Syst. nat., ed. 10, 1:48. Type locality, Pennsylvania.
1815. *Procyon lotor*, Illiger, Abh. preuss. Ahad. Wiss., Berlin, 1804–1811, pp. 70, 74.

Range. Southern Illinois, approximately south of a line extending from Madison County to Clark County (Map 8.55).

Diagnosis and Comparisons. A small subspecies when compared with *P. l. hirtus;* skull smaller, pelage not so long.

Remarks. Size differences between *P. l. lotor* and *P. l. hirtus* are indicated by the average body weights of juvenile raccoons (Sanderson and Hubert, 1981). From the vicinity of Richland County, 316 male *P. l. lotor* have a mean of 4,060 g; of 343 males of *P. l. hirtus* from north central Illinois 5,400 g; for 516 males from west central Illinois, 4,660 g. Comparable statistics for the

three groups of females are 3,920 g for 296 from Richland County; 5,180 g for 300 from north central Illinois; 4,520 g for 519 from west central Illinois.

Records of occurrence. SPECIMENS EXAMINED, 18.
Monroe Co.: [1] 2 mi N Valmeyer, 1 (UI). **St. Clair Co.:** [2] 4 mi N Mascoutah, 1 (UI). **Washington Co.:** [4] no specific locality, 1 (SRL). **Randolph Co.:** [5] Kaskaskia Island, 2 (UI). **Perry Co.:** [6] Pyatts, 1 (SIC). **Williamson Co.:** [7] Cambria, 1 (SRL). **Saline Co.:** [8] no specific locality, 1 (UI). **Gallatin Co.:** [9] 3 mi SW Ridgeway, 1 (SIC). **Union Co.:** [10a] 10 mi S Carbondale [labelled Jackson Co.], 1 (UI); [10b] 3 mi N Cobden, 1 (SIC), 1 (SRL). **Pope Co.:** [12] ½ mi E Dixon Springs, 1 (UI). **Hardin Co.:** [13] Rosiclare, 1 (FM). **Alexander Co.:** [14a] Olive Branch, 3 (FM); [14b] Horseshoe Lake, 1 (UI).

Additional records. **St. Clair Co.:** [3] Belleville, 2 (US). **Union Co.:** [10c] 4 mi NW Cobden, 1 (FS); [11] 4 mi S Jonesboro, 1 (FS).

Procyon lotor hirtus Nelson and Goldman

1930. *Procyon lotor hirtus* Nelson and Goldman, J. Mamm., 11:455. Type from Elk River, Sherburne Co., Minnesota.

Range. North of a line extending from Madison County to Clark County (Map 8.55).

Diagnosis and Comparisons. A subspecies of *P. lotor* of large size, dark color, long fur, and large skull.

Records of occurrence. SPECIMENS EXAMINED, 46.
Jo Daviess Co.: [1] near Apple River Canyon State Park, 1 (UI); [2] 3 mi N Savanna Ordinance Army Depot, 1 (UI). **Stephenson Co.:** [3] ¼ mi S Cedarville, 1 (NIU). **De Kalb Co.:** [4a] 1 mi N De Kalb, 1 (NIU); [4b] De Kalb, 1 (NIU). **Kane Co.:** [5] near St. Charles, 3 (ISM). **Cook Co.:** [6] Evanston, 1 (CAS); [7] Jackson Park, Chicago, 1 (FM). **Bureau Co.:** [8] 1½ mi W, 1 mi S Ohio, 1 (UI). **Will Co.:** [9] Joliet, 1 (FM); [10] Park Forest, 1 (UI); [11] 2 mi E Peotone, 1 (UI). **Henderson Co.:** [12] no specific locality, 1 (US). **Fulton Co.:** [13] Farmington, 1 (UI); [14a] 3 mi W Canton, 1 (UI); [14b] 1½ mi SW Canton, 1 (UI); [15] 3 mi S Little America, 1 (UI). **Peoria Co.:** [16] 1 mi W Peoria, 1 (UI). **Marshall Co.:** [17] Henry, 1 (UI). **Woodford Co.:** [18] Panola, 1 (ISU). **Tazewell Co.:** [19] 2 mi SW Peoria [may be Peoria Co.], 1 (ISU). **McLean Co.:** [20a] 3 mi S Kappa [labelled Woodford Co.], 1 (UI); [20b] Evergreen Lake, 1 (ISU); [20c] Hudson Rd. & Rt 51, 1 (ISU); [22] 2 mi SW Lexington, 1 (ISU). **Mason Co.:** [22] Havana, 1 (UI). **Logan Co.:** [24] 5 mi SE Lincoln, 1 (UI). **De Witt Co.:** [25] 1¼ mi SE Lane, 1 (UI). **Champaign Co.:** [26] 2 mi S, 1 mi W Mahomet, 1 (UI); [27a] 2 mi S Leverett, 1 (UI); [27b] ½ mi E, 3 mi N Mayview, 1 (UI); [28a] 8 mi E Urbana, 1 (UI); [28b] ½ mi N Meyer's [=Mira] Station, 1 (UI); [28c] Urbana Twp. Wildlife Area, 1 (UI); [28d] 5 mi SE Urbana, 1 (UI); [29a] ½ mi N Savoy, 1 (UI); [29b] 2 mi S Savoy, 1 (UI); [29c] 2½ mi W Philo, 1 (UI). **Macoupin Co.:** [30] 5 mi S Carlinville, 1 (UI). **Sangamon Co.:** [31] 10 mi W Springfield, 1 (ISM); [32] Springfield, 1 (ISM); no specific locality [not plotted], 1 (UI). **Macon Co.:** [33] Decatur.

Additional records. **Ford Co.:** [22] 6 mi N Piper City, (Koestner, 1942:228).

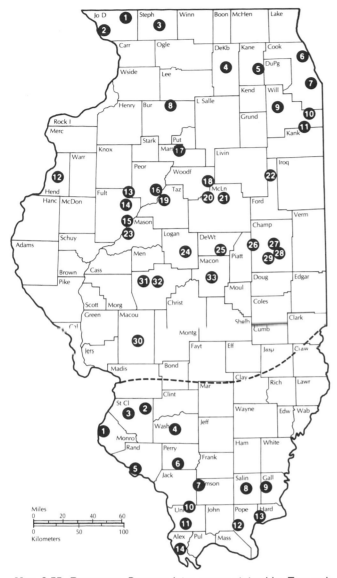

Map 8.55. Raccoons, *Procyon lotor,* occur statewide. Two sub-species are found in Illinois: *P. l. hirtus* north of the broken line; *P. l. lotor,* south. Localities of occurrence as numbered are referenced in *Records of occurrence.* The range of the species in the United States is shaded.

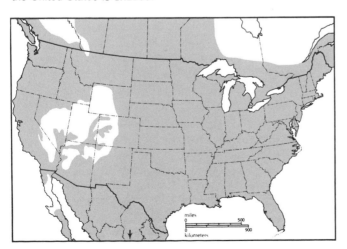

Table 8.40. Harvest of raccoons in Illinois between 1940 and 1980 and estimated by various authorities as given. Data for numbers harvested are missing for some years. (From Sanderson and Hubert, 1981:509-510).

Season	Estimated harvest	Authority	Average pelt price per pelt
1940-41	No data	—	$ 2.15
1941-42	20,245	Anonymous (1946)	$ 3.00
1942-43	27,130	Anonymous (1946)	$ 3.10
1943-44	No data	—	$ 4.40
1944-45	No data	—	$ 2.16
1945-46	No data	—	$ 2.50
1946-47	No data	—	$ 1.50
1947-48	96,936	Ashbrook (1948)	$ 1.00
1948-49	87,046	Ashbrook (1954)	$ 1.00
1949-50	81,818	Ashbrook (1954)	$ 0.90
1950-51	71,040	Ashbrook (1954)	$ 1.80
1951-52	80,807	Ashbrook (1954)	$ 1.70
1952-53	No data	—	$ 1.00
1953-54	No data	—	$ 1.00
1954-55	No data	—	$ 1.00
1955-56	No data	—	$ 1.40
1956-57	No data	—	$ 1.05
1957-58	No data	—	$ 0.91
1958-59	No data	—	$ 0.77
1959-60	No data	—	$ 1.38
1960-61	No data	—	$ 1.41
1961-62	53,763	Anonymous (1963)	$ 1.76
1962-63	88,522	Anonymous (1964)	$ 1.77
1963-64	61,758	Anonymous (1965)	$ 1.28
1964-65	83,066	Anonymous (1966)	$ 1.43
1965-66	109,571	Preno (Unpubl. data)	$ 2.53
1966-67	48,963	Preno (Unpubl. data)	$ 1.60
1967-68	49,135	Preno (Unpubl. data)	$ 1.59
1968-69	49,429	Anonymous (1970)	$ 3.11
1969-70	62,949	Anonymous (1971)	$ 2.44
1970-71	52,866	Preno (Unpubl. data)	$ 1.35
1971-72	68,174	Preno (Unpubl. data)	$ 2.95
1972-73	85,536	Preno (Unpubl. data)	$ 5.37
1973-74	181,776	Ellis (Unpubl. data)	$ 7.36
1974-75	No data	—	No data
1975-76	310,593	Hubert (1977)	$14.00
1976-77	187,377	Hubert (1977)	$17.17
1977-78	237,315	Hubert (1979)	$18.00
1978-79	292,728	Hubert (1979)	$27.25
1979-80	381,006	Hubert (1980c)	$25.50

Family Mustelidae, Weasels, Skunks, and relatives

Carnivores of small to medium size with well-developed anal scent glands, M 1/2, rostrum short, legs short; many have delayed implantation of blastocyst, resulting in a long gestation period. In Illinois, there are four genera: *Mustela, Taxidea, Mephitis, Lutra.*

Mustela, Weasels, minks, ferrets

Diagnosis. Long, thin-bodied mustelids, with short legs; short, rounded ears, auditory bullae greatly inflated and cancellous; paraoccipital processes appressed to bullae, palate extending behind upper molars, postorbital processes relatively well developed; talonid of first lower molar trenchant.

Dentition. 3/3, 1/1, 3/3, 1/2.

Comparisons. Mustela differs from *Mephitis* in having a brownish, brownish black, or white pelage, and no white stripes on back; shorter legs; palate extends much further posteriorly and well behind plane of last upper molar; auditory bullae more greatly inflated, postorbital processes more obvious; talonid of M_1 trenchant rather than basined.

Mustela differs from *Taxidea* in its much smaller size and shorter claws; auditory bullae less well inflated; upper carnassial tooth (Pm^4) more trenchant and less triangular.

Mustela differs from *Lutra* in being much smaller in size, with shorter tail, toes not so extensively webbed, braincase relatively less broadened, three upper premolars rather than four, auditory bullae more inflated.

Secondary sexual variation. In *Mustela frenata,* males are approximately twice as heavy as females, and the skull of the female weighs some 45 percent less than that of the male (E. R. Hall, 1951). The differences are not so pronounced in *M. nivalis.* The sexes are compared separately.

Mustela nivalis, Least weasel

Range. Probably north of an east-west line running through Edgar-Adams counties (Map 8.56).

Diagnosis. A small species of *Mustela,* with total length of males less than 250 mm, females, 225 mm; tail short (less than 20 mm longer than hind foot and less than 25% of the head-body length), tail without a noticeable black tip although there may be a few black hairs; skull with a relatively long braincase and short precranial portion, sagittal crest only minimally developed.

Color. Summer pelage with dorsum, sides, tail, and top of head reddish brown; brown extending on legs to base of toes; tops of toes white; venter, chest, throat, and cheeks white.

Those least weasels that turn white in winter become entirely white except for about 10 black hairs at the tip of the tail. In specimens of the other species, *M. frenata*

Fig. 8.130. Least weasel, *Mustela nivalis.* Note the short tail and overall small size. Photograph by K. Maslowski and W. W. Goodpaster.

and *M. erminea,* that turn white in winter, the tip of the tail—not just a few hairs—remains black.

Fall color for those animals turning white consists of brown hairs that are retained longest on top of the head and down the middle of the back. Tops of the legs seem to turn white first.

Spring color (based on March 8 specimen) has brown hairs on back beginning to extend down toward lateral line. Fur on the back has a salt-and-pepper appearance, with a mixture of brown in the white.

Specimens have been examined in each month of the year for color (winter vs. summer). These are recorded thus: March, 5, 3 W (1–80, 1–50, 1–40), 2 B. This should be interpreted as five having been examined in March, three being white and two, brown; of those that were white, one was 80 percent white, one 50 percent, and one 40 percent. January, 1, 1 W; February 3, 1 W, 2 B; March, 5, 3 W (1–80, 1–50, 1–40), 2 B; April through November, 22, 21 B, 1 W (1–20); December, 3, 1 W, 2 B. Six out of 12 specimens in December through March were white or had some white on the back.

Chromosomes. Diploid number 42; FN = 66.

Comparisons. Mustela nivalis differs from *Mustela frenata* by having a tail that is less than 20 percent of the head-body length and less than 20 mm longer than the hind foot; tail without a concpicuous black tip; basilar length of skull less than 32.5 mm in males and 31.0 mm in females; sagittal crest only weakly developed.

M. nivalis differs from *Mustela erminea,* ermine—a species occurring in southern Wisconsin but not reported to date in Illinois—in the same way that it is described, in the preceding paragraph to differ from *M. frenata.*

M. nivalis is much smaller than *M. vison,* mink, and differs from other mustelids as described in the comparisons given for the genus *Mustela.*

Molt. Information on seasonal changes from summer to winter pelage is discussed under *Color.*

There is the possibility that many specimens never acquire a completely white winter coat in Illinois, but instead retain some brown on top of the head and down the midline of the back. We know, however, that in winter some specimens are all-white, and some remain brown.

Remarks. Hoffmeister (1956) reviewed the records of *M. nivalis* up to 1955. There were five records for the state, but numerous reports followed in the next twenty years. Now some 49 different localities of captures or reports are listed.

A record of *Mustela nivalis* from a prehistoric Indian site at Meyer Cave, about 4 mi SSW Columbia, Monroe County, was reported by Parmalee and Munyer (1966). This locality is not plotted on the Distribution Map. This may represent a resident animal or a specimen carried in by the Indians.

Least weasels have been referred to under the name *Mustela rixosa,* but in the 1960's it was determined that least weasels were of a circumpolar species for which the name *Mustela nivalis* was proper.

Habitat

Least weasels are captured so infrequently in Illinois and in such unlikely places that it is difficult to know their preferred habitat. I suspect that they prefer short-grass fields or fields with taller grass, provided the grass is not too thick. Also, the edges of cultivated fields with corn and soybeans may provide both food and cover.

One specimen was taken in a window well on the western outskirts of Champaign. Fields were present to the west. The window well may have provided a trap for mice, injured birds, or insects, and attracted the least weasel.

The specimen from 2 mi N Normal was taken along a railroad right-of-way, with bluegrass and weeds. Another taken nearby was in a grassy waterway (Schmidt and Lewin, 1968). Near Mayview, Champaign County, a least weasel was taken along a weedy railroad right-of-way. Across the highway was a cemetary. Both habitats probably provided ideal sources of food.

In Indiana, Mumford and Whitaker (1982) reported a least weasel entering a mole tunnel, another caught in a trap set in a vole runway, one living under a slab of concrete, and one that fell into a newly excavated grave.

Habits

Least weasels kill mice and voles by biting into the back of the skull. Like many species of weasels, they may sometimes kill more mice that they can consume at

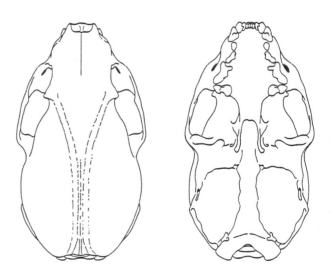

Fig. 8.131. *Mustela nivalis,* dorsal and ventral views of skull; 1 mi S Urbana, Champaign Co., Illinois, 32838 UI. Male, 32.6 mm greatest length.

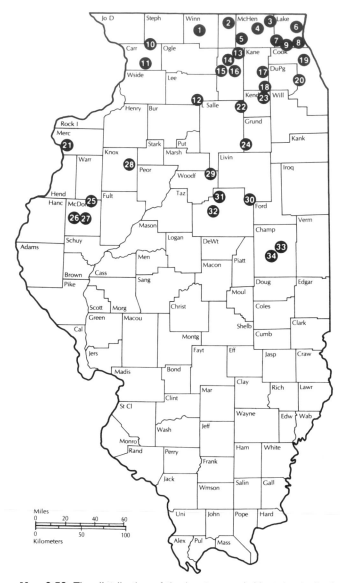

Map 8.56. The distribution of the least weasel, *Mustela nivalis*, in northern Illinois is shown by numbered localities, referenced in *Records of occurrence*. The subspecies is *M. n. allegheniensis*. The range of the species in the United States is shaded.

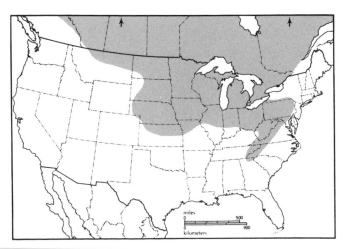

the time; the "extras" are stored, and many of these decay or mummify.

Least weasels frequently take over the nests of meadow voles or other small mammals for their own use. Near the Ohio River near Cincinnati, Ohio, one had taken over the nest of a Norway rat under some roofing paper. The weasel undoubtedly fed on nearby meadow voles, as evidenced by nearly one hundred fragments of skin, feet, and tails of these voles packed in the nest cavity (Goodpaster, 1941).

Woodrow Goodpaster kept a least weasel in a large outdoor cage where it nested in a hollow log. Goodpaster would take the piece of log (and weasel) out of the cage and place it on the lawn. The least weasel would cautiously nose through the grass but never stray far away and would return every so often to its hiding place in the log; once inside, the weasel could be returned to its cage.

E. R. Hall (1951) reported that least weasels will emit a musky odor when annoyed and may give a shrill shriek. Several authors have indicated that these weasels must rely heavily on their sense of smell, for they seemingly have poor eyesight.

Food

Nothing is known of the food habits of the least weasel in Illinois. They probably feed on any kind of mice and voles, young thirteen-lined ground squirrels, young Norway rats, any small birds, insects, and other invertebrates.

Reproduction

Least weasels do not exhibit delayed implantation as do many other mustelids. Young are born at various times throughout the year but probably most are produced in the spring. The gestation period is only about 35 days (in contrast to nearly 270 days in the long-tailed weasel). Two or more litters may be produced a year. Average litter size is around 5 (1–10). At birth, the young are hairless and weigh about 1.4 gm. At 18 weeks of age, females are sexually active; at 32 weeks, males are also. Nests used by least weasels for rearing young are often the appropriated nest of voles.

Variation

On the basis of E. R. Hall's monographic revision of weasels (1951), specimens from Illinois are referred to *M. n. allegheniensis*. Across the Mississippi River in Iowa, specimens have been referred by Hall to *M. n. campestris* (type locality, Beemer, Cuming Co., Nebraska.

Mustela nivalis allegheniensis (Rhoads)

1901. *Putorius allegheniensis* Rhoads, Proc. Acad. Nat. Sci., Phila., 52:751. Type from Beallsville, Washington Co., Pennsylvania.

1959. *Mustela nivalis allegheniensis,* Hall and Kelson, The Mamm. N. Amer., Ronald Press, 1959:1082.

Range. Probably north of an east-west line running through Edgar-Adams counties (Map 8.56).

Diagnosis and Comparisons. A small subspecies with short hind feet and short tail; differs from *M. n. campestris* in being of darker color, having the hind foot less than 25 mm in males, 22 mm in females, and a tail averaging shorter than 34 mm (E. R. Hall, 1951).

Records of occurrence. SPECIMENS EXAMINED, 43.
McHenry Co.: [3] 3 km NE Spring Grove, 1 (ISM). **Lake Co.:** [6] Waukegan, 2 (CAS); [7] Tower Lake, 2 (FM); [8] Deerfield, 1 (CAS), 1 (FM). **Carroll Co.:** [10] T25N, R6E, Sec. 8 [Cherry Grove Twp.], 1 (NHS); [11a] T23N, R5E, Sec. 2 [near Chadwick], 1 (NHS); [11b] 2½ mi S Chadwick, 1 (ISM). **Lee Co.:** [12] Henkel, 1 (NHS). **De Kalb Co.:** [14b] 1 mi NW Glidden Rd. & Rt 64, 1 (UI); [15] ¼ mi S Malta, 1 (UI); [16a] De Kalb, 1 (NIU), 1 (UI); [16b] 5 mi E De Kalb, 1 (NIU); Audubon Sanctuary [location?], 1 (NIU). **Kane Co.:** [17] near St. Charles, 1 (ISM); [18] Aurora, 1 (FM). **Cook Co.:** [19b] Niles Center [=Niles], ? (CAS); [20] La Grange, 1 (CAS). **Mercer Co.:** [21b] 4 mi N Keithsburg, 1 (UI). **La Salle Co.:** [22] 5 mi S Sandwich, 1 (UI). **Grundy Co.:** [24] Kinsman, 1 (SIC). **McDonough Co.:** [26] Lake Argyle State Park, 1 (ISM). **Livingston Co.:** [30] Belle Prairie Township, 1 (NHS). **McLean Co.:** [31a] 6 mi S Gridley, 1 (ISU); [31b] Lake Bloomington, 1 (ISU); [32a] T24N, R2E, Sec. 9 [2 mi N Normal], 1 (ISU); [32b] 2 mi N, ½ mi W Normal, 1 (ISU); [32c] ½ mi N Normal, 1 (ISU); [32d] Normal, 1 (ISU). **Champaign Co.:** [33a] 6 mi NE Urbana, 3 (UI); [33b] 4¼ mi NE Urbana, 1 (UI); [34a] 2 mi W Champaign, 1 (UI); [34b] Champaign, 3 (UI); [34c] Urbana, 1 (ISM), 2 (UI); [34d] 1 mi S Urbana, 1 (UI).

Additional records. **Winnebago Co.:** [1] no specific locality, 2 (BM). **Boone Co.:** [2] 3 mi NE Poplar Grove, (Harty and Thom, 1978:85). **McHenry Co.:** [4a] Wonder Lake, (Harty, 1981 in litt.); [4b] Woodstock, (Harty, 1981 in litt); [5] Marengo, (Harty, 1981 in litt.). **Lake Co.:** [9] Long Grove, (Harty, 1981 in litt.). **De Kalb Co.:** [13] Russel Forest Preserve, (Harty and Thom, 1978:85); [14a] 2 mi E Clare, (Harty and Thom, 1978:85). **Cook Co.:** [19a] Northfield, (E. R. Hall, 1951:190). **Mercer Co.:** [21a] 2 mi W, 1 mi N Joy, 1 (WIU), (Harty and Thom, 1978:85). **Kendall Co.:** [23] Oswego Twp., 1 (WIU), (Warnock and Warnock, 1973:116). **McDonough Co.:** [25] 1 mi W Walnut Grove Village, 1 (WIU), (Harty and Thom, 1978:85); [27] near Macomb, 1 (WIU), (Warnock and Warnock, 1973:116). **Knox Co.:** [28] 4 mi S Victoria, 2 (KC), (Harty and Thom, 1978:85). **Woodford Co.:** [29] 3½ mi E Minonk [from owl stomach], 1 (ISM), (Munyer, 1966:176).

Mustela frenata, Long-tailed weasel

Range. Throughout the state, but records are missing from many central counties (Map 8.57).

Diagnosis. A large species of *Mustela* with a long tail that has a distinct black tip; tail is usually more than 40 percent of the head-body length and usually more than 110 mm in males, more than 80 mm in females; postglenoid length of skull (measured from the glenoid fossa

where the mandible articulates to the posterior margin of the occipital condyle on the same side) less than 46 percent of the condylobasal length in males, 48 percent in females; length of hind foot in males about 45 mm, in females, 35 mm; light-colored underparts orangish, or suffused or washed with orange.

Color. In summer, dorsum reddish brown with feet and tail, except for tip, the same color; brown extending down side of face to throat; venter orangish or whitish, with white extending part way out on underside of legs.

In winter, usually the same color as in summer in Illinois, but some may be white: dorsum, feet, and tail white except for prominent black terminal tip; fur on underside whitish except for a slight orangish frosting which extends onto tail (based on a December 31, 1949, specimen taken 1½ mi W Farmington, Fulton County).

Chromosomes. 2N = 42; 20 acrocentrics, 20 metacentrics and submetacentrics; X and Y submetacentrics (Hsu and Benirschke, 1971d:231).

Comparisons. For a comparison with *Mustela nivalis,* see account of that species (p. 288).

Mustela frenata in Illinois can be confused with *Mustela erminea,* which is known to occur as close to Illinois as Pewaukee, Waukesha Co., Wisconsin, some 40 miles north of the Illinois state line, and near Stockton, Muscatine Co., Iowa, 10 miles northwest of the Illinois state line. When animals of the same sex and adult age are compared, *M. frenata* differs from *M. erminea* as follows: length of tail in males usually more than 105 mm rather than less, in females usually more than 80 mm rather than less than 72 mm; postglenoid length of skull (see *Diagnosis* for measurement procedures) less than 46 percent of condylobasal length of skull in males and less than 48 percent in females, rather than more; length of tail usually more than 44 percent of head-body length (but external measurements are often inaccurately taken).

Some specimens of *M. frenata* which approach the characteristics of, and might be confused with, *Mustela erminea* are worthy of discussion. A female from Vermilion County has a postglenoid/condylobasal length percentage of 48.2; a female from Fulton County, 49.0. On other features, these two specimens are referred to *M. frenata.* A male from 1⅛ mi NW White Heath, Piatt County, is represented by the shriveled and dried parts of the skin and part of the skull. This specimen has the long tail of *M. frenata* but the white lips of *M. erminea.* E. R. Hall examined it and was "95 percent convinced" that on the basis of the short black tip of the tail, the long tail, and the uninflated anterointernal face of the tympanic bulla the specimen was a dwarf *M. frenata.* It is not possible to measure the postglenoid or condylobasal length of this specimen. Nevertheless, small specimens of either sex of *M. frenata* in northern Illinois should be carefully scrutinized to see if they might be *M. erminea.*

Fig. 8.132. Long-tailed weasel, *Mustela frenata*. (From Hoffmeister and Mohr, 1957. Photograph by K. Maslowski and W. W. Goodpaster)

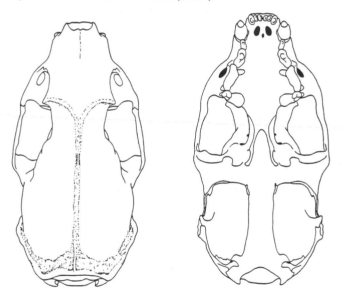

Fig. 8.133. *Mustela frenata*, dorsal and ventral views of skull; 3 mi NW Canton, Fulton Co., Illinois, 952 UI. Male, 47.2 mm greatest length.

Aging. Age groups were defined by E. R. Hall (1951) as follows:

Juvenile, birth to three months, one or more deciduous teeth present.

Young, three to seven-and-one-half months, suture widely open between the maxillae and nasals and between premaxillae and nasals.

Subadult, seven-and-one-half to ten months, sutures between maxillae and nasals visible but indistinct.

Adult, more than ten months, no sutures visible to the naked eye.

Growth. At about one month of age, males weigh about 108 gm.; females, 86; at two months, the weights are about 250 and 175, respectively; at three months, 325 and 220 (Sanderson, 1949:414). Animals attain adult external size by the tenth week of age according to Sanderson (1949:414) although E. R. Hall (1951) regarded animals at this age as "juveniles" (see *Aging*).

Secondary sexual variation. See account of the genus (p. 288).

Molt. Animals that acquire a white winter coat and a brown summer coat undergo two molts a year. It is not clear whether weasels that remain brown all year undergo one or two molts annually.

Remarks. When persons talk about weasels in Illinois they usually are referring to the long-tailed weasel. Although seemingly not abundant in the state, it is encountered more often than the least weasel.

Habitat

Long-tailed weasels are found in a variety of habitats in Illinois but are neither common nor abundant in any one. They are found in brushy areas, open woodlands, grasslands, weedy areas along roads, and on farms often around out-buildings that might harbor rats or mice, or around chicken houses. They are not diggers so they take refuge or nest in the burrows of other similar-sized mammals or in or under brush piles. They avoid places that have insufficient cover.

Robert Kennicott (1858) in writing of this weasel says

> It is said not to burrow readily, but usually to take possession of the burrow of another animal, or to choose its retreat in some natural crevice among rocks, or in slight excavations formed by itself under trees. I have generally found it occupying the burrow of the common ground-squirrel (*Tamias striatus*), and have sometimes known it to live in hollow logs in summer. It often travels under snow, through pathways constructed like those of the shrews and meadow-mice; and I have traced these snow-covered ways for many rods, where the weasel had evidently been in search of prey. Some of these had been travelled repeatedly and for a long time, though few tracks were seen on the surface. In consequence of this habit, the presence of the animal is sometimes not noticed.

Habits

Long-tailed weasels are nocturnal but also far more diurnal than most other Illinois carnivores. It is not unusual for someone to encounter a weasel when tramping through or working in the woods, or hunting. Weasels, when discovered during the daytime, usually do not make a rapid escape, but show an inherent curiosity before retreating.

In winter, long-tailed weasels may not move far from their den area. In central Iowa, the average distance travelled was 312 feet, with a maximum distance of 642 feet (Polderboer et al., 1941). In Pennsylvania, the distance travelled per winter night by males was 704 feet, by females 346 feet (Glover, 1943).

These weasels are good climbers and are known to pursue squirrels into trees. They climb and move about in the branches quite well, considering their short legs.

The hunting behavior of *M. frenata* is summarized by Hoffmeister and Mohr (1957:100):

> A hungry long-tailed weasel, once on the trail of a rabbit, is an intent, relentless pursuer. A healthy rabbit, however, will give the weasel a good run and may cleverly confuse its own trail by hopping back and forth over a small area. Again, the rabbit may freeze motionless and be nearly lost to sight in a tangle of brush so that the weasel may pass it by momentarily. The rabbit may make a confusing maze of tracks before dashing off, and the shorter-legged weasel must hustle to keep up with its prey. But once the gap is sufficiently narrowed between predator and prey, the weasel makes a quick dash and bites the rabbit at the base of the skull. Over and over the two may tumble, the weasel holding on tenaciously until the rabbit ceases to struggle.

Food

Long-tailed weasels feed extensively on a great variety of small and medium-sized mammals, including cotton-tails and jack rabbits. Their diet also includes birds,

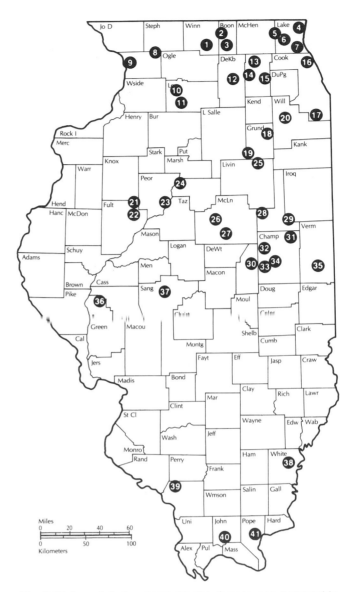

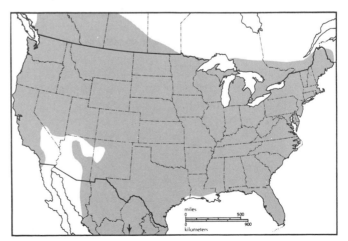

Map 8.57. Long-tailed weasels, *Mustela frenata,* occur statewide. The subspecies is *M. f. noveboracensis.* Numbered localities of occurrence are referenced in *Records of occurrence.* The range of the species in the United States is shaded.

especially ground-dwelling kinds, up to and including domestic chickens. They will also feed on lizards and snakes. In my estimation, weasels are sufficiently good hunters that they do not have to depend on road-kills as a source of food. Rather, weasels that are killed on our roads were probably not scavenging food, but rather in the process of crossing the road.

In Iowa, Polderboer et al. (1941) obtained information on foods eaten by long-tailed weasels in winter and spring by analyzing scats. These scats contained by frequency and percentage (in parentheses) the following: *Microtus,* sp., 71 (43); *Reithrodontomys megalotis,* 36 (22); *Peromyscus* sp., 17 (10); *Sylvilagus floridanus,* 14 (8); shrews, other mice, pocket gophers, and least weasel, 22 (13); tree sparrow, 1 (0.60); grasshoppers, 1 (0.60); unidentified, 3 (1.85).

Weasels are heavy eaters. For example, captive animals that were five to seven weeks old ate 22 percent of their body weight in food each day; from the eighth to tenth weeks, 24 percent; after that, 18 percent daily (Sanderson 1949:413).

Robert Kennicott (1858) in writing about weasels in northern Illinois and Wisconsin observed:

> Meadow-mice are certainly the greatest pests among mammals of Northern Illinois; and of these the weasel destroys great numbers. I am informed that, upon the appearance of a weasel in the field, the army of mice of all kinds begins a precipitate retreat. A gentleman from Wisconsin related to me that, while following a plough, in spring, he noticed a weasel with a mouse in its mouth, running past him. It entered a hollow log. He determined to watch further, if possible, the animal's movements, and presently saw it come out again, hunt about the roots of some stumps, dead trees, and log-heaps, and then enter a hole, from which a mouse ran out. But the weasel had caught one and carried it to the nest. Upon cutting open this log, five young weasels were found, and the remains of a large number of mice, doubtless conveyed there as food. Pleased to learn that his supposed enemy was in fact a friend, and his poultry being at considerable distance, the farmer spared the young ones, intending to continue his observations; but upon examination the next morning, they had disappeared, having probably been carried by the mother to a more secure retreat.

Reproduction

In long-tailed weasels, after mating and impregnation, there is a delay in implantation and arrest of the blastula for a period of time, so that the lapse from fertilization to birth of the young on the average is about 270 days. Young are born in the spring, probably in April. There may be as many as nine in a litter, but usually there are fewer.

Young are hairless at birth. Their eyes open at about the thirty-seventh day. Weaning is accomplished at about this time also. Young males are sexually mature during their first summer, females not until their second summer.

Variation

All specimens from Illinois are referred by E. R. Hall (1951) to the subspecies *M. f. noveboracensis.* Those from Missouri and Iowa, adjacent to Illinois, are referred to *M. f. primulina* (type locality, 5 mi NE Avilla, Jasper Co., Missouri).

Mustela frenata noveboracensis (Emmons)

1840. *Putorius Noveboracensis* Emmons, A report . . . quad. Massachusetts, 1840:45. Type locality, Williamstown, Berkshire Co., Massachusetts.

1936. *Mustela frenata noveboracensis,* Hall, Carnegie Inst. Wash. Publ., 473:104.

Range. Probably throughout the state. After the distribution map was completed, we had a sighting of a long-tailed weasel from near Pecatonica Creek, T27N, R7E, Sec. 11, Stephenson County (Map 8.57).

Diagnosis and Comparisons. A medium-sized subspecies of *M. frenata* with no white markings on side of face or top of head.

Records of occurrence. SPECIMENS EXAMINED, 48. **Winnebago Co.:** [1] Rockford, 1 (NHS). **Boone Co.:** [3] 1 mi NE Belvidere, 1 (NIU). **Lake Co.:** [5a] Pistakee Lake, 1 (CAS); [5b] Volo Bog, T45N, R9E, Sec. 28, 1 (ISM); [6] Fremont Twp., T44N, R10E, Sec. 9, 1 (ISM); [7b] Highland Park, 2 (CAS). **Carroll Co.:** [8] T25N, R6E, Sec. 1, 1 (NHS). **Lee Co.:** [10] 2 mi S Dixon, 1 (UI); [11] T20N, R9E, Sec. 25, 1 (UI). **Kane Co.:** [14] ⅛ mi W Virgil, 1 (NIU); [15] ½ mi W St. Charles, 1 (ISM). **Cook Co.:** [16a] Glencoe, 1 (FM); [16c] Evanston, 1 (CAS); [16d] Niles Center [=Niles], 1 (CAS); [17] Flossmoor, 1 (FM). **Will Co.:** [20] Joliet, 1 (UI). **Fulton Co.:** [21a] 2 mi W Farmington, 1 (UI); [21b] 1½ mi W Farmington, 1 (UI); [21c] 1 mi W Farmington, 1 (UI); [22a] Brereton, 1 (UI); [22b] 3 mi NW Canton, 2 (UI). **Woodford Co.:** [24] Partridge Twp., 1 mi E Illinois River, 1 (ISU). **Livingston Co.:** [25] Dwight, 1 (NHS). **McLean Co.:** [26a] 3.3 mi N Normal, 1 (ISU); [26b] Normal, 1 (NHS); [27] 1 mi E Downs, 1 (ISU). **Ford Co.:** [28] vic Sibley, 1 (UI). **Iroquois Co.:** [29] near Loda, 1 (ISM). **Piatt Co.:** [30] 1⅛ mi NE White Heath, 1 (UI). **Champaign Co.:** [32] 10 mi NW Champaign, 1 (UI); [33a] ½ mi E Bondville, 1 (UI); [33b] Seymour, 1 (UI); [33c] Seymour Prairie, 1 (UI); [34a] 2 mi W Champaign, 1 (UI); [34b] 1 mi S Champaign, 1 (UI). **Vermilion Co.:** [35] Catlin, 1 (UI). **Scott Co.:** [36] 2 mi S Chapin [labelled Morgan Co.], 1 (ISM). **Sangamon Co.:** [37] 1 mi N Springfield, 1 (ISM). **White Co.:** [38] 5 mi NE Carmi, 1 (ISU). **Jackson Co.:** [39] near Ava, 2 (SIC). **Johnson Co.:** [40] 2 mi S Vienna, 1 (ISM). **Pope Co.:** [41a] 6 mi N Golconda, 1 (UI); [41b] Golconda, 3 (US).

Additional records. **Boone Co.:** [2] Caledonia, (Harty, 1981 in litt.). **Lake Co.:** [4] Camp Logan, (E. R. Hall, 1951:228); [7a] Fort Sheridan, (E. R. Hall, 1951:228). **Carroll Co.:** [9] Savanna, (E. R. Hall, 1951:228). **De Kalb Co.:** [12] De Kalb, (Harty, 1981 in litt.). **Kane Co.:** [13] Starks, (Harty, 1981 in litt.). **Cook Co.:** [16b] West Northfield, (E. R. Hall, 1951:228). **Du Page Co.:** Bloomingdale Spg., [location not plotted], (E. R. Hall, 1951:228). **Grundy Co.:** [18] Goose Lake Prairie State Park,

Fig. 8.134. Mink, *Mustela vison.* Photograph by K. Maslowski.

(Harty, 1981 in litt.); [19] Kinsman, (Harty and Stains, 1975:44). **Peoria Co.:** [23] Peoria, 2 (UM). **Champaign Co.:** [31] Harwood Twp., (E. R. Hall, 1951:228).

Mustela vison, Mink

Range. Throughout the state, but associated with water—streams, drainage ditches, ponds, lakes.

Diagnosis. A mustelid specialized for aquatic life (but less so than *Lutra,* river otter), toes connected with a web at their bases; tail bushy, ears small and barely projecting above fur; color dark on dorsum and only slightly lighter ventrally; auditory bullae flattened and wide; length of upper toothrow from canine to last molar more than 18 mm.

Color. Dorsum usually a rich reddish brown with venter nearly the same color, although slightly more reddish; tail gradually darkens toward tip so that the terminal one-third to one-half is black all around.

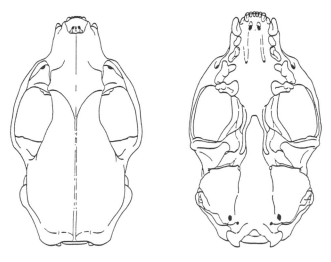

Fig. 8.135. *Mustela vison,* dorsal and ventral views of skull. Rockford, Winnebago Co., Illinois, 33444 UI. Male, 63.4 mm greatest length.

For some Illinois specimens the venter is entirely brown; others have white spotting, usually on the chin and on the chest between the forelegs; sometimes there is a small white spot near the base of the tail.

Chromosomes. 2N = 30; 26 metacentrics, submetacentrics, or subtelocentrics, two acrocentrics; X and Y submetacentric (Hsu and Benirschke, 1968a).

Comparisons. Mustela vison differs from other *Mustela* in Illinois in being of larger size, having a bushier tail, and longer hind feet; underparts nearly same color as dorsum, rather than whitish or white with an orangish wash; auditory bullae less inflated, maxillary toothrow (canine to last molar) more than 18 mm rather than less; webbing between toes more extensive.

Remarks. The mink has a high population in Illinois and—when the value of each fur is considered—it is the second most valuable furbearer, next to the muskrat. The abundance of mink is directly correlated with the large population of muskrats upon which the mink prey.

Habitat

Mink are found where there is a permanent water supply such as streams and rivers, shorelines of lakes, marshes, farm and strip-mine ponds, and ponds frequently called borrow-pits created by removal of earth for road construction. Mink feed extensively on water-dwelling animals and thus are dependent on a water source. They may den in the conical houses built by marsh muskrats or the burrows dug by bank muskrats. They also may den a short distance from water, under either a brush pile or a large stump, for example.

Kennicott (1858:102) in writing about mink in Illinois stated that

> mink sometimes take possession of the house of a muskrat, after devouring or driving off the rightful inhabitants. It appears to be quite as abundant and as much at home about prairie ponds and streams as in the woods. It digs burrows on the dry ground near the water. . . . At the extremity of the burrow is a chamber a foot in diameter, in which is found a globular nest of soft grass, lined with feathers, constructed with considerable art, and entered by an opening on one side. In the northern part of this State, where the climate is more severe, the burrows are deeper, being sometimes eight or ten feet in extent, with the nest two feet below the surface. On the prairie, minks are also found living in burrows, often six or eight rods in length, on high ground, from which long galleries extend to the edge of a slough or pond. These galleries, however, are not formed by the minks, but by musk-rats which dig them in order to place their nests beyond the reach of high water, and yet have subterranean communication with the stream. Though they frequently take possession of the burrows of the musk-rat, and sometimes those of the badger and skunk, when situated in suitable localities, they also excavate them for themselves, but of much less diameter. In the woods, the burrows are generally found under logs or the roots of trees near the water, and in rocky regions they burrow under rocks or stone walls; and I have occasionally discovered them living in the hollow of a fallen tree, or in the decayed roots of large trees growing in the water.

Habits

Mink usually do their feeding and hunting at night, although their foraging may continue into the daytime. Yeager and Anderson (1944:170) gave this account at Lake Chautauqua Refuge, Mason County:

> At daybreak on February 12 the senior writer saw two foraging minks on the forest bordered levee. Snow covered the ground. One of the minks was on the levee proper and appeared to be trailing rabbits; the other was on a jam of floating logs and debris lodged against the levee. At the slow approach of the writer, the former ran down the levee and disappeared under a brush pile; the latter entered the water and swam toward the levee where it was lost to sight. A third mink was seen shortly after daybreak on February 14 in a willow thicket on the opposite side of the refuge. Snow tracking indicated that minks were active nightly and that they foraged over every part of the levee. On ice they traveled at least as far as the inmost fringe of willows, button-bushes, and aquatic vegetation. Food was unquestionably abundant, consisting mainly of crippled ducks and rabbits and muskrats.

Gregory (1936:40) in his account of the mammals of the Chicago area recounted: "I have found one asleep in the sun on the bushy shore of a small island near an active loon's nest. The bow of the boat scraping the bushes awakened him and made him look up. He did not wait long."

Mink are excellent swimmers and while in the water successfully prey upon muskrats and many kinds of fishes. They also move with agility on the land. Gregory (1936:40) described some measure of their stealth:

> The skill with which a mink can hide when following a watercourse, scurrying along the bank much of the time, diving again and again into the water, is quite remarkable. One eluded me this way, almost at my feet, on a chill November day, when the air was full of snow. It reappeared farther down stream, but whether it progressed from its hiding place along the undercut bank or in the water itself, I could not tell.

Food

Mink feed on a variety of animals. Any plant material that they eat is probably accidental. The animals upon which they prey are muskrats, fish, voles, *Peromyscus*, cottontails, crayfish, birds—including waterfowl, domestic chickens, turkeys, and ducks—and a few reptiles, amphibians, and insects. The diet varies, depending upon the availability of food items at different times of the year.

At the Lake Chautauqua Refuge, Mason County, Yeager and Anderson (1944) found that 26 mink scats collected in November and December consisted almost entirely of duck feathers; other items were fish, cottontail, and muskrat. One mink den in this area reportedly contained 13 freshly killed muskrats, two mallards, and one coot (Brown and Yeager, 1943). In Michigan, about one-fourth of the winter food is muskrats.

Kennicott (1858) wrote about the mink as follows:

> Though not so expert as the otter, it frequently succeeds in catching fish in shallow water. In the prairie sloughs it devours at times considerable quantities of cray-fish, tadpoles, and frogs; and when the smaller of these places become nearly dry from evaporation, and are quite alive with tadpoles, and occasionally with mud-fish and sticklebacks, in common with the musk-rat, the raccoon, and reptile-eating birds, it clears these muddy pools entirely of their unfortunate inhabitants, which have no way of escape. The mink, however, does not always confine itself to this kind of prey, for when once it has gained access to the farmyard, stocked with young turkeys, chickens, and ducks, it far prefers taking up its residence near by, where, without the exertion of long journeys and hard chases, it can make a nocturnal feast of its favorite food—blood and brains.

Reproduction

The mating season extends from January through March, and perhaps longer in Wisconsin according to Jackson (1961), and from late February until early April in Missouri (Schwartz and Schwartz, 1981). The gestation period may be variable, anywhere between 40 and 75 days, depending upon when there was implantation of the blastocyst. Young evidently are born over a considerable span in the late spring and early summer but probably most arrive in April and May. One specimen from Fulton County taken on May 30 must be less than one month old. The tail is still nearly hairless and the total length is only 187 mm.

Litters usually number between three and six young, nearly hairless at birth, and pinkish in color. Eyes open at about 3½ weeks and young are weaned at between 1½ and 2 months.

Variation

Since the time that Hollister (1913) reported on the variation in American mink, specimens have been referred to two subspecies in Illinois: *M. v. letifera* north of a line from "the northwestern corner of Indiana to the northeastern corner of Missouri" and *M. v. mink* (under name of *M. v. lutreocephala* by Hollister) south of this line. The southern mink has been considered to be slightly smaller and darker than the northern subspecies.

I am not convinced that two subspecies are present in Illinois; however, until more material has been studied from Illinois and the adjacent states, I follow this earlier arrangement.

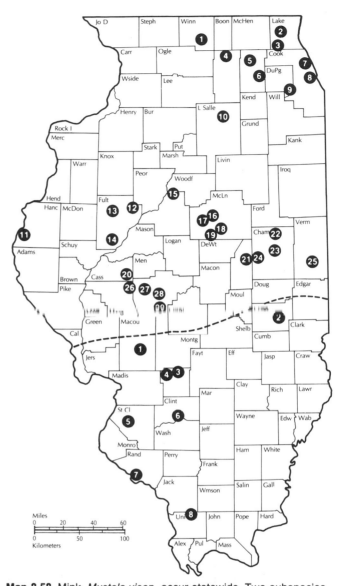

Map 8.58. Mink, *Mustela vison*, occur statewide. Two subspecies occur in Illinois: *M. v. letifera* north of the broken line; *M. v. mink*, south. Numbered localities of occurrence are referenced in *Records of occurrence*. The range of the species in the United States is shaded.

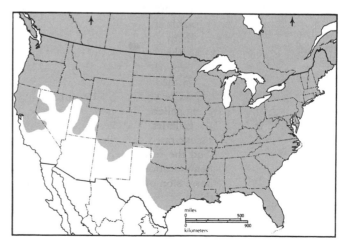

Mustela vison mink Peale and Palisot de Beauvois

1796. *Mustela mink* Peale and Palisot de Beauvois, A sci. and desc. cat. of Peale's mus., Phila., 1796:39. Type locality, Maryland.

1914. *Mustela vison mink,* Hollister, Proc. Biol. Soc. Wash., 27:215.

Range. Southern two-fifths of state south of a line from Calhoun County through Edgar County (Map 8.58).

Diagnosis and Comparisons. A subspecies that is smaller than *M. v. letifera* but darker in color (Hollister, 1913).

Records of occurrence. SPECIMENS EXAMINED, 13. **Macoupin Co.:** [1] 5 mi S Carlinville, 1 (UI). **Bond Co.:** [3] 7 mi N Greenville, 1 (UI); [4] 1 mi W Reno, 2 (UI). **St. Clair Co.:** [5] 3 mi SW Belleville, 1 (UI). **Clinton Co.:** [6] 3 mi W Posey, 1 (ISM). **Randolph Co.:** [7] Kaskaskia Island, 5 (UI). **Union Co.:** [8a] 4 mi N Cobden, 1 (SIC); [8b] 3½ mi E Cobden, 1 (SIC).

Additional records: **Coles Co.:** [2] near Ashmore, (E. R. Hall, 1981:1003).

Mustela vison letifera Hollister

1913. *Mustela vison letifera* Hollister, Proc. U. S. Nat. Mus., 44:475. Type from Elk River, Sherburne Co., Minnesota.

Range. Northern three-fifths of state north of a line from Calhoun County through Edgar County (Map 8.58).

Diagnosis and Comparisons. A large subspecies when compared with *M. v. mink,* but lighter in color (Hollister, 1913).

Records of occurrence. SPECIMENS EXAMINED, 48. **Winnebago Co.:** [1a] Rockford, 13 (UI). **Lake Co.:** [2] Grayslake, 1 (CAS); [3] Lake Zurich, 1 (NIU). **De Kalb Co.:** [4] 1½ mi W, ¾ mi N Kingston, 1 (NIU). **Kane Co.:** [5] 5 mi E Burlington, 1 (NIU); [6] Geneva, 2 (CAS). **Cook Co.:** [7] Evanston, 3 (CAS); [8] Chicago, 1 (CAS). **Du Page Co.:** [9] Willowbrook, 1 (NIU). **La Salle Co.:** [10] Rt 23, 11 mi N Ottawa, 1 (NIU). **Fulton Co.:** [12] 3 mi NE Canton, 1 (UI); [13] 12 mi W Canton, 1 (UI); [14] 6 mi SE Ipava, 1 (UI). **Tazewell Co.:** [15] 3 mi N, 4 mi W Washington, 1 (UI). **McLean Co.:** [16] Normal, 1 (ISU); [17] 4 mi W Bloomington, 1 (ISU); [18] 1 mi E Downs, 1 (ISU); [19] 2 mi N Heyworth, 1 (ISU). **Cass Co.:** [20] 1½ mi W Ashland, 1 (ISM). **Piatt Co.:** [21] ½ mi W White Heath, 1 (UI). **Champaign Co.:** [22] 3 mi N Rantoul, 1 (ISM); [23a] 4 mi E, ¼ mi N Leverett, 1 (UI); [23b] 1 mi E Leverett, 1 (UI); [23c] 3 mi N Urbana, 1 (UI); [24] Seymour, 1 (UI); no specific locality [not plotted], 2 (UI). **Vermilion Co.:** [25] Catlin, 1 (UI). **Morgan Co.:** [26] 3 mi S Ashland, 1 (UI). **Sangamon Co.:** [27] 10 mi W Springfield, 1 (ISM); [28a] 4 mi S Springfield, 1 (ISM); [28b] 7½ mi S Springfield, 1 (ISM); [29] 1½ mi E Glenarm, Sugar Creek, 1 (UI).

Additional records: **Winnebago Co.:** [1b] Rockford, 1 (FSM). **Hancock Co.:** [11] Warsaw, (Necker and Hatfield, 1941:47).

Fig. 8.136A. Badger, *Taxidea taxus.* From Hoffmeister and Mohr, 1957. Photograph by Lorus Milne and Margery Milne, Durham, N.H.

Taxidea, Badger

Diagnosis. A monotypic genus of mustelid of medium to large size, body depressed and broad, legs short but strong, toes of forefeet long-clawed, tail short; white stripe of variable length starting on nose and running posteriorly down middle of back; skull heavy and broad posteriorly, upper molar triangular and slightly smaller than upper carnassial, auditory bullae large; mammary glands comprise one pair pectoral, two pair abdominal, one pair inguinal; baculum long, hooked dorsad distally, and with lateral grooves.

Dental formula. 3/3, 1/1, 3/3, 1/2.

Chromosomes. Diploid number 32; 16 metacentrics and submetacentrics; 14 acrocentrics. X chromosome metacentric; Y, submetacentric.

Comparisons. Taxidea differs from *Mephitis* in color of dorsum, which is basically grayish or grayish red rather than black, venter whitish rather than black, skull much longer and broader, auditory bullae more inflated, upper molar triangular rather than squarish.

Taxidea differs from *Mustela* in its heavier, broader body, white stripe present over head and part way down back; skull longer and broader; color of dorsum more grayish than reddish brown or dark brown (in Illinois species of *Mustela*).

For a comparison with *Lutra,* see account of that genus (p. 305).

Aging. According to Long (1972:725), skulls can be placed in categories as follows: *subadult,* basioccipital-basisphenoid suture obliterated or fused but nasal sutures are open and teeth lack conspicuous wear; *adult,* nasal sutures obliterated and teeth show evidence of wear; *old*

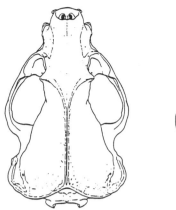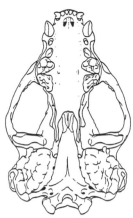

Fig. 8.136B. *Taxidea taxus,* dorsal and ventral views of skull; 4 mi NE Chadwick, Carroll Co., Illinois, 29676 UI. Female, 125.5 mm greatest length.

adult, cranial sutures obliterated and sagittal and postorbital crests frequently are well developed. I have followed this age-classification and use only adults and old adults.

Secondary sexual variation. Males are larger than females, and Long (1972) found that males were significantly larger than females in some measurements.

Taxidea taxus, Badger

Range. Throughout the state except for the southernmost part, from the Ozark Uplift and south (Map 8.59).

Diagnosis. The only species of the genus *Taxidea;* characters in addition to those previously given for the genus are unique facial markings with white on cheeks and behind the eyes; tail length less than 30 percent of the head and body; skull with palate extending posteriorly beyond plane of upper molars.

Color. The dorsum has a grizzled appearance with a mixture of whites, blacks, and ochraceous coloration; this results from hairs that are white-tipped, have a black subterminal band, and are ochraceous at their base, together with underfur that is mostly ochraceous or tan; venter whitish or tan; area between eyes from nose over the top of the head black but bissected by white stripe from the nose over the head, down midline of back; white stripe in Illinois specimens usually extending no further posteriorly than the plane through the base of the forelegs; tops of feet black; tail almost the same color above as the back, below nearly the same as the venter.

Comparisons. For means of distinguishing *Taxidea taxus* from *Mephitis mephitis* and the species of *Mustela* in Illinois, see *Comparisons* for the genus *Taxidea* (p. 298).

Remarks. The badger is thought to have spread southward and eastward in Illinois during the last half-century. The early literature, however, indicates that in the mid-1800's. badgers may have extended entirely across the state (see discussion under Badger [p. 35] in Early History of Mammals in Illinois). Kennicott stated that there were badgers in Cook County in the 1850's but implied that they had been more abundant earlier. With regard to the entire state, he reported that badgers were numerous at least as far as the center of Illinois.

It is my understanding that in northern Illinois in the early 1900's hazards to livestock were created by the holes that badgers dug in the pastures. When a prized horse stepped in such a hole and broke its leg, badgers were placed on an open-season basis. Despite this, they continued to expand their range. In the early 1970's, they were placed on the protected species list for Illinois. As of 1984, they were more widely distributed in the state than ever, perhaps in part because more country has been opened up by the removal of trees.

Habitat

Badgers live in open country — pastures, railroad rights-of-way, roadside shoulders, woodchuck colonies, alfalfa fields, and brushy areas. Digging burrows in which to live is not a problem for them. Actually, burrows for dens are used for only a short time and then the badger moves to another place. They dig many burrows in their search for food — especially ground squirrels or woodchucks. The burrows subsequently are used as temporary shelters.

Badgers cover a large area in their foraging activities. Near Minneapolis, Minnesota, Sargent and Warner (1972) followed a female badger that had a radio transmitter attached. In the summer, she occupied 1,880 acres; in the fall, apparently only 130 acres and re-used dens more often. In the winter, a single den was used and the badger travelled in a five-acre area.

Habits

Badgers can dig rapidly and powerfully and move large obstacles. One badger's burrow in the Savannah Ordinance Depot, Jo Daviess County, lead it to surface from directly beneath a blacktop road that was sufficiently strong to support heavy trucks. The badger proceeded to surface with no difficulty, leaving a hole in the roadway in the process. Perry (1939) found that a badger she kept in the basement of her home dug through the inch-thick concrete floor. Whenever "the badger found a flaw he picked out little pebbles until an opening was afforded for his claws, then jerked out sections of the concrete." Hall (1946) tells of two persons in Nevada who cornered a badger in a three-foot hole. The two tried to dig it

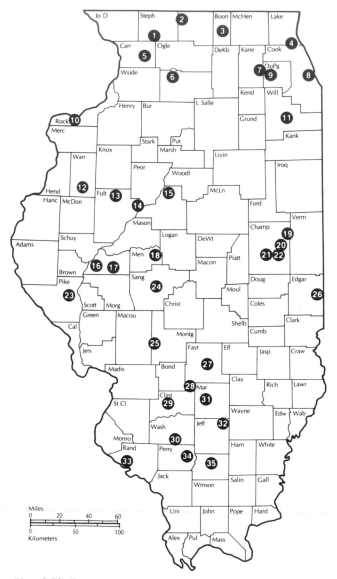

Map 8.59. Records of the badger, *Taxidea taxus,* as numbered, are referenced in *Records of occurrence.* The subspecies is *T. t. taxus.* The range in the United States is shaded.

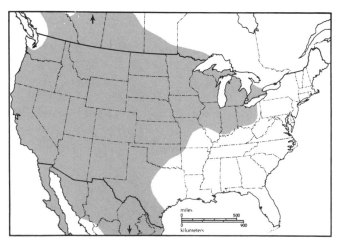

out; they could hear the badger rapidly digging ahead of them, but they were unable to capture it.

When excited, the badger kept by Perry (1939) bobbed up and down on his hind legs and wagged his head vigorously, with mouth open. This badger made sounds that were described as grunts, hisses, breathing hoarsely, yaps, squeals, and purrs, the latter for contentment.

These animals are primarily nocturnal, and their presence is manifest by their burrows and diggings. The dirt removed from a burrow is piled or scattered at the entrance and the burrow entrance is wider than high. Many burrows are less than ten feet long. Only one adult badger occupies a burrow except during the mating season and possibly when the young are in the den.

Food

Foods consumed by badgers in Illinois have not been studied or reported on. Based on their digging sites, one would surmise that they prey upon thirteen-lined ground squirrels, Franklin's ground squirrels, woodchucks, plains pocket gophers, and small, ground-dwelling rodents such as voles and *Peromyscus.* They may even take cottontails if they corner them in burrows. In central Iowa, analysis of 288 badger scats (Table 8.41, Snead and Hendrickson, 1942) indicated that they preyed heavily on ground squirrels, *Peromyscus, Microtus,* and *Sylvilagus.* The authors thought that adult cottontails largely represented carrion. The bird remains consisted partly of domesticated poultry. Identifiable insect remains were of carrot beetles (*Ligyrus gibbosus*), bumblebees, May beetles (*Phyllophaga*), and ground beetles (*Harpalus caliginosus*). In northwestern Iowa, Errington (1937) found that in June and July badgers were feeding on thirteen-lined ground squirrels, meadow voles, white-footed mice, blue-winged teal, grebe, reptilian eggs (probably turtle), and possibly pheasant. He found that 53 percent of the fecal bulk was of ground squirrels and 30 percent of mice.

Reproduction

Mating occurs in late summer. There is a prolonged delay in the implantation of the blastocyst. Young are not born until the following March or April. Young are weaned at about two and one-half to three months. Litters usually comprise one to five young. The body is sparsely covered with fur at birth; eyes open in about one month. Some nest material is in the form of grasses, carried into the underground chamber used for raising the young.

Variation

In his revisionary study of American badgers, Long (1972) regards animals in Illinois as referrable to *T. t. taxus,* but immediately to the north in Wisconsin—as

Table 8.41. Foods eaten by badgers, as determined by scat analysis, in central Iowa (Snead and Hendrickson, 1942). The percentages represent frequency of occurrence in the number of scats (given in parentheses) by seasons.

Food item	Spring (41 scats)	Summer (103 scats)	Autumn (44 scats)
Spermophilus tridecemlineatus	58.5	72.8	47.7
Spermophilus franklinii	22.0	15.5	20.5
Geomys bursarius	2.4	1.9	—
Reithrodontomys megalotis	7.3	3.9	9.1
Peromyscus sp.	39.0	14.6	43.2
Microtus sp.	24.4	9.7	29.5
Undetermined cricetid	2.4	3.9	9.1
Mus musculus	4.9	—	6.8
Sylvilagus floridanus	29.3	20.4	31.8
Undetermined mammal	—	1.0	6.8
Birds	14.6	4.8	13.6
Snakes	—	1.0	2.3
Insects	17.1	43.7	11.4
Plant	7.3	9.7	11.4

close to Illinois as Emerald Grove, Rock County—he refers specimens to *T. t. jacksoni* (type locality 4 mi E Milton, Rock County, Wisconsin).

Taxidea taxus taxus (Shreber)

1778. *Ursus taxus* Schreber, Die Saugthiere . . . 3:520. Type locality, Laborador and Hudson Bay.
1894. *Taxidea taxus*, Rhoads, Amer. Nat., 28:524.

Range. Throughout the state except for the southernmost part, from the Ozark Uplift and south (Map 8.59).

Diagnosis and Comparisons. A large-sized subspecies, pale-colored, with large auditory bullae, large teeth, narrow frontals and frontal processes. Differs from *T. t. jacksoni* in being paler in color; auditory bullae larger, molars larger, and postorbital processes more pronounced (from Long, 1972).

Records of occurrence. SPECIMENS EXAMINED, 26.
Winnebago Co.: [2] 3 mi E Davis, 1 (UI). **Boone Co.:** [3] no specific locality, 1 (NIU). **Carroll Co.:** [5a] 4 mi SE Lanark, 1 (UI); [5b] 4 mi NE Chadwick, 1 (UI). **Kane Co.:** [7] near St. Charles, 1 (ISM). **Cook Co.:** [8] Chicago, 1 (FM); no specific locality [not plotted], 1 (FM). **Du Page Co.:** [9] 4 mi W Rt 59 on Rt 38, 1 (UI). **Will Co.:** [11] no specific locality, 1 (FM). **Warren Co.:** [12] 2 mi E Roseville, 1 (UI). **Fulton Co.:** [13] 3 mi NW Fairview, 1 (UI); [14] 8 mi E Canton, 1 (UI). **Cass Co.:** [17] near Virginia, 1 (ISM). **Menard Co.:** [18a] 2 mi E Greenview, 1 (ISM); [18b] 3 mi E Sweetwater, 1 (ISM). **Champaign Co.:** [19] 1 mi S, 1 mi W Penfield, 1 (UI); [20a] 6½ mi N, 1 mi W St. Joseph, 1 (UI); [20b] 3 mi N, 1 mi W St. Joseph, 1 (UI); [21] 2½ mi S Champaign, 1 (UI); [22] Mayview, 1 (UI). **Sangamon Co.:** [24] 3 mi S Springfield, 1 (ISM). **Montgomery Co.:** [25] 5 mi S Hwy 108 on I-55, 1 (UI). **Edgar Co.:** [26] 9 mi N Vermilion, Brouillett's Creek [labelled Clark Co.], 1 (UI). **Fayette Co.:** [27] Sefton Twp., Sec. 33, 1 (UI); [28] N end Lake Carlyle, 1 (ISM). **Marion Co.:** [31] 4 mi NW Salem, 1 (UI).

Additional records. **Stephenson Co.:** [1] Sec. 17 (NE ¼) T26N, R7E, 1 (ISM). **Lake Co.:** [4] near Halfday (Sanborn, 1930:222). **Lee Co.:** [6] Dixon (Necker and Hatfield, 1941:47). **Rock Island Co.:** [10] Sec. 32, SW ¼, T17N, R3W, road kill, 1 (ISM). **Tazewell Co.:** [15] Sec. 36, T26N, R4W, bluff above Farm Creek, 1 (DOC). **Cass Co.:** [16] 4 mi S Beardstown, road kill, 1 (ISM). **Pike Co.:** [23] road kill on Rt 107 between Pittsfield and Griggsville. **Clinton Co.:** [29] 5 mi W Carlyle on Rt 50, reported pickup of road kill by US Corps of Engineers; supposed to be mounted. **Washington Co.:** [30] 6 mi S Nashville (Klimstra and Roseberry, 1969:414). **Jefferson Co.:** [32] Sec. 17, T1S, R4E, pickup. **Randolph Co.:** [33] 1 mi NW Roots (Klimstra and Roseberry, 1969:413). **Perry Co.:** [34] Sec. 17, T5S, R1W, trapped and released. **Franklin Co.:** [35] 2 mi N Benton, 1 (EIU).

Mephitis, Striped and hooded skunks

Diagnosis. Medium-sized carnivores with fur that is black in color except for two white stripes on the dorsum, or a broad white stripe with intermixed black hairs, or a combination of both dorsal and lateral white stripes; thin white stripe on the nose; tail black with some white, but white not restricted to terminal tip; skull with highest point above orbits, with rostrum depressed; anterior tip of nasals at level of anterior border of alveolus of canine; hard palate ends at about the posterior end of molars; length of P^4 about the same as length of M^1.

Dental formula. 3/3, 1/1, 3/3, 2/1, but in some specimens the upper dentition may be 3-1-2-1.

Comparisons. Spotted skunks, *Spilogale,* may occur sometime in Illinois, either in the past or in the future. At present, they occur in the valley of the Mississippi River in Iowa and Missouri, but no authentic records are available now for Illinois. Means for telling *Mephitis* from *Spilogale* are: narrow white stripe from nose over forehead to plane of the ears rather than a broad nose patch, broad white stripe from ears extends backward, dividing into two stripes near middle of back rather than five or more interrupted or broken stripes on the body, hind foot more than 55 mm in length rather than less, tail more than 75 percent of head and body rather than less, auditory bullae less inflated, condylobasal length more than 60 mm rather than less.

For a comparison with *Taxidea,* see account of that genus (p. 298).

Aging. Animals have been assigned age categories by the degree of closure of three sutures: nasal, presphenoid-basisphenoid, and occipital-basisphenoid. The nasal suture was scored as 1, no fusion; 2, fusing; 3, fused but suture evident; 4, suture obliterated. Presphenoid-basisphenoid: 1, open; 2, fusing; 3, fused. Occipital-basisphenoid; 1, open; 2, fusing; 3, fused. This follows the system devised by Kirkland (1975). Specimens with a summed score of 8 or more were used in the averages. At an earlier time, some specimens we examined at other collections were listed only as adult. I can only assume that they were 8 or more.

Cranial measurements. The cranial measurements as described and illustrated by Van Gelder (1959) for *Spilogale* are used. Nematodes infesting the sinuses have caused abnormal distortions that may have affected the measurement of postorbital breadth.

Remarks. The North American genus *Mephitis* consists of the species *M. mephitis,* striped skunks, and *M. macroura,* hooded skunks. These two species are easily differentiated externally by their different color patterns and differences in proportionate length of the tail, but are most difficult to tell apart on the basis of skull alone.

Mephitis mephitis, Striped skunks

Range. Throughout the state, although some areas are without records (Map 8.60, p. 304).

Diagnosis. A species of *Mephitis* in which the white stripe on the back divides into two and continues part way over back, infrequently reaching the rump; hind feet long; skull large; tail relatively short and bushy; males weigh about 6 lbs, females 4.5 lbs; usually six pairs of mammae but there may be as many as eight on one side, seven on the other (Verts, 1967).

Color. Dorsum and venter black; nose and forehead with narrow white stripe ending at plane of ears; wide, white stripe behind the ears dividing and running backward along each side of midline; paired stripes usually reach halfway down back, sometimes all the way to the rump and onto sides of tail (Figs. 8.140A and 8.140B); tail appears black with a white tip but bases of hairs are white; feet are black. In Illinois only infrequently are specimens found with the broad white stripe just behind the ears without a division.

The variation in black-white color "pattern" for striped skunks in northwestern Illinois has been reviewed by Verts (1967).

Chromosomes. Diploid number 50, FN = 92; 44 metacentrics, 4 acrocentrics, X a medium-sized metacentric, Y a submetacentric (Wade-Smith and Verts, 1982).

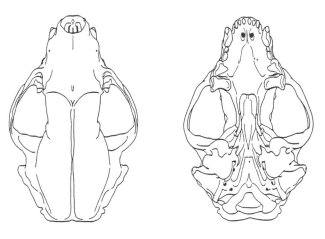

Fig. 8.138. *Mephitis mephitis,* dorsal and ventral views of skull. Rockford, Winnebago Co., Illinois, 33428 UI. Male, 75.5 mm greatest length.

Fig. 8.137. Striped skunk, *Mephitis mephitis.* (Hoffmeister and Mohr, 1957. Photograph by Missouri Conservation Commission, Jefferson City)

Fig. 8.139. Nestling striped skunks, *Mephitis mephitis.* The color pattern is clearly evident at this age. Photograph by K. Maslowski and W. W. Goodpaster.

Comparisons. For a comparison with *Taxidea* and species of *Mustela,* see account of those genera (pp. 298 and 288).

For a comparison with *Lutra,* see that account (p. 305).

Scent glands. Scent glands of varying developmental levels are present in several Illinois mammals, but development is greatest in *Mephitis mephitis.* The glands are situated on both sides of the anus, just inside the anal orifice. When the animal is provoked to secrete material from the scent glands, the nipple-like tips of the glandular ducts are protruded and the yellowish, oily fluid is discharged either in short streams or as a fine, atomized spray. At the age of one month, nursing young already can produce a discharge of musky scent.

Growth. Young at birth weigh about 35 gms, at three weeks about 110 gms, at six weeks, about 220 gms. Animals continue to grow rapidly for the first six months, and there is probably slight growth during the next four months. Adult size should be attained by the tenth month.

Secondary sexual variation. Females are reported to be about 15 percent smaller than males. Verts (1967), however, observed so much variation within each sex that he found it not practical to separate males and females by differences in cranial measurements.

Molt. Molting begins in April. Underfur is molted first. Beginning in July, the guard hairs are molted and both underfur and guard hairs are replaced. Molting and replacement move from anterior to posterior (Verts, 1967).

Remarks. Striped skunks for many years were not sought as fur animals because their pelts had a relatively low monetary value and much work was involved in preparing the hides. Nevertheless, the estimated number of skunks taken annually in Illinois between 1929 and 1961, based on annual reports by trappers, was an average of 15,789 with a low of 182, a high of 40,463. Also see Table 8.42 (p. 305).

Habitat

Striped skunks use a variety of habitats, including pasture lands with grassy fencerows, woody ravines, open woods, or woodlots, and weedy shoulders of roadways. Verts (1967:79) found that they "resided in areas which contained considerable woodland, but in northwestern Illinois highest populations of skunks usually were found in more open country." Some of the best habitat is near major waterways in the rolling hillsides or bluff country where mixed farming is practiced, and where timber and open country as well as a water source are all accessible.

Habits

Skunks for the most part feed and move about at night, but under certain conditions they may be abroad during the daytime. Skunks ordinarily are not distracted

Fig. 8.140A. Variation in color pattern and amount of white striping in adult *Mephitis mephitis,* all from Champaign Co., Illinois. These patterns and stripes would represent approximately what Verts (Fig. 8.140B) refers to as broad stripe, narrow stripe, and short stripe.

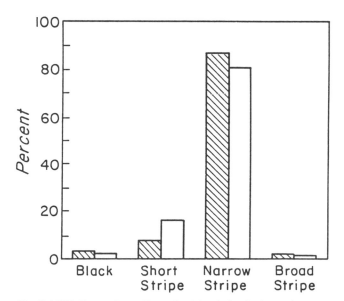

Fig. 8.140B. Four color patterns in striped skunks in northwestern Illinois and the percentage of frequency of each, based upon 130 males (shaded) and 101 females observed between June 1959 and August 1962. (Based on Verts, 1967:16)

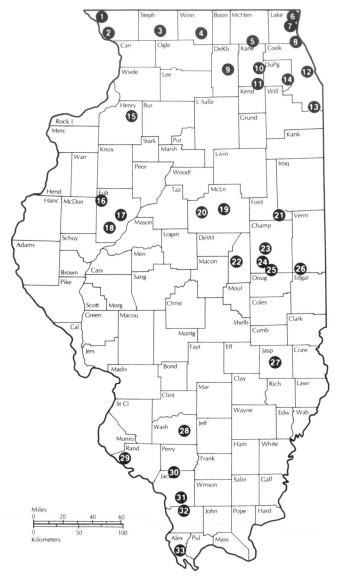

Map 8.60. Striped skunks, *Mephitis mephitis*, occur statewide. The subspecies is *M. m. avia.* Localities of occurrence as numbered are referenced in *Records of occurrence.* The range of the species in the United States is shaded.

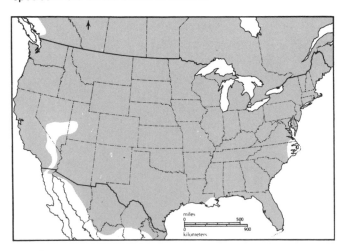

by the presence of humans, but rather avoid them and go about their normal activities. When cornered or harrassed, however, skunks will face the intruder, arch the back, raise the tail and sometimes turn to show the scent glands, and stamp the ground with their front feet. If this fails to discourage the intruder, a skunk may release its malodorous scent in a stream or spray which may travel ten feet or more and can be detected many yards away. However disagreeable the odor, the musky fluid will not harm the skin, but it does cause the eyes to burn and water.

Striped skunks move about by a *pace* or walk, with the front and hind legs on one side alternating with those on the other side, producing a waddle; by *galloping,* with the forelimbs and hindlimbs moving in unison; or *cantering* with hind feet striking the ground alternately between tracks made by the front feet (Verts, 1967:32).

Food

Striped skunks truly eat a great variety of foods that include insects, other invertebrates, fruits, vegetables, small mammals, birds, grasses, roots, amphibians, reptiles, and carrion. Probably the dominant food is insects.

In northwestern Illinois, Verts (1967) analyzed scats, stomachs, and intestinal tracts of striped skunks. Insects were present 88 percent of the time; plant material, 92; animal matter, 95. He thought that the only plant material naturally ingested as food was corn, cherries, nightshade, and ground cherries. The rest was taken while they were in traps.

Reproduction

Mating usually occurs in February or March. The breeding dates in northwestern Illinois, 1960–1962, ranged from February 21 to March 29 (Verts, 1967). The gestation period ranges from 59 to 77 days. Young are born in May or early June. Litter size in northwestern Illinois based on living embryos was 6.3 (1–9). In almost all pregnant females, there is resorption of some embryos.

Young are reared in natal dens. These are usually in burrows dug by other mammals. For example, Verts (1967) found in northwestern Illinois that of the 100 dens occupied by striped skunks, 73 percent were dug by badgers, 17 percent by red foxes, 7 percent by striped skunks, and 3 percent by muskrats. Woodchucks did not occur in the area he studied.

Variation

Striped skunks in Illinois have usually been referred to the subspecies *M. m. avia.* Various workers have assumed, however, that skunks in southernmost Illinois should be referred to *M. m. nigra* (type locality Maryland). Specimens have not been compared in Illinois and adjacent areas to justify the inclusion of *M. m. nigra* in

Table 8.42. Harvest of striped skunks for 25 trapping seasons between 1929 and 1961 in Illinois. Based upon annual reports by trappers to the Illinois Department of Conservation. (Modified from Verts, 1967:24)

Trapping Season	Trappers Reporting Skunk Takes	Average Number of Skunks Per Successful Trapper	Estimate of Skunks Caught in Illinois
1929-30	2,087	5.0	38,255
1930-31	1,158	5.9	40,291
1934-35	865	5.9	21,983
1935-36	907	4.7	13,705
1936-37	1,080	5.3	33,289
1937-38	2,889	3.7	22,770
1938-39	2,306	3.7	22,751
1939-40	1,828	3.7	29,951
1943-44	3,628	3.9	40,463
1944-45	2,150	1.9	18,751
1945-46	2,471	3.0	27,924
1946-47	2,600	2.6	27,440
1947-48	1,864	2.2	13,787
1948-49	1,661	2.2	16,089
1949-50	933	2.2	9,284
1950-51	1,004	2.0	5,040
1951-52	5,085	2.1	4,330
1954-55	405	1.0	1,174
1955-56	343	2.2	2,363
1956-57	329	2.4	1,507
1957-58	254	2.2	601
1958-59	209	1.2	182
1959-60	259	1.8	905
1960-61	185	1.4	741
1961-62	153	1.8	1,172

Illinois. Until a thorough analysis of *Mephitis mephitis* in eastern and central United States has been made, I refer all Illinois specimens to *M. m. avia*.

Mephitis mephitis avia Bangs

1898. *Mephitis avia* Bangs, Proc. Biol. Soc. Wash., 12:32. Type from San Jose, Mason Co., Illinois.

1936. *Mephitis mephitis avia*, Hall, Carnegie Inst. Wash. Publ., 473:65.

Range. Throughout the state although some areas are without records (Map 8.60).

Diagnosis and Comparisons. A subspecies of *Mephitis mephitis* of large size, at least when compared with *M. m. nigra,* from which it differs in average larger size in all external measurements; skull larger, especially across the zygomatic arches.

Records of occurrence. SPECIMENS EXAMINED, 61.
Jo Daviess Co.: [1] Galena, 1 (FM); [2] Savanna Ordinance Depot, 1 (UI). **Winnebago Co.:** [4] Rockford, 5 (UI). **McHenry Co.:** [5] Huntley, 1 (CAS). **Lake Co.:** [6] Camp Logan, 1 (FM); [7] Waukegan, 1 (CAS); [8] Highland Park, 1 (FM). **De Kalb Co.:** [9] 2 mi S De Kalb, 1 (NIU). **Kane Co.:** [10] near St. Charles, 1 (ISM); [11] Jct. US alt. 30 and Ill. 31, 1 (NIU). **Cook Co.:** [12a] Oak Park, 3 (US); [12b] Chicago, 7 (US); 1 (FM); [13] Chicago Heights, 1 (FM). **Du Page Co.:** [14a] Hinsdale, 3 (FM); [14b]

Downers Grove, 1 (FM). **Henry Co.:** [15] Atkinson, 1 (NIU). **Fulton Co.:** [16] 6 mi N Marietta, 1 (UI); [17] 3 mi SW Bryant, 1 (UI); [18a] 2 mi SE Ipava, 1 (UI); [18b] 4 mi S Ipava, 1 (UI). **McLean Co.:** [19] 10 mi E Normal, 1 (ISU); [20] 5 mi W Bloomington, 1 (ISU). **Ford Co.:** [21] 1 mi S Paxton, 1 (UI). **Piatt Co.:** [22] Allerton Park, [near] Monticello, 1 (UI). **Champaign Co.:** [23a] Bondville, 1 (UI); [23b] Champaign, 1 (UI); [24] 2½ mi W Tolono, 1 (UI); [25] 3 mi E Pesotum, 2 (UI). **Vermilion Co.:** [26] 1 mi W Sidell, 1 (UI); Crystal Springs [location?], 1 (UI). **Jasper Co.:** [27] Newton, 2 (UI). **Washington Co.:** [28] T2S, R2W, Sec. 22, 1 (SRL). **Randolph Co.:** [29] near Modo, 1 (ISM). **Jackson Co.:** [30] T7S, R3W, Sec. 15, 1 (SRL). **Union Co.:** [32a] T11S, R2W, Sec. 3, 1 (SIC); [32b] 1½ mi N Cobden, 1 (SRL). **Alexander Co.:** [33] Horseshoe Lake, 8 (UI).

Additional records. **Stephenson Co.:** [3] Freeport, (Necker and Hatfield, 1941:47). **Jackson Co.:** [31] 4 mi N Alto Pass, Rt 127 [labelled Union Co.], 1 (FS).

Lutra, Otters

Diagnosis. Mustelids specialized for aquatic life with toes webbed, ears small and capable of being closed; tail thick at base and tapering to tip; fur a brown color, short but thick; skull flattened, braincase broad, interorbital breadth less than width of muzzle; auditory bullae not inflated; coronoid process of mandible directed dorsad or slightly anterodorsad.

Dental formula. 3/3, 1/1, 4/3, 1/2.

Comparisons. Otters, *Lutra,* differ from other non-oceanic American mustelids in having the toes webbed as far as the terminal phalanx of each digit and the tail thickened at the base and tapering to the tip.

Lutra canadensis, River otter

Range. Formerly along and in major waterways and their tributaries in Illinois; now greatly restricted and only infrequently encountered (Map 8.61).

Diagnosis. A species of *Lutra* with the characters given for the genus; additional characters include color of venter only slightly lighter than dorsum, soles of feet with tufts of hair under the toes, four abdominal mammary glands; weight usually around 20 lbs.

Color. Dorsum dark, being a dark reddish brown with a slight ochraceous frosting, underfur lighter; venter slightly lighter, with underfur much lighter-colored than on dorsum; tail and feet about same color as back; sides of head on cheeks and below ears lighter, almost tan.

Chromosomes. Diploid number 38; FN = 62 (Wurster-Hill, 1968).

Comparisons. *Lutra canadensis* differs from all Illinois carnivores in having webbed feet, a relatively short tapered tail, thick at the base, and haired but not bushy, and a combination of cranial features including the coronoid process of mandible relatively large and directed

Fig. 8.141A. River otter, *Lutra canadensis*. From Hoffmeister and Mohr, 1957. Photograph from New York Zoological Society.

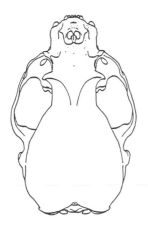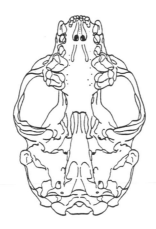

Fig. 8.141B. *Lutra canadensis*, dorsal and ventral views of skull; 2 mi S Albany, Whiteside Co., Illinois, 48112 UI. Female, 108.5 mm greatest length.

dorsad, a broad braincase that is narrow interorbitally (in contrast with *Taxidea*), postorbital processes relatively well developed.

Secondary sexual variation. Evidence from our limited sample from Illinois shows that males are larger than females; the sexes should be compared separately.

Aging. Friley (1949) used a combination of features of the baculum in males from Michigan to place them in age categories. For example, in mature animals, the length times the weight of the baculum gave a value of 400 or more, and usually it was near 500; in immatures it was 399 or less, and usually around 200. Volume of the baculum was also used by Friley as an important feature in some of his values.

Remarks. It is difficult to know how common or abundant river otter were in Illinois. As early as the mid 1800's they were not common, according to Thomas' (1861:655) observation: "Frequently caught in southern Illinois in the last eight years though now becoming much scarcer."

Apparently there was an open season on river otters in Illinois until about 1928–1929 after which they were completely protected.

Reports of River Otter from 1900–1950

1907–1908: Reportedly some remain in southern Illinois. They are taken in cypress swamps in Alexander County.

Early 1900's: In *Outdoors in Illinois* for 1950, there is a letter to the editor with a picture "of the last otter seen in Southern Illinois, about 50 years ago." This picture may be of an otter that was reported to have been taken in "Flat Boat Bend on the Kaskaskia River."

1926: One along Illinois River near Meredosia.

1934: Two taken in the Mississippi River across from Calhoun County.

1939: One taken in net in Little Wabash River, Wayne County. One seen at Big Lake, 2 mi NE Shawneetown, Gallatin County. Some are reportedly still present in Union and Alexander counties.

1940: Supposedly 20 are present in Shawnee National Forest area.

Reports of River Otter since 1970

On November 22, 1972, a female river otter was killed by an automobile on highway No. 84, 2 mi S Albany, one block east of the Mississippi River by the pumping station, Whiteside County.

On March 28, 1976, Drs. L. Scott Ellis and William Severinghaus observed what they regarded as a river otter 3½ mi E, 3½ mi N Havana, Mason County, at a place where Illinois highway 567 crosses Quiver Creek, south of Lake Chautauqua. It was in a swampy area with the water estimated to be less than three feet deep.

A survey by mail of 293 commercial fishermen and 40 Division of Fisheries employees for the year 1977 tallied seven sightings of river otter (Hubert, 1978). Judging from Hubert's map, these were along the Mississippi and Illinois rivers, or major tributaries in the following counties: Carroll (two records), Whiteside, Mercer, Cass, St. Clair, and Randolph.

In 1978, a large river otter was caught in the Illinois River near Spring Valley, Bureau County, in a hoop net (Hubert, 1979b).

Just prior to March 26, 1981, a river otter was caught in a trammel net in the Mississippi River, near the Illinois shore, less than one mile upstream from Lock and Dam 19, Hancock County (letter from John Warnock).

Early November 1982, a male river otter was killed on the truck bypass, west side of the Illinois River at Peoria, Peoria County.

In October 1982, Anderson and Woolf (1987:108) reported that "several otters were using the study area" north of Fulton, Whiteside County. A family group, consisting of at least three individuals, may have been present. Three otters were known to be present in this area until the spring of 1983.

Prior to November 23, 1982, a river otter was found dead on Illinois highway No. 8 where it crosses Bay Creek, Pope County (personal memorandum).

On February 8, 1983, a male river otter was found along Illinois highway 37, 3 mi S La Clede near Dismal Creek, Fayette County (personal memorandum).

Status of the River Otter in Wisconsin

Jackson (1961:383) writes that the river otter in Wisconsin "has continued in varying abundance and distribution . . . since the days of early settlement when it was found throughout the state in favorable habitats. In later years in many counties in the southern part of the state where it was supposed to have been extirpated, a few may have existed, unknown on account of their secretive habits." Jackson stated further (1961:384) that by the time of its legal protection in 1915, the river otter was becoming increasingly uncommon in northern Wisconsin. After the protection, Jackson thought that it increased in numbers and "an occasional otter may be expected in any county, even in the southeastern ones. . . ."

Status of the River Otter in Missouri

Schwartz and Schwartz (1981) related that in 1935 the population of river otters in Missouri was estimated at 70, and they are still rare at the present time. Some live in the Mississippi River Lowland, particularly along the St. Francis River drainage system. Choromanski and Fritzell (1982) reported that otters have increased since 1975 and the total number in 1982 is in excess of 70.

Habitat

River otters require large rivers or lakes for their habitat. They use these waterways as a place to hunt for food, take refuge from danger, to frolic, and as a route of travel. Banks are used as slides and they are used sufficiently often to make a groove in the bank for sliding into the water.

In the delta area of the Mississippi River in Mississippi, Yeager (1938) thought river otters denned in the hollow bases of cypress trees or tupelo gums. Some used hollow logs and a few used bank dens. Yeager also thought that the ideal habitat here was a deep-water swamp adjacent to a large, log-filled, fish-producing lake, which supplied additional food and abundant water for swimming or play.

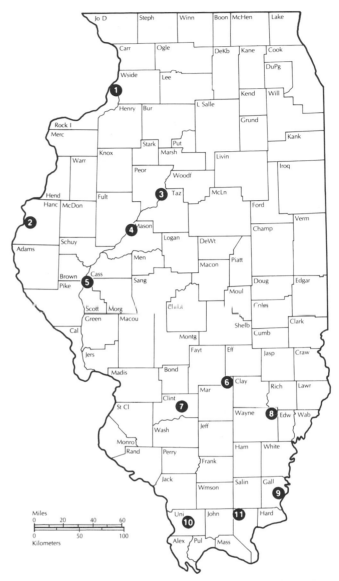

Map 8.61. Known records of the recent occurrence of the river otter, *Lutra canadensis*, as numbered, are referenced in *Records of occurrence*. The subspecies is *L. c. canadensis*. The range of the species in the United States is shaded.

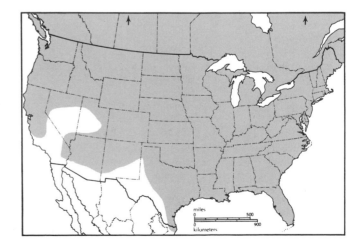

Table 8.43. Measurements (in mm) of male mustelids in Illinois. Mean, minimum-maximum, and one standard deviation are given. Measurements are as taken by E. R. Hall (1951:417 and 1981:1135). Superscripts indicate sample less than N.

Species and locality	N	Total length	Tail length	Head-body length	Hind foot length	Condylo-basal length	Zygo-matic breadth	Mastoidal breadth	Inter-orbital breadth
Mustela nivalis	11	202.2	34.1	168.1	23.3	32.72[9]	16.96[5]	15.65[7]	6.92[7]
Champaign and		180-225	28-43	152-182	20-26	30.7-35.5	16.2-17.6	14.7-16.7	6.4-7.55
McLean cos.		14.06	4.39	10.72	1.42	1.60	0.62	0.66	0.46
Mustela frenata	5	332.3	103.0	229.2	42.2	46.09	24.64	21.58	9.87
Central Illinois		306-373	81-117	184-256	38-47	43.3-48.5	22.55-28.0	19.95-23.3	8.55-10.5
		29.53	15.94	26.92	4.09	1.88	2.03	1.21	0.76
Mustela vison	8	—	—	—	—	68.10	38.32	33.58	15.89
Winnebago Co.						63.4-74.0	35.9-41.35	31.0-37.75	14.8-17.8
						3.82	2.12	2.30	1.07
Central Illinois	*	630	225	405	66	67.96[7]	39.84[7]	34.34[7]	15.36[7]
		632	213	419	73	65.0-71.7	37.65-41.6	33.25-35.3	14.4-16.4
		—	—	380	65	2.67	1.33	0.93	0.82
Taxidea taxus									
Champaign and		732	110	622	103	125.5	83.9	75.6	29.7
Montgomery cos.	*	748	135	613	93	128.4	85.5	74.7	27.6
Mephitis mephitis	*	650	260	390	70	75.94[8]	48.86[8]	40.86[8]	21.54[8]
Northern Illinois		630	210	420	70	70.45-78	46.1-52.65	36.2-43.95	20.0-22.85
		670	270	400	78	3.04	2.37	2.30	1.00
Lutra canadensis									
Peoria Co.	*	1,120	396	724	144	112.7	—	—	24.25

* Individual measurement for three or fewer specimens unless otherwise indicated. ** Measured from sagittal crest to anterior base of bullae.

Table 8.44. Measurements (in mm) of female mustelids in Illinois. Mean, minimum-maximum, and one standard deviation are given. Measurements are as taken by E. R. Hall (1951:417 and 1981:1135). Superscripts indicate sample less than N.

Species and locality	N	Total length	Tail length	Head-body length	Hind foot length	Condylo-basal length	Zygo-matic breadth	Mastoidal breadth	Inter-orbital breadth
Mustela nivalis	*	175	27	148	21	31.2	15.0	14.5	5.9
Champaign Co.		193	30	163	20	31.0	15.9	14.7	6.35
		187	25	162	20	32.05	16.25	15.2	6.2
Mustela frenata									
Fulton Co.	*	—	—	—	32	38.8	19.8	18.4	8.15
Lee Co.		301	64	237	36	41.85	21.3	18.75	8.25
Vermilion Co.		—	—	—	—	39.55	20.2	18.1	8.0
Mustela vison	4	—	—	—	—	59.78	32.90	28.39	13.10
Winnebago Co.						58.5-60.75	31.7-33.6	27.2-29.0	12.65-13.5
						1.00	0.88	0.81	0.39
Central Illinois	*	537	175	362	60	58.79[8]	33.58[8]	28.93[8]	13.21[8]
		563	160	403	40	54.8-62.95	30.85-35.65	26.9-30.65	12.45-14.4
		515	173	342	54	2.64	1.60	1.45	0.58
Taxidea taxus	8	760.0	130.1	629.9	104.5	125.39	81.01	75.98	27.72
No. Illinois		670-902	100-160	555-777	76-125	120.3-131.8	75.7-83.55	73.7-79.0	24.5-29.8
		71.66	19.61	66.28	16.63	3.96	2.39	1.69	1.55
Mephitis mephitis	4	645*	240*	405*	74*	67.69	43.26	36.20	20.08
No. Illinois						66.2-69.7	41.65-45.5	35.65-37.0	19.75-20.4
						1.48	1.66	0.71	0.30
Lutra canadensis									
Whiteside Co.	*	1,037	371	666	121	107.8	71.3	62.3	23.8

* Individual measurement for three or fewer specimens unless otherwise indicated. ** Measured from sagittal crest to anterior base of bullae.

Post-palatal length	Post-glenoid length	Greatest cranium height	Upper toothrow length	Maxillary toothrow length
17.10[8]	16.19[7]	13.10[7]	10.11[7]	8.48[7]
16.0-18.35	15.45-17.4	11.6-14.0	9.6-11.4	8.0-9.2
0.71	0.67	0.78	0.62	0.40
23.16	21.34	17.93	15.94	13.41
21.7-24.1	21.1-21.7	17.4-18.7	15.45-16.3	12.85-14.0
0.91	0.26	0.53	0.41	0.51
32.64		24.20**		20.37
30.4-35.6		23.3-24.95		18.65-22.25
1.77		0.56		1.16
32.11[7]		24.74**[7]		20.37[7]
30.75-34.3		24.0-25.55		19.65-21.4
1.50		0.60		0.57
52.0	40.1	60.5	48.8	39.8
56.85	42.7	56.5	52.4	42.2
38.34[8]		25.43**[8]		22.12[8]
36.0-40.85		24.05-26.0		21.4-22.95
1.93		0.61		0.57
48.8	43.7	—	42.6	37.1

Post-palatal length	Post-glenoid length	Greatest cranium height	Upper toothrow length	Maxillary toothrow length
16.85	16.85	12.6	9.6	7.65
16.8	16.8	12.9	9.5	8.0
17.5	17.5	11.7	9.8	8.4
19.7	19.0	15.2	13.2	11.4
20.85	19.6	15.7	14.0	11.7
20.25	19.05	14.7	13.1	10.9
29.11		21.08**		17.63
28.6-29.55		20.25-21.8		17.2-18.1
0.39		0.66		0.44
28.81[8]		21.46[8]**		17.78[8]
26.8-31.4		20.3-22.35		16.9-18.65
1.46		0.77		0.71
51.70	40.84	58.08	51.24	40.93
48.9-55.5	39.3-44.1	52.8-63.5	48.8-53.2	39.0-41.9
2.20	1.63	2.83	1.67	1.06
34.11		24.03**		20.90
32.8-35.65		23.6-24.3		20.5-21.65
1.18		0.30		0.53
49.2	41.5	42.4	41.4	35.8

Habits

Otters may be active during parts of the day as well as at night. They are excellent swimmers and divers and move more gracefully in water than on land, where they travel by humping their back at each bound.

Food

Food habits of river otters in Illinois have not been studied. There is a report that a pair of otters were watched in southern Illinois as they stalked and hauled out of the water a 38-pound catfish that was still alive when a farmer drove the otters away (*Outdoors in Illinois*, vol. XVI, no. 3, p. 20). They usually feed on a variety of fishes, muskrats, aquatic birds, turtles, frogs, clams, and even aquatic insects.

Reproduction

Young river otters are born in February or March in the Mississippi Valley area of Mississippi. The gestation period is long, about nine months, because of delayed implantation of the blastocyst. Litter size may vary from one to six young.

A den of a male and female with two young of what Yeager (1938) thought was a family group was located in the base of a large, hollow cypress in Mississippi. A hole just above the water level served as the entrance. There was no compact nest but just a few sticks, leaves, and bits of wood.

Variation

At an earlier time, all river otters in Illinois were referred to the subspecies *L. c. canadensis* (type locality Canada, probably Quebec). Van Zyll de Jong (1972) has subsequently reviewed the river otters, and he regards all specimens from central and eastern United States south of the Great Lakes as referable to *L. c. lataxina*. I follow this arrangement.

Lutra canadensis lataxina Cuvier

1823. *Lutra lataxina* F. Cuvier, *in* Dict. de Sci. Nat. . . . , 27:242. Type locality, South Carolina.
1898. *Lutra canadensis lataxina*, J. A. Allen, Bull. Amer. Mus. Nat. Hist., 10:460.

Range. As given for the species (p. 305 and Map 8.61).
Diagnosis and Comparisons. A subspecies of *Lutra canadensis* that is "somewhat larger and lighter in colour than *L. c. canadensis*. Basal length of skull averages greater than 100 mm in males, somewhat less in females; bullae relatively inflated . . ." (Van Zyll de Jong, 1972:85).

Records of occurrence. SPECIMENS EXAMINED, 2. **Whiteside Co.:** [1] 2 mi S Albany on Rt 84, Mississippi R., 1 (UI). **Peoria Co.:** [3] Peoria, 1 (UI).

Additional records. **Hancock Co.:** [2] near Lock and Dam 19, Mississippi R., 1 (WIU), Warnock, 1981, in litt.). **Mason Co.:** [4] 3½ mi E, 3½ mi N Havana (Hwy 567 at Quiver Cr.), [sight record, Severinghaus]. **Morgan Co.:** [5] [near] Meredosia, (Leopold, unpublished manuscript, 1929). **Fayette Co.:** [6] along Rt. 37, 3 mi S La Clede, near Dismal Creek, 1 (DOC), dead on road, found 2/8/83 by Highway Dept. **Clinton Co.:** [7] near Carlyle, Flat Boat Bend, Kaskaskia R., (*Outdoors in Illinois,* 1950). **Wayne Co.:** [8] Little Wabash River, [caught in fish net by H. Griggs]. **Gallatin Co.:** [9] Big Lake, 2 mi NE Shawneetown [=Old Shawneetown], [sight record, Wm. E. Bates]. **Union Co.:** [10] no specific locality, (Leopold, unpublished manuscript, 1929). **Pope Co.:** [11] Rd. 8 near crossing of Bay Cr., Sec. 26, T11S, R5E, on highway, 11/19/82, found by U.S. Forest Service, Biol. M. Spaniel.

Family Felidae, Cats

Carnivores of medium to large size; most species with long, flexible tails (except for bobcats and relatives), short faces, retractile claws (less so in cheetahs); specialized teeth for seizing and cutting, number of premolars-molars reduced, with a maximum of 3-1 above, 2-1 below, often less; carnassials large; auditory bullae inflated. Some workers regard bobcats as members of the genus *Felis;* others, genus *Lynx.* As pointed out under *Remarks* for the bobcat, lynxes and bobcat are placed in the genus *Felis.*

Fig. 8.142A. Bobcat, *Felis rufus.* (From Hoffmeister and Mohr, 1957. Photographs from Illinois Dept. of Conservation)

Felis, Lions, lynxes, et al.

Diagnosis. Much as given above for the family Felidae. See under the species accounts for other information.

Felis rufus, Bobcat

Range. At one time, probably widespread in state; now nearly extirpated and most likely to be encountered in southern third of state.

Diagnosis. A member of the subgenus *Lynx* of the genus *Felis;* tail short, being only about 18 to 22 percent of head-body length, and appearing even shorter; upper premolars two on each side resulting in only three teeth behind upper canine with the third one (first molar) small; ears prominent and with small, black tufts of hair at tips; hair on side of face elongate; underparts whitish with black spots, dorsum brownish gray, but variable, and frequently with dark spots; top of tail black at tip; skull with auditory bullae well inflated; adults may weigh up to 30 pounds, but usually less.

Color. Dorsum mottled with grays, browns, and light tans, and usually darkest along midline; venter with the hair noticeably longer, whitish, or tan, and with conspicuous black spots that extend out onto the legs; back of ears essentially same color as back but with a terminal black patch from which a few hairs protrude to produce small, black tufts; top of tail same color as back, underside of tail whitish, tip of tail on top black and black may extend almost all around.

Chromosomes. 2N = 38, with 32 metacentrics, submetacentrics, or subtelocentrics, four acrocentrics; X and Y submetacentrics (Hsu and Benirschke, 1970a).

Dental formula. 3/3, 1/1, 2/2, 1/1.

Comparisons. Felis (Lynx) rufus is readily distinguished from the mountain lion or puma, *Felis concolor,* by its smaller size, shorter tail, only two upper premolars, and elongated hairs on sides of face.

Felis rufus differs from the Canada lynx, *Felis canadensis,* in having its ear tufts shorter, tip of tail with prominent black area above but not below, tail shorter, hind foot shorter with half of length of hind foot less than tail length; anterior condyloid foramen confluent with foramen lacerum posterius (located between bulla and foramen magnum) rather than separate (Fig. 8.142B).

Felis rufus differs from the domestic house cat in shorter tail, slightly tufted ears, longer hair on sides of face, black spots on light-colored belly, top of tail black at tip, only three rather than four upper premolars-molars, among other features.

Felis rufus differs from other Illinois carnivores by the characters given for the Felidae.

Secondary sexual variation. In 12 of the 14 cranial measurements examined for skulls from Arizona, Hoffmeister (1986) found that males average larger than

females, but the sample is small — eight males, six females. In only four of the measurements are males significantly larger as determined by Student's t-test, and these at the 0.02 level: zygomatic breadth, interorbital breadth, greatest length of nasal, and width of nasals.

Aging. Specimens are compared in the analyses if the basioccipital-basisphenoid suture is closed and obliterated, or nearly so, and if the exoccipital-squamosal suture is closed but not necessarily obliterated, and the sagittal crest is well developed.

Remarks. These felids go by a variety of names: bobcats, wildcats, lynx cats. Mammalogists prefer the name bobcat. Even the scientific name differs with various workers. Most of the literature will refer to the animals under the name *Lynx rufus.*

Although bobcats apparently were never abundant in Illinois, their numbers were reduced by the removal of timber from some of their preferred habitats, because of persecution as a predator, and by an open season for hunting them. Bobcats were decimated first in the northern and central parts of the state. In the early 1900's,

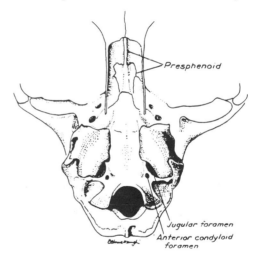

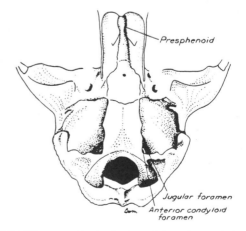

Fig. 8.142B. Differences in the basicranial portions of the skulls of bobcat, *Felis rufus,* above, and lynx, *Felis canadensis,* below. Note the shape and position of the presphenoid and anterior condyloid foramen. (From Jackson, *Mammals of Wisconsin,* 1961)

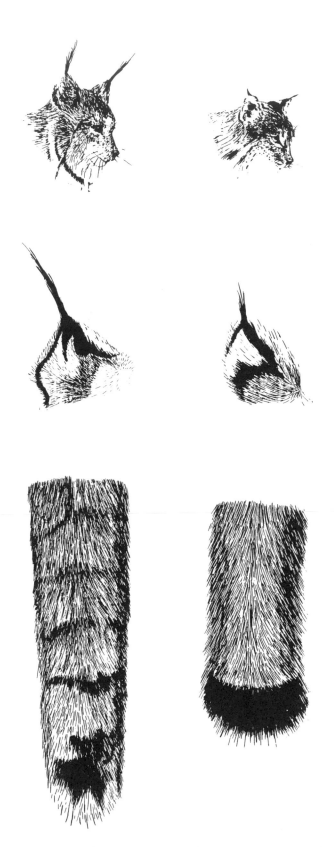

Fig. 8.143. Differences in external features between lynx, *Felis canadensis* (left), and bobcat, *Felis rufus* (right). Upper views contrast profiles of the face; middle contrast ear tufts and color patterns; lower contrast top views of the tail. (From Jackson, *Mammals of Wisconsin*, 1961)

they were still present in several counties bordering the Ohio and Mississippi rivers, and lower parts of the Illinois River. By the mid 1900's or before, the bobcat was nearly extirpated from the state. As shown in the records of occurrence, five records, of which some are sight only, are known since 1970.

By contrast, in Missouri for the late 1970's "a minimum statewide population of 4,200 bobcats is estimated. The population probably does not exceed 10,000 animals" (Erickson et al., 1981:59). These estimates seem high to me. Some of the large populations for Missouri occur along the Mississippi River and from there some individuals should be able to enter Illinois. In Indiana, Mumford and Whitaker (1982) suggested that the species may still persist in the state. They have records thought to be authentic for two bobcats in the 1970's and about five in the 1950's. In Wisconsin, bobcats were found chiefly in the northern two tiers of counties in the 1950's when Jackson (1961) prepared his manuscript for the state. He stated that peaks in abundance occurred in Wisconsin from 1936 to 1938, and in 1946 and 1947.

Some authors regard the bobcats and lynxes as members of the genus *Lynx;* others, the genus *Felis*. Simpson (1945) regarded the lynxes as belonging to a subgenus of *Felis*. Most European workers since the early 1950's have considered the European lynx as of the genus *Felis,* and Kurten and Rausch (1950) have presented evidence that the New World forms should be referred to the same genus as the Old World lynxes. The differences between *Felis* and *Lynx* are relatively minor, especially when the range of variation within each genus is considered. *Felis* has three upper premolars; *Lynx* has two. The tail is short in lynxes but not especially so in caracals, which most authors refer to the genus *Lynx*. These are the major differences between the two groups. Probably the differences between jaguars (*Felis onca*) and pumas (*Felis concolor*) are far greater than those between *Felis* and *Lynx*. Some authors will continue to refer bobcats and lynxes to the genus *Lynx,* possibly because of historical inertia. In this report they are placed in the subgenus *Lynx* of *Felis*.

Habitat

Bobcats prefer the wooded or timbered bluffs, rolling hills that are interspersed with open fields, brushy ravines, or open bottomlands. We know of bobcats seen or taken in swampy lands near Miller City, in the wooded bottomlands along the Little Muddy River, and in a strip-mined area between Pinkneyville and DuQuoin.

Brown and Yeager (1943) point out that the extensive logging of cypress swamps in the southern tip of the state probably destroyed the last good bobcat range.

Habits

Bobcats are usually nocturnal, but in places where they are common it is not unusual to encounter one in the woods during the daytime. Because of their stealth, they will have to be seen, for in all likelihood they will not be heard. They are deliberate, intent stalkers that will not hesitate to remain motionless for long periods of time.

Bobcats have many of the same habits as domestic cats. They are good climbers, quiet hunters, make use of odor posts along routes of travel, and walk and run much like a house cat. They give a variety of calls consisting of snarls, howls, screams, and wails. These may be of such volume that they are attributed to a much larger animal.

Food

Bobcats are known to prey on cottontails, squirrels, mice, and various kinds of birds, including domestic poultry. If necessary, they probably eat other things, such as carrion and invertebrates. Bobcats hunt much the same as do domestic cats, but rarely out in the open.

Reproduction

Mating occurs from February through April, the gestation period is about 62 days, and the newborn are furred. There usually are two or three young per litter. Kittens are spotted. Eyes open at about 1½ weeks; young are weaned at 8 to 10 weeks, at which time the weanlings can effectively hunt for themselves.

Variation

Bobcats in Illinois are referable to the nominate subspecies *F. r. rufus*.

Felis rufus rufus Schreber

1777. *Felis rufa* Schreber, Die Saugthiere . . . 3(95):pl. 109b. Type locality, New York.

Range. As given for the species (p. 311 and Map 8.62).
Diagnosis and Comparisons. A large sized, fairly dark-colored subspecies.

Records of occurrence. SPECIMENS EXAMINED, 1. **Grundy Co.:** [3] 1 mi W Morris [1973], 1 (UI).
Additional records. **Whiteside Co.:** [1] Sterling [1950] one killed, (Rockford Morning Star 2/2/50). **Rock Island Co.:** [2] near Rock Island [no date], 1 (NW) (reported in Cory, 1912:293). **Bond Co.:** [4] near Greenville [no date], 1 killed (Klimstra and Roseberry, 1969). **Clay Co.:** [5] Little Wabash River, near Clay City [1946] one killed, (Olney Daily Mail 12/6/46). **Lawrence Co.:** [6] 5 mi N Lawrenceville [1954, 1956] (sight records L. Tate in Klimstra and Roseberry, 1969). **Jackson Co.:** [7] near Murphysboro [1942–1943], 4 individuals (?) killed. **Williamson Co.:** [8] E boundary Crab Orchard National Wildlife Refuge [1982], 1 (DOC Report), road kill. **Union Co.:** [9] 1 mi N Wolf Lake [1982], 1 (DOC Report, road kill. Pelt to DOC collection, skeleton to SIC collection); [10] Ware [date?], (Mohr, 1943:527); no specific locality [date?, not plotted] (Mohr, 1943:527). **Pope Co.:** [11] near Golconda [1907], (J. C. Baker informed Cory (1912:293) of 2 killed).

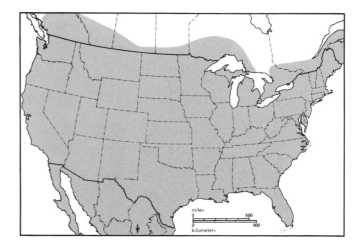

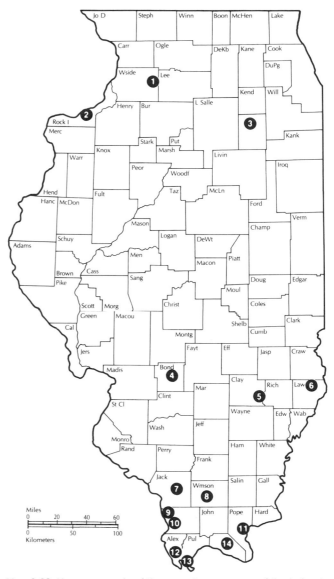

Map 8.62. Known records of the recent occurrence of the bobcat, *Felis rufus*, as numbered, are referenced in *Records of occurrence*. The subspecies is *F. r. rufus*. The range of the species in the United States is shaded.

Order Artiodactyla, Even-toed Ungulates

Hoofed mammals in which the main axis of support is borne between third and fourth toes; usually only two toes in contact with substrate; femur without 3rd trochanter; astragulus with pulleylike surface on two sides; some with no head ornamentation (family Tayassuidae), others with antlers (Cervidae), horns (Bovidae), or pronged horns (Antilocapridae).

Family Cervidae, Deer, wapiti (elk), and relatives

Artiodactyls having antlers that are shed and replaced annually; antlers branched in most species and absent in females; stomach four-chambered, upper canines absent or small (one pair in *Cervus*).

Odocoileus, American deer

Diagnosis. A cervid with beamed, not palmate, antlers; tail conspicuous; tarsal and metatarsal glands usually present; young spotted; upper canines usually absent.

Dental formula. 0/3, 0/0, 3/3, 3/3.

Comparisons. Odocoileus differs from *Cervus* in being of smaller size, having antlers without a brow tine (a branch or tine extending over forehead); absence of upper canine, posterior narial cavity completely divided by vomer; without a large tan-colored rump patch.

Odocoileus virginianus, White-tailed deer

Range. Throughout the state; see *Remarks* (p. 316).

Diagnosis. A species of *Odocoileus* with a relatively broad tail that is white on the underside; dorsum of tail grayish or brownish gray and bordered with white; antlers with one main beam from which tines rise vertically; lacrimal fossa shallow; metatarsal gland short, less than 25 mm.

Color. Somewhat variable with the season and stage of molt, but in general: dorsum grayish or brownish gray, sides tan or light ochraceous, venter whitish, legs nearly same color as sides, insides of ears whitish with backs almost same color as dorsum.

Chromosomes. 2N = 70, with two submetacentrics, 66 acrocentrics; X a submetacentric, Y a metacentric (Hsu and Benirschke, 1967c).

Comparisons. The white-tailed deer is the only native species of deer in Illinois. Mule deer, *Odocoileus hemionus,* have never been closer to Illinois than south central Iowa, and the species is rare or absent in Iowa today. Mule deer differ in having the top of the tail tipped with black and antlers that branch and then branch again (dichotomously); metatarsal gland large (more than 25 mm).

Molt. For white-tailed deer, the spring molt occurs in May and June, the fall molt from around the end of August to mid-October. The summer (red) coat is short, thin, and somewhat wiry and is reddish tan or yellowish brown in color. The relatively longer and thicker winter (blue) coat is a grizzled brown, with a slightly darker streak down the center of the back.

Weight. Weights for different age classes of 451 males and 558 females from southern Illinois were reported by Roseberry and Klimstra (1975). The weight of the males before being dressed averaged as follows: 6 months, 72.5 lb, 32.9 kg; 1½ years, 121 lbs, 54.9 kg; 2½ years, 157.5 lb, 71.4 kg; 3½ years, 173.3 lb, 78.6 kg; 4½ years, 193.4 lb, 87.7 kg; 5½ years or more, 191.8 lb, 87 kg.

The weight of the females before being dressed averaged: 6 months, 65 lb, 29.5 kg; 1½ years, 100.8 lb, 45.7 kg; 2½ years, 110.9 lb, 50.3 kg; 3½ years, 116 lb, 52.6 kg; 4½ years, 120.6 lb, 54.7 kg; 5½ years, 122.8 lb, 55.7 kg.

Antlers. Antlers tend to increase in size and number of points with increasing age, up to a certain period depending on several factors including the physiological condition of the buck. The counting of points is based upon the complete antler set and represents all protuberances other than the brow tines.

In southern Illinois, Roseberry and Klimstra (1975) found that in 1½-year-old bucks, the number of points was 3.7 (2–7) with a standard deviation of ± 1.4; in 2½-year-olds, 6.7 (3–9) ± 1.4; in 3½-year-olds, 7.5 (2–15) ± 2.6; in 4½-year-olds, 8.1 (4–10) ± 1.6; in 5½-year-olds and older, 8.6 (4–13) ± 2.6. There is extensive overlap in number of points at all ages but the differences are more noticeable below and above 2 years of age.

Aging. Various methods can be used for placing deer in age categories but the most reliable are based upon tooth eruption and wear (especially as reported upon by Severinghaus, 1949) and the count of cementum rings in the molars. All of these are based primarily on the teeth in the lower jaw. The latter technique is based on the fact that the cementum layer in the teeth in winter is added to sparingly and this results in a dark-staining zone; in the spring and summer, the cementum layer is

Fig. 8.144. White-tailed deer, *Odocoileus virginianus.* Photograph by W. W. Goodpaster.

added to more rapidly and this results in a pale-staining zone when the teeth are sectioned.

Severinghaus' (1949) study, based on tooth eruption and wear, is quite accurate for animals less than four years; less so for older animals. Briefly, aging based on lower jaws can be summarized as follows:

Fawns: Interior incisors are deciduous (milk teeth) at less than 5 months. Interior incisors replaced with permanent teeth between 5 and 6 months. Other incisors replaced by 12 months.

Second molar is erupting between 7 and 9 months.

Yearling: Third molar erupts between 12 and 16 months.

Premolars are replaced with permanent teeth at about 1½ years. If deciduous premolars are still present, they are badly worn.

At 1 year, 10 months, the lingual crest on the last molar shows no wear.

Adults: 2½-year-olds have the lingual crests of all molars very sharp, with the enamel well above the narrow, brownish dentine line; wear on posterior cusp of M_3 slight.

3½ year-olds with posterior cusp of M_3 worn flat; lingual crests on M_1 blunt; little wear on Pm_1, slight wear on Pm_2, moderate wear on Pm_3.

4½ year-olds with lingual crests of M_1 almost worn away but Pm_1 with very little wear.

5½ year-olds with lingual crests of M_{1-2} worn away; grinding surface of M_1 almost smooth; Pm_1 with some wear.

6½ year-olds with M_1 with grinding surface smooth or nearly so; Pm_1 with moderate wear.

7½ year-olds with gum rolled over M_1; M_2 cupping.

8½ to 9½ year-olds with M_3 cupping.

10½ year and older with all teeth cupping.

Fig. 8.145. Fawns are spotted. Photograph by W. W. Goodpaster.

Remarks. The history of the populations of deer in Illinois is one of extremes. In the early 1800's, deer were abundant. By the late 1800's, deer were exterminated in Illinois, or so reduced as to be absent for all practical purposes (*see also* p. 30). In the 1930's, a program of restocking whitetailed deer was undertaken. By the 1970's, every county in the state had deer and most in good numbers. In a century and a half, it has gone full circle—from many deer to none to many.

Of the early 1800's, reports indicate "Deer are more abundant than at the first settlement of the country. They increase, to a certain extent, with the population. The reason of this appears to be, that they find protection in the neighborhood of man from the beasts of prey that assail them in the wilderness. . . . They suffer most from the wolves. . . . Immense numbers of deer are killed every year by the hunters, who take them for the hams and skins alone. . . ." (Anon., 1837:38–39). Overhunting and the lack of hunting seasons and regulations, in addition to intensive changes in land use, led to the drastic reductions by the turn of the century. The last deer of the original herds were seen in the Ozark Foothills of southern Illinois about 1912 (Pietsch, 1951). Actually, restocking of deer in a small way started in the 1890's in the vicinity of Kishwaukee, near Rockford (Pietsch, 1951). Intensive restocking in many parts of the state occurred in the 1930's. Deer were slow in taking hold because of a number of factors: running by and losses

Table 8.45. Total numbers of deer killed in Illinois between 1957 and 1983. The numbers killed by hunting and road kill are listed here.

	Hunting				Hunting		
Year	Shotgun	Bow & Arrow	Road Kill	Year	Shotgun	Bow & Arrow	Road Kill
1957	1,735	220	329	1971	10,381	566	1,312
1958	2,655	158	349	1972	10,140	552	1,395
1959	2,648	79	477	1973	13,726	960	1,159
1960	2,444	109	523	1974	14,080	1,425	600
1961	4,323	158	710	1975	15,619	1,608	1,358
1962	6,289	168	748	1976	15,370	1,600	*
1963	6,735	225	678	1977	15,760	2,810	2,039
1964	7,087	370	621	1978	19,263	2,241	2.176
1965	7,612	233	1,004	1979	19,975	2,167	1,899
1966	7,367	163	1,012	1980	20,766	2,966	2,175
1967	6,613	316	1,072	1981	20,804	2,678	2,336
1968	8,215	366	1,270	1982	22,657	2,209	2,803
1969	8,370	325	1,475	1983	26,118	*	*
1970	9,104	590	1,350				

* Not known or available

to feral dogs, poaching, mowing operations, and—in the beginning—a negative reaction by the public to the presence of deer.

Once a season was established for the hunting of deer in the state and when farmers were given a freer hand to control packs of wild dogs, deer began to increase in great numbers and spread widely. By 1970, the legal kill of deer in the state was about 1,000; by 1983, about 26,000. In 1950, the estimated total number of deer in the state, not just the ones that were killed, was an estimated 2,870, according to a personal communication from Lysle Pietsch in 1951. This total number of deer is only a little more than 10 percent of the number that was harvested 33 years later.

The attitude of Illinois hunters and sportsmen with regard to problems with deer was lauded by the Wildlife Management Institute in their newsletter of July 1, 1966. This involved a deer-reduction proposal for Crab Orchard National Wildlife Refuge. The plan was to get the number of animals closer to the grazing capacity of their range.

Goals of the hunt was to reduce the deer on the 21,000-acre closed portion of the 43,000-acre waterfowl refuge in southern Illinois. The deer were increasing, the refuge officials were apprehensive that a severe winter plus reduced grain crops in the refuge fields would result in deer-damage to vegetation and perhaps a die-off of deer.

Refuge officials did not want to reduce the deer themselves, but believed that sportsmen could do the job—and would appreciate the opportunity for additional outdoor recreation—if adequate controls were established for the hunt. The two agencies selected dates for the hunt following the regular deer and goose seasons, and the Illinois Legislature authorized the 10-day season. Sportsmen who were unsuc-

cessful in the regular 6-day Illinois deer season were eligible to apply for one of the 3,000 permits.

About 8,500 applications were received, and 3,000 permits were drawn on the basis of 300 hunters for each day of the season. Unsuccessful applicants were permitted to participate on a standby basis, and could go into the field when scheduled hunters failed to appear or when a successful hunter left with his deer.

According to refuge project manager L. A. Mehroff, 1,109 deer were bagged by 3,787 hunters during the special season. Many Illinois hunters bagged their first deer on the hunt, and some of the animals were of trophy quality.

The increase in numbers of deer within the last 27 years is shown by the hunting success in Table 8.45. For example, the deer reportedly taken by conventional hunting in 1983 increased fifteenfold over 1957. By 1977, more deer were killed by car alone in Illinois than were taken by shotgun in 1957. Only 33 counties were open to deer hunting in 1957, and no deer were taken in four of these. By 1976, all counties were open in season to deer hunting. The greatest numbers of deer were harvested in Jo Daviess, Adams, and Pike counties.

Habitat

White-tailed deer in Illinois occur in wooded areas which may be along streams, around swamps, on rolling hillsides, adjacent to fields and pastures, or remnants of more extensive forests. They frequently are found foraging at considerable distances from wooded areas, but they eventually take refuge in such places. For example, at Crab Orchard Refuge where deer do well, the composition of the several thousand acres is as follows: 27 percent deciduous woods, 2 percent pine plantation, 27 percent brush and idle land, 27 percent cropland, 17 percent pasture.

Large numbers of deer are associated with the wooded parts of some of the watersheds of major rivers, especially the Mississippi, Rock, Illinois, and Kaskaskia, and the Ozark Uplift hill-country.

Habits

In Illinois, deer tend to remain together in family groups, consisting of an adult female, a yearling female offspring of the adult, and the adult's fawns, usually two in number. Since males are polygamous, they are not associated with females except at breeding times. Males may form some kind of groups in late winter and early summer, but it is not known how stable these groups are.

The adult does become secretive and seek seclusion at the start of the fawning season. This may last from May through August. Family groups will reform again at that time.

In their study of the social organization of white-tailed deer in the Crab Orchard National Wildlife Refuge,

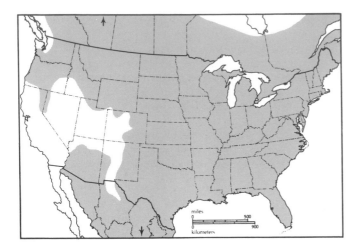

Map 8.63. The range of the white-tailed deer, *Odocoileus virginianus,* in the United States is shaded. In Illinois, it is known from every county. The subspecific status is questionable because of various introductions, but is probably *O. v. virginianus.*

Hawkins and Klimstra (1970) followed 49 family groups, each composed of from two to five marked deer, and these usually consisted of an adult doe, a yearling daughter doe, and two fawns, usually offspring of the adult. A group of three was usually a doe and her two siblings. Sometimes, more than one yearling female may be associated with the older adult.

Deer are most active at night and during the twilight hours. They may be flushed at any time, however, and may even browse during parts of some overcast days.

Food

Deer are basically browsers, that is, they nibble off the tender shoots, twigs, and leaves of trees and shrubs. Also, they are cud-chewers and usually retire to a secluded spot to re-chew the material that they have browsed on earlier. They will feed on grain crops—soybeans, corn, wheat, rye—on gardens, as well as on the leaves and shoots of all kinds of vines including honeysuckle, greenbrier, poison ivy, and grape, on the leaves of maple, sumac, ash, cherry, oak, and others; they will feed on grasses and weeds including plantain, goldenrod, lespedeza, and sweet clover, as evidenced by what Sotala and Kirkpatrick (1973) found in the rumens in 132 deer in Indiana.

In southern Illinois, Ward and Hardin (1977) examined the rumens of 173 deer taken in November and December at Crab Orchard National Wildlife Refuge. These deer were known to make extensive use of milo and corn that was left standing for winter feed for Canada geese. The rumens contained 68 percent by frequency of milo, 34 percent of corn. The volume of each of these was 33 and 11 percent, respectively. Other important food items were honeysuckle, plantago, poison ivy, and *Prunus serotina.*

Foods eaten are dependent upon the season of the year and the availability of the food.

Reproduction

Mating occurs from October through January. This may vary with climatic and social conditions, disturbances, and other factors. The peak is usually in late November. In southern Illinois, Roseberry and Klimstra (1970) found the peak to be between November 22 and 28. Fawns did not breed until 4 or 5 weeks later.

In Illinois nearly 80 percent of the females produce young. In southern Illinois, Roseberry and Klimstra (1970) found that 97 percent of the older does were pregnant, but only 41 percent of the fawns, which are only about 6 months old, were. Does in their second and succeeding years usually produce two young each year. In southern Illinois, adult females had an average of 1.93 embryos and 2.24 corpora lutea. As many as 97 percent of the corpora lutea may represent embryos since preimplantation mortality is low (Dunkeson and Murphy, 1953). Yearling females had an average of 1.76 embryos, 1.94 corpora lutea; fawns, 1.00 embryos, 1.19 corpora lutea.

The gestation period is around seven months. Most young are born in June. At birth, young are precocial and after a few hours can stand and run.

Males do not attain sexual maturity until the second breeding season after birth and are about 18 months old when they undergo their first rutting season. Males in Illinois shed their antlers usually during the period from February through March.

Variation

When Kellogg (1965) reviewed the white-tailed deer in North America, he assigned deer from north of the Ohio and east of the Mississippi river to *O. v. borealis.* The subspecies in Iowa and Missouri has been regarded as *O. v. macroura* (type locality, Kansas River, Douglas Co., Kansas) and from Kentucky as *O. v. virginianus* (type locality, Virginia).

Odocoileus virginianus borealis Miller

1900. *Odocoileus americanus borealis* Miller, Bull. New York State Mus. Nat. Hist., 8:83. Type from Bucksport, Hancock Co., Maine.
1905. [*Odocoileus virginianus*] *borealis,* Trouessart, Catal. Mamm. . . . , supp., fasc. 3:704.

Range. Throughout the state (and see Map 8.63).
Diagnosis and Comparisons. A large-sized subspecies, larger in size than *O. v. virginianus;* cheek teeth lighter than in *O. v. macrourus* (Kellogg, 1965).

Records of occurrence. SPECIMENS EXAMINED, 4. **Champaign Co.:** Champaign, 1 (UI). **Randolph Co.:** 4 mi SE Chester, 1 (UI). **Johnson Co.:** 4 mi SE Ozark, 1 (UI); 7 mi N Vienna, 1 (UI).

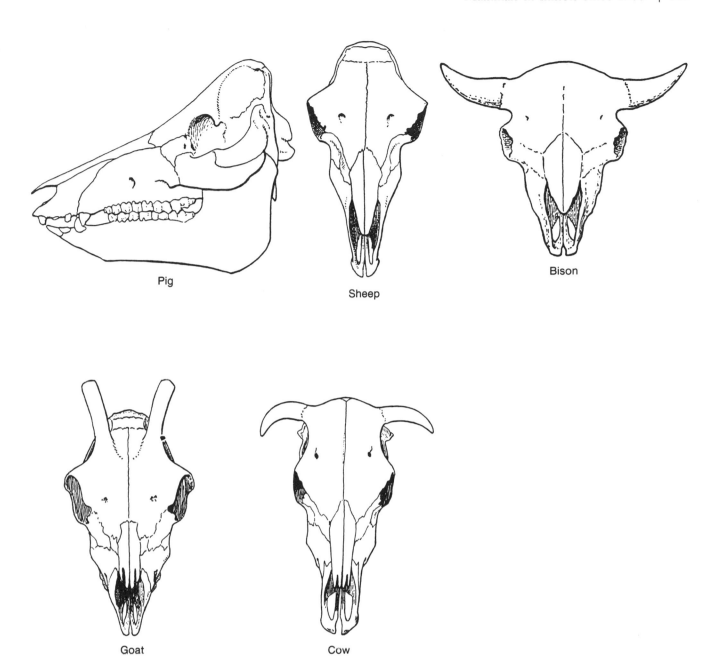

Fig. 8.146. Skulls of some domesticated and semidomesticated hooved mammals in Illinois. (From Hoffmeister and Mohr, 1957. Drawings by Carl O. Mohr)

Glossary

Some textual terms that need further clarification are briefly defined here.

acrocentric. Type of chromosome (Fig. 9.1).

albinism. Lacking pigmentation externally.

altricial. Young that are nearly helpless at birth, eyes not opened, body naked or sparsely haired.

alveolar length. Measurement taken from the alveoli or sockets of teeth.

alveolus. Socket or pit as for a tooth.

ampullary gland. An accessory male sex gland in the wall of the ducti deferentes.

angular process. Posterior projection of lower jaw (Fig. 9.2).

antorbital canal. Canal or passageway below the infraorbital plate (Fig. 9.2).

astragalus. Ankle bone.

auditory bulla. Bony capsule at base of skull enclosing bones of inner ear (Fig. 9.2).

autosomes. Those chromosomes other than the sex (X and Y) chromosomes.

B.P. (= Before Present). Abbreviation for number of years before the present time.

baculum (=os penis). Bone in penis of males of certain species of mammal.

basined. Scooped out, like a basin, as on the occlusal surface of some teeth.

biarmed chromosome. A chromosome with two arms; in contrast to an acrocentric chromosome (Fig. 9.1).

bicolumnar. Consisting of two columns, as the premolar teeth in *Geomys bursarius*.

biota. Flora and fauna of an area or region.

bisulcate. With two grooves, as upper incisors of *Geomys bursarius*.

blastocyst. Arrangement of cells produced by repeated division of fertilized egg.

bony palate. See palate (Fig. 9.2).

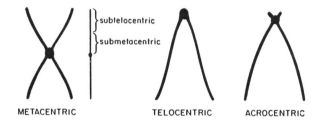

Fig. 9.1. Types of chromosomes referred to in the text. The terminology is based primarily on the position of the centromere (indicated as an enlargement). For submetacentrics and subtelocentrics, the centromere can be anywhere within the area indicated. Many workers would prefer to place all chromosomes in two categories: metacentrics and acrocentrics.

browse. Leaves and twigs of woody vegetation; often consumed by deer and relatives.

brow tine. Branch of antler often extending over the forehead.

buccal. Pertaining to cheek-side; often called labial.

buff-colored. A color that is red-yellow in hue.

calcar. Supporting structure for interfemoral membrane in bats (Fig. 9.5).

canine. Prominent tooth, one on each side of upper and lower jaws, between incisors and premolars (Fig. 9.2).

carnassial. Bladelike cheek tooth; term used for last upper premolar and first lower molar in Carnivora.

caudal. Pertaining to tail.

centromere. A distinct, short region in a chromosome to which the spindle fibers attach during metaphase (Fig. 9.1).

cervid. Any member of the family Cervidae, deer and relatives.

chromosome. Threadlike carrier of genes located in nucleus of cell (See also X chromosome, Y chromosome).

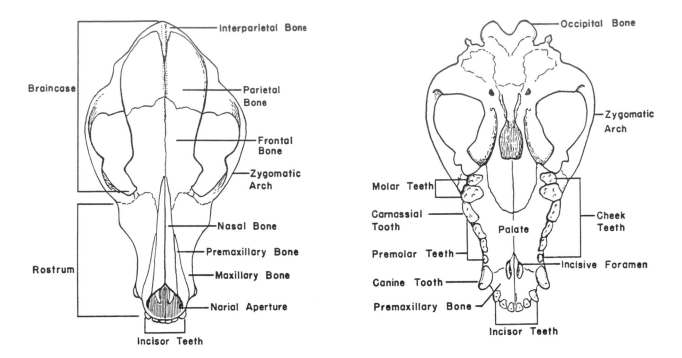

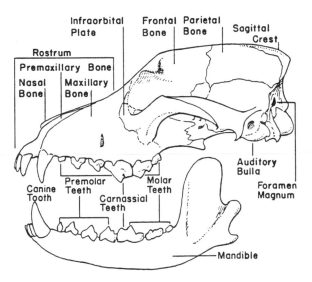

Fig. 9.2. Dorsal, ventral, and lateral views of a mammalian skull to show certain key features. (From Hoffmeister and Mohr, 1957)

cingulum. Shelf around tooth.

cm. Centimeter; 100 cm equals one meter; 2.54 cm equals one inch.

concave. Surface hollowed or curved inward.

coniferous. Pertaining to cone-bearing trees.

convex. Surface vaulted or rounded outward.

coprophagy. Feeding on dung or feces.

coronoid process. See "C" in Fig. 9.2 of lower jaw.

corpora lutea (pl.). Yellowish tissue in Graafian follicle when an ovum is discharged and fertilized.

crepuscular. Active in the twilight.

cricetine. One group of murid rodents, often called New World mice and rats (p. 251).

crown length. Greatest length of the crown (above the alveolus) of a tooth.

cuspidate tooth. A tooth with one or more distinctive cusps.

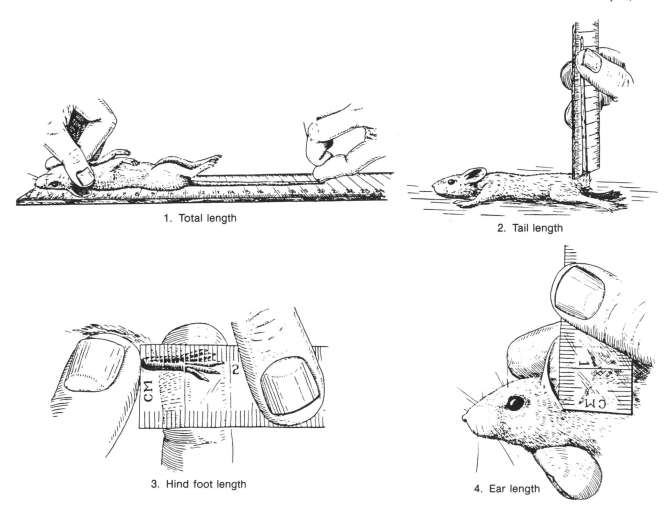

1. Total length

2. Tail length

3. Hind foot length

4. Ear length

Fig. 9.3. External measurements of mammals, frequently referred to in the text, are taken as illustrated, and recorded in millimeters.

deciduous tooth. A milk or first tooth that is replaced with a permanent tooth; applies to all teeth except molars.

dental formula. An abbreviated means of designating the teeth in the upper and lower jaws. Also, see page xv.

dentary. One half of the lower jaw; labeled as mandible in Fig. 9.2.

diastema. The gap or space in the dentition, between the incisors and the premolars or molars.

dicot. Dicotyledon: a plant having two seed leaves, in contrast to grasses, lilies.

diploid (=2N). Total number of chromosomes in a body cell.

dipteran. Pertaining to members of the order Diptera, true flies.

echolocation. Locating objects by the reflected echo. Sometimes called sonar.

ectoparasite. Parasite that occurs externally.

enamel. Hard outer covering on a tooth.

Endogone. A ground-dwelling fungus producing an odor that attracts mammals that, in turn, feed on the fungus.

entolophulid. Fig. 8.88 (p. 208).

epiphysis. Terminal portion of a long bone.

estrus. Mating period of female, marked by intensified sexual urge.

external measurements. Total, tail, hind foot, and ear measured as shown in Fig. 9.3.

extirpated. Completely removed; eradicated.

FN (=fundamental number). The number of biarmed (=2) and acrocentric (=1) elements or autosomal arms of the chromosomes in the diploid set, but not including the sex chromosomes.

falciform. Having the shape of a sickle or scythe.

fenestrated. Having numerous openings, as in the skull of a cottontail.

foramen. An opening in a bone through which blood vessels, nerves, or both pass.

fossorial. Adapted for digging.

gastropod. A univalve mollusk; includes snails, slugs, abalones.

genus. A group of animals consisting of one or more species that are morphologically, ecologically, or genetically (or a combination) separated from other groups.

geomyid. Any rodent with the characteristics of the family Geomyidae (p. 185).

gestation period. The time period of carrying embryos, normally in the uterus from conception to delivery; period of pregnancy.

grizzled. Streaked with gray; resulting in a "grizzled" appearance.

hard palate. Portion of palate supported by bone (Fig. 9.2).

hectare. A metric measure of land equivalent to 2.47 acres.

hibernaculum. Cavity, burrow, cave, or equivalent in which an animal hibernates.

hibernation. Winter torpidity in an animal, when metabolic activities are greatly reduced.

high-crowned tooth. Any cheek tooth that rises noticeably above the gum.

hispid. Referring to pelage; rough, with bristles or stiff hair.

Holocene. Pertaining to the Recent epoch and the time span associated with early man after the Pleistocene.

hypocone. Cusp in upper cheek tooth (Fig. 9.4).

hystricomorph. A major group of rodents with unique masseter muscle arrangement (Fig. 8.53, p. 147).

imbricated. Overlapping, as shingles on a roof.

incisive foramen. Palatine slit (Fig. 9.2).

incisors. Anteriormost teeth (Fig. 9.2).

infraorbital foramen. Small opening on side of rostrum of skull; dark area above third premolar in Fig. 9.2.

infraorbital plate. Anterior part of zygomatic arch (Fig. 9.2).

ingression. Act of entering.

inguinal. Region of the groin.

insectivore. A mammal of the order Insectivora (shrews and moles).

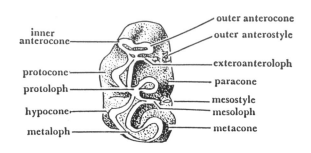

Fig. 9.4. Terminology for cusps and lophs of teeth. Upper (top) and lower molar of *Peromyscus*. (From Hoffmeister 1951, Illinois Biol. Monogr. 21)

insectivorous. Insect-eating.

interfemoral membrane. Tail membrane in bats (Fig. 9.5).

interparietal. Bone of brain case; usually well-developed in rodents (Fig. 9.2).

invertebrate. An animal lacking a dorsal vertebral column.

labial. Lip-side; labial side of tooth is side near lip.

lacrimal. Small bone at anterior angle of eye socket.

lacrimal ridge. Ridge on lacrimal bone.

lambdoidal crest. Ridge at rear of skull mostly between the squamosal and occipital bones.

lepidopteran. Member of the order Lepidoptera, moths and butterflies.

lingual. Tongue-side.

loess. Deposit of yellowish-brown, unstratified loam.

loph. Ridge on occluding surface of tooth formed by elongation or fusion on cusps.

lyrate. Lyre-shaped; spatulate and oblong.

mm. Millimeter; in metric system, equals 1/10th of cm; 25.4 mm equals one inch.

M. Molar tooth; a superior number indicates a particular upper molar; inferior numbers for lower molars.

masseteric tubercle. Elevated area on side of lower jaw for attachment of masseter muscle.

masseter muscle. Used in chewing; raises the lower jaw.

mastoid bone. A part of the temporal bone; a distinct element in embryonic development. Located between bulla and occipital bone; projects over bulla as the mastoid process.

maxillofrontal suture. Suture between maxillary and frontal bones (Fig. 9.2).

medial tine. Reference to small, interior cusplet or spine on upper incisor of shrew (Fig. 8.5).

melanistic. Black or blackish.

mesolophid. An accessory cusp on lower tooth (Fig. 9.4).

mesostylid (Fig. 9.4).

metacentric. A type of chromosome (Fig. 9.1).

metatarsal gland. A small glandular area located in the area of the metatarsal bones of the hind foot; produces scented secretion.

microtine. One group of murid rodents with prismatic teeth (Fig. 8.82, p. 196).

molar. Posteriormost teeth; without a deciduous (milk) tooth precursor (Fig. 9.2).

monocot. Monocotyledon: a plant having only one seed leaf, as the grasses.

monotypic. A taxon with only one immediately subordinate taxon, as a genus with only one species.

moraine. An accumulation of earth and stones deposited by a glacier.

multicuspid tooth. Any tooth with several cusps.

murid. A member of the myomorph rodent family Muridae.

murine. One group of murid rodents often called Old World mice and rats (p. 251).

myomorph. A major group of rodents with masseter muscle and arch as shown in Fig. 8.53.

myriapod. A class of arthropods including centipedes and millipedes.

nematode. Roundworm with unsegmented body; free-living or parasitic.

nictitating membrane. Thin, eyelid-like membrane that can be drawn over the eyeball.

noseleaf. A fleshy growth or flap on snout; especially noticeable in some bats.

occipital condyle. Process labelled "occipital bone" in Fig. 9.2.

ochraceous. Color of ocher, a kind of yellowish brown but with variants including buffy, orangish, or tawny ochraceous.

olive-colored. A dark gray, but variants include a light brownish olive, buffy olive, yellowish olive.

omnivore. Animal that eats a great variety of foods, including plant and animal material.

palatilar length. See Fig. 8.123, A-J.

paracone. Cusp in upper cheek tooth (Fig. 9.4).

parietal. One of a pair of bones on braincase (Fig. 9.2).

parturition. Act of giving birth, delivery of young.

pectoral. Pertaining to chest region.

Pennsylvania sandstone. A special rocky formation in the Carboniferous period, probably 300 million years B.P.

phalanx. Bone in the fingers or toes.

piebald. Of two "colors," usually black and white.

plantar tubercle. Sole of foot and pad or tubercle thereon.

Pleistocene. A period of geological time; about two million years in duration; preceded by the Pliocene, followed by Holocene (Recent).

plumbeous. Lead-colored; some shade of a dark gray.

Pm or P. Premolar tooth.

posterior palatine foramen. Small opening on hard palate located posterior to palatine slits (=anterior palatine foramina).

postglenoid length. A measurement from the glenoid fossa (where the lower jaw articulates) to the posterior margin of the occipital condyle on the same side.

postmandibular foramen. Opening on inside of lower jaw near the condyle; especially noticeable in some shrews.

precocial. Young that shortly after birth are sufficiently developed to run, forage, and eat food items for themselves.

prehensile. Adapted for seizing or grasping.

premolar. Cheek tooth; deciduous or permanent (Fig. 9.2).

preputial gland. Invaginations of the skin forming skin glands near the penis.

prismatic tooth. A cheek tooth that consists of connected, prism-shaped or triangular-shaped sections.

protocone. Cusp in upper cheek tooth (Fig. 9.2).

pubic symphysis. That part of pelvic girdle where two halves come into contact or fuse.

re-entrant angle (fold). Groove or valley on side of prismatic tooth; especially noticeable on grinding surface of tooth.

retractile claws. Claws, as in the cats, that appear to withdraw into sheaths.

rufous. A variation of reddish.

rugose. Wrinkled, rough.

sagittal crest. Ridge along midline of braincase, forming noticeable crest (Fig. 9.2).

scat. Fecal remains or pellet.

sciuromorph. Rodents of the subgroup Sciuromorpha.

sp. = species. A group of populations that can interbreed but are reproductively and morphologically isolated from other species.

standard deviation. A measure of variability or dispersion derived from the squares of the deviation of individuals from the mean.

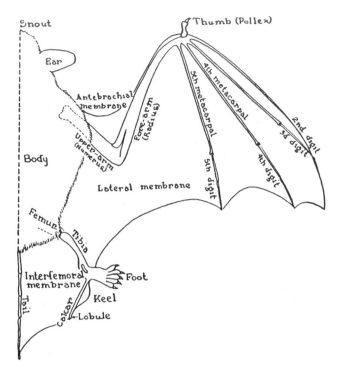

Fig. 9.5. Certain features of the body and wing of a bat. (From Hoffmeister and Mohr, 1957. Charles A. McLaughlin)

strip mine. A mining area that is worked from the surface, where the layers of earth are stripped off to get to underlying coal.

subgenus. A recognized and defined subdivision of a genus; consists of one or more species.

submetacentric. See Fig. 9.1.

subtelocentric. See Fig. 9.1.

supraorbital bead. Ridge of bone on each side of brain case, as in *Oryzomys* (p. 197).

supraorbital process. A bony projection above the orbital region.

talonid. Heel of a lower molariform tooth.

tarsal gland. A gland in deer which is located in the ankle region and produces a scented secretion. In some other mammals, the reference is to sebaceous glands of the eyelid.

temporal ridges. Pair of ridges on roof of braincase, running anteroposteriorly (as seen in *Rattus*, Fig. 8.110).

tragus. Fleshy projection within ear of many bats (Fig. 8.21).

trenchant. Incisive, sharply defined.

trichopteran. Referring to a group of insects, Trichoptera, including the caddisflies.

trochanter. Processes below the head of the femur.

tympanic bone. That part of the temporal bone that forms the wall of the tympanic cavity, which contains the middle ear and ear ossicles.

unicuspid tooth. A simple tooth with only one cusp.

uropatagial membrane. Regarded as same as interfemoral membrane in bats (Fig. 9.5).

X chromosome. Female-determining chromosome.

Y chromosome. Special chromosome only in males.

zygomata. See zygomatic arch, Fig. 9.2.

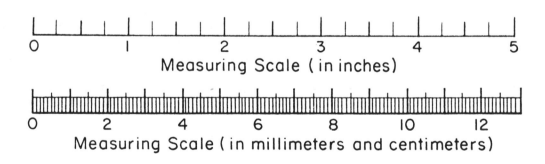

Fig. 9.6. Comparison of inches and millimeters. Scale is to actual size.

Literature Cited

Allen, D. L. 1943. Michigan fox squirrel management. Michigan Dept. Conserv., Game Div. Pub., 100:1–404.

Allen, H. 1893. A monograph of the bats of North America. Bull. U.S. Natl. Mus., 43:1–198.

Allen, J. A. 1876. The American bisons, living and exinct. University Press, Cambridge (Memoirs Mus. Comp. Anat., Harvard). 6 (10), 246 pp.

———. 1877. Monograph of North American Rodentia. XI. Sciuridae. Rept. U.S. Geol. Survey Terr., 11:631–939.

———. 1898. Revision of the chickarees, or North American red squirrels (subgenus Tamiasciurus). Bull. Amer. Mus. Nat. Hist., 10:249–298.

Allen, J. W. 1949. Pope County notes. Mus. Nat. Soc. Sci., State of Illinois. 95 pp.

Alvord, C. W. 1965. The Illinois country 1673–1818 *in* Bannon, J. F., The American west. Loyola Univ. Press, Chicago. 524 pp.

Anderson, E. A., and A. Woolf. 1987. River otter habitat use in northwestern Illinois. Trans. Illinois Acad. Sci., 80:107–114.

Anderson, E. P. 1951. The mammals of Fulton County, Illinois Bull. Chicago Acad. Sci., 9:153–188.

Anderson, R. C. 1970. Prairies in the prairie state. Trans. Illinois St. Acad. Sci., 63:214–221.

Anonymous. 1837. Illinois in 1837; a sketch descriptive of the situation, boundaries, face of the country, prominent districts, prairies, rivers, minerals, animals [*sic*], agricultural productions, public lands, places of internal improvement, manufactures, &c. of the State of Illinois. S. Augustus Mitchell, Philadelphia. 143 pp.

———. 1935. A survey of the annual fur catch of the United States. U.S. Dept. Agric., Bur. Biol. Survey, Wildl. Res. and Mgmt. Leaflet 140: 19 pp.

———. 1939. Survey of the annual fur catch of the United States. U.S. Dept. Agric., Bur. Biol. Surv., Wildl. Res. & Mgmt. Leaflet 170: 21 pp.

———. 1946. Annual fur catch of the United States. U.S. Dept. Agric., Bur. Biol. Surv., Wildl. Res. & Mgmt. Leaflet 290:1–21.

———. 1964. Fur catch in the United States, 1963. U.S. Dept. Interior, Bur. Sports Fisheries, Wildl. Leaflet 460:1–4.

———. 1965. Fur catch in the United States, 1964. U.S. Dept. Interior, Bur. Sports Fisheries, Wildl. Leaflet 471:1–4.

———. 1966. Fur catch in the United States, 1965. U.S. Dept. Interior, Bur. Sports Fisheries, Wildl. Leaflet 471:1–4.

———. 1970. Fur catch in the United States, 1969. U.S. Dept. Interior, Bur. Sports Fisheries, Wildl. Leaflet 493:1–4.

Arata, A. A. 1959. Ecology of muskrats in strip-mine ponds in southern Illinois. J. Wildl. Mgmt., 23:177–186.

Arlton, A. V. 1936. An ecological study of the mole. J. Mamm., 17:349–371.

Armitage, K. B., and K. S. Harris. 1982. Spatial patterning in sympatric populations of fox and gray squirrels. Amer. Midl. Nat., 108:389–397.

Ashbrook, F. G. 1948. Annual fur catch of the United States. U.S. Dept. Interior, Fish & Wild. Serv., Wildl. Leaflet 315:1–24.

———. 1955. Annual fur catch of the United States. U.S. Dept. Interior, Fish & Wildl. Serv., Wildl. Leaflet 367:1–24.

Bader, R. S., and D. Techter. 1959. A list and bibliography of the fossil mammals of Illinois. Nat. Hist. Misc., 172:1–8.

Bailey, B. 1929. Mammals of Sherburne County, Minnesota. J. Mamm., 10:153–164.

Bailey, B. H. 1916. Additional notes on the little spotted skunk, *Spilogale interrupta* Raf. Proc. Iowa Acad. Sci., 23:290.

Bailey, V. 1893. The prairie ground squirrels or spermophiles of the Mississippi Valley. U.S. Dept. Agric., Div. Ornith. & Mamm., Bull. 4:1–69.

Baker, F. C. 1936. Remains of animal life from the Kingston kitchen midden site near Peoria, Illinois. Trans. Illinois St. Acad. Sci., 29:243–246.

———. 1941. A study in ethnozoology of the prehistoric Indians of Illinois. Trans. Amer. Philos. Soc., 32:51–77.

Baker, R. J., and J. T. Mascarello. 1969. Karyotypic analyses of the genus *Neotoma* (Cricetidae, Rodentia). Cytogenetics, 8:187–198.

Baker, R. J., and J. L. Patton. 1967. Karyotypes and karyotypic variation of North American vespertilionid bats. J. Mamm., 48:270–286.

Baldwin, E. 1877. History of LaSalle County. Rand McNally and Co., Chicago. 552 pp.

Bancroft, W. L. 1967. Record fecundity for *Reithrodontomys megalotis*. J. Mamm., 48:306–308.

Barbour, R. W. 1942. Nests and habitat of the golden mouse in eastern Kentucky. J. Mamm., 23:90–91.

Barbour, R. W., and W. H. Davis. 1969. Bats of America. Univ. Press of Kentucky, Lexington. 286 pp.

———. 1974. Mammals of Kentucky. Univ. Press of Kentucky, Lexington. 322 pp.

Barge, W. D. 1918. Early Lee County, Illinois. Chicago. 160 pp.

Bateman, N., and P. Selby, ed. 1902. Historical encyclopedia of Illinois. Munsell Publ. Co., Chicago. 747 pp.

———. 1905. Historical encyclopedia of Illinois. Munsell Publ. Co., Chicago. 1060 pp.

———. 1907. Historical encyclopedia of Illinois and history of St. Clair County. Munsell Publ. Co., Chicago, 2 vols.

———. 1914. Historical encyclopedia of Illinois. History of Kendall County. Munsell Publ. Co., Chicago. 1078 pp.

Batzli, G. O. 1977. Population dynamics of the white-footed mouse in floodplain and upland forests. Amer. Midl. Nat., 97:18–32.

Beasley, L. E. 1978. Demography of southern bog lemmings (*Synaptomys cooperi*) and prairie voles (*Microtus ochrogaster*) in southern Illinois. Ph.D. thesis, Univ. Illinois Library at Urbana-Champaign. 95 pp.

Beck, M. L., and J. T. Mahan. 1978. The chromosomes of *Microtus pinetorum*. J. Hered., 69:343–344.

Becker, C. N. 1975. First record of *Reithrodontomys megalotis* north of the Kankakee River in Illinois. Trans. Illinois St. Acad. Sci., 68:14–16.

Beckwith, H. W. 1879. History of Vermilion County. H. H. Hill & Co., Chicago, Ill. 1,041 pp.

Beer, J. R. 1956. A record of a silver-haired bat in a cave. J. Mamm., 37:282.

Bellrose, F. C., Jr. 1945. Relative values of drained and undrained bottomland in Illinois. J. Wildl. Mgmt., 9:161–182.

———. 1950. The relationship of muskrat populations to various marsh and aquatic plants. J. Wildl. Mgmt., 14:299–315.

Belting, N. M. 1948. Kaskaskia under the French regime. Illinois Studies in Soc. Sci., 29 (3). 140 pp.

Benedict, F. G., and R. C. Lee. 1938. Hibernation and marmot physiology. Carnegie Inst. Washington, Publ. 497:1–239.

Benton, A. H. 1955. Observations on the life history of the northern pine mouse. J. Mamm., 36:52–62.

Bergstrom, B. J. 1984. Morphologic variation between long-established and pioneer populations of the meadow vole (*Microtus pennsylvanicus*) in Illinois. Amer. Midl. Nat., 112:172–177.

Birbeck, M. 1818. Notes on a journey in America. Reprint, Ann Arbor, Mich. 1968. 156 pp.

Birkenholz, D. E. 1967. The harvest mouse (*Reithrodontomys megalotis*) in central Illinois. Trans. Illinois St. Acad. Sci., 60:49–53.

———. 1973. Mammals of Goose Lake Prairie nature preserve. Nat. Hist. Miscell., 191:1–10.

Blatchley, W. S. 1898. Notes on the fauna of Lake and Porter counties. 22nd Annual Report Indiana Dept. Geology and Natural Resources, pp. 89–91.

Blem, L. B., and C. R. Blem. 1975. The effect of flooding on length of residency in the white-footed mouse, Peromyscus leucopus. Amer. Midl. Nat., 94:232–236.

Blus, L. J. 1966. Some aspects of golden mouse ecology in southern Illinois. Trans. Illinois St. Acad. Sci., 59:334–341.

Bond, C. F. 1956. Correlations between reproductive condition and skull characteristics of beaver. J. Mamm., 37:506–512.

Bowles, J. B. 1975. Distribution and biogeography of mammals of Iowa. Spec. Publ. Mus. Texas Tech. Univ., 9:1–184.

Brack, V., Jr. 1979. Determination of presence of habitat suitability for the Indiana bat (*Myotis sodalis*) and gray bat (*Myotis griesescens*) for portions of three ditches, Big Levee and Drainage District, Union and Alexander Counties, Illinois. Unpublished report submitted to U.S. Army Corps of Engineers, Saint Louis District, St. Louis, Mo. 23 pp.

Bradsby, H. C., ed. 1885. History of Bureau County, Illinois. World Publ. Co., Chicago. 710 pp.

Bradshaw, W. N., and T. C. Hsu. 1972. Chromosomes of *Peromyscus* (Rodentia, Cricetidae). Polymorphism in *Peromyscus maniculatus*. Cytogenetics. II:436–451.

Bradt, G. W. 1938. A study of beaver colonies in Michigan. J. Mamm., 19:139–162.

Brenner, F. J. 1975. Effect of previous photoperiodic conditions and visual stimulation on food storage and hibernation in the eastern chipmunk (*Tamias striatus*). Amer. Midl. Nat., 93:227–234.

Brown County. 1972. A history of Brown County, Ill. 1880–1970. Stevens Publ. Co., Astoria. 745 pp.

Brown, L. G., and L. E. Yeager. 1943. Survey of the Illinois fur resource. Bull. Illinois Nat. Hist. Survey, 22:435–504.

———. 1945. Fox squirrels and gray squirrels *in Illinois*. Bull. Illinois Nat. Hist. Survey, 23:449–536.

Burnett, C. D. 1983. Geographic and secondary sexual variation in the morphology of *Eptesicus fuscus*. Ann. Carnegie Mus., 52:139–162.

Burns, J. C., J. R. Choate, and E. G. Zimmerman. 1985. Systematic relationships of pocket gophers (genus *Geomys*) on the central Great Plains. J. Mamm., 66:102–118.

Butler, A. W. 1895. The mammals of Indiana. Proc. Indiana Acad. Sci., 4:81–86.

Cagle, F. R., and L. Cockrum. 1943. Notes on a summer colony of *Myotis lucifugus lucifugus*. J. Mamm., 24:474–492.

Calhoun, J. B. 1941. Distribution and food habits of mammals in the vicinity of the Reelfoot Lake Biological Station. J. Tennessee Acad. Sci., 16:177–225.

Carleton, M. D. 1984. Introduction to rodents. *In* S. Anderson and J. K. Jones, Jr., Orders and families of Recent mammals of the world. Wiley and Sons, N.Y., pp. 255–265.

Casteel, D. A. 1967. Timing of ovulation and implantation in the cottontail rabbit. J. Wildl. Mgmt., 31:194–197.

Choate, J. R. 1970. Systematic and zoogeography of Middle American shrews of the genus Cryptotis. Univ. Kansas Publ. Mus. Nat. Hist., 19:195–317.

———. 1972. Variation within and among populations of the short-tailed shrew in Connecticut. J. Mamm., 53:116–128.

Choromanski, J. F., and E. K. Fritzell. 1982. Status of the river otter (*Lutra canadensis*) in Missouri. Trans. Missouri Acad. Sci., 16:43–48.

Churcher, C. S. 1959. The specific status of the New World red fox. J. Mamm., 40:513–520.

Cockrum, E. L. 1949. Range-extension of the swamp rabbit in Illinois. J. Mamm., 30:427–429.

Cole, F. R. 1977. Nutrition and population dynamics of the prairie vole, Microtus ochrogaster, in central Illinois. Ph.D. thesis, Univ. Illinois Library at Urbana-Champaign. 103 pp.

Collins, H. H. 1918. Studies in normal moult and of artificially induced regeneration of pelage in Peromyscus. J. Exp. Zool., 27:73–99, 15 figs.

———. 1923. Studies of the pelage phases and of the nature and color variation in mice of the genus Peromyscus. J. Exp. Zool., 38:45–107, 57 figs.

Connor, P. F. 1959. The bog lemming Synaptomys cooperi in southern New Jersey. Michigan St. Univ. Publ. Mus., Biol. Ser., 1:161–248.

Cope, J. B., and S. R. Humphrey. 1977. Spring and autumn swarming behavior in the Indiana bat, *Myotis sodalis*. J. Mamm., 58:93–95.

Cory, C. B. 1912. The mammals of Illinois and Wisconsin. Field Mus. Nat. Hist., Zool. Ser., 153:1–505.

Cunningham, J. O., ed. 1905. Historical encyclopedia of Illinois and history of Champaign County. Munsell Publ., Co., Chicago. Vol. 2: 503–1060.

Davis, W. H. 1957. Population dynamics and taxonomy of the bat Pipistrellus subflavus. Ph.D. thesis, Univ. Illinois Library at Urbana-Champaign, pp. 1–87.

———. 1959a. Disproportionate sex ratios in hibernating bats. J. Mamm., 40:16–19.

———. 1959b. Taxonomy of the eastern pipistrel. J. Mamm., 40:521–531.

———. 1966. Population dynamics of the bat Pipistrellus subflavus. J. Mamm., 47:383–396.

Davis, W. H., R. W. Barbour, and M. D. Hassell. 1968. Colonial behavior of Eptesicus fuscus. J. Mamm., 49:44–50.

Davis, W. H., and W. Z. Lidicker, Jr. 1956. Winter range of the red bat, Lasiurus borealis. J. Mamm., 37:280–281.

Diersing, V. E. 1978. A systematic revision of several species of cottontails (Sylvilagus) from North and South America. Ph.D. thesis, Univ. Illinois Library at Urbana-Champaign. 873 pp.

———. 1980. Systematics and evolution of the pygmy shrews (subgenus Microsorex) of North America. J. Mamm., 61:76–101.

Diersing, V. E., and D. F. Hoffmeister. 1981. Distribution and systematics of the masked shrew (Sorex cinereus) in Illinois. Nat. Hist. Misc. 213:1–11.

Diersing, V. E., and D. E. Wilson. 1980. Distribution and systematics of the rabbits (Sylvilagus) of west-central Mexico. Smithsonian Contrib. Zool., 297:1–34.

Downes, W. L., Jr. 1964. Unusual roosting behavior in red bats. J. Mamm., 45:143–144.

Drennan, D. D., and H. B. Broverman, eds. 1968. Illinois sesquicentennial edition of Christian County history. Production Press, Inc., Jacksonville, Ill. Book II [1968]. 693 pp.

Dunkeson, R. L., and D. A. Murphy. 1953. Missouri's deer herd reproduction and checking station data. 1957:1–7, mimeographed.

Ecke, D. H. 1947. The cottontail rabbit in central Illinois. M.S. thesis, Univ. Illinois at Urbana-Champaign Library. 136 pp.

Edgren, R. A., Jr. 1948. Notes on a northern short-tailed shrew. Nat. Hist. Misc., 25:1–2.

Edwards, W. R. 1963. Fifteen cottontails in a nest. J. Mamm., 44:416–417.

Elder, W. H. 1945. Big-eared bat in Illinois. J. Mamm., 26:433–434.

Elder, W. H., and W. J. Gunier. 1978. Sex ratios and seasonal movements of gray bats (Myotis grisescens) in southwestern Missouri and adjacent states. Amer. Midl. Nat., 99:463–472.

Elder, W. H., and C. M. Hayden. 1977. Use of discriminant function in taxonomic determination of canids from Missouri. J. Mamm., 58:17–24.

Elder, W. H., and C. E. Shanks. 1962. Age changes in tooth wear and morphology of the baculum in muskrats. J. Mamm., 43:144–150.

Ellis, L. S. 1979. Systematics and life-history of the eastern chipmunk, *Tamias striatus*. Ph.D. thesis, Univ. Illinois Library at Urbana-Champaign. 1–321 pp.

———. 1982. Life history studies of Franklin's ground squirrel, *Spermophilus franklinii*, in Missouri. Missouri Dept. Conserv., Tech. Rept., 1982:50 MS pp.

Ellis, L. S., V. E. Diersing, and D. F. Hoffmeister. 1978. Taxonomic status of short-tailed shrews (*Blarina*) in Illinois. J. Mamm., 59:305–311.

Erickson, D. W., D. A. Hamilton, and F. B. Samson. 1981. The status of the bobcat in Missouri. Trans. Missouri Acad. Sci., 15:49–59.

Errington, P. L. 1937. Summer food habits of the badger in northwestern Iowa. J. Mamm., 18:213–216.

Esher, R. J., J. L. Wolfe, and J. N. Layne. 1978. Swimming behavior of rice rats (Oryzomys palustris) and cotton rats (Sigmodon hispidus). J. Mamm., 59:551–558.

Evers, R. A., and L. M. Page. 1977. Some unusual natural areas in Illinois. Illinois Nat. Hist. Survey Biol. Notes, 100:1–47.

Fehrenbacher, J. B., G. O. Walker, and H. L. Wascher. 1967. Soils of Illinois. Univ. Illinois Agric. Exp. Sta., Bull. 725:1–47.

Feldhamer, G. A. 1985. A Brazilian free-tailed bat (*Tadarida brasiliensis*) in southern Illinois. Trans. Illinois St. Acad. Sci., 78:103–104.

Fenton, M. B., and R. M. R. Barclay. 1980. Myotis lucifugus. Mamm. Species, 142:1–8.

Fitzpatrick, F. L. 1925. The ecology and economic status of *Citellus tridecemlineatus*. Univ. Iowa Studies Nat. Hist., 11:1–40.

Follman, E. H. 1978. Annual reproductive cycle of the male gray fox. Trans. Illinois St. Acad. Sci., 71:304–411.

French, B. F. 1846. Historical Collection of Louisiana, Part II, Wiley and Putnam, Chicago.

French, T. W. 1980. Sorex longirostris. Mamm. Species, 143:1–3.

Friley, C. E., Jr. 1949. Age determination, by use of the baculum, in the river otter, *Lutra c. canadensis* Schreber. J. Mamm., 30:102–110.

Fritzell, E. K., and K. J. Haroldson. 1982. Urocyon cinereoargenteus. Mamm. Species, 189:1-8.

Frye, J. C., H. B. Willman, and R. F. Black. 1965. Outline of glacial geology of Illinois and Wisconsin. In the Quaternary of the United States, H. E. Wright, Jr., and D. G. Frey, ed., 43-61.

Fryxell, F. M. 1926. A horn of the prong-horn antelope (Antilocapra americana) found at Moline, Illinois. J. Mamm., 7:333-334.

Fuller, G. D. 1939. Interglacial and postglacial vegetation of Illinois. Trans. Illinois St. Acad. Sci., 32:5-15.

Galbreath, E. C. 1938. Post-glacial fossil vertebrates from east-central Illinois. Field Mus. Nat. Hist., Geol. Ser., 6:303-313.

Gallatin County. 1887. History of Gallatin, Saline, Hamilton, Franklin and Williamson counties, Illinois. Goodspeed Publ. Co., Chicago, reprinted 1967. 961 pp.

Gardner, A. L. 1973. The systematics of the genus Didelphis (Marsupialia:Didelphidae) in North and Middle America. Spec. Publ. Museum Texas Tech Univ. 4:81 pp.

Gardner, J. E., and T. L. Gardner. 1980. Determination of presence and habitat suitability for the Indiana bat (Myotis sodalis) and gray bat (Myotis grisescens) for portions of the lower 6.6 miles of McKee Creek, McKee Creek Drainage and Levee District, Pike County, Illinois. Unpublished report submitted to U.S. Army Corps of Engineers, Saint Louis District, St. Louis, Mo. 22 pp.

Garretson, M. S. 1938. The American bison. N.Y. Zoological Society, New York. 254 pp.

Genoways, H. H., J. C. Patton III, and J. R. Choate. 1977. Karyotypes of shrews of the genera Cryptotis and Blarina (Mammalia:Soricidae). Experientia, 33:1294-1295.

George, S. B., J. R. Choate, and H. H. Genoways. 1981. Distribution and taxonomic status of Blarina hylophaga Elliot (Insectivora:Soricidae). Ann. Carnegie Mus., 50:493-513.

George, S. B., H. H. Genoways, J. R. Choate, and R. J. Baker. 1982. Karyotypic relationships within the short-tailed shrews, genus Blarina. J. Mamm., 63:639-645.

George, W. G. 1977. Some recent records of the southeastern shrew in southern Illinois. Nat. Hist. Misc., 200:3 pp.

Getz, L. L. 1960. A population study of the vole, Microtus pennsylvanicus. Amer. Midl. Nat., 64:392-405.

———. 1961a. Responses of small mammals to live-trap and weather conditions. Amer. Midl. Nat., 66:160-170.

———. 1961b. Factors influencing the local distribution of Microtus and Synaptomys in southern Michigan. Ecology, 42:110-119.

———. 1970. Influence of vegetation on the local distribution of the meadow vole in southern Wisconsin. Univ. Connecticut Occas. Papers, Biol. Sci. ser., 1:213-241.

Getz, L. L., F. R. Cole, and D. L. Gates. 1978. Interstate roadsides as dispersal routes for Microtus pennsylvanicus. J. Mamm., 59:208-212.

Getz, L. L., and J. E. Hofmann. 1986. Social organization in free-living prairie voles, Microtus ochrogaster. Behav. Ecol. Sociobiol., 18: 275-282.

Getz, L. L., J. E. Hofmann, B. J. Klatt, L. Verner, F. R. Cole, and R. L. Lindroth. 1987. Fourteen years of population

fluctuations of Microtus ochrogaster and M. pennsylvanicus in east central Illinois. Canadian J. Zool., 65:1317-1325.

Getz, L. L., L. Verner, F. R. Cole, J. E. Hofmann, and D. E. Avalos. 1979. Comparisons of population demography of Microtus ochrogaster and M. pennsylvanicus. Acta Theriol., 24:319-349.

Gipson, P. S., I. K. Gipson, and J. A. Sealander. 1975. Reproductive biology of wild Canis (Canidae) in Arkansas. J. Mamm., 56:605-612.

Gleason, H. A. 1923. The vegetational history of the Middle West. Ann. Assoc. Amer. Geog., 12:39-85.

Glover, F. A. 1943. A study of the winter activities of the New York weasel. Pennsylvania Game News, 14:8,9.

Goldman, E. A. 1918. The rice rats of North America. N. Amer. Fauna, 43:1-100.

———. 1950. Raccoons of North and Middle America. N. Amer. Fauna, 60:1-153.

———. 1969. Classification of wolves, in Young and Goldman, The wolves of North America. Amer. Wildl. Inst., 1944: 387-636.

Goodnight, C. J., and E. J. Koestner, 1942. Comparison of trapping methods in an Illinois prairie. J. Mamm., 23:435-438.

Goodpaster, W. W. 1941. A list of birds and mammals of southwestern Ohio. J. Cincinnati Soc. Nat. Hist., 22:1-47.

Goodpaster, W. W., and D. F. Hoffmeister, 1952. Notes on the mammals of western Tennessee. J. Mamm., 33:362-371.

———. 1954. Life history of the golden mouse, Peromyscus nuttalli, in Kentucky. J. Mamm., 35:16-27.

Goodspeed, W. A., and D. D. Healy, ed. 1909. History of Cook County, The Goodspeed Hist. Assoc., Chicago, vol. 1, 850 pp.; vol. 2, 812 pp.

———. 1909. History of Cook County. Goodspeed Hist. Assn., Chicago, 2 vol. 1,662 pp.

Goodwin, G. G. 1932. New records and some observation on Connecticut mammals. J. Mamm., 13:36-40.

Gosling, N. M. 1977. Winter records of the silver-haired bat, Lasionycteris noctivagans Le Conte, in Michigan. J. Mamm., 58:657.

Gottschang, J. L. 1981. A guide to the mammals of Ohio. Ohio St. Univ. Press. 176 pp.

Graber, R. R., and J. W. Graber. 1963. A comparative study of bird populations in Illinois, 1906-1909 and 1956-1958. Bull. Illinois Nat. Hist. Survey, 28:383-528.

Graham, R. W., and H. A. Semken. 1976. Paleoecological significance of the short-tailed shrew (Blarina), with a systematic discussion of Blarina ozarkensis. J. Mamm., 57:433-449.

Grau, G. A., G. C. Sanderson, and J. P. Rogers. 1970. Age determination of raccoons. J. Wildl. Mgmt., 34:364-372.

Gregory, T. 1936. Mammals of the Chicago region. Program of Activities Chicago Acad. Sci., 7:1-74.

Grizzell, R. A., Jr. 1955. A study of the southern woodchuck, Marmota monax monax. Amer. Midl. Nat., 53:257-293.

Gunderson, H. L., and J. R. Beer. 1953. The mammals of Minnesota. Minnesota Mus. Nat. Hist., Univ. Minnesota, Occas. Paper 6:1-190.

Gunier, W. J. 1971. Long-distance record for movement of the gray bat. Bat Res. News, 12:5.

Gunier, W. J., and W. N. Elder. 1971. Experimental homing of gray bats to a maternity colony in a Missouri barn. Amer. Midl. Nat., 86:502–506.

Hahn, W. L. 1907. Notes on the mammals of the Kankakee Valley. Proc. U.S. Natl. Mus., 32:455–464.

———. 1909. The mammals of Indiana. 33rd Annual Report Indiana Dept. Geol. and Nat. Res. pp. 417–654, 659–663.

Hall, E. R. 1946. Mammals of Nevada. Univ. California Press, Berkeley, 710 pp.

———. 1951. American weasels. Univ. Kansas Publ. Mus. Nat. Hist., 4:1–466.

———. 1981. The mammals of North America. John Wiley & Sons, Inc., N.Y. 1, 181 pp. & Index 90 pp.

Hall, J. S. 1962. A life history and taxonomic study of the Indiana bat, *Myotis sodalis*. Reading [Pa.] Public Mus. & Art Gallery, Sci. Publ., 12:68 pp.

Hall, J. S., and N. Wilson. 1966. Seasonal populations and movements of the gray bat in the Kentucky area. Amer. Midl. Nat., 75:317–324.

Hamilton, W. J., Jr. 1930. The food of the Soricidae. J. Mamm., 11:26–39.

———. 1958. Life history and economic relations of the opossum (*Didelphis marsupialis virginiana*) in New York State. Mem. Cornell Univ. Agric. Exp. Sta., 354:48 pp.

Hancock County. 1968. A history of Hancock County. Publ. by Supervisors of Hancock Co., Illinois. 670 pp.

Handley, C. O., Jr. 1959. A revision of American bats of the genera Euderma and Plecotus. Proc. U.S. Natl. Mus., 110:95–246.

———. 1960. Description of new bats from Panama. Proc. U.S. Natl. Mus., 112:459–479.

Hankinson, T. L. 1915. The vertebrate life of certain prairie and forest regions near Charleston, Illinois. Illinois St. Lab. Nat. Hist. Bull., 11:281:303.

Hansen, L. P. 1977. The influence of food availability on the population dynamics of the white-footed mouse, *Peromyscus leucopus*. Ph.D. thesis, Univ. Illinois. 1–100 pp.

Harnishfeger, R. L., J. L. Roseberry, and D. W. Klimstra. 1978. Reproductive levels in unexploited woodlot fox squirrels. Trans. Illinois St. Acad. Sci., 71:342–355.

Hart, E. B. 1978. Karyology and evolution of the plains pocket gopher, *Geomys bursarius*. Occas. Papers Mus. Nat. Hist., Univ. Kansas, 71:1–20.

Hartman, C. G. 1952. Possums. Univ. Texas Press, Austin. 174 pp.

Harty, F. M., and H. J. Stains. 1975. Least and long-tailed weasels (*Mustela nivalis* and *M. frenata*) collected in Grundy County, Ill. Bull. California Acad. Sci., 74:44.

Harty, F. M., and R. H. Thom. 1978. Distribution of the least weasel (*Mustela nivalis*) in Illinois. Trans. Illinois St. Acad. Sci., 71:81–87.

Havera, S. P., and C. M. Nixon. 1978. Geographic variation of Illinois gray squirrels. Amer. Midl. Nat., 100:396–407.

Hawkins, R. R., and W. D. Klimstra. 1970. A preliminary study of the social organization of white-tailed deer. J. Wildl. Mgmt., 34:407–419.

Hay, O. P. 1914. The Pleistocene mammals of Iowa. Iowa Geol. Survey, 23:1–662.

———. 1923. The Pleistocene of North America and its vertebrated animals from the states east of the Mississippi River. . . . Carnegie Inst. Washington, Publ. 322:1–499.

Hayase, S. 1949. Natural history of the lemming vole (*Synaptomys cooperi*) in central Illinois. M.S. thesis, Univ. Illinois at Urbana-Champaign. 1–55 pp.

Heaney, L. R., and R. M. Timm. 1983. Relationships of pocket gophers of the genus *Geomys* from the central and northern Great Plains. Univ. Kansas Mus. Nat. Hist., Misc. Publ., 74:1–59.

Hendrickson, W. B. 1970. Robert Kennicott, an early professional naturalist in Illinois. Trans. Illinois Acad. Sci., 63:104–106.

Hennepin, Fr. L. 1880. A description of Louisiana. (Translated from 1683 ed. by J. G. Shea). New York, 1880. 407 pp.

Hicks, E. W. 1877. History of Kendall County, Illinois, from the earliest discoveries to the present time. Aurora, Illinois. 438 pp.

Hisaw, F. L. 1924. The absorption of the pubic symphysis of the pocket gopher, Geomys bursarius (Shaw). Amer. Nat., 48:93–96.

———. 1925. The influence of the ovary on the resorption of the pubic bones of the pocket gopher, Geomys bursarius (Shaw). J. Exp. Zool., 42:411–433.

Hofmann, J. E., L. L. Getz, and B. J. Klatt. 1982. Levels of male aggressiveness in fluctuating populations of *Microtus ochrogaster* and *M. pennsylvanicus*. Canadian J. Zool., 60:898–912.

Hoffmann, R. S., and C. F. Nadler. 1968. Chromosomes and systematics of some North American species of the genus Marmota (Rodentia: Sciuridae). Experientia, 24:740–742.

———. 1976. The karyotype of the southern bog lemming, *Synaptomys cooperi* (Rodentia: Cricetidae). Mammalia, 40:79–82.

Hoffmeister, D. F. 1947. A concentration of lemming mice (*Synaptomys cooperi*) in central Illinois. Trans. Illinois St. Acad. Sci., 40:190–193.

———. 1951. A taxonomic and evolutionary study of the piñon mouse, *Peromyscus truei*. Illinois Biol. Monogr., 21(4):1–104.

———. 1954. Distribution of some Illinois mammals. Nat. Hist. Misc., Chicago Acad. Sci., 128:1–4.

———. 1956. Southern limits of the least weasel (*Mustela rixosa*) in central United States. Trans. Illinois St. Acad. Sci., 48:195–196.

———. 1977. Status of the cotton mouse, *Peromyscus gossypinus*, in southern Illinois. Amer. Midl. Nat., 97:222–224.

———. 1986. Mammals of Arizona. Univ. Arizona Press and Arizona Game & Fish Dept., Tucson, 1986:602 pp.

Hoffmeister, D. F., and W. L. Downes, Jr. 1964. Blue jays as predators of red bats. Southw. Nat., 9:102.

Hoffmeister, D. F., and L. L. Getz. 1968. Growth and age-classes in the prairie vole, *Microtus ochrogaster*. Growth, 32:57–69.

Hoffmeister, D. F., and W. W. Goodpaster. 1963. Observations on a colony of big-eared bats, *Plecotus rafinesquii*. Trans. Illinois St. Acad. Sci., 55:87–89.

Hoffmeister, D. F., and M. M. Hensley. 1949. Retention of the "color" pattern in an albino thirteen-lined ground squirrel (*Citellus tridecemlineatus*). Amer. Midl. Nat., 42:403–405.

Hoffmeister, D. F., and C. O. Mohr. 1957. Fieldbook of Illinois mammals. Illinois Nat. Hist. Survey, Manual 4. xi+223 pp.

Hoffmeister, D. F., and J. E. Warnock. 1955. The harvest mouse (*Reithrodontomys megalotis*) in Illinois and its taxonomic status. Trans. Illinois St. Acad. Sci., 47:161–164.

Hoffmeister, D. F., and E. G. Zimmerman. 1967. Growth of the skull in the cottontail (*Sylvilagus floridanus*) and its application to age-determination. Amer. Midl. Nat., 78:198–206.

Holler, N. R., T. S. Baskett, and J. P. Rogers. 1963. Reproduction in confined swamp rabbits. J. Wildl. Mgmt., 27:179–183.

Holler, N. R., and H. M. Marsden. 1970. Onset of evening activity of swamp rabbits and cottontails in relation to sunset. J. Wildl. Mgmt., 34:349–353.

Hollister, N. 1913. A synopsis of the American minks. Proc. U.S. Natl. Mus., 44:471–480.

Holmes, A. C., and G. C. Sanderson. 1965. Populations and movements of opossums in east-central Illinois. J. Wildl. Mgmt., 29:287–295.

Honde, M. J., and J. Klasey. 1968. Of the people—A popular history of Kankakee County, publ. by Kankakee Co. Board of Supervisors, General Printing Co., Chicago, Ill. 436 pp.

Hooper, E. T., and G. G. Musser. 1964. The glans penis in Neotropical cricetines (family Muridae) with comments on classification of muroid rodents. Misc. Publ. Univ. Michigan Mus. Zool., 123:1–57.

Houtcooper, W. C. 1972. Rodent seed supply and burrows of *Peromyscus* in cultivated fields. Proc. Indiana Acad. Sci., 81:384–389.

Howard, W. E. 1949a. Dispersal, amount of inbreeding, and longevity in a local population of prairie deermice on the George Reserve, southern Michigan. Contrib. Lab. Vert. Biol., 43:1–50.

———. 1949b. A means to distinguish skulls of coyotes and domestic dogs. J. Mamm., 30:169–171.

Howell, A. H. 1910. Notes on mammals of the middle Mississippi Valley with description of a new woodrat. Proc. Biol. Soc. Washington, 23:23–33.

———. 1915. Revision of the American marmots. N. Amer. Fauna, 37:1–80.

———. 1918. Revision of the American flying squirrels. N. Amer. Fauna, 44:1–64.

———. 1929. Revision of the American chipmunks (genera *Tamias* and *Eutamias*). N. Amer. Fauna, 52:1–157.

———. 1938. Revision of the North American ground squirrels, with a classification of the North American Sciuridae. N. Amer. Fauna, 56:256 pp.

Hsu, T. C. 1966. Mamm. Chr. Newsl., 19:22.

Hsu, T. C., and F. E. Arrighi. 1968. Chromosomes of *Peromuscus* (Rodentia, Cricetidae). I. Evolutionary trends in 20 species. Cytogenetics, 7:417–446.

Hsu, T. C., and K. Benirschke. 1967a. An atlas of mammalian chromosomes, Mus musculus, vol. 1, folio 17.

———. 1967b. An atlas of mammalian chromosomes, Rattus norvegicus, vol. 1, folio 18.

———. 1967c. An atlas of mammalian chromosomes, Odocoileus virginianus, vol. 1, folio 43.

———. 1968. An atlas of mammalian chromosomes, Mustela vison, vol. 2, folio 81.

———. 1970a. An atlas of mammalian chromosomes, *Cryptotis parva*, vol. 4, folio 155.

———. 1970b. An atlas of mammalian chromosomes, Felis rufus, vol. 4, folio 187.

———. 1971a. An atlas of mammalian chromosomes, Lepus townsendii, vol. 5, folio 211.

———. 1971b. At atlas of mammalian chromosomes, Ondatra zibethicus, vol. 5, folio 224.

———. 1971c. An atlas of mammalian chromosomes, Rattus rattus, vol. 5, folio 229.

———. 1971d. An atlas of mammalian chromosomes, Mustela frenata, vol. 5, folio 231.

———. 1971e. An atlas of mammalian chromosomes, Microtus ochrogaster, vol. 6, folio 272.

———. 1973. An atlas of mammalian chromosomes, Rattus rattus, vol. 7, folio 326.

Hubbard, G. S. 1911. The autobiography of G. S. Hubbard. Lakeside Press, Chicago. 182 pp.

Hubert, G. F., Jr. 1978. River otter status evaluation. Illinois Dept. Conserv., Fed. Aid Proj. 1–8.

———. 1979a. Study I. Population trends and characteristics, Job No. 11: Canid investigations. Illinois Dept. Conserv., Fed. Aid Proj. 1–18.

———. 1979b. River otter status evaluation. Illinois Dept. Conserv., Fed. Aid Proj. 1–8.

———. 1980. Wildlife harvests. Trapper harvest survey, 1979–1980. Illinois Dept. Conserv., Fed. Aid Proj., W-49-R(27), Job 4. 36 pp.

———. 1984. Wildlife harvests: Fur harvest survey, 1983–1984. Illinois Dept. Conserv., Fed. Aid Project, no. W-49-R-31, no. 3. 1–22 pp.

Huish, M. T., and D. F. Hoffmeister, 1947. The short-tailed shrew (*Blarina*) as a source of food for the green sunfish. Copeia, 1947:198.

Hume, C. E., 1949. Factors affecting muskrat populations along stream banks in east-central Illinois. Master's thesis, Univ. Illinois at Urbana-Champaign. 1–49 pp.

Humphrey, S. R., and J. B. Cope. 1976. Population ecology of the little brown bat, *Myotis lucifugus*, in Indiana and north-central Kentucky. Amer. Soc. Mamm., Spec. Publ. 4:1–81.

Humphrey, S. R., A. R. Richter, and J. B. Cope. 1977. Summer habitat and ecology of the endangered Indiana bat, *Myotis sodalis*. J. Mamm., 58:334–346.

Husband, W. W. 1973. Old Brownsville Days. Jackson County Historical Soc. repr. 33 pp.

Izor, R. J. 1979. Winter range of the silver-haired bat. J. Mamm., 60:641–643.

Jackson, H. H. T. 1915. A review of the American moles. N. Amer. Fauna, 38:1–100.

———. 1961. Mammals of Wisconsin. Univ. Wisconsin Press, Madison. 504 pp.

Jones, C. 1967. Growth, development, and wing loading in the evening bat, *Nycticeius humeralis* (Rafinesque). J. Mamm., 48:1–19.

————. 1977. Plecotus rafinesquii. Mamm. Species, 69:1–4.

Jordan, J. S. 1948. A midsummer study of the southern flying squirrel. J. Mamm., 29:44–48.

Junge, R., and D. F. Hoffmeister. 1980. Age determination in raccoons from cranial suture obliteration. J. Wildl. Mgmt., 44:725–729.

Kantak, G. E. 1983. Behavioral, seed preference and habitat selection experiments with two sympatric Peromyscus species. Amer. Midl. Nat., 109:246–252.

Kase, J. C. 1946. Winter food habits of the red foxes in Indiana. Indiana Pittman-Robertson Wildl. Res. Rept., 6:10–27.

Keller, B. L., and C. J. Krebs. 1970. Microtus population biology, III. Reproductive changes in fluctuating populations of M. ochrogaster and M. pennsylvanicus in southern Indiana, 1965–1967. Ecol. Monogr., 40:263–294.

Kellogg, R. 1965. What and where are the whitetails? pp. 31–55, In Taylor, W. P., ed., The deer of North America. Stackpole Co., Harrisburg, Pa., 1965. 668 pp.

Kennicott, R. 1855. Catalogue of animals observed in Cook County, Illinois. Trans. Illinois St. Agric. Soc., 1:577–595.

————. 1857. The quadrupeds of Illinois, injurious and beneficial to the farmer. Trans. Illinois St. Agric. Soc., 2:615–684, pl. V–XIV. See article in Rept. Comm. Patents . . . 1856. Washington, D.C., pp. 52–110, pl. V–XIV.

————. 1858. The quadrupeds of Illinois, injurious and beneficial to the farmer. Agric. Rept. 1857. U.S. Patent Office Rept., 72–107 pp.

————. 1859. The quadrupeds of Illinois, injurious and beneficial to the farmer. Agric. Rept. 1858. U.S. Patent Office Rept., pp. 241–256.

King, D. B., and R. K. Winters. 1952. Forest resources and industries of Illinois. Bull. Illinois Agric. Exp. Sta., 562:1–95.

Kip, W. I. 1866. Early Jesuit missions in North America. Compiled and translated from letters of French Jesuits, with notes. Albany.

Kirkland, G. L., Jr. 1975. Parasitosis of the striped skunk (Mephitis mephitis) in Pennsylvania by the nasal nematode, Skrjabingylus chitwoodorum. Proc. Pennsylvania Acad. Sci., 49:51–53.

Klimstra, W. D. 1957. An additional record of Reithrodontomys in Illinois. J. Mamm., 38:522–523.

————. 1969. Mammals of the Pine Hills–Wolf Lake–La Rue swamp complex. Nat. Hist. Misc., 188:1–10.

Klimstra, W. D., and E. L. Corder. 1957. Food of the cottontail in southern Illinois. Trans. Illinois St. Acad. Sci., 50:247–256.

Klimstra, W. D., and J. L. Roseberry. 1969. Additional observations on some southern Illinois mammals. Trans. Illinois St. Acad. Sci., 62:413–417.

Klimstra, W. D., and T. G. Scott. 1956. Distribution of the rice rat in southern Illinois. Nat. Hist. Misc., 154:1–3.

Klugh, A. B. 1927. Ecology of the red squirrel. J. Mamm., 8:1–32.

Knable, A. E. 1970. Food habits of the red fox (Vulpes fulva) in Union County, Illinois. Trans. Illinois St. Acad. Sci., 63:359–365.

Koestner, E. J. 1942. Noteworthy records of occurrence of mammals in central Illinois. Trans. Illinois St. Acad. Sci., 34:227–229.

Komarek, E. V., and D. A. Spencer. 1931. A new pocket gopher from Illinois and Indiana. J. Mamm., 12:404–408, pl. 14.

Korschgen, L. J. 1957. Food habits of the coyote in Missouri. J. Wildl. Mgmt., 21:424–435.

Krohne, D. T., J. Hauffe, and P. Schramm. 1973. Radio-tracking the Franklin's ground squirrel in a restored prairie. Proc. Third Midwest Prairie Conf., pp. 84–88.

Krull, J. N., and W. S. Bryant. 1972. Ecological distribution of small mammals on the Pine Hills Field Station and environs in southwestern Illinois. Nat. Hist. Misc., 189:1–8.

Krutzsch, P. H. 1954. North American jumping mice (genus Zapus). Univ. Kansas Publ. Mus. Nat. Hist., 7:349–472.

Kunz, T. H. 1971. Reproduction of some vespertilionid bats in central Iowa. Amer. Midl. Nat., 86:477–486.

————. 1973. Resource utilization: temporal and spatial components of bat activity in central Iowa. J. Mamm., 54:14–32.

————. 1974. Reproduction, growth, and mortality of the vespertilionid bat, Eptesicus fuscus, in Kansas. J. Mamm., 55:1–13.

————. 1982. Lasionycteris noctivagans. Mamm. Species, 172:1–5.

Kurten, B., and R. Rausch. 1959. Biometric comparisons between North American and European mammals. II. A comparison between the northern lynxes of Fennoscandia and Alaska. Acta Arctica, fasc. 11:21–44.

LaVal, R. K. 1970. Intraspecific relationships of bats of the species Myotis austroriparius. J. Mamm., 51:542–552.

LaVal, R. K., R. L. Clawson, M. L. LaVal, and W. Caire. 1977. Foraging behavior and nocturnal activity patterns of Missouri bats, with emphasis on the endangered species Myotis grisescens and Myotis sodalis. J. Mamm., 58:592–599.

LaVal, R. K., and M. L. LaVal. 1980. Ecological studies and management of Missouri bats, with emphasis on cave dwelling species. Missouri Dept. Conserv., Terrestrial Ser., 8:1–53.

Lawrence, B., and W. H. Bossert. 1967. Multiple character analysis of Canis lupus, latrans, and familiaris, with a discussion of the relationships of Canis niger. Amer. Zool., 7:223–232.

————. 1969. The cranial evidence for hybridization in New England Canis. Breviora, 330:1–13.

Layne, J. N. 1952. The os genitale of the red squirrel, Tamiasciurus. J. Mamm., 33:457–459.

————. 1954. The biology of the red squirrel, Tamiasciurus hudsonicus loquax (Bangs), in central New York. Ecol. Monogr., 24:227–267.

————. 1958a. Notes on animals of southern Illinois. Amer. Midl. Nat., 60:219–254.

————. 1958b. Reproductive characteristics of the gray fox in southern Illinois. J. Wildl. Mgmt., 22:157–163.

Lee, M. R., and E. G. Zimmerman. 1969. Robertsonian polymorphism in the cotton rat, Sigmodon fulviventer. J. Mamm., 50:333–339.

Leighton, A. H. 1933. Notes on the relations of beavers to one another and to the muskrat. J. Mamm., 14:27–35.

Leopold, A. 1947. The distribution of Wisconsin hares. Trans. Wisconsin Acad. Sci., Arts and Letters, 37:1–14.

Lewis, J. B. 1940. Mammals of Amelia Co., Virginia. J. Mamm., 21:422–428.

Lindroth, R. L., and G. O. Batzli. 1984. Food habits of the meadow vole (*Microtus pennsylvanicus*) in bluegrass and prairie habitats. J. Mamm., 65:600–606.

Lindsay, S. L. 1981. Taxonomic and biogeographic relationships of Baja California chickarees (*Tamiasciurus*). J. Mamm., 62:673–682.

Linsdale, J. 1927. Notes on the life history of *Synaptomys*. J. Mamm., 8:51–54.

Linzey, A. V. 1983. Synaptomys cooperi. Mamm. Species, 210:1–5.

Linzey, D. W., and A. V. Linzey. 1967. Growth and development of the golden mouse, *Ochrotomys nuttalli nuttalli*. J. Mamm., 48:445–458.

Linzey, D. W., and R. L. Packard. 1977. Ochrotomys nuttalli. Mamm. Species, 75:1–6.

Livingston County. 1878. The history of Livingston County, Ill. Wm. LeBaron, Jr., & Co., Chicago. 896 pp.

Long, C. A. 1968. Populations of small mammals on railroad right-of-way in prairie of central Illinois. Trans. Illinois St. Acad. Sci., 61:139–145.

———. 1969. Identity of a short-tailed weasel from central Illinois. Trans. Illinois St. Acad. Sci., 62:334.

———. 1972. Taxonomic revision of the North American badger, *Taxidea taxus*. J. Mamm., 53:725–759.

———. 1974. Microsorex hoyi and Microsorex thompsoni. Mamm. Species, 33:1–4.

Long, C. A., and R. G. Severson. 1969. Geographical variation in the big brown bat in the north-central United States. J. Mamm., 50:621–624.

Lord, R. D., Jr. 1958. The importance of juvenile breeding to the annual cottontail crop. Trans. Twenty-third N. Amer. Wildl. Conf., 269–276.

———. 1959. The lens as an indicator of age in cottontail rabbits. J. Wildl. Mgmt., 23:358–360.

———. 1963. The cottontail rabbit in Illinois. Illinois Dept. Conserv. Tech. Bull., 3:94.

Lowery, G. H., Jr. 1974. The mammals of Louisiana and its adjacent waters. Louisiana St. Univ. Press. 565 pp.

Lyon, M. W., Jr. 1925. Bats caught by burdocks. J. Mamm., 6:280.

———. 1936. Mammals of Indiana. Amer. Midl. Nat., 17:1–384.

McCarley, H. 1966. Annual cycle, population dynamics and adaptive behavior of *Citellus tridecemlineatus*. J. Mamm., 47:294–316.

McLaughlin, C. A. 1951. A natural history and taxonomic study of the pocket gopher, *Geomys bursarius illinoensis* Komarek and Spencer. M.S. thesis, Univ. Illinois, Urbana. 95 pp.

Madison County. 1882. History of Madison County, Illinois. W. R. Brink & Co., Edwardsville, Ill. 603 pp.

Mahan, C. J., and R. R. Heidorn. 1983. The mammals of Iroquois County Conservation Area. 9 MS pp., unpublished.

Mane, A. 1928. History of Will County, Illinois. Hist. Publ. Co., Topeka-Indianapolis, vol. 1, 526 pp.

Mangus, L. H. 1950. Winter food of foxes in Tippecanoe County, Indiana. B.S. thesis, Purdue Univ., June 1950, 31 pp., as cited in Mumford and Whitaker, 1982.

Marsden, H. M., and N. R. Holler. 1964. Social behavior in confined populations of the cottontail and the swamp rabbit. Wildl. Monogr., 13:1–29.

Marsh, F. L. 1978. Prairie tree: Early days on the northern Illinois Prairie, Vantage Press, N.Y. 304 pp.

Martin, E. P. 1956. A population study of the prairie vole (Microtus ochrogaster) in northeastern Kansas. Univ. Kansas Publ. Mus. Nat. Hist., 8:361–416.

Martinson, R. K., J. W. Holten, and G. K. Brakhage. 1961. Age criteria and population dynamics of the swamp rabbit in Missouri. J. Wildl. Mgmt., 25:271–281.

Matson, N. 1867. Map of Bureau County, Illinois, with sketches of its early settlement. Chicago. 88 pp.

———. 1872. Reminiscences of Bureau County. Republican Book & Job Office, Princeton, Ill. 406 pp.

Maurer, F. W., Jr. 1970. Observations of fighting between a vole and a shrew. Amer. Midl. Nat., 84:549.

May, G. W., 1955. History of Massac County, Illinois. Wagoner Printing Co., Galesburg, Ill. 232 pp.

———. 1968. Student's history of Peoria County, Illinois. Wagoner Printing Co., Galesburg, Ill. 321 pp.

Mengel, R. M. 1971. A study of dog-coyote hybrids and implications concerning hybridization in *Canis*. J. Mamm., 52:316–336.

Mercer-Henderson County. 1882. History of Mercer and Henderson County. H. H. Hill & Co., Chicago. 1,414 pp.

Michaux, A. 1795. Journal of Andre Michaux 1793–1795. *In* Thwaites, R. G., 1904. Early western travels 1748–1846. Arthur H. Clark Co., Cleveland. 30 vols.

Miller, D. H., and L. L. Getz. 1969. Life-history notes on *Microtus pinetorum* in central Connecticut. J. Mamm., 50:777–784.

Miller, G. S., Jr., and G. M. Allen. 1928. The American bats of the genera Myotis and Pizonyx. Bull. U.S. Natl. Mus., 144:1–218.

Miller, G. S., Jr., and R. Kellogg. 1955. List of North American Recent mammals. Bull. U.S. Natl. Mus., 205:954 pp.

Mock, O. B., and V. K. Kivett. 1980. The southeastern shrew, *Sorex longirostris,* in northeastern Missouri. Trans. Missouri Acad. Sci., 14:67–68.

Mohr, C. O. 1935. Value of prey-individual analysis of stomach contents of predatory mammals. J. Mamm., 16:323–324.

———. 1941. Distribution of Illinois mammals. Trans. Illinois St. Acad. Sci., 34:229–232.

———. 1943. Illinois furbearer *Distribution and income*. Bull. Illinois Nat. Hist. Survey, 22:505–537.

———. 1946. Distribution of the prairie mole and pocket gopher in Illinois. J. Mamm., 27:390–392.

Mohr, C. O., and W. P. Mohr. 1936. Abundance and digging rate of pocket gophers, *Geomys bursarius*. Ecology, 17:325–327.

Montgomery, G. G. 1964. Tooth eruption in preweaned raccoons. J. Wildl. Mgmt., 28:582–584.

Morgan, J. B. 1968. The good life in Piatt County. Desaulniers & Co., Moline, Ill., 1968:287 pp.

Moyers, W. N. 1931. A story of southern Illinois, the soldier's reservation, including the Indians, French traders and some early Americans. J. Illinois St. Hist. Soc., 24:26–104.

Muul, I. 1968. Behavioral and physiological influences on the distribution of the flying squirrel, *Glaucomys volans.* Misc. Publ. Univ. Michigan Mus. Zool., 134:1–66.

Mumford, R. E. 1969. Distribution of the mammals of Indiana. Indiana Acad. Sci., Monogr. 1:114 pp.

Mumford, R. E., and J. B. Cope. 1964. Distribution and status of the Chiroptera of Indiana. Amer. Midl. Nat., 72:473–489.

Mumford, R., and J. O. Whitaker, Jr. 1982. Mammals of Indiana. Indiana Univ. Press, Bloomington, 537 pp.

Munson, D. J., P. W. Parmalee, and R. A. Yarnell. 1971. Subsistence ecology of Scovill, a Terminal Middle Woodland village. Amer. Antiquity, 30:410–431.

Munyer, E. A. 1966. Winter food of the short-eared owl, *Asio flammeus,* in Illinois. Trans. Illinois St. Acad. Sci., 59:174–180.

———. 1967. A parturition date for the hoary bat, *Lasiurus c. cinereus,* in Illinois and notes on the newborn young. Trans. Illinois St. Acad. Sci., 60:95–97.

Murphy, R. C., and J. T. Nichols. 1913. Long Island fauna and flora. I. The bats. Bull. Mus. Brooklyn Inst. Arts and Sci., 2:1–15.

Myers, P., and L. L. Master. 1983. Reproduction by *Peromyscus maniculatus:* size and compromise. J. Mamm., 64:1–18.

Nadler, C. F. 1966. Chromosomes of *Spermophilus franklinii* and taxonomy of the ground squirrel genus *Spermophilus.* Syst. Zool., 15:199–206.

Nadler, C. F., and C. E. Hughes. 1966. Chromosomes and taxonomy of the ground squirrel subgenus *Ictidomys.* J. Mamm., 47:46–53.

Nadler, C. F., and D. A. Sutton. 1967. Chromosomes of some squirrels (Mammalian-Sciuridae) from the genera *Sciurus* and *Glaucomys.* Experientia, 23(249):1–7.

Nawrot, J. R., and W. D. Klimstra. 1976. Present and past distribution of the endangered southern Illinois woodrat (*Neotoma floridana illinoensis*). Nat. Hist. Misc. 196:1–12.

Necker, W. L., and D. M. Hatfield. 1941. Mammals of Illinois. Chicago Acad. Sci. Bull., 6:17–60.

Negus, N. C. 1958. Pelage stages in the cottontail rabbit. J. Mamm., 39:246–252.

Negus, N. C., E. Gould, and R. K. Chipman. 1961. Ecology of the rice rat, *Oryzomys palustris* (Harlan), on Breton Island, Gulf of Mexico, with a critique of the social stress theory. Tulane Studies Zool., 8:93–123.

Nelson, E. W. 1909. The rabbits of North America. N. Amer. Fauna, 29:1–314.

Nixon, C. M., S. P. Havera, and R. E. Greenberg. 1978. Distribution and abundance of the gray squirrel in Illinois. Illinois Nat. Hist. Survey, Biol. Notes, 105:1–55.

Norton, W. T., ed. 1912. Centennial history of Madison County, Illinois, and its people, 1812–1912. Lewis Publ. Co., Chicago & New York. 1208 pp.

Nowak, R. M. 1979. North American Quaternary *Canis.* Monograph Univ. Kansas Mus. Nat. Hist., 6:154.

Orr, R. T. 1940. The rabbits of Calaifornia. Occas. Papers California Acad. Sci., 29:227 pp.

Packard, R. L. 1956. The tree squirrels of Kansas: Ecology and economic importance. Misc. Publ. Univ. Kansas Mus. Nat. Hist. & St. Biol. Survey Kansas, 11:1–671.

———. 1969. Taxonomic review of the golden mouse, Och-

rotomys nuttalli. Misc. Publ. Univ. Kansas Mus. Nat. Hist., 51:373–406.

Page, O. J. 1900. History of Massac County, Illinois, with life sketches and portraits. Metropolis, Ill., O. J. Page, publisher. 383 pp.

Panuska, J. A., and N. J. Wade. 1956. The burrow of *Tamias striatus.* J. Mamm. 37:23–31.

———. 1957. Field observations on *Tamias striatus.* in Wisconsin. J. Mamm., 38:192–196.

Paradiso, J. L., and R. M. Nowak. 1972. A report on the taxonomic status and distribution of the red wolf. U.S. Bur. Sport Fisheries and Wildl. Spec. Sci. Rept.—Wildl., 145:36.

Parmalee, P. W. 1957. Vertebrate remains from the Cahokia site, Illinois. Trans. Illinois St. Acad. Sci., 50:235–242.

———. 1959. Use of mammalian skulls and mandibles by prehistoric Indians of Illinois. Trans. Illinois St. Acad. Sci., 52:85–95.

———. 1959. Animal remains from the Modoc rock shelter site, Randolph County, Illinois, *in* Fowler, M. L. Illinois St. Mus. Rept. of Investigations, 8:61–65.

———. 1960. Additional fisher records from Illinois. Trans. Illinois St. Acad. Sci., 53:48–49.

———. 1962. A second porcupine record for Illinois. Trans. Illinois St. Acad. Sci., 55:90–91.

———. 1967. A Recent cave bone deposit in southwestern Illinois. Natl. Speleol. Soc. Bull., 29:119–147.

———. 1971. Faunal materials from the Schild Cemetary site, Green County, Illinois, Appendix A, pp. 142–143, *in* G. H. Perino, The Mississippian component at the Schild site (No. 4), Green County, Illinois. Illinois Archaeol. Survey Bull., 8:1–148.

Parmalee, P. W., and D. F. Hoffmeister. 1957. Archaeozoological evidence of the spotted skunk in Illinois. J. Mamm., 38:261.

Parmalee, P. W., and E. A. Munyer. 1966. Range extension of the least weasel and pigmy shrew in Illinois. Trans. Illinois St. Acad. Sci., 59:81–82.

Patton, J. L., and T. C. Hsu. 1967. Chromosomes of the golden mouse, *Peromyscus (Ochrotomys) nuttalli* (Harlan). J. Mamm., 48:637–639.

Pearson, E. W. 1962. Bats hibernating in silica mines in southern Illinois. J. Mamm., 43:27–33.

Pearson, O. P. 1945. Longevity of the short-tailed shrew. Amer. Midl. Nat., 34:531–546.

———. 1950. Keeping shrews in captivity. J. Mamm., 31:351–352.

Perrin, W. H., ed. 1883. History of Crawford and Clark counties, Illinois. O. L. Baskin & Co., Chicago. Vol. 1, 470 pp.

Perry, M. L. 1939. Notes on a captive badger. The Murrelet, 20:49–53.

Peterson, R. L. 1966. The mammals of eastern Canada. Oxford Univ. Press, Toronto, Canada. 465 pp.

Petrides, G. A. 1949. Sex and age determination in the opossum. J. Mamm., 30:364–378.

———. 1951. The determination of sex and age ratios in the cottontail rabbit. Amer. Midl. Nat., 46:312–336.

Pfeiffer, C. J., and G. H. Gass. 1963. Note on the longevity and habits of captive *Cryptotis parva.* J. Mamm., 44:427–428.

Phillips, M. K., and G. F. Hubert, Jr. 1980. Winter food habits of coyotes in southeastern Illinois. Trans. Illinois St. Acad. Sci., 73 (1):80–85.

Piatt, E. C. 1883. History of Piatt County. Unigraphic Press, Evansville, Ill. 1977:714 pp.

Pietsch, L. R. 1951. Is Illinois ready for a deer season? Outdoors in Illinois, 17:5–7.

———. 1956. The beaver in Illinois. Trans. Illinois St. Acad. Sci., 49:193–201.

Pils, C. M., and W. D. Klimstra. 1975. Late fall foods of the gray fox in southern Illinois. Trans. Illinois St. Acad. Sci., 68:255–262.

Polderboer, E. B., L. W. Kuhn, and G. O. Hendrickson. 1941. Winter and spring habits of weasels in central Iowa. J. Wildl. Mgmt., 5:115–119.

Pournelle, G. H. 1950. Mammals of a north Florida swamp. J. Mamm., 31:310–319.

———. 1952. Reproduction and early post-natal development of the cotton mouse, *Peromyscus gossypinus gossypinus.* J. Mamm., 33:120.

Prince, L. A. 1940. Notes on the habits of the pigmy shrew (*Microsorex hoyi*) in captivity. Canadian Field-Nat., 54:97–100.

Provost, E. E., and C. M. Kirkpatrick. 1952. Observations on the hoary bat in Indiana and Illinois. J. Mamm., 33:110–113.

Purdue, J. R., and B. W. Styles. 1986. Dynamics of mammalian distribution in the Holocene of Illinois. Illinois St. Mus. Rept. of Investigations, 41:1–63.

Quaife, M. M., ed. 1947. The western country in the 17th century. "The memoir of Pierre Liette," pp. 85–171, Lakeside Press, Chicago.

Rainey, D. G. 1956. Eastern woodrat, Neotoma floridana: life history and ecology. Univ. Kansas Publ. Mus. Nat. Hist., 8:535–646.

Reich, L. M. 1981. Microtus pennsylvanicus. Mamm. Species, 159:1–8.

Reite, O. B., and W. H. Davis. 1966. Thermoregulation in bats exposed to low ambient temperatures. Proc. Soc. Exp. Biol. Med., 121:1212–1215.

Reynolds, H. C. 1945. Some aspects of the life history and ecology of the opossum in central Missouri. J. Mamm., 26:361–379.

———. 1952. Studies on reproduction in the opossum (Didelphis virginiana virginiana). Univ. California Publ. Zool., 52:223–284.

Rice, D. W. 1955. A new race of *Myotis austroriparius* from the upper Mississippi valley. Quart. J. Florida Acad. Sci., 18:67–68.

———. 1957. Life history and ecology of *Myotis austroriparius* in Florida. J. Mamm., 38:15–32.

Richmond, C. W. 1876. History of Du Page County. Knickerbocker and Hodder, Aurora. 250 pp.

Robinson, T. J., F. F. B. Elder, and J. A. Chapman. 1983. Evolution of chromosomal variation in cottontails, genus *Sylvilagus* (Mammalia:Lagomorpha): *S. aquaticus, S. floridanus,* and *S. transitionalis.* Cytogenet. Cell Genet., 35:216–222.

Rongstad, O. J. 1965. A life history study of thirteen-lined ground squirrels in southern Wisconsin. J. Mamm., 46:76–87.

Roseberry, J. L., and W. D. Klimstra. 1970. Productivity of white-tailed deer on Crab Orchard National Wildlife Refuge. J. Wildl. Mgmt., 34:23–28.

———. 1975. Some morphological characteristics of the Crab Orchard deer herd. J. Wildl. Mgmt, 39:48–58.

Saari, S. 1966. Gray and fox squirrel distribution in towns of Champaign County. Undergrad. Res. Proj., Univ. Illinois at Urbana-Champaign. 16 MS pp.

Sanborn, C. C. 1930. Notes from northern and central Illinois. J. Mamm., 11:222–223.

Sanborn, C. C., and D. Tibbitts. 1949. Hoy's pygmy shrew in Illinois. Chicago Acad. Sci., Nat. Hist. Misc., 36:1–2.

Sanderson, G. C. 1949. Growth and behavior of a litter of captive long-tailed weasels. J. Mamm., 30:412–415.

———. 1961. Estimating opossum populations by marking young. J. Wildl. Mgmt., 25:20–27.

Sanderson, G. C., and G. F. Hubert, Jr. 1981. Selected demographic characteristics of Illinois (U.S.A.) raccoons (*Procyon lotor*), in Chapman, J. A., and D. Pursley, Worldwide Furbearer Conf. Proc., 1:487–513.

Sanderson, G. C., and A. V. Nalbandov. 1973. The reproductive cycle of the raccoon in Illinois. Illinois Nat. Hist. Surv. Bull., 31:29–85.

Sargeant, A. B., and D. W. Warner. 1972. Movements and denning habbits of a badger. J. Mamm., 53:207–210.

Saunders, P. B. 1929. Microsorex hoyi in captivity. J. Mamm., 10:78–79.

Scheffer, T. H. 1940. Excavation of a runway of the pocket gopher (*Geomys bursarius*). Trans. Kansas Acad. Sci., 43:473–478.

Schmidt, N. D., and D. C. Lewin. 1968. First records of the least weasel in McLean County. Trans. Illinois St. Acad. Sci., 61:206.

Schoolcraft, H. R. 1825. Travels in the central portions of the Mississippi Valley. Collins & Hannay, N.Y. 459 pp.

Schuyler-Brown counties. 1882. History of Schuyler and Brown counties, Illinois. Stevens Publ. Co., Astoria, Ill. 412 pp.

Schwartz, C. W. 1941. Home range of the cottontail in central Missouri. J. Mamm., 22:386–392.

Schwartz, C. W., and E. R. Schwartz. 1981. The wild mammals of Missouri. Univ. Missouri Press and Missouri Dept. Conserv., Columbia and London. 356 pp.

Scott, G. W., and K. C. Fisher. 1972. Hibernation of eastern chipmunks (*Tamias striatus*) maintained under controlled conditions. Canadian J. Zool., 50:95–105.

Scott, T. G. 1939. Number of fetuses in the Hoy pigmy shrew. J. Mamm., 20:251.

———. 1943. Some food coactions of the northern plains red fox. Ecol. Monog., 13:427–479.

Seagers, C. B. 1944. The fox in New York. N. Y. Conserv. Dept., Educ. Bull., 1944:1–85.

Severinghaus, C. W. 1949. Tooth development and wear as criteria of age in white-tailed deer. J. Wildl. Mgmt., 13:195–216.

Severinghaus, W. D. 1976. Systematics and ecology of the

subgenus *Pedomys*. Ph.D. thesis, Univ. of Illinois Library. 174 pp.

Severinghaus, W. D., and D. F. Hoffmeister. 1978. Qualitative cranial characters distinguishing *Sigmodon hispidus* and *Sigmodon arizonae* and the distribution of these two species in northern Mexico. J. Mamm., 59:868–70.

Shellhammer, H. S. 1967. Cytogenetic studies of the harvest mice of the San Francisco Bay region. J. Mamm., 48:549–556.

Shump, K. A., Jr. and A. U. Shump. 1982. Lasiurus cinereus. Mamm. Species, 185:1–5.

Simpson, G. G. 1945. The principles of classification and a classification of mammals. Bull. Amer. Mus. Nat. Hist., 85:350 pp.

Singh, R. P., and D. B. McMillan. 1966. Karyotypes of three subspecies of Peromyscus. J. Mamm., 47:261–266.

Skaggs, D. M. 1973. Occurrence of vespertilionid bats in some natural and man-made caverns of west-central Illinois. M.S. thesis, Western Illinois Univ., Macomb.

Slonaker, J. R. 1902. The eyes of the common mole, Scalops aquaticus machrinus. J. Comp. Neurology, 12:335–366.

Smith, P. W., and P. W. Parmalee. 1954. Notes on distribution and habits of some bats from Illinois. Trans. Kansas Acad. Sci., 57:200–205.

Smith, S. G., ed. 1893. Recollections of the pioneers of Lee County, Illinois. Dixon, Ill. 583 pp.

Smolen, M. J. 1981. Microtus pinetorum. Mamm. Species, 147:1–7.

Snead, E., and G. O. Hendrickson. 1942. Food habits of the badger in Iowa. J. Mamm., 23:380–391.

Snyder, D. P. 1947. Winter food and abundance of the short-tailed shrew (Blarina) in east-central Illinois. Honors thesis, Univ. of Illinois at Urbana-Champaign. 19 pp.

———. 1982. Tamias striatus. Mamm. Species, 168:1–8.

Snyder, R. L., and J. J. Christian. 1960. Reproductive cycle and litter size of the woodchuck. Ecology, 41:647–656.

Snyder, R. L., D. E. Davis, and J. J. Christian. 1961. Seasonal changes in the weights of woodchucks. J. Mamm., 42:297–312.

Sowls, L. 1948. The Franklin's ground squirrel, *Citellus franklinii* (Sabine), and its relationship to nesting ducks. J. Mamm., 29:113–137.

Sorensen, M. F., J. P. Rogers, and T. S. Baskett. 1968. Reproduction and development in confined swamp rabbits. J. Wildl. Mgmt., 32:520–531.

———. 1972. Parental behavior in swamp rabbits. J. Mamm., 53:840–849.

Sotala, D. J., and C. M. Kirkpatrick. 1973. Foods of white-tailed deer, *Odocoileus virginianus*, in Martin County, Indiana. Amer. Midl. Nat., 89:281–286.

Sparkes, R. S., and D. T. Arakai. 1966. Intrasubspecific and intersubspecific chromosomal polymorphism in *Peromyscus maniculatus* (deer mouse). Cytogenetics, 5:411–418.

Sparling, D. W., M. Sponsler, and T. Hickman. 1979. Limited biological assessment of Galum Creek. Unpublished report submitted to the Southwestern Illinois Coal Corporation, Perry, Ill. 14 pp.

Spoon River. 1970. Ramblin' through Spoon River Country, via the Rambler's Notes. Committee of the Spoon River Scenic Drive Associates, Canton Daily Ledger, Canton and Morton, Illinois. 107 pp.

Stains, H. J., and R. W. Turner. 1963. Harvest mice south of the Illinois River in Illinois. J. Mamm., 44:274–275.

Stickel, L. F. 1946. Experimental analysis of methods for measuring small mammal populations, J. Wildl. Mgmt., 10:150–159.

Stieglitz, W. O., and W. D. Klimstra. 1962. Dietary pattern of the Virginia opossum, *Didelphis marsupialis virginianus* Kerr, late summer-winter, southern Illinois. Trans. Illinois St. Acad. Sci., 55:198–208.

Stirton, R. A. 1965. Cranial morphology of Castoroides. Dr. D. N. Wadia Commemorative Vol., Mining & Metall. Institute of India, pp. 273–289.

Stone, W. 1908. The mammals of New Jersey. *In* Ann. Rept. New Jersey St. Mus., 1907. Part II:33–110, plus pl. 1–58.

Streubel, D. P., and J. P. Fitzgerald. 1978. Spermophilus tridecemlineatus. Mamm. Species, 103:1–5.

Stupka, R. C., J. E. Brower, and J. Henriksen. 1972. New northeastern Illinois locality records for the western harvest mouse (*Reithrodontomys megalotis dychei*). Trans. Illinois St. Acad. Sci., 65:112–114.

Sudman, P. D., J. C. Burns, and J. R. Choate. 1986. Gestation and postnatal development of the plains pocket gopher. Texas J. Sci., 38:91–94.

Taylor, M. C. 1979. To make a home in pioneer Cass County, Illinois. The Gazette Times, Virginia, Ill. 120 pp.

Taylor, R. J., and H. McCarley. 1963. Vertical distribution of *Peromyscus leucopus* and *P. gossypinus* under experimental conditions. Southw. Nat., 8:107–108.

Taylor, W. P. See Kellogg.

Telford, C. J. 1927. Third report on a forest survey of Illinois. Bull. Illinois St. Nat. Hist. Survey, 16:1–102.

Terrell, T. L. 1972. The swamp rabbit (Sylvilagus aquaticus) in Indiana. Amer. Midl. Nat., 87:283–295.

Thiem, E. G. (ed.). 1968. Carroll County—a goodly heritage. Mt. Morris, Illinois, 485 pp.

Thomas, C. 1861. Mammals of Illinois. Trans. Illinois St. Agric. Soc., 4:651–661.

Thomson, C. E. 1982. Myotis sodalis. Mamm. Species, 168:1–5.

Thwaites, R. G., ed. 1900. The Jesuit relations and allied documents: travels and explorations of the Jesuit missionaries in New France 1610–1791. Cleveland, The Burrows Brothers Co. Vol. 59, 316 pp.

———. 1904. Early western travels, 1748–1846. Arthur H. Clark Co., Cleveland. Vol. 10. *See also* Woods, J. (1822) pp. 177–357; *See also* Michaux, A.

Toll, J. E., T. S. Baskett, and C. H. Conaway. 1960. Home range, reproduction, and foods of the swamp rabbit in Missouri. Amer. Midl. Nat., 63:394–412.

Tomasi, T. E. 1979. Echolocation by the short-tailed shrew *Blarina brevicauda*. J. Mamm., 60:751–759.

Turner, B., S. Iverson, and K. Severson. 1976. Postnatal growth and development of captive Franklin's ground squirrels, *Spermophilus franklinii*. Amer. Midl. Nat., 95:93–102.

Tuttle, M. D. 1975. Population ecology of the gray bat (*Myotis grisescens*): Factors influencing early growth and development. Occas. Papers Univ. Kansas Mus. Nat. Hist., 36:1–24.

[Tuttle], 1976a. Population ecology of the gray bat (*Myotis grisescens*): Philopatry, timing and patterns of movement, weight loss during migration, and seasonal adaptive strategies. Occas. Papers Univ. Kansas Mus. Nat. Hist., 54:1–38.

———. 1976b. Population ecology of the gray bat (*Myotis grisescens*): Factors influencing growth and survival of newly volant young. Ecology, 57:587–595.

Twichell, A. R., and H. H. Dill. 1949. One hundred raccoons from one hundred and two acres. J. Mamm., 30:130–133.

Ullrich, H. S. 1968. This is Grundy County: Its history from beginning to 1968. Rogers Printing Co., Dixon. 338 pp.

Van Gelder, R. G. 1959. A taxonomic revision of the spotted skunks (genus *Spilogale*). Bull. Amer. Mus. Nat. Hist., 117:229–392.

———. 1978. A review of canid classification. Amer. Mus. Novitates, 2646:1–10.

Van Zyll de Jong, C. G. 1972. A systematic review of the Nearctic and Neotropical river otters (genus *Lutra*, Mustelidae, Carnivora). Royal Ontario Mus., Life Sci. Contr., 80:1–104.

———. 1985. Handbook of Canadian mammals. 2. Bats. Natl. Mus. Nat. Sci., Canada. 1–212 pp.

Verts, B. J. 1959. Notes on the ecology of mammals of a stripmined area in southern Illinois. Trans. Illinois St. Acad. Sci., 52:134–139.

———. 1960. Ecological notes on *Reithrodontomys megalotis* in Illinois. Chicago Acad. Sci., Nat. Hist. Misc., 174:1–7.

———. 1963. Movements and populations of opossums in a cultivated area. J. Wildl. Mgmt., 27:127–129.

———. 1967. The biology of the striped skunk. Univ. Illinois Press. 218 pp.

Vestal, A. G. 1931. A preliminary vegetation map of Illinois, Trans. Illinois St. Acad. Sci., 23:204–217.

Wade, O. 1950. Soil temperatures, weather conditions, and emergence of ground squirrels from hibernation. J. Mamm., 31:158–161.

Wade-Smith, J., and B. J. Verts. 1982. Mephitis mephitis. Mamm. Species, 173:1–7.

Walley, H. D. 1970. A brazilian free-tailed bat (*Tadarida brasiliensis*) taken in north-central Illinois. Trans. Illinois St. Acad. Sci., 63:113.

———. 1971a. Movements of *Myotis lucifugus* from a colony in La Salle County, Illinois. Trans. Illinois St. Acad. Sci., 63:409–414.

———. 1971b. A leucistic little brown bat (*Myotis l. lucifugus*). Trans. Illinois St. Acad. Sci., 64:196–197.

Walley, H. D., and W. L. Jarvis. 1971. Longevity record for Pipistrellus subflavus. Trans. Illinois St. Acad. Sci., 64:305.

Walley, H. E., W. E. Southern, and J. H. Zahr. 1969. Big brown bat entangled in burdock. Amer. Midl. Nat., 82:630.

Ward, W. C., and J. W. Hardin. 1977. Milo in the diet of white-tailed deer from southern Illinois, Trans. Illinois St. Acad. Sci., 70:47–56.

Warnock, J. E., and M. J. Warnock. 1973. The least weasel, *Mustela nivalis*, in west-central Illinois. Trans. Illinois St. Acad. Sci., 66:115–116.

Watkins, L. C. 1972. Nycticeius humeralis. Mamm. Species, 23:1–4.

West, J. A. 1914. A study of the food of moles in Illinois. Bull. Illinois St. Lab. Nat. Hist., 9:14–22.

Wetzel, R. M. 1947. Additional records of Illinois mammals. Trans. Illinois St. Acad. Sci., 40:228–233.

———. 1949. Analysis of small mammal populations in the deciduous forest biome. Ph.D. thesis, Univ. Illinois.

———. 1955. Speciation and dispersal of the southern bog lemming, *Synaptomys cooperi* (Baird). J. Mamm., 36:1–20.

———. 1958. Mammalian succession on midwestern floodplains. Ecology, 39:262–271.

Whitaker, J. O., Jr. 1966. Food of *Mus musculus, Peromyscus maniculatus bairdii* and *Peromyscus leucopus* in Vigo County, Indiana. J. Mamm., 47:473–486.

———. 1972a. Food habits of bats from Indiana. Canadian J. Zool., 50:877–883.

———. 1972b. Food and external parasites of *Spermophilus tridecemlineatus* in Vigo County, Indiana. J. Mamm., 53:644–648.

———. 1972c. Zapus hudsonius. Mamm. Species, 11:1–7.

———. 1974. Cryptotis parva. Mamm. Species, 43:1–8.

———. 1977. Bats of the caves and mines of the Shawnee National Forest, southern Illinois. Trans. Illinois St. Acad. Sci., 70:301–313.

Whitaker, J. O., Jr., and W. W. Cudmore. 1988. Food and ectoparasites of shrews of south central Indiana, with emphasis on *Sorex fumeus* and *Sorex hoyi*. Proc. Indiana Acad. Sci., 96: (1987): 543-552.

Whitaker, J. O., Jr., G. S. Jones, and R. J. Goff. 1977. Ectoparasites and food habits of the opossum, *Didelphis virginianus*, in Indiana. Proc. Indiana Acad. Sci., 86:501–507.

Whitaker, J. O., Jr., and R. E. Mumford. 1971. Jumping mice (Zapodidae) in Indiana. Proc. Indiana Acad. Sci., 80:201–209.

———. 1972a. Food and ectoparasites of Indiana shrews. J. Mamm., 53:329–335.

———. 1972b. Ecological studies on Reithrodontomys megalotis in Indiana. J. Mamm., 53:850–860.

Whitaker, J. O., Jr., and L. L. Schmeltz. 1974. Food and external parasites of the eastern mole, *Scalopus aquaticus*, from Indiana. Proc. Indiana Acad. Sci., 83:478–481.

Whitaker, J. O., Jr., and F. A. Winter. 1977. Bats of the caves and mines of the Shawnee National Forest, southern Illinois. Trans. Illinois St. Acad. Sci., 70:301–313.

Wilcox, J. S. 1904. Historical encyclopedia of Illinois and history of Kane County. Munsell. Publ. Co., Chicago. 950 pp.

Will, R. L. 1962. Comparative methods of trapping small mammals in an Illinois woods. Trans. Illinois St. Acad. Sci., 55:21–34.

Willner, G. R., G. A. Feldhamer, E. E. Zucker, and J. A. Chapman. 1980. Ondatra zibethicus. Mamm. Species, 141:1–8.

Wilson, C. E., ed. 1906. History of Coles County, *in* Bateman and Selby, Historical encyclopedia of Illinois, Munsell Publ. Co., Chicago. 886 pp.

Wolfe, J. L., and A. V. Linzey. 1977. *Peromyscus gossypinus*. Mamm. Species, 70:1–5.

Wood, F. E. 1910. A study of the mammals of Champaign County, Illinois. Bull. Illinois St. Lab. Nat. Hist., 8:501–613.

Woods, J. 1822. Two years residence in the settlement on the English prairie. pp. 177–357, *in* Thwaites, R. G. 1904. Early western travels, 1748–1846. Arthur H. Clark Co., Cleveland. Vol 10.

Wrazen, J. A., and G. E. Svendsen. 1978. Feeding ecology of a population of eastern chipmunks (*Tamias striatus*) in southeast Ohio. Amer. Midl. Nat., 100:190–201.

Wurster-Hill, D. H. 1973. Chromosomes of eight species from five families of Carnivora. J. Mamm., 54:753–760.

Wurster-Hill, D. H., and K. Benirschke. 1968. Comparative cytogenetic studies in the order Carnivora. Chromosoma, 24:336–382.

Yahner, R. H. 1978d. The adaptive nature of the social system and behavior in the eastern chipmunk, *Tamias striatus*. Behav. Ecol. Sociobiol., 3:397–427.

Yeager, L. E. 1938. Otters of the Delta Hardwood Region of Mississippi. J. Mamm., 19:195–201.

———. 1945. Cottontails, cane cutters, and jacks--all in Illinois. Illinois Conserv., 10:7–37.

Yeager, L. E., and H. G. Anderson. 1944. Some effects of flooding and waterfowl concentration on mammals of a refuge area in central Illinois. Amer. Midl. Nat., 31:159–178.

Yeager, L. E., and R. G. Rennels. 1943. Fur yield and autumn foods of the raccoon in Illinois River bottom lands. J. Wildl. Mgmt., 7:45–60.

Yeager, L. E., and W. H. Elder. 1945. Pre- and post-hunting season foods of raccoons on an Illinois goose refuge. J. Wildl. Mgmt., 9:48–56.

Young, S. P., and H. H. T. Jackson. 1951. The clever coyote. Stackpole Co., Harrisburg, Pa. xv+411 pp.

Zelley, R. A. 1971. The sounds of the fox squirrel, *Sciurus niger rufiventer*. J. Mamm., 52:597–604.

Zimmerman, E. G. 1965. A comparison of habitat and food of two species of *Microtus*. J. Mamm., 46:605–612.

———. 1972. Growth and age determination in the thirteen-lined ground squirrel, Spermophilus tridecemlineatus. Amer. Midl. Nat., 87:314–325.

Index

Sciuridae, family, 149
Sciuromorph, 147
Sciurus, 166
   carolinensis, 166
     pennsylvanicus, 171
   niger, 171
     rufiventer, 176
seasonal distribution, *Lasionycteris noctivagans*, 109
septentrionalis, Myotis keenii, 103, 106
sex ratio in *Pipistrellus subflavus* (winter), 111
sexual variation, secondary, in:
   bats, 85
   Blarina, 67
   Canis latrans, 271
   Castor canadensis, 191
   Chiroptera, 85
   Cryptotis parva, 75
   Didelphis virginiana, 51
   Eptesicus fuscus, 113
   Felis rufus, 311
   Geomys bursarius, 186
   Glaucomys volans, 182
   Lasiurus borealis, 117
   Lepus townsendii, 143
   Marmota monax, 154
   Mephitis mephitis, 303
   Microtus ochrogaster, 235
   Mustela, 288
   Neotoma floridana, 222
   Ochrotomys nuttalli, 218
   Oryzomys palustris, 196
   Peromyscus, 202
   Plecotus rafinesquii, 129
   Scalopus aquaticus, 79
   Sciurus carolinensis, 167
     niger, 171
   Sorex, 58
   Sylvilagus floridanus, 134
   Tamias striatus, 150
   Tamiasciurus hudsonicus, 176
   Urocyon cinereoargenteus, 279
   Vulpes vulpes, 276
Shawnee Hills division, 6
Shelbyville moraine, 3
shrew, 57
   arctic, 43
   least, 75
   long-tailed, 57
   masked, 11, 58
   northern short-tailed, 67
   pygmy, 11, 64
   short-tailed, 66
   smoky, 43
   southeastern, 61
   southern short-tailed, 72
Sigmodon hispidus, 40, 44
skunk, eastern spotted, 46

striped, 302
sloth, giant ground, 37
sodalis, Myotis, 95
soils of Illinois, 5
Sorex, 57
   arcticus, 43
   cinereus, 11, 58
     cinereus, 60
     lesueurii, 61
   fumeus, 43
   hoyi, 11, 20, 64
     hoyi, 65
     winnemana, 66
   longirostris, 61
     longirostris, 63
Soricidae, family, 57
Southern (vegetative) division, 5
Southern Till Plain division, 5
species extirpated in Illinois:
   bison, 27
   black bear, 31
   elk, 29
   mountain lion, 34
   porcupine, 36
   wolf, 32
species of possible occurrence in Illinois, 43, 50
Spermophilus, 158
   franklinii, 11, 162
   tridecemlineatus, 11, 159
     tridecemlineatus, 162
Spilogale putorius, 40, 46
spotted skunk, eastern, 46
squirrel, family, 149
   flying, 181
   fox, 171
   gray, 166
   migratory, 168
   red, 11, 176, 177
stag-moose, 39
stags (=elk), 29
Subfamily (of Muridae):
   Cricetinae, 196
   Microtinae, 227
   Murinae, 251
Sylvilagus, 133
   aquaticus, 20, 139, 142
   floridanus, 134
     mearnsii, 139
Symbos cavifrons, 39
Synaptomys, 247
   cooperi, 247
     gossii, 250
     saturatus, 250
synonym explained, xv

T

Tadarida, 130
   brasiliensis, 20, 131
     mexicana, 132
Talpidae, family, 78
Tamias, 149
   striatus, 149
     griseus, 153
     striatus, 152
Tamiasciurus, 176
   hudsonicus, 11, 177
     hudsonicus, 180
     loquax, 180
     minnesota, 180
Taxidea, 298
   taxus, 299
     taxus, 301
taxus, Taxidea, 299
Tertiary Border (vegetative) division, 6
Thomas, Cyrus, 1
threatened mammal species in Illinois, 19
townsendii, Lepus, 118
   Plecotus, 44
transplants of *Sylvilagus floridanus*, 138
tridecemlineatus, Spermophilus, 159

U

unglaciated Illinois, 3
Urocyon, 278
   cinereoargenteus, 278
     cinereoargenteus, 281
Ursus americanus, 31, 47

V

vegetative divisions of Illinois, 5
Vespertilionidae, family, 90
Villier, Father, 28, 30, 34
virginiana, Didelphis, 51
virginianus, Odocoileus, 314
vision in *Scalopus aquaticus*, 82
vison, Mustela, 295
volans, Glaucomys, 181
vole fluctuations in Illinois, 23
voles, 227
   meadow, 11, 227
   prairie, 234
   southern red-backed, 45
   woodland, 238
Vulpes, 275
   fulva, 275
   vulpes, 275
     fulva, 277
vulpes, Vulpes, 275